137: defector rate even in cults of 1870

Aspects requiring comment:
① internal discipline
② hostility w/ outside world (and, esp, outsiders causal role in end)
③ emigration to escape persecution

→ 2 aspects
   ⓐ paranoia on inside
   ⓑ real persecution on outside

④ voluntary nature of membership
⑤ high internal commitment resulting from communal life
⑥ role of defectors
210 - carnage a direct result of conflict)
⑦ analogy to family & loyalty to group, even unto death

# GONE FROM THE PROMISED LAND

# GONE FROM THE PROMISED LAND

## Jonestown in American Cultural History

John R. Hall

Transaction Publishers

New Brunswick (U.S.A.) and London (U.K.)

Second printing, 1989
**Paperback edition, 1989**
Copyright © 1987 by Transaction Publishers
New Brunswick, New Jersey 08903

Library of Congress Catalog Number: 86-27253
ISBN: 0-88738-124-3 (cloth)
ISBN: 0-88738-801-9 (paper)
Printed in the United States of America

**Library of Congress Cataloging in Publication Data**

Hall, John R.
  Gone from the promised land.

  Bibliography: p.
  Includes index.
  1. Peoples Temple.   2. United States—Church history—
20th century.   3. United States—Civilization—20th
century.   I. Title.
  BP605.P46H35   1987     289.9      86-27253
  ISBN 0-88738-124-3 (cloth)
  ISBN 0-88738-801-9 (paper)

*And all the children of Israel murmured against Moses and against Aron; and the whole congregation said unto them, Would God that we had died in the land of Egypt! or Would God we had died in this wilderness!*

*And wherefore hath the Lord brought us unto this land, to fall by the sword, that our wives and our children should be a prey? Were it not better for us to return unto Egypt?*

*And they spake unto all the company of the children of Israel, saying, The land, which we passed through to search it, is an exceeding good land.*

*If the Lord delight in us, then he will bring us into this land, and give it to us; a land which floweth with milk and honey.*

—Numbers 14: 2-3, 7-8

# Contents

# Preface

We live with Jonestown in the past. Over the years a parade of books has told the story of the murders and mass suicide that took place there. What more could possibly be learned? The present book will answer that for the people who read it. But I want to say at the outset why I wrote about Peoples Temple, knowing that the shelf already was long, and getting longer.

Jacob Burckhardt admitted in *The Civilization of the Renaissance* that he had written one more book on an already widely studied topic. He knew that previous authors might disagree with what he had to say, but this was the very reason for his effort: "Such indeed is the importance of the subject that it still calls for fresh investigation, and may be studied with advantage from the most varied points of view." So it is with Peoples Temple.

When I first published an article on Jonestown in 1979, a friend asked whether I planned a book on the subject. I did not think so. But it became increasingly clear that justifiable public shock at mass carnage prevented the parade of books from offering anything much deeper than a "devil" or "psycho" story. I realized that the passage of time would increase the problem. It seemed important to set down a reasoned study before the memories of individuals involved became too hazy, before popular histories rendered the primary sources silent.

The further I went with research for this book, the more I became convinced that important aspects of Jonestown's history have been overlooked, poorly understood, or even wildly distorted. Because any new history that tries to remedy these problems may meet controversy, it seems to me that the public is entitled to an account that offers future researchers a thorough guide to the evidence. I therefore have included notes with extensive documentation. So that reference numbers for notes will not overly clutter the text, each note cites all sources relevant to a given topic. The text is self-contained, and most readers will have little occasion to flip back to the notes.

For myself, I have have learned much by this writing, and I am grateful for the help, opportunities, and support that made it possible. Of greatest importance was the willingness of individuals to be interviewed about events that were so tragic to them personally. I appreciate the help of those with whom I talked (whose names appear in the footnotes unless they requested anonymity), and I hope that whether or not they always agree with what I have written, they will understand that I share their sorrow.

Perhaps because the present book deals with a stigmatic event of overwhelming proportions, research for it did not readily attract funding by private foundations or the state. Two sources of financial support thus were all the more critical: a Summer Research Fellowship from the Graduate Research Council and a sabbatical leave from the Department of Sociology, both at the University of Missouri-Columbia. These institutional commitments offer some testament to the possibilities of academic freedom. The cooperation of other organizations also was essential to the present study. The government of Guyana offered me valuable assistance when I visited there. Both the U.S. Federal Bureau of Investigation and Department of State provided me with substantial materials (though they have not yet released all relevant documents that should become public). The relevance of materials that could be obtained only from the U.S. government underscores the importance of the Freedom of Information Act.

In San Francisco, California, the attorney for Peoples Temple during its last years, Charles Garry, allowed me access to Temple files, and he and his investigative assistant Pat Richartz offered valuable background on the documents. Across town, the California Historical Society made available materials still not completely catalogued, and Sandra McCoy Larson brought to my attention documents that I might never have found otherwise.

Finally, my efforts have been eased by support and encouragement from colleagues, secretaries, friends, and relations: Nancy Allen, Michael Barkun, Howard S. Becker, Patty Berns, Lynn Brown, Teri Cone, David De Leon, Michelle Duckett, Michael Flynn, Jane Grieco, Marian Ross Hall, Ted Hall, Gary Hamilton, Michael Hechter, Julie Helming, Irving Louis Horowitz, Ed Kick, Paula McKey, Rebecca Moore, Amanda Noble, Mary Jo Neitz, George Primov, Richard Riddle, Tom Robbins, Guenther Roth, Peter Salter, Francis Shor, Katarina Toll, Gail Ullman, Andy Walker, Brenda Warren, and Sharon Watson. Some of these good people have helped in ways that they might consider incidental. They should know that seemingly casual remarks can have profound effects! Others tried to teach me something, or read and commented on typed drafts of the manuscript, or listened to my ruminations. I thank them all and I am deeply moved by the spirit that animates their lives. The book is stronger for their help. The shortcomings that remain are mine alone. Yet even if scholarship is never without faults, my moral commitment is to truth and light.

JOHN ROSS HALL

# Introduction:
# The Cultural Puzzle of Jonestown

What are we to make of the murders of a congressman and four others and the subsequent mass suicide of over 900 people at Jonestown, Guyana? In the years after November 18, 1978, popular accounts effectively used the events to establish Jim Jones as a scapegoat personifying the alien threat of so-called cults. But that prevailing interpretation has kept us from understanding Peoples Temple as another sort of scapegoat, bearing hidden cultural burdens of U.S. society. If we are to learn anything of value from the tragedy at Jonestown, its history must be salvaged from myth before it passes from our collective memory. In this book I try to reason about what happened, why, and how it was tied to our ideals, our practices, and the tensions of modern culture.

The basic facts are well established. On Monday, November 13, 1978, California congressman Leo Ryan flew from Washington, D.C., to the socialist country of Guyana, on the northeast coast of South America, to visit the large, predominantly Black communal settlement called Jonestown. With Ryan and a press entourage were members of a group called the Concerned Relatives, who charged that the remote jungle community run by Peoples Temple was holding individuals against their will. On Saturday, November 18, gunmen from Jonestown ambushed the group as they were boarding planes at a nearby airstrip after leaving Jonestown. Shot to death were Ryan, three news reporters, and a young woman in a group of fifteen people who had decided to depart from Jonestown with the visitors.

By Tuesday, November 21, the world learned that the Indiana-born Reverend Jim Jones, Peoples Temple's charismatic White leader, had led over 400 residents of Jonestown to drink a poison punch in a cataclysm of murder and mass suicide staged shortly after Ryan and the others had been killed. An initial news story was self-contradictory: "Those who tried to refuse the poison or escape were forced by armed guards to take it," yet somehow there remained hope for several hundred Jonestown residents who "apparently" had fled into the jungle rather than drink the purple Fla-Vor-Aid laced with cyanide and other drugs.[1]

In the following days journalists speculated that survivors had sought refuge in nearby Amerindian villages or fled to Venezuela, about fifteen miles away. Members of the Concerned Relatives meanwhile declared in the press that even from its collective grave Peoples Temple would try to get revenge against its opponents. They feared that Jones's followers in Georgetown, the capital of Guyana, and at the U.S. headquarters of Peoples Temple in San Francisco would organize "hit squads" to assassinate Temple enemies and high-ranking public officials.[2] Not until a week after the event did the truth emerge: initial body counts had been grossly inaccurate. A collective suicide and murder had taken the lives of practically an entire community, leaving only a handful of demoralized survivors. The death toll was over 900.

The question of how many people at Jonestown willingly took the poison always will be open to debate. Certainly young children could not have evaluated very well what their actions would mean. The presence of armed guards shows at least implicit coercion, though the guards themselves reported their intentions to visitors in glorious terms and then took the poison. Nor was the situation structured as one of individual choice. Jim Jones proposed a collective action, and in the discussion that followed only one woman offered extended opposition. No one rushed up to tip over the vat of Fla-Vor-Aid. Wittingly, unknowingly, or reluctantly, they took the poison.[3]

In the United States the news slowly filtering back was a time bomb of horror compounding horror. Amidst a flood of press reports and three "instant books" published by mid-December, the *New Republic* argued that the mass suicide and murder triggered a collective experience of loss and devastation greater than anything concerning the United States since the assassination of President John F. Kennedy in 1963. Large numbers of Americans became emotionally immersed in the tragedy. Even if people did not know exactly what had happened, they knew that, like the Kennedy assassination, it could never be understood.[4]

We are all world spectators to some degree, and we develop a sense of what is plausible both in the drama of everyday life and on an historical scale. But sometimes the curtains that mark the boundaries of the plausible world are drawn back, and beyond them we see things too awesome to contemplate, too unsettling to accept as part of the world's drama. So it is with suicide. We recognize what our popular culture shows, that sometimes people may take their own lives for altruistic reasons, as did Japanese kamikaze pilots during World War II. And we may be dimly aware that some suicides are fulfillments of social codes of honor. But we do not understand the concept of honor in modern Western societies; it seems old fashioned.[5]

Our culture incorporates civic and religious taboos against suicide. Discounting honor and altruism, we regard the act as an affront to a community and society at large, a deliberate and final cutting short of any social intercourse. In religious terms, it often is treated as a sin. In the modern vocabulary of psychiatry, almost by definition, suicide is regarded as a sign of devastating mental disorder. Whether the sources are religious or therapeutic, the conclusion is the same: suicide lies beyond the pale. Thus, in the face of the unthinkable, culture salvages plausible reality by covering the abyss with a curtain circumscribing a world that we can affirm.

From beyond the curtain bordering reality came the photographic images of Jonestown, pictures of all those bodies lying in waste. Why were they there? What could collective death in a single dramatic act like this mean? Was the collective act a response to circumstances in the world the people at Jonestown left behind? This, in fact, is how their leader portrayed the matter. At the meeting held in Jonestown after Ryan's group departed, Jim Jones called the collective poisoning "revolutionary suicide protesting the conditions of an inhumane world."[6]

The viewpoint from the established culture would have to be quite different. The people of Jonestown could not have had a compelling reason for what they did, for the integrity of our own social existence would thereby be placed in doubt. Giving credence to Jones's account would require concluding the unthinkable: that the people of Jonestown were "justified" in taking the action of terminating the lives of an entire community.

Whatever meaning Americans sought for the tragedy could be established only under a contrasting assumption that pointed public discourse in less threatening directions. Because there could be no "reason" for the tragedy, the question of blame became the central issue. Even on this terrain some explanations might be discomfiting in their revelations and conclusions, but at least they would reaffirm the plausibility of a world in which the unnecessary and meaningless deaths of some 918 people might have been prevented.

In the foreign press Jonestown often became a symptom of U.S. malaise. The Soviet news agency Tass took a line not so different from Jones's: the mass suicide somehow reflected life in the United States, where "millions are the victims of an inhumane society." A Tokyo editor saw Blacks and other disenfranchised Americans disappointed by the contradiction between the myth of affluence and their own material circumstances. Others described Jonestown as the natural outgrowth of a permissive society where culturally adrift people confused by the choices of "near total freedom" sometimes opt for the security of commitment to charismatic leaders who offer religious purpose, emotional excitement, and sexual license. This line of interpretation reached its full flower in an engaging book by West-Indian-born author Shiva Naipaul. By recounting his tour of a "New Age" cultural fair, Naipaul aimed to show that Peoples Temple was the likely product of a culture where rational discourse had been engulfed by an orgiastic search for self-fulfillment stemming from naive utopian wishes to transcend confrontation with life in a morally uneven world.[7]

Few American observers took the path of such sweeping cultural criticism. Spokespersons for social groups potentially most "tainted" by the stigma of Jonestown—leftists, Blacks, and Christians, as well as political notables who had lent moral support to the group—sought to put as much distance as possible between themselves and Peoples Temple. Socialists argued that Jones's religious origins and charismatic style belied his radical claims. Black leaders suggested that there was racism in the acts of a White charlatan of a prophet who led their brothers and sisters astray. Chagrined at the Temple's affiliation with the Disciples of Christ, Christian commentators emphasized the blasphemy of Jones's contempt for the Bible.

From the corridors of government offices and the Disciples of Christ came the predictable bureaucratic responses: investigate the adequacy of performance of duty by organizational personnel, reprimand or punish those guilty of malfeasance, and modify policies as if to safeguard against a repeat occurrence. Among a whole raft of such investigations, none found much culpability among the living. Nor, other than the debacle of murder and suicide at the end, did they find much under their jurisdictions that could be counted as crimes by Peoples Temple or its members. And when government reports addressed popular cultural concerns, most of their findings affirmed what had already been reported, both in California in a series of exposés before the Peoples Temple migrated en masse to Guyana in 1977, and in accounts that greeted the public after November 18, 1978.[8]

The mass media, not government reports, shaped public knowledge about Peoples Temple. In the wake of the carnage, media executives apparently could see no end to the public thirst for exposés of what "really happened." Along with all the newspaper and magazine articles, they produced no less than one film, one CBS television docudrama, and sixteen popular books on Peoples Temple in four years. It was by this process that the public cultural meanings of Jonestown became established.

Virtually without exception the popular accounts amounted to morality plays. Collectively they portrayed psychological terror, strange punishments, sexual license, intimidation, and shady economic dealings of Peoples Temple in a way that must come close to defining the "atrocity tale" as a literary genre. Challenging the lurid accounts, religious scholar Jonathan Smith sounded a call for "looking at Jonestown rather than staring or looking away." His "preliminary attempt" at explaining Jonestown reasoned by analogy from Greek antiquity that "the most proximate responsibility for the events of White Night [mass suicide] was [Congressman Leo] Ryan's." But Smith's proposed "quest for intelligibility" did not effectively counter the comforting popular view that neither Jones nor his followers really believed in the religiously founded socialism he claimed to promote. Jones was made out to be a megalomaniac and a madman who compromised his followers through blackmail and brainwashing to obtain their commitment not to a political and religious viewpoint but to his own personal rulership. In this view Jones was a fiend who plotted the deaths of his followers for reasons so perverse as to lie beyond rational discourse. As the most thoroughly researched of the popular books succinctly put it, "Blame for the Jonestown tragedy must ultimately come to rest in the deranged personality of Jim Jones."[9]

Certainly the popular interpreters of Jonestown did not have much difficulty coming up with evidence of the evil they saw in Jim Jones. Let us picture the leader of Peoples Temple seated on his "throne" in the jungle pavilion in the middle of the night, listening to testimonials from Jonestown residents about what they would do if their relatives invaded the community. One man thinks he would butcher his family like hogs; another wants to poison a relative, cut up the body, and feed the poisoned flesh to other relatives so they would die. What kind of leader could put followers up to such improvisation, and whence came his strange and haunting laughter at the recitations? Most people would not have to look for long in the mounds of materials about Peoples Temple to conclude that there was profound evil in Jim Jones. Somehow the popular mind can easily imagine the man, as a 1979 cartoon depicted him, sitting amidst the flames of a fiery hell with Adolf Hitler, the latter exclaiming, "Kool-Aid! Why didn't I think of that!"[10]

Nevertheless, the portrayal of Jones as executioner obscures more than it reveals. To accept at face value the accounts of atrocities served up out of understandable moral outrage at mass death pulls the curtain over Jonestown rather than helping us understand it. There are three basic problems with such an approach.

In the first place, in effect it takes its basic premises from long-standing opponents of Peoples Temple. Their loose-knit organization, eventually called the Concerned Relatives, was tremendously influential in circumscribing the terrain from which the public developed a sustained image of Peoples Temple, beginning in 1977, before the murders and mass suicide. Popular accounts from early reporters onward typically framed interpretations of Peoples Temple in terms of charges by the Concerned Relatives. They thus often uncritically accepted the biases of people who themselves were in bitter conflict with the group, and who, after the mass suicide, had overwhelming interests in absolving themselves of any responsibility for what happened. Such an approach could not succeed in understanding Jonestown in any event, especially because it failed to examine critically the effects of the opponents' actions themselves—including the visit of Ryan and the Concerned Relatives—on the course of history. Moreover, there is the problem of reflexivity: to the extent that early reporters were participants in events, their own actions are part of the story they purported to "cover." For example, a San Francisco reporter covering Peoples Temple, Tim Reiterman, later (with coauthor John Jacobs) wrote the book that blamed Jonestown on Jones's "deranged personality." Despite this analysis, Reiterman admitted that he was emotionally torn by "guilt that somehow my presence had contributed to the terrible outcome." In short, with opponents helping to frame analysis in ways that pinpointed responsibility elsewhere, and with reporters acting in the unfolding drama, the popular exposés are better understood as events in history than as accounts about history.[11]

There is a second major difficulty with the formula of the "atrocity tale." It amounts to a pseudoexplanation based on a logically weak premise: the unequivocally tragic outcome of murder and mass suicide is interpreted as the result of evil. This interpretation in turn provides the warrant for assaying the antecedent evil in Jim Jones and Peoples Temple, and the evil that is identified stands for causal proof about origins of the atrocity. This procedure places a particular interpretation on the outcome, blaming it on the dementia of Jones the Anti-Christ, then drawing on that interpretation to select accounts to be strung together into "history." The problem is this: prior "evil" that may have had little or no causal connection to the outcome is taken to foreshadow the final evil, while the significance of events that fall outside those judged as representatively evil may be completely ignored.

Thus, people who remember the early years of Jim Jones and the Temple are given full opportunity to place their recollections within the context of the murders and mass suicide. We learn from them how as a child Jones conducted sacred last rites for deceased pets, and how, as a teenager, he shot a pistol in the direction of a close friend. We are introduced to the possibility that Jones's moving to Indianapolis with his wife Marceline when they were young, and shifting from unsatisfying job to job, marked a tendency of "running," "one of the classic traits of paranoia."[12] But we never learn about the prevalence of similar actions by other young people who do not grow up to lead socialistic communities to mass suicide in the jungle. Conversely, even the most widespread conventional practices of staging everyday life, like the wearing of ministerial robes, become sinister manipulations of people's perceptions at the hands of the Reverend Jim Jones.

The formula of these discourses holds that sufficient antecedent evil will produce an evil outcome, and a great deal of antecedent evil will produce an enormous evil outcome. The dubious logic of the approach is underscored by the comment of Reiterman and Jacobs on the mass suicide: "The worldwide perception alone would prove the last gesture a failure, Jones's closing act a fraud."[13] In the view of these writers, public "perception" itself is sufficient to establish the nature of events. Thus, public opinion, itself largely dependent on mass media for information, stands as the jury issuing verdicts on history.

The weaknesses of a theory that "evil begets evil" bring us to a third major difficulty. By reducing history to a superficial atrocity tale, the writers who claim to reveal the true story instead place Jonestown beyond the reach of historical analysis. They trivialize an ambiguous tragedy by forcing it into the framework of an "evil-man" theory; then the people who died were simply victims of a "cult." But only at the hands of the Concerned Relatives and the media did Peoples Temple become a "cult." As an Indiana woman whose teenager died at Jonestown remarked, "I can't understand why they call the Peoples Temple a cult. To the people, it was their church."[14]

If the term cult is taken to mean a religious following centered on an individual whose teachings are held to be sacred, then there have been many cults over the centuries, including most prominently the ones that surrounded Jesus, and more recently, Gandhi and Pope John Paul II. Under such a definition, the cult label loses its critical faculty for establishing prima facie evil, for it has to be recognized that there are "good" cults and "bad" cults. But more often, cult is used pejoratively by members of one religion to describe a heretical or competing religion of which they disapprove.[15]

The tale of an evil madman and his cult massacre is simplistic history, nevertheless pregnant with literary possibilities. But we have to wonder why the "atrocity tale" as a literary device of mythmaking has been allowed to substitute for a reasoned analysis of Jonestown and its meaning. Perhaps the events in Jonestown produced unsettling collective questions about cultural dilemmas of the wider society. No doubt there was a strange fascination with mechanisms of seemingly diabolical power and the way the Temple grew like a cancer in the midst of a normal social world. How could the "cancer" feed on normal people, normal organizations and institutions? Did Peoples Temple harness good people to bad ends? Did it "use" organizations by covertly subordinating them to its own purposes? Or,

xviii    **Gone from the Promised Land**

more disturbing to consider, did Peoples Temple partly reflect the society from which it emerged?

There is no easy answer to such questions. Sociologists and historians have long understood that "facts" do not speak for themselves; sometimes the *same* set of facts can be "read off" equally well to support radically different interpretations; *different* sets of facts about the *same* events can support even more disparate accounts. How, then, to make sense of the conflict of interpretations? No simple formula solves the problem, but we do know that the questions we ask frame the relevance of facts and thus shape the range of interpretations. Just sifting through the popular accounts of Peoples Temple shows that not much insight is gained by the atrocity tale. What approach might prove more fruitful?

Perhaps we need to explore the social processes by which Peoples Temple emerged. Perhaps what happened with Jim Jones and his aides, the Peoples Temple as an organization, its interaction with the outside world, and the trajectory of its history can be better explained on the basis of wider social and cultural currents than by the particular personality of the group's leader. I suggest that we at least need to entertain this possibility by letting one question serve as a touchstone: how much of what happened with Peoples Temple is unique to the group and its leader, and how much can be explained by reference to wider social processes?

This question cannot be answered simply by looking at Peoples Temple in isolation. Instead, it is necessary to examine its cultural context and its concrete relationships with other social groups. It also becomes relevant to compare Peoples Temple both to a wide range of parallel social phenomena and to sociohistorical models that clarify distinctive social logics (sociologists sometimes call such models "ideal types"). These sorts of investigations help establish the general social processes and wider cultural currents at work in Peoples Temple. What is left over, that which cannot be explained by such comparisons, is the unique residue of Peoples Temple that requires situational historical explanation.[16] For example, the parallels between the wider U.S. practices of public relations and the practices of Peoples Temple need to be established, so that the degree of deviation from social convention can be stated with precision. Similarly, once we understand the charlatan as an ideal type and American practitioner, it will be possible to ask in what respect Jim Jones was a charlatan, and where other explanations of his actions are required. These sorts of procedures do not insure that all factual controversies can be resolved, nor do they rule out conflict of interpretations, but they do sharpen discussion. And they offer the opportunity to understand Jonestown in a way that allows us to explore its relation to our own society and culture.

As we will see, in diverse ways the growth of Peoples Temple was fueled through its relations to our society. Its cataclysmic end crystallized a particular constellation of forces that exposes to our view social processes otherwise hidden. Looking for the meaning of Jonestown beyond the surface facts of atrocity thus offers a unique opportunity: we can bring to light a complex portion of our cultural world that usually is cloaked in normative perceptions of reality. Such an investigation cannot purport to reveal the "essential" nature of our society, nor does it suggest that Peoples Temple is symptomatic of U.S. culture, for it is not a representative sample subject to generalization. But the simple identification of common and unique cultural pathways is a significant step: an assessment of the degree to which Peoples Temple was truly an aberration or simply a unique conjunctural exaggeration of our society's contradictions permits us to deepen our understanding of a modern scapegoat.

This book proceeds in Part I by asking who Jim Jones was, what ideas he had, where he got them, and how his Peoples Temple became established in Indiana during the 1950s and early 1960s. In these explorations I show the origins of Peoples Temple embedded in the career of a man who tapped three basic streams of U.S. culture: Protestantism's split between fundamentalist and social gospel wings; the quests of Black messiahs to offer a promised land to their dispossessed followers; and the pre-McCarthy era U.S. communist movement. By themselves these cultural origins only chart the cultural pathways of Peoples Temple, not its organizational base or situational causes of its historical development. In Part II, I examine the Temple organization that solidified after a collective migration to California in 1965, through relevant comparisons with modern institutionalized practices in the realms of economics and bureaucracy, social control, and public relations and power. Though the Temple's cultural origins derive largely from the nineteenth century and early twentieth century, I show that its social practices have a distinctly modern cast. Thus, Peoples Temple succeeded in the United States largely *because* it was a distinctly American social movement in its origins and practices. With this recognition, it becomes possible in Part III to trace the situational causes of Peoples Temple's conflict with its detractors, the collective migration to Guyana, and the mass suicide. Both Jones's followers and his opponents sought to act out a drama of history. Examining that history, we can hope to deepen our understandings about the role of myth in modern society. Understanding the role of myth, we can hope to establish Jonestown's cultural significance beyond myth.

Jim Jones has often been dismissed as a madman, but the present study shows that so-called madness, the shared *folie* of nearly a thousand people, took form in tension with social circumstance. In the case of Jones, madness was not a private matter; if nothing else, the devastating events bespeak a madness run rampant on a grand scale. But whence the madness? The fate of Jones's followers obliges us to see if Jonestown is intelligible in something other than a morality tale.

A number of observers have found the prototype for the unveiling of Jim Jones and his jungle autocracy in Joseph Conrad's gripping short story "Heart of Darkness,"[17] but they sometimes missed Conrad's deep sense of irony. On one level "Heart of Darkness" is the tale of a trading company steamship captain sent on an ominous trip up an African jungle river to a remote trading post held against all odds by one Mr. Kurtz. "He drew men towards him by what was best in them," an unrequited lover would later say of Kurtz. The immense personal magnetism of his insight brought native and White "disciples" alike to embrace a grand but empty vision that led to a ghastly reckoning of truth. Chugging slowly up the steamy jungle river toward Kurtz's trading post, the steamboat captain journeyed a soul's voyage into this repulsive, compelling world of evil. Yet it was Kurtz himself who cried with his last breath, "The horror! The horror!"

Jim Jones easily enough can be understood as the source of Peoples Temple's horror, just as there is no difficulty in finding the heart of darkness in Kurtz. But that is not the end of the matter, for in his origins Kurtz represented civilization brought to the jungle. And Kurtz became evil only by wrestling with fate; he therefore knew both fate and evil as few others ever will. With a dark light he cast a shadow on darkness in the world itself.

# PART I

# 1

# Jim Jones

It was Jim Jones who brought people to murder and mass suicide, but who was Jim Jones? Clearly, the man's life and vision raise certain themes that came into play over and over again in the events leading up to the final carnage. By themselves, I argue, these themes do not explain the final debacle. But the outlook of Jones was like a picture frame around a world where a multitude of hopes and fears, plans, ploys, and agendas came to a head.

Some observers would paint a coherent picture of Jones as the Anti-Christ. Others, among them a few followers who survived Jonestown, believe he was a saint. Perhaps Jones was both, for he was no ordinary man, and the multiple facets of his life reflected a volatile set of contradictions onto his followers and detractors alike. This and the following two chapters explore the frame of Peoples Temple's world by considering the early life and ministerial calling of Jones, by asking what, if anything, there was to the philosophy of the would-be messiah, and by pondering claims that he was a charlatan, a fraud, or a madman.[1]

### Hoosier Parents

Some people are born into wealth; others at least inherit a socially defined place in the world. Jim Jones had neither. He was born an outsider at the height of the Great Depression, in the Indiana farm village of Crete, in overwhelmingly rural Randolph County, along the Ohio border.

Randolph County had its origins in the arrival of pioneers who settled the first colony of the United States, the Old Northwest Territory. In the early 1800s they filtered north from Kentucky, Tennessee, and North Carolina, and beginning in the 1820s they streamed west along the National Road. For the most part the settlers were at least nominally Protestant. Sometimes they were self-consciously religious. The very first pioneers to settle Randolph County included Quakers who left the piedmont areas of North and South Carolina. Some of them were proslavery, and other proslavery migrants from the South settled eastern Indiana too, by moving up

3

the valley of the Whitewater River from its mouth at the Ohio River. But in the antebellum years, many Quakers opposed slavery, and some established stations on the Underground Railroad to help slaves escape from their owners.[2]

Underground Railroad activity seems to have had an effect on the composition of the area: by 1860, at the beginning of the Civil War, Randolph County had the highest proportion of Blacks compared to total county population of any county in Indiana, with a total of 825 settled in a series of small communities away from the major towns. After the Civil War the Black population began to decline as younger Blacks abandoned farm life for the cities.

By 1930 the Randolph County population had settled into a relatively stable pattern. The 24,858 inhabitants were 98.9 percent White and native born. Immigrants, mostly from Germany and Canada, made up about half a percent of the population. The remaining half a percent were Blacks, only 136. Even by 1951 there were no Jews, and only a remarkably small 2.6 percent of the population were Catholics. The county where Jim Jones was born thus bore the indelible stamp of a White Protestant culture of Quakers, Methodists, Baptists, and other such denominations, with southern as well as northern origins.[3]

An apocryphal story popular among Kentuckians today has it that the Indiana term *Hoosier* comes from the question posed by early settlers to one another, trying to pin down origins and social position: "*Who's yer parents?*" Perhaps with justification people of the Hoosier State dispute that story, but it is a telling one for Jim Jones, for it underscores his marginal origins. James Warren Jones was born on May 13, 1931, the only child of James T. and Lynetta Putnam Jones. The father was one of twelve children from a prominent Randolph County family of farmers and schoolteachers, descendants of early Baptist settlers from Virginia and Quakers from Pennsylvania. The mother viewed her husband's family as "bigoted" and closed minded. "They were just not broad minded about anything," Lynetta later complained. "They would pick out these facts, and these was the facts and that was the way it was."[4]

For all the resentment Lynetta Jones felt toward pretensions of social position and scholastic elitism in her husband's family, she could not fault her husband on those grounds. Despite his family's upstanding social position, "big Jim" never amounted to much. In the World War he had received a lung injury from mustard gas, and he took up the life of a disabled veteran upon his return. A government check made him a man of meager means, but the war injury left him an "invalid" and a "very bitter, cynical person" in the recollection of his son.

Big Jim, Lynetta, and their only child left their forty- or sixty-acre farm at Crete when they could no longer make a go of it in the height of the Great Depression, probably in 1933 or 1934. They moved to a house next to the railroad tracks in the nearby town of Lynn, which in 1930 had a population of 936, two train lines, and a going casket industry. In these environs James T. Jones spent a good deal of time hanging out at the local pool hall, garnering what respect he could as an old-timer who had served his country. According to a journalism professor who grew up in Lynn, big Jim also belonged to the Ku Klux Klan.[5]

Even before they moved from the farm, the father of Jim Jones seems to have reached the point of life defeat, and it was Lynetta who took responsibility for the family of three, taking what jobs she could pick up, including housework for her neighbors across the Arba Pike. "Finally when everything just seemed to run out" on the farm, she remembers her husband "would slump there, and just, 'I've done all I can do.' He'd burst into tears. 'I've gone as far as I can go.'" The small and wiry Lynetta looked at him with quiet determination: "You cry, my love; I'll whip this [Great Depression] if it's the last thing I ever do."

Lynetta Jones felt little in common with her husband's family: "Some of them harbored a poorly concealed notion that being as fit and able as I was in the skills of survival was unbefitting a female of my size and stature and somehow detracted from the thing they called respectibility." A woman with straight black hair and purported Cherokee Indian blood, she hailed from Gibson County, near the Wabash River in the southwestern corner of Indiana. She was born to Mary Putnam, a woman from Kentucky married to a tenant farmer named Jesse Putnam. When Lynetta's father died, their landlord, a local landowner and stave-mill owner named Lewis Parker became the girl's "foster father," apparently when she was little more than a child.[6]

Always down to earth, Lynetta Jones spoke in the archaic southern piedmont accent prevalent in southern Indiana, with the same colloquial expressions, run-on sentence grammar, and clipped phrasing that were to mark her son's "backstage" voice all his life. She obtained some education, at an Arkansas agricultural college and a business college in Indiana, but neither her formal schooling nor the station she attained in her married life rewarded her with the social position that she felt her due. Trapped in poverty and living with a husband with whom, she later recounted, she did not share a bed, Lynetta worked in tomato fields and at factory jobs. During World War II she began commuting to a job with Perfect Circle Corporation in nearby Hagerstown. There Lynetta not only earned a wage but also helped organize workers in the class struggle of labor by night. Her resentment thus found a focus in the privileges of class and her own low station. She struggled mightily for the only child born to her, for whom she desperately wanted better circumstances: "My ambition for my son knew no bounds!" she once explained. Another of her turns of phrase was more foreboding: "I didn't want him to devote his life to just being a slave to the death interest in people."[7]

Jim Jones's father had little influence on him, except as an example of failure. The boy was reared as Lynetta's son. He picked up a great many of his mother's ways, and carried them with him in his whole life and work. To begin with, Lynetta's religious legacy was less than conventional. She was a rough and ready woman who smoked and cursed and drank. She mocked people like the Joneses' neighbor in Lynn, Mrs. Kennedy, who Lynetta believed took religion too seriously.

Mrs. Kennedy was a member of the Church of the Nazarene, a Holiness sect opposed to consumption of alcohol and use of tobacco. The Nazarenes had formed at the turn of the century by consolidating several Holiness movement groups. These groups had split off earlier from the Methodist Episcopal Church out of dissatisfaction with the Methodists' emphasis on the social gospel and their suppression of the rollicking camp-meeting-revival worship style in vogue since the beginning of the nineteenth century. As Lynetta Jones put it, the Nazarene Mrs. Kennedy believed in "the hellfire and damnation and on all the brimstone that went with it." From that churchly perspective, Lynetta suspected the opinion that she herself "was going to hell straighter than a bird could fly." But Lynetta only laughed at her friend, and tried to set her straight: "Well Myrtle, you're just all tied up with this. . . . No matter what you think it says, it don't say nothing as ignorant as that."[8]

The mother of Jim Jones was not too taken with the idea of a "sky god" in heaven, but she believed in spirits nonetheless. They abounded in the world and its creatures and their visions. Lynetta always had loved the woods and wild animals and she even had been "rather fond of snakes since early childhood." The penchant for animals sometimes shaded off into realms of fantasy. Lynetta lived in a somewhat magical world. No sky god, but in the world enchantment lay in the stories of animals, in visions, and in spirits that possess humans. Jim Jones seems to have picked up his mother's sense of the divine but inexplicable forces of animism. Like her, he was derisive about the "sky god" but believed in forces that shape a world of fate beyond human control.

According to Lynetta's later account, even the birth of her son was shrouded in deep and mystical circumstances. She had been on the verge of death once, before she was married. Typhoid fever took her mother's life in 1925, and attacked Lynetta a year later. Her fever came on in the woods, where she awoke "eyeball to eyeball with snakes of all sizes, with some eggs just hatching." Somehow she made it home, where she lived with her foster father Lewis Parker, by then in his late 60s. When Lynetta's fever peaked four weeks later, she recalled, she "seemed to go down to the Egyptian River of Death and look it over. . . . There was an Egyptian burial box which could be used as a boat, I thought, and a plank that could be used as a paddle. My mother walked out on the other shore." "You are not permitted to cross that river yet," her mother told Lynetta in the dream. "There are two very important things you must do before you come here. Your world is so full of sorrow and sadness, and Lew needs you now that he is old." In the dream, Lynetta recounted, "I turned to retrace my steps," and "came to the bed where the sick woman was and found I was the sick woman."

Lynetta's strength rebounded upon awakening. She took care of the aging Lew Parker, married James T. Jones, and took her foster father to live with her new husband. "My mind was made up long in advance," she later recalled, "that my child should be exactly like Lewis Parker even though he was no blood kin." Five years later Lynetta gave birth to a little boy who had brown eyes just like Parker's, "though both my husband and myself had blue eyes." A little over a year later Lewis Parker died back in southwestern Indiana, and Lynetta Jones provided the information for the death certificate.

Lynetta Jones later said she had not wanted to marry or bear children. In her recollections, she raised innuendoes about the paternity of her son Jim Jones. The child was born of a feverish vision that linked her dead mother's wishes with the fate of Lewis Parker, the family landlord and patron who Lynetta said was "the most outstanding character I had ever met in my life." Her only child had more than the brown eyes of his "godfather"; Lynetta later would proclaim him to reflect the goodness that she saw in Parker: "Nothing was too much for him to do to relieve poverty and need, trouble and unhappiness, wherever he found it," she said of the man nearly fifty years her senior.[9]

## Hoosier Boy

Lynetta Jones had desperately wanted a boy but she was not prepared for the baby who "entered this vale of tears." He "looked like every nation out in the world but his own, and a little bit of his own too." She thought, "God forbid, this is gonna be one of the ugliest children." But she doted over him and indulged him all the same. The child got a bad case of "three months' colic," Lynetta recalled: "I was constantly tormented over him, and the fact is my insecurity because of my fear that I didn't know how to handle him and how to raise him or rear him right or something, and he was so important to me that I was just beside myself in the rearing of him."

Perhaps because of her anxiety, Lynetta Jones did little to bridle the child, and "he just about always got his way about whatever he wanted to do." Around town he had the reputation of a little hellion. He could walk around without clothes. He brought animals home and his mother would care for them. He brought tramps home and she would feed them. Eventually he would charge items at the grocery store without permission and his mother resigned herself to paying the bill. She could not give him a "lickin'" for any of his misdeeds, she said. If she tried, little Jim would let out a screech that brought the household menagerie to his side and bowled her over.

The boy's mother did not have a great deal of time to supervise her child in the first place. She brought her husband and son through the "awful times" of the Depression by working long hours and pinching every penny. As her son put it, "I had less of material comforts, although my mother made every effort to give me what she could." Even in the midst of poverty she managed to save money for young Jim's college, hoping for more for him than she had. Lynetta possessed that old-time virtue of thrift that had been learned of necessity, if nothing else, by the early settlers. Jim admired his mother for it, saying in Jonestown at her death in 1977 that she knew "how to make a dollar go. I learned that from her. . . . You can be sure I learned how to make a dollar stretch, and it's a damn good thing, or we wouldn't all be eating right now." Like his mother, Jones held down consumption and harnessed cash flow to the accumulation of savings all his life, in a way that mimicked what the sociologist Max Weber once termed "the ascetic compulsion to save" among Puritans and Quakers.[10]

Lynetta Jones passed on much of her practical and earthy "religion" of animism, spirit forces, and frugality to her son, but her own ways could not quite contain her son's spiritual odyssey. The Nazarene Mrs. Kennedy and other neighbors exposed the boy to the range of respectable religious experience available in Lynn, including the Methodist Church and the pacifist Quaker meeting of his father's family. Mrs. Kennedy was the mainstay; she would "fox him up and take him to the Sunday school and church and all this sort of thing." But the next thing Lynetta knew, a woman from the local Pentecostal church came calling for young Jim.

The Pentecostal groups had arisen as an almost inevitable extension of the Holiness movement that spawned Mrs. Kennedy's Nazarenes. Waiting for the millennium in the 1890s, Holiness leaders searched for a "new Pentecost," in which believers would receive definitive proof of their own salvation in the Holy Spirit, just as the apostles of Jesus had, according to the New Testament's Acts 2, on the seventh Sunday after Easter. In 1906 in

Los Angeles a Black Baptist preacher named Seymour claimed to re-discover the proof of grace. He promoted a doctrine of glossolalia, or speaking in tongues, originally set forth by the Reverend Charles Fox Parham of Kansas. Seymour thus served as a major catalyst for the Pentecostal movement: in the revival on Los Angeles's Azusa Street that was to continue unabated, sometimes night and day, for three years, speaking in tongues became established as the definitive material sign of salvation.

On Azusa Street the movement was racially integrated: Whites, often putting aside deep racial prejudices, sought the laying on of Black hands in order to become filled with the Holy Spirit. During the early phases of Pentecostalism's rapid growth, interracial worship remained common, but by the 1920s social pressures in the South led to virtually complete segregation of the various Pentecostal denominations.

Pentecostalists were disdained by the more conventional denominations, and sometimes denounced and persecuted, even by fundamentalists, for their immoderate practices, their sometimes outrageous claims about supernatural balls of fire and the like, and their crusades against churches that could not heal, allegedly because they were lost in unbelief. In general the Pentecostal sects attracted the dispossessed and marginal elements of society, sharecroppers, tenant farmers, unorganized factory wage earners, and others who banded together in communities where they could better survive collectively in a changing world from which they often felt excluded.

One of the most interesting analyses of Pentecostal groups, that of W. J. Hollenweger, suggests that they thrived especially among the disenfranchised and the "poor in spirit" who could not easily contend with an increasingly alien, rationalized world. Such people feared being made fun of by outsiders who would be astounded at their inability to contend with modern civilization. In the comfort of their congregations they could express their own social needs "liturgically," that is, in the vocabulary of salvation. While they prayed for the redemption of the Second Coming, Pentecostalists could practice a form of social welfare in a community that operated outside established channels of charity.[11]

As a boy, Jim Jones went to Pentecostal services where they praised God in enthusiastic and unregimented ways, looking to be filled with the Holy Spirit in immediate ecstatic possession of the charismatic gifts described in the book of Acts. Lynetta Jones felt the woman who came to take young Jim to the services was "a zealot" who "got savage in her determination to hang on to" him: she had the boy out at a poor country church "made from scraps o' professionals' [materials]"; she put the boy of eight or ten up in the pulpit, as a "drawing card and a fundraising thing," and she "hauled him all over the country" on the revival circuit. Religious ecstasy took its toll. When Jim Jones began to jerk in agony in his sleep, "felt snakes and things like this," Lynetta decided it was enough of the "holy roller" business. One day when the woman appeared "with the devil looking out of her eyes," to take Jim to services, Lynetta chased her off, and kept her son at home. But for his mother's intervention, young Jim Jones might have lived the life of a child prophet like the boy marvel Marjoe Gortner.

Decisive as it was, Lynetta's rescue of her son from the throes of Pentecostalism came too late: Jim Jones already was long lost to the fascination of religion. "I recognized that my father was infinite spirit," Jones later recalled the revelation to a ten-year-old. As a young boy, Jim imitated his formal religious experiences by conducting play church services in the loft above the garage. There, in what he called "God's House," the boy experienced the awe of personal power that derives from religious office, for he established a realm where he was boss, and he managed to cajole even some of the tougher neighborhood kids into playing the parts of his parishioners. "Those that never went to church anywhere else, they'd come to his church, 'cause he'd tell 'em, that was the thing to do." If they insulted "God's House," or "if they'd get smart with him, he'd just rip the lard out of 'em." Jones's childhood services thus offered full vent to a sense of righteous indignation that warranted the use of force against sinners, recalcitrants, and detractors. Lynetta Jones remembers "doing a little eavesdropping" on Sunday mornings. "He'd point out incidences where they'd done this and that and the other thing. He'd say, 'there ain't no use to deny it; I know y'done it,'" when no one else in town knew. Pushed to explain this kind of divination, Lynetta allowed that her boy "got around like the dandelions do, y'know. But without a doubt he did have these, ah, revelations."

Jim Jones also learned the rewards of acting the cherub. The boy would cut flowers out of a neighbor's yard to place on the altar in "God's House" or to take to the sick. "He could tell when people was troubled, things like that," his mother recalled. One time, she remembered, Jim wandered into a church "half naked and with all his dogs and animals behind him" and presented flowers to a congregation that rippled with laughter at the gesture. "The preacher got so confounded mad, he says, 'I don't want to hear any more funny business. . . . There's more religion in one little finger of this child than there is in the whole town. . . . You have something in your midst that's a crackling gift from heaven.'"[12]

Despite her disdain for the "sky god," Lynetta Jones had enough sense of religion to take pride in her son's precocious gifts of the spirit. Still, she did not think he would be a minister when he grew up. For all her talk of devils and visions, she was a hardheaded woman when it came to the social question. Like other class-conscious members of the industrial proletariat,

Lynetta Jones saw "holy rollers" grasping for salvation in an ecstasy that ignored the real economic forces shaping workers' fate. If she had a faith, it was that of a "humanitarian" labor organizer: "I was never idle under these same principles that he [Jim Jones] would work on today [about 1974]. But I wouldn't put names on it. I saw people being exploited; that's where I was to try and see that didn't happen."

While Lynetta Jones struggled against the interests of management, she refused to acknowledge their superiority; in the little town of Lynn, she supposed "there was even what mighta called theirselves a social elite, which I didn't pay no heed to: who was socially elite and who wasn't." But her son apparently did notice: "He said they always tried to downgrade him." Her own steamy resentment of her supposed betters seems to have rubbed off on him. From all accounts, young Jim Jones did well enough in school, "when he was interested," as Lynetta put it. But he was an outsider, who turned into a rebel because, as he said later, he was born "on the wrong side of the tracks," and therefore "was never accepted."[13]

Jim Jones participated in the evolution of his own alienation. Spoiled and obstinate from infancy, he invited rejection by the cultivation of rude manners and a certain mean streak. By the age of six, he was walking down the streets of Lynn, shouting obscenities. Despite his mother's concern for him and the neighbors' interest in his religious culture, Jones later said he "didn't have any love given to me; I didn't know what the hell love was." With his mother out working to earn their keep, he felt abandoned at a school function when "everybody's fucking parent was there but mine." Likewise, the boy found he was "going to all the churches and still not being accepted."

Only the Pentecostal church impressed him. There he recalled he found something he found nowhere else, a "setting of freedom of emotion." Nor was it lost on Jones that this one source of warmth came from "the most despised rejects of the community." These members of the social outgroup gave him a spiritual home, and though he claimed he "intellectually outgrew" their religion, he recognized their emotional bonds as a haven from the coldness of the world, formed on the basis of a freedom that came from collective alienation from conventional society.

In his high school years Jim Jones dressed decently, succeeded in school, and dated respectable girls. A number of fellow students remember him as "quiet" and "reserved." They knew he was serious about religion, although one girl remembered that "he never tried to push it on anyone. He wasn't a fanatic. He was popular, but he wasn't a leader."

Jim Jones's increasingly studious and upwardly mobile posture promised to fulfill his mother's hopes for her only child. He continued an earlier pattern of reading widely, and he studied religion, medicine, and world affairs. At the end of his junior year, his mother and father finally separated after years of an estranged relationship. Young Jim moved with his mother to Richmond, seventeen miles south of Lynn, where she began dating a mechanic whose marriage was on the skids. From Richmond it seemed Jones eventually would enter into some professional training, perhaps related to medicine. As the Richmond high school yearbook put it when he graduated in 1949, "Jim's six-syllable medical vocabulary astounds us all."[14]

But the outward success in high school belies a consistent inner struggle Jim Jones experienced up to and into those years. Both the accounts of people who knew him and his own reminiscences in the fall of 1977 reveal the meaningful linkages between his character as a youth and the embattled Peoples Temple of the late 1970s. In his memory, while he was growing up there were really only two significant kinds of people—those who were against him, and those who were with him. Apart from his Pentecostal experience, Jones found precious few people who befriended him in a meaningful way. He often got into feuds with authorities. One time, he remembered his first grade teacher's labeling him "abnormal" for having "the hots" for a little girl named Mildred. In the fifth grade, a teacher "shamed" and "berated" him for supposedly cheating.

By both his own account and as others remember him, Jim Jones was an aggressive type: "I was ready to kill by the end of the third grade. I mean, I was so fucking hostile and aggressive, I was ready to kill." By the sixth grade, Jones grandly recalled, he "was considered the big, bad, mean motherfucker." He said that one summer day that year he had found a "rich kid" bullying kids at the swimming hole, holding their heads under water; Jim turned the tables on the boy, and "damned near drowned him."

When people tried to challenge Jim Jones on his conduct, he either turned and amplified aggression against them or he ran away. His recollections made in 1977 suggest that from early in his childhood, he carried a good-sized chip on his shoulder and expected people to mistreat him. When he entered the fourth grade classroom for the first time, he recalled thinking, "Okay bitch, do what all the rest of them do, make an ass out of me." He hated the public embarrassment he felt when teachers faulted him on academic performance, and he sometimes took revenge by devious routes. One opponent seems to have tried to break Jim of his aggression by responding in kind: his male sixth grade teacher supposedly tried to force him out a second-story window; the boy got loose but still received a "whaling" in the principal's office. The whole incident was too much for him, and he ran away to his aunt's in Logansport, only to be confronted with the indignity of parents who did not care to come and get him.

Another time, in high school, Jones said a teacher called him out because his "workbook wasn't neat enough." The woman went on to criticize the girl behind him for being too poor to wear clean socks, and finished up by "bragg[ing] on this prissy assed . . . rich kid: 'His workbook's so neat.'" As Jones later described his own response, he secretly stole all the workbooks to take revenge against a "grading system . . . correlated with the class system."

The incidents may be only isolated, and some of Jones's stories may be apocryphal, but they all fit together in his memory. As a child, Jim was "White trash," suffered for it, and had to fight for the dignity of it, both with his peers and with his teachers. In this alien world inhabited by hostile authority figures and well-to-do sissies and bullies, a few people stood out in his mind as different. Those who complimented him, who supported him, who accepted him, he deemed in memory wise and warm. One teacher did not treat him as an outcast; instead she told him, "if anybody can be a leader, you *must* be." Jones regarded the woman as "a catalyst for a sense of loyalty." Likewise, he remembered the solidarity of his high school gang. "They were the motliest crew in the fucking town. I had the sickest ones, the craziest ones." They were "never invited to any of the socialite affairs," but young Jones stole supplies so they could have parties in style.

Later, when he moved to Richmond before finishing high school, Jim Jones recalled how he worked as an orderly at Reid Memorial Hospital and neglected to charge poor patients for supplies used in their care. He praised the head nurse because "she covered for me, and she *knew* I was doing that shit." Looking back on his youth, Jones thought well of those who stood up for him, stood with him, saw his "true" motives, and covered for him in the face of opponents. He had come to value power and loyalty.[15]

The same concerns marked his youthful sense of international politics. His mother warned him not to "throw your pearls before swine," but her son dabbled with fascist ideas. He also became enamored of Stalin and the Soviets because of their heroic stand against the Nazis at Stalingrad. Jones was led to begin reading about communism when the United States turned against the Soviet government at the end of World War II. As he later described his reaction to the U.S. policy shift, "This is one loyal fucker; you don't just twist me and turn me like that."[16]

The autobiographical accounts of the young Jim Jones's feuds and loyalties on a personal and international scale must be understood as part psychological projection onto his memory by a man who by 1977 was deeply immersed in similar kinds of social struggles. But the accounts also happen to echo similar chords of resentment in Jones's mother about her husband's family, about her proletarian status, and about the social elite of

Lynn. Jones was caught from birth in the modern industrial wasteland of capitalism—the Great Depression. His mother gave him to believe that he was every bit as good as the next person, but his status in the social world of White Protestant Indiana told him otherwise. A world of righteousness could be gauged only by his personal station in it. Like his mother, and even at an early age, Jones deeply resented his social fate. He had no ready place in the world. He did not even have the substantial support of family and community that people of privilege (and even the established poor) could fall back upon when the going got rough. Nor was Lynetta's son predisposed to any kind of physical labor. As his mother put it, "He didn't know nothing about that; if he did, he kept it in the dark."[17]

Jim Jones would have to live by his wits. If he was to fulfill his mother's hopes for him, he would have to pull himself up by the bootstraps. He did so by a route well traveled for such purposes among the wavering masses from the rural mid-South: he became a minister.

# 2

# The Preacher

As a preacher Jim Jones forged a religion for the *déclassé*, people who no longer accepted the existing class and ethnic structuration of U.S. society. To understand what this entailed, we need to consider briefly the social stratification of salvation.

Religions of the privileged classes typically assure their participants that salvation and grace are their due. Their worldly success is taken as a sign of their spiritual grace; charity, as fulfillment of their Christian duty. The less affluent classes may try to mimic these assurances of the more privileged by seeking guarantees of their own salvation in congregations that emphasize sobriety, self-denial, and respectability. By contrast, people who see their status either as beyond personal control or beyond social judgment, especially economically marginal people of the lower classes, may seek spiritual wealth in an ecstatic religion of submission to the instantaneous sense of grace. The spirit in one's heart and the warmth of others in a congregation offer some compensation for the travails of this world. This is what the Pentecostals of Lynn sought.

But there is another path: if the religiously inspired see their material salvation as contingent on altering conditions in this world, they may seek to reconstitute the social order. So it was in Europe during the Middle Ages when scores of messiahs came forward, ready to lead whomever would follow on quests to establish the kingdom of God on earth. In one such case, while Martin Luther took a more politic approach toward the Church, Thomas Münzer received direct revelation from God that the time to prepare for the Second Coming was at hand; the elect, those who felt "the living Christ," were to rise up and vanquish evil so that the Lord could begin his millennial reign. It happened that the elect most easily could be found in the ranks of the poor. The wealthy and powerful princes, on the other hand, were the very embodiment of evil, and as such, in Münzer's view, they had to be exterminated.

In the modern world Münzer's sort of revolutionary attitude has been displaced by revivalism and a more conservative "born-again" movement. Politically, it has given way to secular ideology, predominantly Marxism.

15

But Jim Jones took a different course, one that recombined the previously divergent religious and secular tendencies in a revolutionary religious posture.[1]

## The Call

Childhood experiences served as good schooling for the budding preacher. By his high school days, Jim Jones parlayed the brash self-aggrandizement of his garage-loft "play" services into a more conventional evangelical posture. Sometimes the handsome young man would travel down to Richmond, a much larger industrial and college town seventeen miles south of Lynn, to hold forth on a street corner in a poor neighborhood dotted with factories. There he preached brotherhood to a small crowd, half Blacks, half Whites.

At the hospital orderly job he took after moving to Richmond, Jim Jones met Marceline Baldwin, a young nursing student from a local family of Methodists and Republicans. Marcie was quite taken with the sensitive way the young orderly dealt with the corpse of a deceased patient. Jones then wooed his intended "diligently," as she put it. Later she would tease him that she consented to marriage "to get rid of you." The two were married June 12, 1949, after Jones finished his first semester at Indiana University in Bloomington.

By the time they took up life together in Bloomington, Jim had revealed sacrilege that shocked Marcie and religious conviction that filled her with pride. At a Bloomington church meeting the young college student stood up and railed at the hypocrisy of Christians with Cadillacs. Another time the newlyweds were fighting over religion, and Marcie pleaded, "I love you, but don't you say anything about the Lord anymore." "Fuck the Lord," her husband retorted. Eventually, things came to a head for the young Methodist nurse.

By Jones's account, he was associating with Communists, who told him, "Don't become a member of the Party; work for the Party." Marcie's husband's communist convictions made her think she was "married to the Anti-Christ—personified," her husband later recalled. While they were out driving one day, she demanded, "Either you change your ideology, or get out of this car." Jim Jones opened the door and got out: "I said to myself, 'This marriage is broken. I'm not giving up my ideology for you or anyone else.'" His wife drove up shortly and let him back in the car, perhaps thereby symbolically capitulating to her husband. Jones won the allegiance of his wife, and his marriage took a backseat to his unusual convictions, wherever they might lead.

One place they led was to Indianapolis, where Jim and Marcie moved in 1951 when he shifted from business to a social science emphasis and thought about attending law school. But it would take another ten years before he finally received a college degree, from Butler University.[2]

Another place they led was to Communist rallies, including one in Chicago where the Black singer and Communist party notable Paul Robeson held forth. Both Jim Jones and his mother remember the harassment his mother and his wife's family received in the fever of the McCarthy era because he and Marceline went to the rally. The experience, he recalled, deepened his commitment. The stigma of the "red menace" notwithstanding, he wondered, "How can I demonstrate my Marxism? The thought was, 'infiltrate the church.'"

Though there is no doubt that Jones flirted with communist ideas in his high school and college days, aside from his own accounts, there is no confirmation of the communist inspiration he felt to become a "professional good man." Jones himself remembered that the earthly call came in a used-car lot by way of an invitation from a Methodist district superintendent named Martin. In the summer of 1952 Jones became student pastor at Sommerset Southside Methodist Church on Keystone Avenue in the hillbilly migrant section of Indianapolis. Even though Marcie said her husband "knew the Bible from beginning to end," she recalled a distinctly unorthodox approach. Jim "was eager to awaken people to the humanity of Jesus and to let them know that what Jesus was, they could be also. . . . He said there must be no creed but the helping ministry of Christ and no law but the law of love."

For the new preacher, "an inclusive congregation . . . was the first big issue." He started right out preaching integration, and soon brought Blacks into the church. For some reason Jones thought Pentecostalists would be more accepting of Blacks. He may have been aware of the interracial heritage of the Pentecostal movement. Maybe some of Randolph County's few Blacks had worshiped at the Pentecostal services he attended in his childhood. In any event he attracted some Pentecostalists to his services, and started "preaching integration, against war, mixing in a little Pentecostal crap, . . . and throwing in some communist philosophy." With his new followers, he tried to take the church out of the Methodist Conference, but the Pentecostalists in Indianapolis, many of them postwar migrants from rural Kentucky and Tennessee, were not much more ready for integration than the Methodists, and in the circus that ensued the Methodists kicked him out.

In the aftermath Jones went to a Seventh Day Baptist Church and took in healing services. He thought, "'These assholes, doing nothing with this thing.' I couldn't see nobody healed." But the experience convinced him that healing had its advantages: "You can get the crowd, get some money, and do some good with it." Jones could not believe the Baptists had a monopoly on the power: "If these sons of bitches can do it," he argued to himself, "then I can do it too." His first attempt at healing "didn't work out too well," but he watched closely and somehow developed the necessary techniques and powers.

About a year later Jones was introduced at a Columbus, Indiana, "Latter Rain" Pentecostal church convention. A woman Pentecostal Holiness minister dressed all in white called him out and anointed him with the words: "I perceive that you are a prophet that shall go around the world. . . . And tonight ye shall begin your ministry." His wife was amazed when Jones came forth and "called people out by name and by their Social Security number, and by their disease and their illness, and marvelous healings took place." Here the ministry of Jones really began, but he did not simply adopt one of the ready-made evangelical styles widely available in his day. Instead, he amalgamated diverse techniques and insights and forged a powerful movement out of the contradictions with which he reckoned in his own social milieu.[3]

The Quakers of his father's family always had favored the "inner light" of divine inspiration over dogmatic attachment to doctrine. However little they influenced Jim Jones, his childhood experience of their services could hardly have countered his own aversion toward formal theology. Perhaps his mother inadvertently reinforced the spiritual path of Jones with her denigrations of the "sky god," her world animated by spirit forces, and her seemingly homegrown Puritanism.

For their part, the Pentecostalists offered warmth and dynamism and divine gifts, and Jones took them. But he radicalized Pentecostal theology in two ways. First, he used widespread Pentecostal millennial expectations of the second coming of Christ to proclaim the divinity in himself and, potentially, in those who followed him. He carried the principle of ecstatic faith prevalent in Pentecostalism to its extreme antinomian conclusion, that the person filled of the spirit *is* God and need not be, in fact must not be, subjected to the dead law of morality. Second, he pushed the "holy rollers" out of their own matrix, ostensibly by carrying their legacy to its own (Christian) communalist conclusions.

The real drift of Jones's moves was toward the social question of how this-worldly salvation is dispensed according to race and class in a modern industrial capitalist society. Here Jones transported his mother's political "religion" of class struggle into the particularly potent arena of evangelical religion. By doing so, he capped an already radical approach to religion with a messianic fervor that devolved from his mother's stance of resentment toward the social order.

If resentment is merely personal, it amounts to a particularly bitter form of envy, with little effect beyond the circle of family, friends, and acquaintances who contend with it. But resentment certified with the stamp of religious justification is another matter altogether. As sociologist Max Weber has explained, when personal suffering is no longer explained as "God's will," the religious ethic of the disprivileged "teaches that the unequal distribution of mundane goods is caused by the sinfulness and the illegality of the privileged, and that sooner or later God's wrath will overtake them. In this theodicy of the disprivileged, the moralistic quest serves as a device for compensating a conscious or unconscious desire for vengeance." Thus, Jim Jones channeled personal experiences of resentment into a social movement. He saw himself as an outcast, he saw the poor and Blacks in the United States as outcasts, and he forged a pariah people from among their numbers. Perhaps he sought vengeance all his life.[4]

## The Gifts of Pentecost

Doctrinally, it is fair to say that Jones was a radicalized Pentecostal preacher, conversant with fundamentalist theological debates, proficient in Pentecostal practices. The rage among Pentecostalists (now more widely shared in the "born-again" movement) has always been demonstration of the gifts of the spirit described in 1 Corinthians 12: the word of wisdom, the word of knowledge, faith, gifts of healing, working of miracles, prophecy, discerning of spirits, diverse tongues, and the interpretation of tongues. 1 Corinthians held that "the manifestation of the Spirit is given to every man to profit withal," and that the gifts would devolve "to every man severally as he will." Jim Jones claimed all nine gifts, but he steered away from the Pentecostals' preoccupation with speaking in tongues as the definitive sign of baptism in the Holy Spirit. Mostly he concentrated on discerning, healing, and prophesying.

Discerning of spirits may be understood as knowing the thoughts and dilemmas of others, but from the earliest days of the Pentecostal movement, simple knowledge of concrete but secret facts about an individual, such as a Social Security number, has been taken as sufficient proof of discernment. For this reason, the movement sometimes has provided sanctuary for mediums, mystics, and outright charlatans. But even hardened skeptics sometimes have been impressed by Pentecostalist discernment, eyewashing as it can be.

From the very beginning Jim Jones demonstrated his discernment. At the Columbus, Indiana, convention, Jones later recalled, "I closed my eyes. And all this shit flys through my mind and I call it out. And I had people coming up, screaming and hollering." He did not stop at telling people their

Social Security numbers. "He'd call people out in the crowd and tell them to go down to the corner, make a right turn or something, and there'd be a Nestle wrapper laying in the gutter, and under that Nestle wrapper was some kind of colored stone." Jones admitted that he soon employed deceit, but steadfastly declared that at first he carried the burden alone: "then I didn't have no help. Really. Nothing. Just close my eyes . . . and call. Such a drain. It got so heavy. 'Jesus Christ,' I thought, 'I can't stand this.' Wasn't too long before I started taking little notes. For years and years it was me, and my gift, and whatever [notes] I could take down."

Eventually there would be a special Peoples Temple staff whose job it was to come up with information for "discernment" purposes. They would sift through garbage cans, enter houses under false pretenses, "noting anything personal in the house, like addresses on letters, types of medicine . . . , or pictures of relatives" to obtain information seemingly so obscurely personal that those called out were convinced Jones could not possibly know it, save through true discernment.[5]

Healing also was important. Jim Jones specialized, notably in passed "cancers." From the beginning, he later admitted, deception was a key element: "People pass growths and then by sleight of hand I started doing it—and that would trigger others to get healed. It was kind of a catalyst process, to build faith." Here Jones deviated from conventional Pentecostal practice, though he was certainly not the first to perform dramatic healings. In the early 1900s a more conventional Pentecostalist believer asserted that he had "had the following diseases: cancer, tumor, heart disease, asthma, catarrh of bronchial tubes, rheumatism, and kidney trouble . . . and am now perfectly well." Other healers, too, have caused elderly ladies confined in wheelchairs to jump up and run around tents. Nor was Jones alone in his claims to raise the dead, although he may have been the first to come up with the idea of having a perfectly sound leg bone placed in a plaster cast so that it could be removed after a faith healing.

Turning from the issue of promotional deceit to a consideration of the standards of Pentecostal healing practices, we find that Jones was something of a moderate. Some Pentecostals consider medical treatment taboo, and at least one preacher was convicted of manslaughter by criminal negligence when his healing prayers failed to produce results for a sixteen-year-old diabetic who stated he would rather die if he could not be cured by the power of prayer. Baton Rouge, Louisiana, evangelist Jimmie Swaggart has hedged on the issue, suggesting a spiritually healed person should consult a doctor to confirm the healing before stopping a medical regimen, but also affirming, "Now if God *specifically* says to stop taking medicine, by all means do so and trust the Lord Jesus Christ." Jones was considerably less willing to trust in divine intervention by itself. He eventually followed a carefully constructed legal disclaimer, and he frequently emphasized that spiritual healing was not necessarily a substitute for medical treatment: "If you've got a spiritual healing, go get it confirmed. Keep on with the doctor. If it can stand the test of empiricism, fine. . . ."

Legal niceties aside, the preacher put his all into the healing effort; he recalled, "I was a dogged person; I'd fight every goddamn case. I was different from every other healer because I wouldn't ignore the hardship cases." Even granting his own fraud, Jones was convinced that he had the power of healing, "but," as he said, "how it works, shit, I don't know." Publicly Jones developed a sense of awe about life and its precarious possibilities of accident and disease. He did not claim to be all-powerful, but he understood that many episodes of life lie beyond rational control of modern medicine, and he played upon a similar perception on the part of followers who could not care two whits whether modern science could "explain" the death of loved ones. Jones understood the existential predicaments of life, and acted to intervene on behalf of the afflicted.

Apparently, Jim Jones's techniques brought results. At the very least he convinced people that they had been healed by his hand of everything from bad hearing and poor eyesight to Hodgkin's disease, thrombophlebitis, and breast cancer. Some of the healings undoubtably were simply resuscitations of worshipers who, as sometimes happens in Pentecostal services, became so caught up in the ecstasy that they either suffered catatonic collapses or experienced motor phenomena (sometimes described as being "slain in the spirit" and having "the jerks," at least since the notable outbreak of such phenomena at the Cane Ridge camp meeting that took place in Kentucky in 1800 to 1801).

Most people who spoke publicly about Jim Jones's healing powers either had been gulled by his sleight of hand, or they were making testimonials to promote his ministry, or both. But his mother, who was somewhat cynical about Jones's other "gifts," would readily relate that her son had struggled to pull her out of death's grip once when she was on the hospital operating table. Even Dorothy Hunter, the wife of Disciples of Christ official Barton Hunter, guardedly suggested that Jones's "hokum" aside, he could produce results with a person whose condition "had no major physiological basis." Barton Hunter, somewhat more skeptical, nevertheless agreed that Jones "did make radical changes in the lives of some people."

Some individuals who came to be Jones's strongest detractors also perceived healing powers beyond the fraud. Consider Edith Parks, a woman who defected from Jonestown during Representative Leo Ryan's visit. Even after the mass suicide, she defended Jones on the question. "People laugh about the healing," she admitted. ""But he helped me. I had cancer that had metastasized and the doctor said I had just a matter of months.

But I got stronger and stronger. So you kind of hang around somebody who does something like that for you."[6]

Not only did Jim Jones heal, not only did he discern the past and present, he foretold the future. Here again the preacher used a standard revivalist ploy. He might describe the miracles he had performed elsewhere so that foreseen tragedies could be averted, or *after* events had occurred, he would reveal that he had had "premonitions" about them. Thus, in 1959 his four-year-old adopted Korean daughter and four adult members of Peoples Temple were returning from an exchange service in Cincinnati when they died in a nighttime head-on collision on the highway. To a news reporter Jones remarked, "For some strange reason, I told [the congregation] that some of our people will never be back." Years later, in 1977, Jones could add even more confirmation of his eerie powers by recalling the song they sang at the Cincinnati service: "On up the road/ Far in the distance/ I saw a light, shining in the night . . ./ Then I knew. . . ." As they finished singing, Jones called out a woman named Mabel, and she shot up and rushed to the door in the middle of the service. As she left, Jones remembered calling out "the name of a town, a name that meant nothing to me. It turned out to be the name of the town where the death came. . . ."

Carnival prophecy tricks aside, Jones seems to have had a special knack for "seeing through" people. He developed a sensitivity to their situations, motives, and dilemmas, and he could make predictions about their fortunes by extrapolating from what he knew. Perhaps many of us could do the same, at least with people we know intimately. Indeed, we probably do as much in gossip with friends. Sometimes too, our desire to know the future calls into play less personal, more "rationalized" methods of fortune-telling. Such standardized methods of divination—like astrology, the I Ching, Tarot cards, for example—show that highly relevant individual meaning can be read off from particular constellations of generalized symbols.

Like many Pentecostal preachers before him, Jones harnessed the possibilities inherent in personal knowledge and general symbols in a particularly powerful way by discerning publicly, where others could witness him. The person "called out" would have to struggle with life's dilemmas amidst a community of believers who would witness subsequent events in the context of Jones's prophesy. There was the case, for example, of the spiritually attuned Bonnie Thielmann, who had entertained serious suicidal thoughts. Sometimes on the way to work she would fail to stop at a railroad crossing, hoping a train would hit her. In the middle of a Los Angeles service one day, Jones pointed to her and demanded, "I want you to start stopping at that sign and quit this suicidal death wish."[7]

By taking a position about the future of individuals, Jones came to personify fate, the forces that are taken to determine the outcome of events before they are completed. Persons who fought their destiny would struggle with crystallizations of that destiny formulated by Jones. If it turned out that he had been correct, his psychic powers were demonstrated unequivocally, but whether he was right or wrong in a given case hardly mattered. If he prophesied evil, and evil failed to occur, persons could take heart and perhaps believe that the intervention had shifted the grounds of struggle to their advantage. If he foretold good, and it did not come to pass, they could commiserate together, or maybe wonder whether the person had failed to live up to the possibilities Jones had foreseen. Whatever the outcome, Jones became powerful in people's minds by publicly offering a ritualized dramatization of their personal struggles.

Jim Jones's stock evangelist tricks of discernment, the powers of healing, and the psychic abilities claimed by and for him hardly distinguish this preacher from countless others in the Pentecostal tradition. What set Jones apart was his gift of prophecy concerning the social world and his people in it.

## Beyond Pentecost

For all his gifts, Jones parted company from conventional Pentecostal revivalists by radicalizing their doctrines. Pentecostalists frequently have anticipated Christ's imminent Second Coming, that is, *before* the Millennium (such doctrines are designated "premillennialist" by religious scholars). This stand has helped swell Pentecostal ranks with people who seek the Pentecostal experience of speaking in tongues as a definitive sign of their baptism in the Holy Spirit, in order to be "ready" for Christ's appearance.

Like the Reverend Sun Myung Moon and other would-be modern messiahs, Jones proclaimed the long anticipated Second Coming in himself as the most highly evolved contemporary manifestation of the Spirit of Christ. "I say I am a Savior," he once put it, "but don't make me your creator." Ready dismissals of Jones suggest that his declaration amounted to little more than crude and self-serving blasphemy, but such dismissals seem too facile. It has to be recognized that Jones harnessed Christian theology's revolutionary potential by stripping away conventional doctrines and rationales of worship in favor of a return to the "living" church that is at the historic core of Christianity. In doing so, he took a path used more than once over the centuries, and followed it out of modern Pentecostalism, back to the radical ministry of Jesus and the communalism of apostolic Christianity. By thus establishing a religious social movement, over the years Jones was able to align the intense form of religious zeal prevalent during the primitive Christian era with the central concerns of the modern age: race, class, and nuclear holocaust.

Even in the early years, when many people came for the healing alone, Jim Jones was preaching a "progressive doctrine." As Dorothy Hunter interpreted Jones's strategy, though he did not intellectually believe in the faith healings and other revivalist practices, he used them as a "tool," "to enlarge his following so there would be more money and more people to have an impact on the community, so the poor would be helped, et cetera." A man who left a Pentecostal ministry in the early 1950s to become Jones's associate pastor, Jack Beam, recalled that Jones would "remov[e] people's expectations from heaven into a here and now," emphasizing the passage in the Lord's Prayer, "on Earth as it is in Heaven." "He was bringin' 'em to 'there was a responsibility now,' and you could not use an escape program of heaven to bring about any social change, . . . because we had been conditioned under capitalism to always put off: 'things cannot always be this way; they'll get better.'"

Jones first had become interested in the possibility of a ministerial career when his wife Marcie, born a Methodist, showed him a church bulletin board notice that indicated the denomination's support of racial integration. Jones thereby stumbled onto another horn of the American Protestant dilemma: the counterpoint to Pentecostalism. The Methodist Church (North) in 1908 had been the first denomination to adopt the liberal "Social Creed" formulated out of the social gospel movement efforts to work for a new system called "Christian socialism." Ironically, the liberal Protestant movement toward the social gospel concern with poverty, factory working conditions, and the like as "social sins" may have been among the factors propelling the Holiness movement, foreshadowing Pentecostalism, to depart from the Methodist fold in the first place. Earlier in the nineteenth century, the two doctrines of personal holiness and societal improvement had been linked in the shared theme of "perfectionism," but the Holiness and Pentecostal theologies tended to displace societal perfection until after the Second Coming, while mainstream Methodists rejected the Holiness movement that emerged from within their ranks because it failed to keep abreast of social conditions and modern thought. Yet for all the liberal Protestant concerns about the plight of the poor and destitute, lower-class individuals themselves tended to find the Holiness and Pentecostal person-to-person welfare coupled with promises of future salvation far more attractive than the social gospel that helped shape the bureaucratic welfare state of corporate liberalism.

By the post-World War II period, capitalism had been consolidated anew in the aftermath of the depression and the international war for control of the world economy. By then, with the growth of the atheistic worldwide communist movement, mainstream Protestants themselves were re-evaluating theology.

Preaching the social gospel, Jones personified the worst fears of the more conservative clergy and FBI director J. Edgar Hoover in the McCarthy era: pulpits were being infiltrated by Communists, sometimes using Black rights as a rallying cry for a movement of communist agitation for the cause of a collective society. But Jones did so by reuniting the divergent nineteenth-century streams of social versus individual perfectionism, represented in the schism between the liberal Protestants on the one hand and the Holiness and Pentecostal movements on the other. For Jones, liberal Protestantism itself was inadequate because its very liberality prevented direct intervention in the social struggle on the side of the poor and the dispossessed. Nevertheless, the social gospel would be useful if it could be employed liturgically to radicalize social aspirations of fundamentalist and Holiness and Pentecostal people that long since had been displaced to the expected, but always receding Second Coming.[8]

Jones began his ministerial career in a Methodist church, and he began by emphasizing the social gospel. As Barton and Dorothy Hunter remember him in the 1950s, both behind the pulpit and in their home, Jones was "very much concerned about racial integration, about the poor." According to Dorothy Hunter, "He was strong on peace, even then," and despite his doubts about any supernatural deity, he was "very much committed to the ethic of Jesus."

Like others before him, Jones found that the lofty ideals of a "Social Creed" notwithstanding, poor people's social movements have a different logic. The middle classes may be able to draw on small contributions from a broad spectrum of morally concerned citizens to fund cohesive, professionally administered organizations directed to long-term pursuit of policy goals, but the dispossessed have more pressing needs. If they take part at all in social movements, they seem more attracted to those that offer immediate rewards and the potential for decisive rather than gradual change.[9]

The form that such a movement would take, at the hands of Jim Jones, roughly paralleled the primitive Christian Church. By 1959 Jones was telling his congregation that they should read on in the New Testament's book of Acts, not just stopping in the second chapter, with the gifts of the spirit. Further along, in Acts 4:31–32, they would find "them that believed were of one heart and of one soul: neither said any of them that aught of the things which he possessed were his own; but they had all things in common." The believers were said to have sold their properties and pooled their wealth with the apostles, whereupon "Distribution was made unto every man according as he had need" (Acts 4:35).

Perhaps Karl Marx had read the New Testament as well. Certainly Jones eventually read some Marx; as his wife said, "We live by the rule of from each according to his ability and to each according to his need." In the 1950s Jones was able to legitimate his religious communalist doctrine as a way of fighting the "group mind" of secular communism, in the same stroke using the messianic proclamation of immediate redemption to infuse religion with secular communist and antiestablishment stances on the "political" questions of modern U.S. society. "In the early years," Jones recalled, "I approached Christendom from a communalist standpoint with only intermittant mention of my Marxist views. However, in later years there wasn't a person that attended my meetings that did not hear me say at some time that I was a communist."

It is as though Jones passed "through the looking glass" from ideology to utopia. He jettisoned the ideological use of religion to shore up people's hopes and aspirations in a status quo treated as inevitable, and came to view the world from a "situationally transcendent" utopian perspective. From this alienated platform, Jones was no longer limited by ideological taboos from offering a disenchanted worldview on democratic capitalist culture. Perhaps reaching back to his mother's implicitly Puritan attitude toward earthly existence as a "vale of tears," Jones fostered such a pessimism about this world that in the 1970s a Peoples Temple member could casually describe it as "this miserable damned place." Over the years Jones confronted his followers with radical views on the post-World War II world, from class inequalities, poverty, and persecution of Blacks, gays, and others, to nuclear holocaust and the role of CIA intervention in the Third World.

From the standpoint of Marxists, Jones could best be described as a "crude communist" who had little theoretical understanding of the labor theory of value, class conflict, or a host of other issues that Marxists use as touchstones for their debates and strategies. Indeed, by Jones's own account, he was an outsider: "I shall call myself a Marxist, because no one taught me my brand of Marxism. I read, I listened."[10]

Once Jones became established in his religious calling during the 1950s, his subsequent exposure to communist philosophy and causes was mediated by his religious location. Jones would flirt with radical causes and form coalitions with political groups, but the very success of his own bailiwick would always limit his interest in endorsing a purely political communist movement that would bypass his own expanding patrimonial empire. By the same token, though Jones was exposed to the New Left during the 1960s and 1970s, his own success meant he could incorporate whatever he wanted into a framework largely defined by his crude communism derived from fringe association with the Stalinist-styled pro-Soviet communist movement of the early post-World War II era.

The particular dialectical tension between Jim Jones's religious social movement and wider revolutionary movements gave rise to at least two trademarks of Jones's messianic practices: (1) an ethical orientation whereby "the ends justify the means," and (2) a liturgical style based on revivalistic embellishment of radical social critiques. First, Jones's Marxism, "frozen" in a Leninist-Stalinist orientation, fed his own predispositions, perhaps established by childhood experiences, to forge an intensely loyal, highly disciplined, and tightly controlled organization based on his own personal rulership, and guided by an ethic of total commitment to pursuit of certain ends regarded as moral absolutes, regardless of actions required for their fulfillment. Other ideas, other practices, whatever their source, whatever their utility, were filtered through a screen that separated matters of pragmatic choice from issues of absolute "principle."

Second, because Jones's communism was mediated through a Pentecostalist religious organization, he transformed Marxists' "scientific" argument about social conditions and strategies to a "liturgical" sphere of discourse. His approach was, to say the least, unusual. Most proponents of social change, Methodist ministers and Marxist revolutionaries alike, operate in a rational world of strategy and struggle that lies, as it were, distanced from the realm of everyday life. In marked contrast, Pentecostalism can work, as Hollenweger put it in a revealing analysis, "to restore the power of expression to people without identity and powers of speech, and to heal them from the terror of the loss of speech." Jones came to speak for those who followed him; he manifested their anger, hopes, and fears in witnessed social discourse that transpired on a symbolic and empathic rather than factual and intellectual level.

From the outside, Jones's liturgical discourse sometimes appeared disingenuous, deceitful, paternalistic. At a 1976 Temple demonstration in support of freedom of the press, Jones defended the presence of "elected monitors and spokespersons" because "many members feel they are inarticulate." Much earlier, in the 1950s, Disciples of Christ official Barton Hunter had chided the young preacher after he told his congregation, "God says it's a sin to buy on time." "I cornered him and said, 'Come on, Jim; God didn't speak to you.'" Jones answered, "But you've got to understand these people. If I had said, 'Well, I don't think it's a good idea for you to buy on time,' now, if you're coming up from the mountains [of Appalachia], you get into all sorts of troubles. It wouldn't have meant anything to them. I had to talk their language. Their language is 'God says.'" Hunter allowed that more conventional ministers might make the same argument, as his wife put it, "if you could get them to admit it."

Jim Jones did not abolish religious discourse, but he broke outside the topical boundaries of Pentecostalism. The communist preacher held that "in order to bring people out of their superstition you have to give them a substitute." His solution was similar to one that Black socialist preachers had used at the turn of the twentieth century: because Blacks' primary organizational experience was with the church, the way to mobilize them was through the church. Thus, Jones brought radical ideas into religion by shifting the content of metaphoric discourse away from ideologically safe conventional religious topics. He was able in this way to bend the format of the Pentecostal sermon from typical concerns with personal edification and inspiration to social, political, and economic issues portrayed in the vivid messianic terms that Pentecostalists already understood. By the standards of epic discourse, Jones explored truth by exaggerating reality. He implicitly admitted this by describing his wife in starkly contrasting terms: "Marcie would always play it straight—she was never given to embellishment, even for the sake of dynamism." Himself, Jim Jones never let the truth get in the way of a good story. His rhetorical style of preaching was such that even when his stories were factually based, to the secular ear, their liturgical frame might make them seem concocted.[11] Jones set forth the imagery of apocalypse, a perceptual rather than objective frame, by transferring the radical critique of capitalist society to liturgical statements that brought historical forces to a dramatic level where they could be experienced personally. He wove fact, half-truths, and outright lies about race, class, and the atom bomb into a theological cry for redemption.

# 3

# The Prophet

When the occasion called for it, Jim Jones could deliver his revolutionary religious message in the style of a talented and practiced evangelist. As
the advertisements on the revival circuit say, he was "dynamic," "electrifying." Using the standard device of folk preachers in the United States,
White and Black, Jones spoke extemporaneously, piecing together memo-
rized phrases, hopping from one topic to another, drawing in current
events, relating them back to his basic doctrines. Sometimes he worked off
associate pastors and shills planted in the audience who would shout out
provocations and encouragements. More often the audience itself came
forth with the "amens," the murmers, applause, and the cries that mark the
shifting tempos and spiritual possession of the revival sermon as a social
event. Throughout Jones's career, his "services" kept to this expressive format of Pentecostalism: people in the audience could speak out, in tongues
or otherwise, when they felt "the spirit."[1]

Jim Jones himself felt that spirit so strongly he claimed to be an embodiment of Christ. To others, in part because he declared himself Christ, Jones
was the Anti-Christ. Before we can hope to understand Peoples Temple, we
must explore these conflicting claims about Jones the person.

### Christ

Jones sought to deemphasize concern with the hereafter, even in the
early years, but his initial theology was not a consistent one, partly because
he was still struggling with strategies for reaching fundamentalists with a
message of the social gospel. Sometimes Jones would fall back on traditional concepts to advance his own message, but eventually he became
fairly adept at unveiling his radicalization of Pentecostal ideas, and he did
so by a theology less encumbered with contradictions. A sermon preached
at the branch Peoples Temple in Los Angeles in 1974 exemplifies Jones's
fully developed public theology. Though it has less of the spontaneous
stream-of-consciousness style of earlier or more private events, the 1974

sermon pulled together the multiple strands of discourse in a particularly coherent statement.

The berobed preacher started off that day in Los Angeles by shouting to the crowd of followers and visitors. "Anyone in America who is poor, white, brown, yellow, or black, and does not admit that he is a nigger, is a damn fool," he told them. "Because 'niggardly' means to be treated cheatedly." "You've been cheated," he screamed, and then paused to let the thought reverberate, and added in a quiet voice that broke the tension, "I turned that word around and I made it the proudest word for the chosen people; I said, 'yes, we're niggers, and we're proud.'"

Some people did not yet understand the sources of their oppression, Jones argued. "Baptist and Holiness and Church of God in Christ people" were being ripped off by pastors who pocketed donations for their own personal gain. The worst of it was, the "jackleg" preachers did not just rob their congregations materially; at the same time, they beat them down with the "dead letter" of Bible Christianity. "They won't tell you the truth because the black book is the easiest gravy train that they've ever been on," Jones warned his audience. "That black book is your enemy." Because the Bible was filled with lies and contradictions, he told his listeners again and again, true seekers needed a prophet "sent" to guide them (cf. Romans 10:15), "somebody that's got the goods, [when] all you got is phony loud-mouths, ballooned cisterns filled with hot air; all they got's a black book."

If "slophouse religion" was only a vehicle of fraud and manipulation, Jones asked himself for his listeners, "Well what am I to believe?" "Then listen to me," he replied, and entered a prophetic mode of discourse. "Said God would always speak. . . . He said, 'I will never leave you; I will never forsake you.'" Yet somehow Pentecostalists had been shortchanged; all they received was the gift of tongues, not salvation. "They testify of the living Christ, and you will never recognize him when he comes. You will not come to him, that you might have life. The scriptures are death, but the spirit of Christ. . . ." He shouted, "Hey! Hey! It's ALIVE!"

In the living spirit of the present times, Jim Jones asserted, doctrine, person, Christ all had merged in a constellation whereby he himself became a manifestation of eternal forces. He could heal, he said, as Jesus could heal. But it was not just Jim Jones, it was "the living word." Jim Jones *was* the spirit. How else could anyone "raise the dead and resurrect the people and give them freedom," as he claimed he had done? "No one can do that but God good." Jones took pains to disabuse those in the Los Angeles Temple that day of any deistic conception of God. They should understand God instead as a force manifested in worldly affairs through the agency of humans. "You call it God," he told them. "I prefer liberator, saviour, Immanuel [literally in Hebrew, 'God with us'], the saviour."

Thus, Jones claimed the platform that Jesus occupied almost two millennia earlier. "That's what I am," Jones would burst out, "the word, the spoken word! Say, 'you blasphemer!' I am doing what Jesus got nailed to the cross for doing." As Jones saw it, he was like Jesus, of whom it was said, "We don't stone you for any good work, but because you being a man, make yourself God."

Jones did not reserve the powers of the Spirit wholly to himself. He insisted to the gathered congregation, "You can be fully God; Jesus said you could" (e.g. John 10:34), but he did claim to be first among equals in the quest for the "heaven within." "We don't worship anything in the sky," he announced. "We know that always, someone will speak for God." "Someone will set themselves in the messiah's chair and declare the unsearchable riches." It was Jones himself: "You didn't know anything about a saviour until I came; some of you were living in poverty. You were in jails. You were down with the boot of the oppressor on your neck. You'd better thank Jim for the saviour." Jones proclaimed that eventually, "all shall know, from the least to the greatest, the knowledge of the revolution of God. . . . But first you better follow someone. . . . Can you raise the dead? . . . Then, until you can, follow me! . . . because I have come in the very person, I have come in the very nature, I have come in the person of Christ the Revolution!" he thundered to roaring applause.

Having established his outlook and credentials, the black-haired prophet in dark glasses unveiled the path. The way would not be easy, he allowed. People would oppose what they were doing. Still, it was better, even on rational grounds, to join this cause than to suffer the alternative: "There will be famine where people will be in souplines ten miles long." Chaos and race war were coming to the United States, Jones prophesied, because changes in organization of production meant "they don't need poor workers anymore." Weaving factual information with innuendo, he painted a grim picture. A disproportionate number of Blacks had died in the Vietnam war, he said. Mexican mothers were given a cancer-producing drug as "medicine." The Los Angeles Police Department was filling its street force with "rookies from Mississippi." What about the Jews, Jones asked. "The Jews were chosen people. But seven million of them were exterminated in gas ovens." The preacher would not even authorize ordinary maintenance expenditures for church properties, "'cause trouble's coming to this land." "We've got to get ourselves ready for a great day. We've got no time . . . , 'cause I *know* what's ahead."

In a rising rhythm of joy, he exhorted the congregation to join him, to escape the apocalypse. "I've got shelter for you in depression, food in our warehouses and our storehouses. . . ." "We've got hope," he told them, describing arrangements to escape Babylon. "We've got refuge in the time

of storm! My! Hallelujah! Freedom!" he shouted out, offering his life as
their life, telling them, "whatever I have, you have." A crescendo of the
spirit possessed him as he affirmed again all that he had said: "This has
been the truth. Glory, glory, glory! Once you get it, you'll be thankful in
your heart, you'll be grateful because it'll set you free like you've never been
free in your life." In triumphant tones he affirmed, "You'll come out under
the yoke of bondage, and you'll have to look down to no one. You'll be able
to look everyone straight in the eyes, because you have a city, oh yes you
have! You have a Promised Land!"[2]

Thus in a 1974 Los Angeles service did Jones offer a prophetic account of
the oppressed, their plight, their redemption. Institutionalized religion had
kept them down, blinded them from seeing the salvation that was at hand.
There was no reward in heaven, but the fulfillment of Christ consciousness
on earth. For this simple but radical assertion that threatened established
religions, people of the Spirit would be persecuted, even as poor "niggers"
became economically superfluous. There would be no place for them in
"this" world: they would have to band together and fend for themselves.
Foreclosing the avenue of Bible Christianity, demonstrating the powers that
proved him the modern messiah, warning of troubles to come in the
United States, Jim Jones offered up his own extended family, his Peoples
Temple, as a way out.

Jones was less concerned with the niceties of theology than with persuading those who came into his orb to join his movement. Still, the ideas he
promoted placed him at a critical point of synthesis between the divergent
social gospel and Holiness-Pentecostal strands of Protestant perfectionism.
Jones thereby unleashed latent revolutionary possibilities of Judeo-Christian religion in his own messianic vision of the late capitalist apocalypse.
Somehow, the culture of resentment of his mother and his own youth
would later infuse this synthesis with a quest for religiously sanctified revenge.

## Anti-Christ

Whatever theological coherence may be granted to Jones's preaching, the
man is often characterized as mad, or as a power-hungry pragmatist and a
self-serving cynic and fraud. Many Christians have denounced Jones's con-
ceits, and suggested that his religion was a sham. As Jones prophesied to his
followers, he came to be regarded as the Anti-Christ.[3] This view of the man
himself warrants our attention before we trace the history of his movement, for it has served as a keystone of previous accounts of Jonestown. As
I will suggest, Jones was not a charlatan, and so far as madness and religion
are concerned, what matters is not what labels might be attached to Jones

as a person; rather, we must understand the social consequences of his character for the history of Peoples Temple.

Two broad claims are made about Jones as a person: those about his religion, and more basic suggestions that his actions stem from other than religious provenience in the first place. The latter arguments—that he was a charlatan and a madman—would make consideration of charges about Jones's religiosity moot, and so they need to be addressed first.

Charlatans seem to choose religion as a perennially favored vehicle. The several reasons are transparent. First, religion deals in that which is "sacred" to individuals and communities. Its practitioners thereby gain access to the most intimate knowledge of their clients' situations and help them face the most emotionally disturbing events of life. Religion is thus a "skin trade," that is, an arena in which successful professional activity depends on the lowering of role distance that individuals typically maintain with persons outside their primary groups.[4] Religion, particularly the minister-client relation, permits an unusual form of intimacy based on trust that derives from the presumed sharing of a moral world.

Second, the religious practitioner is granted a legitimacy practically unparalleled in human affairs. Religious practitioners' claims of divine authority have become so completely institutionalized that many believers defer habitually to that authority when it offers pronouncements or makes demands. This tendency varies, of course, with the religion, and is virtually absent in consciously anticlerical organizations such as traditional Quaker meetings. In general, though, when a religious authority issues a command, believers disregard it only at their own hazard, and likely with feelings of anxiety and guilt. Religion thus confers authority otherwise hard to come by.

Third, the con artist can traffic in religious ideas relatively easily because the religious practitioner deals in the most opaque areas of cultural interpretation. Whether the concerns are about "this" world or the "other" world, religion confronts existential problems of meaning that typically lie beyond purely factual adjudication. It is easier to catch a man cheating at poker than it is to bring suit against a religious practitioner for making misleading statements about the Hereafter. What constitutes "fraud" thus is by definition very difficult to pin down.

Fourth, people often are willing to part with significant sums of money in the name of religion for existential reasons—fears concerning salvation, senses of religious responsibility, desires to leave "monuments" to their Godliness, or, under certain Internal Revenue Service codes, as tax deductions. Furthermore, it is possible for those on the receiving end of the offerings to embezzle or "kick back" funds without easily being caught. The Internal Revenue Service has a difficult time keeping track of the flow of "religious" dollars, and religious work thus serves as a convenient "front."

Finally, the con artist can enter the religious trade fairly easily. The tools are not so difficult to come by, especially outside the more centralized denominations and churches. In fact, professing religious expertise without training sometimes is taken as a mark of truly divine inspiration, and numerous religious organizations offer opportunities for lay preaching. In short, the boundaries between authoritative professionals, inspired lay people, and outright pretenders are difficult to establish, and professing religious authority can be based upon little more than a determined shift in one's presentation of self.[5]

Easy as it is to understand how religion affords such opportunities for hustlers, it is equally difficult to spot them, for exactly the same reasons. But the list of swindlers, if it is kept by God's angels someplace, must be a long one! Though most cases are arguable, as a social type the outright charlatan establishes a benchmark of comparison. One Charles Thompson, a nineteenth century self-proclaimed man of God, comes close to the mark. Thompson stumbled upon the possibilities of prophecy in the quasi-Old Testament style of the Church of Jesus Christ of Latter-Day Saints, or Mormons. He then established a communal settlement in Iowa—Preparation—as the vehicle of his schemes. Few religious practitioners have come close to the single-minded persistence that Thompson demonstrated in defrauding hapless followers of their property. He dreamed up a never-ending high-sounding series of revelations that required his settlers to sign over their property and give their savings to their leader. Whatever the occasion, a revelation from Baneemy—Thompson's name for the spirit successor to Joseph Smith—was produced, tailor-made. But the illusion finally stretched too thin, and burst, and the prophet was forced to flee from the outraged victims of his schemes.[6]

Most charlatans are willing to become a bit more sophisticated than Thompson in the promulgation of salvation, and somewhat more solicitous of their flocks' spiritual needs. In many cases it would be difficult to distinguish authentic practitioners from frauds because the same actions (collecting an offering, visiting the sick, establishing a community of goods) can be taken for different reasons. It boils down to the tricky question of motive. Sometimes key events, such as the sudden disappearance of a preacher after a particularly rewarding revival, or the adoption of an increasingly lavish life-style, can be revealing. Even this latter sign is ambiguous, however, as long as religions from Catholicism to the modern Krishna Society insist upon glorifying their leaders and assuring their every creature comfort, much in the way that the mass media public confers "sacred-secular" status on contemporary culture stars—Hollywood actors, politicians, rock musicians, and athletes.

But all such possibilities lie beyond the motive structure of Jim Jones's life. By the standard of personal theft of church funds, or even the more moderate standard of using church resources to live lavishly, Jones simply does not stand out. He did have certain benefits of office, such as a special compartment in the back of a bus used to travel around California and on group vacations in the 1970s. He did eat better than the average person at Jonestown. But these practices add up to nothing compared to a Charles Thompson or modern culture heroes. In the end Jones left this world without making off with any of the Temple's substantial financial assets. Unless new and decisive evidence becomes available, there can be no basis to judge him a swindler out for personal gain.[7]

On the other hand, there is no doubt that Jones indulged in practices of deceit in the practice of the Pentecostal gifts. Some people, of course, do not believe in spiritual healing in the first place, and for them, it is difficult to distinguish Jones from a wide range of quacks. Others argue that faith healing works, and for them, the issue turns on whether Jones had such powers, and whether it is ethical to use deceit to promote them.

Given the centrality of magic and miracles in many religions, it is difficult, if not impossible, to confront the issue in objective terms. Some groups, for example, the Roman Catholic Church, unequivocally assert the power of their practitioners through "office charisma" to transubstantiate bread and wine into the blood and body of Christ. Such bold assertions place miracles beyond the realm of proof, for they are based on the presupposition that external appearances do not always parallel "essential" transformations. In general, rituals—such as the baptism that "washes away" sin—must be understood as magical and miraculous in the way they enact symbolic transformations through material actions. Religion, then, is a dramaturgical practice; as Emile Durkheim argued, ritual offers a way of "making present" the social relations that are charged with religious sanctification.[8] Given that such activity involves "representation," it has a different reality status (or "frame") than other kinds of activity. Ritual self-consciously engages in dramaturgy to achieve results in other spheres of life.

Given the socially constructed nature of religious ritual in general, the claims against Jim Jones's practices really amount to charges of heresy in ritual. Jones, for example, palmed off chicken gizzards to represent "passed" cancers as "real." By adopting "hokey" conventions for representing the miracle of healing, he violated the prevailing dramaturgical rules, the acceptance of which sustains belief in the validity of similarly miraculous activities in other religions. Moreover, Jones did so in ways that threatened established religions' claims to monopolize the paths of personal grace and salvation. Jones faked healings and discernments not only to promote faith that would trigger more miracles but also to groom his own image as the messiah to whom others should look for prophetic leadership. For established religions, this was perhaps Jones's greatest sin: he improvised on the structure of ritualistic practice of conventional religion to lead the faithful into a personally asserted and radically different dispensation.

Jones learned his trade from other preachers on the revival circuit. His practices may have gone beyond the customary degree of contrivance common in public acts of healing, but these were differences of degree rather than kind. Oral Roberts was healing people on television as early as 1956. By 1983 television viewers of a popular religious show could witness the healing power of prayer cause a young girl's shorter leg grow to the length of her other leg in front of their very eyes, albeit with unusual use of camera angles. Such miraculous healings encourage either total wonder at the dynamic power of prayer or suspicion that popular "born-again" television programs resort to what Jones called "embellishments" of reality. It makes little sense to dismiss Jones on the basis of deceit in religious services, so long as fundamentalists and Pentecostals publicly engage in similar practices, even in front of audiences of millions, without controversy. In the absence of public outcry against the others, the charges against the man who claimed himself the Second Coming are uneven. Ironically, they resemble charges against the ministry of Jesus by outsiders who dismissed him as a charlatan and magician who used sleight of hand and staging techniques to perform faked miracles. The issue of divinity aside, such charges likely represent efforts to discredit a religious social movement on "impartial" grounds that are surrogates for deeper, more ideological charges of heresy. Put differently, structurally, Jones's rituals bear the same relation to reality as numerous practices of conventional religion; what differs is the direction in which he took his followers. If Jones was the Anti-Christ, it was not because his concrete practices were those of a charlatan or a fraud.[9]

A parallel interpretation would have it that Jim Jones was not just a con artist, he was fundamentally mad. Clearly he sought power, and presented himself as an embodiment of Christ's spirit. Jones also felt persecuted. He fled his persecutors and fostered in his followers a siege mentality. In the language of psychiatry, the man easily could be diagnosed as having a complex of paranoid thought dynamics that alternated with megalomaniacal delusions of grandeur as a Christ figure.

Psychiatrists perhaps will argue about the appropriateness of this or that classificatory label for Jim Jones. But we need not await the outcome of such debates to determine the significance of Jones's "madness" for history. What is important here is that he was a troubled person. He had an unhappy childhood; he was filled with resentment. According to Barton Hunter, the Disciples of Christ official in Indianapolis, Jones was a ceaselessly active man. As Hunter's wife Dorothy remembers, he was "tense," and "ran uptight." Struggling for the social causes of the day, the young preacher "felt that society was against him." He had "a little streak of paranoia in him."

But Barton Hunter himself knew the civic climate of the 1950s in Indianapolis. Because he served as president of the local American Civil Liberties Union chapter, he had been accused of communist sympathies. Recalling his own "little problems," Hunter would consistently emphasize that Jones experienced real persecution, and sometimes "had reason" for thoughts that might seem paranoid. Though Dorothy Hunter believed that Jones became "insane or sick" at the end, both she and her husband argued that the man they had known intimately in Indianapolis "was not always evil; he became evil."

Jim Jones clearly played out an intense and driven life. By the fall of 1961, he had a stomach ulcer. One history of the Temple implies that Jones "was suffering a mental breakdown" at the time, though the authors themselves acknowledge that Jones's doctor "noted no evidence of psychotic behavior or withdrawal from reality."[10]

Such charges notwithstanding, Jones managed most of his life to steer clear of the label of "mentally ill." Perhaps he was a "borderline personality" who exhibited traits of paranoia and confronted authorities in ways that might preclude release from a mental hospital had he ever been admitted. But Jones did not develop his "sickness" in a "break" from reality, but by bringing reality along with him. If he was crazy, he was crazy like a fox. Like Grigori Rasputin, the "holy devil" who mesmerized the Russian courts through his "occult" powers, Jones established a *grand folie*, not a private one. Though he may have been "possessed," his organizational effectiveness over a span of twenty-five years and even the precision with which he and his staff carried out the murders and mass suicide are testaments to the grim fact that they knew what they were doing. Because Jones, his followers, and his opponents played out the drama of their mental realities through social interaction with one another over an extended period of time, a psychologically reductionist explanation based on labeling Jones as individually insane is inadequate.

This is not to say that Jones was anything less than an intensely driven man who acted out of deep-seated and convoluted motives. But the boundaries between madness and religious possession cannot be defined analytically without presuming the omniscience of the Almighty. The major effort to do so, by the psychologist William James, instead seems to underscore the basic continuities between religious euphoria and psychiatrically defined manic behavior, between religious "melancholy" and depression. Thus, it is not surprising that figures of central importance to the history of religion, such as Martin Luther, were plagued by psychological torment and strange fixations.[11]

By secular standards of everyday life, any form of religious possession outside conventionalized channels stands a good chance of being labeled as insanity. Thus, it might be argued that Jones was not really religious, that he simply used religion's rituals to trap others within his own madness. Jones himself occasionally allowed that he was an atheist, but the self-proclaimed messiah also admitted (as others of considerable religious acumen affirmed) that he acted, as he put it, under "a sort of dual concept—a doubter and yet a believer." Jones clearly did not believe in an anthropomorphic supernatural deity, and he saw existing religious organizations and institutions as "tools" rather than as manifestations of the God they proclaimed.[12] Jones traveled far beyond the bounds of institutionalized religion, but he did so in confrontation with institutionalized religion, establishing a congregation by prophetically infusing everyday life with new and ominous meanings.

With all his tricks and deceits, with all his manipulations and affronts to others' sensibilities, Jim Jones may easily be made out as little more than a caricature of religiosity. His crude use of language and base discussion of taboo subjects strongly contrast with the polished image of the "professional good man." But Jones was cruder than the theology he consolidated. Somehow this man of obscure Hoosier origins stumbled across the keystone of a central contradiction of U.S. Protestantism: the perfectionist schism between the fundamentalist concern with individual salvation and the social gospel emphasis on saving "this" world in God's name. Somehow he inspired others by bringing the overriding social concerns of the day into a millennialist resentment that sought redemption, one way or another. Somehow he convinced those who came to share his views to embark on his religious pilgrimage.

In a way Jones played the part of Anti-Christ simply by presuming the reality of American ideals while walking in the world of its dispossessed. By this practice he brought to the symbolic surface the oppression that his followers had long experienced, thus offering an incontrovertibly religious pathway for the critical deconstruction of sacred elements of U.S. culture.

Before Jim Jones came along, many of those he reached had sublimated their experience one way or another. Jones sought to destroy their "false consciousness," but by doing so, he unveiled an alien new calculus of the sacred. To understand how this occurred is to move beyond Jones's youth, his call, and his prophecy, into the realm of organizational practices, their sources, and Peoples Temple's unfolding relationship to "this vale of tears."

# 4

# The Temple

Attempting to judge Jim Jones as Christ or Anti-Christ would yield only incongruous pieces of seemingly separate puzzles. However they are juxtaposed, the contradictions in Jones do not explain mass suicide. Nor do they reveal the relation of his movement to our culture. An alternative approach is to explore Peoples Temple as an emerging "apocalyptic sect"—a group preoccupied with the final struggle between good and evil and the end of the world in its present form.

Most apocalyptic sects in the Judeo-Christian tradition gravitate toward one of three ways of coming to terms with the "final days." (1) Among *preapocalyptic Adventists*, the Second Coming is taken to be imminent, and all activity is directed toward cleansing self and awakening the world to sanctification in preparation for Christ's appearance. (2) *Preapocalyptic war*, on the other hand, focuses on bringing the apocalypse to a head through a decisive struggle against the forces of evil. (3) Finally, there is the *postapocalyptic* "other-worldly sect," which establishes the spiritual grace of a communal sanctuary "beyond" "this" world, in a "heaven-on-earth" purported to be divorced from the effects of the final days. If the first, Adventist, kind of group takes a communal form, it tends to approximate the postapocalyptic tableau of other-worldly grace.[1]

The history of Peoples Temple can be charted among these possibilities. It had its origins in the vaguely apocalyptic Adventism of the Pentecostal movement, but over the years Jones radicalized Pentecostal theology in ways that pushed in two contradictory directions, toward establishing a "heaven-on-earth" and, less consistently, toward confronting the "forces of evil" that opposed his movement. Eventually, the Temple became caught on the saddle of the apocalypse, that decisive place where the tides of history run in opposite directions at once.

Peoples Temple might have spawned fewer detractors had it arisen outside the matrix of conventional religion, like most of the so-called new religions of the 1970s, but it started as a messianic congregation with roots in amorphous revivalist Christianity, at the same time challenging the proclaimed hypocrisy of the capitalist society that revivalistic Christianity so fervently embraces.[2] In the zeal of its proponents, Peoples Temple stood squarely in the tradition of early Protestants. With its apocalyptic sense about the social order of capitalism as Anti-Christ, the Temple simply radicalized the historic quest of Protestantism to found a "city on the hill." The Temple, too, sought to migrate to a promised land, albeit in a socialist and collective rather than capitalist and individualistic incarnation. Given the alien life-style they forged in the process, given the deep-seated nature of the cultural taboos they violated, the Puritanesque discipline they enforced, and the total commitment they obtained from converts, Jim Jones and Peoples Temple ran into the same sort of opposition that had plagued similar apocalyptic movements.

Thus, the basic history of Peoples Temple must trace its development into a revolutionary religious movement that gave rise to concerted opposition. The present chapter maps the Indianapolis origins of the Temple and the cultural sources of the idea of religious migration. The following chapter explores the religious and social conflicts that ensued in Indianapolis, and it shows how, like certain Protestants before him, in the face of what he deemed "persecution," Jim Jones seized upon migration as a solution, in a 1965 move from Indianapolis to Redwood Valley, California.

## Origins

Peoples Temple was brought to its strange resolution of the apocalyptic dilemma slowly, over a period of some twenty-five years. After Jim Jones was called out as a prophet in Columbus, Indiana, in the early 1950s, his own ministry picked up. The key event came at one of those conventions that are the lifeblood of the far-flung U.S. fundamentalist movement, where preachers meet old friends and make new ones, and observe each other's pulpit skills. Jim took Marcie to such a gathering at the Bethesda Temple in Detroit. The young Indiana preacher was not on the program, but he became so possessed of his calling while watching others preach that he broke out in hives. When the pastor of the church noticed, she told him, "Well, by all means, if you feel you have a ministry to give, feel free to express it." To hear Marcie tell it, Jim was so compelling in his expression of the gifts that he upstaged the convention's star evangelist from Los Angeles.

The inspired performance in Detroit had two consequences of the very sort that make conventions worthwhile. First, Jim Jones met a kindred spirit from Elmwood Temple in Cincinnati; the Reverend Edwin Wilson invited him to hold services there. Thus began a long-term association that gradually burgeoned into a revival circuit of sorts.

Second, and even more important, Jones met several people from the Laurel Street Tabernacle, an Assemblies of God Pentecostal church located in the "Dogpatch" section of southside Indianapolis. The Assemblies of God, an all-White denomination, had split off from the originally integrated Southern U.S. Pentecostal movement at its founding meeting in Hot Springs, Arkansas, in 1914. Not surprisingly, given its denominational affiliation, the Laurel Street congregation counted among its members a sizable proportion of postwar "redneck" migrants to Indianapolis from Kentucky and other mid-South states. The Tabernacle was, in fact, a vivid demonstration of one way the Pentecostal movement grew by following the rural segment of its client population to the North and to the cities.[3]

The Laurel Street Tabernacle connection propelled Jim Jones's ministry into its early small-scale success. Jones already had a small church— "Community Unity"—on Hoyt and Randolph Streets in Indianapolis. After the Detroit convention, some of the Laurel Street folk took in his services. One of them, Edith Cordell, found herself healed of arthritis while one of her pastors, the Reverend Russell Winberg, looked on. Soon thereafter, in September 1954, Jones received an invitation to preach at the Tabernacle, at the very time when the congregation's board was searching out a successor to the retiring minister, John Price. Jones brought along his own congregation, took the pulpit, and gave a couple of guest sermons, even weaving in some social commentaries. Jack Beam, a Laurel Street board member at the time, recalled that Jones "would wrap it up in such a way that you had to look at it. Then he'd heal your ass. And it was the Word accompanied by signs and wonders, which was their scripture; they couldn't get away from it."

Perhaps John Price wanted a "money runner" to guarantee his pension; in any event he had a vision that Jones should be his successor. But board members had different ideas. At a time when church segregation in the United States was practically total, the guest preacher had brought Blacks to the service, and they had not sat just in the back pews. Seeing the need, the board offered to help establish a separate church for Blacks. Jones was outraged by the proposal. "There will be no church in the Black neighborhood," he said. "I will not be a pastor of a Black church or a White church. Wherever I have a church, *all* people will be welcome. . . ." Then he walked out.

The Laurel Street incident unveiled a pattern of action that Jim Jones was to employ successfully again and again over the years. He would become known as a man "who can't compromise with his conscience." Whenever the occasion presented itself, Jones would precipitate a face-to-face dramatization of religious conflict by doggedly taking a stand based on high moral principle. Then he would turn the tables on those who tried to temper his radical commitment to ultimate ends, by exposing their hypocrisy. Time and time again the gambit would pay off, as it did at Laurel Street. In the first (albeit, "mini") migration of Jones's career, a substantial segment of the Tabernacle congregation voted with their feet, leaving their church for Jones's.

Some of the apostates showed the calculation of evangelical entrepreneurs: Rheaviana Beam, the wife of Jack Beam, observed that if the Tabernacle did not have the sense to go with a young draw of a preacher like Jim Jones, it "was never gonna take." Her husband, a man of "backroom" sensibilities, began a lifelong relationship as Jones's friend and trusted associate pastor. The Reverend Russell Winberg's decision was more difficult: he was a strong fundamentalist but he also needed a job, and because he was not in the running for Price's position, he took the opportunity of the Lord's calling and became the second of Jones's associate pastors. Others, like Edith Cordell and her family, the Stahls, Mother LeTourneau's family, Mable Stewart and her daughter Loretta, and Eva Pugh, came as believers, followers, and families, attracted to Jones's dynamism, message, and healing powers. Whatever their reasons for "walking" with Jones, the Whites who left Laurel Street chose in effect to participate in an interracial congregation, even though many of them were, as Beam put it, "tore up on the race issue." Like later migrations over greater distances, the decision would require positive action to go with Jones.[4]

On April 4, 1955, Jones and his new allies founded Wings of Deliverance, the corporate vehicle of what was soon to become Peoples Temple. The group initially listed ten members in the articles of incorporation, including at least five from Laurel Street, who put their faith and a closely held corporation in the hands of Jones, his wife, and his mother as trustees. The group set an early eye on expansion, leaving the door open to accepting other congregations as affiliates.

True to the predispositions of both Jones and the Laurel Street people, the Wings of Deliverance articles of incorporation affirmed basic Pentecostal and Holiness doctrine, with a creed of temperance, abstinence from narcotics and alcohol, modesty, the Christian virtues, and that mainstay of the frugal Jones, "resisting the temptations of worldly gains and material goods." The spirit, and in many respects the letter, of the basic Pentecostal principles would remain important to Jones's movement over its entire history. Its foundation was one of Holiness morality.

Wings of Deliverance hardly had gotten started when it adopted a new name. With an unusual interracial congregation dedicated to healing, Jim Jones "packed out" his own smallish church and borrowed the money to put a down payment on a vacant inner-city church at 15th and New Jersey. Drawing on the widepread Pentecostal use of the term *temple*, and emphasizing the populist orientation of their group, they called themselves Peoples Temple. The Temple took on the typical trappings of church life, including a choir and a youth group. But the head pastor was something else, at least as his followers recall it. Holding forth in a sanctuary with room for 700, Jones acquired quite a reputation for his healing ministry, and attracted large crowds. "Their hopes," one believer recounted, "was to just have his shadow cast on them."[5]

To pack in new faces, Peoples Temple followed a technique not unknown among upstart religious groups in the twentieth century, offering services at times when more established churches were not meeting. The congregation's "foot troops" would fan out across the Black neighborhoods of Indianapolis, inviting the unchurched to join them, and others to visit the 2:30 Sunday afternoon service after they had attended their own services Sunday morning.

Blacks did come, and one of them Jim Jones soon recognized as a man of ministerial promise. He proposed Archie Ijames as his third associate minister. Ijames did not really take to the pastor's theology, but "believed in his honesty" and came on board. Other Blacks were also attracted to the services of the young White man who refused to discriminate on the basis of race.

With the steady increase in Black attendance, Whites who came to regular services found themselves in a quandary. Here was a preacher with the nine gifts of Pentecost holding forth in a racially mixed service. Years later Jack Beam recalled the early days. Jim Jones, he said, was preaching "scorching sermons on 'out of one blood, God made all nations to rule on the face of the earth,' and 'how can you love God whom you have not seen, and not love . . .': you know, the whole racial thing from a Biblical standpoint, boom, boom, boom." As Beam told it, "What he wanted to say, but they was religious people, [was] 'God damn it, you want the fuckin' healing, well stick your fuckin' money up your ass, if you don't love these Black people.' And he'd have to coin it in all loving Biblical words." The Whites "were in awe; they would'a like to kill him, but they thought that they would be touching God's anointed, and at that time, that was one of the scriptures that was used, 'touch not my anointed; do my prophets no harm.'"

Others remembered the beginning in less florid terms. In Rick Cordell's view, Jim Jones "never played any games; he was dealing with a strictly religious crowd, so he had to talk Bible, and he had to talk in the realms they could understand, but when he felt something, he would say it." Even to congregation members who held racially prejudiced views, Jones "was never afraid to speak the truth, right straight forward, never being afraid a minute of the consequences of what anyone would try to do to him because he stood for truth."[6]

There are claims that Jim Jones quickly developed a wide reputation as a spellbinder. The established faith healer Kathryn Kuhlman (once described as "the greatest thing since Christ!") and O. L. Jaggers of California are said to have sought out the Hoosier wonder for tours and guest revival appearances. But mostly the young preacher concentrated his energies in Indiana and Ohio. He and Jack Beam traveled numerous weekends to Elmwood Temple in Cincinnati, trading pulpits with the Reverend Ed Wilson, sometimes preaching elsewhere en route. According to Marcie, Jim could have outdone anyone in drawing crowds on the revival circuit if he had just stuck to healing. But he started preaching that those in the congregation should "feed the hungry, and . . . take care of the sick," and follow Karl Marx's formula, "from each according to his ability, and to each according to his need. . . ." When Jones laid out this gospel, "crowds began to fall off," but Marcie saw a net benefit: "people that did stay were people that wanted to go on to perfection. . . . And so where numbers were sacrificed, quality was gained. . . ."

That was what Jim Jones sought—a strong and loyal commitment—and he was willing to work hard and long hours to get it. He may have disputed the existence of a "sky god," but he pursued his calling under the burden of the Protestant ethic. Even aside from the revival tours, he kept a grueling schedule. Like his wife, in the early years Jones held a regular job, for a time as a social worker for the Marion County (Indianapolis) Welfare Department. He also set up midweek evening meetings with his congregation. All through his years in Indianapolis, he would strike others as an intense yet compassionate man. Some of the many religious functionaries and friends he met over the years found the man "humorless"; in retrospect, one of them believed this was a "fatal flaw" that prevented the preacher from looking at himself objectively. He was too busy. As Jones said in many ways throughout his life, "I only have today." He never kept a schedule if he could avoid it, but he kept to a certain internal discipline. Like other Protestant ascetics, he seems to have been driven by the ethic that "waste of time is . . . the first and in principle the deadliest of sins." His energies grew into an ever-expanding pool of activities.[7]

### Family and Church

To begin with, the Jones family itself was growing. Just as Jim had done with animals in his childhood, he always was ready to take in a waif. In 1952 he and Marcie came upon a ten-year-old girl whose mother had mistreated her, sometimes locking her in a closet all day. Agnes joined the Jones household, received considerable attention to her needs for speech therapy, and was legally adopted in June of 1953. At about the same time, a White woman in her fifties, Esther Mueller, became a follower of Jones. In 1955 she too came into the household, much to the chagrin of her son, who regarded Jones as a con artist.

Then, capitalizing on Marcie's skills as a nurse and the presence of Esther Mueller, the Joneses started what was to become a small home-care fiefdom. One day around 1955 Jim and Marcie Jones visited a follower named Betsy Cooper in a nursing home. When the old woman begged them, "Get me out of here," they "kidnapped" her. Betsy Cooper became the first resident of their first nursing home, which was in fact their own home. By bringing their parsonage up to state standards, the Joneses initiated a formula whereby their ever-widening extended family could be supported in part with cash payments from outside. Eventually, they formed the Jim Lu Mar Company to own their own household nursing home and another one they bought at 2137 Alabama Street.

Gradually a nursing home staff was assembled from Jones relatives and congregation members, and they worked with real pride to offer a standard of "rest-home" care that was probably unusual for its day. The homes, the proprietors remembered later, were well staffed, and featured good meals, fresh daily linen, and a perfectionist effort to keep things "spotless." Barton Hunter, the Disciples of Christ official, visited the homes occasionally. In his recollection, they were crowded by more recent standards, but nevertheless evidenced an emphasis on treatment of residents "with real concern" and "gentleness." "For a while," Hunter indicated, the homes "were the best in the city."

Still, Jones's reported reply to those from other nursing homes who supposedly wondered, "How can you afford to do this?" was a bit coy: "Well, we're not making a profit." Perhaps not, but the homes' care payments met the material needs of those who lived and worked there, and thus served as a sort of working welfare, freeing them from the demands of outside jobs. Operating the facilities on a shoestring budget and keeping personal consumption to a minimum, the frugal preacher was able to avoid drawing a salary from the church, and "use all the church funds to aid the church's social progress."

Because they financed their household from care payments, Jones's extended family hardly could live opulently in Indianapolis. Agnes Jones recalled her adoptive father's rummaging at church sales for clothes to wear. Barton Hunter remembered the Jones household he visited from time to time as "almost barren," and Jones's car as "almost ten years old." But if the Jones home stayed spartan in material comforts, it kept growing as a center of life. With the inclusion of individuals unrelated by blood or marriage, the household amounted to a communal group, even in the mid 1950s. Then Marcie's parents came to live in the bustling household and Mr. Baldwin took on the Alabama Street nursing home. In 1958 Marcie and Jim started what they would call their "rainbow family," adopting two orphans from the aftermath of the Korean War, whom they called Stephanie and Lew Eric. An open-door policy was established. There were always the stray animals, and increasingly, people who needed shelter came to stay with the Joneses, sometimes for short periods, sometimes for months and years. Then Marcie became pregnant. Once, in the early 1950s, she had written her mother-in-law Lynetta that she had "surely accomplished the 'thing' this time," but Marcie would not have her only natural-born child until 1959, at the age of thirty-two, a little over ten years after she first married.[8]

Before Marcie could add a natural child to the growing communal family, tragedy struck. Mable Stewart, a Laurel Street apostate and supervisor in a Jones nursing home, was driving a carload home from Jim's exchange sermon at Elmwood Temple in Cincinnati one night in May 1959. On a wide-open stretch of U.S. 421 near Indianapolis she pulled out to pass, and there was a fatal head-on collision with a car occupied by two local youths. The accident took the life of one of the boys, four church women, and the Jones's adopted child Stephanie. In public Jones managed to put his best pastoral face forward. "We teach others to carry their cross," he told a reporter. "Now we'll take up ours." Years later he would recall facing the dilemma of how to bury Stephanie in keeping with his ethical principles, given the segregation of U.S. cemeteries. Because Blacks could not be buried in areas of cemeteries reserved for Whites, Jones insisted that Stephanie be laid to rest in a section where Blacks were buried. "If that's where you put minority people and Jews, if that's where you put them," he said, "then that's where we all go." Once again, by living his life as though race did not make a difference, Jones stumbled onto the institutionalized racism he resented, knowing full well that his color-blind posture would bring him into confrontation with individuals and social institutions over and over again.

In the wake of the accident, the Joneses reaffirmed their commitment to the "rainbow family," phoning the Buddy McDaniels Orphanage in Seoul to arrange adoption of another Korean girl. Then, the first day of June 1959, Marcie Jones gave birth to Stephan, and she and Jim gave him the middle name Gandhi to honor the nonviolent but confrontational leader of India's independence movement. Two years later the Jones family would take an even more radical step, adopting little Jimmy Jones, Jr., a Black baby about nine months younger than Stephan. By this act the Joneses became the first White couple in Indianapolis, and perhaps in the state, to adopt a Black child. Jim Jones thereby embedded his messianic confrontation with U.S. institutions into his own family. As he remarked at the time, "Integration is a more personal thing with me now. It's a question of my son's future."[9]

Like the Jones household, and over the same years, Peoples Temple became a close-knit community. Rick Cordell recalled Jones's congregation as "a church where people felt closer, more of a family than any other church I have ever been to." With a committed and growing congregation, an income-producing revival circuit, and two nursing homes, Jones and his associates decided to expand. A former synagogue located in the inner city came up for sale when its congregation moved to the suburbs in 1957. Jones bought the building at 975 Delaware Street. Like some previous Pentecostal groups, Jones's drew on the term *apostolic* to reflect identification with the Apostles of the early Christian Church. Temple Bethel became Peoples Temple Apostolic Church and the leader of the integrated, Pentecostal-styled congregation became a crusader who, Louise Moseley remembered, felt a call to "serve these people and meet their needs, and also to change the minds of a lot of White Indianapolis people."

The memories of those who followed Jim Jones from that point on abound with tales of the "good Samaritan." We are told how the young preacher would befriend an old woman who needed money, set up a playground, get his youth group to clean up the neighborhood around his church, and arrange for kids who had never been outside the city to go on hayrides. The catalogue of good works would run on and on. Even when he traveled abroad, Jones was on the job. He and Marcie visited Cuba soon after Castro's revolution to see the social transformation firsthand. Hearing that prostitution had been abolished by decree, Jim took Marcie in a taxi to a brothel and had her ask the ladies of the night if any of them wanted to leave, while the bartender stood in front of the bar mural of nude women with a perplexed look on his face.

Characteristically, when Jim Jones saw a need, an injustice, or an institutional practice that he found ethically reprehensible, he made himself the man of the hour, pouncing on it as an opportunity of service. By doing so, he established both his own reputation as a healer and minister, and a going organization as well. Gradually, he began to look even further for directions to take his work. In his searches Jones came upon a central theme in U.S. culture that more than once before had inspired collective action: the belief that Blacks are God's chosen people.[10]

## The Black Redemptive Quest

Some of the most significant events of religious development have taken place through collective migration. The journey of the Jews under Moses, the European Crusades of the Middle Ages, the Cistercian monastic settlement of Eastern Europe all show how religious migration is bound up in broader processes of history. U.S. Blacks did not have to look so far afield to place themselves in that same tradition. The archetypal case of a latter-day promised land was North America. Just as the New Testament saw a shift from Babylon to Rome as a symbol of evil civilization, so in the Reformation, Rome in particular and Europe as a whole came to represent Babylon to portions of the displaced peasants and craftsmen, independent yeomen, and urban bourgeoisie. Their Protestant religions often reflected class struggles against entrenched feudal interests, and their dissatisfactions often sanctified emigration to the American colonies as a search for the new Jerusalem.[11]

Blacks brought to North America as slaves have had more than good reason to seek a similar way out. Well before the Civil War, an odd alliance of Blacks, Northern White religious liberals, and Southern White racists sought the return of Blacks to Africa. Failing that, desperate slaves fled the plantations via the Underground Railroad run by Quakers and other theologically uncompromising religious liberals. After the Civil War, too, William Jeremiah Moses has observed, "The dominant pattern of Black mass behavior from 1876 to 1925 was migration (and enthusiasm for migration) out of the Old South Black Belt. The rhetoric of this migration was often reminiscent of ante-bellum Black nationalism, with its talk of escape from the land of bondage and quest for a promised land." Like the Jews under Moses, nineteenth-century Black ministers sometimes saw the collective suffering of their people and their quests for redemption as part of a higher religious purpose to history. From time to time former slaves thus received a call to migrate to kingdoms of God under the leadership of Black messiahs. There were three basic migration programs: the internal movement from the South to the states of Kansas and Oklahoma; the less religiously inspired migration to the cities of the North (and more recently the West Coast); and the more radical "back-to-Africa" movement centered on Liberia and Ethiopia.

The culmination of the back-to-Africa fever came in the movement around Marcus Garvey, who, in the first quarter of the twentieth century, proclaimed a movement in support of "the Cause of Africa" and built a far-flung apparatus, the Universal Negro Improvement Association (UNIA), to further his ideas. For his followers, the search for redemption sometimes cast Garvey as the messiah general in a final Armageddon. As one of the faithful put it, "I was born here, but I am not afraid to die in Africa. . . . We must have ships, if the vision of a philosopher called to our service and appointed by Jehovah and his son, the Messiah, will lead us on to victory." Garvey used religious forms to his advantage, but he did more to raise the spirits of Blacks than he did to bring about migration. By the time he was deported from the United States in the wake of FBI investigations of fraud, not one U.S. Black had been repatriated to Africa.

If Garvey did nothing to establish the new Jerusalem, he gave powerful testimony to a vision that kept the nineteenth-century hopes of Black migration alive in the hearts of twentieth-century Blacks all across the United States: the "city on a hill" founded by the Puritans in the seventeenth century was not yet the sanctified church of God on earth, and Black slavery had been the stumbling block in God's plan. Integration was one possible course of redemption in the Promised Land, not just for Blacks but for the nation as a whole. But deep-seated racism in the United States made it easy for Garvey and others to ridicule the prospects of integration and advance the alternative claim that Black redemption could come to pass only with migration to another country.[12]

Jim Jones was exposed to the Black migration legacy through his associations with Garvey's contemporary: self-styled Black messiah Father M. J. Divine. Several times in the late 1950s, Jones visited Father Divine at his Peace Mission in Philadelphia. Though Divine's staff distrusted the visitor, the Indiana pastor was received by Divine as a leader and kindred spirit. Like Jones, but almost fifty years earlier, Divine had rubbed elbows with Pentecostalists during his formative ministry; like Divine, Jones presided over an interracial congregation founded on the ideal of equality. During his visits to Philadelphia, Jones failed to receive the mantle of leadership he sought to have passed from the aging Father Divine. But bit by bit Jim Jones got something for his efforts: he imported Peace Mission religious themes and operational structures into Peoples Temple practically wholesale.

In a speech to a 1958 Peace Mission banquet given in Jim Jones's honor, the visitor put his finger on Father Divine's success: "He shares what he has with you! He wants you to come into his likeness! . . . I have heard him say, 'What I am, you can be!'" Taking the possibility to heart, Jim Jones indeed set out to become what Father Divine was.

Divine presided over a communal and redistributive empire directed to concrete betterment of Black people's lives through material wheeling and dealing. The unorthodox approach often was the object of disdain, ridicule, and active opposition from Whites, but the success of the ministry was phenomenal:

> By the mid-1930s the Peace Mission had become the largest realty holder in Harlem, with three apartment houses, fifteen to twenty flats, and several meeting halls with dormitories on the upper floors. In addition, followers in Harlem operated some twenty-five restaurants, six groceries, ten barber shops, ten cleaning stores, two dozen huckster wagons with clams and oysters or fresh vegetables, and a coal business with three trucks ranging from Harlem to the mines of Pennsylvania.

Some followers worked without wage compensation, and the owners of the businesses typically turned over their net profits to the movement. During the depression of the 1930s, the unschooled cooperativist Divine even associated with the Communist party, which saw oppressed Blacks as a natural organizing target and Divine as a potentially powerful ally. But Divine, like Pentecostalists, was suspicious of the Communists for their atheism and union organizing, and principled Communists could not help but be appalled by Divine's grip on his spiritualistic followers.

As the Communists and Father Divine drifted apart, beginning in 1935, Divine established rural, interracial cooperative communities in upstate New York. For him, they offered a middle road between political communism on the one hand, and symbolically important but unrealistic migration schemes like Garvey's proposal for recolonization of Africa on the other hand. Collectively, the Peace Mission agricultural communities came to be called "The Promised Land." For Divine's poor and dispossessed followers, the movement truly represented an ark of salvation, material as much as spiritual.[13]

Jim Jones had much to learn from a man who had been brought to trial in 1931, found to be living with a woman other than his wife, and declared an immoral menace to society. Three days after Father Divine was sentenced to a year in jail, the judge died of heart failure. From his jail cell, Divine advanced his messianic claims immeasurably by supposedly lamenting, "I hated to do it!"

Indiana's messianic hopeful was suitably inspired. The Peace Mission style offered a theology of spiritual possession in which Jones could assert the divine being of himself, and to a lesser degree, of those who followed him. Second, it offered a way out of the Pentecostalist religious framework: in terms of power, through personal rulership, and in terms of practical theology, through what would be called the "human service ministry." Finally, and most significantly, Jones adopted the promised land as his own motif, at first following the pragmatic "internal migration" approach of Father Divine, later reviving older Black dreams of redemption through colonization beyond the boundaries of the country of their former slave servitude. Over the years Jones would vacillate between two themes: promotion of the largely urban human service ministry, and migration to escape the degradation of racism and poverty.

From the onset of Jones's Philadelphia connection, the Indianapolis church took on many of the trappings of Peace Mission life, themselves often lifted from wider Pentecostal culture. Jim Jones would become "Father" or "Dad," like Father Divine and like many more conventional Black Pentecostal preachers as well. His church would become an extended family, again like the Peace Mission, but also simply an exaggeration of tendencies among Pentecostals. Peoples Temple later took on other little touches,

like using Peace Mission hymns, in part to make the apostates who left the
Peace Mission for Peoples Temple feel that Jones was in fact carrying on
Divine's ministry. The Temple sometimes also followed Divine's lead in
refusing to refer to Negroes or Whites, resorting, if pressed, to terms like
*dark-complexioned* and *light-complexioned.*

Most important, Jones went about the business of building an organization like the Peace Mission. One effort simply did not pan out: when Jim
and Marcie visited Cuba soon after Castro's 1959 revolution, they sought
Blacks who might want to leave behind the left-wing austerity of the new
regime. Jones tried to recruit Cuban families to come to the United States
to establish church-supported communal farms, but the scheme never
took off. He was far more successful at building a human services ministry
from his Indianapolis base.[14]

### Redemption and the Liberal Establishment

In essence, Peoples Temple developed a series of inner-city social service
programs that gave direct fruition to the liberal Protestant ideal of a social
gospel, at a time when the liberal establishment was reawakening to the
existence of poverty in the United States. In 1959 Jones took steps to set up
a church orphan adoption fund to mirror his own "rainbow family." Echoing Father Divine's approach, the fund was to be financed not only from
collections but from church dinners and a church-operated cleaning
agency.

Of much greater significance were the free restaurant and social service
center established by Peoples Temple in the Temple basement. The restaurant, staffed by church women, opened on February 24, 1960, and became
a fast success, soon giving away thousands of meals per month. Peoples
Temple prided itself on giving the destitute some dignity by not forcing
them to pray before they ate, as more traditional religious charity programs
often do. It also sought to ensure a racial mingling at the tables. Gradually
a wide range of people—not just the poor—began taking meals there,
pitching in labor and money, and supporting the church. "You met all
kinds of people. There were people with degrees and people with no education."

It was this tableau of outreach that cemented the first of Jim Jones's
alliances with liberal Protestant denominations and civic leaders. Already
he had met a rabbi through the synagogue building purchase, and when the
congregation moved into the former synagogue, Jones had been introduced to Christian Church (Disciples of Christ) official Barton Hunter and
his family. Jones and Hunter spent many evenings together talking religion, and Jones even broached the subject of affiliating with the Disciples,

a liberal denomination that stressed congregational autonomy and a more social ministry than fundamentalist groups. "You know, our church ought to have an ecumenical outlook," Jones said one evening. "You Disciples of Christ are ecumenical, aren't you?" "In a mild sort of way," Hunter replied, "and kidded [Jones] a bit as I tended to do because I thought he was overly impressed with himself at times." Jones kept pressing Hunter, "How *do* you get to be a Disciple?" Under persistent questioning, Hunter allowed that the Disciples of Christ, like a number of other denominations, let congregations themselves decide whether to affiliate. Then Hunter gave his young friend a book on the history of the Disciples' movement in the United States, promising to introduce him to other Disciples officials, to pave the way for affiliation. The very next Sunday, the week before Easter, probably in 1959, before Hunter and Jones met with any other officials, Jones appeared at the Hunter doorstep late in the evening and announced, "Well, we've joined the Christian Church." Hunter retorted, "Come on, what are you talking about?" "Well," said Jones, "I had a vote of the congregation, and . . . we're putting in our sign, 'Peoples Temple Christian Church Full Gospel.'"

Thus began a tie that was to open many doors for Peoples Temple. Barton Hunter took Jones down to meet the officials, who were impressed by his quick pledge of money to the local association of churches. Peoples Temple began to identify with Disciples' activities in Indianapolis, and Jones sent members to state meetings and gave money to the state organization. The bureaucratic formalities took a little time, but by 1960 Peoples Temple Christian Church was officially part of the Disciples of Christ. Eventually, in 1961, Jones would even take on a "less flamboyant" college-trained Disciples minister, the Reverend Ross Case, whom he had met at a summer church camp in southern Indiana. Over its entire history, Peoples Temple would maintain an active connection to the denomination. Like Father Divine, the Disciples offered the Temple a way out of Pentecostalism, but with far greater public legitimacy, and with ready ties to the community of establishment liberals.

The restaurant in particular established Temple credentials in a way that would remain important in the years to come: Jones's congregation became identified as a viable organization that could work with other civic groups to ameliorate the conditions of the poor. No longer would the sole patrons of Jones's expanding arc of influence come from the ranks of the socially dispossessed. No longer could the social elite dismiss Jones as a somewhat eccentric Pentecostal preacher, disconnected, like the others, from U.S. society's corridors of institutionalized power, for under the shield of what he would call "apostolic socialism," Jones was building a unique, church-based alliance that brought together people from many different stations in life, united not by their class situation or common educational or cultural backgrounds but by their shared commitment to common goals—most prominently, the amelioration of poverty and the sustenance of a community of people who sought to transcend racism in daily life. During the early 1960s, at the dawn of the civil rights movement, Jim Jones secured for himself a local reputation of some notability.

With its "applied Christianity" emphasis, Peoples Temple's Indianapolis basement center looked like just what was needed for the downtown residents whom liberal Disciples officials "didn't know how to reach." Because the restaurant was so successful, it made a good drawing card for other programs. As an outgrowth of Jones's alliances with Barton Hunter and other officials, Disciples volunteers came down to work at an employment desk in Peoples Temple's basement. The church served as an outreach agency, attracting those who were in enough need to come in for a meal, providing clean clothes for the poor who ate there, and sending them to the appropriate welfare agency, to a job interview, or to whatever other service they required.[15]

All this the Disciples regarded with high favor. In the early 1960s, the liberal denominations were beginning to struggle with their own churches' "White flight" to the suburbs, and the Disciples wanted to support congregations that were holding forth in the inner cities while the composition of the communities they served underwent "drastic" change.

But the denomination also was having problems with the headstrong minister and his unusual congregation. Jim Jones always had placed himself at the center of the church, as its shepherd and also the bellwether of the flock. Perhaps with the inspiration of Father Divine, Peoples Temple began to provide a "corrective fellowship" to members who did not live up to Jones's expectations. Associate pastor Ross Case questioned the practice, in which church members were confronted with their shortcomings by a select group of peers, and he even mentioned it to Barton Hunter. But when Hunter confronted Jones about what Peoples Temple was doing, the preacher answered, "Isn't that what its responsibility is, to kind of guide its members?"

Jones attracted more positive attention in governmental circles. By 1960 the Temple was about one-fifth Black. As Jones put it in an interview, "We've made our Negro brothers welcome and they have joined us in proportion to their numbers in the general population." With his integrated congregation, the adoption program reputation, and the free restaurant, Jones probably could lay as much claim as anyone in Indianapolis to a concern for human rights. In February 1961 Mayor Charles Boswell appointed him to fill the vacant position of executive director of the Indianapolis Human Rights Commission. Jones took the job that no one else apparently wanted at $7,000 a year, after a two-year search had failed to uncover a trained professional.

Jones threw himself into the work with characteristic intensity, and he caused more of a stir than most mayors would hope for. The twenty-nine-year-old minister immediately tried to set the community at ease about the most deep-seated taboos of a segregated society. He publicly emphasized that Peoples Temple did not have interracial dating, and he suggested that "the Negro wants to be our brother in privilege, not our brother-in-law." But Jones also assumed an unusually activist role for a salaried public official. Taking the lead from the Reverend Martin Luther King and others beginning to integrate buses and lunch stands in the South, the young preacher sent well-dressed, racially integrated teams from his congregation around to test the racial policies of other Indianapolis churches.

On one occasion, upon hearing that a Black woman had been excluded from a White church's services, Jones brought his own services to a quick halt. He and others from his congregation drove carloads over to the other church, and walked in and sat down in the middle of the service. Another time, after Jones's campaign had attained a public notoriety from press reports, when Jones's integrated team visited the Mount Olive Christian Church, the pastor's wife answered the phone in the middle of the service and received a bomb threat: "I hear you are integrating your church today, and I want to tell you that we put a bomb in the church, and you better be getting your people out, because it will go off in about ten minutes." The worshipers marched out of the sanctuary, carried the pulpit and communion table across the street, and continued services in a football field. At the conclusion, one Mount Olive member told the visitors, "You are welcome back now more than ever."

Jones carried his evangelical style into his political office as well. Instead of working behind the scenes in a conventional bureaucratic capacity, in his first few weeks as Human Rights Commission director he personally persuaded three restaurants to change their segregationist policies. Characteristically with the exploits of Jim Jones, stories abound. One establishment insisted on a widespread segregationist approach: carry-out service only. Jones is said to have integrated the place with a flock of church members who held a sit-in dinner. But Jones also tried to cushion the effects of integration by encouraging prointegration people to eat at places that agreed not to discriminate against Blacks. Peoples Temple old-timers and the then mayor later recalled that the activist minister was successful in integrating other places as well: the telephone company, a theater, an amusement park, and the city's police department.

Jones's most famous success came as he was becoming tense and physically run down from his confrontations with segregationist policies. Not surprisingly, integration did not proceed either as rapidly or as smoothly as he would have hoped. Subjected to intense public pressures from a critical press and segregationists, Jones became exhausted and developed an ulcer, and his physician, E. P. Thomas, ordered him admitted to Methodist Hospital.

The hospital staff, assuming that because Jim Jones's physician was Black, he must also be Black, assigned him to a room in an all-Black ward. When a nurse discovered the "mistake," she reassured him, "Don't worry about a thing; we'll be moving you." "Why?" he wanted to know. When he found out the hospital's policy, Jones displayed his well-rehearsed techniques of confrontation, insisting to the superintendent that Methodist Hospital be integrated immediately. When he asked for a telephone to call the newspapers, he got more response than a conventional approach could have gotten in months. In the press Jones made it clear he did not blame the nurse: "No, as an individual, she was only carrying out her duties. Apparently it is the policy of the hospital that is at fault." Once again Jones had brought institutionalized practices to the surface on a dramatic level that left him with victory.[16]

In more ways than one, the incident at Methodist Hospital was a watershed for Peoples Temple, demonstrating the success of its minister and at the same time bringing to the surface his weaknesses. It was because Peoples Temple merged Pentecostal salvation and a liberal human services ministry that Jones rose to local office in the first place. In turn, Jones's activist style in fulfilling the duties of office led to the decline in health that necessitated his hospitalization. He had not been able to "take the heat" of controversial public moral struggles. Yet even upon entering the hospital, the man could not loosen his grip on the very zeal that had precipitated his admission. He succeeded once again, and yet victory came because he was defeated. Thus began in earnest the search for a promised land.

# 5

# The Ark

In his struggles for integration Jim Jones took personal risks, and he placed his congregation at risk. For their efforts, Jones and his followers suffered considerable harassment from the sizable segment of Indianapolis's population that vehemently opposed "mixing of the races." These difficulties, like Jones's accomplishments as an integrationist, were transported to a mythic level by his followers. Particularly suspect are the recurrent stories of how someone tried to kill Jones by putting crushed glass in his food. To the gullible, the miraculous way the ground glass "passed right through his system" represented sure proof of Jones's divine power.[1] But his power was not quite equal to his confrontations with Indianapolis opponents. Jones began to seek a way out of real, imagined, and staged troubles, and Peoples Temple became an ark of migration: at first stranded in Indianapolis, with its leader adrift in Brazil; then bound for California in 1965; twelve years later, headed for Guyana under the intimidating glare of press exposés.

### Persecution and Flight

Whatever the exaggerations, by 1960 Jim Jones clearly was the object of considerable vengeance. Indianapolis is not a particularly progressive city, and some of its residents did not treat integrationists kindly. Disciples of Christ official Barton Hunter, himself an outspoken man on occasion, received occasional threatening phone calls, and he had "no doubt" that Jones did too. Because Jones was doing extremely unpopular things to promote racial integration, Hunter could understand how he would begin to feel persecuted by those who lashed back. Their actions were not directed only against Jones; he was just one of the objects of a wider campaign of intimidation that prointegration forces underwent in Indianapolis during the early 1960s.

Over the years Peoples Temple and its minister experienced petty harassments, strange plots, and violent threats. One time Jack Beam said he was down in the basement of the church and found dynamite in the automatic

57

coal feeder, ready to explode when it reached the furnace. On more than one occasion, a swastika would be painted on the church door, or a shot fired at the parsonage. After the Joneses adopted little Black Jimmy Jones, antagonists spit on Marcie as she walked her children in the stroller. "People were so prejudiced." Rheaviana Beam recalled. "It was terrible, like you'd done some great crime by adopting children." The Joneses' address was printed often enough in newspaper stories, and they got hate letters and phone calls about little Jimmy, "praying for him to die."

Jones tried to put up a courageous front. Though he may have embellished the accounts of harassment or even contrived certain events for his own purposes, he did not take the heat very well. Even before working at the Human Rights Commission, he was becoming suspicious of outsiders. Once at the free restaurant he found a minister checking out the operation, dressed as a down-and-out tramp. Jones pulled him out of the line, shouting, "You're not one of our fellahs. You're a minister! You're here to spy on us."

In time, the harassment became too much. Growing up White, but taking on the cause of Blacks in a segregated society, Jones perhaps was less equipped to withstand active prejudice than were his Black counterparts. Then too, he received more than his share because of his unequivocal public stances.

In the heat of his struggles against racism, Jones also focused on the "thermonuclear reality." At a time when fallout shelters were popping up in surburban backyards, he wondered, "How could people be mad enough to make such weapons and then sane enough not to use them?" Taking the world's problems as his own cross, the high-strung preacher came to hope that there was someplace else more hospitable than Indianapolis for his interracial family and congregation. "Indianapolis was so bad that he was looking for a better spot."[2]

Jones talked more and more about what Peoples Temple could do to make a decisive difference. "I feel like it's time to do the work of God," he said at one service, discussing a plan inspired by Father Divine. "Some of us are going to sell our property . . . , get a hotel and do mission work." Jones knew that "not everybody's gonna come into this," but prayed that some would, "the few of us that will sell our property and move together and do a common work for God. . . . You say that's not Bible; you don't know your Bible. . . . Says 'sell all you have, live according to his [*sic*] needs.'"

In the same sermon, Jim Jones got carried away on a train of thought that revealed the dramatic proportions of his nascent apocalyptic resentment. He railed against the "conveniences" of contemporary church life and allowed that he would "like to see what men and women would do when they're up against pressure." Something big would have to happen to shake people out of their "complacency," he told the congregation in a quiet voice. Unlike the days when Jesus could awaken the world by his good works and martyrdom, Jones did not "think one man can do it today." "If it's an atomic war," he implored, "then I say, 'God send it,'" as his audience murmured agreement.

After Jones went into the Methodist Hospital for his checkup in October of 1961, his doctor ordered him to take a two-month leave of absence. Jones used the time to check out British Guiana (preindependence Guyana) on the northeast coast of South America as a site for possible pilgrimage. On the visit he lost no time in denouncing the U.S. church establishment as "the most segregated organization in America." The money used for air-conditioned churches and big houses for ministers, he suggested, could be better spent "developing countries such as British Guiana." Back on the Human Rights job in December for only a few days, Jones resigned "for reasons of continuing poor health," receiving an editorial accolade in the Indianapolis *Times* that called him "superb" in "the touchy business of human relations." His doctor insisted that the impassioned minister change his way of life.

Jones flew with his wife and children to Hawaii, "looking for options." But the January 1962 issue of *Esquire* magazine had an article based on the atom bomb scare that offered the preacher what he took to be useful information about escaping the downwind fallout of nuclear war by living in the southern hemisphere. The Jones family departed Hawaii for what Esquire described as the "bustling, progressive" city of Belo Horizonte, Brazil, leaving Peoples Temple's associate pastors—Jack Beam, Russ Winberg, Archie Ijames, and Ross Case—to look after the Indianapolis flock.[3]

The Joneses spent about two years in Brazil. The young preacher worked to serve local orphanages, but he also spent much of his time trying to learn about the social and economic conditions in Brazil, and he searched for possible land to acquire for a colony. Early in his stay Jones met an American Pentecostal missionary, Ed Malmin. Before long Malmin's sixteen-year-old daughter Bonnie, chafing at parental authority, moved in with Jones's "rainbow family." Bonnie found the household eating frugally on a diet of beans, bread, and rice, with occasional vegetables and meat—basically the same diet served at Jonestown years later. The Joneses depended on limited funds sent from nursing home profits back home, but Bonnie saw them feeding poor street children from the common pot, night after night. She enjoyed her stay with the interracial family, though the spiritually oriented young girl wondered why the Joneses, if they really were missionaries, did not have a Bible in the house. And how could Jones ask her father to accompany him to Brazilian spiritist meetings?[4]

In October of 1962 the Jones family was joined by their friends Jack and Rheaviana Beam, who helped with service work for local orphanages, but back home, struggles over nursing home management between Lynetta Jones and Marcie Jones's parents, the Baldwins, were cutting into support from the States. In early 1963 the Beams returned to Indianapolis. They were back only three days when Jones instructed them to go out West to survey the possibilities for migration there. By the end of April 1963 the Beams had set up housekeeping in Hayward, California.

Meanwhile, Jones was still not ready to return from Brazil, but he needed immediate income, so he took his family to Rio de Janeiro, where he had managed to get a job teaching. Jones also continued working to scrape together food supplies for orphanages. As in Belo, he felt the squeeze of limited resources in helping the poor. One time, he told Bonnie years later in front of Marcie, he had even resorted to playing the gigolo for three days to a diplomat's wife, in exchange for $5,000 that went to an orphanage.[5]

Whether or not Jones took money for sexual favors to the well-heeled, his own goal in coming to Brazil—finding a feasible settlement situation—became obviously unrealistic. True, Brazil had an interracial culture with origins in Portuguese enslavement of Amerindians and Africans. Despite some prejudice, people tolerated racial mixing in ways foreign to former British colonies like the United States and areas of the Caribbean, but the non-English culture would have presented difficulties for Jones and his followers. Moreover, hopes of finding a progressive Third World government were dashed as soon as Jones arrived. Brazil had undergone a military coup, and the new leaders were establishing an antidemocratic "bureaucratic-authoritarian" political regime to spearhead economic development.

Of more pressing concern to Jones personally, the associate pastors back in the States could not seem to hold Peoples Temple together without their leader as the driving force, and members of the once solid congregation were drifting away. To top off other problems, the church was split over Black associate minister Archie Ijames's efforts legally to adopt a young White woman. The other associate pastors, Russ Winberg and Ross Case, felt that Indianapolis "crackers" would never stand for Ijames's plan, and they successfully pleaded with Jones against it. But victory was Pyrrhic, for, even from Brazil, the head minister could see which way the chips had fallen on the divisive issue of race. He ordered the oldline Assemblies of God Pentecostalist Winberg out of the church, and Winberg took some presumably more traditional White members of the flock with him. Ross Case also sought less troubled pastures, moving his family to Ukiah, California—a "nuclear-free" zone touted as "upwind" in the 1962 *Esquire* article, west of the Sierra Nevada mountains and considerably north of San Francisco.

In the aftermath of the Ijames adoption crisis, Jones convinced his Pentecostal friend in Brazil, Ed Malmin, to take an upcoming furlough in Indianapolis to provide some stability to Peoples Temple and straighten out finances while Jones remained in Brazil. In Indiana Malmin did his job as any good preacher would, with one eye on doctrine, the other on cash flow. He preached a solid evangelical Christianity, and brought in a Hoosier evangelist, Mrs. Rosa Kemp, to conduct an old-time nightly revival meeting for several weeks.

Down in Brazil, learning about the assassination of John F. Kennedy did not make Jones feel very comfortable about returning to life in the United States, but he finally came to recognize the impracticality of any Brazilian immigration plans. Early in 1964 the Joneses returned to their native state; soon thereafter Ed Malmin returned to missionary pursuits.⁶

### First Migration

With only Archie Ijames to help him with the ministerial duties, Jones plunged back into the Indianapolis scene, but certain actions show that the return to Indianapolis was only a logistical stop on the search that had begun in 1961 for a more hospitable environment. An enigmatic note to Brazil from Lynetta Jones had read, "Remain warm clime til our winter ends. Give me time to arrange 'orderly flight.' Am past point of exploring the *whys*." Before Jones was back in Indianapolis even two months, Peoples Temple sold the 10th and Delaware synagogue building it had used for so many years, relocating a somewhat shrunken congregation, about half Blacks and half Whites, in temporary quarters at the Broadway Christian Center, at 17th and Broadway. There the Reverend James W. Jones finally became officially ordained as a Disciples of Christ minister, some four years after Peoples Temple had become affiliated with the denomination. The connection was to prove immensely useful to Peoples Temple in the long run, but it did little to change the congregation's more immediate situation.

Consistently, Jim Jones had taken ethically uncompromising and "impolitic" positions in the existential crises of racism that arose in his path. Among his followers he had promoted the Father Divine formula of a cooperative mission. The net result was to forge a "born-again" congregation, in the strong sense of that term. Over the years the Temple was shorn of people who lacked strong commitment to the interracial ethic, shorn of liberals who wanted social change but without fundamentally changing their own social status. By falling in with Jones, the people who joined Peoples Temple in the Indianapolis days joined the prophet's cadre in confronting the compelling dilemmas of capitalist society in the modern era: race, class privilege, and the threat of nuclear annihilation. In essence they underwent *metanoia*, a radical break with their previous worldviews. Collectively, they became people of the Apocalypse who acted as if an evil world was coursing on the brink of disaster. They did not thereby become holy persons, cleansed of the ways of sin themselves, but whatever else they did, they lived in opposition to what they perceived as the direction of world history.

The strong ethical position that Jim Jones put forward attracted true believers of sundry origins, but it hardly won him friends in the wider Indianapolis community. After he returned to Indianapolis, Black ministers there continued to see the man who promoted interracial worship as a threat to their own flocks. The Black clergy promoted *de facto* segregation of racial communities (while seeking equal civil rights) by affirming the Black church as an institution that must remain autonomous in order to advance the cause of Blacks. By promoting an alternative approach, Jones upstaged the Black ministers on the sensitive issue of race relations.

Eventually, in the spring of 1965, Jones also managed to provoke the ire of theologically conservative Christians listening to his weekly radio broadcast over WBIC. In his usual iconoclastic style, the preacher waxed ecumenical, defending Mahatma Gandhi as a believer in the teachings of Jesus, adding that perhaps all the great world religions had something to offer. As the coup de grace Jones asserted that he "couldn't see a loving heavenly Father condemning to hell persons because they wouldn't accept some Christian doctrines." The irate calls came cascading in, just as Jones surely knew they would, and his Indianapolis radio preaching career ground to a halt.

By that time plans to leave Indianapolis for California were well under way. The Joneses and those who stood with them already represented a segregated community themselves, cut off from the Black community by their interracial approach, and from the White liberal community by a messianic quest for redemption that went far beyond liberal Protestant ideas about the "social gospel." The Disciples of Christ tried to accommodate the unusual congregation, but Jones was distraught with his situation. At an ecumenical meeting of progressive congregations he "broke down and cried." Covering the meeting for a Disciples of Christ newspaper, Louise Moseley thought, "Well, gee, he is kind of unstable . . . , but he really means well."

Barely back from Brazil, Jones already was moving his congregation elsewhere. He doubted they could survive in Indianapolis, much less prosper. As the Hunters remembered, Jones wanted to "get this interracial family out of this atmosphere," and take his congregation to some sort of haven where "they could develop freely."

Well before the end of 1964, Jim Jones was out in California, visiting Jack Beam in Hayward to see about possible migration sites, but Hayward is on the San Francisco Bay, in the midst of cities and military bases that would be targeted for nuclear attack. An alternative presented itself when Ross Case, the Temple associate minister who had moved to Ukiah, invited Jones to take a look at the Mendocino County seat at the upper end of the Russian River valley, in the heart of logging country. Apparently Jones found the area satisfactory. Some time after he returned to Indianapolis, "he came in the house and started up the stairway and saw a big flash of light . . . ; it was coming from the north, Chicago. . . . It was a picture of a nuclear holocaust; the bomb blasted so bright that he saw it all the way in Indianapolis." Later, Jones "prophesied that we should go to California, and that there would be jobs and a place to stay for all who wanted to come out. He felt we had to come and make this journey."

People who decided to go made preparations, selling their property and closing out their affairs in Indiana, but it does not seem that the income from these transactions was pooled. Jones covered costs of the church's transition with income from the nursing home operations. Members made the move as individuals and in family groups, paying their own way. Some families' members left Indianapolis only grudgingly, and some people were forced to choose between the Temple and relatives who opposed Jones. Family members trying to prevent one woman's departure are said to have sought to have her declared insane so that she would not be legally capable of selling her property to make the move.

Others became head-over-heels enthusiasts. One of them, Rick Cordell, wanted to act on the holocaust prophecy immediately. He sold everything and went ahead west with his family in 1964. Most people waited for the main movement. Marcie Jones headed to California with her preschool children, Jimmy, Jr., and Stephan, in the spring of 1965. The major caravan of around seventy families—half Black, half White, followed them in the summer, with Jones and his mother. By July 15, 1965, Jack and Rheaviana Beam had moved up to Ukiah from Hayward.[7] Jones and his followers had reached what they hoped was their promised land.

### California Sojourn

Promises aside, the beginnings of life in California were not particularly auspicious. To begin with, associate minister Ross Case had a falling out with Peoples Temple over Jones's rejection of conventional Christianity as "pseudo-religious." Despite his differences, or perhaps because of them, the fundamentalist Case remained living in Ukiah—close enough to keep an eye on the Temple's doings.

Peoples Temple did not even complete incorporating in California until November 26, 1966, over a year after the migration. It took another two and a half years before the group could establish itself with a church building of its own. Nor was there any substantial growth in numbers, and at least some of the small increase in members came from Indianapolis families that continued to trickle out to California. Joyce Touchette's family is a case in point. Her parents, Helen and Clive Swinney, were brought to the Temple by the early Laurel Street apostate, Edith Cordell. Joyce took her Methodist-reared husband Charlie Touchette and their four children west from Indianapolis to visit their grandparents in 1966. In 1970 the Touchettes moved from Indianapolis to Stockton, California, and naturally they all went up to Mendocino County for services. Charlie, once a sheet-metal journeyman, then a sales representative for a small heating and air conditioning firm, was not very keen on Jim Jones's talk about sharing the wealth, but his son Mike followed mother and sisters in becoming a believer when Jones discussed with him the racism of professional sports. As Mike remembered, "I was middle class, but my friends were lower class. Rich kids would knock poor kids. That just bugged me, and the race thing even more. So Jim Jones sorta hit me right in what I felt." When Mike joined, he pulled in the remaining family holdouts—his father Charlie and his brother.

Beyond additional migrants, Peoples Temple sought converts from the established churches of Mendocino County. At first the Temple met in a Baptist church in Ukiah and held "fellowship" meetings with a number of local churches. For a while it worshiped with the Golden Rule Church, an established but declining California apostolic communal group that shared some of the less radical of Peoples Temple's socialistic principles. Golden Rule Church had potential converts and a substantial spread of land at Ridgeway Ranch, but a takeover effort by Jones failed, and by 1968 he became more matter-of-fact about secular socialism when speaking to his own congregation.

Nothing else in the way of common fellowship opened any doors for Peoples Temple either, and the group gravitated to the Joneses' home in Redwood Valley, about eight miles north of Ukiah. Other Temple families also settled in the low-rent rural district dotted with rundown houses left over from the logging boom days. Once again, with Blacks moving in, the social boundaries between the church and the outside world became reinforced by external harassment. Eventually a swimming pool was constructed on the Jones land so that church youth would not have to experience the racial insults at more public swimming spots. Then the congregation took an unusual step. Temple workers built a church on top of the pool, so that it could be used not only for recreation, but for immersion baptism as well. The new church opened its doors on February 2, 1969.[8]

Over the years the newcomer congregation gradually managed to establish a solid base, making important alliances in the community of greater Ukiah and attracting some highly dedicated converts to their fellowship. Marceline worked as a public health nurse at the mental hospital, Mendocino State Hospital. Jones taught high school courses for adults for the Ukiah District, served on the board of directors of the Legal Aid Foundation of Mendocino, and in March of 1968 was appointed foreman of a county grand jury.

Even with migrants and community contacts, the Temple grew only slowly in the early years. In 1966, the year the Temple incorporated in California, it reported an adult membership of only eighty-six. By the following year it had gained only twenty new members. Especially important among the new faces were the educated, middle-class Californians who had moved to Mendocino County to pursue careers. Pentecostals from Indiana, likely to hold jobs in services, trades, and sales, found themselves joined by followers from different social strata. One of the new breed was a social worker from San Francisco named Linda Amos, who was quickly to become a trusted Temple operative. Among others were Larry and Carolyn Moore Layton. Larry was the son of a scientist at Berkeley who once had done chemical warfare research. The mother, Lisa, a Jewish emigrant from Nazi Germany, had become a "convinced" Quaker. Larry grew up following her moral aversion to his father's work and to war in general, and he became a conscientious objector when the Vietnam war heated up. In Davis, California, Larry met Carolyn, the daughter of an activist Methodist minister named John Moore. The two were married in 1967 and moved to Mendocino County, where Larry did his alternative service as a conscientious objector at Mendocino State Hospital while Carolyn taught at Potter Valley High School. They joined Peoples Temple in 1968. Even by then, there were still only 136 faithful.

The following year, a slightly older middle-class couple came into the fold. Elmer "Mert" Mertle, a Missouri-born chemical technician with Standard Oil of California, had been attending a Parents without Partners group where he met Deanna, a divorcee raised in the fundamentalist Seventh Day Adventist Church. A year after they married, in November of 1969, their Disciples of Christ minister invited the pair to visit a church he had heard about in Redwood Valley.

Deanna Mertle worried about communism, and she recognized that she held deep-seated racist feelings. Mert, on the other hand, was an agnostic and civil rights activist. Peoples Temple seemed to bridge stressful differences in a marriage based on a romantic notion of second true love. More practically speaking, it seemed that the five children of the two from their previous marriages might thrive in the Temple's clean-cut, drug-free milieu. In spite of misgivings he and his wife had about the faith healings, Elmer Mertle somehow found it in himself to quit his professional job without future employment prospects, sell the family house in Hayward, and move north with Deanna and the children.

The small gains in absolute numbers represented by such newcomers were important ones. Jim Jones drew some key new members into social relationships that fundamentally changed his congregation. Moreover, the organizational skills and social prominence of converts helped propel the group toward an entirely different scale of operations.

The social transformation stemmed from a relationship that developed between Jim Jones and newcomer Carolyn Layton. Until then Jim seemed to have been faithful to Marcie, but he and Carolyn became lovers sometime after Carolyn separated from her husband Larry, in the first part of 1969. Jim complained to Carolyn that Marcie could not respond sexually, and Marcie absented herself from the scene for a while by going down to the Travelodge Motel in Santa Rosa. While there, she wrote to Jim's mother Lynetta that in her depression she had become a "negative stimulus" to Jim. Marcie agonized: she did not see how she could leave the marriage without making the children feel abandoned. Jim convinced both Marcie and Carolyn that Marcie was a mentally unstable person, and Carolyn wrote her parents, explaining that Jim and Marcie would remain married because of "the need for us not to cut her out of our lives." Carolyn and Larry were divorced in 1969, the same year they separated, and the young Methodist minister's daughter became Jones's enduring lover, friend, and associate.

A transformation with more direct organizational consequences came with Jones's prize convert, a bright, ambitious young Stanford Law School graduate named Timothy Oliver Stoen. While still in law school, the student from an affluent Colorado family had planned to "serve man" through theology and the pursuit of political power, still hoping to leave time for the good things in life. By joining Peoples Temple, Stoen offered a mantle of legitimacy to the transplanted congregation, and he marshaled his considerable organizational talents and professional connections to help Jones build a powerful social movement.

In 1965 Stoen had begun working as a prosecuting attorney for the Mendocino County district attorney's office, in an early step of what already had been methodically projected as a long and successful career. His serious Presbyterian upbringing and religiously conservative Wheaton College education had left him grappling with theological matters, and Jim Jones was versed enough in the issues to bring Stoen's more idealistic side to the fore. Stoen was applying for the position of director of Legal Services Foundation of Mendocino in August 1967 when he first met Jones, who was serving on the organization's board of directors. Stoen got the job and participated in Peoples Temple, but left Ukiah in October of 1968 to work as a defense lawyer for the Alameda Legal Aid Society.

Still, the young attorney continued to attend services in Redwood Valley occasionally, and by the end of 1969 he made the commitment "to live up to the standards of the communal Christian church as set forth in [the Bible's book of] Acts, to the best of my ability. . . ." Stanford Law School had steeped the convert in the good life, and he wrote to Jones asking how far he would have to curb the "latent materialism" of his tastes in cars, clothes, and home furniture. Apparently Stoen had little idea about the sacrifices involved in any kind of Christian communalism, for he wanted to know whether it would be permissible to visit nightclubs "assuming there is time to be taken from serving the community." Still, he recognized his conversion would change life in ways he could not anticipate. "I can no longer be the same person, seeking power and pleasure, as I have blueprinted myself to be," he wrote Jim. "I hope you will all bear with me for I have a hell of a lot of growing to do."

On a more practical level, Stoen wanted Jones to advise him: "In your opinion could I do more good for the church by becoming Assistant District Attorney (civil) or by becoming Directing Attorney of Legal Services?" Apparently Jones favored the first option, for Stoen returned to Mendocino County the following year as an assistant district attorney. When he moved to Mendocino County, Stoen brought along a young Catholic woman named Grace Grech, whom he had been courting since the previous fall. Though Grace did not consider herself a true believer, she agreed to join Peoples Temple when she married her love in the summer of 1970, and over the years she took on increasing responsibilities in the growing church.[9]

The influx of a core of White, middle-class California college graduates and professionals like Stoen, social worker Linda Amos, the Mertles, and high school teacher Carolyn Moore Layton attracted others from relatively affluent sectors of society. There was Sandy Bradshaw, the serious young social worker who came to Mendocino County as a juvenile counselor, and later became a deputy probation officer. In 1972 Teri Buford, a quick-witted young hippie, drifted in, just out of a "far Eastern religious type thing." She was hitchhiking through Redwood Valley, came upon Peoples

Temple, and joined, in part on the basis of the Temple's appeal to her Quaker upbringing and antiwar and socialist ideals. There were others, more affluent, but about as aimless. One was Debbie Layton. The attractive eighteen-year-old sister of Larry Layton had grown up in the permissive atmosphere of Berkeley, though she was sent to England for schooling by her establishment father during the height of the hippie and antiwar movements because of the Peoples' Park riot. Debbie explained her 1971 decision: "By joining Peoples Temple, I hoped to help others and in the process to bring structure and self-discipline to my own life."

The Whites like Larry and Carolyn Moore Layton, Debbie Layton, Sandy Bradshaw, and Teri Buford were attracted to the Temple not out of any absolute material deprivation but out of the various strains of alienation that marked the counterculture and the antiwar movement. In the 1960s hundreds of thousands of Americans of the post-World War II baby-boom generation self-consciously "dropped out" of a society that could not seem to accommodate to their life-styles or their idealism, or offer them much other than the opportunity to partake in the material riches of late capitalism. When the heady "crash-pad" days of "flower power" were eclipsed by the late 1960s surge of concern with the Vietnam war, young people sometimes drifted toward structured religious groups, like Hare Krishna and Transcendental Meditation. Others became involved in the social movements of the day, from the antiwar movement to ecology and equal rights. Those who joined Peoples Temple came from diverse counter-cultural paths that all led to the same point, an activist communal group that offered the communion of the family and the social goals of a movement organization.

Other Whites, with already well established career interests, came to Peoples Temple in horizontal career shifts that often would offer increases in career opportunity in an organization that purported to harness vocations not just for personal gain but for the promotion of the common good. One such person was Gene Chaiken, a lawyer who joined in 1972. He began attending services in January, then gave up his job as deputy county counselor for Shasta County, and moved to Redwood Valley to do real estate and legal service law for Peoples Temple.[10]

With the growing number of White middle-class California converts, many of them skilled in professional and bureaucratic vocations, the organizational core of Peoples Temple shifted in a way that facilitated expanding the operation to an entirely different scale. Peoples Temple began using its rural church as a base for concerted "campaign" forays a hundred miles to the south, to the San Francisco Bay area. The large ghetto populations of Blacks there made for more fruitful terrain for radical interracial evangelism than did the overwhelmingly White, predominantly poor rural areas of the Russian River valley, where Peoples Temple was the object of at least some harassment reminiscent of Indianapolis. Though Jones had led his flock to the rural retreat of Redwood Valley in part to escape urban tensions, he said he felt guilty "because there were still kids in the ghetto." Pursuing his self-acclaimed Peace Mission mandate, he declared that he "wanted to get older people and children out of the city—bring them up [to Redwood Valley] every week so they could swim in the pool, get some fresh air." It was also true, of course, that to the degree Jones could enlarge his following, he could increase cash flow, and in turn fund the human service activities that would further enhance his reputation and following.

The Temple initiated its San Francisco efforts sometime in 1968. By April of 1970 the San Francisco Peoples Temple opened in a spacious church building on Geary Street. Peoples Temple blossomed during the early 1970s into a religious movement that could claim success: a growing number of adherents, branch churches in San Francisco and Los Angeles, a nationwide ministry organized through bus tours that doubled as group vacations, and a successful "human service" ministry tied to a string of "care" homes for juveniles and the elderly that served as a nucleus for promoting a communal orientation in Peoples Temple.

Over the years, Tim Stoen later estimated, probably 50,000 to 100,000 people heard Jones speak at one time or another, but the highest active membership, despite exaggerated Temple claims, was around 3,000. Jones followed the Peace Mission formula, seeking out the alienated and dispossessed from every quarter. In June of 1970, just three months after Peoples Temple had opened the San Francisco Temple on Geary Street, it purchased the first bus. All early proceeds must have gone into mortgages and more buses. By November of 1971 Peoples Temple was running a fleet of eleven buses, transporting members among services, and heading for the nation's highways. As it did in so many other ways, Peoples Temple imitated wider evangelical practices, in this case by hauling people around to revival meetings scheduled in one city after another. By the early 1970s weekend bus tours would include stops in Oakland, Richmond, and San Rafael to gather the faithful and transport them to services. Occasionally the entourage would make a weekend campaign tour to the Pacific Northwest. At least every other weekend Jones, his staff, and numerous followers took to a grueling schedule: a Friday evening service in San Francisco, then the nine-hour, night freeway run to Los Angeles for services on Saturday, then back to the San Francisco Temple for a Sunday morning service, and to Redwood Valley for a Sunday evening meeting.

In the summers there were even more ambitious journeys. For $200 (less if they pleaded poverty) Temple members could take nationwide tours with Jones and his staff, seeing the sights and holding services in likely spots like

Kansas City, the South, and Washington, D.C. One time they even visited Jones's hometown of Lynn, Indiana, and paid a call on his early religious "godmother," Mrs. Kennedy.

The summer tours offered an opportunity to seek converts, and among the most important targets were the remaining Philadelphia devotees of the deceased Father Divine. Finally, after one such trip in 1971, Jones sent buses to pick up Philadelphia Peace Mission residents who wished to move out to sunny California. That was enough of Peoples Temple "fellowship" for Mother Divine, Divine's young White widow who ran the Peace Mission after Divine "laid His Body down." "We have entertained Pastor Jones and the People's Temple," she fumed in a public statement in 1972. "We were entertaining angels of the 'other fellow'! (the term followers used to denote the d-v-l) [sic] We no longer extend to them any hospitality whatsoever! . . . They are not welcome!"[11]

By far the larger number of converts came not from summer expeditions but from urban California. As Jones had in Indianapolis, he operated in California in the gulf of urban decay that had come with the transformation of U.S. cities. According to one observer, "Urban renewal . . . had succeeded in reaching into the [San Francisco] Western Addition and totally disrupting a stable and progressive Black community. The redevelopers used meat-ax techniques to dislodge small shopkeepers, Black families, renters, and storefront churches." Conventional Black churches in San Francisco and Los Angeles, like those in other large cities, were finding it difficult to maintain vital connections to their congregations. Moreover, in the era of the Black Power movement, young Blacks across the country were deserting the church in legions.

Jones himself pointed to the problem in his sermons: many Black ministers were still promoting an essentially conservative and spiritualistic theology of heavenly compensation after death, while popular Black sentiments increasingly were directed toward concrete social change in "this" world. By the years Malcolm X and Martin Luther King were assassinated, in 1965 and 1968, Black preachers in the churches and storefront chapels often still were caught up in distinguishing their ministries from competitors' by emphasizing sectarian doctrines like trinitarianism and full immersion baptism. It was into this strain between the congregations of conservative Black churchs and the radical popular movements that Jones inserted his ministry. He ridiculed conservative Black Christianity, telling those who worried about whether the rapture was coming before or after the tribulation, "You strain at gnats and you swallow camels." But he also offered a mainstay of Pentecostal practice, faith healing, in an apostolic socialist dispensation.

In the wake of Martin Luther King's assassination Jim Jones and the Reverend George Bedford, pastor of San Francisco's Macedonia Baptist

Church, began a series of pulpit exchanges. Bedford broke with Jones in 1969, after Jones publicly "extracted" a "cancer" from a young Baptist preacher. But by that time the White Hoosier prophet had done his damage; Jones is said to have gained about 30 per cent of his prey's congregation, one of the largest in San Francisco. He put the Black clergy of urban California on the spot. They could hardly criticize a social action ministry without deepening the gulf between themselves and parts of their own congregations, but few of them were prepared to engage in more militant social activism, and the Temple made steady gains.

Some observers have pointed to the destitution of Blacks whom Jones brought into the fold. John Moore, the Methodist minister and father of Carolyn Moore Layton, talked after Jonestown of how Peoples Temple had carried the ministry of Jesus to its logical conclusion: "They cared for the last and the least of the human family." Jones himself called his followers "the refuse of America." Others were more cynical. Mendocino County Social Services Director Dennis Denny argued, "It was obvious he was building a financial empire from other people's money and that he was taking personalities that were less competent in society and leading and directing their lives."

It is true that Peoples Temple counted the downtrodden among its fold. Some Temple Blacks had worked in mines and northern factories. Others had grown up sharecropping cotton in the South in the early part of the twentieth century. Into their lives had come not only economic hardships but a racial oppression marked by shootings, lynchings, and castrations. Too often family life was full of rape, incest, unwanted pregnancies, and separations. Among these Blacks were some who had participated in Marcus Garvey's back-to-Africa movement. For such people, like the follower who said, "I always wanted to go to a Black country," Jones rekindled a distant dream. Some Temple Blacks had been involved in radical movements like the Southern tenants' unions and the Communist party, studying the *Daily Worker* and taking part in strikes. Many had come out to California after World War II in hopes of a better life. And even some of those born in California knew the harder edges of street life revolving around heroin, pimping, and prostitution.

It was not just Blacks embittered by harsh lives, however, who came to Peoples Temple. Others came from the liberal Black bourgeoisie, many of whom found themselves alienated from politically conservative Black churches. One woman who lost relatives at Jonestown noted that her sister was neither poor nor disadvantaged; in fact, she had given two expensive homes to Peoples Temple.

Along with the range of Blacks, the Temple continued to attract Whites. All told, Peoples Temple gained converts from virtually the entire range of the racial, class, and cultural spectrum of the United States, from poor

Blacks and White fundamentalists to alienated upper-middle-class youth, professional careerists, and affluent members of the Black bourgeoisie. The largest proportion of Jones's followers who eventually went to Guyana, over 40 per cent, were middle-aged and elderly Blacks born in southern states, along with their families. The overall proportion of Blacks was around 70 per cent. Reflecting California's reputation for mobility, less than a third of all Temple members were born in the state. Aside from California, most Whites came from Indiana and nearby midwestern states. A smattering came from all around the United States, most of them young and middle-aged people who presumably joined up with the Temple after they came to California for school or the manifold other attractions of the state.

Despite the disproportionate numbers of older Blacks and young Whites, Peoples Temple was more than an organization built simply on offering either "structure" to "cult-dependent" former hippies and street people or healings and a home to often stereotyped elderly, religiously superstitious Blacks. To suggest as much would promote a subtle form of racial and status-group denigration that insists anyone attracted to someone like Jones must somehow have been deprived and mentally deficient. Peoples Temple offered a formula of communalist activism that brought together diverse people. It offered status passage to a community in which diversity itself marked a gathering of *déclassé* people—those who had abandoned their class and ethnic privilege or stigma, as the case might be, to throw in their lot with people from widely different backgrounds who nevertheless shared their commitment to an interracial society freed of class exploitation.[12]

Both the dispossessed and the relatively affluent often came to the Temple with real misgivings based on their distrust of ministers, but they found Jim Jones was not like others. "Nobody else had ever taken them and looked them in the eye and said, 'I love you,' which Jim would do," remembered Tim Stoen. "When I saw Jim kiss old Black ladies on the cheek and their eyes would light up, I would cry, I was so touched."[13] The preacher did not seem as caught up in the theology of the afterlife as he was concerned with the reconstruction of this life.

Essentially, Jim Jones had begun by taking over Father Divine's Peace Mission model. Success and controversy, however, brought a departure from Father Divine's approach and a return to the foreign colonization dreams of Marcus Garvey. Migration inside the United States to what in 1972 was called the Redwood Valley "heaven-on-earth" was not an entirely satisfactory solution. For all Jones mimicked Father Divine's organizational genius, he could not stomach the idea of developing a rural religious community as the site of a "retreat" from the evils of capitalism and urban racism, as Father Divine had done in upstate New York. Jones was a socialist of sorts, while his mentor mostly had promoted Black capitalism; for a socialist of any provenience, California was hardly the promised land.

Under the scrutiny of a hostile capitalist press, Jones's radical convictions took firmer shape and content in the California years, and he could not rest from an intense preoccupation with getting "out of Egypt . . . , out of Babylon," relocating someplace where interracial socialism could flourish without the stigma it held in a White-dominated, institutionally and socially segregated capitalist society. In 1973 Jones and his staff started to plan for a second emigration. This time they followed the earlier idea of establishing a colony outside the United States. By 1974 an advance crew was in Guyana, on the Caribbean coast of South America, clearing land, constructing facilities, and planting crops for the "Peoples Temple Agricultural Mission." Then, in November of 1976, the corporate headquarters of Peoples Temple were shifted from Redwood Valley to San Francisco, probably to consolidate church operations in preparation for migration.

Soon thereafter, in 1977, a storm of controversy brought Peoples Temple into direct conflict with defectors, relatives, authorities, and religious observers. Those who challenged Jones's activities would capitalize on a public climate of fear concerning "cults" to bring Peoples Temple into the glare of hostile media attention. That spring and summer Jones and his loyal followers departed on a second migration to the next promised land.[14]

In a way the theme of migration was never totally submerged and the search for sanctuary was never totally satisfied during the California years; the stay there represented an extended sojourn for Peoples Temple. But those years can be considered a sojourn only because Jim Jones and his associates successfully built a group and organization that possessed the solidarity, the social control over significant numbers of followers, the material resources, and the organizational and political acumen that made it possible to prosper in California and establish an enterprise on the scale of Jonestown. How they did so not only reveals a great deal about the motivating power of a redemptive myth, but in diverse realms also demonstrates the power of a netherworld of U.S. cultural practices, for Jones was a pragmatic messiah as well as a possessed one. His religion was anything but an ethically purist effort to reach utopian ends by use of utopian means. To the contrary, for Jones, as commentators have said over and over again, "the ends justified the means." He was ready to employ often conventional methods to achieve his unnerving purpose of ridding the world of "complacency." Thus, however much Jones's theology and movement are part of a centuries-long march of millennial dreams, his methods are a catalogue of more modern accomplishments. Many of the strangely awkward practices of Peoples Temple derive from the volatile admixture of primitive charisma with the possibilities of social control, public relations, and politics in a highly bureaucratized and rationalized mass society. To understand the California years thus requires close examination of ends and means, to trace their cultural origins and significance for Peoples Temple.

There is no tidy way approach to this analysis. Jones's charismatic organizational genius often derived from his ability to act in ways that had ramifications in several different institutional spheres at the same time. One event might simultaneously involve administrative practice, public relations, and promotion of social control. Nevertheless, the cultural pattern of ends and means can be explored most efficiently by considering separate spheres in which Jones and his staff operated. The following three chapters therefore consider the administration and financial operations of Peoples Temple, the solidarity and social control of its people, and external politics and public relations during the California "sojourn" of some twelve years.

# PART II

# 6

# The Corporate Conglomerate

Relations between utopian collectivist organizations and modern industrial capitalist societies always have been somewhat strained. For one thing, modern people treat with suspicion true believers who devote themselves to an alien cause larger than themselves. Sometimes the reborn wear odd costumes, and when they come out on the streets seeking converts, they strike a strange contrast to the demeanor and dress of almost any social figure, from the sober but liberal business type to alienated and rebellious youth. Then too, religious revolutionaries act charismatically, that is, without regard to the conventions that govern everyday life, and they therefore inherently challenge an established order, and often, its legal-rational authority. While the state has become the institution that directly or indirectly bestows legitimacy on practically every aspect of social life, at least in the United States, communal groups never have come within this warm orb of government sanction.

But the established order always has held some fascination for utopian deviants too. Especially favored in secular culture is the utopia proclaimed as harbinger of the future. In the progressive vision popularized since the early nineteenth century, society would be organized according to totally rational labor-saving principles that nevertheless maintain individual rights and promote equality of opportunity. From time to time secular communal groups have been established along rationalist lines, to prove the practicality of a philosopher's dream. Thus came Robert Owen from Scotland to New Harmony, Indiana, in 1825, to demonstrate that the benefits of capitalism could be more widely distributed through cooperative enterprise. Religious communities of the day explored the same rational bases of social organization. Upstate New York's Oneida, led by the iconoclastic Yankee preacher John Humphrey Noyes, even dabbled in a rationalistic eugenic experiment for production of children, provoking deep hostility in the society at large. The most apocalyptic of communities, Mother Ann's Shakers, did not practice procreation because the end of the world was at hand. Nevertheless, Shakers developed industries, sales networks, and labor-saving devices to provide an efficient and lucrative basis for sustaining the faithful until the Lord should appear.

Whatever else they did, nineteenth-century U.S. communal groups served as "laboratories" of the new society. At a time when industrial work discipline was hardly well established, they were putting the new rational philosophy to work in every realm of social life. Sometimes they borrowed techniques and practices from the wider culture, using them for their own ends. Sometimes they tinkered with culture, exaggerating it to the point of creating something new. Sometimes their new cultural forms spread to the wider society.[1]

Given these possibilities, communal groups do not exist as entities totally alien from the society at large in which they occur. Instead, they offer refractions of culture, sometimes exposing the dilemmas or developing the unfulfilled possibilities of an era.

Like its less infamous predecessors, Peoples Temple was an organization propelled in part by the dictates of rationality. In many ways the group borrowed tried and true techniques of fundamentalist religion and modern organizational practices. But the Temple's collectivist form and its unusual sense of mission also propelled it toward a new, synthetic bureaucratic form, one that mirrored the logic of the state and large corporations, but with a different orientation. Peoples Temple became a corporation of people.

## The Business of Apostolic Socialism

For complex reasons, connections between religion and economy often define the core of a culture. The classic demonstration by sociologist Max Weber traces the rise of a Protestant ethic of self-discipline for work held by newly autonomous individuals set adrift in an industrializing world of rational capitalism, where cultural requirements differed radically from those of the preceding feudal and mercantilist economies.

If religious values infuse economic life, an era's principles of economic activity also undergird religion. In the modern world, religion itself has come more and more under the sway of rationalistic organization and "marketplace" competition for souls. Even while Protestant theology has promoted the idea that each individual can have a personal relation to God, the organization of Protestantism has tended toward increasingly businesslike rational, bureaucratic, and hierarchical practices.

In the first place, Protestant theology itself strongly promotes rationalization of social relationships, for example, in theologies of salvation, in financial transactions, and in the performance of work obligations of a calling. Applied to churches themselves, the Protestant virtues suggest an efficient form of religious organization, one that maximizes the Lord's return on His work on earth. Second, like other enterprises, churches in the twentieth century have had to become more and more businesslike in order to administer their increasingly complex worldly dealings with banks, lawyers, investment firms, and the like. Third, about the turn of the century, liberal denominations pursued the social gospel at the same time that an emerging philosophy of "corporate liberalism" placed the state in the position of contending with the social problems resulting from industrial capitalism. The convergent interests of the liberal churches and the state in social welfare coupled church agencies with an ever more complicated array of governmental social service bureaucracies, and the churches have had to adopt similar organizational forms and practices to be effective. Finally, in the past century, secular culture itself has undergone a transition from predominantly folk styles to an overwhelmingly mass culture, and some of the churches have succumbed to "fighting fire with fire" by adopting the technology and sensibilities of mass culture to promote their own message.[2] The upshot of "modernization" is that religions today are businesses, often big businesses.

What sort of business, then, was Peoples Temple? Essentially it followed the Peace Mission model, in which Father Divine had placed himself at the center of a vast patrimonial empire of redistribution financed through members' tithing and the profits from numerous Peace Mission businesses. Outsiders long have ridiculed Divine's style and substance, but Robert Weisbrot, a revisionist historian, argues that Divine struggled for dignity and justice for both Blacks and Whites, and offered his followers a road of material as well as spiritual salvation at a time when the Great Depression had laid waste the social landscape all around them.

Like Father Divine, Jim Jones offered an unusual blend of spiritual, social, and material salvation. Like Divine, Jones saw the practical needs of this pastoral program. He seems to have been well aware of his business acumen even in the Indiana years, when he confided to Barton Hunter, "You know, I am embarassed sometimes, because everything I touch turns to money." Yet in the early years in California, the money did not come easily. Peoples Temple members ran the gamut of petty church moneymaking schemes. They had bake sales. They ran clothing drives. They held rummage sales. Every year there was a Christmas drive for the underprivileged. They began selling refreshments at civic events, from a senior citizens dance to the local high school football games. In a modern revival of the Peace Mission approach to free enterprise, the Temple even bought a small shopette on East Road, next to the gas station in the center of Redwood Valley. Administrative offices were set up on the upper level, leaving the ground floor for a Temple laundromat and other small businesses.

The success of small-scale fund-raisers notwithstanding, the key to

Jones's success was converts. The reasoning behind the desire for growth, however, was hardly that of conventional pyramiding evangelical operations. Because Jones always regarded his following as a threat to the established order, he sought safety in numbers: "There was always the object of bringing in more people so we'd have a larger number and maybe wouldn't get harassed as much." In California during the latter part of the 1960s, Peoples Temple had only limited success drawing members from beyond the Indiana circle. By 1969 church membership still was only a reported 300 persons. But after the Temple expanded its activities to San Francisco and Los Angeles, membership shot up, more than doubling to 712 in 1970-71, and climbing to 2,203 in 1972.[3]

## The Home Care Franchise System

The snowballing expansion of Peoples Temple to urban California fueled growth along the lines of the Peace Mission model. Like the Peace Mission, Peoples Temple operated as a redistributive welfare system centered on a man declared to be God in the flesh. Like the Peace Mission, Peoples Temple was founded on the principle of the church as a surrogate extended family that substituted for the natural family. Consonant with its approach, the Temple made familylike demands for economic contribution to the general welfare, and in turn, supported people who took on the communal commitment to the Temple as their family place of work. But there was a decisive difference between the Peace Mission and Peoples Temple. When Father Divine had his heyday during the 1930s, the welfare state was hardly yet established; by the time of Peoples Temple, it was a *fait accompli*. Dealing with the clients of the welfare state became a central business of Peoples Temple.

Modern societies always have been confronted with the poor and the "poor in spirit"—people bereft of the ability to cope with the mental and social challenges of societies undergoing rapid change. According to social critic Michel Foucault, since the seventeenth century the principle of *confinement* has served not only to control criminals but also to segregate from the public world stigmatized people deemed mad, unruly, or simply impoverished. The history of confinement contains the darker side of progress; it includes a compendium of "rational" and "scientific" advances in techniques like lobotomy and shock therapy used in the mass administration of dispossessed lives.

By the 1950s "the great confinement" had packed the back wards of state mental hospitals with row after row of beds filled with the "residual population" of chronic patients—often elderly, some of them abandoned, some too poor to afford private care, many of them members of minority groups.

Juvenile delinquents and "incorrigible" children could be found in similar facilities. Then the advent of psychotherapeutic drugs shifted the boundaries of confinement from physical walls to pills: "acting out" behavior could be prevented through administration of antipsychotic drugs like Thorazine and lithium. The net result was that senile patients, chronic schizophrenics, and juveniles with behavioral disorders often could be discharged from hospitals and detention centers to be maintained in less restrictive facilities: halfway houses, family care homes, and board-and-care homes. But as Segal and Aviram note, progress is laden with the contradictions of creating "new back wards": "to some extent, the community-care system represents a step back to the 'poorhouse' concept, by providing care under the same roof for all types of individuals who are unable to 'make it' in our society."[4]

In the 1960s California pioneered in what came to be called deinstitutionalization. Especially important was federal funding through Supplemental Security Income (SSI) payments, which provided for nonhospital room and board. The emigration from hospitals was phenomenal. At Mendocino State Hospital, where several Peoples Temple members worked, the patient census dropped from 3,000 in the early 1960s to 1,200 in 1969. A number of convalescent homes around Ukiah offered facilities for its former patients.

Peoples Temple itself began organizing care homes for the burgeoning and potentially lucrative market in community care for the "socially dependent." Its members took in not only elderly psychiatric patients but those simply requiring nursing home care, as well as younger mentally retarded people, and minors who had become wards of the state, some after being declared "incorrigible" by their parents.

It has been suggested that Jim Jones led the exodus from Indiana to California not just to escape nuclear holocaust in the "upwind" area north of San Francisco but, more importantly, to cash in on the deinstitutionalization of Mendocino State Hospital. Jones and his followers operated nursing homes in Indianapolis, and before leaving Indiana he promised that his followers would get jobs in California. Marceline Jones and as many as five other Temple members worked on the psychiatric hospital staff, and Marcie was a visiting nurse who looked in on patients placed in care homes. At least eight other Temple members at various times worked for another agency serving care-home residents, Mendocino County's Department of Social Services; among them were some of the Temple's more prominent members: Jim Randolph, Laura Johnston, Grace Stoen, Joyce Shaw, and Linda Amos. These Temple workers provided important liaison between the welfare system and the series of care homes that were established by still other Temple members.

Over the years Temple members acquired houses along and just off East Road, the main thoroughfare through the rural village of Redwood Valley. Facilities with names like Green Acres, Whispering Pines, Fireside Lodge, and Hilltop Haven began to take clients placed through Mendocino State Hospital, the Mendocino County Department of Social Services, and the Juvenile Court. There were no less than nine Temple residential-care homes for the elderly, six homes for foster children, and Happy Acres, a state-licensed forty-acre ranch for mentally retarded persons with developmental special needs. No doubt other Temple family-care homes and individual families took in smaller numbers of clients under less restrictive licensing arrangements and guardianships.

In many cases the Temple itself recruited clients for its care homes, sometimes from the congregations in San Francisco and Los Angeles. Temple members like Carolyn Moore Layton and Tim Stoen were always on hand after services to counsel members of the congregation about everything from automobile accidents to welfare eligibility. Elderly Temple members, children in the juvenile justice system, and others who qualified for welfare asssistance often could have their dealings with the welfare bureaucracy managed by Temple social workers, and Peoples Temple in effect operated a client advocacy program that offered its own facilities to house eligible individuals. Nor is there anything in the least shady about such an operation. It is a formula that has been adopted by other church groups dedicated to serving the poor, for example, the Franciscan Order in New York City.

The Temple's approach to social service delivery nevertheless constituted a threat to the established system, particularly at the county level. Because the Temple cultivated an independent source of clients, to a certain degree it rerouted authority to provide social services outside the established interorganizational social welfare network, thereby challenging existing network organizations. In particular, because Temple members also worked for government agencies, the man in charge of Mendocino County Social Services, Dennis Denny, wondered whether his authority was being undermined. Concerned about the "loyalties" of his staff, Denny smelled the possibility of corruption. Moreover, he did not believe Temple foster children clients would have "freedom of choice" in religious matters. Despite the fact that his Temple employees all did "standard or above-standard work," Denny watched them like a hawk. Even so, he never found them involved in any of the common welfare rackets like creating "dummy" case files. Nor did a 1979 Mendocino County grand jury find any evidence of organized welfare fraud by Peoples Temple.

In an industry plagued with poor care and profiteering among vendors, Temple operators performed practically without malfeasance. Denny maintained "continuous contacts" with Temple facility operators, but even after 1978 he admitted he had found Temple care homes "excellent," with the residents well fed, well clothed, and "always clean." One of the few complaints that led anywhere came from an elderly woman who was described by even a non-Temple member as "aggressive" and "prone to getting into arguments." The woman charged that Temple operators Jim and Eva Pugh were disciplining her by holding back her $30 weekly allowance while other clients received money allotted them. She accepted an out-of-court settlement for $500.[5]

The clients probably did receive reasonably good care, but Peoples Temple still managed to make a tidy profit. In the early California years Temple members operated care homes as individuals, but beginning in 1971 Peoples Temple used debt financing to purchase a series of houses for care facilities, leasing them to the individuals licensed to operate them. Thus, just like private-sector vendors, the Temple built up equity in the homes operated by its members. Moreover, the Temple neglected to pay taxes on its income from rental payments by member operators, though most church income other than donations, including profits from financing care homes for member operators, would have been considered "unrelated business income" falling outside the nonprofit church guidelines of the Internal Revenue Service.

Aside from real estate equity and tax avoidance, there were two additional channels, often intermingled, by which the profits flowed. First, Peoples Temple essentially acted as franchiser of a succession of individual operators, offering them "slots" in a conglomerate that depended on centralized expertise in licensing, care techniques, and so forth. Given the *de facto* administrative control the Temple exercised over care-home operators, it was logical for the Temple to integrate vertically business services to individual vendors as well. The Temple would engage in central purchasing, and scrounge for resources from any quarter, allegedly once even stealing truckloads of federal surplus food from a San Francisco warehouse. Through centralized acquisition and distribution, and by coupling its nursing home operations with other charitable activities such as clothing drives, the Temple was able to introduce franchise-style economies of scale out of the reach of independent operators.

Second, because the Temple care-home operators in effect worked in what was called Peoples Temple's "human services" ministry, they were expected to pay the taxes on their home-care income, live frugally, and tithe the bulk of their profits back to the Temple, so that the Temple's good works could be expanded even further. Sometimes operators simply signed over checks and received all their needs from the central "franchiser." In effect, the operators were treated like members of Catholic lay orders: they were guaranteed a living while they engaged in church service. Thus, Temple profit came from not only franchising and vertical integration but also subordination of individual profit to the collective.

It is difficult to make even an approximate accounting of care-home profits. Apostate Walter Jones said that out of a monthly-care client income of $2,000 on a home he helped run for emotionally disturbed boys, he transferred about $900 to $1,000 to Peoples Temple. But he also received certain noncash supplies from the Temple, so net Temple profit would have been somewhat lower than 50 percent, probably no higher than 40 percent. An October 1972 accounting of another facility, the ranch for the mentally retarded, shows a complicated operation, with basic outlays for food, clothing, allowances, mortgage, entertainment, and doctors' bills. Also listed were expenditures for wages and maintenance service, perhaps indicating that some Temple members were paid (low) wages for their work in Temple-sponsored businesses. When all the expenses were deducted from the $3,333 that apparently came from welfare transfer payments, the net "commitment" turned over to the church was about $800 to $900, or around 25 percent. Social Service Director Denny estimated that over the period from 1966 through 1976, the gross receipts of homes operated by Temple members were approximately $648,000. If the Temple's rate of profit ranged between 25 percent and 40 percent (within industry norms), the church's total net income over the years amounted to between $162,000 and $259,000. Presumably there was more, from other care homes Denny did not realize were run by Temple members.[6]

## Money Schemes and Money Management

The care homes were profitable, but they hardly begin to account for the millions of dollars Peoples Temple amassed. Temple capital formation was not based on windfall profits; it flowed from a multitude of activities, many of them small in scale, conducted over and over again. Transfer payments for welfare clients, for example, did not exhaust income that came from Temple property. Jones's followers cultivated 7,200 grape vines at the ranch, and a smaller number on the land next to the church and parsonage on East Road. The Children's Home October 1972 monthly financial statement reported $2,252 in income from selling the vineyards' harvest to Parducci Wine Cellars. Presumably, church members, including care recipients, worked in the harvest. Then there was $134 in "miscellaneous income," which probably came from one of the panoply of money-making schemes church members operated.

These money-makers, like the home-care operations, often both depended upon and reinforced the flow of believers into Jim Jones's flock.

Deanna Mertle seemed to have a knack for raising money, and Jones asked her to dream up projects. The approach mirrored practices of other media evangelicals who plied similar spiritual waters. Deanna set up sales counters at the San Francisco and Los Angeles Temples where charm photographs of Jim Jones in cheap lockets went for prices from $1.50 to $6. During sermons Jim would tell tales like the one about Sister Turner driving a car

> that was going off into the water with her five children. . . . But bless her heart, she held onto the picture of me that she had on her ignition key, and she said, "Father, for the sake of my children. . . ." And up that car came, as we all know. . . . And when she finally got her five children out, and she stepped out, it rolled back down into that bottomless pit! My, my, my, my!

At the end of a service, Jones would berate people as they departed, "You say you don't need your oil, you don't need the pictures, you don't need the candles? You'd better get them while you can, because they won't always be around." Sales were brisk. Concessions are said to have brought in from $2,000 to $3,000 every weekend.

Together with her husband Mert, Deanna also implemented the mass-mailing scheme. Jim reasoned, "Well, some healers do this. I have a genuine healing ministry; maybe we ought to consider it." Deanna studied what others with the gift of the Spirit were putting out and the Temple mimicked an already flourishing approach to religious financing. Like other mass-mailing operations that included testimonials, Temple monthly mailers proclaimed that "Blessings Are Flowing," and reproduced letters like one from J. Williams, who wrote, "Dear Pastor Jones. . . . I put your Anointed Oil and your picture on my hip as soon as I received it. The picture stuck to my hip. I could walk with it, cook with it, bend down, sit, all with no pain at all. I was healed right then." From their own homes, those on the mailing list could order cuff links with anointed pictures of Jones in them; various lockets with photos for "safety from evil," "safety from attack," or "safety on the road"; anointed oil; and display dinner plates with pictures of the Los Angeles or San Francisco Temple.

What the Temple did with direct mail is hardly a testament to its ingenuity. Instead, it simply reflects extensive wider cultural practices of capital accumulation through direct mail solicitation. There is no way to count the number of charlatans working such operations, but even the more prominent fundamentalist ministries, like the Reverend Jimmie Swaggart's, use the same gift catalogues, the promises of blessings, and sometimes, the same apocalyptic harangues—witness Swaggart's about "THE YEAR OF PERSECUTION," in which, "You see, beloved, the devil is doing everything possible to stop this Ministry." Like Peoples Temple, other direct mail practitioners, for example, "Rev. Ewing's Church-By-Mail" of Atlanta, Georgia, have raised the science of increasing response rates to new heights by including a "prayer cloth" for the addressee to put inside a pillow and sleep with "for 1 night only!" then returning it so that Ewing himself can sleep on it for one night, "AND THEN, BY FAITH, SOMETHING SPECIAL WILL HAPPEN."

Jim Jones claimed reluctance about direct mail schemes, saying, "I'll have the devil to pay," but he did not stop them. He did, however, suspect graft when Deanna began using her own post office box for a return address. Upon this discovery, Jim insisted she use the Temple's address, claiming after the change was made that income from "the damn thing jumped marginally the next month." Even after Deanna and Mert defected in 1976, Jones kept the mailer operation intact, though the content gradually shifted from an emphasis on healing to a description of how the mission at Jonestown reflected "a day of new hope and abundance for all people."

The mailers were not the only source of media income. Like other religious groups, Peoples Temple took to the radio air waves, eventually producing programs in its own Redwood Valley recording studio. Here again, Peoples Temple simply geared into the previously existing institution of radio religion, in which preachers typically buy fifteen-minute time slots on stations like the Mexico-based XRG. Radio ministers run the gamut from mystic Cajun faith healers to anticommunist preachers of civil religion. They use their airtime as they see fit, sometimes offering prophecy, interpreting the Bible, promising healings, always asking at the end for donations or at least a letter of Christian love.

Peoples Temple effectively mimicked other radio religions, many of them small outfits like the Temple, others nationally known operations. One listener who never attended services said of Jim Jones, "He's on there like Oral Roberts, you know, and Reverend Ike." In the 1970s Peoples Temple programs featured Jones expounding on his theory of healing, his denigration of the "sky god" in favor of the God within, apostolic communalism, and the idea of heaven on earth. Jones did not misrepresent his own basic ideas; he simply offered up a less messianic, less prophetic, and less intimate version of them.

Mailer and radio income declined once the Temple's operations shifted to Guyana, but in the early years it must have been substantial. Deanna Mertle said after she left Peoples Temple that they had "averaged about $800 a day." The estimate may be a bit low. At the peak of about 11,000 direct mail pieces per month, Peoples Temple is said to have taken in well over $300,000 a year from the media ministry.[7]

Reaching people was just the beginning. Those who responded to Peoples Temple appeals, either from the mailings or radio ministry, were treated as a valuable resource. Their names found their way onto mailing lists, and logs were created to trace their individual donations, their spiritual and healing needs, Temple return responses, and their potential for becoming Temple members. A crew of Temple corresponding secretaries often would answer letters personally, with a touch sought after but hard to duplicate in the word processing technology of the direct mail industry. By artful use of mass media, the Temple fed cash into a steady stream that grew large by the diversity of its tributaries, and it fed its membership roster on procedures that allowed Temple personnel to size up whether individuals were ripe for Temple membership.

To deal with the flow of seekers, the Mertles proposed a scheme whereby potential members would have to listen to a series of ten tapes that "progressively give the basic indoctrination." Anyone wanting to come to a Sunday Redwood Valley meeting would have to listen to the first tape, reviewing errors in the Bible. Those not put off by a second tape—on social problems, race relations, hunger, and the like—could come to Saturday meetings. Subsequent tapes—on topics like apostolic socialism, the corruption of government and big business, and the necessity of communal government—would pave the way to membership.

In practice member intake depended on various devices to exclude people who did not go out of their way to embrace the Temple. In one approach people on the newsletter mailing list were informed that anyone who did not write back would be assumed no longer interested in the Temple, and dropped from the mailing list. Temple secretaries carefully scrutinized correspondence. If someone asked about attending services, a judgment was made about what type of person was writing, and whether he or she might be receptive to the Temple's unusual theological and social dispensation.

Those who did attend the semipublic services underwent more screening at the door. Jones insisted on the right of his followers to worship in private, and he was more than willing to have his monitors exclude people, including reporters, who might cause the Temple trouble. On one three-by-five-inch card, for example, an elderly woman was listed as "no admit" after she gushed on too much about faith healing and "Christianity in action."

Those who were allowed to enter had to provide basic personal data: name, address, telephone number, and livelihood. The membership secretary, Bea Orsot, would check to see how many times someone came. Following the spirit of the Mertle proposal, she would give the person a membership card after five consecutive meetings, the length of time and level of commitment deemed necessary to understand Jim's social message.

A wide range of Californians attended Temple services only once and never returned. Still others came occasionally; though they never joined, they ended up giving some financial support to the Temple all the same. Aside from the charm photo counter, there was the offering. Jones made sure his audience understood that their donations did not go to support the lavish life-style of some jackleg preacher; instead, the offering was fed into expanding the "human services" ministry, buying buses, care homes, and church buildings, and eventually, developing the Promised Land in Guyana as a refuge available to them all.

The pitch for an offering seems to have been about as "high pressure" as that of more conventional Pentecostal churches. Sometimes Jones would tell his audience the results of an offering. He was known to underestimate substantially the amount taken. And like his Pentecostal brothers, the preacher insisted on a second offering if he deemed the first one insufficient. "That last one only showed $180," Jones would say. "Now folks, I hope you'll just slip something into that envelope." On occasion, he took offerings "by sum," asking first who was willing to give $1,000. Once he even sponsored a tithing competition between the Los Angeles and San Francisco Temples.

People gave and gave, and the income from the offerings was sizable, all the more so when it came in week after week. A defector once told of taking in as much as a total of $37,000 from weekly services in Los Angeles and San Francisco, though elsewhere she described an average 1973 weekend income of around $15,000. Even this more conservative estimate would amount to an income of more than $750,000 every year.

On top of the offering, the Temple took in other valuables and jewelry that people tossed into the bucket in the fervor of support for the cause. To all this would have to be added the monies that members brought in from bake sales and other petty financial schemes, street solicitation activities that Jones assigned occasionally, or wages that were sometimes appropriated as punishment. Then there were the financial opportunities developed by Temple counselors at services in the cities. They could help the congregation's members with tax and welfare matters, and they could encourage those who qualified to live in Redwood Valley care homes. Sometimes they came upon a windfall, like a woman who had an insurance claim that Tim Stoen helped to press. Of the $10,000 due the woman in settlement, $8,000 was to go directly to the Temple.[8]

With Jones and his staff persistently working every possible angle, everything seemed to turn to money. But there were substantial expenses: from $30,000 to $50,000 in vehicle operation and maintenance expenses every month, a small payroll, the various outlays associated with media and other income-producing enterprises, food for communal church meals, and so on. For most of his career, Jones himself received no personal income from Peoples Temple. Instead, for many years Marcie would put her nurse's paycheck into a "special fund" to provide for family needs and possible retirement. Eventually, in 1977, Peoples Temple's Board of Directors voted Jones a yearly salary of $30,000.

The biggest expense was the "agricultural mission." After the decision was made in the fall of 1973 to go ahead with the project in Guyana, a flow of perhaps $3 million went into its development. In November of 1976 alone, the Temple authorized $310,000 in purchases of trucks, a steam generator, agricultural machinery, and other heavy equipment.

All the outlays notwithstanding, the Temple was accumulating a substantial lode of capital. Huge piles of cash on hand represented ready money that could be allocated without anyone's tracing its flow. A whole raft of people were needed to keep track of the Temple's finances, including long-standing member and bookkeeper Harold Cordell and Tim Stoen's wife, Grace. After Grace Stoen defected in July of 1976, Tish Leroy, Debbie Blakey, and Teri Buford took over certain responsibilities. Debbie Blakey began by working on offerings, and took on administering the Needs Department. Carolyn Layton took part in a number of major banking and investment transactions.

Throughout the 1970s, the money kept rolling in. After events in the early 1970s led to development of a plan to migrate from the United States "at the first sign of outright persecution," Jones and his most trusted aides devised an arrangement to act as trustees for the millions of dollars, investing the funds as a cushion against the uncertainty of their future and as a source of capital to finance building a foreign colony for hundreds of people. Following widespread practices of corporations that seek to get out from under IRS regulation by shifting money out of the United States, the Temple placed much of its money in dummy "offshore" accounts in countries with more favorable banking laws.

The international shuffling of millions of dollars was undertaken by people Jones trusted at the time. As Buford put it, "Jim didn't like to have anybody on the money unless you were under Jim's nose." In general the Temple operated on a need-to-know basis, and individuals often participated in transactions without knowing exactly what was happening. At one time or another, Carolyn Layton, Tim Stoen, Maria Katsaris, Teri Buford, Mike Cartmell, and Debbie Blakey deposited money in small private accounts as well as enormous "front organization" accounts with names like "Asociación Evangelica de las Americas." One time, Teri Buford recalled, she and Tim Stoen "smuggled over one million US dollars out of the United States. We had it both packed in our suitcases and strapped to our bodies."

The money from all sources was spread out in banks in the Caribbean, Panama, Venezuela, and Switzerland, as well as Guyana. After November 1978 the Temple's net worth was established by the court-appointed receiver, Robert Fabian. He could not get the government of Guyana to return about $1 million, but by clearing out the foreign accounts and liquidating Temple real assets, Fabian amassed $10 million.

Was that a lot of money? Jones once said, "I have made the poor rich." Not quite. If the value of Temple assets is allocated among the 913 Temple members who died in Guyana, Temple holdings per person in November of 1978 come to around $12,000 per person, even less if allocated among the total number of Temple members. In effect, Jones forged an organization that was wealthier than the sum of its parts, but it was hardly rich, given its size and radical orientation, and its precarious and unknown future.[9]

### The Corporation of People

In essence, all the Peoples Temple capital was for a single cause, bankrolling the Temple as an extended family that was becoming an ark of survival. In turn, the Temple would provide for individual wants on a communal basis.

At the most basic level there was a communistic redistribution of resources, including labor of members. When the Mertles found they needed a new septic system leach line, Temple men did the work in a day. One time Bea Orsot could not meet her rent payment and the Temple came up with the money. Peoples Temple publicly offered services to the needy, from doing laundry and ironing to picking up groceries. The Temple's carehome operators were responsible for arranging medical care for their clients, and they would often rely on the skilled professionals who were Temple members.

In fact, the drive toward group provision of services to members inspired Peoples Temple's college tuition and dormitories program, established by 1971 at Santa Rosa Community College. Temple youth were sent there to gain a practical education that would dovetail into the church's spiraling range of activities. The Santa Rosa suburban duplex "dormitories" were crowded by middle-class standards; the garages served as bunk rooms for eight, leaving bedrooms for study space, so that each resident could have a personal desk. Larry Schacht entered a premed program there. Mike Touchette took college courses before he became disenchanted with school and started doing construction work. Jim Cobb, Jr., began studies for a career in dentistry. When Annie Moore followed her sister Carolyn Moore Layton and joined Peoples Temple, she went to study nursing at Santa

Rosa, where she mounted a Temple-inspired critique of capitalist medicine while she gained skills.

The Santa Rosa College bank account initiated the structure whereby a communal economy eventually became formalized. The Temple began to lay claim to the incomes of members who "went communal," and in turn their needs were paid for out of Temple accounts, at first the college account and later, others. For the people who worked their ways further and further into the organization, apostolic socialism was not a lofty dream. The communal organization of Peoples Temple became their social world.

The care homes provided the household nucleus of the communal system. After the Santa Rosa program was established, non-care-home households in Redwood Valley began to follow the same basic "franchising" model, and people began to live in households in other than nuclear-family patterns. According to an undated proposal developed by Deanna and Mert Mertle, the Temple required what was sometimes called "the commitment" from members of the Temple's inner core. A tithing of 25 percent was expected of those who could afford it, and sometimes the amount went as high as 50 percent. Less financially capable members could make up the difference through organizing bake sales and other money-makers. Sometimes one family member worked full time for the Temple without compensation and another would still contribute 25 percent from an outside job.

The Temple took this general approach even further in San Francisco, when the communal organization expanded rapidly beginning in the winter of 1975. Basically, the scheme was similar to one described by Tim Stoen, in a memorandum titled "Should People's Temple adopt a share-all economic plan?" The Stanford-trained attorney indicated a certain Rotary Club reluctance toward taking a socialist road, but nevertheless proposed that each individual "hold the best job commensurate with his capacity," "assign over [sic] each payday his paycheck . . . with no strings attached (to try to avoid registration under the Securities Acts)," "give all his personal and real property to the church with no strings attached," and "submit a proposed budget as to his needs. . . ."

Those who "went communal" would fill out an application listing their living arrangements and financial data, including sources of income, savings accounts, cash value of life insurance, and real properties. People who entered into this sort of arrangement described it in matter-of-fact terms: "We were communal, and we would cash our check. It was a process of donating our money," said June Crym.[10]

There came to be at least nineteen, and perhaps as many as seventy communal households in San Francisco, plus people living in the Temple church building itself. Substantial numbers of elderly "went communal" under a "life-care" agreement like those used in contemporary profit and nonprofit nursing homes. Peoples Temple offered to take care of an elderly person for life, in exchange for donations of between $30,000 and $40,000. Wrote one woman to Jim: "I have no indebtedness on anything or am I buying anything and with the taxes to come up which or [*sic*] now paid and Just Utility Bills with me and eat out of $117.65 a month I would not fare so well alone I do better living communal as I am now doing."

Many "seniors" simply signed over their Social Security checks to Peoples Temple. The practice eventually fueled charges by opponents, but in March of 1979 the U.S. secretary of health, education, and welfare reported "no basis has been found for concluding that the Peoples Temple stole or fraudulently used Social Security benefits received by its members." Another judgment also came after the mass suicide, when 110 aged former Temple members made effective legal claims against Temple financial assets on the basis of their previous donations, a transaction that underscores the bona fide character of the "life-care" agreements.

Those who went communal not only gave income but also handed over real estate, insurance policies, and other items of value. One woman considered donating her car to the Temple whenever she could not seem to get it to run right. The Temple practiced a sort of spoils communism, taking whatever resources came in, and either converting them to the use of the group or selling them. Thus Temple members would work to fix up cars, furniture, rummage items, and houses.

Real estate was of enough concern by 1974 that the Temple's articles of incorporation were amended specifically to permit real estate transactions to further the primary purposes of the church as a nonprofit religious organization. A special checking account for Valley Enterprises established an "alter ego" to shield the Temple's involvement in property rehabilitation, both to avoid the suspicions of outsiders in Mendocino County and to provide a front in case of IRS investigation. The number of transactions was not very great; even by the time most people had migrated to Jonestown in August of 1977, reporters could find only fifteen properties that had been given to the Temple and sold, for approximately $667,000. Other properties, the Temple bought as a corporation, either for care homes or communal residences, and these too were sold to liquidate the organization's assets in the United States.

In a number of cases the Temple waited until a donor was clearly going to Guyana before processing a gift. "Often people would say, 'Well, I'm going to donate my house,' or whatever, and there would be a deed made, but the deed wouldn't be filed until so-and-so got ready to go to Guyana." The policy may have been motivated by a desire to keep gifts to the Temple out of the public eye until the last possible moment. For example, in the case of Essie Townes, Tim Stoen recommended that the woman get an outside attorney to transfer property to the church, emphasizing "*no* mention that property might eventually go to church." But tardy filing of a deed also allowed donors who changed their minds to withdraw a gift, by executing and filing a subsequent deed, thereby voiding the one to the Temple.[11]

Once donations were processed, they were not considered refundable. But the Temple did not always obtain people's complete financial resources, even if they "went communal." As Teri Buford put it, "I was never under the impression that once you made a donation, you could ever get it back. But I believed I was free to leave with whatever money I didn't turn over." For anyone who decided to hold onto some property so long as he or she remained alive, Tim Stoen could draw up a "last will and testament." On more than one occasion he was named as the executor of a will that left all property to Peoples Temple, or "in any event this gift should be invalid," to "Timothy O. Stoen and Carolyn Layton jointly."

For those who made "the commitment"—the seniors, as well as younger people who tithed—consumption was collectivized, and the net savings due to economies of scale were cycled back into the Temple. Like many features of Temple life, collectivist consumption began in small ways, with the limiting of consumption for birthdays, by buying a smaller number of presents communally, and by holding only one party a month. The logical extension of this approach eventually would have communal Temple members receiving minuscule allowances of $2 per week. If they wanted something not covered by the allowances and the food, clothing, and other resources they received directly from the Temple, individuals would have to submit a "needs envelope" to the Temple "Needs Department," at one time headed by Debbie Blakey. Personal wants thus were subordinated to the collectivity, even while the Temple outwardly operated as a church.

Given that Peoples Temple existed in the midst of a money economy stimulated through advertising of "the American dream," it must have been difficult for members to undergo the transition to communalism. Detractors eventually would apply the standards of a conventional church to argue that the rates of tithing and donation of labor to the Temple were excessive, and the control of consumption, arbitrary; they would even complain about standard business practices to prevent graft, such as the tendering of receipts to account for expenditures. But such protestations ignore the communal nature of the "church": if the journal of one woman is any indication, members committed to a communal lifestyle found the "needs" system neither objectionable nor unduly limiting. One of her journal entries records her satisfaction when the needs envelope came back with money for everything she requested—$30 for clothes and $11 for a MUNI public transportation pass.[12]

The Temple was neither fish nor fowl. Though it gave the external appearance of an unusual but nevertheless conventionally organized religious congregation, the communal commitments made it something quite different. Peoples Temple became what Lewis Coser has called a "greedy institution," a group in which "demands on the individual are omnivorous." In totally communal organizations, undivided commitments are not unusual: individuals often earn no income and sometimes do not even receive allowances, but in the noncommunal outside world people tend to wend their ways among diverse, overlapping, and sometimes conflicting commitments. By embarking on a communalist course while remaining a church, and without establishing a strong physical boundary between the group and the outside, Peoples Temple became "greedy" in precisely the way that would create the greatest conflict with the outside world.

No doubt the communal transition of Peoples Temple caused the organization a good deal of its eventual difficulties, for detractors could claim that a supposed church had subjected people to extortion and false imprisonment. But it must be recognized that Peoples Temple was not a conventional church, and the increased tithing and other money-making activities operated by Temple members were the income side of a communally restructured equation of the relation between a church and its members. For those who were committed to the organization, the sacrifice of "an indulgent lifestyle," the long hours of work without pay, and the shift toward communalism were not in principle problematic. Indeed, they represent the approach often adopted by people who devote their undivided loyalties to a cause they deem just. The results were significant. Because Temple members often were willing to meet the demanding standard of communal religious commitment, working long hours without material compensation, the group had a competitive edge in the marketplace of social service vendors. When asked to explain the group's success, Jim Jones reflected, "I don't honestly know how we got where we are. Hard work, I guess. We are very frugal, and we don't have any paid staff."[13]

In the California years Peoples Temple moved far beyond the realm of care-home vendors. It took the peculiar form of a communal organization loosely coupled to a wide range of social service organizations. The Temple handled cases on a large scale to mobilize the resources due its clients, and it began to front for members as "cases" in the outside world of bureaucracies.

In the conventional modern world, relatively powerless individuals, especially those on welfare, confront bureaucratic demands on their own. With Peoples Temple, they could counter corporations and the state with their *own* bureaucracy that could create and process data for members in much the same manner as other bureaucracies but with more of a personal touch. Seemingly without self-conscious intent Peoples Temple staff stumbled upon the form of a socialist community bureaucracy. To consolidate its own authority, the Temple sought power-of-attorney options to represent its members, and it became, in effect, the clients' counterpart to the array of state welfare and other bureaucracies designed to process individual cases. For those who made the communal commitment, the Temple offered the services of a personal tax consultant, lawyer, and social worker—a sort of diversified, collectivized H. & R. Block.

There were significant consequences of the Peoples Temple bureaucracy. By handling cases on a collective basis, the Temple achieved economies of scale similar to those of state bureaucracies; individuals were thereby freed from deferring to the often confusing and conflicting demands of external authorities. It might even be argued that Peoples Temple offered one solution to a widely recognized problem of modern societies. To some degree, alienation in modern societies is held to stem from the tendency by rationalized bureaucracies toward "one-dimensional" treatment of persons as things. The Temple short-circuited that alienation by establishing an advocate organization that would negotiate the twists and turns of the bureaucratic world. The individual received relief from the often degrading experience of being "processed," and the Temple gained both time and money by serving as a welfare rights organization that specialized in the collective management of individual identity.[14]

Clearly Peoples Temple represented "unfair" competition in the world of modern welfare bureaucracy. In somewhat the same way that the productivity of industrial capitalism depended at its inception on the Protestant work ethic, so Peoples Temple thrived on a "social work" ethic that was connected to a radical redefinition of the relation of individuals to bureaucracy in the modern world. Previously only the state and corporations had subjected individuals to such thoroughgoing rational organization. To the degree that churches and social movements had been rationally organized, they focused on collective pursuits rather than individual ones. Now people who were treated in the language of the state and corporations as clients and consumers became rationally organized as members of Peoples Temple.

If the Temple is a harbinger of things to come, someday the computers of bureaucratic organizations representing legions of citizens will interface with computers of the state and corporations, trading the matrices of personal information needed for adjudication of cases. The work of managing the common person's identity in a bureaucratic world will have become a business itself. Come what may in that regard, it is doubtful that such organizations will take the form of a charismatic bureaucracy like their communal precursor.

## Charisma and Administration

By offering its followers something more concrete than salvation in the afterlife, by taking on a communal form based on an apocalyptic vision, Peoples Temple broke out of the mold of "church" and became a charismatic and communal religious social movement. Jones himself had always asserted his authority in the classic claim of charisma, "It has been written . . . , but *I* say unto you. . . ." He had harped on errors in the Bible and he had surrounded himself with others who conferred legitimacy on his messiahship by believing his vision. But how did such an "unstable" form of authority as charisma become welded to an organization that made part of its business the rational management of bureaucratic identity?

Jim Jones's charismatic authority, already emergent in his Indiana ministry, later became institutionalized in the form of a charismatic community, nevertheless directed to the rational administration of its members' dossiers. Jones always maintained his authority by a charismatic appeal to the popular will of the assembled congregation, in any of a variety of meetings. But the work of the Temple was conducted by a loose but rationally organized bureaucracy directed by Jones's administrative staff—"the leadership," an elite of about thirty people, almost 90 percent White, some 60 percent women, in an organization about three-quarters Black.

The disproportionate participation of Whites in Temple leadership led to persistent charges by defectors and sometimes members that Peoples Temple was as guilty of racism as society at large. In part the issue was not so much the scarcity of Blacks in leadership as the conservatism of the few Blacks who held such positions. Complaining about Blacks like Joyci Clark, Alice Inghram, and Archie Ijames, eight young "revolutionary" defectors held in a 1973 manifesto that "there's no Black people with any discontent for today's evilness that will listen or follow any one of them." White people who came into the Temple—people like Tim Stoen, Mike Prokes, Annie Moore, Gene Chaiken, and Teri Buford—found their ways into the leadership in a matter of weeks. Aside from a few people like Archie Ijames, Blacks rose to leadership status more slowly.

Why the racial imbalance in leadership? In part it seems to reflect previous racial stratification of life chances in the society that spawned Peoples Temple. A number of the Blacks who joined the Temple were virtually illiterate, and not many of the rest had any sort of professional experience in social work, publishing, graphics, public relations, law, or the other administrative, technical, and professional occupations that the Temple depended upon for its successful operation. "From each according to his ability" was the Temple's credo, and those Blacks who did have skills found the Temple ready to utilize them. But the Temple faced the same problem confronted by other organizations with both utopian and operational dictates. The imperatives of administration that promote organizational success tend to conflict with the very goals the social movement purportedly claims to advance. Interestingly enough, Jones's role model, Father Divine, though himself Black, was plagued with hierarchical racial imbalance in his Peace Mission, in part for the same reason: the differential preexisting racial distribution of skills.

Like Father Divine, and following the pattern of Black Pentecostal churches more generally, Jim Jones employed female "secretaries" in the key roles of staff aides, serving as bookkeepers, treasurers, and secretaries. As Divine had done, Jones often assigned White women to these roles. In such "leadership" positions, women with a social-work orientation sometimes saw themselves not as ruling over but as serving clients who were members of the Temple, perhaps even exorcising their own racial guilt. Some of them found the demands placed on them substantial; as Sandy Bradshaw commented, "It was not a PR trip; it was a lot of fucking hard work."

It was also the case that Whites who joined Peoples Temple were socialized to see themselves as "niggers." Some White children sported "Afro" haircuts; White adults in effect renounced their own racial status group by joining a group opposing the color line that had sustained their privileged position in the wider society.

Beyond these considerations, the racially imbalanced leadership necessarily was a product of Jim Jones's choices. His maintenance of charismatic authority had to be based on forging a staff that he could trust. He used all sorts of devices, from love and convincement to blackmail and sex, to maintain allegiances. For whatever reasons, he supposedly was slow to trust men, and regarding his sexual alliances, he said that he wished to avoid perpetuating interracial sexual exploitation and he favored young, White women. The leadership reflected the patterns of his intimate relationships as well as the dictates of effective use of skills, but so long as trust was not problematic, skills, rather than race, gender or friendship, seem to have been the decisive criteria. One young man did not care much for Jones personally, but he worked in a leadership position in public relations because Jones needed his abilities. Over the years, Jones also brought a number of males into the traditionally male role of minister, including Johnny Moss Jones in 1972 and Tim Stoen and Guy Young in 1974.

In historical terms the issue of racism in the Temple was virtually moot for its members. The matter was raised almost exclusively by certain defectors and outside commentators. The internal issue turns on whether followers themselves considered the leadership legitimate. Apparently the vast majority acceded to Jones's interpretation of the situation. They were willing to overlook the race of their leader and members of his staff because he was willing to do the same thing in taking on the stigma of leading an interracial religious organization.[15]

Jones maintained his connection with the mass of followers in meetings ranging from relatively public services to more intimate "family meetings" for "catharsis" and sessions of a "planning commission" that served as a sort of sounding board. The planning commission included up to a hundred people whom Jones, as the charismatic leader, chose to elect to it, and it would meet as often as two or three times a week, with people sometimes staying up all night. "He put anybody there who had any input or anybody he wanted to watch," Teri Buford recalled.

Given the variety of meetings, the Temple took the form of a series of concentric circles. At the innermost circle stood Jim Jones alone; the circle beyond him included a handful of confidants and close working staff; in the next circle outward came the loyal administrative operatives; beyond them was the "working organization" that included many p.c. (planning commission) members; finally, there was the client population, itself often drawn into functional roles. Jones would preside over occasions keyed roughly to each circle. He directed the collective attention where he saw fit, and continued the meeting or dismissed it at will, without reference to any external time system. He did not need to be a total autocrat, however. Given that followers believed in what they thought Jones represented, he would sometimes put questions to the group to try to gauge its sentiments or leave others to make proposals about how to resolve issues. By sharing decision making while retaining the last word, Jones probably enhanced his own charisma.

The public meetings were directed toward maintaining and coordinating the collective life of the group, not to formulating or executing policy per se. The actual administration of Peoples Temple, on the other hand, took place at the behest of Jim Jones in conjunction with "the leadership," his closest aides, and those of the next outermost circle, or others who might be needed to pursue particular issues. The description by Max Weber of such an organization rings true:

> The administrative staff of a charismatic leader does not consist of "officials"; least of all are its members technically trained. . . . There is a call at the instance of the leader on the basis of the charismatic qualification of those he summons. There is no hierarchy; the leader merely intervenes in general or in individual cases when he considers the members of his staff lacking in charismatic qualification for a given task. . . . There may, however, be territorial or functional limits to charismatic powers and to the individual's mission.

So it was with Peoples Temple. As June Crym put it, there were "no formal positions." The participants in the administrative staff varied from time to time, and nonstaff members occasionally were tapped by Jones or his staff for special "missions." Beyond the staff, and organized by them, stood a loosely organized bureaucracy of committees and functional offices that operated by almost anarchic authority. Anyone who had a need for assistance seemingly could draft whomever seemed a logical source of help. But, despite the decentralized and crosscutting web of functional authority relations, the Temple still somehow managed to exercise administrative logic in the organizing of activities and processing of member files for everything from making choir robes and security uniforms and cooking the after-service communal meal to arranging vacation tours, processing income tax and Social Security forms, and buying and selling real estate.

What was Jim Jones's role in relation to all the Temple activities? One staff member, Sandy Bradshaw, later characterized him as "a benevolent dictator, if anything." This view is sustained by an opponent of the Temple who indicated that Jones's staff gave "instructions" rather than direct orders, and couched them in language to the effect that "this is the way we're going to please Father." The few existing tape recordings of staff meetings suggest that Jones felt no compulsion to play the role of autocrat in a private setting.[16]

The Temple was a far-flung operation that succeeded in a variety of arenas, typically with "common people" as its agents. This could occur only because Jones recognized that he did not know everything. There is good evidence that he respected others' expertise so long as it bore fruit, though he was disdainful of failure and incompetence. As an organization, Peoples Temple hardly operated on the basis of a tight chain of command with carefully vested provinces of authority culminating in a central staff presided over by a ruler; to the contrary, various centers of activity functioned with a fair degree of autonomy, based upon their commitment to overall Temple goals. Jones's personal staff then operated as a sort of troubleshooting board that would take on problematic situations, referring to Jones cases they believed he should know about.

Paralleling Weber's description of the charismatic community in general, one member of Jones's staff would be in charge of security; another, counseling; yet another would oversee the Needs Department, and so forth. As Father Divine had done in the Peace Mission, Jones used his personal secretaries as envoys to the wider network. His lover and closest companion, Carolyn Layton, probably was "the top of the line," as Teri Buford later put it. Buford herself worked for years as the liaison between Jones, various departments, and Tim Stoen (for whom she also worked directly). But based on his legal training, Stoen had greater organizational expertise than Carolyn Layton or Teri Buford, and according to various Temple members, including Jones himself, Stoen probably knew more about the operations of Peoples Temple than any single person aside from Jones.

Another central figure was Maria Katsaris, the daughter of Steven Katsaris, a second-generation Greek Orthodox administrator of Trinity School for youth in Ukiah. Maria joined through contacts with a Temple member who worked at her father's school. Like Carolyn Layton, she eventually became one of Jones's lovers; like Layton, she remained as one of his administrative confidentes. Other women, like Grace Stoen and Debbie Blakey, also became close associates of Jones, and in turn acted on his behalf in directing the affairs of the church, sometimes with a good deal of autonomous authority.

Certain areas of Temple operations were "closely held": finances, legal transactions, and a whole range of security practices, clandestine activities, and strategic initiatives. When the Temple leadership wanted to act decisively, it did so by directing operatives who carried out instructions like soldiers. In fact, the tight discipline of the organization and its "ends-justify-the-means" ideology have led some observers to consider the group a model of fascism or a Stalinist approach to Bolshevism. The Temple's own outside attorney beginning in 1977, Charles Garry, was long noted for his support of leftist causes, but even he became frustrated with the Temple. Garry began noticing the leadership operating like a Communist party cell. Once the leaders had come to a decision, on the basis of whatever analysis, Garry found it futile to reason with them. The reason, he surmised, was that he was an outsider, even as their lawyer. "Cell" members acted only on the basis of their internal deliberations, and in the outer world of financial transactions, legal initiatives, or clandestine ploys, they simply implemented a prearranged plan, or, if that was not possible, tried to hold off further developments until they could regroup alone.[17]

### The Legal Office

Emblematic of the style and range of Temple activity was the conduct of legal affairs, an operation central to the success of the Temple on a variety of fronts. The Temple did not always operate precisely within the law, but neither did Temple attorneys disregard it in any wholesale manner. In fact, the effectiveness of the Temple in using the law to "cover" its activities proved frustrating to opponents who judged them morally reprehensible. The Temple was blessed with a viable operation. Tim Stoen provided legal services from the time he joined in 1970 until his defection in June of 1977, and Gene Chaiken became a second Temple counsel when he joined in 1972. With the addition of Hastings Law School graduate Harriet Tropp, who joined in 1970, and a secretary with formal experience in legal work, June Crym, the Temple sustained what amounted to its own legal office.

Jim Jones was not always wholly satisfied with the legal work he got from this crew. Stoen was a well-trained lawyer who offered the Temple and its members legal counsel while also maintaining an accomplished career as a prosecuting attorney in Mendocino County and later in San Francisco. But according to Sandy Bradshaw, Stoen could function effectively for the Temple only at the direction of Jones: "Jim was like a father; he had to guide him, direct him, chastize him." Conforming to the logic of the charismatic community as an organization, Stoen did not receive a salary or retainer, but he was reimbursed as much as $500 a month for his expenses. Gene Chaiken was not as accomplished as Stoen; still, he researched competent legal memos and did a workmanlike job of dealing with routine legal matters like real estate.

The two attorneys handled everything from offering legal services to arranging foreign bank accounts. Editors showed Temple newspaper copy to Tim Stoen so he could give legal clearance. Stoen, and probably Chaiken as well, traveled numerous times on the weekend circuit to counsel Temple members. Both attorneys monitored legal dimensions of Temple actions, and they took effective precautions to stay clear of prosecution. They seem to have performed as other U.S. lawyers tend to do under an adversary legal system, going to great lengths to protect clients' interests, independent of truth or codified law.

Aside from the mundane sort of legal work necessary to keep the corporation functioning, there were those occasional transactions that underscore the social situation of Peoples Temple. As early as 1971 Stoen became concerned with the legal aspects of child custody, writing to the Cecil Johnsons in Indianapolis, seeking permission to appoint a guardian for their daughter Gwendolyn. Another time he wrote to an attorney airing his thoughts about a juvenile probation officer who was to report on a custody dispute in which the father was not a Temple member but the mother was. According to Temple social worker Laura Johnston, when cases came to court, Stoen did what any lawyer would do. He coached those who were to appear on what to say and how to act.

The Temple's lawyers were also careful to nail down a viable legal position on faith healing. In 1972 Stoen traveled to Indianapolis to confer with the Indiana State Board of Psychology examiners on the limits of healing practices by preachers. Chaiken offered a legal memo in June of 1973 advising Jones on the likely limits of prosecution of faith healers. To backstop the standard published legal disclaimer that Jones, like more conservative healers, employed, over the years the Temple compiled a raft of affidavits by those who had benefited from Jim's miraculous powers. "Relatives and friends came to see me that day," one woman affirmed, "thinking I was still paralyzed and expecting me to die. . . . When they returned the next day, I met them at the elevator. I was running and rejoicing in the

corridors. I was so very thankful that Rev. Jones had sent the cloth to me."
The legality of Jones's practice never became an issue, and the affidavits
were quoted in public testimonials.

As with faith healing, so with donations of real estate and other matters
Peoples Temple sought to minimize controversy. In particular, it steered
clear of accepting real estate under clouded circumstances. At one meeting
of the Temple's board of directors, according to the minutes, Tim Stoen
emphasized that donors should be in good physical and mental health, and
that the Temple should make sure that they would suffer no deprivation as
a result of making gifts. The Temple was equally careful with collectively
administered punishment for minors; it was standard practice to obtain an
authorization signed by at least one person legally responsible for each
child, and Temple photographer Mert Myrtle was instructed not to take
pictures of the events. Last but not least, beginning in December of 1976
the Temple used a money order account to operate the Needs Department.
Payments for expenses of people who had "gone communal" thus bypassed
the corporate ledger, and helped to skirt the legal problem with the IRS of a
church's providing private benefits to its members.[18]

Sometimes the Temple's efforts to steer clear of the law were marked by a
less bureaucratic, more clandestine style. Tim Stoen understood quite
clearly what might stand up in court, and Temple members later said he
went to some lengths to advise them on how to avoid creating evidence.
Years later Teri Buford reported that after young Jim Cobb defected from
the Temple in 1973, Stoen informed her about a plan in which he would
write a telephone script intended, Buford quoted Stoen as saying, to "scare
the shit out of Cobb." The handwritten note attributed to Stoen indicated
that the "person who does it should be unknown to subject and should try
to disguise voice and speak to the point. Annie Moore probably good." It
added, "I don't think that the authorities will go to all the trouble to make a
voice print since nothing illegal involved."

Despite efforts to avoid controversy and culpability, Temple lawyers over
the years had to dispose of a number of unseemly matters. At least five
times Temple members became involved in child abuse cases that came to
light as Child Protective Service cases, and once the matter almost came to
court. Knowledgeable about these incidents, Mendocino County Social
Service Director and Temple critic Dennis Denny nevertheless held that
Temple parents engaged in no more child abuse than members of other
religious groups.

There was also a series of deaths that clouded Temple life. In 1970 a
woman named Maxine Harpe was found hanging by a cord from a rafter in
her garage. She had a record of a previous suicide attempt, and a file with
the Department of Mental Health labeled her as depressed, but certain

facts raised eyebrows: Harpe's case workers were Temple members Linda Amos and Jim Randolph. She had talked of marrying Randolph and some $2,500 she had received in a divorce settlement shortly before she died passed through his hands into a Peoples Temple account shortly after her death. Randolph was willing to sign his statement to authorities only "after Tim Stoen of the District Attorney's office reads it." The coroner ruled the death a suicide and the Temple set up a trust fund for Harpe's children and paid for her funeral as well. Whatever the facts, the Temple clearly had concerns about interpretations of its ties to Harpe, and someone drafted a self-serving Temple account of Harpe's suicidal tendencies, claiming that the former husband was "an extreme racist" who "made Maxine commit unnatural sex acts." Over the years there were three other strange deaths— of Robert Houston, of John Head, and of Chris Lewis—all associated with Peoples Temple, that gave grist for detractors' suspicions. But as was the case with Maxine Harpe, Peoples Temple and its members were never indicted, much less convicted, of murdering anyone.

The most delicate matter involved the public reputation of Jim Jones himself. On December 13, 1973, a plainclothes Los Angeles police officer "responded to a vice complaint" from an unknown source, and went to the Rampart area Westlake Theater, where a rendezvous unfolded in the men's room. Jones reportedly ended up "walking toward ofcr. with his erect penis in his hand. Ofcr exited the restroom and signaled his partner of the viola- tion." The minister of churches in Los Angeles and San Francisco was arrested and booked for lewd conduct. Then the Temple went into high gear to submerge the incident. A urologist from San Francisco reported that because Jones had a urinary bladder obstruction, he had been encour- aged to try "jogging or jumping in place" to initiate urination. Tim Stoen called the Ramparts Police Station to tell them the violation could not have occurred because Jones wore a urine bag.

When the case came to its brief trial not even a week later, on motion of the prosecuting attorney, it was dismissed. The next day Stoen was lobby- ing the Los Angeles assistant chief of police to have the arrest record removed from the department's open files. A month and a half later the judge in the case, Clarence Stromwell, indicated the case had been dis- missed for the reason that there was "no evidence of violation based on documents provided to City Atty." In violation of all precedent, he ordered the court records sealed and destroyed, but physical destruction of the records was so antithetical to court procedure that those in charge of the files never carried out the judge's orders. The record of Jones's arrest would have been a substantial embarrassment to him if it had ever come to light, and it remained a potential basis of blackmail against Jones for those few who knew about it. During his life Jones never had to reckon publicly with the shame of the event. How much he privately lived in fear of its revelation can be only a matter of speculation.[19]

All told, the Temple law office handled both routine and extraordinary problems effectively. A series of cases eventually brought by organized opponents of the Temple tell more about the conflict between the Temple and its opponents than about the *modus operandi* of the Temple, and they are discussed later. But it should be noted in the present context that despite the concerted legal opposition the Temple eventually received, its critics never successfully prosecuted the organization for the abuses they charged.

## Conclusion

Given the amount of money the Temple received, the number of real estate deeds it processed, the scale of its operation of care homes, communal households, and Jonestown, what is surprising is how effectively the organization avoided the sorts of shady practices that sometimes have plagued other evangelical and communal religious movements. In its methods of attracting converts and money, the Temple was largely a template of more conservative evangelical practices. Its high rates of tithing were only one part of a more comprehensive communalist equation. Though the Temple was run by a staff subject to the call of a charismatic leader, day-to-day operations were marked by the same administrative logic that structures other modern organizations. The success of the Temple's enterprises reflects not only the zealous energies of members but its adherence to the rational dictates of modern management techniques.

The most significant organizational innovation of Peoples Temple was its creation of a "mirror-image," client-based social welfare advocacy organization. Because the Temple fronted for clients in bureaucratic dealings, it could liberate them from the degrading alienation of being treated as "things" by anonymous bureaucrats. This innovation aside, the overall organization of Peoples Temple reflected widely prevalent organizational forms, from those of religious evangelism to corporate entrepreneurship. Though Jim Jones sometimes advocated a philosophy that "the ends justify the means," in the Temple's money-making activities and daily administration, the Temple's predominant approach depended on marshaling conventional cultural means to sustain an organization devoted to distinctly antiestablishment ends. The significance of this hard-to-accept finding can be understood in light of an earlier and related U.S. menace, Stalinism.

During the McCarthy era of the 1950s, sociologist Philip Selznick completed a study for the Rand Corporation of Bolshevik strategy and tactics. *The Organizational Weapon* described powerseeking by an "elite *in a man-*

*ner unrestrained by the constitutional order of the arena within which the contest takes place.* In this usage, 'weapon' is not meant to denote *any* political tool, but one torn from its normal context and unacceptable to the community as a legitimate mode of action." Selznick noted how the party in the United States operated by persuading people to submit voluntarily to total control by its dictates. He found that the Bolshevik approach necessarily justifies operating outside the law to achieve its ends, given that its ends are illegal in societies committed to the sanctity of private property and free enterprise. But even more disconcerting than illegal party activity was the alternative possibility: cell members with unwavering commitments to the party might use their constitutional freedoms to subvert the Constitution. They might infiltrate perfectly legal organizations that they then would subvert to party ends.[20]

A similar approach marked Peoples Temple as a religious conglomerate. In its wide-ranging operations, from religious mailers and nursing homes to offshore bank accounts and legal defenses, Peoples Temple mirrored the wider U.S. culture. Even in its "infiltration" of other organizations devoted to social work, the Temple simply acted in a long-standing tradition of civil religion: Peoples Temple sought to have its members fulfill their occupational duties in ways consonant with their religious principles that would thus subordinate the state to "sacred" values. But there was a telling difference. Conventional religions seek money for culturally legitimated purposes, or else their entrepreneurs are treated as charlatans. Conventional religions promote a moral basis of action in society that sustains "one nation under God" as the object of civil religion. Conventional corporations use offshore accounts to increase their profits, and even the illegal laundering operations are connected to business quests for profits that, though illegal, nevertheless share a culturally comprehendible rationale.

Peoples Temple, on the other hand, was an alien force outside the matrix of culturally understandable motives, be they illegal or legal. Jones amassed followers and wealth by drawing upon well-worn cultural recipes, but his ends were mysterious; they did not fit within the conventional matrix of religion or of business. He did not want to save souls in the hereafter, and for all the wealth he accumulated, he was not interested in personal material gain in this world. The Temple used the institutions of welfare capitalism to underwrite a charismatic struggle against the capitalist order. In the realm of the Temple's ongoing business operations, the glorious ends of socialism justified the use of means that would require little or no justification, were they directed toward culturally legitimate purposes.

# 7

# The Collectivist Reformation

Peoples Temple offered material benefits and occupational opportunities to Jones's followers, and for many people, once they became committed to the Temple, other options disappeared behind them. But it is just as evident that those who stuck with Jones did so for reasons more compelling than simple economic calculation of the advantages and costs of staying. Sociologist Rosabeth Kanter has argued that successful communal groups are those that foster "total commitment" among their members. Beyond straightforward rational calculation, Kanter theorizes, there are two other central problems of commitment: (1) "social cohesion," a feeling of strong group solidarity in contrast to outside social relationships, and (2) "social control," a willingness to submit to collective authority as legitimate and binding on the actions of the individual.

For French social critic Michel Foucault, the problem translates into one of "confinement" when organizational practices rather than individuals' commitments are emphasized. In Foucault's view, much of the history of Western bureaucratic organization may be written as the continuing development of a fundamental logic based on the power of professional knowledge used to control individuals in even the most intimate ways, that is, in bodily action. Thus, Foucault has examined the history of punishment, madness, and sexuality in Western civilization to unearth the categories, boundaries, and mentalities by which individuals are controlled and, in a broad sense, confined.[1]

If, as was argued in chapter 6, communal groups serve as laboratories of organizational innovation, a major focus of their "researches" has had to do with the structuring of organizational commitment among participants. But communal groups simply confront more directly the same general issues of commitment that arise in all modern organizational management of individuals. Thus, it becomes important to ask about Peoples Temple: What was the calculus of "professional" knowledge undergirding "confinement," and to what extent did this calculus reflect that of other total institutions (monasteries, armies, mental hospitals) or, for that matter, modern organizations more widely? How was Jim Jones able to maintain a cadre of followers, a large number of them loyal to the point of committing suicide? Did he invent a new confinement or use an old iron cage?

### The Cultural Solidarity of Peoples Temple

The push and pull of economic advantages and disadvantages of Temple life are no more sufficient to explain people's commitment there than they are in general. True, Peoples Temple, and by extension its members, succeeded economically. And once people threw in their lot by "going communal," most of them lacked the economic resources that might finance another new beginning. But economic considerations do not explain either the strength of commitment among those who walked with Jones or the traumas others encountered in trying to sever their relationships with the Temple.

An explanation prevalent in the 1970s argued that people who join "cults" are the deceived victims of "coercive persuasion"—mindless zombies who march around like robots, eyes glazed, no longer capable of independent rational judgment. In a word, they have been brainwashed. Proponents of coercive persuasion as a theory detailed the social psychological procedures that unconventional religious groups often bring to bear to keep their converts' commitment strong enough to withstand efforts to "deprogram" them (i.e. break down their beliefs). But critics of the theory have made two telling points. First, coercive persuasion does not seem to have worked very well in the new religious groups; if the rates of defection are any indication, there must be a substantial amount of choice involved or there would not be so many former members. Second, the theory of coercive persuasion discounts the possibility of religious belief, and it disallows the possibility that people may willfully and even rationally choose to submit to external authority, but it does so unevenly. Culturally deviant and unpopular religions are targeted, while the more subtle (and perhaps more effective) coercion in mainstream religion is ignored. To the extent that this is so, the anticult movement was ideological, no matter what its claims to scientific legitimation.[2]

Peoples Temple might seem like the brainwashing cult *par excellence*. Many of its practices demonstrate the chilling possibilities for creating a pervasive and totalistic construction of reality. But we should view with skepticism any explanation based on a general theory of coercive persuasion. A more subtle and more powerful process was at work. People who followed Jones had to exercise a considerable degree of personal choice to enter the "prison camp of the mind." Moreover, they were hardly deceived about the ultimate purposes of the Temple and the ultimate commitment required of them. To the contrary, Jones went to great lengths to warn his followers of their likely fate. However unnerving and futile we may find the gesture of mass suicide, many people in the Temple became committed to sacrificing their own lives for socialism, in whatever way that might come to pass.

Peoples Temple took the widespread religious motif of Babyon's apocalypse to an extreme, cultivating a sense of persecution and siege. It thus accentuated both the boundary between the Temple and society at large and the apocalyptic dilemma of flight versus fight. These motifs created a conflict between contradictory objectives of solidarity. On the one hand, to help his deviant religion survive, Jones sought the power of numbers, and from this point of view, he could not be too discriminating about whom he brought within his fold. Indeed, his power might be enhanced by recruiting not only the weak, the elderly, and the "poor in spirit" but also the unruly, the strong, and the dangerous. Conversely, increased numbers lower the average level of commitment to group ideology; thus, the power of numbers weakens solidarity, and maintenance of control often devolves to manipulating the sentiments of the group as a "crowd."

Jones and his staff used a range of resocialization strategies to promote group solidarity through everyday social intercourse. Yet, as Kanter's theory of commitment suggests, not solidarity alone but social control layered onto solidarity affords a group's leaders the vehicle to shape individuals' actions to collective ends. Peoples Temple consolidated collective control over followers by legitimating Jones's charismatic authority on a mass basis. This authority then instituted practices of surveillance and collective emotional catharsis that turned the group into a crowd. In turn, differing kinds of commitment among members of Peoples Temple became submerged in the crowd, subject to simple yet compelling ideas.[3]

As Peoples Temple began its urban expansion in the 1970s, efforts to screen potential members became increasingly elaborate (see chapter 6). Jones did not shirk from stating his basic position in public services, but staff carefully gauged newcomers before they were ever exposed to more intimate and radical formulations of Jones's message.

Once within the Temple's gates, people became immersed in a comprehensive culture with a distinctive worldview that could frame new interpretations of experiences in the "outer" world. Like many more conventional evangelical groups, the Temple became a "greedy institution" in the most basic sense, by monopolizing time. For the full-fledged member, the weekly round of Temple activities left little time for housework and personal relationships, much less any outside activities. The Temple became a social world. Members who traveled the buses between Redwood Valley, San Francisco, and Los Angeles, including many rank and file, literally spent twenty-four hours a week in transit every other week, eating together, passing nights in other Temple members' homes. They even took vacations together. Faced with the endless stream of activities, some, like Deanna Mertle, wished "we could have some free time"; others lamented the boredom that came when church programs flagged.[4]

The overall schedule of general events was crisscrossed with activities that gave everyone, no matter what his or her station in life, a chance to "be somebody." Temple life essentially replicated the conventional popular culture of Pentecostal and evangelical Christianity. Services boasted a full-fledged choir, a Temple band, and people filling the conventional Black Pentecostal social roles, including ushers and nurses. Then there were auxiliary groups—among them one that discussed issues of "sisterhood," a loose-knit vaudeville company that presented skits, and a Peoples Temple defense group similar to drill team units in wider Black culture.

The various Temple secondary groups in turn offered the backbone of a radicalized church culture. The choir would perform numbers like "The Sympathizing Socialist," or Jack Beam would lead group singing of "The old bullshit religion ain't what it used to be." The theater troup served up skits on venereal disease, slavery, mental illness, the Ku Klux Klan, and concentration camps. Occasionally the Skitsophrenics performed humorous caricatures of Temple members. The functional equivalent of television, the morality plays not only offered a critique of U.S. culture but also cultivated a "patriotic" identification with Peoples Temple's cause. "It was just a way we could project the signs of the times," Jones held, "and much of it was fun. Tremendously entertaining."

Add to the fun the hours Jones himself spent preaching about the horrors of television "brainwashing," the absurdity of Black preachers who were telling their congregations that poverty was God's will, the atrocities of profit-hungry corporations making a buck by cutting corners on safety. Nor did Jones draw his basic points out of thin air. He encouraged followers to read such classics of radical history and theory as Edmund Wilson's *To the Finland Station* and Leo Huberman and Paul Sweezy's *Introduction to Socialism* (foreward by Albert Einstein). He brought in outsiders who spoke with authority, and the Temple screened films that reinforced their outlook. Thus came Daniel Ellsberg, to speak on the Pentagon papers and the Vietnam war, and the avowed Black revolutionary feminist Angela Davis. Occasional evenings, Temple members were treated to screenings of *Z, Joe Hill*, and *State of Siege*.

All was not totally serious in the Temple's cultural world. Sometimes there were dances, and movies like *It's a Mad, Mad, Mad World*. But the overall message was clear. It is not the case that Jones deceived people about his basic orientation. He deemphasized theology, but those who became members in California knew he promoted a communistic "philosophy made into life." Followers were informed that "the most highly evolved person, he who is ready to leave this plane, acts as an atheist. He doesn't ask God for a thing. He lives a life of Principle."

In sermons Jones emphasized, "I cannot impose. I have never made anyone a socialist by my paranormal power. I can't hold a person like that. You've got to get it inside yourself." Like the Quakers, he depended on "convincement," but he gave his audiences the insights with which to convince themselves. People from the Temple walked around in the outer world of California during the Vietnam war years, they saw President Nixon's infamous Watergate fall from power, and they experienced an Arab oil embargo crisis. Like the early Protestants who carried their "cathedral" in their own minds, Jones's followers used his vision as a lens to focus their perceptions of the society he deplored.[5]

## Making Jones's Charisma Valid

If the beliefs of followers depended upon their own conscious will, their willingness to submit to Jim Jones's authority depended on believing that he was a prophet. It was to enhance this image that Jones brought to bear his most elaborate dramaturgical procedures. In turn, the stage work fostered a siege mentality in the group. By projecting himself as a threat to the established order, Jones heightened the gulf between his followers and society at large, and this isolation left the group as the sole collective arbiter of reality. The success of this strategy left Jones in the structural position of a messiah: he was a man without peer among those who knew him, and his position became virtually impossible to challenge.

It would be convenient to assume that Jones was successful because he dealt with mentally incompetent people highly susceptible to the powers of suggestion. Early on, some relatives of Temple members declared their loved ones were uneducated, "mentally retarded," and gullible people who made "easy prey" for a spellbinder like Jones. It is true that Jones's library included a number of books like *Hypnotic Realities: the Induction of Clinical Hypnosis and Forms of Indirect Suggestion*, but he did not just prey upon the gullible. He spun his web around a number of people of substantial sophistication, including Temple attorneys Tim Stoen and Gene Chaiken and a Northern California Disciples of Christ official. Like any effective magic, Jones's did not depend upon ignorance on the part of the "mark"; it was based on the ability to focus attention selectively. "Hypnosis" was just one item in a more comprehensive catalogue of suggestive techniques that sometimes included out-and-out lying. These ploys, in turn, grounded more extensive practices of control, from spying to public humiliation, that were merely legitimated by the charismatic aura of magic.

Jim Jones did much less healing than talking about healing, and he staged other major deceptions only to build the basis for less "fragile" methods of reality construction. On occasion he publicly healed people through the fraudulent passing of cancers (chicken gizzards), but more often he talked about the people he had raised from the dead in the past month or he drew on the time-honored evangelical tradition of letting others offer testimony about his powers. Then there were Jones's own powers of suggestion. With hardly a moment's faltering he could verbally transport himself through time and space, to the site of Jesus's crucifixion, or across town to a supermarket where a fascist thug was taking a gunshot at one of his own sons. Perhaps most disconcerting were the pronouncements based on truth. Jones drew on techniques he apparently had learned from Hoosier evangelist William Branham years earlier, reading off three-by-five-inch member information cards at the pulpit to place facts known by his audience in a prophetic web that supported his own conclusions. Those who knew the truth of the story about Bonnie Thielmann could not fail to share the outrage when Jones talked of the Christian preacher who had propositioned the girl when she came to him with doubts about her Christian faith.[6]

The prophet sometimes seemed omniscient, but he was hardly all-powerful. Jones cultivated the image of fragility along with power, and he led his throng to believe that they were in danger of losing him if they did not respect and care for him. Because Jim sacrificed so much for them, they could hardly complain about the few privileges he took to replenish his spirit of struggle, for when he experienced setbacks, he seemed to become ill, and if he was challenged, he might clutch his chest in heart pain. The antics fostered a fear that "he will die before his time."

In fact, Jim's wife Marcie let it become generally known in the Temple that members were not to disagree publicly with her husband, even if he humiliated them in front of others, as he was known to do. In settings other than public ones, Jones cultivated friendly relations. "He would chastise you in a public meeting, town forum or something, but not one on one," recalled Charlie Touchette. "Then he was always very supportive of you, made you feel good." If, on the other side, Jones wanted to get a private message to someone, "he had you told. He would never say anything bad direct, always through one of his secretaries."

In Jones's view, his relationship with followers was one of uncompromised loyalty: "There's no court in the land that can make me tell what I know about you," he promised from the pulpit. Publicly he suggested that the Temple was a demonstration of "creative individualism, and all that leaves is just that Jim Jones is a friend. Probably in their minds the best friend they've got, but they can disagree with him. And they do." Perhaps, but hardly on equal terms. Jones could use one-on-one friendship to maintain intimacy and monitor his flock, while public channels served to confirm his charismatic authority through his daring and unchallenged admonitions and castigations of others.[7]

Sometimes Jones became much closer than just a friend to his followers. Stephan Jones caught glimpses of his father having sex in the San Francisco Temple apartment, often with a woman, but sometimes with a man. Publicly, Jones allowed that "everybody has all kinds of sexual impulses." But in vague allusions to his own sexual prowess, he also condemned men who jumped from woman to woman as latent homosexuals and promoted himself as the only true heterosexual. He also maintained the public fiction of his fidelity to his estranged wife for years, nevertheless letting it be known that he received notes from women who wanted to see him, and suggesting that wives might well fantasize about him while they made love with their husbands.

A group of Temple insiders bounded at the furthest by the Planning Commission saw a different side. At meetings "Jim would get on that sex kick," Mike Touchette recalled. "People would testify to their homosexual tendencies." Those who felt threatened by such admissions found themselves subjected to collective ridicule led by Jones. At the other extreme, the more zealous p.c. members relished the moment of "confession" as an opportunity to convince Jones of how "upfront" they were.

Jones's sexual predispositions were well enough known by 1973 that Elmer Mertle could write to him, "I admire you greatly to be able to fuck anyone for the cause." Jones once bragged about taking on sixteen people in one day. The women who made love with him would tell others about the unparalleled ecstasy of the experience, but his male partners were not so proud. Thus, Jones sometimes established his sexual superiority over another man both by alienating the affections of the other's female companion and by involving the man himself in homosexual alliances.

In general, Jones claimed to engage in affairs selflessly, and on the basis of his followers' needs. "Nobody got special consideration," according to Bea Orsot. "After he fucked you, that was it. It was for your benefit. . . . He might fuck you because you were ugly or never had much sex." Jones may have had sex with most women and perhaps more than a few men who were part of the innermost circle of the Temple, but for the mass of followers, a mythology of rumors about Jones's sexuality simply contributed to the aura of his charisma, and the substance of that charisma was developed much more along apocalyptic than sexual lines.[8]

Over and over again Jones affirmed the classic trait of charisma, telling his followers, "I can have more power if you give it to me. I'm like a dynamo; I'm like a hydraulic system." The preacher portrayed Christ consciousness as a sort of scaler phenomenon; a person could be thirtyfold, sixtyfold or a hundredfold filled with God. Jones was the fulfillment—a hundredfold god. The personal ego of Jones had died long ago, and now Jim told the assembled, "I'm letting Christ have a body."

But Jim Jones did not simply claim the spirit of Christ in his flesh, he made his proclaimed divinity the basis of struggle. He would stand for righteousness, and he would love love. And for his love he would defend those he loved from attacks. Jones would parlay his stand with "God Socialism" into a transcendent struggle against evil persons who would persecute them who did good. To the faithful, it could only be that others would attack them *because* their cause was just.

From the days of promoting integration in Indianapolis, Jones recognized the value of evil opponents. The doings of racists could demonstrate that his movement was challenging entrenched opposition, and the fact of opposition itself would attract more followers. At some point Jones and his staff entered the fantastic world of dramaturgy. A staged attack was as good as a real one. If there was a lack of boldness on the part of the opposition that surely was out there, Jones and his staff would have to do their duty for them. Even in Indiana some observers had suspected that not all the evil befalling Jones was the work of opponents. Whatever Jones did to contrive events that early, in California he and his staff clearly played up the drama of opposition and learned to exercise the same practices of intimidation they abhorred in their racist detractors.

In the earliest recorded California incident of any significance, a hair stylist angered by a wedding Jones had performed entered the Redwood Valley church building during a service in the spring of 1969, came at Jones, and threatened he would "put a knife through your heart." The assailant later pleaded guilty to misdemeanor charges of disturbing the peace. This sort of harassment justified establishing old-timer Marvin Swinney with a licensed weapon to act as guard at the Temple in Redwood Valley in the same year. A security orientation grew up from there, and was reinforced by incidents at the hands of the pickup-truck crowd in the rural village. Eventually Temple security would establish a guard outpost on the roof of the church, install floodlights, search for bombs, screen visitors, and surround Jones himself with guards. At some point, Tim Stoen would write a memo to Chuck [Chris?] Lewis, asking for a progress report on setting up a "regular training session in defensive tactics" for Temple members.

The *pièce de résistance* of staged events used to justify such measures came with an assassination attempt on Jones that took place in the Redwood Valley church parking lot after services one August Sunday in 1972. The Jones's long-time friend and housekeeper, Esther Mueller, was doing the dishes in the nearby parsonage when "Marcie was told by Jim to come and get me. . . . As soon as I got to the front of the church I heard three shots and he fell to the ground. He immediately got up and walked to the house with the aid of Marcie and two or three close friends and two nurses. They saw the big hole in his chest and he was full of blood. He covered the wounds and went back to the church and preached about two hours after that." The divine had healed himself. Jones thus proved that he could get along without guards, but when it was a matter of guns (and once, even attempted arson, complete with a Jones "premonition"), mere mortals could claim to come up a bit short on faith. Security precautions continued to grow.[9]

In the early 1970s, the seeds of small-town harassment and staged persecution blossomed into a more worthy set of opponents. The press, at least one concerned citizen, and certain local ministers began to see that at a minimum Peoples Temple undermined Christian civilization by making a mockery of its practices. Perhaps, they suspected, the problems ran even deeper. The controversy began in Indianapolis in the fall of 1971, when Temple buses rolled into town to hold services there. Indianapolis *Times* reporter Byron Wells gave the Temple coverage it never had received before, suggesting that some of the very people healed in an afternoon service had a "striking resemblance to those healed at an evening service." The Temple retorted that Wells was a racist who could not tell one Black from another.

After the event another Indianapolis reporter, Carolyn Pickering, eventually hooked up with a San Francisco *Examiner* religion reporter named Lester Kinsolving. Kinsolving was a former Episcopal priest always on the lookout for the more lurid scandals of religious life. Moreover, he shared with Jones a knack for injecting himself into situations in a way that created news out of the dramatic confrontations he provoked. When Kinsolving's interest came to the attention of Peoples Temple, he was inundated with some fifty-five letters from Temple members. One writer, Assistant District Attorney Tim Stoen, offered perhaps overzealous claims about his pastor's healing talents: "Jim has been the means by which more than 40 persons have literally been brought back from the dead this year. . . . I have seen Jim revive people stiff as a board, tongues hanging out, eyes set, skin graying, and all vital signs absent."

After visiting several Temple services, on Sunday, September 17, 1972, Kinsolving led off an *Examiner* series with a story headlined, "The Prophet Who Raises the Dead," noting the presence of armed guards, and featuring quotes from Stoen's letter. The next day's *Examiner* offered up a mocking description of a healing service in which a "woman began leaping wildly and screeching hallelujahs—while an even more elderly woman commenced a frenzied hopping in a corner downstage right." The third installment exposed Jones's methods of discernment by quoting a former member who described how Jones's followers would "visit potential church members, noting anything personal in the house, like addresses on letters, types of medicine in the medicine cabinet, or pictures of relatives." The Temple responded by loading up the buses in Redwood Valley and bringing 150 marchers to San Francisco to demonstrate in front of television cameras against the urban newspaper that disdained religion.

The day of the demonstration Kinsolving was back in print with a Ukiah Baptist minister, the Reverend Richard G. Taylor, wondering whether people at the Redwood Valley church "have ever been threatened and whether instead they have not contrived such reports in order to justify armed guards." Taylor already had urged the state's attorney general to investigate the Temple, Kinsolving reported. "What is of utmost concern," Taylor reportedly wrote the attorney general, "is the atmosphere of terror created in the community by so large and aggressive a group, which effect is implemented by [Tim] Stoen's civil office."

Temple members returned to march at the *Examiner* offices for two more days. The *Examiner* received negative television publicity from the demonstrations, and because Kinsolving's remaining installments might not stand up well in the face of a threatened Temple lawsuit, the newspaper held back on further publication and agreed to run an interview with Jones.

With his exposé series, Kinsolving gave courage to a smattering of Temple opponents outside its walls. David Conn, former member of the Richmond, California, Barret Avenue Christian Church and an old friend of the Mertles, later claimed he had served as a source for the stories. Another man, Ross Case, Jones's former Indiana associate pastor who had moved to Ukiah on his own, now kept tabs on the Temple with at least the fortitude that came from knowing he was not alone. But Kinsolving's series hardly mobilized an outraged general citizenry. And within the Temple the reaction was minimal. Few of Jones's followers ever had an opportunity to read the Kinsolving series, and not a single person left Peoples Temple because of the exposé. Jones himself would use attacks like Kinsolving's to validate his own righteousness, proclaiming, "They that live godly in Christ Jesus shall suffer persecution; you will even be killed. . . . So I'm walking to that old-fashioned persecution that was once delivered to the saints."

The ideology of persecution found ready hearts in Jones's followers. With memories of Mississippi delta plantation life or the streets of San Francisco behind them, Blacks easily could experience the outside world as alien, cold, and evil. They might well regard their isolation from it as pleasant. And once people became accustomed to identifying with Peoples Temple as a surrogate extended, interracial family, attacks like Kinsolving's could be used to validate Jones's claims in a way that further solidified the wall that separated people of the Temple from people of the outer world.[10]

### Monitoring as Confinement

Rarely does the organization that experiences "persecution" from the outside fail to find it within its own ranks as well. As Elias Canetti has observed, people on the inside themselves originally came from the outside. At least some converts faced with the demands of revolutionary commitment will long for the days when they enjoyed simple pleasures and left the world's problems to the shoulders of others. In turn, such backsliding may undermine the commitment of others, for it can raise doubts concerning the sanctity of the cause.

Then too, organizations that offer collective benefits must deal somehow with the problem of freeriders, people who enjoy the benefits of group association without taking on their fair share of its burdens. If such activity becomes widespread, it weakens the commitment of others, and feeds their resentment of the shirkers who get by without contributing. The twin problems of backsliding and freeloading have a common solution: in one way or another, those with the greatest stake in a group try to monitor the beliefs and actions of others.

In communal groups the problems are particularly acute. In principle such groups are voluntary; they have no legal hold on their followers. For this reason, over the centuries communal leaderships have explored a variety of techniques to "confine" their members. They have required those who join to take oaths of loyalty, instituted confession by members, established members' mutual criticism of behavior and attitudes, and developed honor systems or procedures by which members report on one another's conduct. Foreshadowing modern use of television cameras for security monitoring, the nineteenth-century Shaker groups sometimes even installed little windows through which staff could secretly observe the rank and file.

Two polar opposite approaches to the practice of monitoring can be distinguished. On the one hand, some communal groups maintain strict status hierarchies that distribute rewards unequally, typically according to the "spiritual evolution" or ideological commitment of followers. In such groups people of the higher statuses have the greatest vested interest in the group's survival. Alternatively, all group members other than the leadership may derive putatively equal benefits from the group. Under these conditions, no matter what their vocations or roles, all members have a more or less equal interest in collective monitoring of individuals, and the leadership can count on its entire membership to bring to light activities of individuals that threaten the group's solidarity.

Peoples Temple clearly came closer to the latter of the two polar arrangements. No matter that Jones and some of his immediate staff enjoyed slight but symbolically important differences in life-style. No matter that Temple staff sometimes spent thousands of dollars to conduct the business of the group in jet-set style. The rank-and-file Temple member who "went communal" still derived considerable benefits from group life, enough at least to have a personal interest in guarding against threats to the Temple. Jones's staff therefore was able to implement a program of group surveillance that counted on virtually the whole rank and file as its eyes and ears.

The successful infusion of the surveillance orientation into every corner of Temple life had consequences that have been widely noted. In the absence of visible restraints, the Temple could proclaim that its members lived in "one of the freest of atmospheres." Its members could walk in the wider world of California, belying any untoward enslavement. Though one public school teacher noted that Temple children "stayed to themselves and formed their own little groups," another observed, "They didn't seem like they were in any kind of bondage." But appearances were sustained by a thoroughgoing "confinement" that depended on neither isolation nor the sacrifice of individual identity. The program, in turn, was so unrelenting in its demands for loyalty that it helped breed the very betrayal it was supposed to control.

The cultural origins of the Temple approach to monitoring seem most logically connected to counseling, and to Jones's practice of discernment, carried far beyond the traditional evangelical purposes of confirming the psychic abilities of the prophet. Before the Kinsolving series, monitoring rarely was directed to concerns with loyalty. For the most part counselors gathered information about members' bureaucratic snafus with welfare agencies, legal difficulties, problems with spouses undergoing separation, and so forth. Much of the counseling took place privately or with only a few counselors and the party or parties to the situation present.

The lines between surveillance and discernment, threats and prophecy, would be hard to draw. Temple counselors fed information to Jones when they decided it required his attention. Members who requested a private audience could meet with Jones himself, once counselors had screened their concerns to shield him from overburdensome trivialities or irresolvable problems of chronic complainers. On the basis of information brought to his attention, Jones might sermonize on child abuse and then, through "discernment," "call out" a woman, warning her, "You repent of your sins, or Friday night you'll look like you been rolled over by a steamroller."

The Temple monitored members in other obvious ways. Like many types of organizations, including public schools and churches, it subjected members to testimonials and other public ritual affirmations of commitment. It also took attendance. But the Temple eventually went far beyond conventional monitoring in voluntary groups. Deanna Mertle's proposed reorganization plan called for a switchboard operator to serve as "a clearing house for people not going to work, and their reason. . . ." Those who worked full-time outside jobs were to turn in weekly reports on their schedules. "If they fail to turn the schedule in, they will be put on the basis of telephone reporting." Members, even teenagers, filled out forms listing their work schedules, church project commitments, people who lived in their homes, and other basic biographical data.

On other occasions the polling of members gauged far more personal matters. On a form labeled "St. Josephs' Parish Council Questionaire," people were asked who their best friends were, "in and out of the church." What were their jealousies, fears, weaknesses, strengths, temptations? Did they hold "hostilities" or "sexual feelings and attractions to the pastor?" Did they fantasize about leaving the church? Why? What were their thoughts about suicide, and about life after death? "What do you think about church discipline?" the questionaire inquired, and "What criticisms do you have of the church and/or leadership?" Monitoring thus depended heavily on the "confessional" relation that followers maintained with Jones. People in the Temple sometimes used a "My personal message to Pastor Jim Jones" form to reveal their innermost concerns to Jim. Others wrote long letters, detailing everything from problems with spouses, dissatisfactions with communal housemates, and difficulties with hostile outside relatives to apologetic explanations about slow progress with Temple work projects.

The issue of loyalty sometimes shaded monitoring into other realms. In Deanna Mertle's plan, as people became members, they were to sign statements affirming progressively more and more radical positions. "By the time they have signed and had notorized these statements, they will have implicated themselves to beliefs which will cause them to think twice about causing any problems, knowing that we have their statements," she proposed. Practices were much more extensive. Members admitted both to things they had done and things they never did, thus becoming caught in traps of blackmail and pseudoblackmail. Temple staff routinely would have people who were becoming members sign blank pieces of paper, sometimes at the top, in the middle, or at the bottom of the page. The Temple membership file card included checkmarks for "documents signed," including a "blank statement," "resignation," "financial release," and "sheet of paper." "Dear Jim Jones," read "Mert" Mertle's resignation, "I find that my life style has changed so that it demands all of my time now and I no longer wish to be a member of Peoples Temple."

As proof of their "loyalty," the inner circle of Temple members also sometimes wrote "confessions" detailing past offenses and their willingness to perform revolutionary acts. The Mertles's file overflowed with handwritten statements: in one, the couple testified of their "plan to overthrow the government and establish communism in America"; others centered on the sexual topics that preoccupied Jones. Deanna jotted one, a note to Mert, asking him to "please keep Daphene and Eddie away from me, I cannot keep from molesting them so no matter how hard I plead, don't give in—it's for their best good."

Of all the compromising statements and blank sheets that were collected, few were ever put to any public use, nor could they have been in any credible way, but internally they underscored the belief of some members that they had compromised their moral worth in the outer world. With the stigma of soiled identities as confessed homosexuals and revolutionary criminals, they would think twice about leaving the Temple, and with the Temple holding files containing damning statements in their own handwriting, those who did leave would think twice about causing trouble.

The monitoring that bred confinement of Temple members did not depend upon self-reporting alone. In describing their own difficulties, members often revealed a good deal about others as well. Moreover, they were obligated to report about others anything that might be relevant to "the Cause," and in some cases, they purposely took on surveillance under the guise of friendship to probe for specific information deemed essential to Temple interests. Jack Beam "wrote up" a member who stole some jackhammers, suggesting the man was "to [sic] dumb to get away clear." Teri Buford reported on the financial position of the Mertles while she lived with them. By the mid-1970s even children offered up information about their friends, and one actually reported an observed tendency of her parents to talk "real exclusively like in the bedroom." On occasion Tim Stoen phoned teenagers, trying to put together the facts on problematic situations, once encouraging a loyal Temple girl to maintain certain friendships, and coaching her on what to say about their own telephone conversations (wrong number) if she were discovered by her "friends." The committed readily offered voluminous detail on their situations. One Temple member who kept a detailed daily journal clearly did not consider it private, for on February 10, 1976, she dutifully recorded, "I turned in the last journal section I had done to Grace Stoen. . . ."

If Temple members sometimes figured out who had "ratted" on them, Jones would deny it, attributing his seeming omniscience either to psychic powers or bugging devices. But the channels of intelligence made little difference once people became aware of monitoring, for Jones's network left individuals who harbored doubts about Peoples Temple unable to trust their misgivings about the Temple to one another, even parents in front of their children, or spouses with each other.

The confessions similarly left Temple members beholden to a power that compromised their ability to retrace their steps to the world at large. How people viewed the signed statements served as an acid test of commitment, perhaps too well. As one loyalist observed about confessions, "The only people who thought they were important were the people who wanted to leave." Loyalists would have little to fear from subjection to the cult of intelligence. Those truly committed to "the Cause" would have no qualms about signing anything, no matter how absurd or damning, for they construed themselves as having burned their bridges behind them. Therefore, like the witch-hunters of the McCarthy era, Temple staff could note fear of scrutiny itself as a sign of potential disloyalty. Thus, when one woman seemed to complain publicly that Jones had her watched, he "asked if some of her behavior did not justify" his trying to keep an eye on her.[11]

### Catharsis and Punishment

Jim Jones, and counselors as well, became practiced at the art of making their subjects feel guilty for their shortcomings, then alternately showing mercy that proved the Temple's benevolence, or imposing discipline that confirmed a member's sinfulness. Like other religions that hinge a psychic state of grace on the believer's conduct, the Temple became powerful in its capacity to shape the innermost feelings of members so that they became dependent upon the Temple for their sense of well-being. As Jones once told his congregation, "One feels either resentment or guilt, and though it is uncomfortable, it is better to feel guilt."

Nowhere was the psychological domination more effective than in public settings: "deeper life catharsis" meetings, "family nights," planning commission meetings, and once the membership had been pared down to the truly committed, general meetings. At deeper-life-catharsis and family-night meetings beginning in the late 1960s, the inner circle of members gradually became exposed to the church as an intimate family.

Perhaps at the inspiration of its several California-trained social workers, Peoples Temple took up the widespread encounter-group practices of popular culture. In their more extreme formulations, encounter groups were intended to liberate individuals from whatever previous patterns of behavior were deemed inappropriate by confronting them with a noncorruptible "objective" viewpoint on their actions. As the Temple put it (delicately), "members are encouraged to be honest in all situations and

freely discuss problems with one another so as not to nurture any hostilities within the group." Like other encounter groups, the Temple became
a powerful force in defining reality, and leaders became the brokers of
reality.

Jim Jones set himself up as the ultimate authority not only in matters of
theology but in psychological gamesmanship as well. Many followers respected him because he knew ego strategies, and he could produce dramatic changes in attitudes and actions. Even a Temple defector, Mike
Cartmell, would admit that "Jones could be a tremendous counselor," but
Cartmell also held that Jones could be pathologically cruel in the way he
taught lessons, once forcing a child to eat his own vomit. Temple apologists
after 1978 would assert that it was Jones's honesty itself that turned people
against him. "We all had this love/hate thing about him," recounted Bea
Orsot, "because he made us look really hard at ourselves, look at the ways
we were assholes. Nobody likes to admit they're an asshole, but nobody's
perfect. And Jim asked us to face up to ourselves." In general, Temple
practice followed the prevailing pop psychology theory of the day, that
"sitting on" feelings toward others creates barriers. Catharsis, then, offered
a medium for defusing the animosities and dealing with the conflicts that
inevitably emerge in communal situations, where people continue to live
everyday life with others even if they have become emotionally estranged.

From all accounts, through the early 1970s, catharsis sessions approxi-
mated a religious version of the encounter-group model, practiced among
the inner membership at Redwood Valley. One session was described as "a
painful experience, but oh so necessary, in which each member of the body
was encourged to stand and get off his chest everything that was in any way
a hindrance to fellowship between himself and another member or between
himself and the group, or the leader even, Jim in his utter honesty not
desiring nor seeking immunity from the exposure of his own faults. . . . The
catharsis was greatly needed; it opened the clogged channels for the flow of
love."

Even by 1975, when private membership meetings were held at the
urban churches, in dealing with matters like uncooperative adults who
resented communal living, Jones would probe issues, establish a factual
record in courtroom fashion, and make judgments based on the individuals' and the group's welfare. For instance, a child who had become alienated
because of his parents' breakup was discussed in terms concerned simply
with alleviating his difficulties.

In cases of actions judged misdeeds, members sometimes were instructed to raise $100 for the Temple. On occasion Jim Jones directed
whole groups of people to take on some act of penitance to develop their
moral character. The keeper of a journal once duly noted that "every white

person who hasn't known poverty must fast for five days." Another time Jones approvingly read in the meeting a letter from a teenaged girl who had learned the "humiliation" Black people had experienced over the centuries by asking her fellow commune members at the Mertles' home to treat her as a slave.[12]

Jones found that not all individuals responded to catharsis, loving criticism, and requests for penitance. Beginning in the early 1970s, the meetings changed to include explicit use of psychological and physical discipline. As the Temple's operations shifted to urban California, the objects of "catharsis" began to include streetwise young Blacks, some of them youths involved in gangs, petty theft, and the like, others schooled in the tougher lessons of heroin dealing, addiction, and pimping. For these young Blacks and the parents who sometimes brought them there, the Temple represented "structure" designed to jolt them from street patterns of behavior. The Temple's *Peoples Forum* argued, "You don't take people out of a turbulent, hostile environment and set them straight without some discipline or structure."

For behavior modification, verbal castigation was found to be an effective approach. Stephan Jones recalled, "The worst thing anybody could have happen to him was to have Dad chastise him publically. That was the worst fear . . . that you'd be yelled at. I've had guys come to me and say, 'God, I'd rather be beat up than have him yell at me and humiliate me.'"

As early as 1973, especially after eight young Temple members defected in September of that year, Temple catharsis practices included physical punishment. While Grace Stoen served as head counselor, she reported to Jim Jones the names of people to be disciplined. Aside from one incident, middle-aged and older members do not seem to have received any sort of physical punishment. By 1975, however, children sometimes were subjected to extensive paddlings. The collective administration of *in loco parentis* discipline, Temple staff eventually claimed, had grown out of a desire to eliminate child abuse uncovered in homes. According to Tish Leroy, "We found out they [parents] were spanking their children much too severely, and in cases where perhaps it was not warranted. It was decided [with the approval of Jones] any children would be spanked in church if . . . the whole congregation decided that the matter warranted a spanking." The supposed precipitating case Tish Leroy cited, however, likely did not occur until 1975, when physical punishment already was well established.

Whatever the exact genesis of Temple discipline, it effectively substituted collective for familial control and offered the group the opportunity to act as witnesses. If the Temple abused children, it did so publicly. Temple practice differed substantially from the private child abuse marked by parents "losing control" that authorities have estimated to be so widespread in the United States. The Temple's practices were highly regulated. Discipline was administered during the institutionalized catharsis segments of Wednesday night Temple meetings for loyal insiders. Physical punishment took one of two forms: either the person received a set number of swats with a paddle, with the sentence sometimes commuted by a "loving" Jim Jones, or the offender had to box or wrestle against "lesson givers" or "people fighting for the program."

The Temple directed a good deal of discipline toward behavior that was deemed wrong in some moral sense. Children could expect to receive punishment for stealing, for lying, acting "irresponsibly," making fun of people for their handicaps, physically threatening or attacking others, especially adults, associating too intimately with outsiders, and breaking the laws of the larger society, especially in ways that reflected on Peoples Temple. It seems that sexual activities on the part of Temple youth, even homosexuality, were not proscribed, except when they involved people outside the Temple. As the author of the anonymous journal reported one time, "Jim took a casual attitude about the sexual behavior which he said was natural, but was severe about the stealing."

Adults found themselves "on the floor" for such things as violating the Pentecostal and Holiness rules against alcohol, smoking and drugs, using their positions in the Temple hierarchy to "throw . . . weight around," shirking their own responsibilities, practicing personal grooming to the point of "vanity," not getting their offering pledges in, and failing to attend services regularly.

Far more serious than individual weaknesses were the problems involving violations of the Temple's covenant with its members, or actions that undermined that covenant by implicitly asserting the primacy of the individual—an offense that was dubbed "anarchy." At the most fundamental level, Temple staff sought to protect the group from those who would exploit the group for personal gain. One communal member was accused of selling his possessions and keeping for himself money "which should have been turned over to the commune." Another was accused of "freeloading" by consuming Temple resources while failing to turn over money earned at jobs. Like communal groups ever since St. Benedict wrote his *Rule* for a monastic order, the Temple held to the formula "He who does not work, does not eat."

Sometimes punishment was substantial. Young members of a gang were chastised for rebellious behavior and petty theft, and each received "fifty whacks." In 1975 one teenager, Linda Mertle, wrote a letter requesting seventy-five whacks for greeting a lesbian adult friend who had left Peoples Temple several years earlier. "I realize that when people write something up about themselves," she wrote to Jim, "they normally get there [*sic*] discipline lowered but I wish to get all of mine to help make up for all the people I have minipulated [*sic*] over the years." As was uniformly the case when physical punishment was administered to minors, a parent signed a form requesting discipline that held the Temple harmless for administering it. Nor apparently was the husky Linda totally defeated by the experience. To the contrary, she would be found on later occasions serving as a "lesson giver" to those requiring discipline.

In a delinquent vein, several small boys received "twenty-five whacks" for "stealing cookies" in a supermarket. Another time, John Gardner went "on the floor for calling Kirtas Smith a crippled bitch. . . . His mother, Ruby Carroll [who herself had paddled Linda Mertle], cried because he is so bad. . . . One woman said, 'put him on the road.' It was explained that we can't because he is not of age. John screamed as he took 70 whacks; at that point Jim commuted his sentence."

In boxing matches held by 1975, the offender had to take on an opponent like the tough young Chris Lewis, or even a series of such opponents who fought for "the Cause." Opponents supposedly would be roughly matched in age and abilities, but the advantage usually tipped to the Temple. Adults were far more likely to experience this form of punishment rather than the paddlings, and according to an unwritten Temple rule, they were not supposed to fight back. Certainly it would only prolong the experience, because "justice" would have to win out in the end. All the same, some of the more "surly" offenders boxed aggressively. One "cocky" delinquent type "was so hostile that three people had to fight him before one was capable of defeating him." Another time Jones publicly shamed a man who flirted with various Temple women. His brains, Jones said, "had gone into his scrotum." Jones decreed a boxing match, but the man was "unable to return a single blow. Jim's judgement had already taken effect." In a final humiliation the ladies' man was posed with his wife and two other woman so that photographs could be taken.

No matter what the form of punishment—psychological humiliation, paddling, or boxing—the format remained true to one encounter group principle, that such events take place "outside" everyday reality. When Deanna Mertle first witnessed catharsis in 1970, she was amazed to find the next day that even the direct parties to a nasty little cathartic episode were acting as if the event never happened. Jones underscored this approach in 1975, warning followers "that we were not to reflect in any way on anyone who had been disciplined by the group. They were to be treated as kindly as usual."

As for physical punishment, Jones declared in a service, "I cannot wish that any of us will be hurt. I hate these fights." But he did not stop them. On at least one occasion, "Jim Jones insisted on taking ten stripes himself."

Apparently he meant to show that anyone who sinned against the group represented the whole group sinning against itself; for that, he took part of the blame. But Jones had difficulty communicating this strange formulation to the outside. On the last day of his life, he would tell reporters, "I have been beaten too. I live for the people I'm trying to save."[13]

There is no way to estimate the effect of Temple discipline—whether it constrained members from crimes that might have resulted in more confining punishment from the state—but the style can be traced. Physical punishment in the Temple certainly exceeded normative standards of the modern middle class, but Temple members were not predominantly middle class. Disciplinary practices of Peoples Temple more resembled those of stern Protestants, from the Puritans of seventeenth-century New England to some modern fundamentalist sects. The extremes of Protestant discipline are marked by a Michigan sect whose members accidentally beat a child to death for his sins in 1984. More representative of the sensibility is Northeast Kingdom Community, a contemporaneous Christian religious community in Island Pond, Vermont, whose members had no apologies for using rods and switches for "loving correction" of children, even if it left marks on their bodies.

By a Puritan standard like that of Island Pond, Temple discipline was not excessive. Like Puritans, the Temple practiced a regulated penance via the ritual punishment of offenders who demonstrated the boundaries of collective failure. As Kai Erikson has argued for Puritans, "Little attention was paid to the motives of the offender, the grief of the victim, the anger of the community, or any other human emotion: the whole process had a flat, mechanical tone because it dealt with the laws of nature rather than the decisions of men." Just as the Puritans struggled with the contradictions between the doctrine of predestination and holding individuals responsible for their actions, Jim Jones understood individuals' failures as a collective failure to redeem some of his followers from the "predestination" of growing up in the ghetto. Like the Puritans, those in the Temple who sometimes shirked their punishment struggled with internal feelings of guilt, while externally they might be branded as hopeless cases and sometimes banished for failing to adequately represent the ideals of Peoples Temple. By the same token, and as with the Puritans, when individuals did submit to punishment, it reaffirmed the collective sense that the Temple's vision of a moral world was just.[14]

## The Family

The monitoring, the pseudoblackmail of signed "confessions," the seamier kinds of catharsis, and the more humiliating forms of discipline manufactured stigmatized identities. The toll of these practices fell especially heavily upon people who failed to conform, but no matter how defeated the heretics personally became, the possibility remained that they might conspire with one another against the group. The Temple countered this threat by the collective management of interpersonal relationships. Like many other communal groups, both historical and contemporary, the Temple leadership believed intimate monogamous relations between individuals could undermine collective solidarity. Although the Temple did not forbid monogamous pairings, it monitored ones where collective solidarity was at stake, and Jim Jones did his best to undermine them. Conversely, the Temple encouraged a variety of sexual alliances and intimate relations that furthered the collective interest.

In large part the Jones "rainbow family" provided the crucible. It was a collage of people assembled out of Jim's own recruitment, shot through with his son Stephan's resentment of his father's extramarital affairs and Temple demands on his father's time. The family hung together at all only because Marcie swallowed her pride and chose to stay after 1969, when Jim confronted her with the reality of his relationship to Carolyn Moore Layton. Marcie remained in the Temple as a dedicated worker who played the part of pastor's wife when it was required, and tried to use what influence she had with her husband of record to hold him in check for the sake of her children and everyone else.

For her part, Carolyn passed time in the early California years playing with the Jones children; she also sought to nurture a friendship with Marcie and fretted over Karen Layton, the young woman who had married her former husband Larry, for "the countless times she has looked so flirtatiously at Jim." Jim eventually returned the attention, and further emasculated Larry Layton. Like Marcie before her, Carolyn would have to live with Jim's affairs, and she would have to accept a relationship that was not based on exclusivity.

Jim Jones thus stood at the epicenter of a web in which friendships, intimacies, and working relations crosscut and obscured both the legal institution of marriage and the norms that align sexual and companionate dimensions of relationships. In the Temple scheme of things, people could show affection to others, regardless of their primary commitments, and people would have to learn to endure some sort of fairly close relations, even in the wake of sexual and intimate estrangement. As Jeannie Mills commented, "Relationships were just different in Peoples Temple; that's hard to explain."

Emblematic of the alliances and estrangements that flowed from intrigues among Jones and his followers was the case of the child John Victor Stoen, born to Grace Stoen. By the account of both Grace and Tim Stoen, their relationship as husband and wife did not develop conventionally after Jones married them in 1970. In true Temple style, they never went off alone; their house always had other people living in it. By 1971 Tim made it quite clear to his wife that she came second in his life, after Jones and Peoples Temple. By the early summer of 1971, shortly after she had become pregnant, even second place was in doubt to Grace. She tired of feeling that other people were laughing at her marriage. In a "confession" to Jim Jones, Tim Stoen recounted reminding Grace that "the s[ocialist] way was to share husbands and wife." Some seven months before Grace gave birth, Tim was having what he called "outside affairs." In egalitarian fashion, he assured his pastor, he had "told her I would not mind it if she had physical relationships with other men if she felt she was helping them."

The question that has plagued efforts to unravel the story of Peoples Temple since then is whether Grace Stoen herself had a sexual encounter during the times she spent alone with Jim Jones in the spring of 1971, and whether any such encounter might have led to her son's birth on January 25, 1972. Tim Stoen saw his wife through the delivery at Santa Rosa Memorial Hospital, and he is listed as the father on the birth certificate. But less than a week after the Sonoma County Public Health Service gave notification that corrections to the birth certificate should be made "within seven days," Tim Stoen signed a witnessed document. Eventually the statement came to signify everything in Peoples Temple that was alien to the outside world. "To whom it may concern," it read,

> I, Timothy Oliver Stoen, hereby acknowledge that in April, 1971, I entreated my beloved pastor, James W. Jones, to sire a child by my wife, Grace Lucy (Grech) Stoen, who had previously, at my insistence, reluctantly but graciously consented thereto. James W. Jones agreed to do so, reluctantly, after I explained that I very much wished to raise a child, but was unable, after extensive attempts, to sire one myself. My reason for requesting James W. Jones to do this is that I wanted my child to be fathered, if not by me, by the most compassionate, honest, and courageous human being the world contains.

> The child, John Victor Stoen, was born on January 25, 1972. I am privileged beyond words to have the responsibility for caring for him, and I undertake this task humbly with the steadfast hope that said child will become a devoted follower of Jesus Christ and be instrumental in bringing God's kingdom here on earth, as has been his wonderful natural father.

> I declare under penalty of perjury that the foregoing is true and correct.

Underneath Tim Stoen's signature was that of the witness, Jones's estranged wife Marcie, and the date, February 6, 1972.[15]

Documents do little to settle the matter. The birth certificate is not necessarily any more reliable than other papers that Temple members sometimes falsely completed to comply with external norms. By the same token, if Jones was the actual biological father, Stoen's document originally might have been a "cover" to protect Jones in case his act ever became public knowledge. Amazingly enough, such an approach has Christian precedent in Martin Luther's sixteenth century solution to male impotency in marriage: avoid divorce through a secret second sexual relation, preferably with a brother, that is agreed to by the husband. An alternative explanation is that Stoen's signed statement may have been, as he later claimed, false: an "act of trust," and, in case of defection, "a deterrent to my embarrassing the Peoples Temple cause."

Whatever the biological realities, there is no single, objective social truth about the matter. John Victor Stoen did not grow up the child of his legal parents, whoever sired him with Grace Stoen. In the years after John Stoen was born, Grace and Tim became estranged and separated. With Tim's signed statement under his arm, Jones pronounced himself the father. Among others, Carolyn Layton often cared for the boy, and it became widely held Temple lore that John Stoen was Jones's child. The boy referred to Lynetta Jones as "grandma," and she in turn found the boy to be "of sturdy build, deeply bronzed, black eyed, with raven hair."

If Tim Stoen's signing of the document concerning paternity was a statement of faith, the raising of John Stoen went far beyond symbolism. Grace Stoen was made to feel guilty for her possessive motherly attitude, and the child was alienated from her by others who often took care of him. In essence "John John" was groomed as the prodigy who carried the wisdom of Jim Jones.[16]

## Relationships

When it served Jim Jones's purposes, he could quote Bible. On family relations, he would summon up the words of Jesus: "For I am come to set a man at variance against his father, and the daughter against her mother, and the daughter-in-law against her mother-in-law. And a man's foes shall be they of his own household." As it was with Grace, her son, and Tim Stoen, so it was among other Temple members. Jones encouraged people to loosen their family ties and forge new relationships with others in the group. He also encouraged members to weaken ties with family members outside the Temple, and he taught his followers to maintain Temple secrecy toward all outsiders, including family.

The "group mind" was established most directly through the administrative oversight of living arrangements. The communal orientation implicit in foster and elderly-care homes offered a model of the new "family."

Some people received what amounted to "housing assignments," and in general, like more traditional Pentecostal groups, the Temple encouraged parents and children to look beyond biological relations to the entire community as a family. When Bonnie Theilmann came to Peoples Temple with her son, she eventually found him taken away for a night. When she complained, Jim chided her, "He's been spoiled, you know. All he knows is you. You must let him relate to others; this is our socialist way, and you're going to have to conform." Bonnie was distraught and tried to head off the separation, but after her son spent the night with a motherly Black woman, she had to admit that the boy seemed less than upset about the experience.

By the same token, Jones would castigate his followers if they put too much stake in their marriages, or for that matter, any strong dyadic relation. "There's nothing but hell in these marriages," he warned, "because capitalism breeds self-centeredness." To Jones, they signified death. He tried to undermine any relation that he construed as treasonous. In particular, the doubting partner who was considering leaving the church had to be isolated from one who was still faithful. Thus, Jones set Bonnie Thielmann up with a lover, once he sensed her marriage was on the skids. The gigolo for "the Cause" offered her a substitute avenue of affection, while he also informed Jones of her views. This sort of effort to monitor a potential threat to the Temple was the extreme of a more general Temple pattern that favored relationships formed on the basis of the overall collective interest.[17]

Historically, of course, families themselves have served as agencies of social control. More recently, that medium of control has been usurped in many cases by external agencies—therapists, social workers, and others who have developed "professional" knowledge about family problems. The collectively sanctioned relationships of Peoples Temple did not change the fact of control. Instead, they substituted an alternative *basis* of control, that sometimes served different ends.[18]

Take the case of the "intellectual" Bob Houston, his first wife Phyllis, and his lover and eventual wife, Joyce Shaw. Bob and Phyllis were having difficulties with their marriage in 1972, after Joyce Shaw had become attracted to Bob. The problem came under the scrutiny of catharsis sessions, but Joyce Shaw's relation to Houston continued to grow stronger. Eventually, using a typical ploy of his, Jones asked the two to marry so they could become missionaries together. The divorce of Phyllis and Bob was filed in September 1974. Bob Houston and Joyce Shaw married, and went on to head up one of the larger of the Temple's San Francisco communes.

Other couples and lovers found themselves under similar scrutiny of catharsis, and though the directions taken to resolve difficulties conformed to Temple collective interests, the situations of the individuals themselves typically seemed of paramount concern. With Temple counselors present, they "worked through" situations, and came to resolutions that could succeed only with the mutual consent of the parties involved. By counseling over long periods, the collective sought to validate shifts in interpersonal relationships in ways that strengthened the group.

In general, Jones offered counsel, and let people deal with the consequences of their own choices, so long as the "family" came first. As Jones told Grace Stoen after she defected, "The higher relationship of family is preferable to one to one exclusive relationships until at least one gets to the place of peace. When you get yourself situated in the place of peace, then people can have all kinds of relationships—they don't detriment."

Jones's ambivalent prescriptions often contradicted one another. On the one hand, he sometimes held that all relationships should involve partners of different races, apparently envisioning some future "melting pot" of the Temple as a racially blended endogamous sect and proto-ethnic group. On the other hand, he also sensed the difficulties of interracial marriage in the United States from his own experiences with a "rainbow family," and he declaimed the seeking of a sexual partner based on feelings of "racial guilt." Finally, Jones sometimes tried to hold down pregnancies, telling his followers, "Let's wait and do our screwing when we get our freedom."

Given such a tangle of concerns, people often acted on their own predispositions. Probably the vast majority of relationships were not particularly problematic. Many people somehow managed to sidestep the public arena altogether, so long as they got along and did not threaten the Temple as a solidary group. With Jones's blessing, Mike Touchette, the White son of Charlie and Joyce, married Debbie Ijames, the young Black daughter of associate pastor Archie Ijames. If Mike Touchette heard things from Jones that he did not believe in, such as sexual abstinence in marriage, he recalled, "I just didn't listen to it." Most other people who came into the Temple as couples sustained their relationships by demonstrating that they did not threaten the group. Still others, legally married or otherwise, engaged in intimate encounters and alliances as they saw fit.[19]

In short, though strong biological parenting was discouraged as contrary to socialism, and though Temple counselors occasionally tried to regulate social relationships both to settle people's difficulties and to protect the collectivity, not everyone felt obliged to respond to Jim Jones's every whimsical dictate. Aside from the heightened incidence of interracial pairings and the more public airing of troubles, the relations of the Temple's adult members represented the range present in the wider contemporary society.

### First Betrayal

Sexual and social relationships were not monitored to enforce any particular utopian relationship but to promote a fundamental value, loyalty.

After the 1972 Kinsolving exposé, Jones became increasingly concerned about it, for he saw the damage that could be done by those who told tales. His concerns became even more pronounced after the first major defection of members, one that underscored a typical problem of communal groups, that of socializing the second generation to collective goals. In 1973 eight young Temple "revolutionaries" gradually united as a cohesive subgroup. That fall they suddenly left for the Pacific Northwest without telling anyone, fearing, as one of them put it, that their parents "would just fight us and try to make us stay." Jim Cobb, Jr., a Black, and the son of parents who themselves had split apart over the Temple, had studied under a Temple "scholarship" at Santa Rosa College. He left his Temple wife Sharon, and took up with Micki Touchette, another Indiana migrant who had been brought along by parents. They banded together with Jim Cobb's sister, Terri, and her White husband, the politically attuned Wayne Pietla—proud owner of such anti-Vietnam war era classics as *The Anarchist Cookbook*. Four other young Temple friends came along as well.

The youths had found their Temple ideals taking a blow when they began to confront the realities of adult Temple life. They resented the discipline, particularly sexual intimidation based on the assertion that all people repress some homosexual tendencies. However, the eight students and college dropouts did not criticize the Temple on moral grounds; instead they issued a manifesto attacking racist leadership and the antitheoretical socialism grounded in the Temple's religious origins.

The boys had cultivated their radical beliefs and revolutionary fervor growing up in Peoples Temple, participating in paramilitary training sessions that came as an extension of the security force posturing. Jim Jones had called a halt to the drills after Jim Cobb and Wayne Pietla approached assistant pastor Mike Cartmell about buying guns. In youthful proto-Bolshevik rebellion against the more middle-of-the-road or "Menshevik" Temple, the eight styled themselves more "serious" about the revolutionary ideas that Jones promoted in a more guarded style.

When the eight revolutionaries departed, they left Jones and his staff in real fear that they might act on the basis of their heady talk, putting Peoples Temple in serious trouble. The fear was amplified by the defectors' next move. Filled with the exhilaration of their departure and outraged by Jones's dismissals of them as "Coca-Cola revolutionaries," Wayne Pietla and John Biddulph made their way back to Ukiah one night and staged a showdown with Jones in Wayne's mother's house, packing pistols that underscored their message: they wanted their liberty and they wanted to be taken seriously.

To Temple insiders, the intimidation of Jim Jones at Wanda Kice's house was parlayed into an act of near assassination. In the wake of the event, Deanna Mertle wrote, "They believe his death would break the back of our organization." "'God' cannot be killed," Deanna insisted. She proposed that Jim flee to "the field." The gang of eight could then be neutralized by countermoves; "arranging for the disappearance of John B. a few weeks after J leaves might be too risky, but it would certainly cause a great deal of paranoia among the other traitors," Deanna schemed in a memo to Jim. "'With J gone the group is becoming violent' might be a good fear for them to have."

Temple staff did all they could to defuse the defection by alternately intimidating those who left, creating distrust among them, and coaxing selected ones into friendly relations with the Temple. The Temple managed to get the young people to agree that they would stay out of Redwood Valley, and they maintained guarded contact. By 1974 Tim Stoen was on the phone to Wayne Pietla and John Biddulph, offering them a $430 loan if they would somehow compromise members like Sally Stapleton, who "tried to blackmail us." "We don't have any intention of using anything you can get from her," Stoen assured Wayne, "but it would be good to have something, because she's uncontrollable and she's badmouthed not only us but you people up there as well." For his part, Wayne softened his stance: "The agreement I've always wanted to have is: I'll do almost anything for the church. It's just that the hassle was getting too much for me there. . . . But if things come down to a confrontation, I'll be down there."

It was the young people's departure, more than any other event, that changed Temple life. "My love isn't working," Jones argued. "I guess I'll have to start getting hard on people; they seem to respond to it better." According to Bea Orsot, he became more "authoritarian" with people who caused difficulties.

When the eight young people first left, Jones ranted about how they were "going to try bombing" the Temple. For the Temple itself, Jones rejected the supposed terrorist road of the defectors. Instead he reactivated his deep-seated vision of collective migration as the key to liberation from the persecution, capitalist exploitation, and racism of U.S. society. In time Jones fused migration with "revolutionary suicide": together they signified collectively abandoning Babylon in favor of a promised land.[20]

### The Plan for Sanctuary and the Principle of Revolutionary Suicide

For Jim Jones, the ideas of socialist paradise and sanctuary came to the same thing. As late as 1973 he still held out the Redwood Valley enclave as the site of both, where Blacks could escape ghetto life and everyone could endure nuclear holocaust or "a politically inspired emergency," as Tim Stoen casually elaborated. But the Kinsolving exposé series showed the fragility of that particular plan, and the loss of eight key members of the second generation apparently underscored it. Less than a month after the eight Temple members played out their youthful defection as the "true" revolutionaries, the Temple leadersh:p mapped out a response to its perceived situation.

In a memo Tim Stoen sketched both "'immediate action' contingency plans" and "suggested long-range plans." Emphasizing the need to build up skills and offset declines in solidarity, the plan proposed that Peoples Temple develop the capacity to depart for Canada on twenty-four-hours' notice, or "to Canada, thence to Caribbean missionary post" on three weeks' notice, or "to Caribbean missionary post" on six months' notice. "Stay here until enemies lie against us," the plan suggested, but at the same time the group was to "consolidate all property holdings," "prepare powers-of-attorney, legal authorizations, bd. minutes, etc., passports, etc.," "transfer all substantial monies to Int'l banks," and "send team to Caribbean to find mission post." In the long term, Peoples Temple would "stay here in Calif. until first sounds of outright persecution from press or government." Stoen wrote that they should "be upfront about all plans—e.g., establishing mission and retreat," so that when the time came, they could: "1. Start moving all members to mission post—starting with most loyal—to Caribbean or other island—by plane in stages or by boat. 2. Some loyal PC [planning commission] members stay back to protect home front."

Apparently Temple leadership did not take long to investigate possible countries of colonization. In a planning commission meeting, it was concluded that buying an island would be too expensive, Mike Touchette recalled. "Jones remembered this name, 'British something,' he had visited before. Someone looked it up. Jim made it out to be paradise, representing what Peoples Temple represented." On October 8, 1973, the board of directors of Peoples Temple resolved to establish a mission in Guyana.

The following December, not a week after Jim Jones was arrested in Los Angeles on charges of lewd conduct, he led a Temple contingent to Guyana to explore the possibility of settlement, bringing Archie Ijames, Gene Chaiken, and Paula Adams to stay on in the capital of Guyana, Georgetown, to negotiate a long-term lease with the government. Long before the final lease was executed in February 1976, the Temple organized and financed an initial set of pioneers.

The chilling vision of revolutionary suicide emerged from the same quest for redemption of the faithful that informed the search for the promised land after the eight "revolutionaries" defected. To be sure, images of suicide and poisonings had crossed Jim Jones's path before. In Indianapolis in the 1960s, a follower once mentioned rumors that Jones had committed suicide while he was actually in Brazil. And Jones claimed in his *Examiner* interview after the Kinsolving exposé that bigots from the White Citizens

Council in Indianapolis had poisoned his dog with "a good shot of strychnine." More to the point, the preacher already had announced his martyrdom. In May of 1972, paraphrasing Jesus, he prophesied, "Where the eagles gather, there has to be carcass, and where the carcass is, the eagles will gather together, and I am the carcass, willing to die that you could live, willing that you could eat from me that you would know the divine principle that will save you and set you free."

One source for the possibility of collective suicide originated in willingness to commit violent acts for "the Cause." For example, a signed statement from Mert Mertle affirmed in June of 1973, "I have never wanted to hurt or see you hurt and have thought that I could have the courage to die for you if I had the opportunity to defend you." Jones reciprocated a willingness to defend his followers: "I'm gonna knock the shit out of anyone that tries to take my people," he bragged. The loyalty required to take the lives of others amounted to a willingness to give one's own life, and the willingness to give one's own life eventually was transmuted into a capacity to take one's own life.

It was the occasion of the young revolutionaries' defection that aligned the act of suicide for the first time with the full range of meanings that were to become solidified in Jones's mind: the "gang of eight" easily might bring shame on the Temple by terrorist acts; they might as easily expose the Temple for its catharsis and other practices. Either way, the Temple would become subject to "persecution" by those who would use any misstep against it. Collective suicide thus emerged as a proposed collective penance for the failure of the group to succeed with its members, and failure to endure within the wider society, at the same time that it affirmed the sanctity of its members' commitment and beliefs.

After November 1978 Jeannie Mills said that Jones had reacted to the 1973 departure of the eight "revolutionaries" in an emergency meeting the following day by toying with the idea that members of the planning commission take their own lives with poison to show that they were peace-loving apostolic socialists. Soon thereafter, he was announcing to his wider circle of followers that they might have to resettle in Canada or a jungle paradise if a "dictatorship" came to the United States. The Jews should have, he warned, "and they just held on. They thought, 'Oh, it can't happen to us. We're God's chosen people.' Well we niggers know we ain't God's chosen people." When Jones experienced microphone trouble that day, he counted himself the victim of evil forces. But talking of migration, he shouted, "Oh, we'll make it," quickly laughing in his characteristically weird way, "Ha, ha, ha. I've got all kinds of plans. . . ." "Shhh!" he interjected, as if to himself.

The occasion of the young people's defection apparently was the first time Jones put any idea of collective suicide to the p.c. as a concrete proposal, and when he encountered immediate opposition from longtime friend Jack Beam, he quickly dropped the matter. Nevertheless, the seed of the idea no longer lay dormant; it was planted in the fertile soil of a siege mentality that already stressed loyalty in the face of the taunts of Redwood Valley locals and the media exposés of Lester Kinsolving and Carolyn Pickering. It continued to grow.

At least as early as July 1974, a file was kept for Jones on "people who have never felt the need or had the desire to *commit suicide*." In 1975 or early 1976, probably on New Year's Day, 1976, the thematic interest found its way into an ambiguous social test of commitment. Jones talked as he often did about the pain of life, and after a catharsis session, he broke a Pentecostalist taboo by insisting that some thirty people in the planning commission meeting drink Temple vineyard wine that he claimed to have blessed. Carol Stahl had never touched alcohol to her lips in her life, but even she had some. Some p.c. members feared from the way Jones acted that the stuff was poisoned, but nothing happened.

It was this single event that became a "suicide rehearsal" in the lore of defectors, and the stories have it that Jim told his trusted followers assembled for the occasion that the wine contained poison. Jones is said to have had a few shills in the group fall out dead, and then watched others' reactions before reassuring them the event was only a test of their loyalty and an opportunity for them to reflect upon the depth of their commitments. At the time she "passed" the test, Neva Sly remembered she and others "all felt strongly dedicated, proud of ourselves."

Even if Jones did not claim he was poisoning everyone, at the least the event took place as a test of obedience, and at a time when Jones was talking more and more about the collective honor of Peoples Temple and the glory of mass suicide. "I love socialism," Jones said in a sermon. He was willing to die for it, an observer reported, "but if he did, he would take a thousand with him." Jones complained that the Temple could not get newspaper publicity for its beneficial activities. One day things would be different. "When we go into action, you won't be able to open up a newspaper without seeing Peoples Temple on every page," he predicted. Five months later Jones was telling his followers, "The last orgasm I'd like to have is death, if I could take you all with me."[21]

The postures about death and suicide aggregated at least three elements: loyalty, migration, and rebirth. Eventually Jones drew on the ideas of Huey Newton to forge these elements together as a solution to the historic Black American cultural search for redemption. Newton, the author of *Revolutionary Suicide* and *To Die for the People*, had worked with Bobby Seale to found the Black Panther party in Oakland, California, in 1966. In the long tradition of the Black messiahs, and most immediately in the footsteps of Malcolm X, the Black Panthers wrestled with oppression of Blacks and what to do about it. J. Edgar Hoover labeled the Panthers "the No. 1 threat to the internal security of the nation" as they set forth a platform in October 1966 that demanded not only equality but "A United Nations Plebiscite in the Black Colony to Determine the Will of Black People as to Their National Destiny."

For Newton, Blacks faced a choice only between two kinds of "suicide": (1) the slow reactionary suicide of continuing to submit to the life of unemployment, crime, and addiction in the ghetto, and (2) revolutionary suicide. In his view the latter term symbolized the death of the already dead ghetto soul. Out of the ashes of rejecting their oppression, Blacks would be reborn to a revolutionary struggle that could only end in victory or death. Either way, revolutionary suicide would unite Blacks in their historic racial destiny as the liberators.

Jim Jones read *Revolutionary Suicide*. Newton's basic ideas of rebirth to the socialist cause and life as struggle to the death fit well within Jones's own theology of revolution; he must have felt equally comfortable with the Panther's "race-class line" that argued Whites and Blacks should not fight each other when they could direct their revolutionary efforts against their common enemies, the state and the capitalist classes. The questions Jones puzzled over when he eventually met Newton living in exile in Cuba in 1977 revolved around the nature, and site, of the struggle. Jones lectured Newton on the futility of struggling against capitalism on its own turf. "He tried to tell me that I should think of finding some place outside the United States," Newton recalled after the Jonestown mass suicide. "He didn't think there was any hope for the United States or the Third World. He said he saw suicide as the only way out." Newton did not fully understand Jones. For the latter, revolutionary suicide was the emblem of rebirth not to the battle *in* Babylon but through migration to Black redemption *beyond* Babylon. Death in persecution and rebirth in the Promised Land were to form a cycle of incarnations.

Jones gave forth of an awesome vision, and what is even more disconcerting, he followed the advice in Stoen's 1973 memo: he did not try to hide that vision from his followers. Instead, Jones prided himself in driving away people who were "not here for truth." Those who stayed would stubbornly cling to "the truth" the more any outsider might try to dissuade them. Willingness to die for "the Cause" became the acid test of loyalty. Jones painted a terrifying picture of the U.S. apocalypse of race and class war, concentration camps, and genocide, and people who shared that vision came to accept the ultimate commitment to the death as a testament to their solidarity.[22]

Yet, for all the talk of brainwashing, Jones does not seem to have successfully coerced unchoosing followers to accept his vision of the world. True, he tried to tip the wavering toward allegiance, and he used the diverse ploys of "confinement" to do so. When insiders did leave, he sought to intimidate them into silence about the Temple's strange vision. Over and over again Jones emphasized that those who left should move at least five hundred miles away or face the possibility of death. The intimidations were shabby, however, and they lacked substance. As Steve Katsaris, father of young loyalist Maria, put it, "Lots of people thought they'd be dead in a week out of Peoples Temple; but they found themselves alive years later."

Those who thought about leaving experienced the deep conflicts that came with betrayal of a cause depicted as representing the aspirations of the oppressed and downtrodden. "When I became angry with Jim and decided to leave the Temple," said one survivor, "I would immediately have a vision of Christ on the cross, and everyone deserting him, so on I would trudge. . . . " For Stephan Jones, "I would have been doing more than just leaving a family. It would have been like I was a counterrevolutionary, in some sense."

Yet no matter how much Jones played upon deep-seated feelings of guilt that flowed from abandonment of family, friends, and the cause of racial and class justice, in California he would have been foolhardy to try to coerce people. Given the "open" boundaries between the Temple and the outer world, he could hardly hold people against their will, or that of legal guardians. The Temple never tried to retain under-age members without a legal basis. For example, it was quick to yield the Johnson girls to their Indianapolis parents when their mother intervened. In 1972 a prison parolee who could not swallow Temple life was allowed to leave after four hours of intensive counseling that reportedly left him "terrified." Even Bonnie Thielmann, who considered herself Jim's "daughter" harking all the way back to their life in Brazil, found when she defected that once she got past the threat that she would die as a result, there was little to stand in her way. "It was not as painful as I had feared. I had made my move, and that was it."

In the later California years, after key defectors began to make their moves beginning in 1975, a Temple member observed from time to time that one or another of her acquaintances no longer showed up for meetings. At least some people were literally driven out; others drifted away without incident. People who chose not to go to the Promised Land seem to have voted with their feet. The overwhelming evidence is that large numbers of Temple members left the group during the California years, and, as in other so-called cults where the voluntary defection rate runs as high as 78 percent, the departures represent prima facie evidence that people were not held against their will, if their will was to leave. On the other hand, there were many who stayed, and among them substantial numbers who were willing to give up property, live communally, and accept Jones's prophetic vision. Given the possibilities of defection in California, and the potential to choose that route, it must be concluded that for those who stayed, life was not filled with the day to day terror that some defectors felt.[23]

## Reprise

We are left to wonder how chafing and how unusual the Temple's "confinement" of members in California actually was. Clearly, sexual programming, humiliation, and general psychological intimidation occur in communal groups more widely, to say nothing about other kinds of "total institutions," including mental hospitals, prisons, armies, and even nunneries. All communal groups face the problem of confinement more acutely than do other total institutions, because they are in principle voluntary, while prisons, mental institutions, and armies claim legitimate authority for controlling participants. Among the range of commmunal groups, the most strenuous efforts at confinement can be found in what I have termed apocalyptic "other-worldly sects." In such groups, as in Peoples Temple, the world of society at large is seen as totally evil, and in its last days; at the end of history as we know it, the current dispensation is to be replaced by a community of the elect, those who live according to the revelation of God's will. The convert who embraces such a sect must, perforce, abandon any previous understanding of life's meaning and embrace the new worldview, which itself is capable of subsuming the individual's previous life, the actions of opponents to the sect, and the demands that are placed on the convert by the sect's leadership.

It is in other-worldly communal groups, where efforts are made to forge a wholly new version of reality, that the stakes in maintaining confinement are especially high. Among such groups, the Temple had even greater stakes, because of its "secret" alignment with political communism. Thus, Temple practices were something other than the sadistic perversions of an egomaniac.[24]

Like other-worldly groups more widely, Peoples Temple embraced the most effective techniques it could muster. The Temple exercised its confinement by bringing to bear an odd admixture of practices, many of them borrowed and blended from the legacies of Puritanism and contemporary popular psychology. To the extent that Temple techniques were those employed historically and within its contemporary mainstream culture, the confinement by the Temple reveals the soft underbelly of a wider practice of confinement, by families, counseling psychologists, education, religion, and a diffuse array of other social control mechanisms that maintain capitalist society through what sociologist Max Weber once called "masterless slavery." If the Temple did anything to modify the "professional" approach to confinement, it amalgamated the confinement under one roof and one hierarchy, bringing everyday life into the realm of a total institution not unlike other such realms set aside from everyday life.

By the opposite token, it was because Peoples Temple so starkly challenged the sensibilities and legitimacy of that other confinement—of family life and bourgeois individualism in everyday life—that its own resocializaton provoked such strong responses from certain of its members. Perhaps the saddest of these was Bob Houston, who took the Temple ethos so much to heart and allowed himself to become the object of so much castigation. Others, who denied the goals of resocialization, bridled at the means used to implement it, defected, and held after they left that they had been brainwashed.

These alternative responses to resocialization mark out the abyss that comes to exist more generally between other-worldly sects and the world of society at large left behind. Every sectarian action has its benevolent interpretation and legitimation within the sect and a converse interpretation from the outside. Thus, from inside the sect, confession, monitoring and catharsis sessions seem necessary to prevent deviant worldviews from taking hold within the group. From the outside, all this tends to be regarded as brainwashing. But insiders would follow Jim Jones's lead in turning the accusation outward, claiming that it is those in the society at large who are brainwashed.

These charges and countercharges amount to a conflict of interpretations, but one thing is clear. It is the relation of confinement to an apocalyptic goal of struggle with "the forces of evil" that distinguishes the Temple's confinement from other ones. This struggle, not the practices of confinement per se, explains the unique course of Temple history. Perhaps it is appropriate in the modern world that this struggle turned on the Temple's public image.

# 8

# Politics and Public Relations

In the modern era reality has become more and more blurred by the production of images that people experience through mass media. With the development of technologies capable of transmitting sounds, visual images, and in the broadest sense, data, instantaneously and over long distances, the relation between image and reality has shifted in a fundamental way. It is no longer so easy to argue that images distort reality, because images themselves are accorded the status of reality. Today, more and more, news organizations, advertising agencies, and public relations firms have clustered around the media to manufacture material for distribution. Life becomes submerged in the production and consumption of spectacle. Events often are no longer so important for their immediate audiences as they are for mass media audiences, and individuals and groups "in the news" (to say nothing of advertisers) understandably respond to the new circumstances by creating what Daniel Boorstin has called "pseudo-events," living dramas carefully tailored to foster favorable images in the media.[1]

Corporations interested in creating and managing their "identities" originated the "image" as a professional concern. Today politicians and preachers face the same problem. Thus, the old politics based on courting various interest groups becomes remapped onto the grid of mass media and associated polling techniques. Granted that historical forces still drive the political calculus. Granted, too, that politics always has been concerned with staging techniques, publicity ploys, and disinformation about one's opponents. What has changed is that today the political world forms a nearly seamless whole with the institutions of public relations and the media.

Men and women of the cloth, though often more retiring, also have been forced to recognize the power of public relations. As early as 1921 the *Handbook of Church Advertising* warned against making exaggerated advertising claims. But it also listed "things the church has for sale" and it frankly embraced "the power of suggestion." More recently a public relations textbook argued, "The apostles, after all, used the best means of communication they had at hand in their day, and church evangelists in the twentieth century can well do the same."

Today the triumph of the public relations culture in politics and religion is an accomplished fact. Even so, public relations has an "image problem." Phineas T. Barnum (1810–1891) spoke to it as concisely as anyone. Perhaps the true founding father of the field, Barnum pioneered in the art of embellishing the truth. He had, for example, a supposed mermaid depicted in fanciful oil paintings outside his American Museum in New York City, but those who paid to enter the gallery found only a monkey's embalmed head attached to the body of a preserved fish. Barnum reflected, "The public appeared to be satisfied, but . . . some persons always *will* take things literally, and make no allowance for poetic license, even in mermaids. . . ." To this day, unsympathetic portrayals of PR work focus on fraud, hype, distortion, and the sleight of hand involved in papering over disaster, malfeasance, and evil.[2]

Given that images so easily can be seen as distorted, the PR industry carefully promotes a code of ethics to guard against protests of fraud. Actual standards are not well defined, however, and they do not question the *ends* of clients, instead warning against using deceitful *means* to achieve a client's purposes. The prevailing definition would see covert manipulation only "when both the *source* and *intent* of the propaganda are disguised." The classic case came in the 1950s, when civic club circuit speakers from "front organizations" funded by the railroads through a PR firm sought to undermine the public acceptance of highway trucking, while never mentioning railroads and covering up their own connections to the railroad industry.

A stricter definition by Daniel Boorstin regards *all* public relations as manipulative "pseudo-events," and pervasive at that. For Boorstin,

> the fantastic growth of advertising and public relations together with everybody's increasing reliance on dealers in pseudo-events and images cannot—contrary to highbrow cliches—accurately be described as a growing superficiality. Rather these things express a world where the image, more interesting than its original, has itself become the original. The shadow has become the substance.[3]

Like most modern organizations, Peoples Temple sought to maintain certain public images. Like many organizations, its efforts at public relations and its political alliances fed into one another. Compared to other organizations, though, its techniques often seemed clumsy, its press releases, puerile or hysterical. Yet its successes themselves became a target of opponents, and the religious conflict between the Temple and opponents eventually took on the character of a public relations war. In exploring the public trajectory of Peoples Temple prior to this PR war, one question seems paramount: Did Peoples Temple simply mimic conventional public relations and political practices, albeit for culturally deviant purposes, or did it subordinate established institutions of politics and public relations through use of alien tactics? Where was Peoples Temple located in the modern hall of mirrors?

## Goals

Whether or not Jim Jones is judged a fraud who used religion for other purposes (in the sense discussed in chapter 3), he and his staff became crude but effective operators in the worlds of public relations and political influence. Peoples Temple engaged in many activities hidden from public view, and it fostered public images and alliances that sometimes obscured its inner workings. In large part Peoples Temple succeeded by using available institutionalized mechanisms for its own purposes. Jones understood the game, he played it, and he did not so badly, pulling in the accolades of people who sought reciprocal benefits in turn. When outsiders like then Vice President Walter Mondale eventually discovered more about the group with which they had trafficked, they would confront the embarrassment of having endorsed Peoples Temple on the basis of its media image, with no personal knowledge of its "good works."

Alone, Jones could not walk the stage of messianic history. Others would unwittingly help him by performing their conventionalized tasks. To foster its favorable public image, Peoples Temple depended on the netherworld of politics and PR that sustains the spectacle of U.S. popular culture. It is a reality knit together from a web of press releases, on-camera interviews, lobbyists, campaign directors, news directors, ad writers, and television personalities. The spectacle that Jones produced drew in the producers of the standardized spectacle by formatting Peoples Temple within their own framework.

Standards by which the goals and practices of Peoples Temple can be assessed are not easily established. When the PR industry is devoted to fostering public images rather than portraying "reality," the techniques used cannot easily be faulted. Similarly, obfuscation of the true purposes of political actions lies at the heart of a good deal of politics. Perhaps in time Peoples Temple itself will be taken as a standard by which to judge contemporary public culture. But an era that spawned Watergate, a Las Vegas emcee and Hollywood actor named Ronald Reagan in the White House, and the Iran-*contra* scandal offers little in the way of a converse benchmark, and it is best simply to examine the double reflection between politics and public relations in Peoples Temple and in the United States in general.

In the Temple itself, the character of U.S. public relations was hardly lost on believers steeped in a critical attitude toward established culture and the "power elite." Jones went out of his way to accuse the media of "brainwashing" and suppression of information that would make people aware of their true situations. He symbolically took on corporations, government and the media as his protagonists in a capitalist apocalypse, and thus went far beyond the contemporary cultural boundaries of the established churches. Therein lies the public relations anomaly of the Temple: though organizationally a church may well be a logical vehicle of an apocalyptic socialist movement, Peoples Temple often used the image of a more conventional church to hide its own clandestine nature. By turns the Temple offered a radical critique of the culture that sustains churches, and paradoxically drew on that culture to promote its own success. The contrast with other religious media practices is notable.

Conventional local churches, perhaps more than any other users of mass media, have sought to maintain some integrity by using the media simply to convey a reality that is sustained prior to public relations. On the other hand, the mass media ministries, like those of the Reverend Jerry Falwell and the Reverend Jimmie Swaggart, create diverse staged realities to achieve composite images that attain their coherence only in the broadcast. Their main activity involves producing the "pseudo-events" of their public image. They thus need not fear "exposure" of any reality behind the image save the reality behind all images, that is, the "backstage" whereby the images are produced.

Peoples Temple was established on different terrain than either conventional or mass media religion, and its public relations and political goals derive from this fact. Like conventional churches, the Temple possessed substance rather than image alone. But the content—an anticapitalist interracial communalism that involved practices of catharsis and collectively sanctioned physical discipline—was hardly an image they wanted to advertise publicly. On the other hand, like religions more conversant with the mass media, Peoples Temple depended upon public relations to attract followers, grow, and survive financially and politically. But the Temple differed in a basic way from media ministries caught up in the U.S. pyramiding promotional style: for all Jones's use of dramaturgical devices, the Temple was not just produced for public consumption, sustaining itself off that consumption. Instead, the core of Temple reality lay beyond public scrutiny, in an enclave expressly created to withstand its spotlight.

The dual alignment of Peoples Temple—having both a secret inner reality and a promotional need for public relations—locates it in a realm different from that of either mainline or mass media religions, a realm populated by a variety of "deviant" religions with unusual beliefs and practices. Sociologist Charles Selengut has pointed out that such "cognitive minority" religions, from Orthodox Jews to the Unification Church of Reverend Sun Myung Moon, promote public images that disguise inner activity so as to avoid the social stigmatization that occurs when they are exposed to the predominant worldview of "modernity." One "Moonie" explained their deception in the following terms: "Look, the world is so anchored in sin that you cannot tell people that the Messiah is on earth. You cannot, as Niebuhr explained, follow an absolute ethic; what you need to do is to use other than perfectly ethical means to bring people to a situation where they can recognize the truth."

In the conflict between deviant religions and modernity, the capacity to set the tone of reality is overwhelmingly on the side of modernity. The countercultural religion faces an uphill battle in substituting its reality for prevailing ones, even among its own members. To accept the prevailing cultural standards by which reality is "constructed" would doom the effort from the start, because the plausibility of a worldview and the cultural procedures that sustain it form a neat, cohesive circle. For the cognitive minority religion, the problem becomes one of maintaining plausibility without publicly confronting the overwhelming reality made plausible by the institutions of mass culture. The solution, for the cognitive minority, is to construct an ethic of conduct that distinguishes between acts in and toward the "fallen" world and those in the world of believers.[4]

Thus came Jim Jones's first and greatest deception: using the cover of a church to preach that religion was "the opiate of the people." In the United States, serious discussion of socialism effectively has been excluded from mainstream media, and the subject has become virtually taboo for the population at large. One of Jones's converts, Tim Carter, explained, "Telling people about socialism in America, you'd get 20 people. But as a preacher you could get a large audience." In semipublic services in the early 1970s, as a sort of bait to the interested, Jones would allude to deeper truths than those he was presenting, much as gnostics and mystics had done before him. By the mid-1970s, he became more and more explicit about his socialist vision. Like early twentieth-century Black socialist preachers, he used religion as the most straightforward way to inspire followers: both the Blacks he weaned from "jackleg" Christianity, and Whites who were more interested in the "inner light" and the practice of the social gospel.

The deception of using religion to promote socialism dissipated for followers as they came to know their leader more intimately, but the persistence of the church front sustained a public relations facade that legitimated the group within established society and attracted support of politicians and other notables, many of whom might otherwise have steered clear of the socialist messiah. The superficial purposes of the public relations facade differ little from the purposes of all public relations: (1) to protect controversial secrets of an organization, in the Temple, especially the practices of catharsis and group discipline, and the staging techniques of prophecy and faith healing; (2) to shield an organization from adverse publicity that would undermine its claims to legitimacy and destroy its cash flow; and (3) in general, to advance its public reputation and standing.

Jim Jones's concern with exposure went much deeper than most such image maintenance. The man who fancied himself a Stalinist had come of age in the heat of McCarthy anticommunist purges that permeated practically every avenue and level of U.S. life. He believed that what he was doing would provoke public outrage if it ever came to light, and in this he was probably correct. As a writer in the *New Republic* put it, given what Jones was up to, he could not really be labeled as paranoid, for there would have been something seriously amiss if he had *not* been hounded by enemies. Jones was presiding over an emerging apocalyptic socialist movement that depicted the United States as the contemporary Babylon. On the basis of his vision, he had brought converts into a collective life that sealed Peoples Temple as their family and their fate; the stakes were not just personal. Thus, Jones once pinpointed his deepest fear: "my exposure as a communist would affect the lives and well-being of my most precious family and dearest associates, and, in fact, all of my church that have become an extended family."[5]

Even if Jones's familial claims were gratuitous, they point to the precarious position of people who pulled themselves up by the bootstraps to become a highly visible community of fate subject to the vicissitudes of PR. Sometimes Peoples Temple operated as effectively as other groups in the sophisticated world of press releases and fund-raising dinners. All the same, its occasional crypto-Stalinist style of dismissing detractors as "Trotskyites" must have raised the eyebrows of more than one managing editor. Somehow, whether it played the game of PR and alliance building well or poorly, Peoples Temple played on the basis of an underlying program that would make no sense if it ever surfaced in the world of pseudo-events. Given the Temple's deeper commitments, it is no wonder that others sometimes could not "read" its image.

### The Facade

If we are to believe Jim Jones, his wife, and his early associates, although Jones used religion as a vehicle, his identification with a crude version of political communism came at the onset of his career, in the early 1950s. All the same, it was not until the late 1960s that he was willing to reveal to the California migrants that "apostolic socialism" was the collective goal. In pronouncements to the broad Temple membership, he continued to use the "apostolic" characterization until the mid-1970s. Similarly, there was hardly what could be called a political origin of the term *promised land*, lifted from Father Divine's ministry, and reinforced by Martin Luther King's famous "I have been to the mountain top" speech. Jones used the term to characterize the agricultural mission in Guyana even after he arrived there in mid-1977. Thus, though Jones often denounced conventional religion, he continued to draw on religious images in the company of his followers until the end.

On another level Jones cloaked the Temple in the public imagery of conventional religion to protect it from unwanted publicity. Over the years, however, the public images and alliances of Peoples Temple changed, and plotting their benchmarks helps establish the sources and purposes of the Temple's facade, as well as its inner character.

During the initial phase of Jones's Indianapolis ministry, it seems he kept whatever latent purposes he had to himself, letting healing, the social gospel, and interracial worship serve as surrogates. Jones's success in the early years was predicated on his seemingly native PR talents. He consistently drew matters of ethical principle (such as interracial worship) to a head in concretely dramatized events that established the righteousness of his own position, often in contrast to pious but apparently hypocritical Christians. For outsiders, Jones's ministry itself testified of a rare capacity to combine ministering to dispossessed populations with a progressive approach to the social gospel. His capacity for taking symbolically infused concrete action attracted some of his earliest followers, the interest of the Disciples of Christ, and civic recognition. Public relations amounted to little more than dramatizing the reality of tangible accomplishments to a wider audience, and pursuing the opportunities that arose from the ascending spiral of publicity.

Jones did not content himself with letting good works stand for themselves. Just as he embellished sermons with a liturgical discourse that cast apparently factual reality into a highly charged theatrical form, just as he propped up native faith-healing abilities with fakery and testimonials, he developed a similar capacity to resurrect stories with some factual basis, raising them to the level of myth among his followers and in the mass media. Whether they were true or not, Jones's tales about walking out of a Bloomington, Indiana, barbershop because of racist practices became legend. Whether or not Jones's father had been a member of the Ku Klux Klan, the preacher would cite the "fact" as a shorthand way of portraying racist attitudes in his hometown of Lynn, Indiana. Whatever harassment Jones and his family experienced during his stint on the Indianapolis Human Rights Commission (and there is little doubt such harassment occurred), Jones fed the stories to the press in a way that built up his image as a crusader.

In the end, the style of discourse that Jones used to present such tales probably created difficulties for him with the press: his liturgical dramatizations did not have the ring of "modern" truth for reporters, and his stories were sometimes dismissed out of hand. Thus, the old saw that Negroes "have to be out of town by sundown" probably held sway in the culture of thousands of small towns from the Great Depression at least through mid-century. Nevertheless, Jones's apocryphal accounts of racism in Lynn, Indiana, were discounted by California reporters Reiterman and Jacobs: "There were no Blacks to speak of, few Catholics—and no reason for the Knights of the Ku Klux Klan to raise their sinister white-sheeted ranks there." Still, a Florida journalism professor born in Lynn also remembered the "sundown" warning to Blacks. This example suggests that at least to some extent, Jones's eventual problems with the media derived from the incongruity between his evangelical promotional style and the interactional codes of the modern world of mass media.[6]

If certain elements of Jones's style lacked credibility with reporters, other motifs represented out-and-out red herrings, crudely designed to throw the curious off his trail. Early on Jones hit upon a strategy of what I will call "counterposturing"—a way of displaying a dialectic of polar opposites, typically communism and capitalism. In a cloud of obfuscation he could use convoluted support of one pole to evidence its limitations, or a back-handed critique to establish his position publicly, even while he hinted at a different stance. Jones went beyond what his one-time associate pastor Mike Cartmell called "the big lie" to the emphatic posturing of ambiguity.

The approach surfaced in Jones's efforts to portray himself and his organization as anticommunist. In the earliest documented sermon in which he advocated a communalist direction, he did so under the auspices of fighting godless communism. Similarly, as he traveled through British Guiana in 1961, the Guiana *Graphic* reported that Jones "accused the Church of being greatly responsible for the spread of Communism." The same ploy would pop up over and over again during the 1970s, as when Peoples Temple promoted a Jones sermon topic, "Apostolic socialism is the only hope against communism."

There were much more bizarre twists. In 1971 the Ukiah *Daily Journal* indicated that Peoples Temple had written both the USSR and President Nixon to propose that Black U.S. communist Angela Davis (later a Temple ally) be exchanged "for the Russians being persecuted." The Temple added an even more convoluted angle to the playing off of the communist/capitalist opposition during the 1974 saga of the would-be revolutionary cell called the Symbionese Liberation Army (SLA). After the SLA kidnapped heiress Patricia Hearst in Berkeley, there was nationwide news coverage of an offer by Jim Jones, Tim Stoen, Mike Prokes, Carolyn Layton, and Karen Layton to be "hostages for the safe conduct out of this country for SLA members involved," arguing, according to Stoen, that the plan might help safeguard Hearst's life. If the offer had been taken up, the Temple would have had its cake and eaten it too, saving Hearst and facilitating sanctuary for the SLA self-styled revolutionaries whom Jones did not entirely repudiate in Temple sermons. As it was, the Temple simply basked in the glow of an irrelevant humanitarian gesture.

The SLA incident demonstrates an uncanny ability to mingle elements of dialectical opposites. It thus offers a distant clue to the mental struggles of Jim Jones. Sometimes when depicting the threats of facism and anticommunism, recounting horrors of concentration camps in Germany or the grim purges that took place after the CIA-backed coup against the elected communist Allende in Chile in 1973, Jones seemed almost to warn about himself. Even as he steeled his followers against the totalitarian forces of the Right, Jones brought them into a counterpart regime on the Left, by promoting solidarity against the forces that opposed him. Similar contortions were used in a parallel way in public. Peoples Temple obscured its developmental course by registering opposition to the very ideology it espoused, communism, and advocating the very rights it would suppress more and more in the face of external opposition: freedom of speech and civil liberties. Jones's public relations efforts thus mapped the forces of good and evil onto the cultural grids of anticommunism, capitalism, fascism, and "apostolic" socialism in convoluted and contradictory ways.[7]

During the time the Indiana migrants established themselves in Redwood Valley, the latent structure of Jones's machinations remained buried in routine public relations efforts of the sort found in more conventional churches. It was no easy task in the mid-1960s for the Hoosiers to gain acceptance in largely White Mendocino County, but the Temple soon found a friend in Kathie Hunter, a reporter and wife of Ukiah *Daily Journal* editor George Hunter. She introduced the newcomers to the community by announcing in the paper that "far from being a closed, tightly-knit group living a communal existence, members of the church live their own lives as part of the community as a whole. . . ." Jones built on this public image by cultivating his emergence as a civic leader, just as he had with White liberals in Indianapolis. By 1967, only two years after arriving in California, he was appointed to a Mendocino County grand jury. In the late 1960s he served with the Juvenile Justice Commission, the Mendocino County Legal Aid Foundation, and the Citizens' School Commission.

During the same period, the Temple courted law enforcement officials by writing letters to newspaper editors commending the Highway Patrol for its good works, donating money that Mendocino County Sheriff Bartolomie used for a piped-in music system for jail prisoners, and inviting the Ukiah police chief to speak at the Temple on the drug problem. By September of 1970 the San Francisco *Chronicle* reported that Peoples Temple was starting a fund for the family of a slain Berkeley policeman, a publicity move that was to be repeated over the years.[8]

In one of the letters to editors supporting law enforcement, published June 5, 1969, came first public mention of a slogan that was to become a trademark of the Temple and its pastor. Like others in need of an image, Peoples Temple staff sought that perfect phrase to solidify public group identity. They seem to have followed prevailing advertising wisdom.

In the heyday of Madison Avenue self-confidence, advertising man Mack Hanan once observed that although an image should not be "wishy-washy, vague, or unplanned," it nevertheless must be "open-ended." A "neutral corporate image" is superior to a "positive corporate image," he held, because it serves as "an invitation to management's public for a suspension of their critical judgement."

The Temple's "open-ended" image derived from its budding social work orientation. The 1969 letter to an editor captured the Temple with the catchy phrase, "the highest worship to God is service to our fellow man." In later years God was dropped, and with greater sensitivity to sexism and agism, the slogan was slightly retooled: "The highest form of worship is service to our fellow man, woman, and child." The "human services ministry," sometimes expanded to the "interracial, interfaith human services ministry," drew on the formula found in Matthew 25: 35, to feed the hungry, clothe the naked, take in strangers, and minister to those in prison.

To foster good community relations in the early California years, Peoples Temple already was engaging in a highly organized rendition of the old-fashioned Christian charity denoted in the motto. As Rick Cordell recalled,

> we had a committee of several people, dozens of people, in fact, to take cakes, send cards and letters, do special humanitarian things to help people in the community. Like for instance . . . every time there was a baby born, there would be gifts, cards and cakes sent to those who had the newborn child; every time there was a death, there would be cards and letters sent in condolence, and if there was a family left, we would move in to help the family.

When the charity went to community leaders and political contacts, it amounted to a form of petty bribery akin to the Christmas gifts that some corporations give out to clients. Thus, after Peoples Temple had gone to California, the people in the Indianapolis Disciples of Christ office would find themselves at Christmastime eating "marvelous fudge" that Jones had some of his followers make. Eventually, as the Temple became more financially affluent, the cakes and pies turned into dollars donated to the favorite causes of people the Temple wished to subordinate. A case in point involved the $200 Tim Stoen sent in 1973 to Steven Katsaris, director of Ukiah's Trinity School for Children. In reply, Katsaris wrote, "Your contribution moved me deeply. Tell Jim that I opened your letter minutes after a meeting with our head teacher, who asked me if I could find someone to donate enough money to purchase . . . encyclopedias for our library. The cost, he said, would be $200. God works in strange ways. . . ." Indeed.

Media publicity compounded the efforts at goodwill. The local newspaper reprinted the periodic news releases typical of many churches. There, Peoples Temple announced various charitable activities and reported on Temple events, weddings, guest speakers, and awards received by the church choir. One theme always good for a "puff" piece was Jim Jones's collection of pets saved from an uncertain fate at the pound.

For all the upbeat press, however, the Temple was hardly without public controversy. Partly it was a result of the Temple's public stances. In 1966, on Good Friday, Temple members staged Ukiah's first demonstration against the Vietnam war. Other early public reports alluded to Jones's concern with racism and nuclear war, and to the long-standing Temple position against drugs and narcotics.

Along with controversial public stands, there must have been town gossip and rumors as well. From the beginning, the Temple reacted strongly when it was cast in a negative light. On May 10, 1968, a group of self-proclaimed "private citizens" (who nevertheless professed church membership), took out a large advertisement in the Ukiah *Daily Journal* to offer a detailed rebuttal to "rumors" they deemed false. Jones, they held, favored increasing taxes for schools, but without overburdening the average citizen; Jones opposed drug use, but did not think marijuana the greatest evil, and proposed treatment rather than punishment. And despite his opposition to the "senseless war" in Vietnam, the preacher did not believe in demonstrations because he felt that they could be used by people "to avoid making a commitment about Jesus Christ's teachings on peace." Even this early the Temple had a tendency to react to its reputation on the grapevine in ways that may have deepened controversy about it.

Still, Jones attracted allies. On July 8, 1968, a second advertisement defended Peoples Temple in the local paper. Signed only by nonmembers, among them Tim Stoen, this one deplored "unseemly words and actions of a small segment of this community." Kathie Hunter also affirmed her staunch friendship by becoming a one-woman "truth squad." In a longish article she revealed that the group and its pastor had suffered "terror in the night." "Are they a secret cell of Communists sent here to subvert good old fashioned American beliefs with their doctrine of 'love thy neighbor'?" she asked rhetorically. With the naive cooperation of Kathie Hunter, the Temple planted a statement artfully raising the issue of communism, while presenting itself as communism's antithesis.[9]

Temple public relations and cultivation of civic allies during the early years remained at a sophomoric level, but the early efforts set the basic boundaries of practices that were to persist throughout the group's history. Exaggerations, embellishments, apocryphal stories, counterposturing, controversial public stands, and planted disinformation became stocks-in-trade. Efforts to cultivate friends through charity flowered into what amounted to petty bribes.

### Public Relations and Civic Alliances in the Expansionary Phase

Like other Temple operations, public relations changed with the influx of California converts in the late 1960s. It is not always possible to identify the direct connections between individuals and particular shifts in style. Still, taken as a whole, the arrival of new blood in the persons of upper-middle-class Whites like Carolyn Moore Layton, Tim Stoen, the Mertles, the Tropps, and television newsman Mike Prokes marked a shift in the entire scale of Temple PR efforts in the media, the community, and the Disciples of Christ.

When the Temple expanded its operations from Redwood Valley down to the Bay area and Los Angeles in the early 1970s, its staff concentrated on advertising the bus caravans to attract new converts, and offering those who came to the Temple physical tokens of group belonging, from trinkets and anointed pictures to religious tract materials. In their wake came the radio programs, the leaflets announcing special services, the mailers, the newsletters, the letters to editors, and the cultivation of external allies.

Emblematic of the Peoples Temple approach was its managed letter-writing enterprise. Over the years members often dashed off letters supporting one cause or another, sometimes crudely promoting the Temple ministry at the same time. Jones's mother, Lynetta, could find time to send off a long handwritten message to a prisoner who had written the *Examiner* in search of pen pals. Tim Stoen would draft a letter to Richard Nixon in the midst of the Watergate scandal. Describing Temple members as "heart-sick and outraged" at the abuse the president was receiving, Stoen pleaded with him, "Never resign, never."

Other letter writing was organized more along what is known in the PR business as "campaign mail." One early large-scale effort, following a televised appeal of the National Safety Council for mail on drunk driving, came up with four hundred letters. Another occurred much later, when Tim Stoen resigned his Mendocino County assistant district attorney post in 1976 to prosecute vote fraud for the San Francisco district attorney. Temple letter writers received a Xerox copy of a newspaper article about his departure, with typed instructions:

> Write the following letters for final draft not later than Saturday at bus time. Clear your original draft with the Letters Office. . . . Some write as members who know him. . . . Some write as non-members who know him. *Don't* say you are not a member, just don't say you are. . . . When writing the *Journal*, . . . talk about the church (especially the local church) in a favorable light. . . . Thank you.

Such Temple public relations practices were not entirely without precedent, as Temple staff well understood. In their files could be found a 1956 magazine account of how a New York *Times* columnist had criticized the television industry for showing preacher Oral Roberts's healing services; the columnist received over 1,450 letters as a result of a protest "organized by Mr. Roberts, who urged his backers to write." The Temple took the practice a step further, to the borderlands of PR ethics about concealing people's true identities and intentions.

Other Temple efforts followed a similar trajectory, moving exponentially from humble beginnings in typically conventional practices to dizzying heights of mind-boggling aggrandizement. Most early Temple PR materials were crudely produced, even by church standards of the day. Materials were often mimeographed, like the 1971 newsletters. In these publications the Temple's distinctive style of grandiose logorrhea began to surface. The reader was subjected to an "urgent request" to support a "vast human service ministry." An explicit warning indicated that failure to write back would mean no longer receiving the "LIFE-SAVING PROTECTION" of the newsletter. "Astounding healings" were described. Publications began to affirm the legitimacy of Jim Jones's ministry by reeling off litanies of his accomplishments. "We have rehabilitated over sixty young people from a meaningless life of drug use to the Christian life of service to mankind," they would trumpet. What would become a (longer and longer) stock phrase listed "an aged home, two college dormitories in Santa Rosa, a fellowship hall and manse . . . in which we minister to the needs of hundreds." Somehow, beneath the hype, Temple editors managed to serve up features like an analysis proclaiming the absurdity of the virgin birth, and a "message from the prophet" decrying corporate fascists as the real radicals.

By 1972 Temple staff experimented with publishing *The Living Word: an Apostolic Monthly* to emphasize the healing side of the ministry. Jam-packed photographs and testimonials documented the stories of people like young Chris Lewis ("Free from heroin! Free at last!") and twelve-year-old Mark Cordell, who revealed how Jim had saved him after he fell off a forty-foot cliff. Captions carefully and discreetly explained Jones's strange appearance, claiming, "the sunglasses Pastor Jones wears during meetings are not special in any way. He uses them to minimize distraction during meditation." Jones must have done a great deal of meditation, in a host of situations, for he always seemed to be wearing them. Another caption would inform, as did signs in the sanctuary, that "Pastor Jones wears a used choir robe to cover his modest clothing. . . . His robe is not symbolic of any special glory or honor."[10]

In publicity materials for members and potential converts, the Temple drew on the "apostolic Christian socialist" image as a convenient frame to align fundamentalists and liberal Christians together under the same rubric. In a similar way for the community at large, Jones elaborated a populist and paranoid antigovernment stand that found favor with arch conservatives as well as radicals. The Temple cultivated friends from all parts of the political spectrum, and found that its friends' influence helped shield the group from scrutiny while elevating its prestige by association.

In Mendocino County this involved currying favor with the Republicans, not a difficult task, given Tim Stoen's position as assistant district attorney, and his Rotary Club and Republican party activities. Marge Boynton, chairman of the Mendocino County Republican Central Committee, courted Jim Jones in a 1970 letter. Mentioning her interest in talking personally with Jones, she offered the "hope that you will be able to support a majority of our candidates this year, because I firmly believe our party philosophy is very closely akin to yours." Later, schoolteacher and Temple member Jean Brown ended up serving on the county's Republican Central Committee.

Jones has been described as opportunistic for seeking out conservative ties among the Mendocino County community elite. He formed alliances with successful politicians of whatever persuasion. He even became friends with the local head of the John Birch Society, who lived on a neighboring ranch. Temple loyalist Sandy Bradshaw would grant that "we courted people we didn't agree with in order to survive. We were trying to keep our heads above water." Nevertheless, she dismissed opportunists as people, unlike Jones, who "take advantage of others for their own gain, without being committed to any single principle." The strategy of survival brought the Temple into alliances with people of all political stripes, but given that Jones played his cards so close, both the Mendocino conservatives and

Jones's eventual liberal allies were to remain ignorant of his deeper program.[11]

The same was true of the other major front on which Peoples Temple
strived to maintain good relations, the Protestant denomination that sustained its legitimacy. Temple publicity often cited their pastor as "an officially ordained minister of the 1.4 million member Christian Church
(Disciples of Christ) denomination." Eventually the nebulous association
would become truly far-fetched, with Temple publicity listing people like
President Lyndon Johnson and FBI Director Clarence Kelly as members of
their denomination.

As they would with other notables, Peoples Temple staff found ways to
set up eminent Disciples professionals to defend the Temple. Without identifying himself as a member, someone might write a minister, enclosing
news releases about the Temple. If the minister responded with trusting
Christian charity, the reply might go to the attention of Tim Stoen with the
notation, "Jim said this guy is a conservative and might be good to quote."

Peoples Temple had continued its affiliation with the Disciples of Christ
after moving to California, formally affiliating with the Northern California-Nevada regional conference. It also maintained good relations with
Jones's old Indianapolis Disciples friend Barton Hunter. In 1970 the congregation participated in voting for the head of the Disciples region, and
the candidate it supported, Karl Irvin, won.

By 1971 the Temple's influence within the denomination was rising
rapidly. Star Temple notable Tim Stoen was elected to serve on the govern-
ing board of trustees of the regional conference. With participation at key
regional events, growing donations reflecting a growing membership, choir
exchanges, and friends cultivated among the denomination's leadership,
Peoples Temple established itself as a force to be reckoned with in denominational affairs. By 1973 the Los Angeles branch of the Temple affiliated with the Southern California regional Disciples conference, giving the
Temple an alternate channel of denominational leverage.

In fact, the Southern California affiliation came about in the aftermath
of the September 1972 Kinsolving exposé in the San Francisco *Examiner*.
How useful the Disciples of Christ could be to Peoples Temple was demonstrated by the way it responded to Kinsolving's series. In the face of questions posed to the national Disciples office after Kinsolving published his
stories, Disciples President Dale Fiers consulted with the regional office. At
the time Peoples Temple was seeking Southern California affiliation for its
Los Angeles branch, and Northern California-Nevada Regional President
Karl Irvin was passing on a $1,000 Temple donation to the Southern Cal-
ifornia region, calling the Temple "a very hard working and committed
group of people." Disciples President Fiers was hardly put off by Jones's

claims to the gift of healing, for he believed in healing by faith himself. After Jones categorically denied claiming to be the reincarnation of Jesus Christ, Fiers issued a form letter dated February 8, 1973. He supported what seemed to be an active and viable congregation, calling the stories "inaccurate, prejudicial and misleading."

Peoples Temple rewarded the denomination with generosity that exceeded even its previous rather high rate of tithing; acting in his capacity as Temple board chairman, Tim Stoen sent off $3,000 more in checks to Irvin to underwrite the "pressing needs" of the denomination. In July of 1973 the Los Angeles Temple was accepted into the Southern California Disciples region. As it would on other occasions, Peoples Temple had deflected criticism by using political and financial support to cultivate alliances that would bring prominent people to its defense.

Some Disciples executives sensed problems with the Temple, but they were no more effective than other outsiders in breaking the boundaries of group secrecy. After a 1974 visit to Redwood Valley, Disciples general counsel Wade Rubick wrote a carefully crafted report. He admitted that the Temple "does not follow in the traditional Disciple mold . . . and in many respects proved to be an enigma to me." In the end Rubick argued that the Temple's very differences were what made its unusual outreach ministry effective. As for Jones, he was "very humble, unpretentious, self-sacrificing, completely dedicated and committed to the fulfillment of the Gospel as he understands it." Masters of monitoring themselves, Jones and his staff effectively ducked attempts at monitoring by others. The Temple was emerging as a power beholden to no higher worldly power. It acted on an equal footing with its denomination, with newspapers, with political parties, and even with governments.[12]

### The Golden Age of Temple Public Relations

The Kinsolving exposé spurred the Temple to improve its image by launching intensified public relations efforts. Independent of its occasional efforts at reasoned discourse, the Temple went the conventional PR route of creating pseudoevents to serve as counterpoint to the bad publicity. The sophistication of these efforts picked up dramatically when KXTV-TV Stockton news bureau chief Mike Prokes joined forces with the Temple after first encountering the group while starting out to follow up on Kinsolving's stories.

While they were busy firming up Disciples denominational support after the *Examiner* exposé, Temple staff took time to organize a stunt that was bound to get some positive press: they donated $4,400 to twelve news media organizations "in the defense of a free press." By capitalizing on a topic of current media concern, Peoples Temple was able to "put its own spin" on stories about itself. Trustee Jim Pugh would be quoted on his concern about "recent jailings of news reporters." Papers carried Tim Stoen's remarks calling for "the church to become the conscience for its social order [so that] government will not have to." The good works of Peoples Temple—its drug rehabilitation program, care homes, the whole list—could be portrayed as the hidden story, obscured by Kinsolving's infamous slurs. Attacked in the press, Peoples Temple defended the rights of a free press, at the same time weaning news organizations away from a negative approach to its doings.

The efforts began to snowball. A congressman inserted remarks in the *Congressional Record* praising Peoples Temple for its stand on freedom of the press. The Temple put out one issue of a newspaper, *The Temple Reporter*, and reprinted the *Congressional Record* remarks in it on page 1. Then Temple staff started collecting reminiscences of Jim Jones's life ("When Jim was pulling weeds, he took them and transplanted them. . . .") in order to write a magazine article in the "style of *New Yorker* (voice of writer very much present; lots of interview-type quotes)." Tim Stoen suggested in his proposal for contingency plans that Peoples Temple review tapes and writings and "select portions for retention." In the long run, he projected putting out two books with "J's message—broke down into various parts; a) 1st book—to Bible-oriented people; b) 2nd book—to human-itarian-oriented people." By such moves, Jones's long-standing personal knack for appealing to different audiences became grafted onto self-conscious PR tactics.

Stoen also wanted to see "good pictures of every facility and every activity." Temple photographers clicked away. Hundreds of visuals were produced, filed under categories like "Jim and animals," "Jim and children," "Jim and important people," "sensitive pictures—plays and skits," "P.L. [Promised Land, i.e. the agricultural project]—good for outsiders," and "Additional P.L. (for family viewing)." Sometimes decked out in a country-and-western leisure suit, other times in suits or casual clothes, the prophet always seemed a bit stiff in the posed pictures, as though he felt self-conscious summoning up the facial gestures to portray benevolence, charity, sincerity, and other Christian virtues. In candid shots taken at services or in public publicity events, he looked somewhat more at ease.

Out of the hundreds of shots, publications staff picked out the best, and they employed the same darkroom techniques of touching up photographs as their media nemesis the San Francisco *Examiner* uses to highlight desired features and obscure irrelevant background details. Temple publications came alive with pictures of rest homes, church buildings, communion feasts, happy Temple children, and most of all, Jones anointing ecstatic crowds with his spirit.

Professional PR efforts surfaced in other ways as well. Temple submissions to newspapers were issued under an official looking "news release" letterhead of a "front organization," California Sun-times. And the Temple began to more self-consciously produce its activities in ways that would result in favorable coverage. On a bus trip to Washington, D.C., Temple tourists were detailed to an hour of cleaning up the Capitol grounds (presumably with adequate PR advance work) that netted a laudatory editorial in the Washington *Post*. In conservative Indiana, Jones splashed into the newspaper praising "the Jeffersonian ideal that the government governs best which governs least." For San Francisco, the Temple would score a KGO-TV special feature on its drug rehabilitation program. To the anti-establishment Berkeley *Barb* the Temple could emphasize its human service ministry and donations to progressive organizations needing funds. To media outlets always on the lookout for human-interest stories, Peoples Temple offered a treasure trove of story angles.

Once the sundry puff pieces saw print, Temple staff could recycle them. They assembled a set of newspaper reprints to be distributed along with Temple-produced information sheets, leaflets, and pamphlets filled with photos and testimonials, some of them by Temple members whose affiliation was not noted. In turn, the reprints and PR materials could be collected in packets that accented the Temple's image in different ways to different "markets." The main problem, Jim Jones understood, was taking care to insure that any given packet did not contain accounts that contradicted one another. Once, while instructing a secretary to get some publicity flyers out to a progressive ally, he cautioned, "Don't send him Andersonville, because it says something about the Lord, loving the Lord, and a bunch of bullshit. . . . Be sure to give him material with numbers that impress, but with," Jones paused to laugh, "some sort of statistical consistency."

Sometimes the press followed up on Kinsolving's exposé angle. But sufficient doses of what sometimes in the PR business is frankly called "press management" usually carried the day. In services closed to the public, Jones told his audiences he was shielding them from the press because "they'll make fun of people." He tried to dissuade followers from telling people outside the group that "Jim Jones is God," carefully shading his position as prophet, messiah, and embodiment of good as distinct from a "sky god" that he never aspired to anyway. He would instruct his audience on the proper image to project when strangers of any significance were to be present. He decried the press for biases based on publishers' desires not to offend readers and advertisers, and then bragged about manipulating the press on the basis of those same interests. A reporter would look around the audience, Jones claimed, and think, "'That's an advertiser here,' or 'that's that many people that might not take our paper.'"[13]

Even an iconoclast like Kinsolving could be headed off the second time around. The cleric turned journalist kept alive the animosity between himself and Peoples Temple with a January 1974 KGO radio comment about the "Ukiah messiah," and his "men armed with .357 magnums." "So we're keeping an eye on the people in Ukiah," Kinsolving boasted. Apparently the Temple was keeping tabs on Kinsolving too, for Tim Stoen got a transcript of the radio broadcast and drafted a letter demanding that the station disavow it. Then in 1975 the Temple received enough information on Kinsolving's statements about it that a Temple lawyer could file a libel suit against Kinsolving, ruining the latter's possibilities for publishing news articles on it. Like other objects of media scrutiny in recent years, Peoples Temple used the libel laws to "chill" efforts at news reporting, albeit against a man whom even a clearheaded outsider, Methodist minister John Moore, found "obviously hostile towards . . . Peoples Temple."

Eventually, Peoples Temple would parade the "smoking gun" of Lester Kinsolving's alleged racism: he had been booted from the U.S. Congress galleries by fellow reporters on grounds that he unethically accepted payments to promote the interests of the government of South Africa. From the voluminous files the Temple kept on Kinsolving, Temple staff would conclude that the man was not just another muckraking reporter; given his stories on the World Council of Churches and on Black religious activist Jesse Jackson (to name two of his targets), Kinsolving fit nicely into the Temple pantheon as a bona fide enemy. During the 1975 Kinsolving "crisis," Jim would proudly report to his followers that he had been seven days without sleep successfully fighting a battle against "a media campaign initiated by Lester Kinsolving and backed by the CIA."

With grist like Kinsolving for his mill, Jones increasingly refined and publicized his particular version of a U.S. political stance that historian Richard Hofstadter has called the "paranoid style." As Hofstadter observed in his seminal 1950s essay, whether a person may be diagnosed as *clinically* paranoid is beside the point; what matters in politics is the successful public promotion of a theory that grandiosely links the disparate threads of history into an organized, hostile, and conspiratorial effort to undermine a people representing principles of truth, justice, and the good. When opponents like Kinsolving surfaced, when staged and actual events "confirmed" the intentions of the Temple's opponents, when former followers turned on Jones, and when the press sought to uncover the "real" Peoples Temple behind the image, Jones and his staff would link the events together, sometimes in fantastic ways, sometimes with strong evidential basis, into a sinister conspiracy that was trying to destroy a radical social movement dedicated to class and racial justice.

As the rhythm of "conspiracy" picked up in 1975, Temple operatives worked even harder at PR. The widely read San Francisco *Chronicle* columnist Herb Caen took a shine to the Temple and graced his chatty column with an occasional upbeat note. After considerable pressure that quite unnerved her, *Chronicle* reporter Julie Smith filed a story that called the services "a bit on the unconventional side," but added, "On the other hand, they are by no means the razzledazzle lovefests Glide Memorial Church is famous for."

One event gives a particularly clear picture of the tangled web of media and PR connections that the Temple drew on to maintain its image. Mike Prokes and a KDKI radio personality talked one time, ostensibly about the Temple's financial underwriting of airtime for a Peoples Temple Christmas show. Prokes managed to get in a word of thanks for the station's help with "our recent ordeal." The radio man was probably happy to get the underwriting and he did his best to assure Prokes that the station would not tolerate negative call-ins about the Temple on its talk show. "When it starts sticking people in the eye, it's no fun at all," he maintained. Thus relied Peoples Temple on the upbeat radio ideology that sustains an "easy-listening" format.

In perhaps its most successful PR ploy, the Peoples Temple marched in defense of freedom of the press, in the instance of four Fresno *Bee* reporters jailed for refusing to reveal their news sources. How could newspapers fail to carry the story? The ultimate payoff was a 1977 Freedom of the Press Award from the National Newspaper Publishers' Association.[14]

Peoples Temple became fairly adept at managing public relations, largely by using practices that are commonplace in the corridors of the profession devoted to managing images of business and government. The extensive PR developed a life of its own, independent of the Temple's California activities. No doubt the clearest proof of this was Jones's invitation to the "Religion in American Life" (RIAL) twenty-eighth anniversary dinner held in March of 1977. RIAL, a public service advertising organization, was launching "a multi-media campaign, making use not only of television spots, or billboards—but of all the available media, making a single integrated impact" to promote religion. The corporate and advertising elite, from American Can Company to Young & Rubicam, gave generous, tax-deductible dollars to support the public service work carried out by advertising agencies, and they gathered at New York's Waldorf-Astoria Hotel for a banquet dinner honoring the cream of U.S. religious leaders. Men like multimillionaire Peter Grace and the president of AT&T, William

Lindholm, rubbed shoulders with the senior bishop of the African Methodist Episcopal Church and the presiding bishop of the U.S. Episcopal Church. On the third tier of the dais could be found the pastor of Peoples Temple of the Disciples of Christ, with Robert Beusse from the U.S. Catholic Conference on his left, between Jones and the chairman of the J. Walter Thompson Agency. Mike Prokes watched from a table in the audience that he shared with the head of the largest U.S. polling organization, George Gallup, Jr.

Jim Jones's presence would seem less a testament to his good works than to the way guests were selected. As befits the U.S. pseudoevent, Jones could have been chosen only by reference to the superficial image that he and his staff publicly cultivated, not on the basis of his congregation's "apostolic socialism." It all began in 1975, when RIAL Business Advisory Council secretary Newton Hudson sought to recruit one hundred clergymen from "the most influential and effective congregations across the country." Hudson wrote Jim Jones, "Your name came up again and again." Jones accepted the honor, and in 1976 Peoples Temple sent off $2,500 to support the organization's work. The following year came the invitation to be seated on the dais at the banquet. The man behind the image never would have been elevated to these heights, no doubt. Thus are exposed the lengths to which Jones and his public relations staff would go to cultivate influence. By the same token, Jones's success also points to the vulnerability of our public images, and adds substance to the view that the United States no longer has heroes, only celebrities.[15]

Peoples Temple marshaled the power of PR to shield an apocalyptic socialist movement in opposition to the capitalist culture that had spawned PR, but the Temple could not both use the mainstream media to maintain a front and at the same time use it to reach the organization's target audiences. In the mid-1970s, the Temple therefore launched concerted efforts to bypass the channels of established mass media. The most ambitious project was a mass distributed newspaper, *Peoples Forum*. The first issue hit the streets in April of 1976, announcing a nonsectarian, nonpartisan editorial policy that was directed to "a better realization of our common goals." As an eye-catcher, *Peoples Forum* typically headlined some sort of natural disaster or social outrage, in the frame of the sensationalist *National Enquirer*. Other content was more focused. Editors wove in news stories on the Temple and Jim Jones, along with a potpourri of short pieces on racism and various progressive political struggles, such as that of radical American Indian leader Dennis Banks. Though the politics were never made explicit, a careful reader could find code words and stories that displayed a distinctive leftist, racially egalitarian tilt.

The Temple inflated *Forum* circulation claims to the lofty figure of

600,000. No matter what the true press run, copies got around: the average San Franciscan of the day saw issues of the paper floating along with the other litter of the streets. People from all walks of life looked over *Peoples Forum*, and Temple staff took on a thousand errands spawned by the paper's circulation, taking time to place a cat for a reader who could not care for it any longer, and meeting a financial district "pigeon woman" to receive a partially tamed bird that needed care.

Whatever it accomplished in acts of charity, *Peoples Forum* somehow touched the raw nerve ends of a diverse multitude, electrifying them into writing feverish letters that went beyond the formatted responses of polling operations like the Gallup Poll. Temple worker Jean Brown fielded correspondence from every quarter, from gay activists and hard-hat communists to a proponent of space colonization and a man advocating formation of the "Democratic Free Enterprise Socialist Party," from proto-Nazis to liberals decrying socialism as a fascism of the Left. As it always had, Peoples Temple somehow catalyzed extreme responses. During the years *Peoples Forum* was published, 1976 and 1977, the lines of controversy were becoming more publicly drawn. Peoples Temple emerged from its political closet.[16]

### The Progressive Urban Coalition

Essentially, in the 1970s Peoples Temple brought to urban California its successful Mendocino County political strategy. Because it was able to find more congenial allies than Republicans in the cities, the alliances became more ideological, less pragmatic. For this reason, the Temple was somewhat more successful in politics in San Francisco than Mendocino County. By August 1975 Jim Jones had abandoned conceiving of Redwood Valley as an "internal" promised land, and was reversing the direction of migration from rural back to urban areas, arguing that the Temple was safer in San Francisco because of its good relations with police and politicians. The Temple continued to litter its trail of obfuscation with public relations ploys and inverted public stands on communism. The difference was that in San Francisco the possibilities of coalition politics offered potentially significant rewards—the spoils of office, as they say, and the coalitions the Temple entered into revealed its true political stripes for all to see.

San Francisco in the 1970s was crisscrossed with radical organizations of all persuasions, and Peoples Temple became one of the progressive churches, like Glide Memorial, that allied with New Left and counterculture politics. Indeed, Jim Jones became that rare White person who could be accepted by segments of the progressive Black community. True, when he first came into San Francisco in the late 1960s, Jones had raised eyebrows with his healing hoopla and raids on other pastors' congregations, and some fellow preachers continued to feel threatened by the growing influence of a charismatic pastor who was syphoning off their own members. Ministers like Hannibal Williams and Amos Brown met with other Black leaders in Williams's Third Baptist Church in late 1976 to discuss the threat Jones posed to the Black church. The result was a decision to bar him from membership in the somewhat conservative Black Leadership Forum by requiring a potential member to be an "adult person of African descent." For his efforts, Williams found himself the subject of some cheap threats from the Temple "diversions" squad. They seemed to have a knack for raising the possibility of death, without giving their names or threatening murder. Williams complained to the police, but felt he got nowhere.

Though Jones offended some Black leaders, he also made lasting friendships in the community. Dr. Carlton Goodlett acted as Jones's personal physician, and offered the paper he published, the *Sun Reporter*, as an outlet for practically every item the Temple sent him, beginning in 1970. Jones met Glide Memorial Methodist Church minister Cecil Williams, who presided over unconventional "be-in" services. Eventually the two began appearing together on the podium in support of the progressive causes they shared. And Jones also elbowed his way onto the NAACP board, partly by having Temple members enroll in the organization and vote for him. Cultivating cooperative endeavors with other groups, Peoples Temple became a firm fixture in the pantheon of organizations mobilizing for social change in the United States in the aftermath of the antiwar movement.[17]

The Temple was too devoted to its own capitalization to free up much in the way of financial support for the causes of the day. Still, sometimes it would make substantial contributions for publicity purposes, such as the $6,000 it sent to a federally sponsored effort, the Seniors' Assistant Program, when the program ran out of funds, and the $1,500 it reportedly gave to the Telegraph Hill Neighborhood Center and Health Clinic to wipe out its deficit and help keep its doors open. In one case the objective was more than publicity: Jim Jones evidenced strong commitment to the plight of American Indian Movement leader Dennis Banks, and he put substantial financial and other resources into the fight to stave off Banks's extradition to South Dakota, where he had been convicted in 1975 of assault charges stemming from a confrontation between Indians and government agents.

More often, financial contributions to all kinds of groups were of token size. Still, sometimes even a small sum (like the $100 Jones donated for a Christmas party for Indian children) could make a difference for a struggling organization. Hungry organizations and politicians cannot look even a Trojan gift horse in the mouth, and the Temple might be seen as at least friendly by everyone from Tom Hayden's Campaign for Economic Democracy (which received $15) to the Berkeley anti-nuclear-power group, Science for the People (which wrote seeking support).[18]

If the Temple did not donate much money, it had other things to offer: the symbolic support marked by a Jones appearance (along with the hundreds of Temple members who would come to assure him an audience), media promotion, and the "foot troops" that are essential to machine politics. Perhaps because by 1975 the agricultural mission in Guyana had become a viable location to colonize, Jones began taking a visible role in leftist politics. He let Temple ideology become known to the point that by December of 1976 the San Francisco *Chronicle* was quoting him as favoring "some kind of democratic socialism." Though his own formative communist ideology emerged out of Stalinism, Jones thus identified with New Left culture. He even privately questioned why Angela Davis stayed "in that old Communist Party bag," charitably concluding, "I suppose we need mobilization in all segments." Jones also made sure that his own promotion of leftist causes elevated his own position in the coalition. Like Father Divine in the struggles of the 1930s, he put his own movement first. Nevertheless, the newspapers of the Left for the most part welcomed Jones to the scene, and his New Left approach to mobilization did not differ so much from that of other progressive groups trying to avoid the stigma of Stalin associated with a largely discredited Soviet model of communism.

Jones was especially adept at making public symbolic stands. He, Cecil Williams, and state Assemblyman Willie Brown appeared together with Kathleen Cleaver at a press conference in July of 1976, urging amnesty for Eldridge Cleaver after Cleaver disavowed the Black Panther party and returned to the United States. In October 1976 Jones, Dennis Banks, and Cecil Williams appeared together at a rally protesting the *Bakke* decision by the California Supreme Court, a decision that held unconstitutional a special program giving minority applicants to the University of California preferential treatment. The next month Jones rallied with members of the Socialist Workers party. In 1977 he joined others at Kimball Park, denouncing the racism of South Africa. When World Peace Council representatives came to town, they were invited to speak at the San Francisco Temple about ending the arms race. Jones also brought to the Temple Chilean refugees who talked of the anti-Allende right-wing coup backed by the CIA, offering chilling accounts of seeing "their wives and loved ones tortured to death in front of their very eyes." Through its political activities on the Left, the Temple hooked up with the famous leftist lawyer Charles Garry, who came to speak to Temple members on the "San Quentin six" sometime after he had heard about the Temple's demonstrations in support of the Fresno *Bee* reporters.[19]

Because members came from so many segments of the population, someone in the Temple could resonate with the concerns of any group in the spectrum of potential political allies, and the group pursued a series of alliances with individuals and other organizations. In Los Angeles the Temple established a "defense alliance" with the Black Muslims, culminating in a May 1976 "spiritual jubilee" that brought together a pantheon of political luminaries from Black leaders like Los Angeles Mayor Tom Bradley and Assemblyman Willie Brown, and White liberals like San Francisco District Attorney Joe Freitas, to Communist party member Angela Davis. The friendship between the Temple and the Muslims, both Jones and Muslim chief Imam Wallace Muhammed agreed, underscored their commitment not to let scriptural and doctrinal differences create disunity in the face of what Jim Jones pegged as "resurgent, viscious racism and oppression."

The theme of persecution also offered bridges to the community that had perhaps the best understanding of it. Temple member Harriet Tropp, herself Jewish by birth, believed it important to emphasize the solidarity the Temple felt with Jews in their "age-old struggle." The Temple drafted a letter to rabbis and Jewish organizations in the Bay area, calling for a "unified, broadly based resistance to a very evident resurgence of Nazism and its insidious, intolerable doctrines of racism and genocidal 'solutions' which, once again, are being openly proclaimed, and are beginning to take hold like a disease in our midst." In December of 1976 Mike Prokes and other Temple staff met with staff members of the Jewish Community Relations Council about ways of combating the increase in Nazi propaganda in the Bay area.

On another front Jim Jones and Cecil Williams urged followers to support a boycott of Florida orange juice because its advertising celebrity, Anita Bryant, was taking nationwide tours fanning the flames of antigay sentiment. A Temple member gave out remarks on behalf of Jones, supporting rights of gays, and calling Bryant's attacks a "marriage of pseudo-Christian morality and patriotism, backed up by corporate money." Bryant's campaign, the Temple held, was "giving birth to a new wave of facism . . . , spreading its poison in attacking anything that's not straight, white and conservative."

With its support of gay rights and Jews, the Temple fashioned its coalition stance under an anti-Nazi imagery. At rally after rally during 1976 Jones would retell the German clergyman Martin Niemöller's account of how he fell into the Nazi trap: "When they came for the Communists, I didn't do anything, for I wasn't a Communist. When they came for the Jews, I didn't do anything, for I wasn't Jewish. . . . But when they came for me, I realized that there was nobody left to do anything on my behalf."[20]

The peculiar character of Temple imagery traces not simply to its communist alliances and strategies or to its religious provenience but to the fusion of the two. By establishing affinities on common ground, the Temple came close to adopting a conventional leftist mobilization organizing strategy of drawing people into a coalition by interpreting their individual struggles as part of a more fundamental struggle between the oppressed and the capitalist establishment. The only difference was that the Temple cast oppression in more messianic religious terms of fascist persecution. However slight the shift in emphasis from the more straightforward, if sometimes equally paranoid, leftist political approach, it was to have profound consequences.

### Party Politics and the Liberal Surge

Like other left-leaning organizations, historically and at the time, the Temple played a double game. It worked "underground" and among progressive circles on the presumption that the entire establishment political apparatus was oppressive, corrupt, and, in a word, the "enemy." At the same time, on the public level it strived to maintain legitimacy and exert leverage in traditional political channels, both for its own protection, and to advance its cause. As Jones put it in one of those frank, behind-the-scenes political conversations with a radical ally, "My feeling is that our relationship to the people is that: while we're working for the good man or woman [candidate] to come that we can support—who we feel will make real changes, is to be manipulative on their [the people's] behalf, and to tie the enemy up, so to speak, in minor debts here and minor debts there, and pin them down." Like other progressive groups, Peoples Temple made effective alliances with the Democratic party establishment, participating in the broad coalition of the mid-1970s that was to put George Moscone in power as mayor of San Francisco.

Already in Mendocino County, the Republican party had cultivated Jones's support, for he controlled enough votes, 300 to 400, to make or break victory in an off-year election in which Jones's cadre might amount to over 10 per cent of the total turnout, around 2,500 voters. Jones bragged over the phone to Dennis Denny: "When people want votes, they don't hesitate to ask me for consideration, and I have produced. And I have brought some good people into government in this county."

Jones's efforts would be equally successful in San Francisco, where a coalition group version of old-fashioned machine politics counted on the ability of ward heelers and big-time politicos to deliver votes. Those who could claim some credit participated in the rewards of victory, cashing in their political debts. As Dennis Denny described it, "In the arena down south [San Francisco], that's an acceptable practice."

Whoever had power in San Francisco, Temple members made sure to write to impress upon them the good works of their pastor, and they received letters back from Board of Supervisors members Terry Francois and John Barbagelata, thanking them for their support. Like corporations that donate money to political candidates, Peoples Temple hedged its bets by offering support to both sides, and gravitating to the winning one. In terms of real leverage, however, Peoples Temple could expect to affect politics only on the side of progressives, and it embraced the San Francisco coalition that was emerging in the mid-1970s. Jones and his staff made inflated claims about the size of Temple membership, no doubt in part to impress politicians with Jones's power base. Nevertheless, it was not uncommon for 3,000 people to show up for special Temple services in the period, and whether they were committed members or not, those who visited the Temple were ripe targets for any voter mobilization activity. Moreover, as a leader, Jones had an asset of particular value: the color of his skin helped him to mediate between a largely Black constituency and a largely White political establishment in a way that may have seemed less threatening to the politicians. By the same token, some Blacks convinced of Jones's sympathies may have felt he was more effective fronting for them than a person of their own race.

Eventually some former Temple members, along with San Francisco Supervisor John Barbagelata, would accuse the Temple of practicing voter fraud, busing members back and forth on election days between San Francisco and Mendocino County, where Temple members like Wanda Johnson and Lynetta Jones had served as deputy county clerks for registering voters. But the voting clout of actual Temple members in San Francisco seems to have been grossly misperceived, at least if many of the people who eventually went to Jonestown were followers registered to vote in San Francisco in 1975. That was the year of the watershed election between Moscone and other liberals who ran against Barbagelata, a conservative real estate man. Of the 913 Temple people who died at Jonestown, only "several dozen" were registered in San Francisco for the election. Actually, it seems that Jones's concerted effort to register Temple members in the fifth assembly district came *after* the election of Moscone, in preparation for the Democratic party caucuses of 1976. Even then, Jones seems to have played it fairly straight, privately acknowledging to a political ally that party rules about residence during the previous election would limit the number of Temple members participating. He did, however, plan to deliver the votes for the fall 1976 election.

It would be a mistake to gauge the significance of Temple support only on the basis of actual Temple votes. State Assemblyman Willie Brown, no doubt aware of Peoples Temple's profile in the Black community, suggested to Democratic party notables the possibility of recruiting Temple members as political workers. Through the political legwork of members, Peoples Temple, along with similar and allied groups like the Delancey Street Foundation and the Black Panther party, managed to obtain clout out of proportion to actual numbers. That, of course, is precisely the enterprise of political party struggle, not only among so-called fringe groups but within political establishments as well. As one of Jones's political allies put it in a phone-session mapping strategy, "A couple of hundred people could take both parties over, because they become dependent on you."

Reporters Reiterman and Jacobs argued that Jones could produce political workers because of the "communal and authoritarian structure" of the Temple, but such an explanation does not acknowledge the degree of commitment all sorts of political parties and other groups are able to exact of volunteers, without any substantial pressure. Jeannie Mills explained members' obedience to orders in the Temple's political mobilization by commenting, "You don't understand. We wanted to do what he told us to." Reiterman and Jacobs interpreted Jones's expanding political clout as the product of "illusion, public relations, misrepresentations and exploitation of political greed." If so, it was part and parcel of the political process, not an aberrant invention of Peoples Temple.[21]

Urban politics in the United States underwent a transformation as early as the 1960s. Republicans had been able to make inroads in some traditional Democratic party urban strongholds because of migration to the suburbs by working-class Whites, and on the basis of decreasing voter turnout among the poor. With the decline of urban machine politics based on ward-heeling empires, the patronage-guaranteed bloc of voters has become a rarity in politics. In the contemporary era of voter mobilization via interest groups and the mass media, Jones controlled a resource practically as important. He had lists of people who attended Temple services, and he had a ready legion of workers who could carry out the essential activities of urban machine politics—canvassing, getting voters registered, and getting them to the polls with slate lists in their hands. In a close race the margin of victory can depend upon such activities. The 1975 San Francisco elections were that close. In a city where average turnout was around 200,000, the first liberal mayor in memory, George Moscone, won a runoff by only 4,000 votes, a margin of around 2 per cent, and a number that would have been critically affected by Peoples Temple efforts. Fellow liberals Joe Freitas, running for district attorney, and Richard Hongisto, candidate for sheriff, also were listed on the Temple slate, and they won by somewhat wider margins.

The liberal victory at the polls in 1975 became the Temple's springboard to substantially increased political clout in San Francisco. Jones used the victory to propel himself toward center stage of the Democratic party. He worked with others on the Democratic caucuses. He bused in Temple members for Rosalynn Carter's opening of Democratic campaign headquarters when her husband Jimmie was making his first presidential bid. The move saved Mrs. Carter from the embarrassment of facing a half-empty hall, and in the words of a local campaign official, the rally "proved to the [national] press that Carter can turn out 'the folks.'" As a side benefit, the occasion gave Jim Jones the opportunity to sidle up next to Mrs. Carter while Temple photographers tried to get some decent shots. Later in the campaign Jones could be counted among the few notables invited aboard vice presidential candidate Walter Mondale's chartered jet for a private visit.

Jones's hobnobbing with big shots paid off. He pursued his contact with Mrs. Carter by writing her to urge a rapprochement with Cuba. The reward was a handwritten note. "Dear Jim," it went, "Thank you for your letter. I enjoyed being with you during the campaign—and do hope you can meet Ruth [Carter Stapleton, Mrs. Carter's born-again evangelist sister-in-law] soon. Your comments about Cuba are helpful. I hope your suggestion can be acted on in the near future." The Temple made a fetish of collecting dozens of such letters written by everyone from Temple members to Vice President Mondale and Mrs. Carter. As the New York *Times* noted after the Guyana tragedy, the letters lauding "high principles of morality and humanity" are "the sort any preacher with even minimum respectibility— and a large congregation—could obtain from almost any politician."

For much the same reason, the Temple was able to stage a huge testimonial dinner during the 1976 election campaign, ostensibly because of the Temple's support for the "Fresno Four" newspaper reporters. No political hopeful could miss the chance to appear before all those voters, but to do so, they would have to pay homage to Pastor Jones. They did so. Mayor Moscone gave Jones a plaque thanking him for support, and Lieutenant Governer Mervyn Dymally paid tribute to him, as did Board of Supervisors member Bob Mendelsohn. Even conservative politicians attended, for Peoples Temple never wanted any faction to assume it had the Temple in its hip pocket.

In all this, it must be understood, Jim Jones did not just use politicians for legitimacy and political leverage. He returned favors by working for certain changes in the system. Along with other progressives, Peoples Temple backed the San Francisco ballot initiative known as Proposition T, which called for election to the Board of Supervisors by individual election district rather than by the city at large. The proposition was widely seen as an effort to defuse conservative influence on the board, by preventing voters from outside the poorer districts from tipping the balance of power in those districts by their disproportionate rates of voting. The proposition was passed, much to the disappointment of John Barbagelata and his conservative allies.

From the beginning Jones's efforts were not lost on Mayor Moscone. As one Democratic political worker put it, "Moscone had created a lot of obligations in his coming to power, and he was very good about repaying political debts." Although District Attorney Joe Freitas later claimed to have been unaware of the benefits of Temple support at the time of the election, at the initiation of state Assemblyman Willie Brown, and with strong recommendations from Mendocino County officials, Freitas tapped Tim Stoen to run an investigation into San Francisco voter fraud. The man who also served as a Temple attorney left his district attorney's office job in Ukiah in May of 1976 to mount a successful effort that resulted in some fifty indictments.[22]

Though Stoen's appointment offered him an important opportunity to advance in his career, the real political plum eventually went to Jim Jones. Temple member Mike Cartmell served on the forty-eight-member committee to nominate candidates for San Francisco's various commissions, and he and others pressured the Moscone administration to appoint Jones to a position that adequately rewarded Temple election work and befitted Jones's purported position as a leader in the Black community and an advocate of the rights of the poor. Initially, in March of 1976, Jones was to be put on the Human Rights Commission, but he declined to serve in a role that repeated his Indianapolis position of fifteen years earlier, and it was announced that Moscone was "urging him to reconsider and take another post" in the city's administration. The following October, Moscone appointed Jones to the commission regulating the government agency responsible for administration of public housing, the San Francisco Housing Authority. Perhaps it was an appropriate appointment for a man who had devoted considerable efforts toward putting a roof over peoples' heads, albeit under his own organization's auspices. Perhaps that was the point, for two years earlier Jones already had been scheming with Dr. Carlton Goodlett about obtaining a redevelopment project grant to build communal housing for Temple members in the Western Addition.

When Jim Jones was sworn in late in November of 1976, he affirmed to his honor the Mayor, "I think what you want from us is action, not words. I will vote my conscience." Action Jones gave them. He went to bat for the tenants' association of the International Hotel. The seedy, low-rent residence hotel was owned by the Four Seas Investment Corporation, which sought to raze the structure to make way for progress near increasingly fashionable North Beach, long a haven of Orientals, Italians, and the remnants of the beatnik era, tucked amidst a strip of topless bars. The Temple's *Peoples Forum* carefully avoided the hint of favoring one side or the other in a dispute that would require Housing Authority action. On the street things were different: in early January 1977, at the time when the Housing Authority was seeking to purchase the hotel by using $1.3 million in federal funds, a crowd of some 300 demonstrators chanted a militant cadence outside the hotel: "Low income housing is our right. Stop the eviction: stand and fight." Sheriff Hongisto's deputies elbowed their way through the hubbub to the building to post eviction notices for some eighty elderly Orientals. Ten days later a crowd of 5,000 people, including busloads from Peoples Temple and Glide Memorial Church, formed a human wall to prevent the anticipated eviction effort. The eviction order was stayed for a while, though the battle was ultimately lost in June, when courts prevented the Housing Authority from acquiring the structure through eminent domain. Seven years later Four Seas still had done nothing with the property.

The emotional January demonstrations pitted the liberal establishment, in the instance of its Human Rights Commission and its Housing Authority, against its own sheriff. Through all the commotion, Jones gained political ground. When the Housing Authority Commission chair position opened up and the obvious candidate bowed out, Jones ran and won, reportedly with the help of a few well-placed phone calls by Mayor Moscone. The eighty-odd supporters of Jones who were regularly bused in to the meetings cheered; some twenty people mobilized in the same way by the losing candidate left the meeting dejected.[23]

In the Housing Authority election, as with so much of its efforts in public relations and politics, Jim Jones and People's Temple staff played the game. Sometimes they played fairly well for an upstart group, and they often came out on top. The Temple used all sorts of contrived techniques to promote its image and gain political clout. The techniques—orchestrated letter-writing campaigns, canned press releases ready for newspapers to print, cultivating friends in the press, bargaining for political spoils, and garnering testimonials from political notables—were not inventions of Peoples Temple but a compendium of techniques that mark the underside of U.S. political culture.

To be effective, the Temple used stratagems precisely because they involved playing the conventional games of politics and public relations in ways that others understood. If the Temple used public relations to create images that differed from reality, that must be recognized as the very nature of public relations. If Peoples Temple got on politically through superficial alliances and political horse trading, the fact that it was successful offers a certain testament to the nature of the political process more widely. What

Peoples Temple did reveals as much about the conventional worlds of public relations and politics as it does about Peoples Temple. It underscores the constructed artificiality of our mediated public domain, its vulnerability to propaganda, disinformation, and political aggrandizement from any quarter. Thus, the practices of Peoples Temple reflect back upon the conventional techniques by which the spectacle of U.S. public life is sustained.

This is not to say that all public relations and politics are characterized by the same distortions and ploys, but that the Temple operated well within the range of institutional practices. The significance of politics and public relations for the history of Peoples Temple lies not in the nature of the widely practiced techniques it used to achieve public notability in California. It lies instead in the fact that the Temple was able to employ such mainstream public relations and political stratagems to survive as a disestablishmentarian group.

Practitioners of politics and public relations pride themselves on understanding the tension between image and truth, and they try to work it to their own advantage. This activity depends on carefully negotiating the conventions by which previously nonexistent images are created. It is the negotiated conventions used to construct images, not any simple correspondence of image to reality, that give images their "plausibility." What Peoples Temple did was to break the conventions that give images plausibility. It did so by representing a deviant reality through the use of image conventions that had been reserved for other forms of image construction.

Peoples Temple thus "misused" a conventionalized form of "fraud": it entered the realm of PR pseudoevents for the purposes of promoting an apparently mainstream church ministry that was, in reality, something else. Accustomed as the denizens of political and public promotion were to creating images to sustain the wavering masses' senses of reality, they could only be outraged at a group that would use their practices in the same way, but against them, and for alien purposes.

# PART III

# 9

# From the Promised Land
# to the Promised Land

The public relations and political successes of Peoples Temple give cause
to wonder why Jim Jones did not move from a religious base directly into
the realm of politics, as the Reverend Adam Clayton Powell had done, from
his Harlem Abyssinian Baptist Church to the U.S. House of Representatives. The answer to that question has to do with the battles that took
place between the Temple and its opponents. For all the political support
Jones peddled in California, for all the Temple's PR finesses, they also
cultivated opposition. Apostates and their allies in turn harnessed their
own PR, media and political connections to a conflict that confirmed
Jones's prophecy of "persecution" and precipitated the collective migration
of Peoples Temple to its Promised Land.

By early 1977, in the afterglow of the previous fall's Democratic victories,
Jones was considered a potential political candidate. Indicative of his climb
to dizzying heights of notability was the Reverend Martin Luther King
birthday celebration staged by the San Francisco Council of Churches at
Peoples Temple. On January 15, 1977, more than 4,000 people jammed the
sanctuary, and any politician who thought the votes of Blacks and the poor
were important put in an appearance. Mayor Moscone was there, as was
California Governor Jerry Brown. Jim Jones used the occasion to align
King with a radical legacy: "It is interesting that Martin Luther King was
assassinated," he told the crowd, "just when he was making the connection
between racial exploitation and economic exploitation. He was a threat to
the capitalists' drive for profits and exploitation." In spite of all the political
backslapping, no, the noncandidate coyly emphasized, "I have no political
ambitions. I'd never make it." Perhaps he was correct.

Jones's foreboding prophecies directed his movement along a path different from "worldly" politics. For all his support of progressive causes,
Jones shared the pessimism of Pentecostals and other Adventists who take
seriously the Book of Revelation prophecies about the apocalyptic down-
fall of the present evil world order as a prelude to the Second Coming. With

175

such a worldview, plans to reform social institutions in "this" world (for Jones, the capitalist world of the United States) seem irrelevant.

Jim Jones, moreover, found concrete events he could point to as evidence that the Temple was the object of a campaign of harassment. If the apocalypse was not coming for everyone, it certainly was for the people of Peoples Temple. The most striking "proof event" came in November of 1976, when Unita Blackwell Wright, a Black woman mayor from a small Mississippi town, spoke at Peoples Temple about her 1973 trip with the first delegation of U.S. women to the People's Republic of China. As she spoke, ever watchful Temple security staff noticed a man skulking about the side of the building with electronic equipment. They followed him to a parked car, got the license number, and traced the car to a rental agency. Temple intelligence staff quickly (and correctly) ascertained that the man, one Thomas Dawsey, was an electronics expert who worked for an Air Force communications team ostensibly devoted to checking out possible interference with national defense radar. Years later Dawsey would claim he had just been cruising around, but to the Temple, the incident proved persecution to be considerably more than a fantasy.

Such events fed a messianic vision that was far more politically radical than those of contemporary religious Adventists: Jim Jones focused on imminent apocalypse rather than Christ's heavenly salvation, and his eschatology had to resolve a choice between preapocalyptic struggle with "the beast" versus flight to an "other-worldly" haven beyond the tentacles of the apocalypse. For all his coalition politics in urban California, Jones projected images of economic catastrophe, class persecution, and Nazi-like extermination of Blacks and gays. To him, the convergence of different oppressed people's plights underscored the need for flight to a safe haven.

As a path of redemption, Black migration had laid dormant for years. Marcus Garvey had passed from the scene, Father Divine arrived at the more conservative solution of creating his promised lands within the boundaries of the United States, and the Reverend Martin Luther King had told his followers he had "seen the promised land" coming with societal changes in the United States. At first for Jones's followers, the promised land was merely a remote image, but in the heady revolutionary climate of the 1970s, Jones was able to reinvoke the radical alternative to Divine and King, based on the premise that Blacks are a stateless nation, and that radical revolutionary movements in the United States are subjected to relentless repression in both subtle and violent forms. The vacuum of Black leadership that followed the slayings of Martin Luther King and Malcolm X offered the Temple's leader the opportunity to reestablish forcefully the promised land as a dream of migration. The image grew in its attraction when the "persecution" Jones always prophesied came crashing in around Peoples Temple.[1]

Somehow, in an era of the pseudoevent, it is fitting that the "persecution" of Peoples Temple unfolded largely as a struggle about the validity of another Temple image, the one fostered by public relations. The Temple fostered its public image partly by cultivating political connections. Because of the particular Left-liberal alignment of Peoples Temple in San Francisco, a struggle between conservatives and liberals for political power there during the mid-1970s became focused on a narrower struggle of increasingly vocal detractors against the Temple. The focused struggle attracted the resources of combat from the larger struggle. It was, in fact, in the spotlight of a partly politically motivated "exposé" that the Temple's public image shattered, and the faithful who had long prepared for some such event departed for the Promised Land.

While Jones was serving as head of the Housing Authority Commission, the Temple got wind of a potentially damaging reporter's investigation. Marshall Kilduff, who followed the Housing Authority meetings for the San Francisco *Chronicle*, wanted to do a story on the increasingly influential leader of an unusual congregation. Kilduff's editor nixed the story idea, pointing to similar coverage not long before, but the minister who came to Housing Authority meetings with bodyguards intrigued Kilduff, and he started to look for someone else to publish his account. In March of 1977 he signed on to do the story with *New West*, but editor Kevin Starr received a Temple delegation that convinced him to drop the project. Kilduff then turned to *San Francisco* magazine. The editors expressed interest, even though they received a long treatise from Temple publicist Dick Tropp requesting assurance that they not consider the story. But when Marshall Kilduff submitted his manuscript on an odd and powerful public official, the editors rejected it as lacking in focus and evidence.

In the meantime, *New West* was purchased by Australian publisher Rupert Murdoch, who was beginning to build his empire of U.S. publications, including the *National Star*, the *Village Voice*, and the New York *Post*. When Kilduff came back to *New West* the new editor, Rosalie Wright, agreed to a Temple story beefed up with fresh material. To help Kilduff with the job, Wright assigned Phil Tracy, a contributing editor. Tracy had a masterful touch at writing sober scandal. Already he had sensationalized the San Francisco conservatives' "law-and-order" issue with an article describing incidents of "random violence" that epitomized "San Francisco's current crime wave." His next story, "The Broken Promises of George Moscone," was a hatchet job on the liberal mayor of San Francisco. Moscone was characterized as "usually uninformed and incredibly ineffective," a man who "may well be the worst political disappointment in the west." Tracy did not concoct this account on his own; apparently he had the help of conservative San Francisco city Supervisor John Barbagelata. A biography of Moscone later observed, "The people around George began to feel that the reporter was the instrument of a reactionary cabal."

The logical next step for Tracy and *New West* was a look at Moscone's associates. Kilduff's story on Jim Jones fit the bill quite well. The project became, in effect, an investigation of a group that did not want publicity. Why, the two reporters would ask, was Jones important enough to require protection? What, they wanted to know, did Peoples Temple have to hide?[2]

## Threads of Opposition: Defectors from the Temple

For all Kilduff and Tracy might find out about Jim Jones's politics, they would not be able to reveal the secret life of Peoples Temple without access to informed sources. While Kilduff and Tracy remained on the outside, another reporter also was on the trail of Peoples Temple and he knew people with inside information, ready to talk. George Klineman, a free-lance writer and Sebastapol stringer for the Santa Rosa *Press-Democrat*, had been approached by his girlfriend's father (and future father-in-law), David Conn, with unnerving stories about a group that amounted to "an armed camp of blindly loyal followers."

David Conn had been a member of the Barrett Avenue Christian Church in Richmond, California, in 1969 when minister Bob Lemon first took Mert and Deanna Mertle to visit Peoples Temple. Soon after the Mertles moved up to Ukiah, two Richmond church members, Mert's former wife Zoe, and Larry Tupper, the former husband of Temple member Rita Tupper, confided to Conn concerns about their children. The young ones had gone with the two Richmond church members' former spouses to live in Redwood Valley under communal arrangements presided over by a faith healer. Conn went up to see Peoples Temple for himself in the summer of 1970. He came away amazed that the Disciples of Christ numbered a charlatan like Jones among the ranks of its pastorate, and he set about ferreting out evidence of Temple doings. In Ukiah a small group of Temple protagonists led by former Temple associate minister Ross Case was sharing similar concerns in Bible study meetings. But Conn was more the activist. He later claimed to have contributed to the first exposé of the Temple, Lester Kinsolving's 1972 series. Over the years he held steadfast in his determination to force Peoples Temple to a public reckoning, and eventually he was successful. The opening came after the Mertles defected from Peoples Temple in October of 1975.

Deanna and Mert Mertle were high-ranking members of the Temple's leadership and well acquainted with Jones's "revolutionary message." Deanna was not always satisfied with the recognition she received for her efforts, and her attempt to convince Jones to "go to the field" in 1973, after the defection of the "gang of eight," was seen by some as a crude effort to restructure the leadership of the organization, and to her own benefit. She created other storms as well, sometimes calling her staff in the publications office on the carpet, sometimes trying to "fire" those who disagreed with her style of administration. Perhaps underscoring a change in Deanna's status, around early 1974 the planning commission talked of sending her and Mert as missionaries to Chile, probably as a gentle way of easing them out of positions of power.[3]

Years later Deanna Mertle admitted to confidants that she became disillusioned with the Temple only after she lost out in her power struggle to take the organization in a different direction from that intended by its leader. Once she made her move, Deanna and her husband were no longer trusted. They began to see the Temple in a light less filled with commitment, and it looked very different. In particular, Mert objected to the seventy-five smacks his daughter Linda received as punishment in 1975. That year the Mertles moved from Redwood Valley to Berkeley and started a nursing home, and Deanna and Mert stopped attending services. After a while the Mertles would link their departure directly to Linda Mertle's beating, though the event occurred some months before they actually departed, and Linda remained in the Temple after the rest of her family left. Originally, the Mertles claimed their motives in leaving were strictly economic.

To give themselves a little leverage in any conflicts that might develop with the Temple, the Mertles held onto some items they claimed as their own and other things they thought might help them in court some day, should the occasion ever arise. In the year that followed, a series of squabbles left them the targets of Temple surveillance as well as some settling of accounts by the Temple's "diversions" group. Linda Mertle helped other Temple people enter the Mertles' Berkeley house to retrieve photographic equipment, sensitive photographs, and membership files the Temple claimed as its property. With coaching from the Temple leadership, Linda also took steps to try to drive a wedge between her mother, Zoe Kille, and Zoe's former husband Mert.[4]

In mid-December 1975 the Temple formed a "Mertle Committee" to keep track of the hot-headed Deanna and her husband. They learned a great deal about the Mertles' old circle of friends. Mert once had listed the Conns as his intimate friends. A Temple member who had lived with Deanna and Mert back in Redwood Valley let the Temple leadership know that she had seen David Conn visit Elmer Mertle sometime before the fall of 1975. "Deanna Mertle will do anything to get her way," another claimed. "She doesn't care who she hurts and she will walk over anyone and use everyone. A treacherous bitch! Mert will follow all the way."

A whole range of unsettled issues fueled distrust between the Mertles and Peoples Temple. The Mertles suggested a meeting at Arthur's Coffee Shop in the South Shore Center on New Year's Eve to carry out a series of trades of property and money, and signing of papers for Linda to be adopted by Temple members. Part of the deal would be a guarantee by themselves "to not contact any other person in or out of the church in any negative manner about the church." But the meeting failed to resolve the issue of an unrecorded deed to Richmond property that the Mertles had signed over to Peoples Temple.

By February of 1976 the unresolved conflict and the memories of all the blank sheets of paper they had signed left the Mertles so distraught that they changed their names to Al and Jeannie Mills. Eventually they made contact with other Temple members who defected, among them, Grace Stoen.

Even though Grace had risen to a position of major responsibility as head counselor and was tremendously popular with other members, she would claim later that she had never been committed to Peoples Temple, and had participated because of her husband Tim. In 1976, as Grace became increasingly dissatisfied, she became friends with Walter "Smitty" Jones, who worked as a mechanic maintaining Temple buses. For reasons that are unclear, perhaps because of her affair with Smitty, Grace began to feel that people were muttering about her behind her back and that Jim Jones was about to come down on her. In July of 1976 she and Smitty drove off from Redwood Valley, heading to Lake Tahoe, leaving her son John Victor Stoen behind. Four months earlier, along with Tim, Grace had signed a release (Temple form 8) authorizing her son's travel to Guyana under the authority of Temple leadership. She probably would have had great difficulty bringing her son on her July "elopement" anyway, because by then John Stoen already was enveloped in the Jones family communal living network.

The same month as her departure, Grace was on the phone with Jim, talking as intimates, frankly and without obvious fear, about whether she would return, as Jones wanted her to, how she would explain to her parents that she had left her husband and child, and whether she could come visit her son. Jones praised Grace for leaving her son behind, saying, "You were bright enough to know you couldn't take John without there being repercussions for him." In a concrete reference to Tim in at least the social role of father, Jim told Grace of the efforts to put the child at ease about his mother's departure. "It's something that his dad and I have to deal with," Jim said.

Three months after Grace and Smitty left, Tim Stoen signed a notorized pqwer of attorney for his son, appointing Jim Jones, Maria Katsaris, and others, "jointly and severally," "to take all steps, exercise all powers and rights, that I might do in connection with said minor." In the fall of 1976 the four-and-a-half-year-old was trundled off to Guyana to live at the agricultural mission. Even before the boy ever left the United States, Tim Stoen was on the phone to an angry and depressed Grace, telling her that it already was a *fait accompli*, and that "John just insisted on going." Asked if she had any regrets about her son's moving to the Promised Land, Grace replied with a barely inaudible "no." "I mean, do you think it's the right thing?" Tim pressed. "Sure," came the listless reply. Grace could visit the child any time, her husband of record assured her, but her son John could not return. "He said," Tim recounted, "'I'd rather die than come back there.'"

That same fall the Millses, Grace and Smitty, the Purifoy family, and others began to meet to share the camaraderie of escape, the sadness about relatives and friends left behind, and the secrets that few outsiders possessed about the inside of Peoples Temple. With awe they watched as Jones continued his political ascendency in San Francisco. But because Al's daughter Linda chose to remain in the Temple, Jones had an effective hostage against the Millses' making any public efforts to discredit the group. Nor did the small band of defectors really believe that they could get outsiders to accept their farfetched tales of beatings and intimidations. All this changed in November of 1976 when Linda Mills followed the rest of her family out of the Temple.

To make sense of their experience, the reunited Mills family picked up on a prevailing tide of public fear about "cults" like Sun Myung Moon's Unification Church and the Hare Krishnas. They began to account for Peoples Temple as a "cult." In particular, the Millses were following the public controversies of the day about religious group members' families' seeking court-ordered conservatorships for custody over family members lost to strange messiahs. Then too, the centerpiece of "cult" hysteria—the "coercive-persuasion" explanation of conversion and commitment—offered a ready vehicle for the Millses to distance themselves from actions they had taken in the name of "the Cause." As one Mills daughter explained to her sister, "We were all brainwashed in there, Linda. The one thing we have learned is not to blame ourselves for the things Jim made us do."[5]

In late 1976, with her daughter Linda no longer in jeopardy, Al Mills's former wife, Zoe Kille, talked with her longtime confidant, David Conn. She suggested he meet with her former husband, whom Conn had known as a Richmond Disciples congregation friend and fellow chemical analyst at the Chevron Oil refinery. When Conn talked to the Millses, he sought to convince them to protect themselves from unknown threats by establishing a journalistic record. They agreed, and Conn then brought in his daughter's boyfriend, Santa Rosa *Press-Democrat* reporter George Klineman, who met a group of some six Temple defectors, led by the Millses.

For years former Temple members had suffered their resentment quietly, at most sharing experiences with each other. Now things changed: the alliance between the Millses, David Conn, and George Klineman consolidated an activist opposition of key former Temple members that in turn fueled a U.S. Treasury Department probe, and tipped outside reporters to inside sources.

In a conversation with a Treasury agent he knew in the Customs Service, George Klineman tried to tease out whether the department was aware of the group his sources said was shipping weapons to South America. As the Customs Service described it, "an unpaid informant . . . offered to arrange a meeting between special agents and a group of former Temple members." Days later the agent called to tell Klineman that he wanted to talk with the reporter's sources. Al Mills checked out the possibility with the others, and they agreed, on the condition they be granted immunity from prosecution for acts they had committed in Peoples Temple. A group of thirteen Temple opponents met with the agent on February 24, 1977. Thus began an investigation that the agent (referred to as "James" by Jeannie Mills, perhaps the same man as James Hubert, a Treasury agent Steve Katsaris met later) assured the opponents would be a full-scale effort involving all levels of government.[6]

With the Treasury agent talking to the defectors, reporter Klineman belatedly sought to dissociate himself from the investigation for ethical reasons, even while he quietly maintained contact with both the agent and former Temple members. As a reporter he hoped someday to break a big story. David Conn was less careful. Though he had been told by a defector that Jones would "kill us if he finds out we're talking," Conn passed the story on Peoples Temple to a Seminole named George Coker who worked with him at the Chevron refinery. George Coker in turn carried the tale to Lehman (Lee) Brightman, a Sioux Indian and a friend and associate of Dennis Banks. Brightman, in fact, had shared a platform with Jones at the April 1976 rally supporting Banks, and he raised with Banks his concern that their cause might be tarnished by association with the preacher who was about to receive unfavorable press exposure.

Soon the word came back to David Conn that Dennis Banks wanted to know more. Perhaps Conn believed he could help his Indian friends avoid bad associations. Perhaps he wanted to "turn" Banks to his cause. Whatever his motive, Conn was ready to talk, and he did so, seriously misjudging the effect it would have on an Indian leader who, unbeknownst to Conn, had received a loan of $19,000 from Jones to bail his wife out of prison.

On March 23, 1977, at around 12:30 A.M., Dennis Banks met at Lee Brightman's house with George Coker and David Conn, and the latter poured out what he knew—the defectors' stories of faked healings, beatings, property extortion, threats and intimidations, the fact he was working with a reporter, and the U.S. Treasury investigation. Banks acted incredulous at the revelations, pumping Conn for more details. Conn kept pressing him to meet with a federal agent to prepare a statement denouncing Jones, Banks later recalled. Conn put it differently: he had wanted the Indian leader to sign a notarized affidavit dissociating himself from the Temple. Months later Banks would say Conn intimated that his own cooperation in discrediting Jones could hardly hurt his chances of winning his struggle against extradition to South Dakota, where Banks believed he faced a trial that would end in a death sentence. What Banks took to be blackmail Conn would describe as an effort to warn Banks of pending trouble.

The meeting ended without Banks's making commitments to David Conn. Within hours the leader of the American Indian Movement apparently told all to Jones, including the existence of a Treasury agent on the trail, a man whom Banks could get Conn to identify only by the first name Jim. The Temple wheeled into action with its well-practiced procedures of discernment and surveillance.

The Temple *modus operandi* did not change much over the years, but when the group started dealing with the Millses and other political defectors, the techniques began finding application to increasingly serious intelligence, disinformation, and covert action. Temple members went through the garbage can of Donna Conn, David Conn's former wife, got her phone number, and gave her an anonymous threatening phone call when her former husband was there on one of his frequent visits. While the phone call was put through, two Temple members lay under her house, ready to monitor the subsequent response to the conversation. It confirmed the suspicions raised by Banks: Donna Conn demanded that her former husband seek help from "the agent." The story checked out.

When Conn had talked to Dennis Banks, he coyly concealed the names of the reporter and defectors, but the nature of his stories and the clue of his employment at Chevron were enough to tip off Jones as to the source of the information. Jones's operatives fired back with a salvo of scare messages to Al and Jeannie Mills, and Grace Stoen, telling them, "I know of everything D. Conn boasts of having," and "You should know that one hundred will be staying back." Belatedly, it dawned on David Conn that he had been set up, and probably tape recorded during his rendezvous to warn Dennis Banks about Jim Jones.

Jones's intelligence net worked well, but there was one wrong inference. Knowing that Marshall Kilduff was trying to sell a story on them, Temple leaders assumed that he was the reporter Conn and the defectors had met. In fact, however, Kilduff was working in total ignorance of Klineman. Kilduff had an outlet, but he lacked the inside sources who would backstop his political sketch. Klineman had the sources, but not the channels or rationale to market the story. After the incident with Dennis Banks, the defectors clammed up for fear of revenge, but Jones's camp was just getting started. Not only did it continue surveillance of the Millses, Grace Stoen, and David Conn's former wife Donna, it moved into high gear in a campaign against Kilduff's article. Notes in Tim Stoen's handwriting listed a host of Temple friends next to a reference to Kilduff as "bigoted." *New West* was deluged with letters from both everyday folk and eminent politicians like the well-known San Francisco homosexual Harvey Milk and Black Lieutenant Governor Mervyn Dymally.[7]

### The Fusion of Political and Defector Opposition in Exposé Journalism

Finally, the Temple's efforts to suppress the story became a story itself, and its hypersensitivity to the press became the bridge between the *New West* reporters and the loose network of people who had left the Temple over the years. On June 7, 1977, the newspaper at which Kilduff worked, the San Francisco *Chronicle*, published an article by W. E. Barnes about the Temple's efforts to dissuade *New West* from publishing. Kilduff and Tracy reaped instant benefits. Conn, Klineman, and the Millses made contact with Kilduff, and offered the inside information that would make his as-yet merely political analysis "work" as a publishable story. In his initial meeting with Klineman, Kilduff admitted, "I don't have much of anything on Jones. I was hoping the Barnes article would flush people out, people with knowledge of what's really going on at Peoples Temple. Looks like the ploy worked."

At first the new sources were reluctant; Jones would discern the origins of any material published. Jeannie Mills still continued to feed information to the Treasury agent, and she took encouragement that San Francisco Supervisor John Barbagelata had spoken out against Peoples Temple at a meeting of San Francisco's top business leaders' organization, the Downtown Association. But she presumed, she later said, that the decision to serve as a public source in exposing Jim Jones was a "decision to be willing to die."

The decision came after *New West* staff reported a burglary of their editorial offices on June 17, 1977. The only thing allegedly touched was a file containing a draft of the Temple story, but a police investigation failed to substantiate that any forced entry through a window actually occurred. In fact, the only fingerprints on the supposedly jimmied window were those of a *New West* employee who had locked himself out of the office on a trip to the men's room four days earlier. Enraged staff at Peoples Temple dismissed the claims as a publicity stunt to promote the Temple exposé before publication.

The night after the burglary was reported, Phil Tracy convinced Jeannie Mills of the need for her to go public as a source, and Tracy, Kilduff, and Klineman met with David Conn, Jeannie and Al Mills, their daughter Linda Mertle, and Grace Stoen and her boyfriend Smitty Jones. Days later George Klineman drove up to Ukiah to take up an offer that Ukiah preacher and former Temple minister Ross Case made to Phil Tracy after the Barnes article appeared. Klineman interviewed Case, along with several of the Temple defectors whom Case had counseled over the years.

As the newsmen worked with the defectors, they became subject to much the same spirit of paranoia that animated some of their sources, who in turn reflected the paranoia of the Temple itself. Because of his personal ties with David Conn, Klineman was ripe for this sort of viewpoint. He knew that the Temple was trying to suppress the story, and he took covert actions of his own to cover the trail of his research. One time he went to an office of the California Department of Public Health and requested files on Temple care homes under a phony name; on his departure from the office, he stole the request form on the outside chance that Temple intelligence operatives were everywhere. Marshall Kilduff tried to maintain a cooler perspective. When Klineman wanted him to pretend to be visiting the elderly on a trip to the Mertle's care home, Kilduff told him, "I don't go for that cloak-and-dagger stuff." For his part, Phil Tracy one day convinced himself that he had spotted a Temple spy lurking near the editorial offices. He leaned out the window with a camera and snapped away at the individual, shouting, "I got you, motherfucker." In such episodes the journalists became personally infused with the mentality that marked both the Temple and their own sources.[8]

Finally the *New West* exposé, "Inside Peoples Temple," hit the newsstands the week of July 17, 1977. Its authors took the unusual step of parading their sources at a press conference to promote the story. The article itself led off with the subhead "Jim Jones is one of the state's most politically potent leaders. But who is he? And what's going on behind his church's locked doors?" It then noted the socialist tilt of the Temple newspaper and sketched Jones's rise to political influence. With this introduction, the article announced "Ten Who Quit the Temple Speak Out." Those who finally came forward gave the authors the impression that Temple life consisted of "a mixture of Spartan regimentation, fear, and self-imposed humiliation."

Kilduff and Tracy then recounted atrocities: the catharsis meetings, the punishment, the faked discernment and healings, the financial operations and offering collections, property transfers, and the inability of Grace Stoen to obtain custody of her own child from her husband Tim. The reporters went on to point out that hundreds of Temple members were preparing to move to Guyana, where "the option of ever leaving is questionable." At the close of the piece, they summed up "Why Jim Jones Should Be Investigated," and offered their report as a warrant for official probes of potential Temple child abuse, care-home fraud, and real estate misdealings. "The story of Jim Jones and his Peoples Temple is not over," Kilduff and Tracy argued. "In fact, it has only begun to be told. . . . If Jones is ever to be stripped of his power, it will not be because of vendetta or persecution, but rather because of the courage of these people who stepped forward and spoke out."

At the Temple, the courage of the defectors did amount to a vendetta, and the adoption by the journalists of the defectors' view of reality was seen as organized persecution. Kilduff and Tracy had relied entirely on defectors as substantive sources. Though the reporters had conducted a two-hour interview with Temple officials, they printed only Mike Prokes's and Gene Chaiken's blanket denials of the opponents' allegations. The *New West* article offered a one-sided view of Peoples Temple, by airing the perspective of the people who opposed it.

The public snapped up the shocking account, and the press and electronic news media milked the defectors for a steady flow of similar stories. George Klineman fed material to Steve Hart, a reporter who worked for the paper where Klineman was a stringer. Tim Reiterman of the San Francisco *Examiner* interviewed the *New West* sources and ferreted out other defectors who would detail more atrocities. Newspapers like the *Mendocino Grapevine* and the Santa Rosa *Press-Democrat* offered stories behind the story, about freelancer George Klineman, and human interest stories about the local people who had come forward. New allegations kept surfacing, and sidebars unveiled dramas of parents seeking custody under the threat of imminent migration to Guyana. As reporters began to delve further into allegations made at the end of the *New West* article, they promised, "Some of the stuff that's still to come make [*sic*] *New West*'s story seem tame." It was a reporters' field day.

All the coverage presented only one thorny problem to the defectors, that of credibility. A fundamental question was seldom raised explicitly: What had been the role of the defectors themselves in the activities of Peoples Temple? Kilduff and Tracy did try to confront one obvious issue: Why had the defectors taken so long to come forward? "Their answers were the same—they feared reprisal, and that their stories would not be believed." As the flood of stories continued for a month, this response was grafted onto the rhetoric of the anticult movement. In a July 28 *Mendocino Grapevine* story, a Temple defector named Rich Schroeder described "constant brainwashing" comparable to practices of the Unification Church. Reiterman and his *Examiner* colleague Nancy Dooley echoed the explicit connection: "When asked why they submitted, usually without question, to such a bizarre lifestyle, the former members explained that Jones' rules and rituals left them terrified, emotionally confused, and, in the words of many of them, brainwashed." By August 18, 1977, Santa Rosa *Press-Democrat* reporter Steve Hart was calling the group a "controversial cult."

Sociologically, it is questionable whether the term *cult* has any analytic usefulness, but intellectual distinctions are beside the point. In popular discourse, *cult* is a pejorative term used by adherents of one religious viewpoint to denigrate an alternative one. It is in this sense, not in any carefully framed intellectual argument, that news stories based on defectors' accounts began to treat People's Temple as a "cult."[9]

Like the sermons of the man they were exposing, the defectors' own revelations were not necessarily lies, but they were not the whole truth either. Many of the charges amounted to an ideological denigration of communalism and a community of goods as such, mapped onto the activities of Peoples Temple. Such charges did not reveal the violation of any law; rather, they conveyed the righteous anticult outrage of a culture that places high value on private property and individualism. The articles' potentially more serious allegations—about real estate, nursing homes, physical punishment, and the like—skirted serious inquiry into whether the Temple's practices were legal, and few of the stories that followed the *New West* piece bothered to balance their accounts with the Temple side of the story.

Even when reporters were confronted with information that did not fit their story line, they could frame the contradictory material in innuendo that discounted it. The *Examiner*, for example, reported that an elderly woman wrote from Guyana to her sister in the States that she was "real happy" when she found out the Temple had succeeded in selling her property "because we need that money over here to live on, since we are not intending to work [i.e. for wages] any more." The reporter added, "It is not known, however, what has become of the money. Temple officials in recent weeks have refused to comment on almost anything connected with Temple business." Another story looked into accusations about two deaths, those of Maxine Harpe and John Head, that had been investigated years earlier and officially ruled suicides. The effect of such stories admittedly based on no more than "accusations" was to vaguely associate Peoples Temple with events that might involve extortion and murder.

To some degree the very nature of "scandal" drove the style of reporting. Reporters would seize upon the most extreme statements in efforts to outdo one another. "Pack journalism" forced any self-respecting media outlet to print puffed-up, ever more scandalous revelations just to keep up with the competition. Ironically, the hyperbole, embellishments, and apocryphal stories of the defectors mirrored the style of the organization that had spawned them, that they now opposed. This does not take away from Jones and his staff whatever is their due based on duplicity, bizarre sexual and psychological intimidations, and other affronts. By the same token, if these practices of Peoples Temple were so clearly reprehensible, why was it necessary to exaggerate them in order to expose the group? The answer partly lies in the tension that exists between reality and its reflected image in a society that has come to accept the mediated version as reality itself. Like Peoples Temple, in their public relations activities the defectors and the press created embellished images in order to sustain the public interest that would give credibility to the media reality.

But there was also a moral dimension to the coverage. After the murders and mass suicide in Guyana, Tim Reiterman's managing editor at the San Francisco *Examiner*, David Halvorsen, affirmed that his paper had not been "morally neutral" in reporting on Peoples Temple. To the degree that news coverage was tipped toward defectors, and to the degree that the scandals reported had a moral, rather than legal, basis, the media effectively took one side of a religious conflict between Peoples Temple and its detractors. As we will see, the religious conflict itself set the stage for the murders and mass suicide at Jonestown; thus, the press in fact played a reflexive role, actually affecting events it purported to cover, helping shape their particular course of development.

Temple staff responded to the bad press much as others might: they worked with their friends in the media and with lawyers to counteract it. Temple writers wrote letters to local newspapers claiming that detractors were either liberal humanists opposed to religion or racists seeking to discredit them because of the progress they were making toward racial reconciliation. Even before the *New West* story came out, the Temple was laying the groundwork for the exodus to Guyana by releasing stories about the "kibbutz-style" agricultural mission "where San Francisco misfits can get away from their pressures." When the *New West* story broke, the Temple's own *Peoples Forum* offered a rebuttal, and the paper owned by Jim Jones's friend Dr. Carlton Goodlett, the *Sun Reporter*, ran a story in which Mike Prokes wondered aloud, "Why did they use only sources hostile to us?" *New West* sources, the Temple claimed, counted among themselves radical extremists and provocateurs. "When we combine the nature of the charges, the character of those making them, and the misrepresentations of the magazine itself about the church," one Temple statement went, "we realize that we are indeed up against a concerted effort to destroy us."

The Temple also sought legal help. On July 17 it paid a $10,000 retainer to San Francisco lawyer Charles Garry, a man already famous for his defense of leftists, including members of the Black Panther party. Originally Temple leaders wanted Garry to pursue a libel suit against *New West*, but when Garry was interviewed on the radio in August, he defended free speech, saying, "I personally don't like libel suits." The reporter retorted, "You know that transacts into a bottom line: you don't have a case. That's what that really sounds like." As the barrage of accusations continued day after day, Garry took on the general task of ferreting out what he said "looks like a conspiracy" against Peoples Temple. In September he told the Berkeley *Barb* that two months of charges in the media looked like "an orchestrated, premeditated government campaign to destroy a politically progressive organization."[10]

Whatever the validity of Garry's early assessment, the Peoples Temple exposé was borne of a complex alliance that included individuals with agendas other than "straight" news. Even authors of the *New West* article itself had diverse interests. George Klineman, who was listed on the first page as having assisted Kilduff and Tracy, had a personal tie to David Conn that filled him with the zeal of a crusade shared by the people he interviewed. Kilduff clearly became interested in the first place because of Jones's political power. Tracy had an axe to grind with the political associates of Mayor Moscone, and he quickly became caught up in the shadowy struggle between the Temple and its dissidents. With the reporters' range of interests, the article united the dual wings of opposition to Peoples Temple: personal/cultural and political. The defectors' revelations in the article could then be used by politicians who opposed not just Peoples Temple but the entire progressive coalition that put Moscone in office. Even a defector interviewed on KNBR said he was "very concerned, as are a number of others who have left the Temple, that the issue of the Temple is going to become a hot political football, which is going to be used by the political right in the city, in the Bay area, particularly by Barbagelata and his crew."

The *New West* article created a storm of controversy about Peoples Temple just at the time when the progressive coalition that included the Temple was being challenged by conservative-backed election initiatives,

Propositions A and B, that would recall Moscone and provide for citywide voting on city supervisors from each election district. When Phil Tracy was asked whether he and the other exposé authors were on a crusade against Peoples Temple, he cited their procedure of two-source corroboration, and demurred: "We don't feel we're attacking Peoples Temple. We're simply making public certain allegations by former members of the Temple." But Tracy added, he "would be foolish not to recognize that some people will use this story to attack the mayor, the sheriff and the district attorney." The article's publication dovetailed nicely with the campaign of Barbagelata and others to undo the liberal restructuring of electoral procedures, Tracy insisted, purely by chance.

Yet Tracy himself suggested at the press conference held to promote the article that because Jones worked with the Housing Authority, Mayor Moscone "ought to issue a statement on the matter immediately." About a week later, with the special election of August 2 a week away, conservative Board of Supervisors President Quentin Kopp echoed Tracy's call for a city investigation. Mayor Moscone responded that he had found absolutely no hard evidence in the *New West* article, and he urged anyone with allegations that laws had been broken to take their information to law enforcement officials.

The San Francisco liberals beat back the conservative Propositions A and B despite the uproar about Jim Jones, and two days after the election the mayor received a resignation from the controversial head of his Housing Authority Commission. Jim Jones already had left for Guyana; he departed in mid-June, well before the *New West* article came out, telling his friend Cecil Williams that he was not going to stay around to be abused first by the media, and eventually, he suspected, by the government as well.

With Jones gone and the election over, the intense news coverage still continued for a good two months. As the initial scandals waned, the press kept public interest high by turning to the migration that already had been under way for some time.[11]

## Guyana and the Mission Post

The country of Peoples Temple's Promised Land was hardly paradise, and historically, most colonists had purely economic motives. For centuries major European colonial powers—the Dutch, the French, and the English—had fought for control of both the Caribbean coastline of South America and the river trade routes that led upstream into the Guiana jungle highlands, south toward Brazil. They wanted the coastal land to grow sugarcane, and they wanted to use the rivers to exploit a handy smuggling trade that sidestepped Brazil. The jungle started a mere ten miles back from the fertile swamplands along the coast, and as far as the European adventurers were concerned, the Indians could have it. The climate was not much to brag about either. What with hot, muggy weather and a rainy "season" that had no predictable beginning or end, most Europeans hardly considered the Guianas a garden spot for colonization.

True, Puritans leaving England to escape persecution seriously considered the Guianas as a possible promised land themselves, enticed by Sir Walter Raleigh's description of a "countrie . . . rich, fruitful and blessed with a perpetual spring, where nature brought forth all things in abundance without any great labor or art of man." But the sober-minded pilgrims worried about the inhospitable Spanish and about "hot countries," and they chose to migrate to New England instead. By the time Britain consolidated political control over its share of the Guianas in 1814, it was abundantly clear that the land would not become a colony for smallholder settlers of English stock. Instead the small elite class of English plantation owners at first used Indians, then African slaves, and finally indentured East Indian "servants" to work the cane fields. The sleepy political economy of British Guiana was disturbed only by a nagging border dispute with Spanish-settled Venezuela to the west. Despite the fact that the colonial backwater was located on the continent of South America, it developed the ethnic and cultural diversity of the Caribbean islands it faced to the north; it was, above all, a British colony.

Like most great powers, Britain gave way to the post-World War II drive for independence in its colonies. The vast majority of the former colonial rulers deserted the new nation called Guyana. As in many other parts of the Third World, political activity fell to the agricultural working classes, and in this case they took socialist and communist directions, split along the ethnic cleavages established by the phases of British colonialism. The less radical socialist party, the People's National Congress (PNC), was overwhelmingly dominated by Guyanese of African descent, led by Forbes Burnham. The more radical Marxist-Leninist party, the Peoples Progressive party (PPP), included most of the approximately 54 percent of the population of East Indian descent, led by Cheddi Jagan.

After Guyana attained independence in 1964, the PNC consolidated effective monopoly power through a series of maneuvers, some of them shady, that marginalized the more radical PPP. British and U.S. intelligence agencies were faced with a distasteful choice between the lesser of two evils, and they gave crucial support to PNC leader Forbes Burnham, who established virtual one-party rule through development of a "soft" state socialist regime. The PNC regime developed a bureaucracy built upon patrimonial rewards to the party faithful, and it deployed sometimes ruthless parapolitical and paramilitary cadres to silence the opposition.

Like many Third World governments, the Guyanese state shielded somewhat shady capitalistic ventures of its protégés (including the venerable
Guianas tradition of smuggling), but it did so in the name of a patrimonial
socialism that brought sectors of the economy directly under state control.[12]

The politics and ideology of Jim Jones and his Peoples Temple
dovetailed nicely with the PNC regime. Even Jones's style of charismatic
quasi-religious politics had its kindred spirits among charismatic Caribbean leaders. They spoke a common language that understood money,
power, and the accommodation by the state of "feudal" rulers who swore
political loyalty in return for territorial power. For its part, Peoples Temple
favored the Caribbean Black Christian and reggae cultural styles and the
drama of socialist politics as welcome changes from the White-dominated
culture of the United States. Guyanese politicians wore revolutionary uni-
form "jac-shirts" instead of suits, they called each other "comrade," and
they preferred steel drum bands over symphony. Anyway, Jonestown would
be in the jungle, far away from the desperate urban poverty and
Georgetown's crime problem, sometimes summed up with the apt Caribbean phrase "choke and rob."

The Guyanese government found that the Temple's colonization project
offered diverse benefits. At a material level, the immigrants proposed to
embark on an important experiment of jungle agricultural development. If
successful, the project would provide a working demonstration of how the
jungle could be harnessed to help move Guyana's fragile economy away
from dependence on foreign imports, relieve its balance of payments crisis,
and offer economic opportunities to its immiserated and ever-growing population. At a time when many Guyanese were trying to migrate to the
United States to escape Guyana's poverty and its heavy-handed political
regime, here was a group of mainly Black Americans who saw more opportunity for themselves in Guyana than in the land of opportunity to the
north. Moreover, the Temple would bring much needed hard currency
dollars to fund its project, and it proposed to establish a community along
the lines of "cooperative socialism" that already served as Guyana's model
of development.

In geopolitical terms, the agricultural mission would place settlers on
land that was in the region where Venezuela had reopened its old territorial
claims. The Venezuelan government well understood that such "third flag
nationals" would be hard to displace. As immigrants do for many regimes,
those from Peoples Temple offered Guyana's rulers a peculiar kind of political benefit: totally dependent on the state for their continued existence,
they could be brought to the service of the state as political cadre.

Before independence, British Guiana had a long tradition of harboring criminals who had escaped from the nearby prison in French Guiana. Such hospitality always has had its price. Those who received asylum could be called upon to act as though with autonomy, to do the dirty work of state domination without staining the state itself. In postindependence Guyana, the tradition continued with the "House of Israel," a Black liberation religious sect drawing substantial numbers of tough young men from Guyana's poor urban Black districts. The group was led by one "Rabbi Washington," a man who had jumped $50,000 bail on a corporate blackmail charge in Cleveland, Ohio, and fled to Guyana. The sect did more than hold Pentecostalist services; its members carried out paramilitary actions like strikebreaking in the sugarcane fields worked by East Indians. The U.S. government, ever mindful of its reliance on the Burnham regime to forestall an even more radical regime in Guyana, left Rabbi Washington to his intrigues rather than seek extradition.[13]

Following in the political footsteps of the House of Israel, Peoples Temple established a communal settlement under one of the few diplomatic situations in which a socialist regime enjoyed the tacit support of the U.S. government. The Peoples Temple Agricultural Mission, as it was called formally, was eventually named Jonestown after its founder. Whether the Guyanese government or the egotistical Jones chose the name remains in doubt.

The settlement grew up gradually, on the basis of hard work by early pioneers who labored alongside Amerindians employed to help clear land and establish agricultural activities. A crew of six Temple men, all Whites except one, arrived in the Temple's rented Georgetown house in March 1974. Then Mike Touchette, Lester Matheson, Greg Frost, and Georgetown-based Temple liaison Paula Adams headed out to the Northwest District village of Port Kaituma. There they established a base of operations until land could be cleared and facilities built at the chosen settlement site, some six miles away in the midst of tropical jungle. In June of 1974 Tim Sweeny and Mike Touchette headed to Miami on the Temple's recently acquired fishing boat, the *Cudjoe*, to pick up fourteen additional settlers and a thirty-ton load of supplies and heavy equipment to ship directly up the Kaituma River to Port Kaituma. On this trip they established a strategy for dealing with customs. Stopping for an inspection in Georgetown, they took the customs agent out for drinks beforehand, and received nothing more than a cursory look.

Arriving with the *Cudjoe* was a mixed bag including Jones's most trusted followers and young men who were to be kept out of trouble on the streets of San Francisco. Mike Touchette, his father and mother (Tim Sweeny's sister), and another Touchette son, Albert, left to avoid contact with Mike's sister Micki, who had defected with the "gang of eight" in 1973. Archie

Ijames, the Temple associate minister since Indiana days, and his wife Rosie and daughter Debbie (Mike Touchette's wife) also came as Temple leaders. Others, like agriculturalist Jim Bogue, offered specific skills. Still others, like Jerry Livingston, Jeff Carey, and the most renowned drug reform case, Chris Lewis, came under a sort of delinquency reform program.

From the beginning the settlers understood that Peoples Temple eventually would relocate from California to Guyana. They worked almost entirely at constructing housing, and by the end of 1974 people began living at the agricultural mission site itself. Up through 1977 the community grew only slowly, to about 50 people, probably 90 percent of them under thirty years old. Guided by an esprit de corps based on serving people back in the States, the crew worked long hours preparing for the expected influx. They put up pole-style buildings similar to those used elsewhere in the warm tropical climate of Guyana, and they built a warehouse, communal kitchen, laundry, bathhouse, and other facilties to accommodate a community that at various times was projected to reach 500 or even 700 people.

The U.S. ambassador to Guyana at the time, Max Krebs, visited the outpost in March of 1975, and found a crew about two-thirds White and one-third Black living in two "very primitive combination dormitory-kitchen-storage structures" near "the comparatively sumptuous roofed cage in which was housed a chimpanzee." "The atmosphere was quite relaxed and informal," Krebs recalled. "We talked freely with several of the 'pioneers' about their living conditions (uncomfortable), work (tough), aspirations (high), etc." In May of that year a U.S. embassy official, Wade Matthews, found a "frontier-type, active, new agricultural settlement with perhaps half a dozen rustic buildings and metal-roofed open-sides sheds," along with about a hundred cleared acres planted mostly in cassava, the starchy staple of the South American peasant diet.

With the mission settlement under construction in the jungle, Peoples Temple staff worked to consolidate relations with the government in Guyana in the capital of Georgetown. It was a steamy, sleepy, rundown city, filled with aging frame Victorian buildings inherited from the colonial era facing on streets that constantly flooded from the tropical rains. Initially, Paula Adams returned from Port Kaituma to Georgetown to maintain the Temple's presence, working with Debbie Touchette. Eventually the Temple purchased a comfortable contemporary house over in fashionable Lamaha Gardens, and they outfitted it with the sophisticated radio equipment needed to communicate with San Francisco. Paula Adams was replaced after the Temple's mass migration by another Temple woman, Linda (Sharon) Amos. One of the most zealous of Temple members, Amos marched around the streets of Georgetown, gathering information needed for Temple projects, writing it all in her notebooks, sometimes even soliciting people for donations to the church's agricultural project.

For her part, Paula Adams cultivated an important contact with the Guyanese government. She developed an intimate friendship with Laurence "Bunny" Mann, the Guyanese ambassador to the United States, and she lived in the residence in which Mann stayed on his trips to Georgetown. The two could be seen together at social events held for the diplomatic community in the capital, and when Mann was in Washington, Adams would talk with him in personal ways using Temple radio hookups. Transcripts of the conversations occasionally might end up in the hands of other Guyanese officials whose favor the Temple sought. Temple operatives like Tim Stoen, Linda Amos, Debbie Touchette, and Paula Adams took pains to emphasize Peoples Temple's loyalty to members of the ruling PNC party. And they made sure that Temple members could be found at government rallies. Jones and his staff thus played the diplomatic and governmental networks in Guyana much as they had monitored and influenced members of the Temple and public officials back in the United States.[14]

The U.S. embassy in Georgetown took almost as much interest in Peoples Temple as Peoples Temple did in the government of Guyana. The United States had no official role in establishing the settlement, but embassy officers visited the actual site at a time when it was hardly begun, in July of 1974. Because ambassadors usually favor the good life, the subsequent visit to the remote pioneering settlement by Ambassador Krebs in March of 1975 can only be considered unusual. The trip by Wade Matthews in May of 1976 effectively amounted to monitoring activity, a point underscored by Matthews's description of a "working vacation." Some twenty-five miles away from the Temple settlement stood another of Matthews's touring interests: a "Guyanese National Service training camp . . . which," he reported, "was alleged to have a contingent of Cuban military personnel among the cadre." The man who checked out rumors about Cuban troops based in territory disputed with Venezuela also found it worth his while to "drop in" at the agricultural mission, though the trip was so difficult that it left little time to visit.

Granted that Guyana is a small country with few U.S. citizens, nevertheless, the official U.S. attention bestowed on Peoples Temple suggests that its presence was of significance to U.S. interests. After the Jonestown murders and suicides in 1978, discussion of whether Peoples Temple was monitored or infiltrated by the CIA often focused on fingering this person or that as an "agent." Such searches may miss the forest for the trees. It is known that the CIA had at least one "field installation" in Guyana. In the way that U.S. missions abroad are typically structured, one person occupying a "cover" role serves as the CIA desk officer. However, the activities of the CIA and the rest of the mission are not sharply divided; they form a continuum. Activities undertaken for other reasons may yield "intelligence," and people other than the CIA desk officer may undertake actions at the initiation of the desk officer, without necessarily even knowing their purpose. By the same token, some non-CIA actions of a mission in relation to a host country may not require cloak-and-dagger strategies but nevertheless depend upon secrecy and the use of intermediaries for their success. To a significant degree, especially in a small country like Guyana, the U.S. mission is a unified presence that transcends distinctions between agencies, desks, and individuals.

The U.S. embassy was even willing to capitalize on Peoples Temple's dealings with the Guyanese government, as is revealed by the December 1976 visit to Guyana of Jim Jones, accompanied by his friend, the Black lieutenant governor of California, Mervyn Dymally. With Jimmie Carter just elected president a month before, Democrat Dymally urged a stronger State Department effort toward good relations with Caribbean countries. Dymally and Jones had just come from a session with Guyana Foreign Minister Fred Wills when they met with U.S. embassy consul Richard McCoy. The two visitors took the opportunity to convey to McCoy the Guyanese foreign minister's "fear that USG [U.S. government] would destabilize Guyana like we did Chile." Jones reported a real belief among Guyanese officials that the CIA was trying to act against the Guyanese government, though he recalled his own assurances months earlier from then vice-presidential candidate Walter Mondale that a Carter administration would not interfere in Guyana's internal affairs. A U.S. embassy cable about the visit by Jones and Dymally reported, "Jones intends to pass this message to [Guyana Prime Minister] Burnham today (Dec. 29) when he sees him."

With the California lieutenant governor adding an official sheen to the event, Jim Jones went to meet Prime Minister Forbes Burnham for the first and only time. Dymally and Jones then attended a luncheon hosted by Comrade Deputy Prime Minister Ptolemy A. Reid, one of the Temple's strongest supporters in the government of Guyana.

Whether the embassy official, Richard McCoy, encouraged Jim Jones to pass the "message" to Burnham is not clear; what is clear is that McCoy wanted to make the same point about noninterference to Guyanese officials, and was frustrated in his efforts to do so. The fact that Jones planned to reassure the prime minister about U.S. intentions, McCoy took to be of enough significance to include in a cable to the State Department. Clearly, the embassy could find it useful to maintain intercourse with a group of Americans who held the apparent favor of the Guyanese government and the ear of its highest officials.

What Jones got out of the December 1976 exchanges is another matter. At that date no firm timetable had been set for the long anticipated resettlement of Peoples Temple, but certain events made Temple leaders believe that departure from the United States would come soon. During his stay in Guyana, Jones solidified alliances with the highest echelon Guyanese government ministers. To the press he offered an oblique comment, apparently about U.S.-Guyanese relations, that reversed the valence on the noninterference "message" he had taken to Comrade Prime Minister Forbes Burnham. "Considering the situation today," Jones said, "your government has been very tolerant in allowing Americans to settle here."[15]

### The Tax Crisis

The genesis of the decision to migrate to Guyana did not come from Temple concerns about the defectors' meetings with David Conn, the Treasury agent, and a reporter. Instead, Temple intelligence information on these contacts consolidated already-established Temple fears about government investigations into the legality of the Temple's operations. The revelations from Dennis Banks simply confirmed Jones's oft-stated prophecies of persecution, and proved to the faithful that their plans to flee were not without basis.

In a 1975 resolution concerning the Guyana mission, the Temple board had authorized certain transfers of corporate assets and liabilities "forever" to a corporation established under Guyana law, i.e. beyond the legal reach of U.S. authorities. How to keep "Black people's money" out of the hands of the IRS, that was the problem. The Temple did pay property taxes on buildings not used for religious purposes, but in certain other matters it operated at or beyond the borderlands of religious tax exemption, especially with its "franchised" nursing homes run by members who tithed profits to the Temple, with its communal organization offering "private benefits" to individuals, and with its substantial real estate holdings received under "life-care" agreements and held by a fictitious "front" operation, Valley Enterprises. Jones knew his political activities could cause problems, and he complained about how the government effectively could "bribe the church into silence" by holding out the carrot of tax exemption.

The solution to the problem of the Temple's providing "private benefits" was the Apostolic Corporation, a legal entity created in February of 1976 to hold the communal wealth of Temple members. Temple hopes rested on establishing the tax-exempt status of the corporation as a religious communal group under section 501(d) of the Internal Revenue Service tax code. After a prolonged exchange of letters, the IRS finally denied tax-exempt status on March 4, 1977. The Apostolic Corporation, it held, was not designed to be "internally self-sustaining by virtue of agriculture or other small businesses." The Apostolic Corporation was a legal dodge anyway. As Temple attorney Gene Chaiken put it in a July 1976, memo, the Temple needed to hold the IRS at bay "until we are in the P.L. [Promised Land] and the whole thing is closed down."

There were other tax difficulties, too. In April of 1976 the Temple drew attention to itself with an ill-conceived letter to the IRS. Tim Carter inquired at the San Francisco office as to whether Temple members were operating within the law when they wrote letters concerning various quasi-political issues, such as USSR emigration policies for Jews or support of the police. Tim Stoen feared such a letter might raise controversy at the IRS, and he fired off trailing letters to assure the IRS that "we always . . . in every way . . . comply with the law." But Carter and Stoen had opened Pandora's box.

Stan Long of the IRS answered Stoen by suggesting a meeting "to resolve any questions you may have." This invitation threw the Temple into a true panic. Stoen responded with a long, carefully crafted epistle emphasizing that church members had been set straight on the limits to church lobbying activities, and assuring Long, "A meeting with you will not be necessary." Thus, he tried to lay to rest a sticky issue that could only get stickier if the IRS pursued it. Stoen covered all bets: sometime later in the year, he prepared a Temple memo posing the question of whether Peoples Temple could finance legal defense for its officers without losing its tax exempt status. Stoen's tentative answer was hardly reassuring: yes, the church could pay legal expenses for actions of Temple staff arising from "recognized traditional-type church/ministerial duties." However, he also suggested that if Temple officials broke the law in other than tax-exempt religious activities, they would have to fend for themselves.[16]

It was in the shadow of these ominous signs that Jim Jones visited Guyana in December of 1976. At a time when Marshall Kilduff was only beginning to explore doing an article on Jones, the Temple was proceeding with increased urgency to complete preparations for migration. There could hardly have been more added impetus than a February 1977 memo from Gene Chaiken on the Temple's tax situation. Chaiken held that nursing home profits since 1971 clearly constituted "unrelated business income," and were taxable. Second, whether the communal program begun in 1972 violated the IRS private benefit rule was, at best, an "open question." Then there were the highly visible activities beginning around 1975 that "might be construed as 'political.'" In Chaiken's opinion, the Temple needed contingency plans. The Temple's initial plan amounted to deciding for the first time, five days later, to pay Pastor Jim Jones a salary, in the amount of $30,000.

Adding to the threat of tax problems and a possible newspaper exposé were the rumblings Grace Stoen was making about her son. On the phone with her estranged husband Tim on February 2, 1977, Grace complained that John was in Guyana, beyond her reach. Tim replied, "Well, his dad isn't seeing him either, you know. He's sacrificing." Apparently Grace took Tim's third-person allusion to "his dad" as a reference to Jim Jones; she retorted, "He told me just the last phone call he goes down there quite often." The sensitive young mother could not stomach John's departure for Guyana: "That's what really got me thinking—what a sucker I've been." Then she told Tim what she wanted: "I would like him to come back to San Francisco and live here." The Temple's solution? The father of legal record would go to Guyana to live with John; if Grace decided to press the issue, Guyanese courts surely would side with the resident parent, particularly when he was involved with a group so closely allied with the ruling Peoples National Congress. Three days after the February board meeting, young Temple attorney Tim Stoen was on the plane down to the agricultural mission.

In his first weeks in Guyana Tim Stoen brought his considerable organizational skills to bear on preparing Jonestown for an expected large influx of immigrants. He sketched a crash program for constructing housing to accommodate 500 people, the target planning number for the size of the community. Three dormitories, each projected to hold forty-two people with space that amounted to a six-by-six-foot area per person, would be done in a month. Two similar-sized dorms, one of them for couples, would house fewer people. Because "people can live better in smaller units," Stoen proposed that the remainder of housing consist of twenty-six cabins, twenty-five by eighteen feet, to house twelve people each, to be built on a modular system of construction at the rate of one per week.

As Stoen envisioned it, the round of life for immigrants would be demanding. Work would run from 6:30 A.M. to 6:00 P.M., seven days a week. There would be an hour for lunch, "but try to limit to ½," he suggested. Those who misbehaved would reap the rewards: "If on discipline, do bad work." To top off a day's hard work, people in Jonestown would have to attend a general meeting, a movie, socialist class, children's night, or a farm meeting. The evening sessions were to end at 11:00 P.M., and typically there would be a night of free time, but "sometimes," the plan suggested, "mtg every night."

By the time of Tim Stoen's survey, Jonestown was on its way to becoming a small town, a fact that Peoples Temple staff in San Francisco had difficulty comprehending. Joyce and Charlie Touchette were serving as overall administrators, Joyce in her "mother-figure" role, while foremen Charlie Touchette, Albert Touchette, and Tom Kice directed a crew of ten who worked with six Guyanese nationals to construct buildings. Tom Grubbs and Becky Beikman worked hard at establishing a school. A Temple Amerindian woman, Jan Wilsey, helped coordinate the agricultural work, which still required the contributions of some forty-eight Guyanese nationals in land clearing. Then there was a chicken coop, a piggery, and cassava cultivation, along with a kitchen garden, kitchen, and a laundry facility.[17]

For all the plans and progress, Tim Stoen did not see himself in Jonestown; he would be the attorney based in more hospitable Georgetown. In fact, Stoen did not necessarily see himself continuing to participate in Peoples Temple at all. Years later he would assert the turning point came in 1976 when he was subjected to a "hazing" that other Temple men had undergone, a catharsis session focusing on whether he had homosexual tendencies. Perhaps as a result, perhaps because of the rumblings of tax problems, or for other reasons, in 1976 Stoen began to keep a lower profile within the Temple. On December 18, 1976, fellow Temple attorney Gene Chaiken typed out a memo to Jim Jones, questioning whether Stoen was making extra work for himself at his district attorney job "so he 'has' to stay in the office." "Perhaps Tim could speak to his motivation," Chaiken suggested.

Stoen did speak to his motivation. Before leaving the States in February, he instructed his father in Colorado to open bank accounts in his name at the Continental National Bank in the Denver area. Unfortunately for Stoen, Temple staff intercepted a note from Stoen's father about the accounts a few days after his departure to Guyana. In March Stoen departed from Guyana for Trinidad and Barbados, ostensibly on a trip to explore admission to the Caribbean bar, but he really wanted to investigate joining the bar in New York, Washington, or Colorado, and to rendezvous with a woman friend named "Bev," apparently a fellow attorney from California. The explanation Stoen would give for his unanticipated departure from Guyana? His notes laid out the planned excuse: "I have gone to States—own $; am planning to return to teach at Univ end of Sept; am in love wth a Black woman—must *see* her and handle on own." Ten days later a telegram sent March 25 to Paula Adams in Georgetown announced, "MUST STAY 9 MORE DAYS DUE TIMEHRI [Georgetown's airport] SUNDAY 2 APRIL 1905 BRITISH AIRWAYS TIMOTHY."

Paula Adams and Debbie Touchette sprang into action, informing San Francisco of Stoen's disappearance. The Temple already was having a difficult week of it. Two days before, in the early hours of March 23, Dennis Banks had met with Temple opponent David Conn, taking the information about defectors, a reporter, and a Treasury agent to Peoples Temple at the conclusion of the meeting. The next day, at a Housing Authority commission meeting, Jim Jones collapsed, "from apparent exhaustion," as the

*Chronicle* put it. Jones's aides claimed his dedication to parishioners knew no bounds: he had stayed up all night supervising a drug counseling session. Jones may well have been losing sleep, but the likely reason was Banks's information about a Treasury agent. Jones's "collapse" probably was staged. Even if it was not, it offered a public rationale for dropping out of sight for a while.

That Jim Jones needed time and freedom of movement became even more apparent when he learned within the next two days of Tim Stoen's disappearance. On Monday, March 28, Jones headed for Georgetown. Meanwhile, Stoen had arranged for his San Francisco friend Bill Hunter to send some belongings to his ultimate destination, London, England. Temple members trying to trace Stoen discovered the plan, and generously told Hunter they would take care of the matter. In fact, Sandy Bradshaw and Mike Prokes personally escorted the luggage to London and waited for Stoen. When he finally appeared to claim his bag, Prokes and Bradshaw approached him. "Go ahead, shoot," Stoen said, "You got me." The other two convinced him to phone Jones in Guyana, and Jones talked the recalcitrant lawyer into flying to Guyana for more talks. Stoen took off from Heathrow Airport on April 3.

There is no direct evidence as to why Tim Stoen remained with Peoples Temple at this juncture. Journalists Reiterman and Jacobs suggest that Jones and his staff placed "unrelenting pressure" on him, but they fail to indicate the substance of the pressure, instead citing an idealistic appeal by Jones to Stoen's socialistically egalitarian side. Yet we have to assume that the revelations by Dennis Banks about his meeting with David Conn were discussed. Surely Jones mentioned the matter of the Treasury agent whose ear Conn claimed to have, along with the fact that the Apostolic Corporation tax exemption finally had been rejected by the IRS. Did Stoen then stay because he believed he and other Temple officials were the objects of a Treasury Department investigation? Or was he only biding his time?

Whatever the pressure, whatever Tim Stoen's motives, after he talked with Jim Jones, he was not quite as anxious to depart Guyana. In fact, he threw himself back into the Temple's work with an increased sense of urgency, making notes about salvaging his own character in the eyes of the IRS, preparing Peoples Temple for defense against the presumed IRS investigation, and taking care of PR with Temple friends in the States who might be contacted by the press.[18]

## From California to Jonestown

Plans for migration were stepped up the week of March 28, 1977. Even before Stoen returned to Guyana from England, Jim Jones was busy in the country's capital, as U.S. embassy staff learned from Guyana Foreign Minister Fred Wills. To the Temple's leader, what was happening in California was a rerun of the events that pushed him out of Indiana, but on a much larger scale. So overwhelmed was Jones by the previous week's events that he asked the Guyanese government to approve immigration of 380 members of the Temple on April 3 via two chartered planes. Waving an envelope he claimed contained a check for $500,000, Jones reportedly told Guyana officials that the prospective colonists "represent some of the most skilled and progressive elements of his organization, and as such are most vulnerable to State repression on the part of American authorities."

Elements of the Guyanese government were voicing concerns about Peoples Temple's alliances and the planned large-scale migration, the embassy learned from Wills, but politics prevailed. The Temple's close ally Deputy Prime Minister and Minister of National Economic Development Ptolemy Reid told Vibert Mingo, whose Ministry of Home Affairs handled immigrants, to process the Peoples Temple settlers. By April 6, when the migration was approved, Jones apparently had calmed down a bit, and migration lost some of its urgency. On April 7, Tim Stoen received a phone call from "Comrade Codette" (the Temple's code name for a high ranking government official). Stoen assured him that they were "as loyal to the PNC as to God." The official seemed more interested in coordinating lists of Peoples Temple members settling in Guyana, so that the government "could determine how it . . . might be able to 'use' some of our members," Stoen reported.

Deputy Minister Reid encouraged a migration of from 500 to 800 people. Tim Stoen detailed procedures to help the government expedite processing of immigrants. He seemed to sense the importance of getting and keeping Peoples Temple members out from under U.S. press scrutiny, scribbling to himself, "Do not let people go back [i.e. to the United States] until interest of press has dissipated." Stoen also drafted a rationale for Jones to resign his Housing Commission post, and he set forth a general rationale for the migration of the elderly. Because they could not be justified as contributing a great deal to the mission work, seniors were to be depicted as tired of the general public's racism in the United States.

While migration planning proceeded in Guyana, Peoples Temple in California began poking into the purported Treasury investigation. Based on a statement by former Temple member J. R. Purifoy that he had been contacted by someone representing himself as a Treasury agent, Gene Chaiken and Dick Tropp wrote letters to government agencies alleging that David Conn had represented himself as a Treasury agent. Mike Prokes met with an IRS man under Freedom of Information Act procedures to determine whether the Temple actually was under investigation.[19]

All the issues were laid on the table in day and night meetings held at the Temple's Lamaha Garden house in Georgetown beginning April 27, 1977. The night before Jim Jones offered up "psychic" revelations, while Tim Stoen dutifully noted them. During the "seance," journalist Marshall Kilduff's name surfaced; he was "not acting alone," Jones discerned. "I think we are up against a major conspiracy." Harriet Tropp, Gene Chaiken, and others met with Jones and Stoen the next day. By that time the issues before the group were manifold, even beyond the tax and reporters' investigations. Temple staff had followed the difficulties of the Unification Church since at least the fall of 1975, and they knew of the temporary conservatorships by which outside relatives sometimes obtained custody over "brainwashed" adult sect members. They feared the same possibilities for Temple members, notably Maria, the daughter of Steve Katsaris.

Gene Chaiken also reported on Grace Stoen's actions against her estranged husband. Grace had filed for divorce and custody of John Victor shortly after Tim left for Guyana. Eventually, Chaiken reasoned, Grace would learn, if she had not already learned, that Tim "plans to stay [in Guyana] for an extended period." This strategy would make Grace's claim that Peoples Temple held her child irrelevant.

Tim Stoen wrote out a draft statement. It declared himself the legal father, and went on to argue that Grace was an unfit mother who abandoned the child, and "ran off with another man." Probably for the benefit of Guyana's socialist government, the statement noted that Grace was "a dangerous reactionary who has indicated she would work with the Central Intelligence Agency to 'make things rough' for any socialist country." To underscore his de facto custody, Tim Stoen cited a postcard apparently sent earlier to Gene Chaiken in California: "My son, John Victor, is with me and doing *great*. . . . He is receiving lots of love and affection, and is happy as a lark."

On May 5, at the conclusion of the Lamaha Gardens meeting, the mostly White covey of Temple leaders—Jim Jones, Marceline Jones, Tim Stoen, Carolyn Layton, Johnny Moss Jones, Terry Buford, Gene Chaiken, and Harriet Tropp—flew to the island of Grenada to explore the possibilities of establishing an alternative Caribbean settlement location there, but the main thrust was toward defense of the Temple in the States and preparation for migrating to Guyana. During the legal conference, Stoen drafted yet another list, indicating himself as in charge of "central coordination." He laid out plans to counter the investigation of "alleged tax fraud" and the receipt by himself and Carolyn Layton of properties from Temple members without paying any gift or trust taxes. He also plotted the posture for Temple members to take. They were to go around ranting, "I'm mad, I'm mad. If weren't for JT [Jonestown] to give me a chance to build, I don't know what I would do." But Stoen did not want matters taken too far; he noted a "P.S. to Terri's letter," a caution to the Temple's enforcer, Chris Lewis: "We don't want you to resolve the problem with our people [i.e. defectors] that we've had. You have far more important things to do, and some of them, if confronted beforehand, might try to sabotage the move."

Stoen also pondered the migration itself. Apparently the number of people interested in coming was on the increase, for he puzzled over strategies to bring over 900 people in two quick trips, versus spreading the migration out at a rate of 100 per month through February 1, 1978. "Should we move our people now as fast as can be organized?" Stoen jotted in his notes, "Get people on fixed incomes 1st." At another juncture, he suggested that children and children's workers be brought, and then noted, "People should be told to come abruptly."

Stoen saw disadvantages to a rapid exodus. The Temple would lose money by trying to sell real estate too quickly in the United States. It might precipitate an international incident detrimental to Guyana by "Inciting Ty [Treasury] people/military frameup." On the other hand, if Temple staff dawdled too long, the Treasury Department might freeze Temple assets in the United States. Moreover, "bad PR" would surface, and this could result in authorities, relatives, and reporters acting to "discourage *workers* from coming." Worse, Jim Jones himself might be arrested in the United States. If Jones was situated permanently in Guyana, he would act as a beacon drawing others to migrate, and he would be able to "cushion shock of immigrants."

In practice the Temple followed a mixed strategy. After Stoen's arrival in February, there was a steady trickle of migrants, most of them young, all capable of working to build the community. Many who came were held to be in danger of getting into trouble in the States, and *Peoples Forum* trumpeted the success of the Guyana mission in reforming the criminal element. Mike Touchette seconded the argument about an almost blissful socialist work communion. "We really could turn kids around," he claimed. "They couldn't get away with the shit down here [in Guyana] they could when they came out of Watts, Fillmore and like that."[20]

In San Francisco migration plans proceeded apace. Jean Brown presided over a "Guyana coordinating committee." Jim Randolph worked feverishly on organizing the massive shipment of materials to Guyana, everything from bed sheets to be sold on the black market and dye for the forty-six-year-old Jim Jones's graying hair to spare chainsaw parts and 10,000 toothbrushes. Paula Adams and Mary Ann Casanova coordinated receiving shipments on the Guyana end. Broadcasting equipment, boxes of rummaged clothing materials, chalkboard paint, agricultural implements—the material goods to supply an entire town were sent wholesale. In 1975 the

Guyanese government had given the Temple permission to bring two shot-guns, "for use on the farm." Somewhere amidst the huge crates of goods or on the ship *Cudjo* went some thirty pistols, shotguns and rifles procured by Temple members in the United States. In Georgetown, Temple women would flirt with customs agents while "cripples" in wheelchairs rolled by with guns in their duffle bags.

The preparations for migration of followers were as involved as the shipping of equipment and goods. People took their smallpox and yellow fever shots. Bringing to bear social work skills, Temple staff drew up a roster indicating whether a person's change of address had been filed, what had been done with pets, whether relatives had been notified, house keys transferred—all the host of details required to get each person ready with a "go file" that contained passport, birth certificate, immigration forms, Temple authorization forms required for both adults and children, and if required, a guardianship letter. From all appearances, Temple staff tried to operate with considerable care in handling legal and bureaucratic aspects of the migration.

In May Jim Jones returned to the United States to help prepare for the mass migration. His discussions in Cuba with Huey Newton some four months behind him, Jones turned away from Newton's revolutionary sui-cide of struggle against the state, a path already seemingly exhausted by the Black Panthers, the Symbionese Liberation Army, and others. Nor could he countenance personal suicide. While back in San Francisco, he man-aged to work into his schedule an appearance with other community lead-ers at Golden Gate Bridge. From the heights where so many have jumped to their deaths into the bay, Jones reaffirmed life over death from personal despair. Facing tax investigations and bad publicity, he chose instead an-other, symbolic, "suicide": departing Babylon. The "death" of the individ-ual's life in the world of the capitalist United States made possible redemption in a world where a socialist community could be built. Rebirth awaited in the Promised Land.

Jones departed San Francisco for the last time, apparently on June 17, well before the appearance of the *New West* article. He left behind a series of tape-recorded interjections ("I need Johnny on '5'"), to be played over the Temple public address system, so that it would seem that he was still in San Francisco, just too busy with church affairs to perform public duties. In July, with the *New West* article's appearance, the mass exodus began in earnest. The Temple bought airline tickets for some 137 of the faithful to leave California that month. An even larger number, 348, departed during August, when the press was pumping out *New West* spinoff stories. By September the migration of Peoples Temple as an entity was effectively completed; remaining in San Francisco were the staff required to take care of business, people who held jobs with good salaries, and others who either had not made the final decision to migrate, or who found themselves held up by the seemingly endless bureaucratic details.

In at least one conservatorship case, a senior citizen named Washington Sanders was complaining to his nephew about Temple communal life in the United States. Temple staff held back on sending the man. A woman who wanted to go kept delaying her departure in hopes of getting her delinquent son to come along before he landed back in jail. But the young man "hated the church," and Jean Brown told the woman that if her son "didn't like our meetings here, he wouldn't like them there." Such incidents suggest that people were actively encouraged but hardly forced to go to Guyana. To the contrary, they needed to take personal initiative to assure they would be among the emigrants.

Even with all the negative publicity, the Temple continued a steady flow of migration. Some twenty people per month left from September through February of 1978, and in March a larger contingent of fifty-four embarked. When the Concerned Relatives mounted a new PR campaign against Peoples Temple beginning in the spring of 1978, the trickle of migrants still continued, with slightly more than ten people a month leaving the United States through October of 1978. People in the Temple followed the negative news stories closely. When they were faced with choosing to understand events from the viewpoint of Peoples Temple or its detractors, many still chose to see things the Temple's way, even with their purportedly authoritarian leader gone to an isolated jungle town thousands of miles away.[21]

### Religious Migration and Jonestown

Religious migration resulting from cultural conflict is not a new phenomenon, nor, for marginal religious groups, is it an unreasoned choice. For Peoples Temple, the idea lay deeply embedded in its claim to the historical legacy of Marcus Garvey and Father Divine, of Black redemption through migration to a promised land. Jones long had promoted an apocalyptic vision of U.S. history. His followers shared his pessimism about the United States; many of them had dreamed the dreams of Black redemption in a promised land before Jim Jones was ever born. For them, Jones became the liturgical spokesman who could voice a collective despair about racial and class justice under capitalism in the United States. To his followers, Jones's faults looked hardly any worse than those of his establishment peers, and at least he stood, as he kept emphasizing, "for principle."

Ever since the defection of the "gang of eight" in 1973, Jones and his staff had prepared for the day when Temple life in the United States would end.

As they became aware in 1976 that their tax practices might be scrutinized, they proceeded with a new sense of their preparations' wisdom. Concrete planning for departure was actually carried out only when events came to a head during the week of March 21, 1977, with the rejection of the Apostolic Corporation's application for tax exemption and the news from Dennis Banks about David Conn's contacts with defectors and a Treasury agent. True, Jones and his inner circle mistakenly connected reporter Kilduff with Conn and the defectors, but it could not have been concern about bad publicity alone that propelled migration plans, for Temple leaders already were well aware of Kilduff's interests before the week of March 21, and they had not initiated an exodus because of them.

The tax and Treasury problems were another matter altogether. Beginning the week of March 21, first on an emergency basis, then in a more deliberate manner, Temple staff mapped out the logistics of collective migration, before their collective assets (and with them, the dreams of migration) could be seized by the IRS—a government entity known by Peoples Temple staff for its hostility toward new religious groups like the Unification Church. In the view of the Temple's leadership, the capacity of the Temple to exist as a group was in serious jeopardy in the United States. They chose to err on the margin of safety by planning an emigration, rather than risk losing all Temple members had worked toward for so many years simply to remain for another six months in the land they had come to hate.[22]

The circumstances under which Peoples Temple departed for Guyana are no doubt unique, yet there are striking historical parallels. Insofar as dynamics of religious conflict and migration recur, I argue that the general social dynamics, rather than the unique features of Peoples Temple or any "contagious paranoia" of Jim Jones, explain the group's departure.

A general theory of religious migration suggests that a deviant and "persecuted" religious group may attempt to solve the problem of its persistence through collective migration, an act that breaks any conflicting social ties and achieves a heightened sense of commitment among the faithful who embark on the journey. The general tendencies of religious migration thus can be anticipated by the structure of the collective action.

Some of the most significant events of religious development have taken place through collective migration. The quest of the Jews under Moses, the European Crusades of the Middle Ages, the Cistercian monastic settlement of Eastern Europe—all underscore the way in which religious migration is bound up in broader processes of history. The archetypal case was North America, settled by Puritans, Quakers, French Huguenots, and a host of other groups that migrated in search of the freedom to practice their religion without being subjected to persecution.

Many religious groups migrated from Europe to North America or across North America under circumstances like those faced by Peoples Temple. The Puritans, Swedish Janssonists, the German Lutherans who came to Missouri, the Mormons—to name a few—all experienced religious conflict over their transgressions of established sacred values. Just as the primitive Christian Church became the sword that cut through the ancient world, rearranging its social relationships, in post-Reformation Europe, and in North America, religious migration became an equally decisive sword. In the midst of legal controversies, heated charges of heresy, and struggles among families over the allegiances of converts, a sect's faithful might use migration to escape the theological and mundane controversies that boiled up around them, at the same time consolidating a community of people who cast their lot with the hope of a new world.

It was hardly unusual for Protestant groups migrating to North America to leave Europe amidst storms of controversy. Some of their leaders were accused of sexual seduction, of proclaiming themselves God, even of causing insanity among their followers. Others used deceit and treachery to help faithful followers escape from the clutches of their families, while European newspapers bemoaned the loss of anyone, "misled by fantasy," who would "surrender himself to the martyrdom." The "martyrs" who forsook the comforts of Europe in turn founded the pioneering colonies of a New Jerusalem.

For all those who actually embarked on such journeys, the chances of ever returning to the former homeland were marginal. Such an act of apostasy brought judgments of personal dishonor from their former comrades, and required traveling a considerable distance. Only the very few individuals with strong personal fortitude and resourcefulness, and perhaps some independent financial means, were likely to reach the dramatic point of turning their backs on their communities and returning home. More likely was the choice of drifting away from the group to establish a nearby individual homestead.

The case of Peoples Temple is not so different from previous religious migrations. In the Temple, as with others, charges of "heresy," difficulties with the law, and interests in building solidarity inspired flight to a Zion in the wilderness. Against the others, as against the Temple, detractors brought charges of sexual abuses, property rip-offs, kidnapping, and the use of ungentle persuasion that played upon naive victims of false prophets. Many members of Peoples Temple, like religious migrants of other sects, counted themselves lucky at falling in with a true avatar, and they relished the victories of escape from the clutching hands of relatives they regarded as perhaps sincere but spiritually dead. Nor did controversial and putatively disreputable prophetic origins always spell doom for long-term prospects. In fact, the reverse was sometimes true: the more that outsiders might raise doubts about the authenticity of the Book of Mormon given to Joseph Smith by angels in 1830, the more conviction the Latter-day Saints mustered to defend him. Today, whatever the historical facts concerning Smith, his legacy is a social fact of no small magnitude.

Both the Mormons and Peoples Temple are notable for the persistence of their opponents. Most migrating religious groups succeed in leaving controversy behind; their success or failure in the promised land typically depends on how well they shift from the charismatic phase of migration under the leadership of a prophet to the more routine everyday demands of pioneer life. But Mormons faced nagging conflict with opponents because they migrated by land, rather than sea, and they could not easily stake out a territory unclaimed by previous pioneers. The followers of Joseph Smith seemed to provoke outrage wherever they fled after having been hounded out of their previous encampments. Their reputation traveled like a brushfire that swept around their own journeys, from New York to Ohio, to Missouri, back to Illinois, whence they fled to their final Zion around the Great Salt Lake, to become what historian Thomas O'Dea called a "near-nation."[23]

Peoples Temple fled not by land but over the sea, and by a method unavailable to earlier religious migrants—air travel. Their exodus occurred in an era when the world had become a smaller place by virtue of the speed of travel and communication and the more routinized diplomatic relations among governments. Earlier opponents of religious migrants from Europe were hardly prepared to venture on some wild chase to a foreign land, no matter how much they missed their loved ones. But the flight time on Pan American airlines from New York to Guyana is a matter of hours. No matter how far from civilization Peoples Temple went, in the modern era their detractors were not far behind.

# 10

# The Concerned Relatives, the "Concentration Camp," and the "Conspiracy"

In a venture on the scale of Jonestown, founded through a mass exodus of mostly city dwellers, the material problems could be expected to be significant. But two things are certain: first, whether or not Jonestown ever would have succeeded, the exodus brought to Guyana a group of people who possessed "appropriate technology" for pioneering on an industrial scale in the Third World. Jonestown catalyzed the energies of people who cleared land, planted crops, built buildings, and sheltered and clothed and fed a community of nearly a thousand people, all in the kind of remote jungle terrain where similar attempts had ground to a halt much sooner.

Second, the causes of the murders and mass suicide in November of 1978 had nothing to do with material problems per se. Instead, the carnage has to be understood as a product of the conflict that emerged between Peoples Temple and the people who came to call themselves the "Concerned Relatives." That struggle quickly overshadowed daily life in Jonestown, and ironically, it intensified the very conditions—maintenance of a facade, infringement of individual liberties, and discipline—that the Temple's opponents declaimed.

Lines of religious conflict became drawn gradually. Jim Jones had set forth a stark messianic vision in California as part of an unrelenting effort to ferret out backsliders. The approach hounded out many (though not all) people of lukewarm commitment, but it also alienated certain members of the inner circle, individuals who possessed the "secrets" of the organizaton. In part because "true believers" who defected became the objects of intimidations they once had helped promote, their zealousness sometimes underwent a phase shift from advancing "the Cause" to destroying it. Most notable was Jeannie Mills, who seems to have psychologically compensated for her own earlier role in Peoples Temple through a reaction formation in which the cause of exposing Jim Jones became every bit as compelling as "the Cause" was to its members. Her efforts are emblematic

210

of how a wider group of former members became, as one reporter observed, "fanatical" in their opposition. In Jeannie Mills's vision, the threat of Jim Jones reached grandiose proportions that ultimately threatened the entire nation. "What recourse would we have," she inquired, "if he became president?"[1]

### The Turning of Timothy Stoen

The hinge upon which the history of Peoples Temple turned was Tim Stoen. So long as he remained in Guyana, the Temple likely would win custody of his legal son, John Victor, in the courts of its adopted homeland. But Tim Stoen departed Guyana in June of 1977, leaving his son behind in Jonestown. The aide once closest to Jim Jones eventually became one of his most bitter enemies, and the struggle for the "child-god" became a powerful symbol of the conflict between Peoples Temple and its opponents.

For all the struggle over John Stoen, Tim Stoen's motives in leaving Jonestown and joining the opposition remain opaque to adequate understanding. Given that Stoen left without young John, any commitment he had to custody at that time could not have been so strong as his own desire to leave. Probably Stoen was less than enchanted with settling into a poor, backwater Third World country as the lawyer for a group that was fleeing legal problems in the United States. Still, when Jim Jones talked him into staying in March of 1977, the young lawyer threw himself into dealing with threats posed to Peoples Temple by the Treasury Department and the press. Stoen's notes indicate a pressing concern for his own legal problems in operating trusts for real estate, and for a while he remained in Guyana, with Peoples Temple, and beyond the prosecutor's reach. But other factors pulled him away. Perhaps, as Stoen later held, he resented a 1976 public confrontation on the subject of homosexuality. Whatever the specifics, answers to a Role Construct Repertory test in Tim's notes designated Jim as a "threatening person." Perhaps Stoen also saw the possibility of distancing himself from the Temple's tax situation before any legal actions took place. If the threats to the Temple in the States were serious, his good name would suffer by continued association. If he bailed out, he still might salvage his reputation.

Finally, there was the question of whether Stoen any longer could claim an inside position in the Temple's leadership. While he was in Guyana, Temple members went through his briefcase one day and found notes written in 1961, when he had gone to East Berlin during a high school Rotary Club travel fellowship. The young American student had been taken into East German police custody for photographing the Berlin wall, and afterwards, he jotted out thoughts about "a police state."

The notes discovered at Jonestown were the last tumbler falling in place in a lock that opened the door to a revised perception of Tim Stoen. Perhaps his years of "fronting" Peoples Temple to conservative audiences had come too naturally. Perhaps he was a CIA agent. Though he was an asset for dealing with Grace Stoen concerning John's custody, the lawyer never again could claim quite the trust he once had.

The question of commitment was at hand. Tim Stoen wrote to himself, "In 6 months I can turn image around. Less ideological." On Sunday, June 12, 1977, he slipped out of the Temple's Lamaha Gardens house at 4:30 A.M., leaving a message that he was off on business and would be back soon. He then caught the Pan Am flight to Port of Spain and New York, and disappeared.[2]

Whether Stoen intended to return after a six-week vacation, as he later asserted, is unclear. He did nothing to confront Jim Jones, but events caught up with him. As Stoen recalled, "In the first part of July I met with my estranged wife, Grace, and others who had left Peoples Temple." They laid out their case against Peoples Temple, and apparently Tim underwent a conversion experience: "I realized the charges were substantially true," he recounted, "and that I could no longer defend Peoples Temple or Jim Jones."

On Wednesday, July 13, at his brother's house in Colorado, Tim Stoen was served notice of Grace's legal actions for dissolution of the marriage and custody of John Stoen. The same day, someone telephoned Peoples Temple in Tim's name. "He is working for you desperately," the caller reported. "He is being watched and cannot make direct contact. He unfortunately is the only one that can help you at this stage. . . . He wanted you to know that if you go down that he will go down with you."

Later Grace Stoen reported that her husband "indicated that he believed that custody should be split between the Temple and myself." Tim Stoen did not want any custody rights, but he offered to try to get John Victor back to live with Grace for six months a year. If he failed to negotiate such an arrangement, he would go to Guyana to institute legal proceedings. Apparently Stoen hoped to serve only as a mediator. Actually siding with the opposition would just create more trouble for him. Defection was one thing; becoming a traitor, quite another.

Once again Tim Stoen was under pressure, but this time not from Peoples Temple. In the *New West* stories that then came crashing into the public arena, comments that associated him with the "good works" of a group under a barrage of bad publicity certainly would not contribute to turning his image around. The lawyer next surfaced for press interviews in Ukiah the weekend of August 20. He took great offense at the *New West* attacks on himself and the Temple, declaring, "It is essential that I clear my name." In particular, he denied that he was "afraid" of Jim Jones. "I want to dispel that allegation," Stoen told the press. He announced that he would take the bar in New York in order to "form a national law firm to help people who are prosecuted, on some pretext, for their religious beliefs."

The Temple could not afford the departure of a man who held so many of its secrets, but just as Tim Stoen knew the Temple's secrets, key defectors knew the secrets of Tim Stoen. In fact, the *New West* article mentioned "irregularities" in real estate transactions involving the lawyer. Grace, for one, claimed she had been "pressured" by her husband to sign a deed long before it was notarized. Tim Stoen would invite revenge by the Temple if he sided with its opponents, but he could refuse to cooperate with the opponents only at a certain risk.

The possibilities became abundantly clear when the San Francisco *Examiner* headlined a story, "Deputy DA tied to Temple deal." A former convict turned private eye, Joe Mazor, had followed Peoples Temple since late 1976, when a government detective friend had drawn him into checking out accusations against Jim Jones by a Black minister. Mazor discovered, "Hey, this guy is not the Pope." Still, there was no solid case either. After the *New West* article, Mazor hooked up with Temple defectors, and turned over to the California attorney general a tape recording with a voice that sounded like Stoen's discussing a controversial Temple real estate transaction. One August day a district attorney investigator spotted Stoen back in the city. "He was told that we'd like to talk to him, and he indicated that he'd have to talk to his attorney." The other shoe dropped on August 30, 1977, when Stoen was named along with other Temple officials in a real estate fraud and false imprisonment suit filed by none other than Al and Jeannie Mills. The Millses did a great deal to oppose Peoples Temple in the next year and a half, but they let the suit sit like an unexploded bomb.

Pending legal prosecution could only encourage Tim Stoen in a direction that reinforced his desire to turn his image around. The more Stoen worked to counter the Temple, the more he could cleanse himself of the sins of complicity, and the less likely he was to be prosecuted for its crimes. Though he left Peoples Temple in June hoping to be a mediator, Stoen eventually cast his lot with the opponents.[3]

### Investigations, "Conspiracy," and Custody

By the time the Millses filed suit against Peoples Temple and Tim Stoen, the *New West* story had led to a spate of investigations of Peoples Temple. But bureaucratic wheels turn slowly, when they turn at all. Frustrated defectors began to focus on a central issue of the wider anticult movement:

whether people in Jonestown were being held against their will. For their part, Peoples Temple staff began to piece together the puzzle of how the blitz of media and government inquiries had fallen into place so neatly.

Government investigations of Peoples Temple seemed to feed on one another as bureaucrats took up Kilduff and Tracy's call for official inquiries. Opponents like Ross Case repeated allegations about Temple involvement in murder. District Attorney Joe Freitas ordered an investigation of his one-time allies. The California secretary of state looked into abuses by notary publics. California's Department of Health pursued possible nursing home scandals. And the superintendent of San Francisco's schools ordered an investigation of whether Peoples Temple students attended a special school without going through proper admission procedures.

In at least one case bureaucrats were reluctant to waste resources on a "big-name political-type" group, but less tainted investigations came up with little in the way of a "smoking gun," and the scandalous charges by Temple opponents never translated into any significant criminal prosecution. A report to District Attorney Freitas summed up the situation. If substantiated, abuses by Temple notary publics would amount to misdemeanors. The most damning charges lacked credible evidence. "Obviously," the report added, after surveying the donations of property and the public punishments of children with legal consent of their parents or guardians, "nothing in this memorandum should be read as approving of the practices of Peoples Temple, many of which are at least unsavory, and raise substantial moral and non-criminal legal questions."

Temple staff believed more was going on than public investigations, and it turned out they were correct. They wrote various government agencies, asking whether the Temple was under investigation. One reply, from the U.S. Treasury Department's Customs Service, denied "any activity in this Region of the Customs Service which would be in the nature of a 'fishing expedition.'" At best, the statement was not the whole truth. Unknown to Temple staff, the "Treasury agent" whom Dennis Banks had told them about in March of 1977 was a Customs agent. The opponents had told him that approximately 170 firearms, once stored in Ukiah, had been sent to San Francisco's Peoples Temple, and might be smuggled into Guyana. Customs officials passed the allegations on to other government agencies: the State Department, the Secret Service, and the FBI. Jeannie Mills continued to report to the Customs agent. In early August, after she drove past Peoples Temple in San Francisco and saw workers loading a flatbed truck with crates for Guyana, she called the agent and told him she believed the crates might contain weapons or unreported currency.

On August 19, seven Customs officials swooped down on cargo sitting at a Miami dock. They searched one of ninety Temple crates about to be loaded on the S.S. *Atlantic Comet*, but found nothing. Temple attorney Charles Garry shot off a letter on October 3 to argue that Customs would not take the time of seven agents without some sort of "prior information." The reply from Customs indicated that "examinations . . . are conducted on a routine basis," but it added, "any information which might have prompted an examination would be of the type which would be exempt from disclosure . . . to your clients."

Peoples Temple soon learned through its own channels that the search was not "routine." The Customs Service informed the International Police organization, Interpol, of its activities, and Interpol in turn shared its information with Guyana police. Guyanese Police Chief C. A. ("Skip") Roberts then reportedly showed a copy of an Interpol report to either Paula Adams or Carolyn Layton. The report revealed much to the Temple. It confirmed Dennis Banks's statement that defectors had met with a government agent, and it indicated that they had accused the Temple of smuggling weapons and money to Guyana. But the Interpol report did not stop there. It alluded to use of secret codes in Temple radio traffic between San Francisco and Guyana, thus showing that Temple communications were being monitored. Jim Jones was even made out as a provocateur who had been "seen throwing tear gas into a demonstration" in Guyana in 1975. Opponents of the Temple apparently were not above the sort of embellishment Jones practiced in his sermons, even in making allegations to government agents.

With the Interpol report, Temple staff pieced together a picture of surveillance on Peoples Temple, serious and purely fabricated allegations against it, and contacts among several U.S. government agencies. All of the charges, moreover, were in the hands of the Guyanese govenment.[4]

By the fall of 1977 any psychological tendency toward paranoia in Jim Jones was nurtured by valid fears. Jones *was* the object of a network of opposition that included defectors, reporters, and government agencies. Whether the opposition could be termed a "conspiracy" minces words. News of "nefarious acts" percolated through investigatory offices from the San Francisco Police Department to the Federal Communications Commission. To be sure, government agencies on the whole seem simply to have pursued their mandates, sometimes not so effectively, sometimes on the basis of false leads. On the other hand, certain defectors and key reporters with extrajournalistic commitments to family, friends, or to latent political agendas, did "conspire": they worked together and in secrecy to plan actions against Peoples Temple, and they effectively drew the press and government agencies to their side.[5]

Though Temple opponents did not get far with the exposé-driven governmental investigations of Peoples Temple, they did succeed in arousing relatives and the general public to a powerful and emotional issue: whether people had been taken to Jonestown against their will, and, in the case of children, without permission of parents or guardians. Newspapers portrayed the exodus as an exercise of abduction. Al and Jeannie Mills employed private investigator Joe Mazor to determine where two children once in the Millses' custody had gone, only to have Temple attorney Charles Garry point the private eye in the direction of San Francisco's mission district, where the children were living with their natural mother.

Some families of Temple members had granted legal permission for children to go, but later argued they were duped by claims that the trip was to last only two weeks. The San Francisco district attorney investigated the charges, and found, "in no case in which we had the name of such a child was the allegation borne out." Still, with the opportunistic entrepreneurial streak of a man who once served prison time for check fraud, Joe Mazor saw a gold mine of business in the dissatisfactions of relatives, and in the fall of 1977 he lined up clients by promising to get their loved ones back from Guyana, by hook or crook.

Mazor telephoned U.S. embassy consul Richard McCoy in Georgetown. The investigator said he had court orders for seven children whose parents initially had allowed them to go to Jonestown but now wanted them back, and he requested "welfare-and-whereabouts" checks on twelve people. Around the same time, in Jonestown, thirty-four-year-old Caroline Looman received a message that her mother was seriously ill; then a plane ticket came in the mail. But when Looman called her mother, she found her in reasonably good health. The U.S. embassy reported, "Family concerned that Caroline being kept against her will and that she is afraid of reaction of group should she leave." McCoy traveled out to Jonestown to talk to people who were objects of stateside concern. There he took Caroline Looman aside and asked a series of questions. Are you being ill-treated? Do you wish to leave? Are you being held against your will? No, she told him.

Jim Jones resented the U.S. government's entry into the community, but in the coming year McCoy or other embassy staff were to conduct four more visits to Jonestown. They even arranged with Guyanese officials in the nearby towns of Port Kaituma and Matthews Ridge to keep an eye on Jonestown and offer onward transportation to Georgetown for any defector.

In three separate visits McCoy interviewed seventy-five people, each time looking for physical signs that they had been mistreated, each time trying to assure privacy in his interviews, each time meeting refusals of his offers to assist in leaving Jonestown in an Guyanese government vehicle to Port Kaituma, then on to the United States. He recognized that an "attempt might have been made to stage a favorable scenario" for his visits, but he noted that the five to six hundred residents he saw "appeared adequately fed, and expressed satisfaction with their lives." He never could determine beyond doubt that people were not being held against their will, but he believed that someone who truly wanted to depart, especially a young adult, could fade into the jungle, and make for Port Kaituma.

Perhaps this belief was underscored by an event during McCoy's first visit. En route to Jonestown, he encountered a young man named Leon Broussard who had fled the agricultural mission and headed for Matthews Ridge. Broussard had cuts on his shoulder that came from Temple punishment, he had told a Guyanese official. But to McCoy, he denied mistreatment, instead claiming that he had been working with heavy lumber. Still, Broussard wanted to go back to the United States. McCoy raised the issue with Jim Jones later in the day, and the leader of Jonestown agreed to pay Broussard's airfare. The incident failed to settle reports to the embassy about brutality, but it did show two things: first, it was possible for a young man to "escape"; second, in the only case in which someone actually stated to an embassy official a desire to leave Guyana, Jones cooperated in effecting the repatriation.[6]

### The Case of the "Child-God"

Broussard was not aligned with the Temple's opponents, and his departure represented no defeat for Jonestown, but other people at Jonestown became caught up in the unfolding conflict. The central case was John Victor Stoen's. In August 1977 Grace Stoen and her lawyer, Jeffrey Haas, learned from Charles Garry that Jim Jones claimed the right to custody of the boy. Then on August 26 a California court preliminary ruling granted custody to Grace. By August 30, Haas was en route to Guyana with the court order and claims that Tim Stoen had withdrawn his permission for John to stay with Peoples Temple.

Haas and a Guyanese court marshal traveled to Jonestown September 6 to serve the summons for Jim Jones to appear in court with the Stoen boy, but Jonestown residents said their leader was not around. Then Temple members ripped down summons notices Haas posted on three buildings, tore them up, and tossed them into the marshal's vehicle. The Guyanese Supreme Court judge hearing the case was outraged to learn of the actions, and he issued an arrest order to take John Victor Stoen into custody, and an order for Jones to appear and show why he should not be judged in contempt.

Some people at Jonestown already had been up four days and nights when the news came that John Victor Stoen and Jim Jones might be taken away by police. The arrest and contempt orders met pitched resistance. Jones claimed to his son Stephan that he had been shot at, and the youth went charging out into the bush to ward off attackers. A dramaturgical state of siege followed. Brandishing hoes, picks, and other garden tools, the inhabitants of Jonestown—seniors, children, and the rest—confronted the perimeter of a green velvet jungle canopy that seemed to shadow unknown alien forces.

In the months just before the September crisis, Jim Jones had seemed happy and involved, touring the grounds, taking an interest in the housing construction, people's problems, the life of the community. Now he could not spit out his rage quickly enough. Like other modern communal settlements, Jonestown was wired for sound. On the day Jones heard of the arrest order, September 10, he worked back and forth between the radio to San Francisco and the loudspeakers to his followers in Jonestown. Jones's long laid plans to escape the clutches of opponents in the United States symbolically shattered, his understanding of revolutionary suicide took a new turn. Following the logic of Huey Newton's book, Jones asserted that he had already died to the cause: "It's been twenty-five years I've lived as a revolutionary suicide." Now Jones said he did not care whether he died the next day. He said that he and the assembled plebiscite of Jonestown had decided the point at which living for "principle" would become transformed into dying for "principle." "I related to Grace, and out of that came a son," Jones recounted. "That's part of the deal. The way to get to Jim Jones is through his son. They think that will suck me back or cause me to die before I'll give him up. And that's what we'll do, we'll die." The crowd's support could be heard all the way back in San Francisco.

Temple staff at the radio in San Francisco agreed that it would be bad to set a "precedent . . . of giving anyone back." In the face of all the negative publicity, there might be a flood of such efforts. Jones himself half feared that the arrest order was part of some larger *putsch*. He knew that not all Guyanese officials looked favorably on Peoples Temple. Maybe the people of Jonestown should seek collective asylum in another country, but Jones insisted, "We will not move separately."

In San Franciso Marceline sobbed over the radio to her husband, "I know all about the beautiful child-god, and I know why he was conceived, and I was very much involved with it. I know the pain that you've suffered, and as painful as it would be for me not to see any of you again, I would not ask you to change your stand." Meanwhile, stateside Temple staffers worked feverishly to defuse the crisis. Finally, outside Chicago, they tracked down the wife of their good friend Guyanese Deputy Prime Minister Ptolemy Reid, and they received assurances that the Guyanese would not invade Jonestown to get Jones. The crisis abated.

In Georgetown the legal process seemed to stall. On September 17 the U.S. embassy sent a note to the foreign minister of Guyana, observing that the arrest order of a week earlier had not been signed, "apparently" because of interference by Guyanese authorities (later alleged by Temple opponents to be Dr. Ptolemy Reid). The United States was not taking sides in the case, but it expected due process in Guyana courts for U.S. citizens. Foreign Minister Wills replied that Guyana would enforce its court orders, but he also reported that Jones had retained internationally known Guyanese attorney Sir Lionel Luckhoo, and Luckhoo was challenging the legality of the summons. The following Friday Luckhoo informed the embassy that Grace Stoen's lawyer had made substantial mistakes in preparing her case, as had the judge. In an October 6 hearing Luckhoo argued that the court lacked any evidence that Grace Stoen and her husband Tim ever had revoked their standing grant of custody to Joyce Touchette, and the court had erred by issuing the arrest order in the absence of such revocation. The judge ruled in favor of Luckhoo on the very grounds of due process insisted upon by the U.S. embassy. Later, the embassy agreed. "Frankly," it cabled the State Department, "our opinion is that Mrs. Stoen and U.S. attorney hurt their case by not revoking custody order earlier."

As Haas left Guyana empty-handed, faced with the task of straightening matters out in the California court, Temple attorney Charles Garry flew from San Francisco to Jonestown, partly to try to get to the bottom of the September crisis. Jones mollified him with the story that there really had been an attack on Jonestown, but the crisis had been overplayed. The Temple's attorney recommended a security step sometimes used by large communal organizations in the United States: a security gate three or four miles from the community's center. Jonestown would have advance warning of any "guests," and kidnapping would be no easy matter. When Garry returned to the United States, he admitted to being favorably impressed with his first visit to Jonestown. "I told my partners in the office that I had seen paradise," he informed a local reporter.[7]

In early October the legal process moved ahead in California. Debbie Blakey and other Temple members waited in front of the divorce court to try to dissuade Tim Stoen from appearing under court order. Nonetheless, the former aide to Jim Jones took his first public step to side with his estranged wife, joining her in John Stoen's custody proceedings some four months after he left the child in Jonestown. He also began meeting with the other defectors, including the Millses and Grace, who were actively discussing steps to advance their own cause against Peoples Temple. By the latter part of November Stoen had turned his back on Peoples Temple completely. His new stand, he recognized, "puts me on a collision course with a man I was so fiercely loyal to. But I'm doing it because it is right." Friday,

November 18, 1977, the California court issued an order revoking all previous custody grants and powers of attorney, awarding custody to Grace and Tim Stoen.

Attorney Haas then followed a plan of action reminiscent of Peoples Temple PR moves: he transmitted certified copies of the court order directly to congressmen and senators, from Phil Burton and Leo Ryan of California to Indiana's Birch Bayh and Idaho's Frank Church. Tim Stoen's old friend San Francisco District Attorney Joe Freitas also wrote U.S. and Guyanese officeholders, requesting that they "use whatever influence you have to help obtain Rev. Jones's compliance."

Members of Congress typically pass such requests on to a government agency, asking about appropriate action. The State Department received a barrage of congressional inquiries about John Stoen, but Leo Ryan was different. The twice-divorced maverick suburban Democratic congressman from middle-American San Mateo already had aligned with the "anticult" movement, partly on the basis of his own relatives' involvement with groups like the Unification Church. A Roman Catholic, Representative Ryan made his most notable early anticult efforts in an investigation of the Reverend Sun Myung Moon's Unification Church, and in an alliance with conservative Congressman Robert Giamo from Connecticut. The two congressmen once held a briefing for the Justice Department with the noted anticult intellectual, Margaret Singer, but the Justice Department was not receptive. Absent a specific offense, it held, "religious proselytizing and the recruitment and maintenance of a belief through a strict regimen, meditation, chanting, self-denial and the communication of other religious teachings cannot under our laws—as presently enacted—be construed as criminal in nature and serve as the basis for criminal indictments."[8]

If the arguments of Margaret Singer were lost on the Justice Department, they found a sympathetic ear in Congressman Ryan. He continued to follow the "cult" news. In November of 1977 Ryan read San Francisco *Examiner* reporter Tim Reiterman's article about the plight of Ryan's old friend "Sammy" Houston. First the veteran Associated Press photographer lost his son Bob, a member of Peoples Temple, to a mysterious Southern Pacific Railroad yard death; later his son's former wife, Phyllis, bundled Houston's two grandchildren off to Jonestown.

With an interest in "cults" and a personal friendship with a distraught grandfather of children at Jonestown, Leo Ryan responded decisively to the situation. Secretary of State Cyrus Vance received a December 8, 1977, letter from the representative about a man who "refers to himself as the Reverend Jim Jones." Ryan wrote, "Please consider this letter to be a request to investigate what action might be taken in connection with Mr. Jones in regard to his passport or other means to obtain his presence here in this country before courts which may wish to question him."

The State Department demurred, calling Jones's situation a legal question that did not warrant any "political action without justification." Moreover, in terms of international law on what is called "comity," the State Department pointed out that a California court custody order was not directly enforcable overseas. Although State Department officer Elizabeth Powers thought the California court order "may be useful" in the Guyana court, she added that the boy's "family and their attorneys must . . . not expect that court to accept the decisions of a foreign (U.S.) court at face value." In the case of a young boy who had lived in Guyana for over a year, sent and later left there by his legal father, the outcome in a Guyana court was far from a foregone conclusion.

Tim Stoen and Grace Stoen flew to Georgetown in early January 1978 with Grace's attorney, Jeff Haas. Once again Haas would press for a ruling on the arrest order for Jim Jones, but before the court hearing, the three American visitors met with U.S. officials in the embassy's neatly preserved Victorian colonial clapboard townhouse. Consul McCoy reported that Haas argued, "There was no way, on the basis of the evidence that would be presented, that his clients could possibly lose the case." Therefore, should the judge rule against them, the attorney would suspect government interference.

Haas warned embassy officials John Blacken and Richard McCoy that Leo Ryan and other congressmen were very interested in the case, and told them that "should his clients lose their case, he intended to direct as much publicity and pressure as he could on the State Department and the GOG [Government of Guyana] to rectify any adverse decision. . . ." What, Haas wanted to know, did the embassy intend to do if the Guyanese government would not enforce its court order? Blacken would not countenance the question, and in his memo McCoy concluded, "Obviously, Haas wants the embassy to take sides, which we believe would be improper." Consistently, the embassy and the State Department viewed Haas's tactics as an effort to salvage the case he had prepared so poorly the previous September, in part by drawing the embassy into support of activities aimed at establishing that "court proceedings [were] not being handled in fair and impartial manner."

Things did not go well for Haas and his clients in the next few days. At closing arguments on January 10, the high court judge took the matter under submission to consider the complex legal issues involved. He noted that he had received derogatory phone calls from people at Georgetown's finest hotel, the Pegasus, and he emphasized that he would decide the case solely on law and the facts presented in court. He then withdrew from his chambers to his contemplation, where he was to remain for months.

The day after closing arguments, McCoy traveled from Georgetown to Jonestown for his scheduled consular visit. For the consul's benefit, Jim Jones trotted out his ace in the hole, a copy of Tim Stoen's statement dated

February 6, 1972, affirming Jones as the natural father of John Victor Stoen. Jones then told the consul he would appeal any decision of the court that favored returning John Stoen to Grace and Tim. Whoever won the current pleadings, the next phase of the legal battle promised even more controversy.[9]

The next round in court did not come quickly, and a new phase in the struggle for custody began: pursuit of legal victory became subordinated to public relations by both sides. In San Francisco the *Chronicle*'s famed Herb Caen was always ready to foment scandal. He printed Tim Stoen's 1972 statement and explained that Jim Jones would not return to the United States for fear "my son" would be taken away. A Temple member sent the U.S. ambassador in Georgetown a long letter full of lewd accusations that Stoen's wife Grace once had been concerned about her husband's "compulsive pattern of transvestitism." Such people were "using the child as a means of harassment trying to provoke us to action even if it means our death and the child's death," said the letter bearing the signature of sixty-four-year-old Lenora Perkins.

Grace Stoen had struggled consistently to regain custody of her son John. Tim, on the other hand, came around only by degrees, but the surfacing of his statement affirming Jones's paternity was the final turn of the screw. The lawyer who was trying to salvage his reputation in the public eye looked to be either a sexually impotent male pursuing a legal case to salvage his own sense of honor or a reformed zealot who once had foolishly signed a false document. Tim Stoen proclaimed himself the latter man. "I love my son so much I am willing to go through whatever humiliation Jim puts me through to get my son back. I just wish Jim to get well," Stoen told the California press in February. If the Temple claimed that the Stoens were using the child as a pawn, Stoen turned the tables, claiming that Jones was using the boy to punish the Stoens for defecting.[10]

For Peoples Temple, the issue involved politics and precedent. Whatever the claims to biological or legal paternity, John Stoen had been raised communally for more than half his life. Peoples Temple, now Jonestown, was his world. Like other communal groups, Peoples Temple altered the social claims of biological parenthood. The communal logic held that John Stoen's family was the group of people who raised him, and that he had a right to a destiny in the world where he was growing up.

On the other hand, defectors, when they left the communal organization, confronted the awesome gap between the communal ideology of an extended, nonblood "family" and the conventional ideology of the nuclear family. In the calculus of the nuclear family, for biological parents to abandon a child to rearing by others in a communal group was inexplicable. And in the United States, the law was on the side of the nuclear family.

California law holds that the child has a right to *legal* legitimacy independent of biological paternity, and that right is sustained only if the legal father is presumed to be the biological father, no matter what the actual circumstances. In California, a wedded woman cannot give birth to a bastard son.

In the communalist view, wrenching children from their ongoing lives, even on the basis of biological claims—much less other ones concerned with the legal sanctioning of civic rights to legitimacy—seemed to place abstract principles, individualistic at that, ahead of children's welfare. Nor was John Victor Stoen alone in this situation. He was just the most celebrated of some twenty-two children who had come to Jonestown under non-joint-custody legal arrangements ranging from the custody of one natural parent to court-appointed guardianship of an unrelated adult. Carolyn Layton held that Jonestown would "defend even to death" its right to custody in such cases because "no child here would ever again feel secure if we handed over John Stoen."[11]

### The Concerned Relatives and Their Relatives

If John Stoen had been the only focus of concern, legal channels might have contained the conflict, but relatives back in the United States who read about the horrors of Peoples Temple worried about other children, and adults as well. Parents, brothers, sisters, grandparents gravitated toward Al and Jeannie Mills and the core group of defectors. Gradually they became linked into a cohesive group, and fed by fears concerning events in Jonestown, they became ever more desperate to force a public reckoning. They did not just want their relatives back. They sought, as the father of Maria Katsaris has put it, to "dismantle" Jones's system of intimidation and oppression.

Though Joe Mazor had been involved in the first efforts to obtain the return of children, the former convict become private investigator also was developing evidence about Tim Stoen's role in real estate transactions, and he may have seen a lucrative lawsuit in the making. His clients saw it differently. With Stoen in alliance with other defectors, the Millses parted ways with Mazor in early 1978 when Stoen returned from the legal proceedings in Guyana to live next door to them. Mazor could not understand: were they not out to get Stoen?[12]

The embassy itself checked out "welfare-and-whereabouts" requests, but it operated under constraints. Legally, U.S. citizens in a foreign country have the right to privacy. This meant that the embassy could come to Jonestown only with the consent of the people there, and that Jonestown residents legally could choose to cut off communication with other individ-

uals, including relatives. Embassy visits to Jonestown depended upon
maintaining a reasonably good working relation with Peoples Temple, and
this the embassy clearly wanted, for a variety of reasons. There was not
only the need to monitor the welfare of relatives but probably an intelligence interest in keeping tabs on the delicate relation of Peoples Temple
to the Guyana government and its possible impact on U.S. relations with
Guyana. The deputy chief of mission (DCM) at the embassy during the
early phases of Temple settlement, John Blacken, wrote a memo concerning the Temple that remains classified because it "contains material
relating to the Government of Guyana which might affect relations between the U.S. Government and the Government of Guyana if it were
disclosed." Richard McCoy, who visited Jonestown more than anyone else
at the embassy, had a background of involvement with U.S. intelligence
organizations. So did U.S. Ambassador to Guyana John Burke and the
deputy chief of mission (DCM) who served from early 1978 onward,
Richard Dwyer. Upon their return from Jonestown consular visits, McCoy
and other staff invariably met with the ambassador, the deputy chief of
mission, and others. The very highest officials at the U.S. mission in
Guyana kept abreast of the controversies surrounding Peoples Temple.
From September 1977 onward the embassy knew that Jones believed in a
CIA plot against him, and the State Department advised the embassy to
avoid creating the impression that they were "checking up on Jones or on
the Peoples Temple."[13]

Relatives could not be satisfied with embassy efforts, no matter what the
legal niceties or intelligence interests. Howard and Beverly Oliver came to
believe that their two teenaged sons were being abused, and they petitioned
the courts to have the boys returned, but the boys came of legal age before
the matter was resolved. Other *New West* relatives also made their sentiments known. Micki Touchette got a phone patch to Jonestown through
the good offices of Charles Garry. She accused Jones of breaking up her
family, and pleaded over and over for them to return to the United States.
Her relatives in Jonestown retorted that she had left her family, not the
other way around. Micki was not dissuaded. "Tell Jim Jones," she warned,
"that we are not going to give up. And he can sit back there and he can
laugh and laugh and laugh, because we in the U.S. are going to continue
until our families are returned to us."

"Micki, are you going to kidnap us?" her father wanted to know.

"No Daddy, that is your word," she came back. "Everything will be done
legally. And like I said, Jim Jones will not be able to continue ripping up
families and controlling peoples' minds the way he does it." To which her
father replied, "Micki, I am an adult and I have made up my own mind."

Scores of Jonestown residents made similar statements over the coming months. Leanne Harris established that she was of legal age, and wanted her father to leave her alone. Magnolia Harris reported that she did not want her daughter bothering her. Children were orchestrated to tape statements and write letters to Charles Garry saying they preferred their present custody arrangements with whomever had brought them to Jonestown. The efforts by relatives to talk with people at Jonestown and learn of their welfare through the embassy consul widened the gulf between the opposed camps. Once Jonestown staff found out which outsiders were seeking to contact relatives while at the same time working against Peoples Temple, they monitored and censored those particular communications. The decision came most graphically in the case of fifteen-year-old Donna Ponts. She concluded a friendly but seemingly "canned" letter, "I am sorry to hear that you called the radio station, but since you did, I will not be writing you anymore. I don't know what you think—all I know is that *I love* it in *Guyana* and I *truly* am *happy*."[14]

Relatives in the United States found it difficult to accept rejection from Temple members who said they were more committed to Jonestown than to their own families. Perhaps the most tragic struggle saw Steve Katsaris try to bring back his daughter Maria, by then a Jones intimate and one of his closest aides. A Greek Orthodox upbringing made the father suspicious of "tight-knit" groups; nevertheless, he retained the strong faith of a committed religious liberal. With his life of service as director of Ukiah's Trinity School for developmentally disabled children, Katsaris could see that Peoples Temple reached people otherwise forgotten, but he asked one thing of his daughter above all else, "Don't cut yourself off."

Maria warned her father about the forthcoming *New West* article as she departed for Guyana for a stay of "several weeks." Then she called from Guyana to ask if she could stay several weeks longer. "This is strange," Katsaris said to himself. "She knows she doesn't have to ask me." He resolved the puzzle by concluding that his daughter might have been sending him a call for help. On September 26, Katsaris flew to Georgetown, only to receive a transcript of a taped radio conversation between Maria at Jonestown and Temple Georgetown staffer Paula Adams that Adams had brought to the embassy. In it, Maria asserted that she was twenty-four years old, happy, and not interested in seeing her father, who, she asserted, had sexually molested her as a child.

Emotionally wrenched by his daughter's refusal to see him, Katsaris returned to California and started trying to learn more about Peoples Temple. He called Grace Stoen, and then talked with Jeannie Mills. A meeting was arranged with the Millses, Grace, Neva Sly, Micki Touchette, and several of the government people interested in the Temple, including the Treasury agent. Steve learned that Maria had become a central member of Jones's staff, handling huge sums of money. One defector even recounted witnessing her sign an undated suicide note. Those who had exposed the Temple in *New West* told Katsaris that Maria's very life could be in danger if Temple staff thought she was defecting.

The defectors' claims left Katsaris with a gnawing fear about his daughter's safety, and he took steps to stage a situation where Maria could freely choose whether to stay in Jonestown or leave. In November he flew to Washington, D.C., and talked with Guyanese Ambassador Laurence Mann, who set up a meeting in Guyana between Katsaris and the daughter, and flew to Georgetown with the distraught father.

The encounter was tense. On the balcony of the house where Laurence Mann stayed when he visited Georgetown, Richard McCoy and Maria's lawyer, Sir Lionel Luckhoo, looked on while Steve Katsaris asked his daughter whether she had accused him of sexually molesting her, and whether she had signed an undated suicide note. He also made the mistake of telling Maria that Grace Stoen wanted to convey a message of love for her son John. His confirmation of contacts with opponents was thrown back in his face by his daughter. Maria told him that *she* was now John's mother, and she accused him of joining the conspiracy against Peoples Temple. If she ever wanted to return, Steve told his daughter, McCoy held a plane ticket for her. His daughter was obviously agitated, Katsaris concluded from the encounter. Secretly, she wanted out, he had to tell himself, if he wanted to believe that the real Maria was still alive in that body. Unable to countenance the idea that Maria wanted to cut herself off from him, Katsaris left Guyana a dejected but somehow determined man, all the more disillusioned when officials in Washington pointed out that his daughter was twenty-four, and had the legal right to privacy, even from her father.

"To get the best of the devil," Steve Katsaris's immigrant father once told him, "you have to be a devil and a half." Katsaris feared that he had jeopardized an imprisoned daughter's welfare by his visit, and his own mistake made freeing her all the more urgent. He decided to kidnap his daughter. "If I can get Maria out," he thought, "even if she's crazy, I can deprogram her. If we can't deprogram her, she'll go back, and at least I can say I have been who I can be for her." He was convinced that God guides our lives. Why am I an airplane pilot? he pondered. The answer: his skill might prove instrumental not just in getting his own daughter out but perhaps in freeing one thousand people.

Katsaris sounded out State Department officials on what would happen if he brought Maria to Puerto Rico or Trinidad. They assured him they would accept her into the United States on the basis of her citizenship. Katsaris then slipped into Guyana secretly, avoiding immigration authorities. He planned to wait until Maria was in Georgetown, kidnap her, get her to an airplane, and fly her out of the country. But the "go" signal never came from Katsaris's confederates. Instead they told him that Peoples Temple was onto him. He left Guyana once again empty-handed, without ever learning whether he had been taken in by those who helped him plan the mission. Altogether the ill-fated effort cost upwards of $5,000. To Katsaris, it would have been a small price to pay to assure that his daughter had a choice. He hoped against all hope that he could redeem the love of family in Maria's heart, and he was willing even to break the law to give her that opportunity.[15]

## The Concerned Relatives Go Public

When Tim Stoen returned from Georgetown to Washington, D.C., in January, 1978, he believed he and Grace would win custody of John; the problem was, how to get the child. He went to members of Congress with a "white paper" that described John Stoen as being held by Jim Jones "illegally," even though proceedings in the court with jurisdiction had not been completed. "The court is expected to award custody to the Stoens," the document reported, "but enforcement may require a political decision to use the Guyanese Army and could result in harm to John Victor or other innocent persons." Before a legal decision was reached, some ninety-one members of Congress were asked to communicate their concerns to Forbes Burnham, the prime minister of Guyana, "pointing out that it is in the best interests of the Stoens, the Peoples Temple Agricultural Mission, and the Cooperative Republic of Guyana that the child be safely returned so as to avoid dangers inherent in a confrontation."

At the end of January, Tim Stoen and Steve Katsaris met in Washington with State Department officials. A State Department officer later wrote that Stoen "fears Jones mental deterioration. Unsubstantiated rumors of contact w/Mid-East terrorists. Paranoid megalomania." Stoen also pushed the State Department to request that the government of Guyana guarantee that any custody order be "speedily enforced." State cabled the embassy, "Dept. believes this not unreasonable method to express USG [U.S. government] concern." The embassy replied by reiterating its position that such a move might buy into attorney Haas's effort to have the U.S. government take sides. This the government could not afford to do. The State Department received a letter from Charles Garry arguing, "There is no reason whatsoever for any interference in this case from parties acting in any governmental capacity from the U.S." Under the circumstances the embassy's argument won the day, and the enforcement issue was put off until a decision in the case actually came out.

In the next few months the embassy did try to gauge how soon a decision might reasonably be expected. Guyana Minister of Justice Mohamed Shahabudeen told Richard McCoy that custody suits were civil in nature, and under no specific time requirements for swift resolution. Moreover, the decision of a judge could take four months to compose and release. A local attorney was even less encouraging. The whole matter might take up to two years to conclude!

The State Department had to weigh the situation carefully. A briefing paper prepared for a State Department official's trip to Guyana noted that the legal parents' inherent claim had to be balanced against the fact that "the Stoens effectively abandoned the child" when they left the group. The briefing paper concluded that "custody of John Victor very likely could be awarded to Jim Jones." If that happened, or if Jones lost but failed to hand over the child, Tim Stoen could be expected to "demand that the Department intervene with the government of Guyana to force the return of his child. This demand undoubtedly will be accompanied by strong Congressional pressure on the Department." "In your conversations with Ambassador Burke," the briefing papers advised, "we recommend that you discuss fully the domestic [U.S.] consequences of such adverse results [i.e. apparently, pressure from Congress on the State Department] as opposed to the consequences in Guyana should the Stoens be granted custody." Though the department insisted that "failing clear proof of outside interference," it would "decline to intervene in behalf of either party," it certainly saw that alternative outcomes would affect either department dealings with Congress or U.S. interests in Guyana.

The cause of the Temple opponents was too urgent to wait out the wheels of Guyana justice. Faced with the evenhanded dealings of the embassy, Tim Stoen apparently considered plans for a Katsaris-style rescue mission, for he sent a plane ticket, along with a notarized authorization to the embassy to repatriate John Victor, "in the event any person appears with said minor in his or her physical custody." Whatever the plan, in early April the embassy vetoed it, noting that under a Guyanese court order, "John Stoen cannot utilize airline ticket and leave Guyana with anyone including his parents," until the conclusion of the case.[16]

Frustrated opponents of the Temple turned their appeals to the court of public opinion. Steve Katsaris reasoned that Jim Jones survived only on the basis of secrecy and intimidation. The solution was to lift the veil of secrecy and refuse to be intimidated. The opponents moved on two fronts: publicity efforts about human rights issues, and a series of "show" trials. For over a year a core of Temple opponents had been meeting. Now, for the first time, a public group—the Concerned Relatives—would demand accountability for what was happening in Jonestown. A publicity event was planned to draw maximum media exposure. On Tuesday, April 11, about fifty people showed up at the San Francisco Peoples Temple. Barred at the iron front gate from entering the Temple, the demonstrators made their way around to the rear to present a petition through the chain-link fence to a young man working in the parking lot. The petition accused Peoples Temple of "employing physical intimidation and psychological coercion as part of a mind-programming campaign aimed at destroying family ties, discrediting belief in God, and causing contempt for the United States of America." It maintained that Jonestown residents had been deprived of their rights guaranteed under the United Nations Universal Declaration of 1948: the people of Jonestown could not be reached by telephone or by uncensored mail, and they could not leave the community because of armed guards.

Last, the Concerned Relatives' petition made public a letter sent to Congress March 14 on Peoples Temple stationary under Pamela Moton's signature. After the letter reviewed a long string of alleged conspiracies against Peoples Temple, it concluded, "I can say without hesitation that we are devoted to a decision that it is better even to die than to be constantly harassed from one continent to the next. I hope you can . . . protect the right of over 1,000 people from the U.S. to live in peace." The Concerned Relatives dissected the statement in their petition. "When you say you are 'devoted' to this decision, does that mean it is irreversible?" they asked Jones rhetorically. "If irreversible, at what point will the alleged 'harassment' have gotten so great as to make death 'better'?" They suggested possible circumstances: "Would it be an International Human Rights Commission investigation, or an on-premises investigation of your operations by the U.S. Government?" The Concerned Relatives left interpretation open. "We frankly do not know if you have become so corrupted by power that you would actually allow a collective 'decision' to die, or whether your letter is simply a bluff designed to deter investigations into your practices."

Tim Stoen called around to relatives of Temple members, trying to garner support for the opposition. As early as May 7, 1978, Frances Muchnick reported to Temple staff that Stoen told her, "If things don't go Jim's way, Jim could get his followers to partake in a mass suicide action if he so decreed." Temple stalwart Jessie McNeal posed as a "Mrs. McCormick" worrying about her nineteen-year-old grandson, and called Stoen to sound out his strategy. She reported to Temple staff why Stoen told her to write Guyana's prime minister, Forbes Burnham. "The more letters that keep coming in," Mrs. McNeal said Stoen argued, "the more one could be the straw that breaks the camel's back." As he envisioned it, she recounted, the names of Jonestown relatives should be given to the Guyanese government, "so that if something ever happens and Jim Jones has disorganization, and the government, they'll have the list before them, and say, 'we want these people sent back to the States right away.'" How would that happen? "Jim Jones is not going to be able to last much longer, because he's doing so many stupid things. Like every time we have a demonstration against him, he overreacts, okay?" "My God, my God," replied Mrs. McNeal, as the other continued, "So when he overreacts, then we will . . . , the government down there will see that things are amiss." Jessie McNeal's phone call report unveiled to Peoples Temple the kernel of a strategy its opponents might follow, but the Temple leadership would brook no scenario to destabilize Jonestown. If it came to that, Jones would choose another climax. Word was passed to attorney Charles Garry: "Jim thinks they are trying to provoke us to suicide."

Above all else, the Concerned Relatives kept the pressure up. They added names to the list Tim Stoen reportedly mentioned. On May 10, fifty-seven petitioners forwarded the names of eighty-two relatives to U.S. Secretary of State Cyrus Vance and Guyana Prime Minister Forbes Burnham. The largely White leadership of the Concerned Relatives had gotten a number of Blacks to join with them. Still, in all, 58 percent of the Jonestown residents claimed as relatives were White, considerably higher than Jonestown's proportion of Whites, which was less than 30 percent. Sixty-eight percent of the Jonestown people listed as objects of concern in the petition were adults, and only three of the twenty-six children, John Stoen, Donna Ponts, and Mark Wagner, were actually subjects of custody suits.

The petition shifted the issues about both adulthood and custody. It no longer mattered what legal rights people in Jonestown had, or what they said. If they really were cut off from outside communication, if their mail was censored, if they were intimidated, then it could be argued they did not have free will. Effectively, the Concerned Relatives dismissed their loved ones' capacity for rational decision making. In the words of Steve Katsaris, talking about Maria, they had been "mind-programmed." As a remedy, the Concerned Relatives asked that Jim Jones "permit and encourage" people at Jonestown to come back to the United States for one-week visits at the expense of their relatives in the United States, with free return to Guyana guaranteed. The proposal amounted to a voluntary version of the temporary-conservatorship plan then being advanced in U.S. courts as a solution to purported coercive persuasion at the hands of "cults" like the Unification Church.[17]

The other prong of the spring offensive was a series of show trials. The Concerned Relatives sought to bring court cases against Peoples Temple as a way of forcing the Temple to submit to the legal process and adverse publicity. In mid-May Steve Katsaris filed the first suit in Mendocino County Superior Court, for libel and slander against Jim Jones and others whom he charged had spread rumors he was a child molester. Perhaps Peoples Temple could be forced to produce Maria to testify, and if so, Katsaris harbored hopes he could kidnap her. Katsaris's lawyer? Tim Stoen, the very man who had met with other Temple members little more than a year before to discuss Maria Katsaris and her father's possible conservatorship efforts. Stoen had stayed in the background at the public demonstrations, but Katsaris believed he was the logical choice for a lawyer. Stoen was news: here was a defector from Peoples Temple serving as the legal counsel for its opponents!

In meetings of the Concerned Relatives other potential cases surfaced. "Gang-of-eight" defector Jim Cobb used a Temple publicity effort as the basis for his case. Had not the Temple's March 14 letter to members of Congress referred to him as part of the "radical Trotskyite elements which defected from our organization"? Had not Teri Buford headed up a "Diversions Department" designed to intimidate defectors like himself? Tim Stoen filed suit for Cobb, charging Jones and the Temple with libel and "intentional infliction of emotional distress." Wade and Mabel Medlock filed a third suit, again with Stoen as attorney. It claimed that Temple officials used the death of Chris Lewis to threaten their lives when they balked at signing over property. A young streetwise Black, Lewis had returned from Jonestown in December 1977, only to be gunned down in the streets of San Francisco by unknown assailants. Whoever was responsible for his death, the Medlocks alleged it was waved in front of their faces: a Temple member told them, "You know what happened to Chris. Jim wants you to come to Guyana."[18]

Peoples Temple tried to respond to the attacks with logorrheic press releases rebutting charges by the Concerned Relatives, with "campaign mail" letters to the State Department and members of Congress, with well-argued essays by house intellectuals like Richard Tropp, with slurs about defectors "leaked" to newspapers, with Freedom of Information Act requests to the government, and with court strategies to deal with the lawsuits. The Temple pounced on rumors that the Concerned Relatives were willing to hire mercenaries to capture their loved ones, and prodded the press and the public to see the irony. "Concerned Parents or PROVOCATEURS?" their leaflet asked.[19]

When the press carried Temple statements at all, they often focused on flamboyant assertions like one about defectors who "advocated ridiculous and mad schemes of violence in order to achieve revolutionary 'ends' in the classic manner of agent provocateurs." The hyperbolic style of the Temple press releases often overshadowed their content, which had a factual basis on a rough par with statements by their opponents, and Temple staff continued to find themselves frustrated by the way the press discounted assertions that contradicted the thesis of the Concerned Relatives.

But Temple staff did not flinch from the "decision that it is better even to die than to be constantly harassed from one continent to the next." On April 18, 1978, Harriet Tropp spoke to assembled reporters over a phone patch from Guyana into Charles Garry's Market Street law offices. She quoted Martin Luther King on the need to "develop the courage of dying for a cause." "He later said," she recounted, "that he hoped no one had to die as a result of the struggle, but, 'If anyone has to go, let it be me.'" As for Jonestown, "we, likewise, affirm that before we will submit quietly to the interminable plotting and persecution of this politically motivated conspiracy, we will resist actively, putting our lives on the line, if it comes to that. This has been the unanimous vote of the collective community here in Guyana." Lest people think they were zealots seeking martyrdom, Tropp concluded, "It is not our purpose to die; we believe deeply in the celebration of life."

On the legal front, Charles Garry parried the pending cases by a series of procedural ploys that would take a year or more for opponents to untangle. The legal prong of the Concerned Relatives' spring offensive thus failed to accomplish what Steve Katsaris had sought: to keep the Temple in the public eye. In fact, Garry filed suit against Tim Stoen, arguing that he could not legally represent the opponents without breaching a previous attorney-client relation, because he had served as the Temple's lawyer. The move thus turned the focus back on Stoen, and offered a possible basis to obtain evidence about whether he had embezzled money from Peoples Temple, as Garry began to suspect.

The publicity and legal responses by Peoples Temple did little to convince its opponents. If anything, the Temple elaborations about "putting our lives on the line" fed the Concerned Relatives' worst fears, but the opponents apparently did not take Jones's threats seriously. Instead they adopted Steve Katsaris's view that the "posturing" and "intimidation" were just hot air meant to throw opponents off the track. With this interpretation, the Concerned Relatives simply redoubled their efforts. They distributed leaflets showing a little child behind wood stick bars, they called Jonestown a "concentration camp," and they asked "concerned citizens" to pray, to write Forbes Burnham and Cyrus Vance, and to send money to "Concerned Relatives and Citizens" at Tim Stoen's law offices. On August 3, 1978, Stoen signed a declaration stating his belief that Jim Jones "is willing to murder all 1100 people now living under his dictatorial control in Jonestown, Guyana."

Over and over again the Concerned Relatives promoted a threat of mass death that they believed was Jim Jones's biggest bluff. In effect, they bet that they could drive him to foolish and insane acts that would be his own undoing while causing no harm to others. With the demonstrations and lawsuits, they launched themselves into a full-fledged public "anticult" movement. They adopted "mind programming" as the motif for explaining why their relatives stayed in Jonestown, and they steadfastly and courageously marched toward a confrontation that was no longer just an effort on behalf of relatives who might reject their efforts to "save" them. If Jonestown was a "concentration camp," the movement became an effort to "dismantle" it. The Concerned Relatives demanded nothing less than that Jonestown cease to exist as a bounded communal society. Conversely, Peoples Temple would want to know what the prospects were for people who had staked their lives on a migration to a foreign country thousands of miles from California, only to find their opponents hell-bent on shutting down the community they had sacrificed so much to build. Contradictory fears drove the conflict over whether Jonestown was to survive.[20]

We will never know what course Jonestown would have taken in the absence of the Concerned Relatives' crusade. The mass migration to Guyana began even as the controversy started to build, and life in Jonestown was never established independently of the custody suit, the "welfare-and-whereabouts" requests, and all that followed. The opposition played a double game. On the one hand, they would insist on nothing more controversial than internationally affirmed human rights. On the other hand, they tried to cast as wide a net as possible to monitor Peoples Temple, they planned and tried to execute illegal abductions, and they used what little communication they had with Jonestown to their own strategic advantage.

The tactics of the Concerned Relatives became the basis of further tightening of social control, and the efforts to open up Jonestown had the opposite effect. The conflict between Peoples Temple and its opponents came to be understood by both sides as the moral equivalent of war, and the Temple took the step of censorship ("screening") as a wartime measure that staff argued was necessary to avoid spreading either Marxist-Leninist talk that would "throw a bourgeois relative into a frenzy" or the the occasional "transient gripe" that could be misconstrued by opponents and a hostile media. The same strategic considerations marked the implementation of Garry's proposal for a security gate on the road into Jonestown. The September 1977 "attack" on Jonestown was staged, but it rehearsed valid fears that "mercenaries" would attack and take away the "child-god."

A fortress is also a kind of prison, and the soldiers behind its barricades are also its inmates. For Jonestown, opponents' depiction of a "concentration camp" was not just a label, it was a self-fulfilling prophecy. The crusade against Jonestown itself precipitated the efforts at Jonestown to minimize contacts with relatives, but every action taken at Jonestown to defend against opponents in turn was used by opponents to confirm their thesis. Thus developed the odd dialectic whereby actions on both sides amplified the worldview and determination of the opposing side. Convinced of the virtue of their position, the Concerned Relatives blinded themselves to any evidence that they could not psychologically support, for example, that their relatives were willing to abandon their previous lives for a cause. Much like apocalyptic sects, families would suffer a loss of legitimacy in the "defection" of one of their own. On the other side, every action by the opponents was used at Jonestown to prove the existence of "conspiracy." This dynamic of oppositional posturing by both sides did not go unnoticed. The chair of a Disciples of Christ review committee on Peoples Temple observed, "I never got into a situation so paranoid on both sides."

In an odd way the *modus operandi* of the Concerned Relatives mirrored that of the group they hoped to dismantle. They too came to believe that certain ends (freeing their relatives) would justify means of doubtful legality. They too were willing to overlook their relatives' rights to privacy because of an overriding concern for their welfare. They too would embellish accounts for public relations purposes. If the facts about life at Jonestown were not compelling enough to excite the public outrage the Concerned Relatives deemed necessary, they used the hyperbolic symbol of concentration camp barbed wire and atrocity tales about starvation to arouse the proper outcry.

The Concerned Relatives fell prey to the same trap that had tripped up Peoples Temple with the press the previous year. No doubt appearances were staged when embassy staff visited Jonestown, but it would have been impossible to hide mass starvation, and whatever "bondage" existed seemed to have the most amiable support of its victims. Consul Richard McCoy observed, "The Concerned Relatives had a credibility problem, since so many of their claims were untrue." The embassy and the State Department came to wonder about the Concerned Relatives in the same way they wondered about Peoples Temple. After dealing with Tim Stoen for a while, a departmental officer began to feel "a degree of wariness and uncertainty about whether he had purposes beyond his parental concerns."

The difficulties of dealing with Tim Stoen marked a problem the department faced both with the Concerned Relatives more generally and with Peoples Temple. "Because of the starkly conflicting, emotional and, in some respects, bizarre nature of the information provided by the Concerned Relatives and the Temple, and because of the deep bitterness and suspicion that the two groups exhibited toward each other," the State Department recounted, "doubts inevitably arose about the motives and credibility of either side."[21]

## Life in the "Concentration Camp"

Jonestown did not offer much in the way of civilized amenities. It was a pioneer settlement, not an established community. For the Jonestown immigrants, add to the "balmy" climate and cultural shocks of Guyana the extreme isolation of jungle life and exhausting work under a hot sun, and it is easy to imagine that even if Jim Jones had not become caught up in the intrigues of conspiracy, many city people, or those with bourgeois sensibilities in general, would not have found Jonestown their cup of tea. Like most communards of both the nineteenth century and the counterculture of the 1960s and 1970s, Jonestown residents lived a spartan style of life that contrasted sharply with that of the society from which they had isolated themselves. Like other communards, or any group with 600 acres devoted to intensive agriculture, the people of Jonestown toiled long hours, often at physically demanding work. Still, U.S. Consul Richard McCoy did not sense that the labor requirements of Jonestown were beyond the capabilities of its residents.

Again like other communards (not the least of them the Peace Mission followers of Jones's early mentor, Father Divine), the settlers lived in crowded facilities. There were only 847 beds for over 900 people, and Jones's cabin was furnished with the only double bed. Though every adult had a bed, some children had to double up. Both the crowding and the very ideology of communalism dictated that housing facilities were places to sleep, not "homes." The whole of Jonestown was their home, and like most communal settlements, it was mostly public space, with little opportunity for privacy.

The people of Jonestown developed the agricultural effort as best they could under adverse conditions, and they continued constructing housing for an immigrant population that mushroomed beyond original expectations. As with other large-scale communal settlements (such as The Farm in Tennessee), there was little free time once the work, the meetings, and the planned recreation were done. Given the sense of crisis at Jonestown, the number of meetings tended to increase over time, and with the tropical absence of seasons, the passage of days and weeks sometimes seemed to blur.

Whatever their burdens from Jones and the "conspiracy," some people got very frustrated by Jonestown. When they first arrived, even skilled workers put in two weeks in the fields, so that they would maintain respect for all types of workers. Jones also implemented a "participatory" approach to decision making. Committees like the farm analysis board monitoring various agriculture and food preparation "departments" included people who lacked technical knowledge of the issues. For all the socialistic idealism that legitimated this approach, people with expertise found frustration in their efforts to plan and operate effectively. To top it off, there was an overall steering committee and Jones himself reserved the right to sign off on even petty decisions, subjecting the already hobbled decision-making process to his second guessing. That way, everyone would have to thank "Dad" for their blessings. For both the elite and the masses who had to bow to this self-aggrandizement, living under the patrimonial administration of a large communal society had its frustrations, even aside from the hard work and the concerns of the Concerned Relatives.

The food was not all that good either. In letters home, Jonestowners would brag about bananas falling off trees, and they raved at the starchy South American staple, the cassava root. When guests came, the community's image was at stake and they put meat on the table, but just as other communards typically have survived on limited diets, for the most part the people of Jonestown ate a simple diet of rice, sometimes with a meat sauce, beans and greens, and occasional eggs. Agricultural manager Jim Bogue complained, "We weren't getting enough protein," and he reported that people had boils and blisters popping out from malnutrition. But outside observers discredited such charges, failing to find that "the members of the comunity were receiving anything below normal Guyanese standards of food, clothing, shelter, and medical assistance." Their view was reinforced by an elderly survivor, who maintained, "We had food aplenty. A lot of people are not satisfied with whatever you give them."

Even getting basic meals on the table for over 900 people three times a day was no small trick, but Jonestown workers made sincere efforts to improve the situation. Egg production gradually was increased, and the piggery promised to add another source of protein. Even a visiting U.S. Agency for International Development officer gave a glowing assessment of Jonestown agriculture: "Crops have been planted and harvested of all indigenous foods," he reported, adding, "the level of operations, the quality of field work performed and results being achieved will serve as a model for similar development efforts in the hinterland." True, Jonestown had to import huge quantities of commodities like wheat, and it was far from self-sufficient. In this, however, it differed little from other utopian communities of the 1970s. The Jonestown leadership recognized the limits of self-sufficiency in the need to buy commercial goods; they saw the necessity of generating a cash flow in order to survive; and they explored possibilities of manufacturing and a cash-cropping scheme for the lucrative spice trade.

Some 400 of Jonestown's residents were a dependent population, either old or young. Seniors did not have to work at all, Mike Touchette pointed out, and he sneered at reporters' concerns that other people were overworked: "They [the reporters] never worked a day in their lives!" The people of Jonestown were putting their sweat into building a jungle community as few had done before them. Those who built Jonestown—who grew its food, fed its people, schooled its children, cared for its sick—are due some recognition for real successes."[22]

Human rights are another question. Again, like many of the larger and more successful utopian communities, both historical and contemporary, Jonestown was isolated from the world around it. In the first place, the community lay seven muddy miles from the nearest governmental outpost, Port Kaituma. In the rainy season the Port Kaituma airstrip could close for weeks and the most direct access to the larger world was by boat. But Jonestown was isolated as much psychologically and socially as it was physically. Jonestowners had little contact even with nearby Guyanese and Amerindian communities. As in other utopian communities, the boundaries between the project and the "outside" made Jonestown a world unto itself, and people there passed their lives at their own duties and with their friends. This isolation did not depend entirely on physical separation. Numerous trusted residents not under the threat of kidnapping traveled back and forth to Port Kaituma, Matthews Ridge, and even to Georgetown for such sundry purposes as making business arrangements, receiving medical care, and participating in cultural exhibitions.

The people of Jonestown are also supposed to have been isolated from world events, cut off from the news, and beholden to Jim Jones as their only source of information. But Jones did not filter what people heard about so much as the slant with which they heard it. In Jonestown he took on the task of resocializing his followers to a leftist perspective on world events.

Interrupting the soul music or classical concertos broadcast over the Jonestown P.A. system, Jones sometimes held forth from the microphone in his cabin for hours, serving up a mixture of news, commmentary, and readings from leftist analyses of capitalism and revolution. Sometimes he read from U.S. left-wing sources like the Black Panther party newsletter. Occasionally he added comments about the "thousands" of poor people in the United States who had died from lack of heat during the winter. With subtle exaggerations and "straight" news accounts of events like the pogrom against the Philadelphia Black anarchist group MOVE, Jones portrayed the United States as beset by racial and economic problems that his followers had escaped by coming to Jonestown. Other times he read from the Guyana *Chronicle*, Radio Cuba, and the Soviet press, from a lengthy account of the CIA-backed coup against Allende in Chile, or from heady

Marxist academic studies of the connection between fascism and racism. Some of what Jones read about economic dependency of the Third World reflected little more than contemporaneous scholarly views on the mechanisms by which poor countries are exploited economically by the core countries of the capitalist world economy. With such materials, Jones effectively reoriented his followers toward a Third World liberation perspective that portrayed their former homeland as the imperialist whore of capitalism to the north. Jonestowners were not totally isolated from the mainstream U.S. press either, but when Jones read accounts from the New York *Times*, he told people, "I am giving you capitalist news. And you have to understand, I interpret it as much as I can."

Jones became a Paul Harvey of the Left. Like the conservative noontime radio commentator, Jones did not just read the news, he gave it life and meaning from a particular political perspective. The occasional embellishments were layered onto a steady diet of information, from a greater variety of sources, let it be said, than reaches the average U.S. citizen. Jones seems to have been positively determined that his followers would be informed on a wealth of subjects. Objections to news quizzes notwithstanding, the people of Jonestown developed, on average, a more sophisticated understanding of world events than did their counterparts in the United States, albeit from a different political viewpoint. Thus it was that an older man could pester Charles Garry during one of his visits for his opinion on Marx's labor theory of value.

The reoriented worldview of the news reinforced the effort to foster Jonestown's strength in the solidarity of its people. Briefing people about the politics of Guyana and the activities of Temple opponents, Jones would say, "We gotta keep this movement strong. Our first loyalty is to *this* movement, to *our* leader, to *this* movement, not to some communist movement outside of this movement, but to us first." He warned people not to split off. "If we start to try to make individual compromises," he told the assembled community, "you'll *all* lose in the process." Faced with what he called the "conspiracy" originating in the activities of David Conn, George Klineman, and the Millses, Jones insisted time and again, "Obviously, we will fight for our freedom." "They have to come through all of us to get any one of us," he argued, "and that's our key: one thousand strong, united we stand."

In Guyana, Jones thus built upon the siege mentality established in the United States. The need for solidarity against an external enemy was used to justify strong security and disciplinary measures meant to counter the "conspiracy" and keep dissidents from escaping. Consul McCoy did not see how the broad tableau of Jonestown life could be staged if people truly were being held in bondage, but he did not understand the pervasiveness of the internal social control procedures Jones employed, or the cooperation Jones could exact from the vast majority of Jonestown residents. McCoy, Jones told his captive audience, was under Peoples Temple control, and any attempt to leave with him would just mean coming up for discipline. Jones also told people that if they tried to escape they could be accidentally shot by security personnel who had the authority of the Guyana government behind them. People came to understand that the guards were there to keep them in as much as to prevent mercenary invasion.

Some people became disgruntled early on, but not always for the reasons or with the intensity that the Concerned Relatives promoted. Workers sometimes thought their skills were not used effectively. True believers lamented the decline of faith healing and religion, and they faced the disappointment of coming to terms with the less than perfect Jones as someone other than "god." Others found the work too demanding, or they longed for the light and life of the city. Whatever the complaints, Jonestown staff feared any dissatisfied person who left would be recruited by their opponents. Jonestown could not control people once they left, so its operatives tightened the confinement. Under regimens akin to corporation ploys originally used to discourage labor organizing, staff rotated the assignments, breaks, and days off of workers, so as to prevent "conspiracies" or escapes. When someone had to go to Georgetown on business, a loved one remained in Jonestown as a hostage of sorts.

Jones openly demanded that people monitor themselves and one another, and his defenders in Jonestown made no apologies. "In a Communist collective, it is necessary to have some internal safeguards, and so it is true," they admitted, "that one has a duty to report behavior or attitudes that are potentially harmful to the collective, so that such behavior, etc. may be dealt with *openly* in our public meetings." Jones was more emphatic. "There's no way we can help but have a Committee for the Defense of the Revolution, and look at *every* person," he announced. "It is your duty to see any strange behavior and negative talk from anyone—leadership, top leadership makes no difference, and all echelons of this egalitarian society." The difficulties of flight resigned even dissidents to remaining. Once they developed the capacity to role play in the face of the controls, they found that on a day-to-day basis, things did not seem so bad.

Jones backstopped the threats and the surveillance by giving his followers to believe that their continued existence as a community depended on not caving in to their opponents. A tape was prepared on what to say to outsiders, and Jones told people, "Listen to that tape damn, damn closely, because you make a mistake, you are hurting yourself very desperately, and you are hurting a lot of innocent children." "We work eight hours a day," he coached. "We have the best foods. We have meats, fruits, vegetables, and you live in a house where you have four people besides yourself. Or some people can say, 'five.' Say we are building more, and we will point them to the fact that we *are* building more."

The people of Jonestown either believed in the need to present a united front or feared the consequences of challenging the collective, and they presented a relaxed, affable image to a steady stream of visitors. Their public ease suggests that large numbers of residents did not see themselves as living in bondage; instead, they engaged in public relations efforts to maintain the community's standing in outside opinion. Those who felt themselves trapped in Jonestown, on the other hand, knew of the consequences of making "mistakes."[23]

The leadership of Jonestown brought the disciplinary procedures from the United States to the Promised Land. At evening "town forum" meetings, Jones and the assembled crowd "brought up" and passed judgment on people for such diverse offenses as trying to escape, violence, stealing, and making fun of others. "Sentences" were handed down, commuted, or lifted, according to the remorse and rehabilitation or repeated offenses of the guilty party. But the nature of punishment shifted somewhat. Slackers and other offenders were assigned to a crew that did the heaviest and dirtiest work, digging ditches, building latrines. Over the microphone from his house, Jones exhorted people, "Step up your production, so you are not brought up for the New Brigade tonight, because we are observing some that are not producing as they ought to be producing." "I love you very much," he added.

Other approaches supplanted heavy work as punishment. Soon after the mass exodus, Jones lauded "public humiliation" as "a good form of discipline." "It's better than boxing. It's better than spanking," he argued. "We'd rather compliment and humiliate one another so that we can grow, than to get into physical violence with one another, wouldn't we?" Humiliation sometimes seemed boundless. In late 1977 fourteen-year-old Tommy Bogue came up for unauthorized use of building materials. His hair reportedly was shaved off, he was forbidden to talk with others, he had to run everywhere he went, and he was assigned to build a huge hole for a latrine one night, and forced to work in the fields the next day. Adults were occasionally pressured by Jones to mock Pentecostal religion as the price for getting out of more stringent punishments. In general, the meting out of humiliation in public forums served as a spectacle that offered entertainment at the expense of those who had offended the body politic.

If humiliation and discipline proved insufficient, more bizarre punishments might be employed. One defector reported incidents in which a terrified child might be lowered into a pit with greased ropes made to seem like snakes. Other survivors say a seldom-used underground isolation box was based on a theory of "sensory deprivation" developed by a teacher of handicapped children named Tom Grubbs. This sort of solitary confinement, which might last a whole day, he saw as a "humane" form of social control.

Jonestown also employed more conventional modern means of social control—the administration of psychotherapeutic drugs like Thorazine—for those who, as Jones put it, "have proved themselves incapable of their own controls." In modern psychiatric practice the boundary between therapy and confinement is a thin one, and advertisements for psychotherapeutic drugs blatantly advertise ease of patient management as a marketing plus. After November of 1978 newspapers reported on a huge cache of drugs at Jonestown: Demerol, Valium, Quaalude, and 11,000 doses of the tranquilizer Thorazine. Given the difficulty of supply, the quantities stocked in Jonestown were not excessive, at least in the view of a doctor otherwise totally critical of Jonestown, Dr. Leslie Mootoo, of Georgetown. Moreover, the bonded pharmacy records of nurse Annie Moore indicate only moderate drug dispensing. The uses ranged from clearly therapeutic applications to administration for purposes of "resocialization."

Nursing supervisor and eventual defector Dale Parks gave Larry Layton psychotherapeutic drugs after the death of his mother, Lisa Layton, to help him through his depression. Another time, someone who physically attacked Stephan Jones was given Thorazine to calm him down. According to Parks, "on an extremely small scale," far smaller than the inventory would suggest, drugs also were used to control a handful of potential defectors in the Jonestown clinic's "Extended Care Unit," a ward separate from other medical facilities. Parks described the unit's purpose: "If a person wanted to leave Jonestown, or if there was a breach of the rules, one was taken to the Extended Care Unit. It was a rehabilitation place, where one would be reintegrated back into the community. The people were given drugs to keep them under control." A persistent case was attorney Gene Chaikin, who became outraged at the death threat during the September 1977 crisis. Chaiken was not so heavily or constantly sedated that he could not do legal work. But he lived under what amounted to house arrest.

On the whole, Jonestown is less striking for the severity of punishment than for its forms. Though our ideology of liberty does not make us prone to discussing social control, even Congressman Leo Ryan accepted the need for it. Just before his trip to Jonestown, Ryan acknowledged, "You can't put 1,200 people in the middle of a jungle without some damn tight discipline." The point is all the more compelling given that a number of people who had "done time" lived at Jonestown. In the United States persons sentenced to prison might face abuses by guards and inmates that would make practices at Jonestown seem tame, yet Jonestown did not have a jail. Punishment amounted to work, humiliation, a rarely used form of solitary confinement ("sensory deprivation"), and, for dissidents, a pseudotherapeutic resocialization.

Before Peoples Temple ever left California, Jones railed at prisons in the United States and praised practices of socialist countries where offenders received work sentences. At Jonestown he kept to this vision for the most part, at least in dealing with freeriders and petty offenders. The more vexatious problem, and the more disturbing solutions, centered on dissidents. In the California days, Jones somehow managed to live with the departure of hundreds who did not share his vision. At Jonestown the stakes seemed much higher, and Jones and his staff held certain people against their will in order to prevent them from joining the "conspiracy." By trying to undermine their opponents' efforts, Jones and his staff created the very conditions that gave them ammunition for their attacks. As a result, the people who did manage to leave were among the most disenchanted, and they abandoned Jonestown brimming with tales of atrocities.[24]

### Reports from the Tropics

By the middle of May 1978 the Concerned Relatives' evidence about Jonestown was based largely on their own shortwave radio monitoring and their experiences trying to reach their relatives. The mosaic convinced Representative Leo Ryan that he wanted to visit the jungle camp, and the maverick congressman became the vehicle by which the Concerned Relatives would try to open up Jonestown. By the end of May 1978, at the time when Tim Stoen reportedly outlined the circumstances in which Jones might "overreact," Leo Ryan already had written the San Francisco Peoples Temple. "Please be advised that Tim Stoen does have my support in the effort to return his son from Guyana," he informed the Temple, adding that his long-term friend Bob Houston "has told me his grandaughters [sic] are being held in Guyana." Ryan added a request: "Please let me know if I may visit your camp in Guyana as a part of my official oversight plans for this year."

To the Temple, Ryan's letter "declared his sympathy for Mr. Tim Stoen" in a case still pending in the Guyana courts, and took the side of a grandfather against a mother who was living in Jonestown with legal custody of her children. No matter what Ryan claimed to the contrary, Temple staff would see him as working for the cause of the Concerned Relatives. To the Temple, as Ryan's plans unfolded, "the feeling of being entrapped turned to belief—it had to be a setup."

The mutual "paranoia" of the Temple and the Concerned Relatives intensified as a result of two events during late spring—the defection of Debbie Blakey, and the visit to Guyana of reporter Kathie Hunter. Blakey had brought her cancer-stricken mother, Lisa Layton, to Guyana in December of 1977. After a series of attempts to leave, in May she prevailed upon the good offices of Consul Richard McCoy.

As it happened, McCoy had just made his third visit to Jonestown several days earlier, touring with the new deputy chief of mission, Richard Dwyer. He and Dwyer had one of those odd encounters with Jim Jones. Sitting around the pavilion eating lunch with about fifteen people, Dwyer and McCoy listened to the leader rail on about "Trotskyites" amidst discussions ranging from the difficulties of maintaining motivation in cashless societies to the problems of leadership that would occur if Jones should ever "pass from the scene." By this visit, it was clear to McCoy that Jones was using drugs. Though McCoy did not know the specifics, the delicate balance of Jones's constitution was affected by his use of "uppers" like amphetamines and "downers" like the addictive opiate, Percodan. Jones might break into a rage, only to calm down moments later. Sometimes he slurred his words badly. Mostly, he maintained a delicate balance marked by a substantial degree of coherence. In general, Jones's pattern of drug use does not seem to have affected his moment-to-moment thinking during "balanced" periods, but if he responded to opiates like heavy users, the drug may have increased his day-to-day tolerance for adversity by allowing him to sublimate ever-growing resentment.

Jones's erratic ramblings offered striking contrast to the tableau that surrounded him, a thriving community that DCM Dwyer concluded was "much more than a Potemkin village." But deeper concerns also groped for expression; embassy staff entertained a "persistent uneasiness" about Jonestown. On departing from the May visit, even though Temple member Tim Carter was accompanying them back to Georgetown, after they took off from the Port Kaituma airstrip, the embassy officers had the plane "circle slowly over the community in order to permit the DCM to take photographs at an angle to try to locate any roadways or buildings at the settlement's periphery." The films revealed none.

Two days after the visit, Debbie Blakey showed up at the U.S. embassy. After less than six months in Guyana, the upper-middle-class young woman wanted out. She harbored no ill will toward the group, she told McCoy, but she was frightened by threats of mass suicide. Her mother living in Jonestown was going to die of lung cancer anyway, she reasoned, and she herself "had to leave when I could." Blakey picked up a ticket her sister had sent to the embassy, got an emergency passport, and prepared to depart Guyana on May 13.

What Blakey told McCoy about suicide was so damning an indictment that McCoy briefed Ambassador Burke, who directed him to write down the substance of it. Debbie Blakey signed a handwritten statement that read:

> I am afraid that Jim Jones will carry out his threat to force all members of the organization in Guyana to commit suicide if a decision is made in Guyana by the Court to have John Stoen returned to his mother. I know that plans are being made to carry out this mass suicide by poison that is presently at Jonestown. I also know that plans are made to kill those members who are unwilling to voluntarily commit suicide.

When questioned, Blakey could not say whether the threat was real or just a scare tactic.

Perhaps fortuitously, Richard McCoy shared the flight to the United States with Blakey, on his way to attend a consular conference in Washington. As the Pan Am jet headed to New York, McCoy quizzed the defector on what was really going on in Jonestown. Debbie told him about armed guards, smuggled firearms, the diversion of capital to foreign banks, and how Jones had made people feel that even consular officers could not escort them out. McCoy thought the revelations might offer the basis for an official investigation of Jonestown by the Guyanese government, but that could happen only if the State Department received enough corroboration of allegations to justify a request to the Guyanese government. He urged Debbie Blakey to go to Customs, and to Alcohol, Firearms and Tobacco Control at the Treasury Department. As they were flying along the Atlantic coast to New York, Blakey asked what McCoy thought about going to the press. He did not see it as accomplishing very much. Government investigations, he emphasized, would be the key. But Blakey was persistent; after they arrived in the United States, she phoned McCoy, again asking about going to the press. He repeated his advice about going to authorities, and in the end he decided that Blakey's credibility would be tested by what she did.

When McCoy returned to Guyana, he met a senior Guyanese government official who was suspicious of Peoples Temple. The embassy had known for nine months that working-level Guyana police and other agency officials harbored concerns that Jonestown effectively lay beyond their jurisdiction. When McCoy unloaded Blakey's charges, the official shot back, "We have heard the allegations. What have *you* found?" Aside from his own inconclusive visits, McCoy had only the initial and uncorroborated reports of a defector. Still, he sought to take some action.

On June 6, a cable prepared with the help of McCoy and DCM Dwyer was sent from Georgetown to the State Department under Ambassador Burke's signature. "It has been observed that the local Guyanese administration exercises little or no control over the Jonestown community, and that the settlement's autonomy seems virtually total," Burke informed Washington. Without saying as much, the cable portrayed Jonestown as a "state within a state." The embassy wanted to "approach the government of Guyana at an appropriate level to discuss the Peoples Temple community and request that the Government exercise normal administrative jurisdiction over the community," letting the people of Jonestown know that they "enjoy the protection of the Guyanese legal system."

State Department officials later held that they "had not the slightest notion of what lay behind the embassy's telegram." McCoy thought they should have fully understood it, he later said, because "the people who received that telegram had been personally briefed by me regarding Jonestown for several hours," three and a half weeks earlier. State Department officials would say that the cable belabored the obvious, that people in Guyana were subject to the laws of Guyana. Their response? "Department at present of view that any action initiated by the embassy to approach the GOG [Government of Guyana] concerning matters raised in reftel [referenced telegram] could be construed by some as interference, unless Amcit [American Citizen] member or family requests assistance or there is evidence of lawlessness. . . ." Constrained by legalistic considerations, the State Department and embassy backed off and Blakey's statement about mass suicide was left to sit in the embassy safe.[25]

Nor did Debbie Blakey ever go to government officials, as Consul McCoy twice advised, so as to give a defensible basis for approaching Guyanese officials. Instead, she went to the Concerned Relatives, giving them substantiation of suicide drills. Following their strategy and her early predispositions, Blakey ended up going to the press. In a matter of days after she flew to California, Blakey met with Grace Stoen. She then talked with Tim Stoen and Al and Jeannie Mills. The Millses were starting what would be called the Human Freedom Center, a sort of halfway house where they planned to provide voluntary deprogramming counseling and shelter to defecting Temple members. Tim Stoen saw Blakey's accounts of life at Jonestown as very important. Perhaps, he told her, it would be the beginning of a "Watergate of the cults." More concretely, Stoen and Jeffrey Haas hoped that Blakey's eyewitness account would bring a breakthrough in the John Victor Stoen custody case, and they helped her prepare a detailed affidavit describing the suicide threat, gun smuggling, the September 1977 arrest-order crisis, a community "swarming" with armed guards, and a "woefully inadequate" diet.

Blakey also described "white-night" emergency meetings that began to occur monthly or more often in the wake of the arrest-order crisis. In these paramilitary exercises, people were mobilized to defend the community against mercenaries. During one white night just before Blakey left

Jonestown for Georgetown in March, the people of Jonestown were told that their situation,

> had become hopeless and the only course of action open to us was a mass suicide for the glory of socialism. We were told we would be tortured by mercenaries if we were taken alive. Everyone, including the children, was told to line up. As we passed through the line, we were given a small glass of red liquid to drink. We were told that the liquid contained poison and that we would die within 45 minutes. When the time came when we should have dropped dead, Rev. Jones explained that the poison was not real and that we had just been through a loyalty test. He warned us that the time was not far off when it would become necessary for us to die by our own hands.

Blakey portrayed herself as steeled to the loyalty drill. "I had become indifferent as to whether I lived or died." To underscore that the welfare of John Victor Stoen was affected by all this, Blakey reported that during one white night, Carolyn Layton gave the child sleeping pills, saying she probably would have to shoot him, and it would be easier for the child if he were asleep.

Jeffrey Haas saw the Blakey affidavit as a way to connect the long delays in the Stoen custody case with outrageous and unconscionable threats, and he forwarded copies to several contacts at the State Department. In perhaps its most inept moment, the State Department bureaucratically mishandled and substantively ignored Haas's letter. He never got a reply, and only one person in Washington even absorbed the Blakey affidavit's foreboding doom.[26]

The State Department would have performed better if its officials read the California newspapers, for Blakey offered interviews to the press via telephone from Haas's San Francisco office. If her affidavit contained allegations she had not mentioned to McCoy, her statements to reporters went even further. Jones, she said, had described his September threat as "the crazy nigger approach." John Victor Stoen believed he had come from the womb of Maria Katsaris. The "Security Alert Teams" of fifty armed guards drew on an arsenal that included between two and three hundred rifles, twenty-five pistols, and a homemade bazooka. "Everyone wants to leave," Blakey said, "I'm sure of it." Tim Reiterman of the *Examiner* did not know whether to believe the young woman or not, but Marshall Kilduff and George Klineman, who had worked on the *New West* story, carried the accounts in the *Chronicle* and the Santa Rosa *Press-Democrat*.

Blakey's press splash came on the heels of a saga involving Kathie Hunter, the reporter who originally had introduced Peoples Temple to the Ukiah community in the 1960s. In May 1978, less than a week after the Concerned Relatives' human rights demonstration, Hunter flew to Guyana to get the real story on Jonestown on the basis of a phone call invitation from Guyana Prime Minister Forbes Burnham, a call she later called a "hoax." Before leaving the United States, Hunter tried to sell her firsthand account, but the best she could get were "freelance" arrangements with the Santa Rosa *Press-Democrat* that if she came back with a story it could use, the paper would buy it.

Hunter's trip brought nothing but trouble, and whatever happened is shrouded in a mist of accusations and counteraccusations. She held forth from the Pegasus, the nicest hotel in Georgetown, facing the Caribbean on the very shores of the sea. Apparently she talked with Peoples Temple Georgetown staff about a story, and at first she was invited to Jonestown. When her mission to Jonestown was vetoed because of her connections to the anti-Temple *Press-Democrat*, Hunter characterized Temple members as a "squad of interrogators." Five fire alarms went off in her hotel in one day. In Hunter's stories to the press back home, hotel security guard patrols became "protective custody," even though she continued to move freely about Georgetown. Then the government accused the reporter of misrepresenting herself to gain entry into Guyana, and asked her to leave. The *Examiner* headlined its initial account, "Report of Peoples Temple terror," and Hunter arrived at San Francisco's International Airport to the glare of television lights. She was also greeted by Tim Stoen. Whether or not the Concerned Relatives had inspired Hunter's ill-fated trip to Georgetown, they could not have but savored the uproar it created.

A month later, even as the Santa Rosa *Press-Democrat* was publishing a detailed Temple rebuttal to media coverage of Hunter's strange voyage, she was back in the news again. The same sorts of mysterious events that sometimes plagued Peoples Temple years before now besieged her. It was, she informed the papers, a "campaign of terror." There was an anonymous phone call. Then came crashing through her window a rock wrapped in a note composed of newspaper-letter cutouts: "Hey white trash, we know where you live! We're watching you all the time, we know where you work, we know your home number, we know your trashy life honkey. . . . Keep your ass clean and your mouth clamed [*sic*] up." The final outrage came when the reporter, a woman known for drinking heavily, said she was confronted by two Black men who entered her kitchen, poured a bottle of alcohol down her throat, and then left without being seen by anyone else. Ukiah police told the press, "We're taking it at face value."[27]

## Uncovering "Conspiracy"

Peoples Temple did not sit still for all the allegations, but somehow Temple PR efforts never captured the limelight the way stories against it did. Jim Jones became increasingly obsessed with his enemies, and Temple staff began a major initiative, bringing Kennedy assassination conspiracy theorist Mark Lane to their cause. The trail to that effort marked the decline of Charles Garry's influence as the U.S. attorney for Peoples Temple.

Garry was doing a lawyer's job of dealing with the Temple's problems, but without scoring major victories. He insisted on controlling all Temple contacts with the press, to try to filter out some of the more rabid Temple statements. He wrote to newspapers, demanding that they retract headlines describing "terror." The papers did so. Garry ran an advertisement in the Ukiah newspaper offering a reward for information leading to the arrest and conviction of persons who allegedly assaulted Kathie Hunter. He tried to shift the balance of public initiative by filing suit against Tim Stoen. And he proceeded with efforts to unmask any conspiracy by filing Freedom of Information Act requests.

But Garry did not live up to Temple hopes. He demanded that Peoples Temple staff tell him whether Blakey's affidavit was true. More telling was his inability to nail down the conspiracy. From his Privacy Act and Freedom of Information Act requests, all Garry ever turned up were a few letters Jones and Gene Chaiken had sent to government officials. By May of 1978 he was assuring Peoples Temple that there was no government conspiracy against it. Temple staff hoped for something different. The defection of Blakey had been a particularly crushing blow, and the Hunter flap consolidated Temple fears about the pervasive network of their enemies. Peoples Temple staff saw themselves as victims of an exposé like the one against Synanon then unfolding in the California press, and as targets of a government vendetta like the one against the Church of Scientology, a group that had done a great deal to detail the FBI practices of using infiltrators and agents provocateurs.

Jim Jones had faced personal doubts at least since the death of his mother Lynetta on December 9, 1977. Maybe he should not have taken on responsibility for so many people. His mother he could eulogize for her spunk and her steadfast support for his struggles. "Oh God," he sobbed on the day of her death, as he spoke to the people of Jonestown, "you don't know how good somebody is until they're gone. For that, I cry for the human race." The grave marker read, "Lynetta P. Jones, In commemoration of the true fighter for justice; who gave the ultimate, who gave up her son so he could serve the people in the struggle for justice, for freedom from oppression and for the foundation of socialism."

About Debbie Blakey, Jones felt much differently. As he saw it, he had never let her down. He believed that people would use him and discard him when their own interests were no longer served. But a woman whom he had trusted had done far worse. She had joined those out to destroy Jonestown. For Jones, it was "the final blow"; he became disheartened, started to withdraw more from his followers, and began intensifying demands on them.[28]

Jones and his staff hoped for more than a war of attrition with their opponents. They sought vindication. One battle the Temple won respite from, at least temporarily. On August 12, Guyanese High Court Justice Audrey Bishop announced that he would step aside instead of ruling on the custody of John Stoen. "Citing pressure tactics mounted upon the government and the court," the embassy reported, the judge returned the case to the chief justice for reassignment. Once a new judge was picked, the case would have to be heard from the beginning, as though no previous record existed. The pressures, the judge said, were "persistent efforts of an extralegal or opprobrious nature, in the form of letters and other documents, as well as telephone calls." They had come, he made clear, from both sides. Whatever the Concerned Relatives achieved in the way of publicity, they, along with Peoples Temple, had become parties to a mistrial that stalled their efforts to win the custody battle.

But Peoples Temple won only a skirmish, not the war. The case would go another round, and then what? Clearly, if Jones lost the custody case, the embassy would insist that the custody order be enforced. Perhaps Jones and his followers should spirit John Stoen out of Guyana to the next haven. Perhaps Jones should martyr himself for his community by returning to the States to face trial. Airing the possibilities established at least one thing for Temple leaders: freedom might not be achieved in Guyana. For all the government's socialist talk, for all the alliances the Temple had forged, the government clearly harbored Temple opponents, and the United States apparently had considerable influence, which staff feared it was using against the Temple. The border dispute between Guyana and Venezuela added another element of instability, and Peoples Temple also was torn between its pragmatic alliance with the Guyanese party of power, the PNC, and its own communist ideology, which more readily aligned with the People's Progressive party, the Soviets, and the Cubans. In Guyana Peoples Temple stood at the confluence of international political crosscurrents.

After the September 1977 crisis, Temple staff made serious efforts to establish yet another haven for flight in case the situation in Guyana became untenable. In the waning months of 1978 they continued negotiations that centered on Cuba and the Soviet Union. Despite extensive discussions, however, neither the Soviets nor Cuba moved to resolve the Jonestown crisis by encouraging an early migration. Still, the possibility of migration changed things in Jonestown. Some projects continued to develop as though Guyana would remain the home of Jim Jones's people, but agriculture began to decline after the Soviet migration scheme was first discussed publicly in the summer of 1978, and the uncertainties contributed to an unsettled mood within the community.

If the legal and geopolitical troubles were not enough, the media hounds seemed ever at the doorsteps. In June 1978 came Gordon Lindsay, a British stringer for the *National Enquirer* scandal tabloid. The reporter buzzed the Jonestown settlement in a small plane, without contacting Temple staff in Georgetown to arrange a visit. Two months later he called the Reverend John Moore in California. Moore found Lindsay's questions displayed prejudices of the Concerned Relatives and disbelief that the paternity of John Stoen could be a legitimate issue.[29]

Staff sought to turn Jonestown's situation around with the same strategy favored by its opponents: public relations. If they could just get out the truth about Jonestown, if they could just expose the conspiracy that sought to undo the community's brave venture into egalitarian socialism, perhaps all else would fall in place. The plan was to get a major writer to do a book on Jonestown. Attorney Charles Garry's assistant Pat Richartz suggested the Temple call on Don Freed, a progressive and a member of Citizens Commission of Inquiry—a group headed by noted conspiracy theorist Mark Lane. In late August 1978 Freed journeyed to Jonestown ("New heaven, new earth," he called it in the guest book). On his return Freed linked activities against Peoples Temple with other "attempts to criminalize political people" like the Black Panthers and the Communist party of the 1950s. "The murder of Martin Luther King has echoes for Jonestown," he said. He told Richartz there would be no book, just some occasional free-lance publicity efforts.

The public relations effort Freed pursued had as its centerpiece Joe Mazor, the private investigator who had worked with opponents to rescue people from Jonestown a year earlier. Freed set up a meeting at San Francisco's posh St. Francis Hotel to discuss Jonestown, inviting Mazor, Pat Richartz, and Mark Lane to engage in a freewheeling discussion of plot alternatives for a bogus movie scheme. Supposedly the group would piece together a film proposal for some interested investors.

Shakespeare himself would have been impressed with the charade. The talk about a plot was a plot itself, tape recorded at that. Each of the actors read, as it were, from a script from a different play, but each script somehow grew heavy with the others' distorted perceptions as the hotel room drama unfolded. Mazor waxed eager to convince of his irreplaceable role as a for-fee consultant. At the outset he weighed in with a bombshell: he had just collected from an insurance company on bonds for fraud and forgery tied to Tim Stoen's actions in Temple property transfers. Mazor also spewed out apocryphal tales about his daring exploits as a mercenary who had crept around the edge of Jonestown during the crisis the previous September.

In a brief timeout from the drama of Peoples Temple and the Concerned Relatives, those gathered in the St. Francis Hotel debated the content of the movie as a way of fleshing out the play of real life. Was John Victor Stoen really conceived by Jim Jones in Bus #7, as Mazor claimed? Had Tim Stoen really been in "deep cover" from his past associations with U.S. intelligence, Lane wondered. Did Stoen advocate fraud and intimidation as a provocateur? Was the CIA really behind it all? In the middle of history they stopped to write the end of history. How would it all turn out? Who really should be cast as the villain? Tim Stoen? Jim Jones? "I don't know who you are talking about making martyrs out of in the drama, if anyone," Mazor allowed, "but you better be careful, because it's unfolding day by day."

Amidst the clatter of dishes from a room service lunch, Mazor made it clear that he had no love lost for either Tim Stoen or Jim Jones, but he was more than willing to help with the film. Freed suggested that they try to visit Jonestown to answer some of Mazor's questions. Mazor had the ear of reporter Tim Reiterman, and maybe his views would count for something. After the meeting, Freed dashed off a memo to Charles Garry and Jim Jones. If Mazor could satisfy himself that children were not being held against their will in Jonestown, he would confront the Millses on their vendetta against Jones and go to the media with the truth. "Personal recommendation: Bring Mazor to Jonestown at once. He is ready to turn around."[30]

Within days Mazor traveled down to Guyana with Garry, who needed to go there to gather affidavits for court cases. At Jonestown Garry saw Jim Jones's obvious physical deterioration. The man was running a high fever, and seemed delirious much of the time. He had lost thirty pounds since the only other time Garry had visited, a year earlier. Back in Georgetown, Garry obtained judicial assurances that Jones could feel free to come to Georgetown without fear of being arrested on the basis of the writ of habeas corpus issued a year earlier. Garry also talked with the chief justice of the Supreme Court, who agreed with the Temple's local counsel, Sir Lionel Luckhoo, that the judge who heard the custody case had botched the trial terribly. If anyone followed the chief justice's opinion, the entire matter would be dropped. Garry related all this good news to Jones in a taped message, insisting that the leader of Jonestown should take the risk of opening up Jonestown, and telling him, "You must get some medical evaluation."

But the St. Francis Hotel one-act play was seeping back into the historical drama. Events were to follow a different track, one that capitalized on

Jones's fears. Mazor would "turn around" almost effortlessly, and Mark Lane would follow his trail. At Jonestown Mazor "confessed" to possibly concocted mercenary activities the previous fall, when he claimed to have led a band that planned to enter Jonestown, blow up the generators, and take the kids out in the ensuing confusion. He became an instant hero, playing into Temple charades with his own.

On the heels of Mazor's departure from Jonestown came the man who had made a big name for himself by promoting conspiracy theories in the deaths of John F. Kennedy and Martin Luther King. Mark Lane left for Guyana September 12, running into Charles Garry as the Temple attorney was returning to the States. Without telling Garry why he was in Guyana, Lane went out to Jonestown to drape Mazor's tales with an aura of legitimacy that would seal his own role in the unfolding drama. Lane put together a series of suppositions: the right-wing Rotary Club and Campus Crusade for Christ connections of Tim Stoen, Stoen's financing by neo-Nazis holed up in Venezuela, the CIA lines of influence in the Caribbean converging on Jonestown as a bone of contention in U.S. alliances with Guyana and Venezuela. If Jim Jones was an Elmer Gantry, was Tim Stoen a Lee Harvey Oswald, the shadowy figure pegged with the assassination of President Kennedy? Ideas like these had fed Lane's fertile imagination in the Hollywood-style brainstorming session at the St. Francis Hotel, and at Jonestown he fed the imaginations of others with a palatable plot line. Jones and his associates ate it up.

Here at last was someone who knew how to unearth conspiracies and manage press relations at the same time. Here was an expert on conspiracies who could sort through the shreds of evidence collected by Temple staff and see the same pattern they saw. From a Jonestown meeting with Mark Lane on September 17 came a decision to have the lawyer work full time on the case for at least three months. Lane talked in Jonestown about preparing a complaint in a conspiracy case, and about doing a book. He proposed putting together a team out of his Memphis law office: himself, Don Freed, a researcher, an archivist, perhaps an undercover agent. They would hope to work closely with Teri Buford, the Temple aide being sent to San Francisco to coordinate with Charles Garry. The cost of Lane's operation? Around $6,000 a month, and Freed and Lane would be available for speeches and fund-raisers under the auspices of something like a "Jonestown Support Committee." From Lane's visit came a memo that proposed a legal, public relations and congressional "counteroffensive." In it he held, "even a cursory examination reveals that there has been a coordinated campaign to destroy the Peoples Temple and to impugn the reputation of its leader." Whatever the validity of Lane's assertions, Jones received substantiation of his sense of persecution from a man who had seen what happened to Martin Luther King.

On his way back through Georgetown after the deal had been struck, Lane showed off his adroit ability. Honing up a presentation for later use in the United States, he held a press conference at the Temple's Lamaha Gardens house. Lane announced to the world that "a key witness [Mazor] who was one of the key people who had made the charges . . . now has made in essence a full confession to us." He then expounded the view that the U.S. government was conspiring to destroy Jones and Peoples Temple because they represented a powerful force for social change in the United States. Within ninety days, he promised, a law suit for damages in the millions of dollars would name the U.S. attorney general, the FBI, and the CIA, among others.

Jim Jones was inspired. He or his staff composed a letter to President Jimmie Carter that cataloged the whole sordid story of how the "MASSIVE CONSPIRACY" uncovered by Mark Lane had emerged out of the acts of agents provocateurs, Trotskyite elements, and a man who had asked him to father a child for his wife years ago, and then turned on him, "attempting to use a child as a pawn in a plot to discredit and ruin my work." Several weeks later, Marceline Jones brought back to Jonestown a tape of the San Francisco Temple meeting at which Mark Lane had spoken upon his return to the States. "The offensive must begin," Lane affirmed. To cries of "Tell us, brother!" and "All right!" he shouted out, "We can begin to confront the evil and horrible charges that have been made against Jonestown in Guyana . . . , just the same way we have won every other battle that we have ever been involved in." The group closed with an emotional rendition of the old civil rights standard "We Shall Overcome." At Jonestown, the tape was played on the public address system over and over again.[31]

# 11

# The Apocalypse at Jonestown

Temple PR man Mike Prokes sent a letter to San Francisco *Chronicle* columnist Herb Caen in the summer of 1978. "We have found something to die for," he wrote, "and it's called social justice. We will at least have had the satisfaction of living that principle, not because it promised success or reward, but simply because we felt it was the right thing to do." Children in Jonestown mouthed the same viewpoint. A boy named Clifford Gieg vowed, "If I could die, I would like it to be a revolutionary death where I would take some enemies down with me." Eleven-year-old Mark Fields worried about falling into the hands of the enemy: "If the capitalists came over the hill, I'd just drink the potion as fast as I could do it. I wouldn't let the capitalists get me."

Jim Jones feared he was dying anyway. His friend and physician, Dr. Carlton Goodlett, diagnosed a fungal disease in the lungs, progressive coccidioidomycosis. Jones ran fevers, and he withdrew to the cottage he shared with Maria Katsaris, Carolyn Layton Prokes, and the two boys—one, Kimo Prokes, Carolyn's son fathered by Jones, the other, John Stoen. No one would see Jones out and about for days at a time, but they could hear him coming over the P.A. sounding "planted," slurring out a jumble of ramblings. He fumed about their enemies. And he warned people not to trigger the hidden security devices meant for "mercenaries."

In spite of Jones's threats and his orders to security personnel, during his withdrawal, the web of surveillance at Jonestown loosened up a bit. Scores of visitors streamed through an alleged prison camp, sensing nothing. Young people who tired of seeing their hard efforts undone by others stopped being so zealous in their work. As they recounted later, the Jones boys and Mike Touchette began talking, questioning whether one or another had informed to Jones about offhand remarks. Like Elmer and Deanna Mertle years earlier, the youths forged an alliance that evaded surveillance. Each in his own time "came around to seeing how phoney everything was." They supposedly talked about a possible coup, and even about assassinating Jones, making it look like a hero's death or the result of his shadowy illnesses. But Lew Eric and Jimmie Junior apparently opposed the plan, and Stephan himself had doubts because of the seniors: "I just felt like this was all they had. They just needed this messiah, this purpose. They had nothing to go back to [in the United States]." As life in Jonestown became a tableau of decline, the boys waited, and hoped that things would fall apart.[1]

### Mission to Jonestown

The Concerned Relatives would wait no more. Frustrated by the slow and presumably corrupt legal process in Guyana, shut out by the embassy's respect for privacy and its demand for evidence before proceeding against Peoples Temple, the Concerned Relatives put their stake in Leo Ryan, the suburban San Mateo congressman who had informed Peoples Temple of his sympathies for their opponents in May of 1978. One summer day a White woman named Clare Bouquet came to Ryan's office. She had gotten in touch with Tim Stoen after her son married a Black woman and departed for Guyana without saying goodbye. Ryan told her he shared her frustration. "I'd even go down to check it out," he said. She went to the Concerned Relatives with the news, and a meeting was set up with Ryan, Clare Bouquet, Tim Stoen, Jim Cobb, and Steve Katsaris and two of Katsaris's children, Elaine and Anthony. Al and Jeannie Mills, Sam Houston, and the Olivers joined subsequent meetings. Over the summer plans were firmed up for a visit to Jonestown by Ryan and a group of the Concerned Relatives.

From what Debbie Blakey had told them, everyone would want to leave. And so the Concerned Relatives prepared for a mission that would help those who wanted to return. To aid the liberated cultists who no doubt would be coming back to the States, Jeannie and Al Mills set up a sort of halfway house in a rambling yellow house on Regent Street in Berkeley. Mimicking names of other groups dedicated to freeing individuals from "cults" (like Citizens' Freedom Foundation), the Millses called their organization the "Human Freedom Center." They operated it on a shoestring budget. Partly the center drew support from profits the Millses siphoned off from a nursing home they operated, partly from the charity of a Los Angeles banker, and partly from donated labor. Workers lived at the center, wrote funding grants to try to support it, and prepared for the anticipated influx of Jonestown defectors who would need food, shelter, and counseling to help them reintegrate into U.S. society.

The Guyana expedition can either be construed as a kidnapping mission in the mold of self-styled U.S. "deprogrammer" Ted Patrick or as a less clandestine effort to have Congressman Ryan orchestrate a legitimate occasion for offering people at Jonestown the chance to leave. The goals of each relative probably differed somewhat, and each perceived the strategy of journeying to Jonestown according to those goals. Some relatives had heard such alarming tales that they simply wanted to see that their flesh and blood were all right, and not confined in some concentration camp.

For others, the fear was much stronger. Steve Katsaris could not comprehend his daughter's changing to the person he had seen the year before, and he worried that she was ignorant of the dangers at Jonestown. He believed that Maria would come to her senses if she could just get out from under the Jonestown regime, and he forged yet another plan to kidnap her, this time during the Ryan expedition.

Tim Stoen was of a similar mind. In the fall, with the custody case scheduled to begin anew, he waxed impatient about the legal process. On October 3, he sent a telegram to the State Department in Washington: "You are hereby advised I will retrieve my son John Victor Stoen by any means necessary. State Department conduct inexcusable. Ignoring mass suicide rehearsals documented by Blakey affadavit." In a phone conversation, Stoen told the department he planned to use "self-help" to "retrieve" the boy within two months, "by force if necessary." After he got his son back, he warned, he would announce the lack of cooperation by the State Department in his case, and its failure to make a full investigation of Jonestown.

Beyond the schemes that individual relatives forged secretly, the surface aspects of the trip would force Jones's hand. Either he would refuse to allow a U.S. congressman to visit Jonestown after the congressman had traveled all the way to Guyana, or the congressman would gain access. In the former case the Concerned Relatives would obtain damning proof about prison-like conditions at the mysterious cult on the Kaituma River. In the latter case, they would be able to establish the principle of access to Jonestown by its opponents from the outside world. If Debbie Blakey was correct, they would fill the Human Freedom Center and more with defectors. Victory was within reach.

Officially, Leo Ryan's expedition would be billed as an objective, fact-finding "congressional delegation" totally independent of the Concerned Relatives' travels to Guyana. But Ryan's public posture was a facade that obscured a working alliance with the Concerned Relatives. The plan for the visit to Guyana was formulated in discussions between them during the summer of 1978, and Ryan received substantial information from them about Peoples Temple. He even learned from Tim Stoen about Jim Jones's 1973 morals arrest in Los Angeles. From his meetings with the relatives, Ryan also learned about the rational side of Jim Jones. Under pressure, the man was known to strike deals. Ryan hoped to confront him about a number of issues: armed guards, custody, freedom of movement. Perhaps

Jones would negotiate if he realized that the alternative was simply more trouble.

Effectively, Ryan acted on behalf of the Concerned Relatives. How intimately he was aware of certain relatives' schemes remains controversial. Ryan's staff assistant, Jackie Speier, later said that she witnessed no discussion whatsoever of plans to bring people back from Jonestown, but others suggest at the very least that Ryan was open to the possibility that some people from Jonestown might want to return with him. Whatever victory was to be won would be achieved for distraught citizens who believed that niceties of due process and privacy rights were compromising more fundamental human rights—the freedom to choose one's associates, and the freedom to escape a life of domination under a madman.

On September 15, Congressman Ryan went to the State Department for an initial meeting to discuss the trip. He told Assistant Secretary Vaky and Richard McCoy that he planned to go to Guyana sometime after November 10 with a party of about eight people, including a doctor, a member of the press, and possibly some relatives. McCoy and others briefed the congressman on Jonestown, a group that McCoy characterized as a "pseudo-religious organization" that "espouses socialist philosophy." Was there anything to the threat of mass suicide reported by Debbie Blakey, Ryan wanted to know. "Nonsense," he was told. But in view of all the accusations of mind control, it was suggested that a clinical psychologist might be included in the party. Vaky assured Ryan that the State Department would offer all possible assistance for a trip, but he discouraged Ryan from including friends and relatives of Jonestown residents in the group, "at least on the first visit."[2]

With plans for the trip proceeding apace, the press started jockeying to cover it. Gordon Lindsay of the *National Enquirer* wanted to follow through on a story he had been pursuing for months with the help of Concerned Relatives. Lindsay was not sure his editors would publish his work, however, and he went to NBC reporter Don Harris, a Georgia-born soldier of fortune of a journalist. Would Harris be interested in making the trip to do a piece about people trapped in a jungle commune?

Harris approached an NBC cameraman, Leigh Wilson, about the expedition. The two sat in Harris's Burbank office while the reporter told Wilson he had a list of names of people who wanted to leave Jonestown. The plan, he said, was to play "the nice reporters" until they were ready to leave. Then he would sit down and do a final interview with Jim Jones. Harris traced the script: "I'm gonna pull out this list at the end of the interview with Jim Jones, and I'm gonna say, 'I got these names from families, and I know they want to come home,' and 'can they?' Whether he says 'yes' or 'no,' I'm going to tell him, 'We're leaving, and these people are free to come with us if they want to.'"

Harris made it clear to Wilson that people in Jonestown carried guns, and that if he followed his plan, they would not be very happy. "There could be trouble," he acknowledged. Harris had done some dangerous and controversial television reporting before. He was a gutsy newsman, often confrontational in his interviewing technique, but always careful to work up a defensible story. Still, this project sounded to Wilson as much like a commando mission as television journalism. "Thanks," Wilson told Harris, "but no thanks." Harris instead recruited cameraman Bob Brown and soundman Steve Sung. He warned them, "It's more than just going out and doing a story." Before they left, Brown told his wife he had "a funny feeling something was going to go wrong."

In Washington Ryan's staff assistant, Jackie Speier, kept in touch with the State Department, where staff briefed her on the logistical and legal issues of the trip and told her of the need to obtain advance permission to visit Jonestown. Speier doubted that Ryan would agree to such a procedure, for fear that people in Jonestown would be subjected to psychological intimidation prior to their arrival. Speier's reaction suggests that at this stage Ryan's plan was to show up without permission, cutting red tape by taking matters into his own hands. This was his style as a congressman, someone who would get things done by his own intervention on a personal basis.

During October Ryan yielded to more diplomatic procedures. The chairman of the House Committee on International Relations, Clement Zablocki, Jr., withheld authorization for the trip until Ryan conformed with committee travel guidelines that favored multiple rather than solo committee member trips. By October 18, Ryan was able to report that Republican Congressman Ed Derwinski from Illinois had agreed to accompany him, and Zablocki gave the green light for the delegation's trip.

Ryan also came around to the State Department's position that he should notify Jim Jones in advance of a visit, but he wanted a procedure that brought people from Jonestown to the more neutral turf of Georgetown. Speier told the department that Ryan planned to request the physical presence of around twenty-nine people from Jonestown, including Maria Katsaris and John Victor Stoen, for private interviews with the congressional delegation. There might also be Concerned Relatives and members of the press along. Richard McCoy knew how the people at Jonestown would handle such proposals. The congressmen could be told that the twenty-nine people did not want to travel to Georgetown. As for the Concerned Relatives and the press, McCoy warned Speier that they could pose a liability in gaining access to Jonestown, and in any event, they were private citizens, and the embassy would not try to force the Temple to receive them.

Moreover, because the relatives and the press were not part of the official congressional delegation (CODEL), the embassy should not be expected to arrange transportation for them. Speier agreed that the relatives would not be part of the official CODEL, but she was blunt in expressing to State Department staff her concerns about young Americans taken in by people like the Reverend Sun Myung Moon and Jim Jones, and she received with distaste State Department arguments that presence of media and the Concerned Relatives could only complicate access to Jonestown.

Ryan did not finalize his fast-breaking plans until shortly before departing. On November 1, some five months after he began planning for the trip, and fourteen days before he was to arrive in Georgetown, Ryan finally cabled Jim Jones via the embassy about his delegation's proposed visit. His cable noted the "anxiety" of constituents about their relatives and the statements of other people who said that "such concerns are exaggerated." His trip to Guyana would be "an effort to be responsive to these constituents with differing perspectives and to learn more about your church and its work." But Ryan did not ask Jones for an invitation. He simply announced that while he and Congressman Derwinski were in Guyana, "I have asked our Ambassador, John Burke, to make arrangements for transportation to visit your church and agricultural station at Jonestown. It goes without saying that I am most interested in a visit to Jonestown, and would appreciate whatever courtesies you can extend to our Congressional delegation."

By their own means Peoples Temple staff picked up a radically different view of the trip from that suggested in Ryan's cable. While Teri Buford was back in San Francisco working with the Temple's lawyers, she signed off on all Temple money connections and wrote a letter to Jean Brown. She explained that she had already discussed with Jim Jones the potential need for the project she was about to undertake, and it had been left up to her as to when to act. Her plan? In an attached "confidential" letter to Jim Jones, Teri set the stage for playing double agent by "defecting" and waiting for Tim Stoen to seek her out. "If you try to interfere," she concluded, "you will just have a suicide." With that, Buford disappeared from the Temple scene on October 26, leaving the letter for Brown to find the next day.

Apparently Jim Jones did not really buy Teri Buford's five-page single-spaced epistle. He tried to track her down. Among those put on the lookout for Buford was Tim Carter, the son of an Internal Revenue Service agent, and from Burlingame, the same town as Concerned Relative Clare Bouquet. Carter managed to "escape" from Jonestown and resurface at the Millses' Human Freedom Center in Berkeley. He was to contact Pat

Richartz at Garry's office with any information about Buford. But Carter came up with something different from that. Having left Jonestown himself, he told people at the Human Freedom Center he wanted to get his wife and child out too. Carter was accepted into the ranks of those discussing Ryan's planned expedition. His wife and son would be saved, Concerned Relatives assured the young man. They told him that Ryan had been briefed by Debbie Blakey. "Wow, that's a coup!" exclaimed Carter. "If you think that's a coup, wait 'til you see what happens when Ryan gets to Jonestown," he says he was told. What that meant, Carter did not really know, but on November 8 he used Pat Richartz's phone to pass the information on to Sharon Amos in Georgetown, and from there, it was relayed to Jones in Jonestown.

The word? Tim Carter later recounted, "I learned [the group's] strategy for coming down. Tim Stoen expected Jones to overreact." The Concerned Relatives knew about the mass suicide plan, but they believed that "either Ryan would come down and get refused entrance to Jonestown, make a media circus out of it, and hold congressional hearings, or he would come to Jonestown, bring people back with him, and get his investigation started that way." Several days after Carter's revelation, Pat Richartz wrote to Jones that the key to the conflict was Tim Stoen. "His ax is with you—and your fatherhood," she wrote. "It has become clear to me that anything Stoen's involved in has as its goal the destruction of you (Jim Jones) and ultimately the organization."

Earlier Peoples Temple had reacted with some favor toward the congressman's proposed visit, but in early November the Temple stance shifted dramatically. On November 4, U.S. Ambassador John Burke discussed the whole matter with Laurence Mann, the Guyanese ambassador to the United States, who happened to be in Guyana. By Mann's account, Peoples Temple seemed convinced that the CODEL was hostile and prejudiced, and that an on-the-spot visit simply would be used to enable the delegation to return to the United States and propagate a prejudiced view with greater authority than before. Apparently NBC had approached the Guyanese embassy in Washington about taking a crew down with Ryan, and Mann had tipped off Temple staff in Georgetown. Now Temple staff were insisting to Mann that Jonestown would not receive the congressman.

No more than an hour after Burke finished talking with Mann, the embassy received a call from one of the Temple staff. They had not definitely closed the door to a visit, but there were three conditions. First, they insisted that the CODEL be balanced by the presence of someone sympathetic to Peoples Temple. Second, there should be no media coverage of Jonestown. Third, attorney Mark Lane would have to be present. Peoples

Temple told the consul that Ryan would receive a response to his cable through Mark Lane.[3]

In Los Angeles, Lane apparently had developed some new information. For some time, he had been negotiating with the *National Enquirer* to suppress a negative story on Peoples Temple. Jean Brown reported by radio to Jonestown on November 8 that the lawyer was now worried that the *National Enquirer* was working with the Los Angeles district attorney, Congressman Ryan, and the Concerned Relatives. Ryan's trip to Jonestown might be used as the occasion to bring forth another round of charges against Peoples Temple, perhaps even surfacing the sealed court records from Jim Jones's 1973 morals arrest. Brown radioed that Mark Lane needed $10,000 to buy a draft copy of the *Enquirer* article and research its assertions to work up a detailed rebuttal. Oddly enough, he also wanted the right to represent Teri Buford rather than the Temple, should she become involved in a legal conflict with the Temple. Jones did not answer the request about Buford. But he approved the expenditure for the article.

Congressman Ryan was growing impatient waiting to hear. A week before his scheduled November 14 departure, he decided to apply pressure through the press, and he phoned the *New West* nemesis of Peoples Temple, Marshall Kilduff, to air his dissatisfaction. By the time Ryan talked with Kilduff, Congressman Derwinski had backed out of the trip six days earlier, but Ryan did not correct Kilduff's impression that Derwinski was part of the CODEL, and on November 8 the San Francisco *Chronicle* reported the flap about Ryan and Derwinski's planned trip. Don Edwards, another congressman from California, knew of Derwinski's pulling out and advised Ryan that taking the trip under such conditions "was not the right thing to do." Edwards remembers, "I said congressmen are ill-advised to take such matters into their own hands." But Ryan was not to be turned back. In fact, he was particularly incensed by a patronizing reply to his original request that he finally received from Mark Lane.

On November 6, Lane wrote Ryan at great length on the basic Temple insistence that he, Mark Lane, "be present while you make that tour." He informed Ryan that he had not been able to get in touch earlier. Now, unfortunately, Lane was to be tied up with witnesses testifying before the House Select Committee on Assassinations "from the middle to the end of November." Then came the kicker: Lane warned Ryan against any "witch hunt," and informed him that Peoples Temple had standing offers to take refuge in two countries, "neither of which has entirely friendly relations with the U.S." "You should be informed that various agencies of the U.S. Government have somewhat consistently oppressed the Peoples Temple," he went on. "You may judge, therefore, the important consequences which may flow from further persecution of Peoples Temple and which might very well result in the creation of a most embarrassing situation for the U.S. Government."

Ryan's response was pointed. With disdainful thanks for Lane's "offer of assistance . . . on behalf of the Peoples Temple," Ryan told Lane that his policy as a congressman was "to deal with the principals in a given situation," i.e. Jim Jones. Ryan regretted that Lane would not be able to come to Guyana, but he found it necessary to put the official business of the House of Representatives first rather than cooperating with preconditions set by the subjects of his inquiry. Finally, Ryan expressed deep offense at Mark Lane's closing remarks:

> No "persecution," as you put it, is intended, Mr. Lane. But your vague reference to the "the [sic] creation of the [sic] most embarrassing situation for the American government" does not impress me at all. If the comment is intended as a threat, I believe it reveals more than may have been intended.

Ryan's decision was clear. He could not operate on the basis of preconditions or threats. He could not wait for a direct response from Jones. He would go to Guyana, he told State Department officials, without Mark Lane, and without any assurances that his delegation could visit Jonestown.

In California, Concerned Relatives scurried to prepare for the expedition. In Ukiah the Reverend Ross Case even convinced the old friend of the Jones family, Bonnie Theilmann, that she should come along. Though Bonnie had remained friendly with Marceline Jones after leaving the Temple, she decided to go, as Case put it, for "whatever purposes God might want to use you." Two patrons came forward with $1,200 for her plane ticket, the San Francisco passport agent rushed her application through, and Bonnie ran errands for the trip organizer Ross Case put her in touch with, Tim Stoen, to help get John Stoen's custody papers in order.

Meanwhile, NBC reporter Don Harris did a pretrip story at the San Francisco Peoples Temple. As the camera was being set up, he denied a Temple accusation he was out to do an exposé. "I have absolutely no idea, at this point, what the story will look like," he assured the Temple. "And I must tell you in all honesty, I really don't give a damn."

In Washington the State Department kept pointing out that Ryan would have "no official status" or investigating rights in a self-governing foreign country. On Monday, November 13, the day before Ryan was to depart to Guyana, the State Department held a last briefing with Ryan, his staff, and several of the Concerned Relatives.

Steve Katsaris was offended by the event. Here State Department staff were being briefed by Grace Stoen and Debbie Blakey. If anyone knew of the trip's potential dangers, it was the Concerned Relatives. But despite all of their earlier efforts to alert authorities, it seemed that when the two women described the threats of mass suicide at the briefing, few of the department's staff had ever heard the allegations before. The Concerned Relatives knew more than the people holding the briefing!

State Department staff seemed preoccupied with lecturing their guests on their relatives' rights to privacy and the logistical difficulties of getting to Jonestown, if such a trip even could be arranged. They cautioned Ryan not to bring the press to Jonestown, but they did not say much about the trip's possibly involving danger. When Blakey described the presence of armed guards, a department representative asked whether the guards ever drew their weapons to intimidate or injure people. Blakey replied that they had not. Still, with the Concerned Relatives going along, State Department and embassy staff foresaw the possibility of "friction" between the two groups, some arguments and shouting, maybe even someone's getting "punched in the mouth." That was the limit of "friction" the State Department staff anticipated, but then, that projection may have been based on limited information. There is no evidence that the Concerned Relatives ever informed State Department officials either about their expectation that Jones would overreact, or about their plans to offer Jonestown relatives the opportunity to return to the United States.

Members of the delegation and relatives knew more than State Department staff about the trip, and some of them held stronger views of the dangers. Jackie Speier had enough of a premonition to write out a will before she left, as did Bonnie Theilmann, but overall, the travelers thought they would be safe. The Concerned Relatives believed that Leo Ryan was their shield, and so did the members of the press. Ryan regarded the press as offering a public accountability that would keep Jim Jones from any missteps.

Ryan and his staffers flew to New York and checked in for the Pan American flight to Georgetown, along with fourteen hopeful Concerned Relatives, Don Harris's four-man NBC crew, Gordon Lindsay of the *National Enquirer*, and three journalists from San Francisco—Tim Reiterman and photographer Greg Robinson from the *Examiner*, and Ron Javers of the *Chronicle*. As they boarded the Tuesday afternoon flight, Speier and the other congressional staffer talked. Perhaps explosives lay hidden in the luggage on the plane. One of them raised the possibility with Pan Am officials, but a search was dismissed as too time-consuming. The plane took off into the night falling along the eastern coast of the United States. Finally, the North American continent drifted away to the rear, and the Caribbean waters shining darkly against the scattered lights of island civilization announced their approach to Guyana, the land of many rivers.[4]

## CODEL and Concerned Relatives in Georgetown

The plane touched down at Timehri Airport shortly after midnight Wednesday morning, November 15, and the press immediately began running into problems. Some news people had not obtained visas for the trip, and the embassy had to intervene with the government to allow them to stay. Everyone finally made it through immigration except Ron Javers, who was importing Guyanese currency in violation of the law.

Leo Ryan went off to stay as the guest of Ambassador Burke, and his staff members rode to the Pegasus Hotel with Deputy Chief of Mission (DCM) Richard Dwyer. Jolting along on the straight, flat, but perilously narrow road to Georgetown, Dwyer complained to Jackie Speier and Jim Schollaert. The influx of media personnel had not been anticipated and lack of preparations in the United States was creating extra work for the embassy, he told them. The congressman's staff members found themselves annoyed.

Later Wednesday morning, after some sleep, the ambassador and other embassy staff gave a briefing to Ryan, Speier and Schollaert. The embassy had not been able to arrange its quarterly visit to Jonestown since May because of scheduling conflicts and the deterioration of the runway at Port Kaituma during the rainy season. But on Tuesday, November 7, in the midst of all the negotiations concerning Ryan's proposed visit, Consul Doug Ellice had made the trip to Jonestown with a vice-consul.

The embassy staffers briefly reported that they had found their welfare-and-whereabouts cases in Jonestown about the same as previous ones: all stating that they were fine. One couple, the Goodspeeds, remarked to Vice-consul Reece that the relatives inquiring after them "were never particularly interested in their welfare before the Goodspeeds went to Jonestown," the vice-consul later reported. Beyond their casework, the two embassy staffers took note of two things: the road from the front gate of the project's property to the center of Jonestown had become so eroded that it could be traveled only in a large dump truck. Second, Jim Jones seemed in a poor state: he slurred his speech, he could not spell a word that he did not want a child to overhear, and he complained of a high fever, even though he did not appear to be perspiring. To underscore his fragile health, the leader wore a surgical mask when not eating and had two aides help him away from the table when he finished dining with his guests.

After listening to the consular officers' report, Ryan and his staff watched slides that Richard Dwyer had taken of Jonestown, and they discussed the State Department view of the Privacy Act, by then a sore subject for Speier.

The discussion centered on whether Ryan would be able to get to Jonestown. According a fresh Temple press release, the answer was a flat no. Ryan was hardly the liberal he styled himself to be, the Temple claimed, and he was coming to Guyana with members of the press who "have taken part in the vendetta against Jim Jones." In the Temple view, the trip was nothing more than "a contrived media event" that was "being staged for the purpose of manufacturing adverse publicity for the Jonestown community, hopefully by provoking some kind of incident." According to the release, the residents of Jonestown had signed a statement "refusing to see Congressman Ryan and those accompanying him." They were prepared to request Guyana police protection if attempts were made to enter Jonestown.

While the ambassador, Ryan, and the others talked about the Temple's press release, five thousand miles away trucks sped around San Francisco delivering the *Chronicle* with a report by Ron Javers filed the day before. Javers described Ryan (and Congressman Ed Derwinski, who had not made the trip!) as "leading" the group of Concerned Relatives, and he quoted Tim Stoen on the expedition's objectives. "We hope to liberate at least some of the people who are down here against their will," Stoen announced. Attorney Charles Garry was quoted as opposing the visit: "For a congressman to barge in there is not the proper way. This is these people's home."

Ambassador Burke suggested that Ryan's best hope of getting to Jonestown was to persuade Temple representatives in Georgetown. Ryan aide Schollaert followed up on the ambassador's suggestion, while Ryan himself spent the rest of Wednesday lunching with Burke, paying a courtesy call on Guyana's foreign minister, and attending a small cocktail and dinner party at the ambassador's house. After dinner Ryan went over to the Pegasus Hotel to talk with the relatives and the press. The relatives had had a rough day of it. When they went to the Temple house in Lamaha Gardens, they were told, "None of you are welcome. Go see the American ambassador." Ryan tried to muster optimism. "They seek to delay us and wait us out," he told the reporters, and he announced he would consider extending his visit past his scheduled departure the following Sunday, if he felt it necessary to accomplish his goals.

From the Pegasus, Ryan went to engage in what had become a trademark for him: person-to-person diplomacy. He showed up at the Lamaha Gardens Temple house unannounced. "Hi, I'm Leo Ryan," he told the residents. "I'm the bad guy. Does anyone want to talk?" Sharon Amos and others found Ryan friendly, and they talked for several hours. The congressman wanted to fly to Jonestown the next day and make arrangements for the others in his group to follow. He was informed that Mark Lane was on his way down from Washington. The Georgetown Temple staff left the door open to negotiations, once Lane arrived. But the congressman would not be allowed to visit Jonestown without their attorney.

In San Francisco earlier the same day, Charles Garry received a message from Peoples Temple: "There is some sort of emergency in Guyana, and Jim requested you come right away." Until then he had been bypassed. On November 8, Garry had picked up the *Chronicle* and learned for the first time that Mark Lane was playing a role in arranging Ryan's visit. He had demanded an explanation. Jean Brown tried to reassure him that Lane was only a friend. But then the outspoken Garry learned about the content of Lane's letter to Ryan, and he hit the ceiling. The way Lane raved about government persecution and witch hunts was not going to go far with a congressman, Garry knew. He phoned Brown on Friday, November 10 to tell her that unless Lane was repudiated by the following Monday, Garry would no longer offer legal representation to Peoples Temple. In Jonestown, Temple attorney Gene Chaiken was not so clouded by tran-quilizers that he could not offer an opinion in a memo to Jones. Noting their own dissatisfaction with Garry, Chaiken advised that "a rupture is inevitable" and suggested that they "work through Mark to get a S.F. law-yer." But Jim Jones wanted Charles Garry in Guyana, and the "street-fighting" attorney dropped his work to travel there, despite his flap over Lane.

The next morning, Thursday, November 16, Leo Ryan held an informal press conference at the Pegasus. The trip to Jonestown remained elusive. Bonnie Thielmann observed that Ryan "continued to sound neutral and dispassionate so as not to jeopardize his image with anyone, but under-neath, we knew what he was feeling." In fact, Ryan was turning up the heat on the Temple. He indicated to reporters that Jonestown might be a "prison," and he told them he wanted to look into what sorts of U.S. government checks were being received at the mission, and whether Tem-ple members were being coerced into signing those checks over to Jones. It was an issue that the embassy had settled nearly a year earlier.

At the Lamaha Gardens house, Temple operative Sharon Amos took Ryan's statements as an affront. When Jonestown received word of the press conference over the shortwave, Lamaha Gardens got back orders not to allow the congressman to come. Jim Jones also got on the radio to try to convince the members of Jonestown's basketball team to come home; they were needed in the crisis. But Stephan Jones refused to follow his father's orders. He and the others were in Georgetown to play the Guyanese na-tional team the next day, and they were up for it. To return to Jonestown for the Ryan showdown promised only the tensions of one more staged crisis.

The Concerned Relatives were as frustrated as Ryan at all the delays and negotiations. They demanded a meeting with Ambassador Burke, open to the press. But Burke would not allow the embassy to be used as a platform on which the relatives could air their grievances and accusations in front of television cameras, and he insisted that press access be limited to a brief photo opportunity. The relatives begrudgingly agreed to Burke's limitation and used the afternoon's closed meeting to voice their allegations of physical abuse and denial of freedoms in Jonestown.

With Ryan and his staff members looking on, one relative told the ambassador that the group would get their kin out of Jonestown one way or another, by force if necessary. The relatives were tired of hearing the State Department's Privacy Act interpretation that "the embassy has no authority to require contacts between members of the Peoples Temple and persons whom they do not wish to receive." Ryan already had gone on record with an opposite view the day before. "In a free society," he held, "you can't deny access to relatives, either here or in the U.S." To the relatives, the carefully weighed State Department opinion amounted to "the same old embassy runaround," in the words of Howard Oliver, or "bullshit," as his wife Beverley put it.

Thursday evening, Ryan threw a dinner for the relatives and reporters, and he got a ray of encouraging news. Some Concerned Relatives had met people from Jonestown while walking along the seawall behind the Pegasus Hotel, near where the slow muddy Demerara River widens into the Caribbean. On a human level, beyond the eye of the media, away from Jonestown, there had been some friendly exchanges, but nothing more.

The next day, Friday, would be the point of no return, for the logistics of travel would make a one-day trip nearly worthless. Air Guyana interrupted its commercial schedule to provide a plane, a twin-engine Otter. When DCM Dwyer walked into the Pegasus Hotel around noon, Mark Lane and Charles Garry finally had arrived from the States, and they were about to leave for Peoples Temple's Lamaha Gardens house to try to set up the visit via shortwave. But Dwyer explained that even if the two lawyers returned by 2:00 P.M., it would be too late to make it to the airport and fly out that day because the Otter had to be back before dark. At this point, Ryan, Garry, and Lane huddled in a third-floor hotel room. Garry later said he accused Ryan: "You've got a prejudgement," and heard Ryan reply, "I've already got a prejudgement, but I've got an open mind." But he did not have an open mind about negotiating entry to Jonestown before leaving. Ryan decided to short circuit the lawyers' efforts and proceed with the flight to Port Kaituma. He informed the Lamaha Gardens staff of his plan and then posed some tough choices to the Concerned Relatives. Space on the plane would be tight. The Temple's lawyers would make the trip with

Ryan, as would Jackie Speier, DCM Dwyer, Guyanese Ministry of Information officer Neville Annibourne, and nine members of the press (Charles Krause, working Latin America for the Washington *Post*, had flown in on assignment). That left room for just four more people.

The Concerned Relatives had only a matter of minutes to decide which of them would make the trip. They chose each representative for different reasons. Carol Boyd was to go simply because she was one of the few relatives who actually lived in Ryan's congressional district. Young Jim Cobb went partly because he was Black, and the Concerned Relatives wanted to avoid the impression that they were a basically White organization opposing an overwhelmingly Black organization. The last two people were chosen partly because it was thought they could bring about defections. Mrs. Oliver was Black, and her presence would assure racial balance. More important, everyone knew that her sons loved her, and maybe she would be able to prevail upon them to return. Finally, Steve Katsaris's son Anthony was chosen because Maria was such a key person at Jonestown that, as her father put it, her defection "would unravel the whole thing." The other relatives who had hoped to go—Tim Stoen, Nadyne Houston, Wayne Pietla, Micki Touchette, Grace Stoen, Clare Bouquet, Bonnie Theilmann, Sherwin Harris, and Howard Oliver—would have to stay back in Georgetown. Three of them, Tim Stoen, Bonnie, and Howard Oliver, went off to the Guyana police to request protection for the expedition, for fear of "bloodshed."

Steve Katsaris originally had planned to go up with Anthony. They were going to abduct Maria to the airport just after they arrived. A private plane would be waiting there to spirit them off. Don Harris had assured Katsaris, "We'll film every goddamned step." Katsaris had believed "God has given you this opportunity, not just to get your daughter out, but to free 1,000 people," but now he needed to change plans quickly. He told Anthony just to try to get Maria to come to the airstrip; they would have to hope that she would board the plane, and the presence of the NBC crew would protect them. With a ticket for Maria to fly to San Francisco in his pocket, Steve Katsaris wished Anthony luck and handed his son a silver cross that his own father had passed on to him. "I know she still loves us," he said. "Give her this cross."

The entourage headed out to the airport. Lane and Garry stopped by the Lamaha Gardens house and talked with Jim Jones on the shortwave, briefing him on the alternatives of shutting out the congressman or opening up Jonestown. "I don't know what I'm going to do," Jones's voice crackled back over the speaker. He acquiesced. "Come on down." The lawyers sped out to the airport to catch up with Ryan and the others already boarding. Around 2:15 P.M. the chartered Guyana Airways Twin Otter roared down the old U.S. Air Force base runway at Timehri Airport, cleared the palm trees, and banked west for the hour flight over the velvet rainforest canopy cut by jungle streams flowing into the sea.[5]

## Into Jonestown

As the plane approached Port Kaituma, the pilot announced that the airstrip was bad, and they would not be able to land. Disappointed relatives asked him to fly over the community at least, and he winged over the dense forests that suddenly fell away to a clearing. As cameras clicked, the pilot decided to go back and try the runway again, and he brought the plane in and landed it. The entourage was met by a Guyana police corporal who informed them of the instructions he had received from his superiors. He was not to allow anyone to go to Jonestown without permission from Jim Jones.

Charles Garry and Mark Lane conferred with some Temple members who had come to Port Kaituma in a dump truck. They were to ride to Jonestown to discuss entry with Jim Jones. But as the truck headed off, they met up with Harriet Tropp on a tractor. "Go back and get the congressman and the ambassador," she told them. Five minutes later the dump truck reappeared at the airstrip, and Ryan was told he, his aides, DCM Dwyer, and Guyana Information Officer Annibourne could proceed to Jonestown. "What about the media and the other people?" Ryan demanded. Garry bristled, "It's none of your goddamned business. Do you want to come or don't you want to come?" Ryan would come. The truck made it to the Jonestown front gate in less than ten minutes. Then it headed slowly up the rough, muddy road to the settlement. As they passed a trailer that seemed stuck in the mud, Garry remarked to Johnny Jones, "If I didn't know better, I'd think you put that there on purpose."

In the center of Jonestown, Marceline Jones came out to meet the travelers. She told Ryan that Jim Jones was not in the best of health, and she gave a short guided tour while they waited for her husband to appear on the scene. Back at the pavilion they found Jones sitting at a table near a large sign hand-lettered with the words, "THOSE WHO DO NOT REMEMBER THE PAST ARE CONDEMNED TO REPEAT IT." Ryan joined Jones at the head of the table and entered a plea on behalf of the press and relatives: "This place is much too important, much too alive to be jeopardized by misinformation." Jones said he was "fed up" with the "lies" from the press, and disturbed that Ryan had not brought along journalists from Third World countries. Garry counseled him that the press would do more good than harm, and Jones relented, agreeing to let in all the press except Gordon Lindsay, the *Enquirer* reporter. The Concerned Relatives' delegation could come too.

How would the people of Jonestown handle such a visit? The evening before, in front of the assembled throng, Jones had threatened the life of Ryan, saying, "I want to shoot someone in the ass like him so bad, so long, I'm not going to pass this opportunity up. Now if they come in . . . they come in at their own risk." Jones also tried to prepare his followers for scrutiny, and told them, "Relax, we could come through this." The next morning, the microphone was on in the radio room, and around noon, people at Jonestown could hear Jim Jones arguing with Sharon Amos in Georgetown about the projected visit. If the group tried to come, he told Georgetown, the plane would fall out of the sky. After the plane took off, Jones's aides apparently persuaded him to prepare to contain the damage of the unwelcome guests, should they come in. Jones announced that everyone should behave so that the Ryan party could visit without incident and leave as soon as possible. Jann Gurvitch went around coaching people who might be subjected to questions about leaving. By one estimate, about 150 people were to coordinate the staging of Ryan's visit, keeping tabs on reporters and relatives, making sure no one broached the subject of departing when the visitors left.

With his defenses in place, Jones feigned openness to the congressman. When Ryan gave Jones a list of the people he wanted to interview during his visit, Jones told him, "See what you want to see. Talk to whom you want to talk." If people wanted to leave, he informed Ryan, they could.

Soon the journalists and relatives arrived, and the photographers started snapping away while reporters fired questions to Jones. The Jonestown kitchen served up its standard dinner for important guests: pork, this time served in sloppy joes with greens and potatoes. With the dinner came a preview of the program Jonestown was to put on in the Guyana capital for the upcoming Christmas holidays. There were singers and dancers, with jazz and disco music performed by "The Jonestown Express." Amidst the infectious air of hospitality, Marceline Jones asked Ryan if he would care to address the crowd. Ryan walked up to the stage, greeted the throng of nearly a thousand, and told them he was happy to be there. "From what I have seen," he chose his words carefully, "there are some people here who believe that this is the best thing that has happened in their lives." The corrugated steel roof reverberated with cheers and applause that seemed to last too long. Ryan joked that he would not mind signing up the people of Jonestown to vote in San Mateo. But then he turned serious. "I may as well tell you why I am here," he announced. "I am here to carry out a congressional inquiry into allegations made about the activities of your organization."

In the midst of partying to the band after dinner, Jackie Speier spotted

Tim Carter. The defector who had shown up at the Human Freedom Center several weeks earlier was back in Jonestown! Elsewhere in the crowd, a young man serving as part of the monitoring crew for Ryan's visit went up to NBC reporter Don Harris and managed to pass him a note. As soon as Harris got the chance, he read the words: "Help us get out of Jonestown." It was signed "Vern Gosney." On the reverse side was the name "Monica Bagby."

Over at a table, Charles Garry sat between Tim Reiterman and Jim Jones while Reiterman continued to interview Jones, even after the music ended around 11:30. The *Examiner* reporter asked all about the custody case, the conspiracy, the Social Security checks, all the allegations. Reiterman found Jones slurring words, incoherent in his answers, and preoccupied with death. Garry, on the other hand, thought Jones's fever had abated that evening and he saw Jones's interview performance as "very frank" and "very rational."

While Jones submitted to the exhaustive questioning, Ryan went to mingle with some of the people of Jonestown. Harris got word to Ryan about the note and the congressman sought out Vern Gosney. Did he really want to leave Jonestown, Ryan asked. Yes, Gosney answered. Then Gosney told Ryan that the congressman had reason to fear for his life. For the first time, perhaps, Leo Ryan could fully sense the vulnerability of his own position.

As the hour grew late, Jones cut off the reporters' questions: "We are not seeking accolades," he summed up. "All we want is to live in peace. I do hope after I have been gone, justice will be seen." Tim Reiterman asked Jones whether the reporters could spend the night. They did not need beds, they could sleep on benches in the pavilion. No, he was told, unlike the official delegation, the reporters would have to return to Port Kaituma, along with the visiting relatives, and come back the next day.

Around 1:00 A.M., after Mark Lane headed for the cot set up for him in the radio shack, Charles Garry talked with Jim Jones alone. What was Lane up to, Garry wanted to know. Who was going to be the Temple lawyer? They talked about Teri Buford. What did Jim think? He told Charles he believed the letter was a lie, that she had defected. Whatever Buford's game, Jones did not admit to being in on it. The leader of Jonestown also assured Garry that there was no way in the world he would want him to resign as counsel. Around 3 A.M. Garry went off to the radio shack to sleep on the cot next to the window.

### Exodus

The next morning dawned November 18, a year to the day after Grace Stoen and her estranged husband Tim won a ruling from a California court awarding them joint custody of John Victor. The reporters had passed the night with a little recreation and not much rest at a dayglow Rasta bar and weekender in Port Kaituma. In the midst of the reporters' late-night confab, NBC reporter Don Harris shared with his colleagues the note from Vern Gosney. The event seemed to confirm what the Concerned Relatives always had claimed, and it promised a hot story back in Jonestown the next morning. The dump truck scheduled to pick them up at 8:30 was slow arriving, and they did not make it back to the settlement until around 10:30.

Marceline Jones began leading reporters on a tour of the community, but the public relations effort quickly fell apart. The reporters sensed that they were missing crucial events and they wanted to stay close to any potential defectors to document what transpired. They also suspected a whitewash and their attention came to rest on Jane Pittman Gardens, a dormitory for elderly people. Jonestown staffers tried to dissuade them from entering. The elderly people who resided there were not all dressed and they did not want visitors, Jonestown staff said. The more interference the reporters received, the more they demanded to enter. Perhaps, they suspected, people who wanted to leave were being held inside. Finally, Mark Lane told them why all the evasion. Housing construction at Jonestown had not yet been completed and Jane Pittman Gardens was overcrowded. The reporters insisted on seeing for themselves, and Jonestown staff begrudgingly took them inside.

Earlier in the morning security staff had been sent around to people's quarters. They were going to have a good breakfast, they were told. People should dress for the occasion, they should be at their best, and they should look happy. Wending his way through this tableau of coached dramaturgy, Ryan had already been about his business for over an hour when the reporters arrived, talking with Jones first, then interviewing the people on his list.

Some people who wanted to leave Ryan would never meet. Diane Louie had arrived the previous May only to find people "living like dogs, like slaves." Julius Evans and Richard Clark had wanted out for months. They all decided the commotion created by a dignitary's visit would be as good a chance as any. The next dignitary happened to be Leo Ryan. To get Evans's children out of Jonestown school, they told the teachers, "We want to go on a picnic." Then the small band made its way down the Jonestown road and hightailed it thirty-seven miles along the railroad tracks to Matthews Ridge. Paradoxically, they proved on a day when a 150-person Ryan-visit staging team supposedly was in full force what former Consul Richard McCoy always had believed—that able-bodied people could fade into the jungle if they truly wanted to leave Jonestown.

In the meantime Ryan found that some people wanted to leave Jonestown under more official auspices. Vern Gosney and Monica Bagby came to Dick Dwyer around 11:00 that morning, and he told them they would depart with the Ryan delegation. Around noon Ryan recorded oral statements by people who intended to leave. When Monica Bagby finished speaking into the cassette recorder, the congressman informed her, "You are under the protection of the United States government." Jackie Speier took Monica to her dormitory to pick up what worldly possessions she wanted. A guard followed them and tried to force his way in. Fear shot through Jackie as she wedged her body against the door and gestured to Monica to scoop together what she had. They burst from the dorm and hurried back to the pavilion.

In the early afternoon NBC reporter Don Harris walked up to Ryan's assistant with another lead. Jackie might want to talk with an elderly White woman named Edith Parks, he told her. Some of the Parks family members had come to Jonestown in the spring of 1978, and they immediately saw it as a mistake. For the last few months they had discussed a secret plan to escape with the Bogue family, along with Richard Clark and his wife. Today was the day they were to disappear into the jungle. Clark, in fact, had already departed. But Gerald Parks, the father of the family, saw someone near where they had hidden clothes in the jungle, and he worried that their plan had been uncovered. Now grandmother Edith feared her son himself was in trouble. When she went to talk to Speier and Dwyer, the issue was forced. Once Jonestown staff definitely knew of their intentions, they would never get another chance to escape and they would face punishment to boot. Edith's move left the family members in a confused disarray. They told Ryan that they were debating whether to leave individually while some stayed, or depart as a group.

Sharon Swaney and Jones's adopted son Johnny tried to talk the family out of leaving. "No way," retorted Gerry Parks. "It's nothing but a communist prison camp." Jones came over and begged them at least not to leave with Ryan's group. "Why give in to people who want to destroy me and lie and come over and harass me and imprison me, and the threats of arrest and all this, just—and come into it and verify and go back and let them have their heyday on me in the States?" Jones pleaded. He claimed the Parks family was free to leave if they wanted, if they just would not associate their departure with his enemies. He even offered $5,000 to cover their transportation if they would wait to leave two or three days later.

Edith Parks went back a long way with Jim Jones and he had her wavering, but her grandson Dale did not trust Jones and he insisted they leave there and then. They decided to leave together. "I have failed," muttered Jones. Garry saw him go through a horrible reaction. "These traitors,"

Jones faltered. "All is lost," he agonized. "I live for my people because they need me. But whenever they leave, they tell lies about the place." Nonsense, Garry told him. If they want to leave, let them go and wish them well.

On top of the Parks family, who practically ran the medical clinic, Jones had to confront the loss of his agricultural manager, Jim Bogue, who declared his intentions to Ryan after the Parks family made their move. Bogue's estranged wife Edith would leave too, along with her male companion, Harold Cordell, an old-timer like the Parks family members. Young Thom Bogue wandered over from playing basketball to find out what the ruckus was about and learned that he too could leave, as he always had wanted. He spoke into Ryan's cassette recorder and went to join his parents, two sisters, Harold Cordell, and the Parks family waiting around the pavilion to go down to the truck. His nineteen-year-old sister Marilee refused to join them.

Just as some families had been split apart by the migration to Guyana, others were parting ways during the liberation. But none of the seventy-five people Richard McCoy had interviewed during consular visits planned to leave; nor did any of the people Debbie Blakey had told McCoy wanted to escape. All the same, the growing cluster of defectors in the center of Jonestown stood as a living testimony to a breach in the solidarity of the community in the face of a visit forced upon them by their enemies. It showed others that they too might leave. It showed Jones that his struggles with the Concerned Relatives would take new directions. The commotion of people planning to leave Jonestown was compounded by the reporters, who finally saw their story taking shape. The day's mood took a heavy and ominous turn.

Night nursing orderly Odell Rhoades was puttering around in his cottage when Jonestown security man Joe Wilson came in to ask him for help moving a heavy locker from the nurses' cottage to a shed. Rhoades always suspected the locker contained weapons, and when they lifted it and moved out, the former soldier thought he heard the sound of ammunition clicking against itself as the two men jostled down the path with their load. Did Joe say something about getting a move on, before they were gone? Rhoades had just woken up a few hours earlier and he could make no sense of what Wilson was saying.

At the pavilion Jones himself became increasingly distraught. The NBC camera played up close on him for a parting interview. Don Harris sensed news in the making. The other reporters waited with their heaviest questions, the ones they had saved until last when they no longer needed to cultivate the relationship. Harris waved the note from Vern Gosney and Monica Bagby in Jones's face, telling him he had received it the night before, probing Jones into a reaction for the camera.

Charles Garry thought Harris was "brutal" in his technique. Even Dale Parks, who had insisted on the Parks family exodus, saw the reporters throwing caution to the winds. They could have done something with Jones other than "hassle with the camera and the [defection] notes, and 'people want to leave,' and lead him to believe that you're going to broadcast this all over America." Jones reacted, Garry thought, "as though he were in a panic."

Finally, with some farewells, the relatives visiting Jonestown, several of the reporters, Garry and Lane, Jackie Speier, and the Parks family and others departing Jonestown started bringing their baggage down to the dump truck parked at the beginning of the Port Kaituma road. Loading seemed to take a long time. The mission had not been as successful as they had hoped. Anthony Katsaris, for one, never really got to talk openly with Maria. As he headed toward the truck, he made one last effort. Pulling out the silver cross Steve Katsaris had given him, Anthony tried to place it in his sister's hands. "What's this?" Maria demanded. "Just take it," Anthony pleaded, and turned away knowing he had not broken the hold on her. As Tim Reiterman walked by, Maria hurled the cross into the moist dirt, along with the words, "Tell Steve I don't believe in God."

At the truck, Speier sent Garry and Lane back to the pavilion to deal with another family disagreement that seemed to have erupted. Bonny Simon stood screaming that her husband Al was leaving with her children. The custody fight would have to be settled in court. But Ryan was planning to stay in Jonestown one more night anyway, and he could make sure Al Simon would be able to leave the next day if he wanted. The lawyers decided to stay back, too, to represent Jonestown should any legal difficulties arise.

With the logistics settled, Ryan stood chatting at the pavilion with Garry, Lane, and Jones. Turning to the lawyers, he told them, "I want to thank you two for making it possible for us to come down here and to be able to accomplish what we have been able to accomplish." The congressman then previewed what he would report to his colleagues when he got back to Washington. He would describe Jonestown in basically positive terms; no force was being used, he would say. Only a few people wanted to leave, he pointed out, and none of the sixty people named by the dissident families wanted out. "If 200 people wanted to leave," Ryan told Jim Jones, "I would still say you have a beautiful place here." The sense of imprisonment, he went on, he would explain as the result of peer pressure and lack of physical transportation. He would argue for more interchange with the outside world, and he would suggest that people should be able to come and go freely when they . . .

Suddenly the strong arm of a tall man slipped under Ryan's arm and grabbed down behind his neck. The voice screamed in his ear, "Congressman Ryan—you motherfucker!" A knife flashed into the muggy air. Charles Garry was not a young man, but he put a half nelson of his own on the assailant, while Mark Lane seized the man's hand flailing with the knife. Blood spurted across Ryan's shirt as Tim Carter rushed forward and pried the knife away from the man. Now Garry recognized it was Don Sly, the former husband of a Concerned Relative named Neva Sly. Jones stood about four feet away, impassive, detached.

Ryan picked himself up and gradually composed himself. The blood across his white shirt had come from Sly's wrist. The congressman was shaken but unhurt. Jones turned his gaze to Ryan. "Does this change everything?" "It doesn't change everything," Ryan answered, "but it changes things." He demanded, "You get that man arrested." Garry agreed. Sly's treacherous breach of civility might be patched over by the exercise of government jurisdiction. In his mind's eye, Jim Jones saw the Guyanese police coming into Jonestown to arrest one of his people.

The incident put a quick end to the congressman's visit. DCM Dwyer talked Ryan out of staying another night. "I want you to go with us," Dwyer told him, against Ryan's objections that he still wanted to stay to straighten out the Simons' custody dispute the next day. "I'll return," Dwyer assured him, "after we take you down to Port Kaituma." As a light drizzle fell, Dwyer, Garry, and Lane led Ryan down to the dump truck and packed him in.

A last straggler, a young man wearing a green rain poncho, came down to the truck as Ryan boarded. Like some of the others before him, the man had gone up to Jones and shared a farewell embrace before going to get his things and heading for the truck. Now Carolyn Layton's husband before she turned to Jones ten years earlier, the brother of defector Debbie Blakey, the son of the Jonestown loyalist Lisa Layton who died of cancer a few months after her daughter's defection, a man whose entire adult life had been buffeted by the travails of Temple life—Larry Layton was getting out of Jonestown.

The others already were edgy, and they received the latecomer as less than a comrade. Dale Parks, for one, did not trust Layton; he had been too close to Jones. Parks told Jackie Speier that Layton might not be a real defector. She wondered the same thing. Had not Layton talked to her earlier, denouncing his sister Debbie as the root of evil? The disconcerting juxtaposition lingered in Speier's mind.

A young man who once had thought about defecting himself, Wesley Breidenbach, climbed aboard the truck to act as a security escort for the trip to Port Kaituma. People perched around the center of Jonestown, standing in small circles, leaning up against the fences. It was a quarter after three or later. They watched the dump truck lurch into first gear and down the muddy road out of Jonestown, jammed with the media men, the Concerned Relatives' four representatives, sixteen people from Jonestown, and the official Ryan delegation.[6]

## Death in the Afternoon

No one talked much during the ride down the rutted road, but it was not an easy silence. The tensions of the day had piled up. There had been some successes in finding people who wanted to leave, but the delegation of Concerned Relatives had failed to "liberate" key people, much less "unravel" the entire operation. In fact, none of the people who chose to leave Jonestown were related to any of the Concerned Relatives who had come to Guyana. At the end Don Sly's strange attack on Ryan crystalized the departure as a less than triumphant escape, but at least they were leaving. Cameraman Bob Brown tried to inject his usual good humor into the thick feelings. "No wonder those people want to stay there," he joked. "Anything is better than this truck ride." A good three-quarters of an hour had passed when driver Ed Crenshaw pulled the truck up to Jonestown's front gate, three miles away from the center of the community. Big burly security man Joe Wilson came up, cast a menacing glare at the defectors, and searched the truck, claiming to look for his wife and child among the bags, packs, and people. Then Wilson hopped up to hang from the side of the truck and motioned Ed Crenshaw to head out. Off again, they roared onto the main road, and reached the airstrip at Port Kaituma around four thirty.

The travelers unloaded their belongings near a shed. The dump truck turned around to take Dick Dwyer and Guyana information officer Neville Annibourne back to the office of the Guyanese government's administrator for Port Kaituma, so that Dwyer could report the attempt on Ryan's life and have the police sent into Jonestown to arrest Don Sly. Dwyer planned to return to Jonestown to look after the people who had declared their intention to leave, but could not be accommodated by the two planes flying out that day. As he was making arrangements, a tractor pulling a trailer passed by the administrator's building and the Jonestown dump truck pulled out with it, leaving Dwyer behind. His plans changed abruptly. He and Annibourne hurried back to the airstrip along with several soldiers from the G.D.F. (Guyanese Defense Forces).

At the airstrip Jackie Speier was taking charge of assigning seats even though the planes had not yet arrived. She decided to put unmarried adults from Jonestown on the six-seater Cessna and the families and delegation of Concerned Relatives on the Twin Otter, along with Leo. The newsmen would have to fight it out for the seats left over, precious slots for reporters anxious to file stories. The small single-engined Cessna finally touched down at the airstrip, and soon after, the twin-engine Otter swooped in behind it. In the hubbub of loading, Dale Parks again asked Speier not to let Larry Layton board either plane. Jackie Speier was scared. She went over to Leo Ryan. "Why don't you just let him go on the first aircraft and you can come on the larger aircraft?" Leo asked her. Jackie agreed.

As they began to load, the Jonestown dump truck reappeared down the field, with the tractor and trailer behind it. Joe Wilson hopped down from the truck, and walked over to chat with some of the people who were leaving Jonestown. Which plane was he going on, Wilson asked Gerry Parks. Parks motioned to the larger one. Wilson then went over and talked with Larry Layton. When the two parted, they shook hands under Layton's green poncho. Ryan frisked the people from Jonestown as they boarded the Cessna, searching for the bogus defector they had come to fear might be carrying a weapon, but Layton already had hopped into the plane, ready to go. San Francisco *Chronicle* reporter Tim Reiterman blew the whistle on him, and Ryan insisted Layton get out and be searched. He was clean.

Once the Cessna was squared away, Ryan and the others moved over to the Twin Otter, where the reporters were still debating seat allocations. They looked down the field and saw the red tractor and trailer moving toward them. It looked as though the men from Jonestown had some final business to take care of, and somehow they did not seem friendly. Speier tried to hurry people aboard.

The Cessna six-seater was ready to take off, with Monica Bagby next to the pilot, Larry Layton behind him, and Vern Gosney next to Layton. In the back sat Dale and Tracy Parks. Around five o'clock the pilot finally started the engine, taxied the plane around to the head of the runway, revved to full bore, and headed for takeoff. Suddenly the plane lurched to one side and braked to a halt. The pilot had been cut off by the tractor pulling the trailer with a cluster of men—Whites and Blacks—standing in it. Vern Gosney peered out the Cessna window.

Young Stanley Gieg was steering the tractor across the runway and around the side where the Air Guyana Otter still was being loaded. In the trailer pulled by the tractor stood some of Jones's most trusted security men, his "Red Brigade": Tom Kice, Ronnie Dennis, Bob Kice, Anthony Simon, and maybe two or three other men. Joe Wilson and Wesley Breidenbach were there too. NBC cameraman Bob Brown filmed the tractor as it approached. Anthony Simon and another man jumped out of the trailer and walked beside it. The Jonestown men pulled to within about thirty feet of the Twin Otter and the G.D.F. men Dwyer had brought to the airstrip faded out of harm's way. As if by signal, the Jonestown men suddenly reached down into the trailer bed, picked up rifles, and started shoot-ing at the people still clustered outside the plane.

"They're killing everyone. They're killing everyone," gasped Vern Gos-ney. Then an explosion rang out right next to him. Inside the Cessna, Larry Layton had pulled out a .38 special. Monica Bagby was hit, now Gosney felt the dull thud of one, then another bullet tear pain into his own body. He reeled around and saw Layton point the gun to the rear seats, and he reached to wrench the gun out of Layton's hands. Dale Parks grabbed the gun. Gosney wrestled out of Layton's clutching arms, jumped from the plane and ran for the jungle past a panorama of destruction.

"Let's spread out!" yelled Bob Brown to soundman Steve Sung, as he tried to continue filming. Reporters, Ryan, Dwyer, Speier, the relatives still boarding flew in all directions as the crack of rifle fire rang out. Some dove for shelter behind the landing wheels of the plane. Others fell in place, spurting blood from the ripping flesh as the riflemen found their marks. Speier played dead, and NBC producer Bob Flick watched in horror as a man walked up and shoved a shotgun toward Leo Ryan's face. The gun exploded in a coup de grace that splattered red specks and bits of flesh across the ground where the bodies slumped into awkward stillness. There was a short lull, then more shots. Finally, an eternity of minutes after the attack began, the gunfire stopped, and the tractor hauled the men in the trailer away. The survivors gradually pulled together to care for some ten wounded and count the dead: Congressman Leo Ryan, NBC reporter Don Harris, cameraman Bob Brown, San Francisco *Examiner* photographer Greg Robinson, and defector Patricia Parks.[7]

***

An hour and a half earlier, after the dump truck had whined through the gears down the muddy road, the tense hostility that had fallen over the onlookers in Jonestown gradually faded. Not everyone even knew that people had defected, and only a handful were aware that a tractor and trailer had left following the dump truck. Marcie Jones came on the P.A. system and announced that people should all go to their quarters and rest. Everything would be fine, she assured them.

While they waited for DCM Dick Dwyer to return from Port Kaituma, Mark Lane and Charles Garry wandered out toward the cottages for about an hour. Together they recapped what Garry deemed a rather successful day. Up walked Jim McElvane, a large Black man who handled real estate in California for the Temple. He had arrived at Jonestown only two days earlier. With him was Jack Beam, the jocular White man from Kentucky who had been Jones's confidant for almost twenty-five years. What did the lawyers think about the defections, the two wanted to know. As they talked it over, the P.A. sounded out an announcement: "Everybody come to the pavilion." Hundreds of people began to pour out of the dormitories and cottages, many of them still dressed in their Sunday best for the visitors. They laughed and kidded each other. "We like it here. We're not going to go any place," came a shout as they streamed past the lawyers toward the center of Jonestown.

Beam and McElvane walked the lawyers along with the crowd, then shunted them into the school shelter near the pavilion. There sat Jim Jones on a carpenter's sawhorse. Harriet Tropp was next to him, and Maria Katsaris hovered behind. "All is lost," Jones announced. "Every gun in this place is gone." Larry Layton and Gerry Parks were not really defectors, Jones informed them. In fact, when Larry had embraced Jim before leaving, he had whispered in his leader's ear, Jones recounted, "You will be proud of me." But Jones told the others, "I did not detect any weapons on him." Garry asked Jones about Don Sly's attack: "This was the act of an agent provocateur, Jim." "Oh no," Jones replied, "I don't believe so. People are so upset and angry." Then he spat out, "Why would that damned fool come in here from Congress without any security?" Garry told him it would have been an insult to Jonestown.

As Garry absorbed the omens of the conversation, his thoughts wandered to the people sitting over in the pavilion. They had not seemed angry to him. "They ought to have some music or something; somebody ought to say something to them," he told Jones. "The hell with them," Jones replied, "It will do them good to do some thinking."

It was well after five o'clock, moving on toward six. Maria Katsaris came up: "Jim, I want to talk to you for a second." She pulled him away. After a moment's whispering, Jones returned. "Charles, you and Mark will have to go up to the east guest house. Your life is not safe here. People are angry at you," he told the lawyers in an oddly matter-of-fact way. He reached down to pick up an empty cigarette pack someone had tossed on the floor during the visit, and threw it in the trash. Lew Eric, the Joneses' adopted Korean son, grabbed Lane's duffle bag and Garry's briefcase, and walked them over to their quarters.

Back at Jones's cabin, Maria Katsaris prepared suitcases jammed with currency, passports, and last wills of bank account holders to be given over to the Communist party of the Soviet Union. "I am doing this on behalf of Peoples Temple because we, as communists, want our money to be of benefit to oppressed peoples all over the world," read the note signed by Annie J. McGowan, an elderly woman who had been made an account signatory after Debbie Blakey defected. Mike Prokes and Tim and Mike

Carter were told to lug the Temple's assets through the jungle and eventually get them to the Soviet embassy in Georgetown.

Garry and Lane sat alone in the east guest house waiting, wondering. About a dozen men came up to a shed about forty feet away, opened it up, and started pulling rifles and ammo boxes out. Then Don Sly sauntered up and sat on the stoop of the guest house. "Don, what happened to you? Did you freak out this afternoon?" Garry called out. "Mr. Garry, in all deference to you, I'd rather not discuss it." Sly watched as the other men carried the guns and ammo away. "When do you want me up there?" he called out. Then he left.

A little later two youths came up, grinning, even laughing. They had guns, but they did not point them. Garry recognized one of them as the Johnson teenager who had come to trials of Black Panther party members Garry had defended back in the States. "What's going on?" Garry asked Johnson. "We're committing revolutionary suicide," they announced. Lane carefully sized up the situation. "Is there no other alternative?" he probed. "No." Lane held steady. He offered, "Well, Charles and I will stay back and tell the story to the world." The four men embraced. Then the young men gave the revolutionary fist salute. "How do we get out of here?" Lane asked them. "You take the plane." "We don't have a plane," Lane pointed out. "What you do is go around up there, walk up there and go into the bushes, and from the bushes go on to the Jonestown road and go into Port Kaituma." The two youths turned and left.

Garry and Lane wasted no time in heading out. As they moved along, they could hear shouts coming from the pavilion. "Let's not be divisive," someone cried. The two lawyers slipped toward the bush, and made their way between the cassava fields and the jungle toward the Jonestown road. As they approached the edge of cleared land, two or three men came into view ahead carrying boxes, moving toward the jungle themselves. Garry and Lane froze, dropped to the ground, then gradually crept toward the comparative sanctuary of green canopy. By the falling dusk's light they waded into the jungle about a hundred feet before stopping in the growing darkness.

\*\*\*

Months earlier, after the one suicide poison ritual, someone who still remembered Coca-Cola ads about "the real thing" wrote "Dad":

> If the potion we drank had been the real thing, then it would have been the end of Dad's pain. He would not have to suffer for us anymore. Just like last night, the more he talked, the more pain in his tongue. The rest of the people

would be in peace with our loving leader if it was the real thing there would be
no more pain and no more suffering. We would be in peace today. That would
have been the best way to die. Everyone wouldn't have to go to the pavilion.
There would be no more toots of the horn or talking about strategy. If it was
real, of course we would have been free. We would have died the best way. Any
other way we wouldn't be sure if it would work or not and we would have
suffered. I know that Dad wouldn't let us suffer like that. Thank you Dad for
the test and not letting us suffer. Thank-you Dad.

Soon there would be incalculable suffering, then no more. At the schoolhouse, some of Jones's aides and medical staff stood around a table, preparing a liquid according to a recipe that already had been tested. Within the
last month, perhaps only four days earlier, a hundred-pound container of
deadly potassium cyanide had been brought to Jonestown. No one dealing
with herbicides knew why it was there. Now the container was opened up.
The smell like bitter almonds drifted out. A case of Fla-Vor-Aid packets
had been brought from the warehouse where it had sat for seven months,
never used. A melange of tranquilizers and sedatives—Valium, Penegram,
chloral hydrate—came from the bonded pharmacy that had always been
under the lock and key control of Annie Moore. The crystal cyanide was
poured along with other drugs into the purple liquid in a large vat.

Nursing aide Odell Rhoades saw guards armed with guns and crossbows
take up positions around the pavilion, with nearly the entire population of
Jonestown jammed inside. This was no charade: even the kitchen workers
had been pulled in. One girl leaped up on the stage and started dancing and
screaming, "I'm going to be a freedom fighter."

Now Jim Jones was ready to hold forth to the assembled throng. The
tape recorder often used at Temple meetings was running. "How very
much I've tried my best to give you a good life," Jones started off to the
crowd's shouts. "In spite of all that I've tried, a handful of our people, with
their lies, have made our life impossible. There's no way to detach ourself
from what's happened today." The people who had left Jonestown, he told
the assembly, had betrayed them. "Some have stolen children from others
and they are in pursuit right now to kill them, because they stole their
children," he maintained. "I don't think this is what we want to do with
our babies."

Jones went straight to his call, paraphrasing the words of Jesus he had
quoted before: "It was said by the greatest of prophets from time imme-
morial: no man . . . takes my life from me. I lay my life down." He
prophesied a catastrophe was "going to happen on that airplane," and to
cheers and short applause, he cried, "If we can't live in peace, then let's die
in peace." The alternative?

They'll parachute in here on us. . . . So my opinion is that you be kind to children, and be kind to seniors, and take the potion like they used to take in ancient Greece, and step over quietly; because we are not committing suicide—it's a revolutionary act. We can't go back; they won't leave us alone. They're now going back to tell more lies, which means more congressmen. And there's no way, no way we can survive.

Jones asked for dissent and answered a question by saying there was no point in striking out against innocent people, and no easy way to get to Timothy Stoen in Georgetown. "He's responsible for it; he brought these people to us," Jones fumed. "He and Deanna Mertle. The people in San Francisco will not be idle over this. They'll not take our death in vain."

A woman named Christine Miller stepped to the microphone to argue with Jones. Maybe they could get to Russia. Jones countered that emigration to Russia was only a contingency plan in case the socialist government of Guyana fell. Besides, it was too late. People from Jonestown had left with guns. "They started to kill," he reported. "If one of my people do something, that's me. And they say I don't have to take the blame for this," Jones said, of Don Sly's attack on Congressman Ryan,

> but I don't live that way. They said, "deliver up Udjara [the Jonestown nickname for Don Sly]," who tried to get the man [Ryan] back here. —Udjara, whose wi.., mother's been lying on him, and lying on him, and trying to break up this family. And they've all agreed to kill us by any means necessary. Do you think I'm going to deliver them Udjara? Not on your life.

Christine Miller broke in, "I think that there were too few who left for 1,200 people to give their lives."

That was not the point, Jones came back. "There's one man there who blames, and rightfully so, Debbie Blakey for the murder, for the murder of his mother." "He'll stop that pilot by any means necessary. He'll do it. That plane'll come out of the air." What was happening at the airstrip would soil Jonestown's existence forever. "You think Russia's gonna want us with all this stigma?" Jones stammered.

"As long as there's life, there's hope. That's my faith," replied Miller.

"Well . . . , everybody dies," Jones countered. "Some place that hope runs out, because everybody dies. I haven't seen anybody yet didn't die."

Miller insisted, "I'm not ready to die."

"I don't think you are," Jones said.

"I look at all the babies and I think they deserve to live," Miller went on.

"I agree with you. But don't they deserve much more? They deserve peace." Tim Stoen finally would reach his goal, Jones continued. "He has done the thing he wanted to do—have us destroyed."

That meant they were defeated, Miller reasoned: "We let them, the enemy, destroy us."

Not so, said Jones. "We win when we go down. Tim Stoen has nobody else to hate. . . . Then he'll destroy himself."

But Miller held out. "We all have a right to our own destiny as individuals," she said. Jones agreed.

Then Jim McElvane broke in. "Christine," he counseled, "you're only standing here because *he* was here in the first place. So I don't know what you're talking about, having an individual life." The momentum changed. Jones invoked an aspostle of Jesus: "Paul said 'I was a man born out of due season.' I've been born out of due season, just like we all are. And the best testimony we can make is to leave this goddamn world." The meeting broke into shouting. "You must prepare to die," intoned one old woman. Jones mouthed old gospel phrases, "Lay down your burdens, I'm gonna lay down my burden—down by the riverside."

Then someone asked how Jones could let little John Victor die. "Do you think I'd put John's life above others'?" Jones answered. "I don't prefer one above another. I don't prefer him above Udjara. I can't do that. I can't separate myself from your actions or his actions. If you done something wrong, I'd stand with you. If they wanted to come and get you, they'd have to take me." For the children, Jones held, life was worse than death: "we give them our children, then our children will suffer forever."

Others in the crowd were making up their minds. A man came to the microphone. "We're all ready to go," came the resonant words. "If you tell us we have to give our lives now, we're ready. All the rest of the sisters and brothers are with me."

"Several months I've tried to keep this thing from happening," Jones responded, as low wails began to rise above the sobbing. "But I now see it's the will of Sovereign Being that this happened to us, that we lay down our lives in protest against what's been done." Mostly White people went with Ryan, he pointed out. "I'm so grateful for the ones that didn't—those who know who they are." To the people who stayed in Jonestown, he argued, "if you'd wanted to run, you'd 've run with them today, because anybody could have run today."

A commotion: "What comes now, folks, what comes now?" Jones asked. In filed the men who had gone to Port Kaituma. "Say peace. Say peace. Say peace." Thinking Dick Dwyer had come back on the truck as he had planned, Jones insisted, "Take Dwyer on down to the east house."

"Sit down," someone shouted.

Jones tried to reassure people. "Tell 'em, folks. It's easy. It's easy. Yes, my love," he turned to a woman. Someone else denounced the White people who left. "They're not a part of us."

"Quit talking," Jones interjected. "The Congressman's been murdered." The crowd quieted; the organ music droned on in the background. "What a legacy. What a legacy," Jones mused. "They invaded our privacy. They came into our home. They followed us 6,000 miles away. Red Brigade showed them justice. The Congressman's dead."

"Please get us some medication. It's simple, it's simple. There's no convulsions with it." His voice pitched higher and more intense. "Just, please, get it. Before it's too late. The G.D.F. will be here, I tell you, get movin', get movin', get movin'."

Two nurses brought out the "potion." Judy Ijames came to the mike to try to organize the milling crowd. "The people that are standing there in the aisle, go stand in regular lines. Everybody get behind a table and back this way, O.K.? There's nothing to worry about." The children were brought to their death first. Two young women with babies came forward to begin. Ruletta Paul picked up a cup of poison and poured some down her own child's throat, then downed the remainder herself and walked out of the pavilion. The woman behind her followed suit with her own baby.

Confusion reigned. People ran around, trying to find their families, hugging friends. Lines began to form. Did any one-time fundamentalists remember the quotation from Mark 16:18? "They shall take up serpents," it went, "and if they drink any deadly thing, it shall not hurt them." Judy Ijames continued her instructions, "The older children'll help love the little children and reassure them. They're not crying from any pain; it's just a little bitter tasting." Then "Mac" McElvane came to the mike again and told a story about how he had used reincarnation therapy to follow clients through past lives. "And everybody was *so* happy when they made that step to the other side," he added. The shrieks of children yelling "Noooo!" swallowed up his words.

An elderly Black woman named Irene Edwards came up and reprimanded the others over the P.A. "I just want to say something for everyone that I see that is standing around crying. This is nothing to cry about. This is something we could all rejoice about." "I was just thinking about Jim Jones," she went on. "He just has suffered and suffered and *suffered*." Amid the clamor and sobbing there was clapping. Then Jones took the mike: "Please, for God's sake, let's get on with it. We've lived. We've lived as no other people lived and loved. We've had as much of this world as you're gonna get. . . . Let's be done with the agony of it." People clapped even harder. "They'll pay for it," he went on. "This is a revolutionary suicide. This is not a self-destructive suicide. So they'll pay for this. They brought this upon us. And they'll pay for that. I leave that destiny to them."

One man brought up the fate of the Jews in Germany. "The way the children are laying there now, I'd rather see them lay like that than to see them have to die like the Jews did, which was pitiful anyhow." The wailing of the boys and girls wore on. The man finished: he thanked "Dad" "for giving us life, and also death."

"We tried to find a new beginning," Jim told them as they passed through the lines to receive the poisoned Fla-Vor-Aid, "but it's too late. You can't separate yourself from your brother and your sister. . . . I don't know who fired the shot. I don't know who killed the Congressman. But as far as I'm concerned, I killed him. You understand what I'm saying? I killed him." He measured out the words. "He had no business coming. I told him not to come."

A child bawled out. "It's just something to put you to rest," Jones shouted. "Oh God," he moaned himself as he tried to talk people through death. "Free at last," he claimed, echoing Martin Luther King's words cut into the Black preacher's gravestone. On Jones went:

> I call on you to quit exciting your children, when all they're doing is going to a quiet rest. . . . Are we Black, proud, and socialists, or what are we? Now stop this nonsense. . . . Hurry. Hurry, my children. All I say, let's not fall in the hands of the enemy. . . . Hurry, I don't want to leave my seniors to this mess. Quickly, quickly, quickly.

Jones gave a farewell to someone: "Good knowing you." Then he told the cheering crowd that Jim Cobb lay dead on the airstrip, though the young man had survived.

The green vat was brought out for the rest of the adults. A man passed by the mike as he no doubt had done before, denouncing his relatives. Now he would shut the door on them forever:

> I'd like to say that my . . . my so-called parents are filled with so much hate and treachery. I think you people out here should think about how your relatives was, and be glad about that the children are being laid to rest. And I'd like to say that I thank Dad for making me strong to stand with it all and make me ready for it. Thank you.

A young woman followed. "It's been a pleasure walking with all of you in this revolutionary struggle. No other way I would rather go than to give my life for socialism, communism, and I thank Dad very, very much."

Odell Rhoades already had decided he did not want to die for what others had done. In the hubbub as the lines formed, he helped carry a young boy out to the yard and gently laid down the life jerking with convulsions. He walked about the field, trying to comfort the people walking from the pavilion into the spasmed clutches of death. Marceline Jones came over and hugged Rhoades, and thanked him for his acts of mercy.

Then the Jonestown doctor, Larry Schacht, called from the schoolhouse. He needed a stethoscope. Rhoades leaped forward and told Phyllis Chaiken, and the two walked past a guard to the medical area. While Phyllis looked in Schacht's office, Rhoades feigned searching another building. Then he dove under the building and hid, and waited. Later he would head for the jungle.

Another streetwise young Black, Stanley Clayton, was equally determined not to die. He sauntered out to the perimeter of the pavilion, pretended to look for a friend, and slipped past a guard or two by telling them he was heading back, then disappeared behind a building and tore off toward the bush. An elderly Black man, seventy-eight-year-old Grover Davis, managed to hide in a ditch.

No one else left. As the tape ran out, Jones begged, "Take our life from us. We laid it down. We got tired. We didn't commit suicide. We committed an act of revolutionary suicide protesting the conditions of an inhumane world."

\*\*\*

Crouched back in the jungle with Mark Lane, Charles Garry thought he heard three shots ring out after a while. Stanley Clayton heard gunfire too. Having fled in the opposite direction from the road to Port Kaituma, he prowled back to Jonestown, hoping to collect his passport on the way through. He heard four shots ring out. Jonestown's pet chimp, Mr. Muggs, cried out after one of them. Clayton froze in the silence. A fifth shot. Silence. Clayton came on again. He reached the center of Jonestown and slipped into the office where the box of passports was kept. An explosion stopped him in his tracks—another gunshot, he realized as he stood motionless. Silence. Clayton riffled through the passports, found his, and headed out down the road. The quiet crescendo of the jungle insects' night drone swallowed the curtain of silence behind him.

In Jones's cottage lay twelve poisoned bodies of the inner circle: Carolyn Layton Prokes, Karen Layton, Maria Katsaris, Jim McElvane, six other adults, and two children Jones claimed as his own—Carolyn's son Kimo, and next to Maria, Grace Stoen's son John. On the stage back in the pavilion lay the body of a man who had sought to shake the world out of "complacency" since his preaching days in Indianapolis. His head rested on a pillow. There was a small hole on the right side of his skull, just above the ear, and a larger, rougher hole on the left side. This would be the trajectory of a bullet fired by Jones if he took his own life. But the gun that shot the man lay some twenty feet away. Thus Jones probably was not the last person to die at Jonestown. Had someone else killed him? No one will ever know.

Back at Jones's cabin, slumped next to the door was one more body, Annie Moore's. Next to her was a note to posterity in blue ballpoint ink:

I am twenty-four years of age right now, and don't expect to live through the end of this book. I thought I should at least make some attempt to let the world know what Jim Jones and the Peoples Temple is—OR WAS—all about. It seems that some people—and perhaps the majority of people—would like to destroy the best thing that ever happened to the 1,200 or so of us who have followed Jim. I am at a point right now so embittered against the world that I don't know why I am writing this. . . . Where can I begin—JONESTOWN— the most peaceful, loving community that ever existed, JIM JONES—the one who made this paradise possible—much to the contrary of the lies stated about Jim Jones being a power-hungry, sadistic mean person who thought he was God—of all things. I want you who reads this to know Jim was the most honest, loving, caring, concerned person whom I ever met and knew.

Annie finished her note, scrawling a sentence with a different pen, in different ink. "We died because you would not let us live in peace." Beside her body rested a .357 Magnum. The bullet wound to her head was consistent with suicide. In and around Jonestown lay 912 other bodies—men, women, children, mostly Black, some White, the hopes and burdens of this world's life stilled in their silent hearts.[8]

# 12

# After Jonestown

The murders and suicides of a muggy jungle afternoon ended Jonestown as a living community. But Jonestown became something else, a grotesque symbol of devastated human life. The gruesome piles of bodies huddled next to one another attained an instant place in the U.S. collective consciousness. By February of 1979, 98 per cent of Americans polled said they had heard of the tragedy. George Gallup observed, "Few events, in fact, in the entire history of the Gallup Poll have been known to such a high proportion of the U.S. public."

The tide of mass media attention to Jonestown did more to create myths than to help us understand the tragedy. In turn, historical analysis has faced an unusual burden, for mythology has a curious and uneven connection to historical events. It often is built up out of them, but it easily can displace history by ripping events from the realm of causal understanding and placing them in a different context. Myth draws on facts, half-truths, conjecture, and conventional wisdom to fictionalize events in a way that effectively cordons off history itself. In the case of Jonestown there is not a compelling cultural demand to know, in any historical sense, the causes of the deaths. The horror could never be understood in historical terms, for history has an uneven relation to the moral distinction between good and evil. Thus, the task of myth is to close the curtain on a tragedy steeped in stigma so as to reaffirm the normal social world.

The present study of Peoples Temple and its connections to our culture is necessarily flawed to the degree that it depends on mythological accounts. All the same, it has been able to reveal a history that was previously submerged in myth. Historical analysis has shown that the popular mythological accounts failed to offer causally adequate understanding of the cultural origins of Peoples Temple, its societal affinities, the circumstances under which the exodus to Guyana occurred, the extent of coordination between defectors and relatives, journalists, and politicians, or the degree to which Ryan's delegation to Guyana shielded a clandestine goal of "dismantling" Jonestown. It is no longer possible to understand Peoples Temple apart from the actions of its detractors. However powerhungry and

289

insecure Jones was, he did not act simply in the psychotic isolation of paranoia but in an historical conflict against equally dedicated opponents, who sometimes acted under the ethic, as Jones sometimes did, that "the ends justify the means."

Yet even a close study of Peoples Temple's history does not undo myth, for as Roland Barthes has observed, myth neither hides history nor unmasks it. Instead myth "naturalizes" history by simplifying the uneven paradoxes of real life at the same time that it strips events from their historical connections. In Barthes's words, "The reader lives the myth as a story at once true and unreal."[1]

Thus, myth has a power that is sustained independently of history. In the case of Peoples Temple, the myth is more compelling than history ever could be, and perhaps rightfully so. The present investigation shows that there is considerable historical basis for the mythological treatment of Jim Jones as Anti-Christ. He gained control over others in diverse and unseemly ways, he sometimes "imprisoned" or blackmailed into silence those who would not wholeheartedly submit, and he pulled the strings of a puppeteer to stage the circumstances in which he could use murder and mass suicide as revenge against the enemies of Peoples Temple. The myth of Jonestown portrays a cult centered on an insane totalitarian megalomaniac. It succeeds in part because there is a wealth of information to sustain it. No historical analysis will displace a myth grounded on facts as stark and awesome as those of Jonestown.

So it is that we face a cultural impasse. Whatever the truth in myth, it shields us from history in a way that emasculates reason. We remain prisoners of myth, and the historical study of events, by itself, cannot set us free. To do that, to "demythologize" (as Barthes called it), requires a different tack. The development of myth after Jonestown must itself become an object of cultural analysis.

### Burying the Dead

Even after the deaths at Jonestown, the alien and enigmatic forces that propelled the collective doom could not be contained within the rational social order. To be sure, Larry Layton was arrested at the airstrip, and Michael and Tim Carter and Mike Prokes were detained before they ever made it to the Soviet embassy with the Temple's money. However, at the Lamaha Gardens house in Georgetown, Linda Amos got wind of what was happening in Jonestown, slit the throats of her own children, and then took her own life with a butcher knife. Apparently she feared that her former husband, Concerned Relative Sherwin Harris, would gain custody of their children. She would not yield to the Temple's opponents, when her comrades in Jonestown had not done so.

Months later Mike Prokes followed. At first he had wanted to seek revenge against the Temple's enemies, but other survivors convinced him it would accomplish nothing. After arriving back in California, Prokes withdrew from socializing with other survivors who were receiving counseling, and started to write a book that would tell what Jonestown was "really" like. One day the former Temple PR man called a press conference at a motel on Kansas Avenue in Modesto. "I can't disassociate myself from the people who died, nor do I want to. The people weren't brainwashed fanatics or cultists; the Temple was not a cult," he told the gathered reporters. Then he handed them a sheaf of his writings on the subject, went in the motel room bathroom, put a .38 Smith and Wesson to his head, and pulled the trigger.

A few other surviving followers of Jim Jones remained faithful to the cause in the wake of Jonestown; they even declared they would have drunk the poison if they had been with their comrades that Saturday. But most survivors gradually adopted the outsider's perspective on Peoples Temple: that they had been duped by Jim Jones. To believe otherwise bordered on a suicidal impulse. Still, some of them would try to distinguish between Jones as madman and Jonestown as a positive accomplishment. To Debbie Touchette, the evil in Jones did not discredit his view that U.S. society is racist. Similarly, Jones's only surviving natural son, Stephan, initially denounced his father but not the socialist vision he tried to advance. Stephan Jones tried to convince himself that he would not have allowed the suicide ritual to take place, but as the years passed he wondered whether he might have taken the poison, too, if he had not been quick enough to stop it at the very beginning: "I would have had to, especially if I saw other people doing it."[2]

More than former members of other failed modern religious movement groups, the survivors of Jonestown became members of a community of fate who stayed in touch with one another. The Concerned Relatives sensed this strangely compelling bond among the survivors from the beginning. Whatever the degree of coercion involved in the deaths at Jonestown, the simple fact that the event was brought to completion offered grim testimony to the power of Jim Jones. When the Concerned Relatives waiting in Georgetown and the United States heard on Saturday, November 18, that Leo Ryan and the others had been attacked, they could not help suspecting what they had always claimed but refused to believe themselves—that Jones could be pushed to the mad act of leading his community through mass suicide. As the Concerned Relatives saw it, they finally had exposed the machinations of a madman to a world that had never fully taken them seriously, and in turn, they felt the chilling vulnerability of a group whose loved ones would die at the behest of Jones, by force, acquiescence, or commitment. In the shadow of the murders and suicides, the Concerned Relatives could see the Jonestown basketball team in Georgetown as a "hit squad" and themselves as the next targets of a madness that could not be quelled even by the death of Jim Jones.

The fears of Jones's enemies testified to their awe of his charisma and cunning. Was Jones really dead? "I don't believe it," Holly Morton stated flatly at Jeannie Mills's Human Freedom Center in Berkeley. Mass murder was not beyond the evil design of the man the Concerned Relatives had worked tirelessly to expose, but for Jones to kill himself did not quite align with *New West* accounts of the supposed preacher as a greedy and self-indulgent madman who robbed people of their personal identities and material wealth for his own personal gain. The Jim Jones of *New West* must have survived and escaped.

Thus, during the first few days when news reports theorized that hundreds of people had fled from Jonestown to the jungle, there emerged a theory from the Human Freedom Center. Jim Jones sometimes had look-alikes who would stand in for him in dangerous situations. The body that was supposed to be Jones was actually a guard who had been murdered to serve as a foil. Jones had fled, planning to meet up with the young men with the money—Prokes and the Carter brothers—and other survivors to seek revenge on their enemies.

The apparent death of a person imbued with historically potent charisma has never been a question that the living could leave unresolved. It is, after all, the most decisive event whereby the divine authenticity or hoax of reputed transcendent powers are established or dismissed. In the Gospels, the accounts of Jesus rising from the dead infuse his life story with the triumph of vindication and the hope of redemption, at the same time that they confirm his superhuman nature.

Somehow the deaths of heroes, saviors, tyrants, and devils—from Jesus to Jesse James and Adolf Hitler—require more evidence than deaths of lesser mortals. So it was with one of Jim Jones's early mentors, William Branham, whose followers believed him the Second Coming. After Branham's death in late 1965, his body was rumored to have been "embalmed and refrigerated" by followers in hopes of a resurrection. Burial, in fact, did not take place until after the following Easter, when all hopes of resurrection had faded.

Authorities took no chances in the case of Jim Jones either. Guyanese officials assured the world that they would get fingerprints for positive identification. If the corpse's prints were too badly decomposed from exposure to the jungle sun, the teeth from the apparent body of Jim Jones would be compared to dental records.

Dealing with the rest of the carnage presented major logistical problems, and these were compounded by the overwhelming shame that quickly settled on the mass suicide. The Guyanese and U.S. forces entered Jonestown as a military expedition, not as detectives or pathologists. They originally undercounted the number of bodies by 500, and did not know whom they would find among the living. But they found no enemy—only a seventy-six-year-old woman named Hyacinth Thrush who had slept through the suicide ritual, and Grover Davis, the elderly man who avoided drinking the poison by hiding in a ditch. Nor did they find the two hundred guns the Concerned Relatives insisted had been smuggled into Jonestown. The arsenal of a town of over 950 amounted to ten pistols, thirteen small-calibre rifles, seven shotguns, and a flare gun.

Counting guns was a far easier task than dealing with the bodies. Authorities initially assumed that a graveyard would be established near Jonestown, for Guyanese law requires burial within thirty-six hours after death. But the stigma became too much, and the government of Guyana insisted that the U.S. government return the bodies to their homeland. Initial identifications of some of the bodies were made at Jonestown with the help of survivors Stanley Clayton and Odell Rhoades; U.S. soldiers placed the tagged corpses in body bags that were then airlifted to the U.S. Air Force Base at Dover, Maryland. There, relatives faced the wrenching task of retrieving their loved ones' remains from a government that seemed indifferent to their grief. Some bodies never could be identified, and some people of Jonestown had no concerned relatives willing to claim their bodies or able to pay the costs of funerals.

The Temple's reputedly fantastic monetary assets, on the other hand, had no shortage of claimants. Even before the dead were buried, the living—from former members of Peoples Temple and Leo Ryan's next of kin to the U.S. government—pressed to receive a portion of the money. When distribution of $10 million in Temple assets finally was completed nearly five years later, court-appointed receiver Robert Fabian himself received a fee of $480,000 for his efforts at tracking down Temple assets and processing claims. In the meantime, a mass burial was held at Evergreen Cemetery in Oakland, California with caskets stacked two deep to hold the bodies of over two hundred dead—the unknown and the unwanted of Jonestown.

The body of Jim Jones (it was not a stand-in) presented a different problem. Once, years earlier, Jones had told his congregation in San Francisco, "I'll not be in a graveyard." Other prophecies failed, but this one was fulfilled. Jones's parents-in-law, Walter and Charlotte Baldwin, wanted to bury Jones and his wife Marcie in Earlham Cemetery near the Quaker college in Richmond, Indiana, but Richmond would not stand for the infamy. The Baldwins changed their plans, as the local funeral home director put it, to reflect "what they felt was best for the community of Richmond and all concerned." The body of Jim Jones was cremated, the ashes spread into the choppy waters of the Atlantic Ocean one spring day in 1979.

Yet even with Jones certified dead and his remains cast to the depths, he would not be gone, at least in a mythic sense. A Guyanese policeman who patrolled Jonestown told a *National Enquirer* reporter that he had seen the ghost of Jim Jones not once but three times. Twelve-year police veteran Corporal Abdullah Inshan was quoted as saying the apparition "seemed to be smiling, a twisted, cruel smile."[3]

## The Spectre of Martyrdom

The emergence of a ghost story suggests that disposing of the physical remains of Jim Jones was easier than exorcising the world of his "spirit." The problem was simple but formidable. No doubt Jones was a flawed prophet, but he drew people into a movement that claimed to confront the central dilemmas of the modern capitalist world: racial justice, class conflict, and the rationalized madness of the nuclear arms race. However awkwardly, sometimes with deceitful and repressive methods of social control, Jones consolidated a band of followers who would act out his dramatization of a messianic struggle for the vindication of "principle." Together they lifted themselves and their opponents from the world of everyday life into a Shakespearean realm where the moral contradictions of an era became crystalized in persons who acted out history as spectacle.

What was the "moral" of the spectacle from the vantage point of Jonestown? For however many inhabitants of Jonestown took "the potion" willingly, the act of collective suicide irreversibly shut out the relatives concerned enough to try to save them. Implicitly, the mass suicide casts the opponents of Jonestown and the social web of mass media and government personnel as moral hypocrites with whom the faithful of Jonestown could brook no accommodation or compromise.

The doctrine of revolutionary suicide established the groundwork for this final solution. Jim Jones sought to differentiate the deaths at Jonestown from individual suicide, which, despite his own death wish, he had opposed at various points in his life ("Duty keeps us from there," he once told Grace Stoen). To make the distinction, Jones followed the classic analysis of French sociologist Emile Durkheim, who identified three types of suicide: egoistic, anomic, and altruistic.

The first two of Durkheim's types describe ways in which individuals become so misaligned with an encompassing community that life no longer matters. The third type of suicide in Durkheim's theory depends not on a failure of personal justification or a loosening of moral bonds but on precisely the opposite. Altruistic suicide occurs in conformity with normative cultural expectations. Its quintessence may be found in the Japanese kamikaze pilots who sacrificed their own lives *for* the community. Under such conditions, from the viewpoint of the community, suicide is an honorable act. While egoistic and anomic suicide breach the social order, altruistic suicide affirms it.

For years Jones and some of his followers had puzzled over the logic and practices of martyrdom. A surviving Peoples Temples document about their researches suggests that one source—and perhaps the original Temple idea of mass suicide—derived from an obscure event described by a Greek historian. In *The Peloponnesian War* Thucydides recounted how, during the fifth century B.C., certain people of Corcyra took their own lives at the temple of Juno when they saw their cause was lost. For Peoples Temple, this page of Greek history was transposed into a modern framework through the concept of revolutionary suicide—Black Panther Huey Newton's term for dying from the life of oppression under capitalism, becoming "reborn" to the revolutionary struggle. The death that Newton envisioned was not personal suicide but at least symbolic, and potentially real, martyrdom, the altruistic sacrifice of one's social biography, and perhaps physical life, for a cause. Insofar as the revolutionary individual accepts death as the potential ultimate consequence of commitment, altruistic suicide becomes indistinguishable from martyrdom.[4]

At Jonestown the initially metaphoric revolutionary suicide—commitment to a transcendent cause—became transformed into actual mass suicide through struggle with the opposition, a dynamic that brought into play the crisis of a lost cause described by Thucydides. Without a decisive showdown with forsworn opponents, like the face-to-face confrontation involved in the visit to Jonestown by Leo Ryan and those who traveled with him, it is much less likely that the deaths would have occurred. The people of Jonestown already had undergone a series of figurative deaths and rebirths by the time that Ryan, the Concerned Relatives, and the press visited Jonestown. For years Jim Jones had demanded that his followers put "principle" ahead of personal interest or desire. He advanced not only a figurative vision of individual death and rebirth but a societal one as well. Preaching political apocalypse, he argued that U.S. society was in its death throes. Salvation could occur only through collective transcendence. The migration to Guyana underscored the death of the capitalist self through the foreclosing of life in a dying capitalist society. Rebirth came in a new world, one where utopian commitment to socialist principle was held up as the very axis on which the sanctity of the community turned.

In the migration to Jonestown, revolutionary suicide initially framed a "postapocalyptic" vision of moving to an autonomous sanctuary beyond the old order, much as it had for earlier other-worldly sects that had escaped persecution in Europe by establishing religious communities in North America. The key to understanding mass suicide at Jonestown lies in the recurrent dynamics of conflict between religious communities claiming autonomy and external political orders. In the general case a demand to submit to the external order forces a choice within the community between the sacred and evil. The choice brings religious conviction to a question of honor, and it is the seedbed of martyrdom. It is worthwhile to consider in some detail the sociology of such circumstances.

W. H. C. Frend, the religious historian, traces the changing motifs of martyrdom that originated in ancient Judaism and shifted in their meanings for the early Christians. Martyrdom, Frend argues, is one of the basic continuities that binds the New Testament world to the Old. Under each covenant the believers would embrace death rather than foresake their religion, and in each case, under certain conditions, the affirmation of faith effectively amounted to altruistic suicide.

In the wake of Jonestown a television docudrama popularized the story of the A.D. 73 Jewish mass suicide at Masada under siege by Roman troops, first described by Josephus. At Masada the Jews faced a choice of death by their own hands or rape and slavery at the hands of the Romans. But such relatively unambiguous choices were not always the case, either among the Jews or the early Christians. A Jewish delegation that met the Roman Patronius in A.D. 40 *asked* that they and the rest of their people all be killed, "in order that we may not live to see an evil worse than death." Similarly, a group of Christians came to the Proconsul of Asia in A.D. 185, wearing halters around their necks, insisting that they be put to death; only then, they believed, would they become "perfected" martyrs.

For both the Jews and the early Christians, death was not usually inevitable. They could avoid martyrdom through infamy or face-saving gestures—either by feigning worship of Greco-Roman idols or by publicly recanting their beliefs—but for the true believers, it was a matter of honor to face up to the consequences of their commitment. Among Christians, apostates who abandoned the covenant were the objects of the deepest scorn, and over the centuries tens of thousands of believers died as testaments to their faith. The historical records of this zealous martyrdom clearly show that it did not spring forth as the personal choice of individuals acting on their own. To the contrary, the attitudes and behavior that would be necessary to stage one's martyrdom were shaped through social control practices of reward and punishment instilled by religious communities to insure an incontrovertible sense of honor, practices that bear a striking resemblance to the ones used by Jim Jones to create group solidarity and commitment among the people of Jonestown. The suicidal impulse effected by practices of social control among the early Christians raged to the point of group or mass suicide, and it likely led Augustine to his strong injunction against suicide.[5]

Despite continuities between Jewish and Christian martyrdom, there were subtle yet important developments in the practice, and they may be used to pinpoint the emergent self-definition of revolutionary suicide by whatever number of people willingly submitted to it at Jonestown. For the Jews, martyrdom served as a testament to the evil of those who persecuted them at the same time that it represented a sin-offering of the martyr's life as an act of collective atonement for whatever shortcomings of the Jews were responsible for the sufferings God had imposed on them. These two themes were fused in *ressentiment*, the resentment of a disprivileged religious community whose members hope for God's revenge against their enemies and await their own promised land.

As Frend argues, Jewish martyrs did *not* understand their acts as a way to bring *nearer* the day of God's reckoning. They were simply testaments symbolizing the apocalyptic Jewish faith that God ultimately would redeem the suffering of God's chosen people. Jewish martyrs were not heroes so much as they were people who became caught up in the vortex of history and died in fulfillment of their fidelity to God's covenant with the Jewish people. They had to endure suffering without the hope that the suffering itself would hasten the day of redemption for the Jewish nation. All the same, as Max Weber suggests, the hope of ultimate victory often "serves as a device for compensating a conscious or unconscious desire for vengeance" against the forces of persecution. In the Jewish struggles, martyrs lived side by side with others who fought back against oppressors of the Jews. Martyrdom, resentment, and struggle were fused in a vision of ultimate triumph.[6]

The crucifixion of Jesus followed in the established tradition of Jewish martyrdom, but for early Christians, probably influenced by Greek conceptions of heroism, the death of Jesus altered the meaning of martyrdom in important ways. Like Jewish martyrs, Jesus could have avoided his death by recanting his beliefs; in the archetypal mode of martyrdom, he chose death rather than the abandonment of faith. Like Jewish martyrs, Jesus died as a sin-offering atoning for the acts of his opponents, the apostasy of doubters, and the failings of his followers. But in a crucial account, Romans 3: 19–26, the martyrdom of Jesus in crucifixion was interpreted as *more* than either a way of attesting Jewish faith in God despite earthly travails or an act appeasing God for Jewish sin. It became a shedding of blood through which God offered redemption from the guilt of sin to all humankind who testified to faith in Jesus. Hence the formula, "Christ died for our sins."

The Resurrection then showed the promise of Jesus's ministry in the hope of triumph over death. In the crucifixion of Jesus, martyrdom was turned from the test of faith for the Jewish nation to the vessel of hope for those with faith in Jesus, Jew and gentile alike. After Jesus's death, martyrdom of his followers developed in a way that diverged from Jewish martyrdom. It came to be regarded as an event that might actually *quicken* the coming of the apocalypse that would establish the Kingdom of God on earth, at the same time offering the martyred one immediate heavenly salvation.[7]

How do these distinctions about martyrdom help us understand what happened at Jonestown? It might be argued that Jonestown was not a religious community, at least in any conventional sense (the same could be said about its socialist claims), but in the final analysis, Jonestown approximates the religious socialism of the "other-worldly sect" ruled in a theocratic style. The relative absence of rituals of worship should not deflect us from this understanding. As Frend notes, the Romans attacked the early Christians as atheists because they lacked the conventional features of worship. Similarly, in the United States today, communism is popularly depicted as irreligious. But Jones made secular communist ideology over into the faith of a community. He charismatically abandoned the conventional notions of religiosity so that he could try to infuse the world with a new dispensation of "religious" meaning.[8]

What, then, of martyrdom at Jonestown? Ross Case, Jim Jones's early fundamentalist associate Temple pastor in Indiana and later apostate cell leader in California, recognizes the general parallel of martyrdom between the death of Jesus and the mass suicide at Jonestown: neither Jesus nor the people of Jonestown had to die. But there is a decisive difference, Case argues: the crucifixion of Jesus offered hope for the future of mankind; Jonestown did not. Case is essentially correct. The martyrs of Jonestown—that is, those who willingly died—regarded their fate as connected to the honor of their struggle, not to its hope of triumph.[9]

Jones had based Peoples Temple as a movement on an apocalyptic vision that vacillated between a preapocalyptic ethic of confrontation and a postapocalyptic ethos of sanctuary. In the end Jones succumbed to the fate of other failed revolutionary millenarians.[10] Rather than successfully establishing the other-worldly sanctuary of a promised land, he could only declaim the web of "evil" powers in which he was ensnared and search with chiliastic expectation for the imminent cataclysm that would affirm the integrity of his cause.

Other-worldly sects have a sense of the eternal about them. Claiming to have escaped from the apocalypse of "this" world to a sanctuary beyond the reach of society at large, they adopt the temporal tableau of "heaven," which amounts to a timeless bliss of immortality. But the sanctuary of Jonestown was punctured with external threats to its existence by the forces of "persecution" that followed Peoples Temple to Guyana. Thus, Jones and his followers remained caught in the struggles of the apocalypse. As they conceived it, they were forced to continue their fight against the evil and conspiratorial world that could not tolerate a successful racially integrated U.S. expatriate socialist utopia.

In the struggle Jones and his true believers took on the character of what I have termed an apocalyptic "warring sect," fighting a decisive Manichean struggle with the forces of evil. The struggle of a warring sect takes place in historical time, where one action builds on another, where decisive outcomes of previous events shape future possibilities.[11] The contradiction between this earthly struggle and the timeless sanctuary Jones would have liked to proclaim gave Jonestown many of its strange juxtapositions—of heaven and hell, of suffering and happiness, of love and coercion.

In effect, Jones could not really claim to bring his flock to sanctuary beyond the apocalypse. If he were indeed a messianic prophet of God, as he sometimes claimed, Jones might be expected either to win the struggle of the warring sect against its evil persecutors or to deliver his people to the bliss of another world. Had he established his colony cut off from the unsympathetic purview of defectors, Concerned Relatives, investigative reporters, governmental agencies, and a congressman, the postapocalyptic other-worldly tableau perhaps could have been sustained with less repressive methods of social control. As it was, the leaders of Jonestown took their most extreme steps of increased surveillance and control in order to maintain boundaries between the group and its opponents, but the efforts to cordon off Jonestown from external threats themselves fueled internal dissension.

Robert Lifton argues that revolutionaries inherently are engaged in quests for immortality.[12] Other-worldly sectarians in a way short-circuit this quest by the fiat of asserting their immortality, positing their everyday life as the timeless "heavenly" plateau that exists beyond history. But under the persistent eyes of external critics, and because Jones himself increased his social control through the "paranoid syle" of focusing on "persecution," Jonestown could not sustain the other-worldly culture of a group that had escaped apocalyptic history.

On the other hand, Peoples Temple was equally incapable of achieving the sort of political victory that would have been the goal of a warring sect. Because revolutionary war involves a struggle against an established political order in unfolding historical time, revolutionaries can attain immortality only in the wide-scale victory of the revolution over the "forces of reaction." Peoples Temple could not begin to achieve this sort of revolutionary immortality, for it could not even pretend to achieve a victory against its enemies. If it had come to a pitched battle, the Jonestown defenders—like warring sects such as the Symbionese Liberation Army against the Los Angeles Police Department S.W.A.T. (strategic weapons and tactics) Team in 1974 and MOVE in Philadelphia in 1985—would have been wiped out.

But Jones's followers could create a kind of "immortality" that is not really a possibility for political revolutionaries. They could abandon apocalyptic hell by the act of mass suicide.[13] This would shut out the opponents of the Temple: the Concerned Relatives could not be the undoing of what was already undone, and there could be no recriminations against the dead. By Jones's assertion that reincarnation resulted from "revolutionary" as opposed to other forms of suicide, the act could also be claimed to achieve the other-worldly salvation Jones had promised his more religious followers, their final promised land. Mass suicide would unite the divergent public threads of meaningful existence at Jonestown, those of political revolution and religious salvation. It would be an awesome vehicle for a powerful statement of collective solidarity by the true believers among the people of Jonestown: they would rather die together than find their life together subjected to decimation and dishonor at the hands of opponents and authorities they regarded as illegitimate.

Jim Jones always tried to encapsulate symbolic conflict within the dramaturgy of everyday life. The visit by Congressman Ryan offered an event that could be fitted into the mold of provocation. Here was an occasion that drew together all the elements of the conflict with the Concerned Relatives that had continued unabated for a year and a half. The leaders at Jonestown set the stage carefully. They obtained advance intelligence information about the latent purposes surrounding Ryan's visit and they tried to prevent the showdown. Despite their efforts to negotiate the terms of a visit, they essentially were confronted with a *fait accompli* of an unwanted tour, to which they acquiesced. They then coached people to try to prevent the dishonor of defections, nevertheless preparing to take the community down in mass suicide if circumstances "required" it.[14]

On November 18, as the defectors headed for the truck that would take them out of Jonestown, Temple attorney Charles Garry advised Jim Jones to accept the departures gracefully. Garry and others have since emphasized, and rightly so, that the "victory" of Ryan and the Concerned Relatives in departing from Jonestown with some of its people hardly "justified" mass suicide. The community could have endured the loss of a handful of defectors. But from Jones's viewpoint, the congressman and the Concerned Relatives did succeed in driving a first wedge in their efforts to open up Jonestown; Ryan promised Jones that this was just the beginning of Jonestown's loss of autonomy, and arch-enemy Tim Stoen awaited the developments in Georgetown. The leadership at Jonestown saw Ryan's visit as a turning point toward defeat in the struggle to avoid becoming subordinated to the Concerned Relatives and their allies.

Concerned Relative Steve Katsaris reflected that Jim Jones "couldn't afford at that point to have even sixteen people leave and tell their story." Jones himself agreed, though he put it differently: "Whenever people leave, they tell lies about the place." Either way, in the eyes of Jonestown's leaders, the Concerned Relatives' interpretation of Jonestown and its atrocities would win out, and their own claims to serve as a righteous beacon for justice and social change would be exhausted.[15]

The attack on Congressman Ryan and others at the Port Kaituma airstrip short-circuited the process of official investigation and fulfilled the worst fears of Jonestown's detractors, but it did so on Jones's terms. It is not impossible, of course, that Don Sly's attack on Ryan and the murders at the airstrip came as acts of outrage and revenge by people from Jonestown acting with Jones's knowledge but not under his direct orders. One surviving resident of Jonestown observed that there were always some people there who sought to unleash revenge upon their enemies. However, such an hypothesis flies in the face of the way Jonestown worked as a disciplined organization. It seems much more probable that Jones and his associates saw Ryan's departure with Jonestown residents as the dramatic symbol of Peoples Temple's "defeat." It also was the best chance for revenge against the congressman himself, something Jones savored as a possibility before Ryan ever set foot in Jonestown.

The strong likelihood that Jones ordered the murders at the airstrip serves as an index of how far the leaders of Jonestown were willing to go to stage the circumstances wherein they would choose death. The attack in turn became the dramatic pretext for proclaiming a mass suicide. Just as those who commit murder under other circumstances (for example, within their families) occasionally take their own lives afterwards, Jones could justify suicide to the assembled community as the only option in the wake of the murder stigma, partly on the basis of circumstances that it seems quite likely he helped to stage. We may never know whether Jones actually ordered the murders at the airstrip, but for Jones such a question was moot. In his last speech before the people of Jonestown, he again affirmed the "principle" that he had always emphasized: they all were responsible for the acts of one another. "It doesn't matter who killed the Congressman," he maintained. "As far as I'm concerned, I killed him."

In their search for an occasion to justify martyrdom, Jones and his supporters closely resemble some of the Old Believers in seventeenth-century Russia who gathered thousands of the devout, innocent children too, into church sanctuaries, and set them ablaze to die in fiery protests against reforms imposed in the Russian Orthodox Church. Like some of the more zealous of the Old Believers, Jim Jones based his career on provoking outrage from his antagonists, trying to manipulate the confrontations to further his cause. Now, as it is said about some of the Old Believers, Jones and his associates "were willing to go to great lengths to organize suitable circumstances" for martyrdom.[16]

Awkwardly and through contrivance, Jones aligned the circumstances of Ryan's visit with a tradition of heroic martyrdom. The world would never accept the people of Jonestown, Jones told his audience, for they had been "born out of due season." The honorable thing to do, he argued, was to "take the potion, like they used to take in ancient Greece." Jones described mass suicide as a "protest against what's been done." "Take our life from us," he cried, "We laid it down. We got tired." This despair of a failed cause is echoed in the final message of Jones's personal nurse, Annie Moore, who wrote, "We die because you would not let us live in peace."[17]

The images of heroic desperation at the end of Jonestown hold out martyrdom as a vessel, not of transcendence but of submission to what Jones called "the will of Sovereign Being." Even the revenge against Ryan and other opponents and the promise of further retribution come closer to the resentment of Jewish martyrdom than to the pacifistic acceptance and hope-filled anticipation of early Christian martyrdom. Jones and his followers had failed, but they would not allow their enemies to gloat in their failure. Thus, their very self-image echoed the pre-Christian martyrdom of the Jews. Nor is this connection accidental. The whole tradition of Black messiahs in the United States out of which Peoples Temple sprung was itself founded on an existential predicament that became identified with that of the Jews. Blacks suffered oppression, it was held, because God had made them a bellwether of His divine purpose in the unfolding of world history.[18] Like the Jewish martyrs, Jones and his followers saw themselves as the victims of an uneven historical process of change, not as the avatars who had succeeded in testifying to the hope of the New Age. They could not say that on earth the Promised Land was theirs.

Most warring apocalyptic sects reach a grisly end. Their unchallenged extermination is used by the state as proof of its monopoly on the legitimate use of force. For Peoples Temple, revolutionary suicide was a victory by comparison. The event, sculpted into myth, can be drawn upon for moral didactics, but this will not erase the stigma that Jonestown implicitly places on the world that its members left behind. Nor can the state punish the dead who are guilty, among other things, of murdering a U.S. congressman, three newsmen, a defector, and however many Jonestown residents did not willingly commit suicide. Though they paid the total price of death for their ultimate commitment, and though they achieved little except perhaps, as they saw it, vindication of their own collective sense of honor, still those who won this hollow victory cannot have it taken away from them. In the absence of effective retribution, the state search for living guilty in the person of Larry Layton, as well as the widespread outcry against "cults," took on the character of scapegoating.[19] Those most responsible rest beyond the reach of the law, beyond the grasp of revenge by Concerned Relatives. Unable to escape the hell of their own lives by creating an other-worldly socialist existence on earth, they instead sought their "immortality" in death.

### Peoples Temple and Evil

The failure of Jonestown was more than the collapse of a community. Jim Jones and those who followed him established a movement that fused the central dilemmas of modern Christianity: personal salvation versus the social gospel, with the philosophical antithesis of Christianity, a "godless" yet prophetic vision of communism. These ideological themes found their concrete expression in a movement of *déclassé* true believers—Black, White, poor, working class, and professional—who renounced their previous lives for a cause. In life, they adopted the legacy of Black suffering as the vehicle that carried forward their quest for redemption. In death, they relinquished the burden of history to those of us who live on.

In our culture, we have not done well in coming to grips with the legacy of Jonestown. The mass suicide left behind the most awesome issue of stigma in the apparently desperate act of people who blamed others for their own actions inflicted upon their enemies, friends, loved ones, and themselves. The leaders of Jonestown styled their act in the traditions of pre-Christian Jewish martyrdom and ancient Greek heroism, mediated through the Black-Power concept of revolutionary suicide. But understanding their construction of their actions still leaves open the issue of Jonestown's cultural significance, for Jewish and early Christian martyrdom as "sin sacrifice" may stand for sin located variously in the acts (1) of the martyred group itself, (2) of its apostates, or (3) of the world against which it struggled.

The interpretation from the self-proclaimed martyrs of Jonestown is clear enough. They had died to anything but "principle" long before. In their view, those who had not been able to rise up to principle—traitors like the Mertles/Millses, Grace Stoen, Tim Stoen—had tried to purge themselves of their own guilt for abandoning the cause by mounting a holy war to vindicate their defections. In turn, the Temple accused its opponents of using falsehood and innuendo to subordinate others to their side. Predisposed toward harassing socialists and cult organizations anyway, the press, government agencies, and politicians pounced on scandals that, Temple staff claimed, would be dismissed as petty if they were raised against establishment persons and institutions. The followers of Jones could conclude only that they were singled out for persecution because they stood for principles that revealed the failure of the American dream.[20] For the faithful of Jonestown, it was the sin of hypocrisy by their opponents, borne up by a hostile world, that led them to accept martyrdom as their fate.

Certain events in the wake of Jonestown's deathly collapse would be taken by those who died as evidence to uphold their view. They might point to how Debbie Blakey became reborn to the bourgeois life of a stockbroker married to a banker, who could affirm, "We are conservative people. We voted for Ronald Reagan." They might wonder how Jeannie Mills could create an "anticult" center that some people found to mirror organizational practices in Peoples Temple. How could she denounce the group she had fled with such conviction, at the same time deploying a patronage system demanding absolute loyalty without pay at her Human Freedom Center, while building up family real estate holdings worth over $700,000? The dead of Jonestown probably would have found the luxurious Mercedes-Benz she eventually purchased a fitting symbol of her true commitments.

Finally, the Jonestown dead would wonder about John Victor Stoen's paternity—a matter even today not resolved by public evidence. In the Temple view, the custody struggle involved a child whom Jim Jones fathered, abandoned by his mother. Tim Stoen could not leave matters to a legal solution. He mounted a public relations campaign when the courtroom process failed to go his way, and he threatened to retrieve John Victor by force. Yet years earlier Stoen had been aware of the Temple interest in heroic Greek martyrdom that refuses to countenance enemies. Somehow, the Temple faithful concluded, the man who helped establish Jonestown in the very form he later opposed, the man who reportedly envisioned the occasion when Jim Jones would "overreact," had wanted to drive them to their last-ditch plan.

When Grace Stoen was questioned after the mass suicide about whether she ever had been physically drawn to Jim Jones, whether he had been attracted to women like her, she replied, "I don't really care to get into it. I don't think that's important at all." It was not important to Grace Stoen. She would have deserved consideration by a court concerning custody rights no matter who the biological father was. But if it is ever established that Jim Jones sired John Stoen, then a central Concerned Relatives atrocity contention—Grace and Tim Stoen as the presumptive suffering parties locked in a struggle against a man who amounted to a kidnapper—would lose considerable of its moral, if not legal force, and the supporters of Jonestown would find substantiation of their argument that the child had been used as a pawn for a vendetta with Jim Jones by a man trying to salvage his sexual and marital honor. But today this issue, and with it our understanding of the motives and methods of Tim Stoen, remains very much unresolved. Until compelling evidence surfaces—if the parties with knowledge ever come forward—public understanding rests on a central ambiguity that renders any claim to definitive interpretation at best premature, more likely, mythical.[21]

Myth, of course, is not made by the dead. The living, on the other hand, hold vested interests in what interpretation holds sway. In the struggle to come to grips with the carnage at Jonestown, some searched for scapegoats: most prominently attorney Mark Lane, sometimes Temple attorney Charles Garry, or officers at the CIA and the State Department who are supposed to have had "guilty knowledge" of what might happen in Jonestown when Ryan visited. Ryan himself was also the target of suggestions that the entire staging of the investigative trip was ill-advised, and involved prejudgment and the conflation of fact-finding and executive activities.[22]

The search for scapegoats also produced what amount to assorted reincarnations of the "conspiracy" theory advanced by Peoples Temple. The most farfetched of these was the claim of Black comedian Dick Gregory that CIA-FBI commandos killed the people of Jonestown so that their bodies could be used to smuggle heroin into the United States. A slightly less grandiose theory depicted Jones as a long-time CIA employee who used Peoples Temple to amass socialists and then wipe them out. A less flamboyant theory holds that the United States sought to undermine Jonestown because the government could not tolerate the success of Jonestown as an example of what people out from under the yoke of capitalist oppression could do once they took control of their own lives. A final type of government conspiracy theory attributes the motive to international intrigues deriving from the triangle of fragile alliances among the government of Guyana's ruling PNC socialist party, Peoples Temple, and U.S. geopolitical interests. These theories, it seems to me, elevate an apparent U.S. government quasi-intelligence activity of monitoring Jonestown (possibly through infiltration as well as external monitoring) to a more clandestine intervention, but without any substantial evidence. It is important to continue to probe questions that have not been given the full light of unreleased evidence held by the U.S. government: what did the government know, why did it not intervene? But other than any forthcoming evidence about Jones as a CIA agent, evidence about CIA objectives in relation to Jonestown would not contradict the present study's depiction of a basically coherent Temple history in its own terms, and the way in which that history aligns with the actions of Jones and his followers at the end.[23]

The search for scapegoats hardly need range so far. The most prevalent public approach treated the mass suicide as the result of evil (or, in more modern parlance, mental illness) in Jim Jones.[24] In this frame, Jones became a modern embodiment of the Devil, and the story of his undoing amounts to a heroic tragedy. Courageous apostates and relatives who claimed to recognize the hidden concentration camp that was Jonestown in turn awakened a vigilant press and a congressman who posthumously was awarded a Congressional Gold Medal for his sacrifice. Jones defeated the heroes, even as he substantiated their claims.

The popular indictment against Jim Jones and Peoples Temple would do well to paint a portrait of a man who began his life with ideals born out of resentment against an established order from which he was alienated. On the basis of his ideals, Jones provoked hypocrisy in his opponents and bound to himself people who shared his convictions. He elevated those ideals to "ultimate ends" that justified sacrificing other ethics: honesty, fair play, individual self-determination. He cultivated his own opposition through arbitrary and excessive practices, then took "persecution" at the hands of his opponents as proof of his righteousness, and ultimately, as justification of a mass martyrdom he orchestrated. It is the unity of this perverse double game, binding perhaps noble ideals with resentment-breeding "persecution," that sustains the popular view of Peoples Temple. In all of this the terror belongs to Jim Jones. No matter what his ideals, no matter how much his more devoted followers believed in his love, Jones was a man who succeeded as a prophet only insofar as he failed, by taking a tortuous path that buried his ideals and accomplishments in needless martyrdom.

But that is not the end of the matter. In the flood of mass media stories on Peoples Temple, the stigmata of evil in Jim Jones enveloped a much longer compendium of sins. The popular accounts recounted a series of atrocities in Peoples Temple—how Jim Jones and Peoples Temple misrepresented their movement through public relations, how they compromised and subordinated politicians, how they squeezed money out of believers and intimidated them in the United States, how they shattered families in the demands for establishment of a group mind that suppressed individual freedom, how they then tricked the unsuspecting into going to Guyana, and how in Jonestown they held dissidents and believers alike as hostages until the moment of their collective martyrdom arrived. That a small number of people wanted to leave with Congressman Ryan was taken as proof that Jonestown as a whole was a prison. That the people of Jonestown took poison after the murders at the airstrip was taken as proof that Jones was a coward who could not face the harsh light of the defectors' revelations.

A counterfactual theory about the end of Jonestown promoted by the Concerned Relatives extended the formula of pervasive evil. The thesis in some quarters was that Jim Jones did not really plan to die, that he was murdered by someone else against his will. How could the executioner, the egotistical coward take his own life? The logic of an internally coherent myth demanded that a power-hungry charlatan would have tried to save his own skin and make off with the money. This, despite contradictory evidence: Jones's death by a gunshot consistent with suicide, and the bequeathing of Temple assets to the Communist party of the Soviet Union. The conjectures that Jones wanted to prevent Ryan and the others from telling their story, and that he planned to survive the deaths of his followers seem farfetched. No matter how many people Jonestown sharpshooters had assassinated, they would only have fueled the exposé, not cut it off. And the counterfactual theory ignores the words of lost hope, revenge, and martyrdom that pervaded Jonestown's last hours. Such evidence notwithstanding, "unconfirmed reports" were used to advance claims that the Anti-Christ intended to live on.[25]

That opponents and observers would cling to a counterfactual theory about Jones's death reveals an ideological interest in forcing the evils of Jonestown into a mold in which they do not fit. No doubt Jones tried to infuse his followers with the resentment of the dispossessed. But defectors from the Temple became equally possessed of another resentment: as apostates they tried to redeem their own spiritual past by mounting a crusade against Peoples Temple's devaluation of sexual monogamy, the family, individualism, and the U.S. way of life in general. By embarking on a public symbolic attack on such scandals in 1977, the Temple's opponents offered their mass media audience the opportunity to experience taboo ways of life vicariously while they themselves regained moral respectibility in the process.[26]

After the mass suicide the stakes became considerably higher for the Concerned Relatives and their allies in the press and government. Jim Jones had to become so manifestly evil that there could be absolutely no question about the justification for the crusade the Concerned Relatives had taken up against him, the tactics they had used in their struggle, or the promotion by certain reporters of their cause. If the Concerned Relatives' efforts at each step were understood as unequivocally justified by the evil in Jones, then responsibility for the murders and mass suicide could rest with Jones alone and not be seen as partly a consequence of the campaign by the Concerned Relatives, supported through the activities of the press, government agencies, and Congressman Ryan. Though a "mental experiment" cannot definitively establish what would have happened under different circumstances, the Concerned Relatives had to believe that if Ryan's visit had not triggered mass suicide, Jones would have found another pretext.[27]

Effectively, the crusade by the Concerned Relatives served as the basis for the popular view of Peoples Temple as the embodiment of evil. In the aftermath of Jonestown, the stark vision of this overwhelming evil reaffirmed the sanctity of U.S. culture by comparison. The Concerned Relatives' scapegoating of Jim Jones thus became transposed into a vehicle of societal exorcism. The thoroughgoing evil of Peoples Temple was traced to the group's character as a "cult" alien to the U.S. way of life. The mass suicide became the outcome of a diabolical plan perpetrated by a madman who acted in psychotic isolation from the world. Because this view prevailed, the mass suicide could not be understood as a more complex product of the struggles between Peoples Temple and its opponents. Any historically adequate explanation was overwhelmed by the interest among the living in avoiding stigma attached to the carnage of death.

Ideological procedures of interpretation in the aftermath of disaster serve not just the self-interests of involved individuals; they also realize a basic capacity of religion, namely, the reaffirmation of the sanctity of a social order. The French sociologist Emile Durkheim first described the process. Modern society is cleansed from any connection to Peoples Temple by the specification of what Durkheim termed a "negative cult." Identifying the negative cult as a social aberration effectively establishes a contrast with what Durkheim called the "positive cult," the idealized conception of society as the embodiment of a consensual morality. Such a symbolic differentiation cannot be so easily accomplished when what is socially defined as evil emerges within the sanctified centers of a culture, in its established political, religious, or cultural institutions. But Jim Jones founded his movement in opposition to the established order. The circle of exorcism thus could be completed by straightforward contrast of the "positive cult" with the cancerous evil of Peoples Temple, a group that cast itself off by migration, murder, and mass suicide.[28]

We must recognize, however, the potential gap between sanctifying a social order and deepening the public understanding of that order. The painting of a positive and negative cult will not carry the burden of historical interpretation, for it proceeds on the basis of an overdrawn mythic simplification that must ignore the ambiguities of history. The logic of the process demands that evil be loaded onto the negative cult, no matter what its source. Beyond the evil posited in Jim Jones's quest for socialist martyrdom, two other standards of evil were used to establish Jonestown as a negative cult. One is based on a suspicion of communalism in general; the other judges as evil the techniques that Jones and his followers used to achieve their evil ends.

The first standard simply reads onto Peoples Temple a particular ideological judgment about the relative values of communal versus individualist approaches to life. The critique of an organization that takes possessions from its members, "brainwashing" them into a "group mind" in the process, hardly distinguishes Peoples Temple from a long list of religious communal organizations such as Hare Krishna, the Unification Church of Sun Myung Moon, the now-collapsed "cult" around Bhagwhan Shree Rajneesh (which Leo Ryan's daughter Shannon joined after her father's murder), and various nineteenth-century communal sects like Oneida, the Shakers, and some Mormon groups. The opponents of the Temple simply borrowed a culturally available "anticult" critique and applied it to Peoples Temple. To this extent, the "evil" in Peoples Temple is nothing other than an ideological critique of communalism as a form of heretical deviance.[29]

The second standard for establishing the negative cult of Jonestown focuses on Temple methods: healings, money-making schemes, glorification of a prophet, intimidation and punishment, public relations, and political manipulations. But this auto-da-fé can proceed only by the device of projecting onto Jones the burden of carrying evils that are widespread and sometimes institutionalized practices in the wider society, for, as we have seen, Jones was hardly a creative man, at least when it came to his methods. To the contrary, he learned by watching others. However crudely, he mimicked their practices and used them to establish an organization that owed its success in no small part to the fact that its cultural inventory reflected the pathways of the wider world. At his most perverse, Jones manifested the dialectical psychology of resentment: he not only struggled against the forces against which he sought revenge; he also secretly respected their power and emulated their ways, even as he claimed to oppose them.[30]

Thus the Temple's world of opposition to the world at large often enough was but a mirror of it, sometimes a grotesque reflection of its seamier side. In much of what they did, Jones and his followers relied on disarmingly familiar cultural recipes. Jones's faith healing claims seem conservative by comparison to the current practices of other, more prominent evangelists.

So it was with his financial schemes, politics, public relations, even the techniques of confinement and social control. Each finds its application not just in "shady" enterprises but in mainstream social institutions: the advertising, public relations, and monitoring practices of corporations; the bureaucratic, confinement, and control techniques of prisons, mental hospitals, and schools, the "dirty tricks" of politicians and security agencies like the FBI and CIA; and the money-making gimmicks of evangelical religious movements. The most ironic testament to the compelling attraction of Jones's techniques in the arenas of communal economics, politics, and public relations is that his own opponents—the Concerned Relatives and the Human Freedom Center—used similar tactics.[31]

The stigma of Jonestown thus stems in part from its uneven reflection of society at large. If the claims of his opponents are accepted, Jim Jones carried a triple burden. Not only did he carry his own unique evil; not only did he embody the evil of communalism; he also shouldered a sin-offering for evils he shared with the world he left behind. To the degree that the evil in Peoples Temple was transferred to it by Jones's resentment-driven secret desires of emulation, he caricatured and sometimes intensified sinister tendencies in modern society. The "negative cult" of Jonestown stands as an ominous monument to an arsenal of manipulations in a netherworld of institutional practice that has not left us with the death of Jonestown.

Jones's goal of martyrdom hardly justifies his means, but his actions face us with an ethical challenge. Are the acts of Jim Jones to be judged evil only because they were practiced within a realm beyond the legitimate auspices of society? Or are they intrinsically evil? If they are taken as the latter, exorcism cannot proceed on the basis of singling out a fringe religious "cult." It must cast a wider net. We must search out how widely the evils of Jonestown permeate our world. The alternative to a judgment of intrinsic evil is to adopt the line of argument used by Jones himself, namely, that "the ends justify the means." Insofar as the means that propelled Jonestown are more widely shared, we are then left to ponder: what ends justify them in our world?

The death of over 900 people on November 18, 1978, was a tragedy of an immensity beyond words. But the past cannot be undone, and the great tragedy in the wake of tragedy would be to move beyond that moment driven solely by stigmatic urges to submerge it. Neither the Jonestown view of justified martyrdom nor the identification of Jonestown as a negative cult achieves adequate understanding. Each projects evil in an opposite direction, reserving righteousness for its own. But oddly enough, for Jones's followers, the sin-sacrifice of collective martyrdom was only the fulfillment of a covenant, not an effective act. They did not believe it cleansed anyone of sin and they did not believe it brought the world any closer to redemption. Ironically, Jones has become far more important for the society at large as a symbolic personification of evil than he is in any way to those who share some of the concerns that animated his movement. It is the opponents of Jim Jones who infused him with a charisma powerful enough to make him play the mythic role of scapegoat that cleanses the world of sin, even if they failed to acknowledge that the sin-offering of Jonestown had wider sources than the evil in Jim Jones.[32]

Whatever their directions, such symbolic transformations leave elements of Jonestown culture still alive in our world, in our techniques of social control, our religious practices, our politics, our public relations. And in the wake of Jonestown, the major dilemmas that brought forth the wave of commitment to Peoples Temple are hardly closer to resolution. In the Promised Land, the poor still live among us, even more so in the Third World to which Peoples Temple fled. Racial equality, much less community, remains elusive. And we have not yet defused the nuclear holocaust that haunts us as the final mass suicide. Despite the uneven, flawed character of Jim Jones, I believe that many who joined him were people of good will who cared about these things in ways that led them to concrete action. In the end, many of them shared his resentment. They became reduced to shadows of Jim Jones who could not rise up against him. Came the silent cry of nightmare across the ocean: "The horror. The horror."[33] We hear the screams, but we do not entirely understand them, and we will continue to wrestle with the apocalypse that they unveiled.

# Appendix:
# A Comment on Methodology

The present book is a project in the historical sociology of culture that attempts to offer a coherent general understanding of Peoples Temple as a social phenomenon of cultural significance. It draws on the classic approach of Max Weber (1977: 4–22) to construct a methodological strategy that is carried out through four interrelated analytic frames: historical narrative, sociological analysis, causal historical analysis, and cultural interpretation.

At the most basic level, the text unfolds as a narrative history of what happened with Peoples Temple and Jim Jones. I do not claim, however, that there is only one "correct" history. In the first place, the available information on Peoples Temple is so voluminous that some practices of selection must be involved in the construction of all narratives. Any narrative is therefore incomplete. Moreover, narrative in general proceeds on the basis of a framing of subject that cannot be derived from the raw stuff of the historical flux. For example, in the present study, I have tried to depict "what life was really like" for the people of Peoples Temple only insofar as it seemed relevant to other issues. This choice in no way invalidates the possibility of a deeper inquiry along such lines, but there was a limit to how far I could go in that direction and still maintain an investigatory momentum toward my principal purpose.

The second analytic frame, that of sociological causation, in part dictates the structure of the first frame, of narrative discourse. The sociological analysis proceeds through use of ideal types, sometimes called "socio-historical models" (Roth, 1971, 1976) to emphasize their parallels with empirical social phenomena. What Weber referred to as "average types"—empirical modalities or averages—are also employed. In either case, to the degree that a particular phenomenon related to Peoples Temple can be subsumed under a more general concept, the social dynamics related to that concept are taken to be explanatory. For example, a sociohistorical model of the "charlatan" offers a basis for exploring whether Jones's actions can be subsumed under such a motive structure. On another front, contemporary practice within the public relations industry in the United States offers an empirical type as a baseline of comparison for

313

Temple practices. In general, comparison with abstract and empirical models offers the opportunity to ferret out the more general social and cultural dynamics in Peoples Temple, leaving a residue of unexplained phenomena to be submitted to situational causal historical analysis.

The third frame, causal historical analysis, thus also shapes in part the choices of narrative. In brief, the narrative itself is embedded with explorations surrounding theories (or plots) about the unique causal sequences that ultimately led to mass suicide. A number of questions about historical actions and events were crucial to that analysis. Was Jim Jones really the biological father of his aide Tim Stoen's legal son John Victor Stoen? When did Jones first learn that his opponents had gone to a Treasury agent? These questions and others like them are focused on the "break points" of Temple history in an attempt to base a situational causal analysis on the interrelations of events in the unfolding drama itself. Documentary evidence thus is brought to bear on the testing of alternative theories of plot (cf. Veyne, 1984).

Finally, the book offers a cultural interpretation of Jonestown that is built up from the other frames: narrative, sociological analysis, and causal history. In one sense this interpretation turns to the realm of sociological theory insofar as it explores how, in the postmodern era, individuals pursuing realization of ultimate values became the protagonists in a societal drama of mythic proportions. This analysis in turn permits an effort to strip away myth from Jonestown, so that its cultural significance can be more clearly considered.

These four frames were not kept neatly separated during the course of research nor are they separated in the book; they were interwoven with one another both in the process of gathering materials and in writing.

I began thinking about the topic of Peoples Temple immediately after I learned of the mass suicide in November of 1978. The event seemed to me to pose an extreme test for the interpretational usefulness of my (1978) typology of communal groups. I immediately began a clipping file, and as a mosaic of information about events began to fall in place, in early January of 1979, I completed the draft of an initial article (1979). The article draft set forth a basic analytic framework, and it used available information from news sources and several "instant" books to offer a historical sketch in terms of the framework.

News reports continued to pour in during the first half of 1979, and a number of investigations were set in motion by various governmental agencies, both in the United States and in Guyana. Newspapers reported that Peoples Temple had kept extensive documents and tape recordings of various events, including the mass suicide. A New York business named Creative Arts Guild briefly offered copies of a pirated cassette tape recording of the mass suicide, and I managed to obtain one before it closed shop. I also began to learn enough about the principals involved in Temple history to decide to try to interview certain people. Because the article on Jonestown was to be published in the fall of 1979, it was critical to weigh each new piece of information against what I already had written. For this same reason, I decided to travel to Guyana with a colleague in May of 1979 and to visit San Francisco the following month.

In Guyana, based at Palm Court, across the main street from the U.S. AID mission, I was able to interview certain Guyanese officials through the good offices of a high-ranking member of the government whom I had contacted through mutual personal acquaintances. Although Guyanese officials were not particularly forthcoming about the relation of Jonestown to their government, they did offer other information, and I gained a sense of their style of operation. More important, the trip allowed me to talk with various unofficial observers of the Guyana scene and to visit the Lamaha Gardens house still occupied by a few former Temple members. There I found former Jonestown residents, somewhat disenchanted by reporters who refused to eat or drink anything offered by survivors of mass suicide. Nevertheless, the people at Lamaha Gardens spent hours responding to my questions and offering their oral histories.

In California I met with former Temple attorney Charles Garry in June of 1979 after doing nothing more complicated than calling him by telephone, and in the same way I contacted and interviewed key informants from the ranks of Peoples Temple and the oppositional group, the Concerned Relatives. Garry offered me access to Temple archives in his possession, including tape recordings, files, letters, photographs, and videotapes. The individuals I interviewed often put me in contact with others who they thought might offer additional information. In a sense I entered a still somewhat coherent social world, a world whose inhabitants often still carried agonies, doubts, stigma, bitter anger, ideological self-justifications. In only one case did an individual I approached refuse to be interviewed: when I was in Ukiah, California, one summer day in 1984, an intermediary asked Tim Stoen if he would meet with me, and he declined.

Slowly I began puzzling though a maze of often contradictory information. In all I traveled to California on four occasions, through the summer of 1984, conducting follow-up interviews, and engaging in an exhaustive analysis of the archives in Charles Garry's possession and those at the California Historical Society, once they became available.

Government agencies were other major sources of information. When the U.S. Department of State, the California Attorney General, and similar offices issued reports of their investigations, I wrote and obtained copies. It also became apparent that the FBI and the Department of State held

316 Gone from the Promised Land

substantial archives, and I initiated requests for any and all such materials by writing letters under the Freedom of Information Act. These requests initially were denied because of the first U.S. trial of Larry Layton, charged as the lone surviving conspirator in the death of Congressman Leo Ryan, but beginning in 1981, I received copies of hundreds of tapes and documents from the two agencies. Still, neither the State Department nor the FBI, the CIA, or other federal agencies has yet released all the relevant documents in their possession, citing interests of national security and individuals' rights to privacy. Similarly, the Committee on Foreign Affairs of the U.S. House of Representatives refused to release any materials not included in its public final report (1979), and to my knowledge, portions of the report, for example, one entitled "Conspiracy against Jim Jones and Peoples Temple?" remain classified today. Aside from these prohibitions against seeing certain documents, the federal agencies responded to my requests in a timely way.

Over the course of some six years, I gathered five major types of data: (1) original documents of Peoples Temple, its members, and other groups (e.g. the Concerned Relatives; the U.S. Department of State) and individuals, including personal journals, correspondence, reports, financial records, public relations materials, and miscellaneous other materials; (2) original tape recordings of Temple meetings, telephone conversations, interviews, sermons, staff meetings, and other events recorded by Temple staff; (3) personal interviews I undertook in Georgetown, Guyana; San Francisco; Washington, D.C.; and elsewhere after November 1978, with certain surviving members of Peoples Temple, certain members of the Concerned Relatives, and various other informed sources such as government officials in the United States and Guyana, church officials, and so forth; (4) news accounts, both prior to and after November 1978; and (5) various books and other secondary source materials published after November 1978.

The draft of the text was written from September 1983 to September 1984, during a sabbatical year leave from the University of Missouri at Columbia. The structure of the book was derived from the intersection of data with the four frames described above, via topics clustered in chapters. The four frames were used to identify a series of topical concerns, from Jim Jones's social origins to the events of November 18, 1978, and after. An outline of the topical concerns grouped in chapters ordered the text, while leaving conclusions from any one topic and their implications for other topics open to the analysis of data itself. Whatever their sources, materials were screened for their relevance to the text's chapters, and within chapters, to topics. Analysis and drafting of the text then proceeded by reference to the topically relevant materials.

In general, given the conflicting and oppositional versions of many events, I did not rely only on the two-source corroboration technique of verification so favored by journalists: two mutually confirming datums could not be assumed to hold greater validity than another one that contradicted them both, simply because two allies easily could coordinate their versions of events with each another, creating a verifiable falsehood. Given this problem, I sought to weigh the data with a scholar's balance, trying to reconstruct the historical situations of their intentionalities and production, weighing the plausibility of assertions, puzzling through chains of inference, triangulating data from alternative sources, building up mosaics of situations from disparate pieces of information. Information that seemed anomalous I kept aside, waiting for other data to help identify it, trying relentlessly to force it back upon the text to clarify further the emergent plots.

Such techniques of historical investigation are well known (Barzun and Grath, 1985) and need no great elaboration, but I should indicate that I consistently tried to employ Alfred Lindesmith's (1947) method of negative evidence analysis, paying more attention to data that contradicted a line of argument than to data further confirming it, trying to learn the source of the conflict and whether it required a reformulation, and in what direction.

The present study offers an interpretation based on careful and recursive examination of a wide range of data. Though historical truth may be an elusive thing, I believe that the broad structure of a complex set of events is clear. Nonetheless, it is the burden of the historian to know that some information that could shed further light on events lies beyond reach. In the case of Peoples Temple, survivors, opponents, and governments might yet surprise us with revelations previously withheld to protect various interests. I hope they do so.

# Abbreviations

AI: Author's interview

CAG: California Attorney General (1980)

CAG/PT: *California Attorney General* vs. *Peoples Temple*, California Superior Court, San Francisco, case #746571

CCR: Crimmins, John Hugh, and Stanley S. Carpenter (1979)

CDT: Columbia (Mo.) *Daily Tribune*

CFA: Committee on Foreign Affairs (1979)

CFAH: Committee on Foreign Affairs Hearing (1979)

CGA: Charles Garry, Attorney-at-law, Peoples Temple archives, San Francisco

CHS: California Historical Society, Peoples Temple archives, San Francisco. (N.B.: All archive citations with a F, G, P, or CHS number currently may be found in a separate CHS archive containing the author's research documents; all other CHS documents are contained in the society's general Peoples Temple archive.)

CIA: U.S. Central Intelligence Agency

CIR: Committee on International Relations, U.S. House of Representatives

CSC: California Superior Court

CSS: California Department of Social Services (1979)

DOS log: Department of State Peoples Temple Freedom of Information Act archive document number

FBI: U.S. Federal Bureau of Investigation

GC: Guyana *Chronicle*

GS/TOS: *Grace Stoen* vs. *Timothy O. Stoen*, California Superior Court, San Francisco, case #719147

GUSEC: Georgetown, Guyana U.S. Embassy cable (log number refers to State Department Peoples Temple Freedom of Information Act archive)

IR: Indianapolis *Recorder*

IS: Indianapolis *Star*

IT: Indianapolis *Times*

ITT: *In These Times* (Chicago)

JC/PT: *James Cobb, Jr.* vs. *Peoples Temple*, California Superior Court, San Francisco, case #739907

JM/PT: *Jeannie Mills et al.* vs. *Peoples Temple et al.*, California Superior Court, San Francisco, case #727–517, filed August 30, 1977.

LA: Los Angeles

LACA: George Eskin, report to Los Angeles City Attorney (1979)

LAT: Los Angeles *Times*

LCJ: Louisville (Ky.) *Courier-Journal*

MG: *Mendocino* (Calif.) *Grapevine*

NYT: New York *Times*

p.c.: Peoples Temple Planning Commission

PF: *Peoples Forum* (Peoples Temple, San Francisco)

PT/TOS: Peoples Temple vs. Timothy Oliver Stoen, California Superior Court, San Francisco, case #740531

q.: Quoted

RPI: Richmond (Ind.) *Palladium-Item*

SF: San Francisco

SFB: San Francisco *Banner*

SFC: San Francisco *Chronicle*

SFE: San Francisco *Examiner*

SFP: San Francisco *Progress*

SFSR: San Francisco *Sun Reporter*

SK/JJ: *Steven Katsaris* vs. *Jim Jones et al.*, California Superior Court, Mendocino County, case #45373; *Steven Katsaris* vs. *Jim Jones et al.*, First Appelate District Court, California, case #1CIV45373

SRPD: Santa Rosa *Press-Democrat*

UDJ: Ukiah *Daily Journal*

USSDC: U.S. State Department Cable (log number refers to State Department Peoples Temple Freedom of Information Act archive)

WM/PT: *Wade and Mabel Medlock* vs. *Peoples Temple*, California Superior Court, Los Angeles, case #C243292

WP: Washington *Post*

WPW: Washington *Post Weekly*

# Notes

*Introduction: The Cultural Puzzle of Jonestown*

1. The group often is referred to in print as "People's Temple" or "the Peoples' Temple." The present book consistently follows the usage "Peoples Temple" because it is more often found in statements of participants, and because it is part of the official name of the group, "Peoples Temple of the Disciples of Christ," under which it was incorporated. Washington *Post* (hereafter cited as WP), 11/21/78.
2. San Francisco *Chronicle* (hereafter cited as SFC), 11/22/78; New York *Times* (hereafter cited as NYT), 12/11/78.
3. Guards' accounts: Louisville *Courier-Journal* (hereafter cited as LCJ), 11/21/78. Tape recording of 11/18/78 Jonestown pavilion meeting: Peoples Temple (1979), reprinted in Zaniello (1987). For strikingly differing opinions of survivors on degree of coercion, see, e.g., Thom Bogue and Chuck Kirkendale, depositions for *California Attorney General* vs. *Peoples Temple* (hereafter cited as CAG/PT), California Historical Society, Peoples Temple Archives, San Francisco (hereafter cited as CHS).
4. Two of the instant books offered on-the-scene accounts: Kilduff and Javers (1978) and Krause (1978). One, Maguire and Dunn (1978), was put together by a "quicky" research network. *New Republic*, 12/9/78, p. 9.
5. On plausibility structures: Berger and Luckmann (1966), Berger (1967), and Goffman (1974). On honor: Berger (1974: 83ff.)
6. Jim Jones, November 18, 1978, in Peoples Temple (1979).
7. Foreign press commentaries quoted from LCJ, 11/23/78. Naipaul (1981: 187–214) is a skilled and engaging writer, but his moral outrage at the suicides and murders sometimes misses its mark because his general disdain for the United States seems to blind him to the nuances of its culture.
8. One of the most extensive considerations of socialist and Black-community reactions to Jonestown is the series by David Moberg in *In These Times* (hereafter cited as ITT), 12/6–12, 13–19, 20–26/78. An early Christian reaction is contained in the Christian college campus newspaper *Today's Student* (Ames, Ia.), which devoted most of its 12/6/78 issue to coverage of Peoples Temple as a "cult." On the reaction of the denomination with which Peoples Temple affiliated, see "Press release 78a–188," Christian Church (Disciples of Christ), Indianapolis, November 22, 1978, reprinted in Rose (1979: 176–78), itself a Christian inquiry. The official investigations include California Department of Social Services (1979; hereafter cited as CSS), George Eskin, report to Los Angeles City Attorney (1979; hereafter cited as LACA), California Attorney General (1980; hereafter cited as CAG), John Hugh Crimmins and Stanley S. Carpenter (1979; hereafter cited as CCR), Committee on Foreign Affairs (1979; hereafter cited as CFA), Committee on Foreign Affairs Hearing (1979; hereafter cited as CFAH), and General Accounting Office (1980).

9. Smith (1982: esp. 112, 120). For a well-reasoned essay from a Caribbean perspective: Lewis (1979); a sociological survey is provided by Levi (1982). The popular accounts include that of a defector, Mills (1979). Other popular accounts include White, Scotchman, and Shuster (1979), Klineman, Butler, and Conn (1980), an eyewitness account of the mass suicide (Feinsod, 1981), Theilmann and Merrill (1979), Dem (1979), Tello (1979), Santos (1979), Nichols (1979?), Ahlberg (1980), Syski (1980), Yee and Layton (1981), Kern and Wead (1979), Lane (1980), Nugent (1979), Reston's (1981) self-described (on a National Public Radio call-in show, 4/23/81) "novel in reality," Reston and Adams (1981), Wooden (1981), and Reiterman and Jacobs (1982). For an informed discussion of the popular literature, see Weightman (1983: 165ff.). On atrocity tales, see Bromley (1982). "Blame for the Jonestown tragedy," Reiterman and Jacobs (1982: 577).

10. Throne scene: Jonestown Tape 1 Side 1," tape cassette, Charles Garry, attorney-at-law, Peoples Temple archives, San Francisco (hereafter cited as CGA), apparently recorded the same night as a cassette of radio transmissions with Jonestown recorded at the San Francisco Peoples Temple offices during a September 10, 1977, Jonestown "white night" (emergency related to external threats). Cartoon magazine source unknown; copy: F655, CHS.

11. Reiterman and Jacobs (1982: 4).

12. Reiterman and Jacobs (1982: 19, 27, 583).

13. Reiterman and Jacobs (1982: 572).

14. LCJ, 11/23/78.

15. Fallding (1974: 27).

16. The procedure is a longstanding one in the analysis of social action; see Weber (1977: 4–22).

17. Conrad (1967).

## Chapter 1: Jim Jones

1. The "frame" terminology of Goffman (1974) suggests a set of boundaries by which reality is perceived.

2. Jones's hometown: Richmond *Palladium-Item* (hereafter cited as RPI), 11/26/78. The Old Northwest: Rohrbough (1978: 146–47, 164). Randolph County settlers and the Quakers: Buley (1950: I, 25–26; II, 50, 474–75); Knollenberg (1945: 18ff.); Smith and Driver (1914: 753); and Henry (1908:388–89).

3. Randolph County demographics: Thornbrough (1947: 49, 228); Tucker (1882); U.S. Census (1930: tables 11, 14, 18, 19); Whitman and Trimble (1954–1957: table 39).

4. On *hoosier*: Dunn (1907). Jones's birthdate: NYT, 11/26/78. James T. Jones almost surely was the son of John Henry Jones and Mary C. Shank. The enumerator's manuscript census sheet, 12th U.S. Census, 1900, Indiana, vol. 64, enumeration district 125, sheet 12 (Washington Township, Randolph County), lists John Henry Jones's family with a son, James T., born in October 1887, that is, the correct age to have been approximately sixteen years older than Lynetta Jones, as she said her husband was, in FBI file BB18Z30. (There is a slight discrepancy, for Lynetta Jones was born around 1901, according to the enumerator's manuscript census sheet, Patoka Township, Gibson County, Indi-

ana, 13th U.S. Census, 1910.) Biographic sketches of Jones family ancestors: Smith and Driver (1914: 1474–75); John Henry Jones's father's first name was Warren, the middle name given to Jim Jones. John Henry Jones started out as a schoolteacher and turned to farming in 1880, "specializing in hogs which he fattens for the market, shipping from his place about six hundred dollars' worth annually, and no small portion of his income is derived from this source." The 280 acres of Jones family holdings are shown on the Washington Township map in Lake (1874). See also Lynetta Jones, U.S. Federal Bureau of Investigation Peoples Temple tape recording (cited hereafter as FBI tape) Q761, made in the 1970s in Redwood Valley, California. This is one of a series of tape recordings about Peoples Temple, most of them found at Jonestown. This and other FBI and U.S. Department of State materials were obtained by the author through Freedom of Information Act requests.

5. "Big Jim" Jones: FBI file O1A1. Lynetta Jones, FBI tape Q761, declared the Crete farmstead had a mortgage, but a neighbor said the house was rented; RPI, 11/26/78. U.S. Census, Indiana (1930: vol. 1, table 4). Blacks in Lynn and Jones's father in KKK: George Southworth, LCJ, 11/23/78, who grew up in Lynn, "a stone's throw" from Jim Jones. Apparently this story that Jones himself often used, e.g., Indianapolis *Recorder* (hereafter cited as IR), 7/25/64, was culturally shared in the wider population. On Jones's father in KKK, cf. Jim Jones, FBI tape Q967.

6. RPI, 11/26/78; FBI tape Q761; Lynetta Jones, FBI file BB18Z2–3. Lynetta's family: enumerator's manuscript census sheet, Patoka Township, Gibson County, Indiana, 13th U.S. Census, 1910. Barbara Shaffer, a cousin of Jim Jones on his father's side, says Lynetta was Welsh, in David Johnston, Los Angeles *Times* (hereafter cited as LAT) News Service, in Columbia (Mo.) *Daily Tribune* (hereafter cited as CDT), 12/3/78; Crete neighbor Alicia Heck recalled talk of Lynetta Jones's Indian background, RPI, 11/26/78; Barton Hunter, author's interview (hereafter cited as AI), also talked of "Indian blood"; and *Newsweek*, December 7, 1978, asserted that when Jim Jones was young, he claimed Lynetta was part Cherokee. Parker as foster father: Lynetta Jones, FBI file BB18Z25. Lewis Parker is listed in the 1910 enumerator's manuscript census sheet for Patoka Township in the residence next to the Jesse Putnam residence, and he is the only person enumerated on the sheet as owning land. Listed living with the fifty-eight-year-old man in 1910 is Flora Putnam, a fifty-six-year-old widow, presumably the mother of Jesse, the only living one of her four children. Her household status is given as "servant" and her occupation as "housekeeper." Apparently Parker was less a "foster father," as Lynetta Jones remembers him, and more the patron of his tenants. Still, the relationship between the Putnams and Parker was a close one; given Lynetta Jones's account and census records, we may infer that Parker took in Putnam and her children when her husband died, and provided a tenancy for her only surviving son, Jesse, his wife, and their children.

7. On the pioneer language from which Jones's speech patterns derived: Buley (1950: 350ff.). Lynetta Jones's education: Reiterman and Jacobs (1982: 10). Lynetta, her husband, and her son: Lynetta Jones, FBI file BB18Z30 (not sleeping with husband), 37; Thelma Manning (childhood neighbor), RPI, 11/22/78; letter to Lynetta Jones from Perfect Circle Corp., 12/1/52, Lynetta Jones file, CGA; Lynetta Jones, letter about Taft-Hartley Law to Indiana Representative Ralph Harvey, 11/18/48, Lynetta Jones—correspondence, CHS. On Jones and his father: Lynetta Jones FBI tape Q761; Jim Jones FBI file O1B5.

8. On Nazarenes: Mead (1975: 105); Synan (1971: 60). Lynetta Jones and religion: FBI tape Q761; LCJ, 11/25/78; Lynetta Jones, FBI file BB18Z3, 25.
9. Lynetta Jones, FBI tape Q761, and FBI file BB18Z5 (animals), 25–27. Parker's death is given as June 10, 1932, at the age of seventy-three, Gibson County, Indiana, Department of Health, Book H–42, p. 29.
10. "Aweful times" description of Great Depression: Lewis Parker, letter to Lynetta Jones, 1/17/32, Lynetta Jones file, CGA. Lynetta Jones on her son: FBI file BB18Z30; FBI tape Q761. Jim Jones on comforts: FBI file O1A1a. Frontier: Rohrbough (1978: 165). Jim Jones on thrift: December 9, 1977, FBI file O1B13. Weber (1958: 172).
11. Synan (1971: 123, ch. 8, 182, 185ff.); Hollenweger (1972: 459ff.).
12. Jones's religious experiences: Lynetta Jones, FBI tape Q761; cf. Vera Price, letter to Jim Jones, 10/26/71, Operations, correspondence—general, CHS. On Marjoe: Hal Wingo, "The confessions of Marjoe," *Life* September 8, 1972, p. 60; Gaines (1973). Jim Jones's recollection of revelation, FBI tape Q967 (1972).
13. The forces promoting irreligiosity of nonprivileged strata are described by Weber (1977: 481). Lynetta Jones, FBI tape Q761. Jim Jones, FBI file O1A1a (late 1977).
14. On obscenities: George Southworth, LCJ, 11/23/78. Jones's youth: Jim Jones, FBI file O1B5, 7 (September 1977); Lynetta Jones, FBI tape Q761; Jim Jones, FBI file O1A1–a, –f (late 1977). Difference between the emotional atmosphere of Pentecostal and other church services: Synan (1971); Hollenweger (1972).
15. Jones's alienation: Reiterman and Jacobs (1982: 24–26); LCJ, 11/22/78; NYT, 11/26/78. Jim Jones, FBI file O1B1, 2, 5–7 (late 1977). The elder Jim Jones died several years after the separation, in 1951. Reiterman and Jacobs (1982: 582) treat Jones's account as his attempt "to recast his youth" so as to appear a "rogue." Probably the account was a mixture of fact and some embellishment, although in certain minute details, such as the distance from Lynn to the town where he went when he ran away, Jones exhibited a strikingly accurate memory.
16. Jim Jones and fascism: Lynetta Jones, FBI tape Q762. Jim Jones on World War II: FBI file O1B2. For an account of the glowing war-era press stance toward the then-U.S. ally, the USSR, to which young Jim Jones probably was exposed, see Howe and Coser (1957: 431–32).
17. Lynetta Jones, FBI tape Q761.

## Chapter 2: The Preacher

1. Weber (1977: 486–87). On revolutionary religion: Knox (1956); Cohn (1970: 243ff.); Lewy (1974: 110ff.). For a Marxist view, see Engels (1964).
2. Street preaching: Reiterman and Jacobs (1982: 26). Courtship: Marcie Jones and Lynetta Jones, 5/10/75, FBI file HH6A17; Marcie Jones, FBI file BB18Z63; Marcie Jones, 8/10/77, F146, CHS. Communism and religion: Jim Jones, FBI file O1B214 (at this point the Communist party was on the verge of going underground; see Howe and Coser [1957: 478]). Marcie Jones, FBI file BB18Z64. Move to Indianapolis: Reiterman and Jacobs (1982: 38); NYT, 11/26/78.
3. Communist contacts: Jim Jones, FBI files O1A1c–d and O1B4; Lynetta Jones, FBI tape Q762. "Professional good man" is Sinclair Lewis's (1927) term. Ministerial call: Jim Jones, FBI files O1A1d and O1B8; Marcie Jones, F338, CHS;

Indianapolis *Star* (hereafter cited as IS), 11/20/78. Jones's theology: Marcie Jones, FBI file BB18Z70. Early ministry: Jim Jones, FBI file O1B8, FBI file HH6A18; Marcie Jones, FBI file BB18Z64.

4. Max Weber (1977: 494).

5. Pentecostalism's theology and history: Hollenweger (1972); Synan (1971); and Clark (1949: ch. 4). Jim Jones's claim of the gifts: FBI tape Q612; FBI tapes Q976 and Q1016 include antinomian assertions; on the former, Jones also claims that the revelation came to him that he was God when he was ten years old. On discernment: Hollenweger (1972: 3–4); Synan (1971: 111). Jones's discernment: Jim Jones, FBI file O1B9; Jack Beam, FBI tape Q777; Mr. and Mrs. Cecil Johnson of Indianapolis, San Francisco *Examiner* (hereafter cited as SFE), 9/19/72; Temple notes on individuals for discernment use: F236, CHS; young woman, FBI tape Q761.

6. Jim Jones, quoted (hereafter, q.), FBI file O1B9. Testimonial: Synan (1971: 188–89). Pentecostal faithhealing: Hollenweger (1972: 358–60, 366–67). Cast "healing" incident: Theilmann and Merrill (1979: 78). Healing descriptions: FBI tape Q1055 pt. 7. Jones's claims to raise dead: SFE, 9/17/72. Pentecostal healing practices and problems: Hollenweger (1972: 369); Washington *Post Weekly* (hereafter cited as WPW), 10/15/84. Recently, a Tennessee preacher's daughter sought to refuse medical treatment on religious grounds but was forced by a court order to undergo chemotherapy: CDT, 9/22/83. Temple disclaimers: SFE, 9/24/72; *Peoples Forum* (hereafter cited as PF) 1, no. 12 (November 1976); see also Marcie Jones, FBI file BB18Z66. Jimmie Swaggart (1983: 40–41, original emphasis). Jones discussion of limitations of his powers and the limitations of medicine: SFE, 9/24/72. Temple healings described in affidavits: F280, CHS. Raising of dead by Jones: SFE, 9/18/72. Testimonials: letters to IS by Temple member Jim Randolph, 11/12/71, and by a Christian Theological Seminary (Indianapolis) professor, James Carley, who had attended Peoples Temple services, 12/22/71, both in response to an IS article, 10/1/71. Lynetta Jones on healing: FBI tape Q762. Dorothy Hunter, AI; Barton Hunter, AI. Edith Parks, q. ITT, 12/13/78.

7. Miracles described: FBI tapes Q1020 pt. 1; Q1055 pt. 3. Exchange accident: Jim Jones, q. in Indianapolis newspaper, probably IS, about 5/12/59, undated copy in G3A–1, CHS. Police described the collision as the result of a driver's error in trying to pass in the face of oncoming traffic. Jim Jones, September 1977 recollection: FBI file O1B10. Pentecostals' similar prophesies: Hollenweger (1972: 345ff.). On Bonnie Thielmann: Thielmann and Merrill (1979: 87–88).

8. On Pentecostal beliefs: Durasoff (1972: 243) gives an insider's view. Jones's approach to religion: Dorothy Hunter, AI.; Jack Beam, FBI tape Q777; Jones's earliest printed statement, "As a man thinketh, so is he," *Herald of Faith* (Chicago), May 1956, F170, CHS. Jones's savior statement: FBI tape Q1055 pt. 3. Anti-communism fears: Hoover (1958: 243ff.). Jones and Methodists: Jim Jones, FBI file O1B8; Marcie Jones, FBI file BB18Z70. On the social gospel and Pentecostalism: Ahlstrom (1972: 802); Synan (1971: 56–58); Smith (1965); cf. Hofstadter (1963: pt. II); Hunter (1983); Smith (1950).

9. Barton Hunter, AI; Dorothy Hunter, AI. On poor people's movements: Piven and Cloward (1979); on the outcomes of different forms of collective action: Olson (1968).

10. Jones on primitive Christianity: Reiterman and Jacobs (1982: 60–63); FBI tape Q1059 pt. 5; Marcie Jones, q. NYT, 9/2/77. Jim Jones on communism: FBI

tape Q134. Mannheim (1936) offers the classic theory of ideological and uto-pian worldviews. Worldly pessimism: Lynetta Jones, FBI file BB18Z44; un-named woman, FBI tape Q762. The Jonestown shipping inventory lists, CHS, include books by Karl Marx and V.I. Lenin, as well as an introduction to socialism by Huberman and Sweezy. In Jonestown Jones occasionally read over the P.A. works on communist strategy and on dependency theory and their application to current events; see FBI tapes Q197, Q235, Q253. Peoples Temple was not the only popular movement to fail to conform to theoretical dictates of radical movement organization; see Piven and Cloward (1979). Jim Jones on his Marxism: FBI tape Q134.

11. On value-rational action: Weber (1977: 24–26, 153–54); Sorel (1961). Jim Jones on his value-rational action: FBI file O1B4. On Pentecostal functions: Hollenweger (1972: 459). Paris (1982) convincingly shows that Pentecostal dis-course and practice, far from involving "escapism," offers a meaningful vehicle for personal and community affirmation. On Black fears of wider world: Julian Mayfield, WPW, 5/7/84; and in Peoples Temple, Michael Prokes, F116, CHS. Jim Jones on inarticulate followers: q. Fresno (Calif.) *Bee*, 9/19/76. Jones's liturgical discourse: Barton Hunter, AI; Dorothy Hunter, AI. Jim Jones on getting out of superstition: q. by Marcie Jones, NYT, 9/2/77. On Black socialist preachers: Foner (1977: 151ff.); Wilmore (1983). Jones portraying the religious image of a "God within" as a message opposed by capitalism: FBI tape Q967. On the Pentecostal sermon: Paris (1982: 63ff., 160). Jim Jones on Marcie: FBI file O1B10; his description is corroborated by Dorothy Hunter, AI. For a litur-gically framed story with a known factual base, see Thielmann and Merrill (1979: 77).

## Chapter 3: The Prophet

1. On the general format, see Raboteau, quoted in Paris (1982: 64). Example of an early service of Jones's: FBI tape Q1017; even the Jonestown pavilion meetings had the same relatively "open" format of communication.

2. All sermon quotations taken from, and description based on, FBI tape Q612, recorded at Peoples Temple in Los Angeles, sometime in 1974. Jones's suspi-cions about "jackleg" preachers echoed those of others; see Paris (1982: 30). On the "jackleg" Black minister as a social type: Childs (1980: 18–19). Black con-cern with the parallel of the Jewish holocaust: Moses (1982: 170–229). A refer-ence by Jones to the United States as "Babylon": FBI tape Q1058 pt. 1.

3. Characterizations of Jones: e.g. Mills (1979); Kerns (1979); Rose (1979); Reiter-man and Jacobs (1982). Jones's prophecy: FBI tape Q612.

4. O'Neill (1972: 6) describes the features of "skin trades."

5. On the general topic: Goffman (1959). I am reminded of an episode in my own youth in Louisville, Kentucky, when a smooth-talking rock-and-roll radio disk jockey dressed in a leopardskin tuxedo jacket approached me with a proposal to "do tent revivals" one summer, assuring me that we could "pull in some good money." In the thinly veiled guise of a novel, Sinclair Lewis's *Elmer Gantry* (1927) offers a vivid sociological composite of U.S. popular religion via the odyssey of one "professional good man" who pursued an ambiguous call.

6. On Charles Thompson: Marks (1906).

7. On lavish life-styles: e.g. "Oral Roberts' critics fault kingly lifestyle," LAT News

Service, in CDT, 3/3/84. Counterfactual conjecture that Jones intended to survive the mass suicide and make off with the money is discussed in chapter 12. Whether Peoples Temple defrauded individuals of their property for collective reasons is a separate question, and it is considered in chapter 6.
8. Durkheim (1947).
9. On Oral Roberts: *America*, 3/17/56. On Jesus: Smith (1978)
10. Barton Hunter, AI; Dorothy Hunter, AI. Ulcer: IR, 10/7/61; undated IS article, probably 12/15 or 12/16/61, G3A12, CHS. Innuendo of mental illness: Reiterman and Jacobs (1982: 75).
11. On Rasputin: Wilson (1964). On mental illness and religion: James (1929). On Luther: Erikson (1958).
12. Jim Jones, FBI file O1A1d; Barton Hunter, AI; Dorothy Hunter, AI.

## *Chapter 4: The Temple*

1. Hall (1978: 68ff.).
2. On "new religions": Glock and Bellah (1976); Hall (1978); Robbins and Anthony (1981); Tipton (1982).
3. Jones's ministry: Jack Beam, FBI tape Q777. Assemblies of God: Synan (1971: 152–53, 203).
4. Jones's reference to Community Unity Church: IR, 7/25/64. There is also evidence of association with the Assemblies of God in 1954, during the "Community Unity" phase; see Peoples Temple Operations—correspondence, CHS. Laurel Street Tabernacle: Marcie Jones, F338A, CHS; IS, 11/20/78; Jack Beam, FBI tape Q777; Marcie Jones, FBI file BB18Z66–8. Substantial congregational movement from one church to others has been a sign of religious ferment in other contexts; see Zaret (1980: 93ff.).
5. Wings of Deliverance, Inc., articles of incorporation, CHS. The group's rules for the "Apostolic Corporation" it tried to establish in the 1970s as a communal organization and tax-avoidance scheme similarly emphasize prohibition of smoking, drugs, and alcohol, and go on to legislate against a number of "street" problems, namely, "possession of . . . guns, knives, nunchucks, brass knuckles, billy clubs, or other weapons," as well as "illegal drugs"; see draft of rules for Apostolic Corporation, F350, CHS. New Jersey Street building as first "Peoples Temple": Rick Cordell, FBI file HH6A4; cf. *The Herald of Faith* (Chicago) 2 (May 1956), F70, CHS. Apparently the name "Peoples Temple Full Gospel Church" was used while Jones was in Brazil in the early 1960s by the fundamentalist preacher he sent from Brazil to take charge; see undated 1963 Indianapolis newspaper article, G3A–15, CHS; IS, 11/20/78. Choir and youth group: FBI file BB18Z80.
6. On competition by timing of services: Weisbrot (1983:24). Recruitment and Archie Ijames: Lynetta and Marcie Jones, 5/20/75 talk, FBI file HH6A19–20; Marcie Jones, FBI file BB18Z67; cf. Jack Beam, FBI tape Q777; apparently Reiterman and Jacobs (1982: 52) misread FBI file HH6A20 when they stated that Jones's theological views "jibed with Ijames's personal philosophy." Jones's preaching: Jack Beam, FBI tape Q777; Rick Cordell, FBI file HH6A4–5; cf. Lynetta and Marcy Jones, FBI file HH6A20.
7. Established faith healers and Jones: FBI tape Q777; FBI file BB18Z66. Description of Kuhlman: Dorough (1974), which cites religion reporter Lester Kinsolv-

ing. Revival circuit: Jack Beam, FBI tape Q777; Rick Cordell, FBI file HH6A19; undated 1961 Indianapolis newspaper article, FBI file HH6A42; Marcie Jones, FBI file BB18Z65–6. Others' views of Jones: Louise Moseley, Indianapolis Central Christian Church Social Action Committee member in the 1960s, AI; Barton Hunter, AI; Dorothy Hunter, AI; Rabbi Maurice Davis, LCJ 11/22/78. Jones interview quote: Guyana *Chonicle* (hereafter cited as GC), 12/6/78. Other details: Rick Cordell, FBI file HH6A13, 15; Lynetta and Marcie Jones, FBI file HH6A21. Waste of time: Weber (1957: 157).

8. Additions to Jones household: FBI files BB18Z85, –97, HH6A38; Edward Mueller, in LCJ, 11/22/78, and CDT, 12/3/78. Nursing homes: Louise Moseley, AI; FBI files HH6A19, BB18Z93–6, –114; Barton Hunter, AI; Barton Hunter, q. in NYT, 11/22/78; FBI file HH6A31. Household life-style: Agnes Jones, FBI file BB18Z98; Barton Hunter, AI; Edward Mueller, q. in LAT News Service, in CDT, 12/3/78. According to Mueller, Jones drove a Cadillac, but this is the only notable assertion contradicting an otherwise consistent picture of household thrift. Adoptions: Mary Touchette, FBI file BB18Z111; note on letter from governor of Indiana, 1/21/61, Peoples Temple Operations—correspondence, CHS; undated Indianapolis newspaper article, probably 5/12/59, G3A–1, CHS. House guests: Rick Cordell, HH6A8; Judy McNulty, former Peoples Temple member, LCJ, 11/22/78. Pregnancy: Marcie Jones, F338B, CHS.

9. Accident and burial: undated Indianapolis newspaper articles, probably circa 5/12/59, G3A1, CHS; Jim Jones, FBI file O1B11; cf. Thielmann and Merrill (1979: 22). Adoptions: note on letter from governor of Indiana, 1/21/61, Peoples Temple Operations—correspondence, CHS; Mary Touchette, FBI file BB18Z111; Jim Jones, FBI file O1B12; Rheaviana Beam, FBI file BB18Z85; Jim Jones, q. in FBI file HH6A42 (reprint of Butler (University) *Collegian* Indianapolis, 5/10/61); NYT, 11/26/78.

10. Rick Cordell quote: FBI file HH6a3. Pentecostalists would always deride the "coldness" and "formality" of mainline churches; see Synan (1971: 177). Date of move into synagogue inferred from statements by Rabbi Maurice Davis, LCJ, 11/22/78; it may have been as early as 1956; cf. Peoples Temple Operations—correspondence, CHS; and IS, 11/20/78. On the term *apostolic*: Synan (1971). Description of Jones's calling: Louise Moseley, AI. Good works: FBI file BB18Z87–8, 93. Brothel visit: Barton Hunter, AI; Louise Moseley, AI; Rick Cordell, FBI file HH6A6; Jim Jones, FBI tape Q1059, pt 5. Role of Blacks: e.g. on FBI tape Q1058, pt. 1, circa 1975, Jones commented on "the special privilege of being Black in this generation."

11. On North America as a promised land: Niebuhr (1937); Sanford (1961: esp. chs. 3, 6). For a detailed case study of a migration, see Moltmann (1983).

12. The classic inspirational novel on escape from the South is Stowe (1981). On abolitionism and the controversial antebellum African colonization movement: Staudenraus (1961); Miller (1975); Quarles (1969); McKivigan (1984); Dick (1974); Moses (1982: 127). On nineteenth–century emigration schemes after the Civil War: Bittle and Geis (1964); Redkey (1969). On Garvey: Moses (1982: 124ff.); James Robert Lincoln Diggs, q. in Moses (1982: 135); cf. Burkett (1978); Ahlstrom (1972: 1066). Jones on Blacks as a chosen people escaping bondage: FBI tape Q1058, pt. 1, on Peoples Temple as a "city set on a hill": FBI tape Q1016.

13. Jones's visits to Divine: Jim Jones, about 1974, FBI tape Q1059, pt. 5; Divine (1982: 137); cf. Maurice Kleineibst, a Peace Mission defector who gives a

doubtful early date—1952—for the first meeting, FBI file HH6A39. Jones Philadelphia banquet speech: q. in Weisbrot (1983: 218). Peace Mission enterprises: Weisbrot (1983: 122–23). On Pentecostal views of communism: Pope (1942); cf. Paris (1982) on political involvement in general. On Divine, communism, and immigration: Weisbrot (1983: 125–26); cf. Moses (1982).

14. On Pentecostal, Peace Mission, and Peoples Temple cultures: Clark (1949: 124ff.); NYT, 11/26/78; Paris (1982: 115 and passim); Thielmann and Merrill (1979: 74). Jones on skin-color terms: IR, 7/25/64; 1970s sermon, FBI tape Q1054, pt. 4. On other occasions, Peoples Temple made finer distinctions of ethnicity than others would, to emphasize its interracial character; see the Peoples Temple list of immigrants to Guyana, F656, CHS. Peace Mission avoidance of race terms: Weisbrot (1983: 78). Jones and Cuba: NYT, 3/25/79.

15. Harrington's (1962) book on poverty in the United States captured the imagination of President John F. Kennedy and a generation of liberals. Adoption plans: Indianapolis newspaper account, 2/25/60, in FBI file HH6A43. Free restaurant and social services: FBI file BB18Z76, 77, 82, 88, 91, 92; LCJ, 11/21, 22/78. Affiliation with the Disciples of Christ: Barton Hunter, AI; Ross Case, AI; Louise Moseley, AI; cf. Reiterman and Jacobs (1982: 67), who attribute the idea of affiliation to Jones's associate minister, Archie Ijames.

16. Disciples' support of Temple as inner-city church: undated newspaper article, probably a Disciples of Christ publication, G3A–11, CHS. "Corrective fellowship": Barton Hunter, AI; Ross Case, AI; IS, 11/20/78. Human Rights Commission: undated IR article around February 1961, G3A–2, CHS; Indianapolis *Times* (hereafter cited as IT), 12/16/61; IS, 11/20/78. Jones allaying segregationist fears: Butler (University) *Collegian*, 5/10/61. Church integration incidents: Barton Hunter, AI; IT, 9/8/61. Integration of other public facilities and organizations: FBI files BB18Z91, –102; HH6A12, –41, –42; LCJ, 11/21/78. Tensions, ulcer, Methodist Hospital incident: Jack Beam, FBI tape Q777; Agnes Jones, FBI file BB18Z98; Barton Hunter, AI; Dorothy Hunter, AI; Louise Moseley, AI; IR, 10/7/61; Mrs. Robert D. Venner, letter to Jim Jones, 6/5/62, Peoples Temple Operations—correspondence, CHS.

## Chapter 5: The Ark

1. Esther Mueller, FBI file HH6A38.
2. Anonymous phone calls and hostile press: Barton Hunter, AI; Rick Cordell, FBI file HH6A12; see also Dan Burros, American Nazi party, 7/23/61 letter to Jones, CHS. On generalized racism: undated (probably shortly before a 5/19/61 article in the same newspaper) IT article, G3A–10, CHS, and a briefer account, IT, 5/11/61. Dynamite: Jack Beam, FBI tape Q777; cf. Esther Mueller, FBI file HH6A38. Marcie's experiences and other events: Rheaviana Beam, FBI file BB18Z83, –85–6; cf. FBI file BB18Z90–91B, –102A–3: Rick Cordell, FBI file HH6A12–3; IT, 7/29/61. Early suspicion of exaggeration and invention of stories: Dorothy Hunter, AI. Minister spy: FBI file BB18Z92. Nuclear weapons concern: Jim Jones, FBI file O1B14. Motives for leaving Indianapolis: Barton Hunter, AI; Dorothy Hunter, AI; Louise Moseley, AI.
3. Sermon: Jim Jones, FBI tape Q1017. Jim Jones, q. in Guiana *Graphic*, 10/26/61. Human rights resignation: undated Indianapolis newspaper article, December 1961, G3A–12, CHS; IT, 12/16/61; IR, 7/25/64. Move to Hawaii

and Brazil: Jim Jones, FBI file O1B16; power of attorney executed in Hawaii, 1/31/62, Legal Counsel—Jim and Marceline Jones, CHS; Joseph Bevilacqua, United Church of Christ, Hawaii, letter of 11/13/64 recruiting Jones, Peoples Temple Operations file, CHS. *Esquire* article: Bird (1962).

4. Search for land: Jim Jones, FBI file 01B13. On the Joneses in Brazil in general: Thielmann and Merrill (1979: 19–30). Jones probably attended meetings of the Umbanda sect, a "civilized" version of the *macumba* survivals of African religions. Umbanda was popular among the dislocated Black and Amerindian urban migrants who wanted to rise above the animistic magic of *macumba* while continuing to assert the special place of their dispossessed groups. Spiritism and healings thus took a more rationalized form, based in part of theologies about psychic planes, astral energy, reincarnation, and the like. Such ideas began to filter into Jones's discourses in the California years, though it is of course possible that he derived them from Californian, rather than Brazilian sources. On Umbanda and *macumba*: Bastide (1978: 304ff.). (Jones's activities in Brazil have been used by some authors, e.g. Moore [1985: 409], citing a GC article of 11/25/78 to support the theory that Jones was connected to the CIA at the time. But the article provides only conjecture by Jones's neighbors who saw him not gainfully employed but nevertheless disappearing daily with a briefcase. For the rest, the article uses information provided by Jones himself in his memoirs, now located in FBI file O1B15–6, about his encounters with the family of Dan Mitrione. Jones had known Mitrione when they were young, in Richmond, Indiana. Jones asserted that in Brazil Mitrione supposedly was serving as a "traffic advisor," but rumors suggested that "he participated with the military even then, doing strange things to dissenters." Because Jones himself would seem to be the only source of this information, and because he describes Mitrione's activities in negative terms, the incident is not a strong basis to establish a CIA connection of Jones. Eventually Mitrione was sentenced to ten years in prison in 1985 for using his position as an FBI agent to collude with an informer in a $850,000 cocaine deal; see WPW, 12/16/85.)

5. The Beams' trip and the Joneses in Rio: Rheaviana Beam, FBI files BB18Z84 and HH6A22; Jim Jones, FBI file O1B13; Peoples Temple operations file, CHS; Thielmann and Merrill (1979: 34); Bonnie Thielmann remembers Jones's job as being at "the American school," but her father, Ed Malmin, mentioned Sao Fernando University in a 1963 Indianapolis newspaper article, G3A–15, CHS. Jones as gigolo: Jim Jones, FBI file O1B14; Thielmann and Merrill (1979: 47).

6. On Brazil: Rodrigues (1965) and works cited in Hall (1984). For a review of state and development: Canak (1984). Jones's view of Brazil's political situation: FBI file O1B14–5. Ijames adoption proposal and aftermath: Jim Jones, FBI file O1B13; IR, 7/25/64; Reiterman and Jacobs (1982: 93–7). Malmin in Indianapolis and the Joneses' return: Thielmann and Merrill (1979: 35); Ed Malmin, letter of 11/7/63, CHS 40; undated Indianapolis newspaper article, 1963, G3A–15, CHS. Ed Malmin expected Jones to return in December 1963, but IR, 7/25/64, and Thielmann and Merrill (1979: 35) place the date between January and June 1964.

7. Lynetta Jones note: F338C, CHS. Congregational racial balance: LCJ, 11/22/78. Building sale, ordination, and congregation: IR, 7/25/64; FBI file HH6A38; Barton Hunter, AI; Dorothy Hunter, AI. On concept of *metanoia*: Hall (1978: 68ff.). Black leaders and Jones: IR, 6/25/64; Jim Jones, FBI file O1B16; Mrs. Jackie Swinney, letter to IR, 5/22/65. Radio flap: Indianapolis

*News*, 4/12/65; Jim Jones, FBI file O1B17; the sources are unclear as to whether Jones, the radio station, or advertisers initiated the cancellation of programming. Motives for leaving Indianapolis: Louise Moseley, AI; Barton Hunter, AI; Dorothy Hunter, AI. NYT, 11/26/78, probably is incorrect about investigations in Indianapolis spurring Jones's departure, though Jones himself did recall the Internal Revenue Service investigating him on his return from Brazil; see FBI file O1B16. The Hunters remember no such difficulties; though Barton Hunter did talk informally with Jones on various occasions about Jones's activities, the Disciples of Christ did not investigate him. Whatever investigations may have occurred, they would have only reinforced the previously established motives for migration. California site location and prophecy: Ross Case, AI; Harold Cordell, 2/18/65 letter to Ross Case, F661, CHS. Financing of migration: Jim Jones, FBI file HH6A13, –17; Rick Cordell, FBI file HH6A10. Mr. and Mrs. Cecil Johnson, former members who remained in Indianapolis, claimed that Jones "encouraged the congregation to pool their money" for the move, but Peoples Temple denied the migration involved turning over property to the church (FBI file HH6A35), and there is no evidence that the migration involved any substantial transfers of real estate. Cobb family conflict over migration: Reiterman and Jacobs (1982: 98). Insanity story: FBI file HH6A35; the story may involve Esther Mueller, whose son charged that Jones defrauded her of $25,000, CDT, 12/3/78. Migration: Rick Cordell, FBI file HH6A4; Esther Mueller, FBI file HH6A38; Rheaviana Beam, FBI file HH6A22. NYT, 11/26/78, gives the number migrating as 70 families; IS, 11/20/78, counted 145; NYT, 9/2/77, gave the number as 120 people; SFE, 9/17/72, reported 165 immigrants. Ross Case falling out: Harold Cordell, letter of 2/18/65, F661, CHS; Ross Case, letter of 3/3/65, F662, CHS; Ross Case, AI.

8. California incorporation: William Traylor, 6/7/65 letter, Legal Department files, CHS. Peoples Temple of the Disciples of Christ California corporate seal, CGA. Touchette family: Mike Touchette, AI; IS, 11/20/78. Golden Rule takeover attempt: Jones remembrances, FBI tape Q1055 pt. 3; Reiterman and Jacob (1982: 100). Socialism in 1968: Rick Cordell, FBI file HH6A4. The Redwood Valley church: Rick Cordell, FBI file HH6A11; Rheaviana Bean, FBI file HH6A22; Barton Hunter, AI; Dorothy Hunter, AI; Reiterman and Jacobs (1982: 183).

9. Activities of Marceline and Jim Jones: FBI file HH6A53; Ukiah *Daily Journal* (hereafter cited as UDJ), 8/21/69. Linda Amos's conversion: NYT, 2/25/79. Church membership data: SFC, 4/8/79. Layton's family: Yee and Layton (1981); Rebecca Moore, personal communication to author. Elmer and Deanna Mertle: Jeannie Mills (the former Deanna Mertle; 1979: 113ff.). Carolyn Layton and Jones as lovers: Marcie Jones, letter, 7/10/69, F335, CHS; 4/2/69 letter from "Louise" to John Moore, and Carolyn Moore Layton, letter to John and Barbara Moore, 11/28/69, Carolyn Moore Layton (Prokes) file, CGA. Tim Stoen and Grace Grech Stoen: UDJ, 5/18/76; Tim Stoen, handwritten notes, apparently written 1963, F117C, CHS; Tim Stoen, letter to Jim Jones, 1/9/70, F101B, CHS; San Francisco *Banner* (hereafter cited as SFB), 11/9/79; Kilduff and Tracy (1979: 324).

10. Biographies of joining: Sandy Bradshaw, declaration for *Steven Katsaris* vs. *Jim Jones et al.*, California Superior Court, Mendocino County, case #45373; *Steven Katsaris* vs. *Jim Jones et al.*, First Appellate District Court, California, case #1CIV45373 (hereafter cited as SK/JJ); Buford affidavit for *Peoples Temple* vs.

*Timothy Oliver Stoen*, California Superior Court, San Francisco, case #740531 (hereafter cited as PT/TOS); Buford, deposition, CAG/PT, CHS; "Affidavit of Deborah Layton Blakey re the threat and possibility of mass suicide by members of the People's Temple," 6/1978, reprinted in CFA (1979: 308); Blakey, deposition, CAG/PT, CHS; Eugene Chaiken, affidavit, PT/TOS.

11. Expansion of activities to San Francisco: Jim Jones, FBI file O1B18; cf. Dorothy Hunter, AI; Major (1979: 21); UDJ, 8/1/69, 3/20/70. Exposure to Jones: Tim Stoen, NYT, 2/29/79. Bus purchase dates: UDJ, 6/24/70, 11/12/71. The latter-day evangelist Jimmie Swaggart has done Jones one better by entreating his followers to charter buses themselves to attend his crusades. See *The Evangelist* (Baton Rouge, La.) 16 (February 1984): 34. Service schedule described by Jim Jones: SFE, 9/24/72. Seattle tour: Kilduff and Tracy (1979: 323). Seattle sermon: FBI tape Q1020, pt. 1. Lynn, Indiana, stopover: RPI undated article, probably summer 1976, G3A–49, CHS. Mother Divine (1982: 99, 140).

12. San Francisco's Western Addition and Macedonia Baptist foray: Major (1979: 21). On the parallel predicament of Black Pentecostal churches in Boston during the era of "urban renewal" programs: Paris (1982). Ferment in Black churches: Childs (1980: 1, 16–19); Washington (1967); Jim Jones, FBI tape Q1020, pt. 1. Views of Jones's ministry: John Moore, NYT, 1/6/79; Jones, 2/25/79; Dennis Denny, UDJ, 3/7/79. Social origins of Temple Blacks: Lane (1979: 61ff.); NYT, 12/29/78; San Francisco *Sun Reporter* (hereafter cited as SFSR), 2/8/79. The point about diversity is made by Chris Hatcher, of Langley Porter Psychiatric Institute, University of California, San Francisco, who organized the counseling services for those associated with the Temple who survived Jonestown, q. in CDT, 11/18/79. Demographic data are based on analysis of a list of Guyana migrants compiled by Peoples Temple, CHS, and a partial list of Jonestown dead, NYT, 12/18/78.

13. Tim Stoen, NYT, 2/25/79.

14. A Peoples Temple radio program in about 1972 referred to the Redwood Valley operation as a "heaven-on-earth," public relations file, CGA. Limitations of Redwood Valley: Jim Jones, FBI tape Q1058, pt. 1. U.S. as Egypt, Babylon: Jim Jones, FBI tape Q 1058, pt. 1.

## *Chapter 6: The Corporate Conglomerate*

1. For an ideal typical description of the rationalist "intentional association" as a communal group: Hall (1978: 204–5). On nineteenth-century secular and religious communal groups: Bestor (1970); Noyes (1966); Andrews (1972). On work discipline: E. P. Thompson (1967); Bendix (1974). On utopian diffusion: Hall (1978: 208ff.).

2. General sources: Max Weber (1958); Marshall (1982); Berger (1967); Hunter (1983). The classic study of tensions between congregational and bureaucratic religious organization is Harrison (1959). On rationalization in religion: Weber (1958; 1977: esp. 538). On mass culture and religion: Hadden and Swanson (1981).

3. Revisionist view of Divine: Weisbrot (1983). Jones on business skill: q. by Barton Hunter, AI. Temple money-makers: FBI file HH6A30; UDJ, 8/11/67, 12/13/68, 6/20/69, 6/30/69, 7/18/69, 8/1/69, 10/30/70, 5/14/71. Safety in numbers: Jim Jones, FBI file O1B18. Membership size: SFC, 4/8/79.

4. Foucault (1965). On psychiatric care in the United States: Chu and Trotter (1974: 30–31, 43); Segal and Aviram (1978: 37, 40, 43, 64 [quotation], 106).

5. Temple welfare organization: UDJ, 3/5, 3/7/79; CHS 39; guardianship files, #5427–5458, CHS. Counseling: Carolyn Layton Prokes, deposition for PT/TOS, 10/10/78, P9–1, CHS; SFC, 8/19/77. Franciscan care home: ABC network news, 1/25/84. Interorganizational analysis based on Benson (1975). Absence of fraud: Dennis Denny, q. in UDJ, 3/5/79; CSS, 12, 16; CAG, 61. On care-quality problems of the home care industry: Chu and Trotter (1974); Segal and Aviram (1978); WPW 4/15/85, p. 34. Anecdotal accusations of defectors and apparent Temple home care performance: Santa Rosa *Press-Democrat* (hereafter cited as SRPD), 8/1/77; Dennis Denny, q. in UDJ, 3/5 and 3/8/79; *Mendocino* (Calif.) *Grapevine* (hereafter cited as MG), 7/27/77.

6. Care-home financing and tax guidance: Gene Chaiken, F66, CHS. A contract between Peoples Temple and operators Helen and Cleve Swinney, executed 1/29/72, gave complete responsibility for operation to the Swinneys and specified a monthly rent of $500, care home file, CGA. Series of home care operators: Kilduff and Tracy (1979: 325). Stolen food allegation, never further documented: Dennis Denny, UDJ, 3/6/79. Frugality: Debbie Blakey, deposition for CAG/PT, CHS. Walter Jones's accounting: Kilduff and Tracy (1979: 323–24). "Children's home monthly report for October 1972": F490, CHS. Denny's estimate: UDJ, 3/8/79.

7. Vineyard income: F490, CHS. Counter sales and promotion: Sandy Bradshaw, AI; SFE 9/17/72, 8/14/77; Thielmann and Merrill (1979: 72); FBI tapes Q612, Q1020, pt. 1, and Q1058, pt. 1. Mailing schemes: Jim Jones, F156, CHS; SFC, 8/19/77; "Blessings are flowing" and prayer cloth mailers, F332, F336, CHS; Jim Jones, tape cassette marked "Garry discuss with Tish, Chaiken, Harriet, JJ, Lee, properties, defenses," CGA; "Special anniversary medallion," Jonestown mailer, 1978, F105, CHS. Other mail ministries: Jimmie Swaggart Ministries, Baton Rouge, La., mailer of 12/24/83; Rev. Ewing's Church-By-Mail, Atlanta, Ga., undated mailer of January 1984. Temple radio religion: LAT News Service, in CDT, 12/18/78; FBI tape Q1056, pt. 1, contains a series of the short programs. Income from the mail: the October 1975 mailer went to 9,250 people; in July of 1976, 10,848 pieces were sent out; the final Temple mailer, in November of 1978, was sent to the "main file only," with a distribution of 7,800; Mailer file, CGA; F465, CHS; Deanna Mertle's estimate, SFC, 8/19/77; annual income estimated by Pat Richartz, of Charles Garry's law office, AI.

8. Membership stages and screening: F362, CHS; Jean Brown correspondence file, CGA; Deanna Mertle, F257, CHS. "Feeler" approach: Mike Prokes correspondence file, CGA. 1971 newsletter requiring correspondence: F453, CHS; Jones on right to private worhip: FBI tape Q1054, pt. 4. "No admit": F373, CHS. Membership cards: Bea Orsot, AI. One-time attenders: David DeLeon, AI; Orunamamu, AI. On equivalent offering strategies in other churches: Paris (1982: 61ff.). Low-key offertories reported: SFE, 9/18/72. Offering pitch: FBI tape Q1055, pt. 3; FBI tape Q1054, pt. 4; FBI tape Q 1058, pt. 1. Repeated offerings and income estimates: Micki Touchette, SFE, 8/14/77 and q. in Kilduff and Tracy (1979: 323). Offerings by sum: FBI tape Q958. Competitive offerings, street solicitations, and extra wage labor: FBI file HH2. Insurance settlement for Mrs. Polla Mattarras: circa 2/73, F494, CHS.

9. Expenses: Grace Stoen, q. in Kilduff and Tracy (1979: 325); Moore (1985: 350ff.); NYT, 9/2/77. Jones salary proposal passed: 2/14/77 minutes, Peoples

Temple board of directors, CHS. Estimate of capitalization of Jonestown: Laurie B. Efrein, letter, 4/22/80, F153, CHS; equipment purchase authorization, 11/8/76 minutes, Peoples Temple board of directors, CHS. Finance management: Pat Richartz, AI; depositions for PT/TOS, F189 to F202, P2–9, CHS; Teresa Buford, deposition for CAG/PT, CHS; James Randolph, deposition for CAG/PT, CHS; WP, 12/6/78; Deborah Blakey, deposition for CAG/PT, CHS; Tim Stoen, notes, P2–4–16, CHS; Banking file, CGA; "Finances: Peoples Temple," 8/3/79, F127, CHS. On use of offshore accounts by multinational corporations and drug traffickers to shield money from U.S. taxation: WPW, 2/20/84, pp. 6–7. "Need-to-know" basis of Temple information: Jim Randolph, deposition for CAG/PT, CHS; Teri Buford, deposition for CAG/PT, CHS. Smuggling of money: Teri Buford, declaration, 10/23/78, F80, CHS. Jones q.: member's journal, FBI file HH2: II, 124.

10. Temple help for people: Jeannie Mills (1979: 132); NYT, 2/25/79; UDJ, 12/2/66. Santa Rosa college program: SFE, 8/14/77; Rebecca Moore (1985: 95, 140–41, 240ff.). Emergence of communal economy: Gene Chaiken, F66, CHS; Deanna Mertle, F257, CHS; Laura Cornelious, q. in Kilduff and Tracy (1979: 324); Sally Stapleton, q. in SRPD, 8/1/77; Thielmann and Merrill (1979: 71); Tim Stoen, F211, CHS. June Crym deposition for CAG/PT, CHS. On economics of "going communal": CHS 33.

11. Communalism: 11/24/76 minutes, Peoples Temple board of directors, CHS; SFE, 8/14/77; larger number of San Francisco communes given by Michael Prokes, F116, CHS, p. 20. Essie Townes letter to Jones: Essie Townes property file, CGA. Life care agreements: CFA (33–34, 710ff.). Life care arrangements: SFC, 7/11/83; Rebecca Moore (1985: 353ff.), who cites an undated issue of the *Western Law Journal*. Car donation: member's journal, FBI file HH2. On charismatic spoils want satisfaction: Weber (1977: 243ff., 1119–20). Valley Enterprises and the real estate amendment: CHS 59; 5/10/76 and 6/30/74 minutes, Peoples Temple board of directors, CHS. Lawyer Eugene Chaiken used the term "alter ego": F156, CHS. Jack Beam, declaration for PT/TOS, F193, CHS; SFE, 8/19/77. Most real estate was owned privately and collectively managed; see real estate tax roster, CHS 2. Note of Tim Stoen on memo to him from Harold Cordell: Essie Townes property file, 1975, CHS. Delay of deed filing: SFE, 8/19/77; Enola "Kay" Nelson, deposition for PT/TOS, CGA; Jim Randolph, deposition for CAG/PT, CHS.

12. Nature of donations: Teresa Buford, deposition for CAG/PT, CHS. Legal wills: F351, F489, CHS. Communalism and conserving resources: Rick Cordell, FBI file HH6A7. Communal want satisfaction in general: Hall (1978: 120ff.). Allowance amount: defector Micki Touchette, SFE, 8/14/77. Needs Department headed by Blakey: Teresa Buford, deposition for CAG/PT, CHS. Needs envelope: FBI file HH2. Sample needs form: CHS 61.

13. Coser (1974: 4). "Lifestyle" explanation: undated Temple working memo, probably 1977, F58, CHS. Jones q.: Berkeley (Calif.) *Barb*, 7/9/76.

14. Power-of-attorney arrangements and other collective mangagement of identity: SFC, 8/19/77. Peoples Temple files on taxes, pensions, bank loans, migration applications, etc.: F66B, CHS. On alienation: Marcuse (1964).

15. Weber (1977: 1111ff.). On the charismatic community, bureaucracy, and the plebiscite: Weber (1977: 219, 241ff., 262ff.). Number of Temple elite: estimate by Stephan Jones, WP, 11/7/83; this number compares roughly to the list of twenty-six persons, other than Jones, for whom Temple attorney Charles Garry

sought U.S. Department of State files in Privacy Act requests beginning in October 1977; see CFA (692–95). The first recorded charge of racism was the manifesto of the eight young defectors in 1973, q. in Moore (1985: 174–75). Another time, a man complained about the White leadership and was forced to take part in a boxing match with three other people in punishment for a "surly attitude": member's journal, FBI file HH2, I,77. Racial imbalance of Peace Mission leadership: Weisbrot (1983: 77–78). Role of secretary in Black Pentecostal churches: Paris (1982: 109). Temple Whites as sociologically Blacks: Jim Jones, sermon, FBI tape Q958. Sandy Bradshaw, AI. Sexual predispositions of Jones: Mills (1979: 249). Public relations work: Mike Prokes, F116, CHS. New ministers: Johnny Moss Jones, declaration for PT/TOS, F198, CHS. Ordination of Stoen and Young: Disciples of Christ file, CHS.

16. Planning commission: Teri Buford, deposition for CAG/PT, CHS. Belief in what Jones was thought to represent: Mike Touchette, AI. Posing questions to the congregation: for example, the various tape-recorded sermons and a member's journal, FBI file HH2. Description of inner group: Gene Chaiken, declaration for PT/TOS, F195, CHS. On charismatic organization in general: Weber (1977: 243). Organization of Peoples Temple: June Crym, deposition for CAG/PT, CHS; public relations draft in FBI file HH6A27; FBI file HH2; Temple opponent, requesting anonymity, AI; Bill Purifoy, F370, CHS; Dale Parks, deposition for CAG/PT, CHS. Private staff meeting, including Jones conferring with Temple lawyer Charles Garry: F156, CHS. Bureaucratic processing forms: "Data slips" F362, F532, CHS; "Daily report," F501, CHS; "Information sheet for healing medical reports," F250, CHS; typical handling of a mailer respondent file, F336, CHS; preparation of taxes, F66B, CHS; formats, orders, and items for shipping goods to Jonestown, F343, CHS.

17. Jones's staff: Buford quoted in Moore (1985: 345–49); Teresa Buford, deposition for CAG/PT, CHS; declarations in support of injunction, PT/TOS, P2–12, CHS, and Jim Jones, deposition, PT/TOS file, CGA; minutes, Peoples Temple board of directors, CHS; Steven Katsaris, AI; Reiterman and Jacobs (1982: 188ff.). On the limits to domination of a leader in social interaction: Simmel (1950). Stalinist characterization: Robert Scheer, *New Times*, 1/8/79; ITT, 12/20/78; Charles Garry, AI. Robert Lifton, "The appeal of the death trip," NYT Magazine, 1/7/79, characterizes Peoples Temple as internally fascist.

18. Law office staff: F87, CHS; Jim Jones, deposition, PT/TOS file, CGA; June Crym, depositions for PT/TOS, P2–13, CHS; LAT News Service, in CDT, 11/25/78. Stoen as attorney: F94, CHS; Sandy Bradshaw, AI; Carolyn Layton, deposition for PT/TOS, P9–1–4, CHS; John Harris, Eugene Chaiken, Richard Tropp, depositions for PT/TOS, F191, F195, F201, CHS. On Chaiken: Debbie Blakey, deposition for CAG/PT, CHS. Jones q.: Teri Buford, deposition for CAG/PT, CHS. Example of legal counseling: John Anderson property file, CGA. Clearing news copy: declaration of Richard Tropp, for PT/TOS, F201, CHS. Stoen's legal services: Carolyn Layton Prokes, deposition for PT/TOS, P9–1, CHS. Custody case: FBI file HH6A32; SFE, 9/19/72; San Francisco *Progress* (hereafter cited as SFP), 7/31/77; Stoen letter concerning Lawrence and Rita Tupper, 2/15/71, F344, CHS; Laura Johnston, declaration for PT/TOS, F199, CHS. Files on faith healing: F601, CHS. Faith healing affidavits: F75 (quotation), F76, F279, F280, CHS, and legal disclaimer in PF, 11/1/76; Gene Chaiken, memo, 6/12/73, F150, CHS. Stoen's discussion of real estate: 5/10/76 minutes, Peoples Temple board of directors, CHS. Permission ob-

tained for punishment: SFE, 8/14/77; FBI file HH2; signed permission statement by Elmer Mertle and letter by Linda Mertle, Mertle file, CGA. Account of instruction to Mertle by lawyers: Tish LeRoy and Harriet Tropp, F156, CHS. Peoples Temple migration forms, F243, F342, CHS. Needs Department: Teresa Buford, deposition for CAG/PT, CHS; 12/13/76 minutes, Peoples Temple board of directors, CHS.

19. Note concerning Cobb: Teresa Buford: declaration with copy of note, 10/11/78, P11-1, CHS; anonymous memo, "These are things that I would not necesarily [*sic*] want to use in court," F95, CHS, describes similar practices by Stoen. Maxine Harpe death: Mendocino County, California, sheriff's report on Maxine Harpe, 1970, Harpe file, CGA; anonymous account about Maxine Harpe, F46, CHS; cancelled checks for Harpe funeral expense, Harpe file, CGA. Jones arrest, including copies of arrest reports and letters: LACA.

20. Selznick (1952: 2; italics in original); the book is not without insight but, nevertheless, must be taken as a sad commentary on the sociological response to McCarthy era fears of communist infiltration. Howe and Coser (1957: 501) note the limitations of Selznick's ahistorical approach, which fails to differentiate Stalinism from Leninist Bolshevism.

## *Chapter 7: The Collectivist Reformation*

1. On commitment: Kanter (1972); I have explored Kanter's theory elsewhere (1978: 224–26; 1983). Foucault (1965; 1973; 1978; 1979).

2. For the perspective of opponents to "cults": e.g. Patrick (1976); Edwards (1979); Enroth (1977); Appel (1983). On substantial defection rates: Bird and Reimer (1982). See also: Robbins and Anthony (1982); Anthony and Robbins (1981); Shupe and Bromley (1980); Bromley and Shupe (1981).

3. Characterization as "prison camp of the mind": ITT, 12/13/78. Jones explicitly referred to the United States as Babylon in at least one sermon: FBI tape Q1058, pt. 1. For a more detailed exploration of apocalyptic communal groups: Hall (1978). Jones's interest in building numbers for a sense of security: FBI file O1B18. On the power of numbers: Canetti (1978), Simmel (1950: 34ff., 93ff.).

4. Example of a semipublic sermon: FBI tape Q1059, pt. 5. Deanna Mertle, F257, CHS; cf. "The Letter Killeth, but the Spirit Giveth Life," F469, CHS. Attendance, Bea Orsot, AI. A member's journal, FBI file HH2, gives a running account of the services, banquets, bus trips, and secondary groups, and it laments the boredom that came after the main group of Temple members left for Guyana; Deanna Mertle, F253, CHS.

5. On other groups that parallel Temple organization: Weisbrot (1983); Paris (1982: 71ff., 107ff.). Singing: FBI tape Q967, and mentioned in member's journal, FBI file HH2, II, 411. Skit topics: Thielmann and Merrill (1979: 102–3); a Temple file marked "Sensitive pictures plays and skits," CGA; UDJ, 5/14/71; Jim Jones, p. 5, F156, CHS. Sermon topics hardly begin to exhaust the range; the ones mentioned are from FBI tapes Q967, Q973; Q1016 (quotation); Q1020, pt. 1. Books: Wilson (1940); Huberman and Sweezy (1968). Visitors and films described in SFSR, 1975, passim, and member's journal, FBI file HH2, II, 134. Members' perceptions: Mike Touchette, AI; Debbie Blakey, deposition for CAG/PT, CHS. Acting as though an atheist: "A follower of this activist ministry aspires to become," undated mimeo, CHS 53. Jones's advocacy of

freedom of conscience: FBI tape Q967; FBI file HH6A23, 25. On the resilience of unconventional beliefs in the face of the everyday world: Snow and Machalek (1982). On the early Protestants' "cathedral": Hall (1978: 41).

6. On incompetent relatives: Eugene Cordell, interviewed in IS, undated article by Carolyn Pickering, third in a series, fall 1972, G3A26, CHS; SFP, 7/31/77, 8/14/77. Book title: Guyana shipping book inventory, CHS. Sophisticated people and Jones's healing: Barton Hunter, AI; Dorothy Hunter, AI; Pat Richartz, AI. On the form of evangelical testimonials: Ingram (1983). Jones as liar: Stephan Jones (1979); Phil Kerns, q. in *Today's Student* (Ames, Ia.), 2/28/79. Member information cards: F236, CHS. On Bonnie Thielmann: Thielmann and Merrill (1979: 77).

7. Jones's claim of equality: Fresno *Bee*, 9/19/76; versus dietary privilege, Stephan Jones, q. in WP, 11/7/83. On a feigned heart attack: Mike Cartmell, q. in CDT, 11/25/78. Fear that Jones would die: Deanna Mertle, F253, CHS. Marcie Jones's admonition: Thielmann and Merrill (1979: 86); cf. Bea Orsot, AI, and member's journal, FBI file HH2, II, 161. Jones as father figure: F58, CHS; Tim Carter, after Jonestown, NYT, 11/27/78. Charles Touchette, AI. Jones's view of relationship with followers: FBI tape Q973; Fresno *Bee*, 9/19/76.

8. Jones's sex life: Stephan Jones, WP, 11/7/83; Sally Stapleton, SRPD, 8/1/77; Reiterman and Jacobs (1982: 176–77, 222–23). Jones on homosexuality: FBI tape Q1055, pt 3. Jones's claim of fidelity: FBI tape Q1059, pt. 5. Jones's suggestions about his desirability and women's fantasies: Fannie Mobley, q. in NYT, 11/26/78. Mike Touchette, AI; cf. Moore (1985: 175). Elmer Mertle note, 6/4/73: F237, CHS. Jones's bragging: Stephan Jones, WP, 11/7/83; Charles Garry, q. in LAT, 11/26/78. Women's sexual praise for Jones and men's emasculation: Tim Carter, NYT, 11/27/78. On Jones giving sex: Bea Orsot, AI.

9. Charismatic assertions: sermons on FBI tapes Q1055, pt. 3 (quotation), Q973. Jones as Christ in the flesh and followers' similar potential: FBI tape Q1020, pt. 1. On the sociological importance of opposition as a basis of group solidarity: Coser (1956). Reports of intimidation of Blacks and Jones's concern as Human Rights Commission executive director: IT, 5/11/61, 5/19/61, 7/29/61, 9/8/61; IR, 7/25/64. Suspicions voiced by Dorothy Hunter, AI. Hairdresser's attack: UDJ, 3/31/69, 4/8/69, and undated UDJ article soon thereafter, G3A21, CHS. Redwood Valley security procedures memos: CHS 23, 24. Guard tower: member's journal, FBI file HH2, II, 161. Tim Stoen memo to Chuck Lewis: Apostolic Corp. tax file, document 05 7520, CHS. "Assassination" described: Esther Mueller, FBI file HH6A38. Arson attempt and Jones's premonition: SFC, 8/24/73. Jones was not the first to have guards; cf. Daddy Grace's uniformed bodyguard: St. Louis *Post-Dispatch*, 1/12/60; SFE, 9/24/72.

10. Brian Wells's article and Temple responses: IT, 10/14/71, 11/12/71, 12/22/71; letter of response by Tim Stoen, 10/24/71, F518, CHS. Tim Stoen, letter to Kinsolving, 9/12/72, CHS. Kinsolving series: SFE, 9/17, 18, 19, 20, 24/72; the IS carried a parallel series by Carolyn Pickering at the same time. On the Temple response: Jeannie Mills (1979: 181–83); Reiterman and Jacob (1982: 214); Tim Stoen, draft of memo to Jeff Parish, "Re: Jim Jones and Tim Stoen, libel . . . ," F531, CHS. Results of Kinsolving series: Jeannie Mills (1979: 183). Conn as a source: Klineman, Butler, and Conn (1980: 250). Case's activities: Reiterman and Jacobs (1982: 217). Jones on persecution: sermon on FBI tape Q1054, pt. 4; the New Testament is filled with passages where Jesus foretells the persecution of his followers; Jones may have been alluding to either Matthew

24:8 or Luke 6:22. On Blacks' experience of isolation as pleasant: Barton Hunter, AI.

11. Canetti (1978: 23). On freeriders: Olson (1968). On monitoring: Hechter (1983; 1984). On communal monitoring: Kanter (1972: 112, 124–25). Communal group role strategies in monitoring: Hall (1983). Quotation on atmosphere of Temple: Peoples Temple, unpublished response to Carolyn Pickering's articles, FBI file HH6A29. Quotations on school children: SRPD, 8/1/77; SFP, 8/3/77. NYT, 12/29/78; Kilduff and Tracy (1979: 331). On counselors dismissing problems and shielding Jones: member's journal, FBI file HH2, II, 137; Thielmann and Merrill (1979: 93). Jones's request to repent: FBI tape Q1054, pt. 4. Handclapping ritual: FBI tape Q1020, pt. 1. Meeting attendance suggested in Tim Stoen, 10/1/(probably 1973) memo, F159, CHS. Attendance sheets, 197(3?), F517, CHS. Deanna Mertle, F257, CHS. "Work schedule" form, completed by Linda Mertle, age 14: F248, CHS. "St. Joseph's Parish Council Questionaire": F253, CHS. "My personal message to Pastor Jim Jones": F336, CHS. Other letters to Jones: F241, F256, F370, CHS. Confessions and pseudoconfessions: Deanna Myrtle, F257, CHS; Kilduff and Tracy (1979: 322); Debbie Blakey, declaration for CAG/PT, CHS; Theilmann and Merrill (1979: 85); Mertles' confessions and membership form, F99, F254, F260-2, CHS. Surveillance accounts: Jack Beam, F31, CHS; Teri Buford, p. 13, "Tish," p. 23, F156, CHS; Tim Stoen, tape cassette of phone conversation with Lena, another, with Wayne P., CGA; report on "exclusive" parental conversation, Linda Mertle, 11/19/75, F246, CHS. Turning in of journal: member's journal, FBI file HH2, II, 406. Jones's explanation of omniscience: Stephan Jones (1979: 88). Loyalist: q. in Moore (1985: 131). Jones justifying surveillance: member's journal, FBI file HH2, II, 402.

12. The practice of "psychic domination by distributing or denying religious benefits" is called "hierocratic domination" by Weber (1977: 54, 56), and it is taken as a defining characteristic of a "church." Jones on resentment and guilt: member's journal, FBI file HH2, II, 150. Mention of catharsis: F453, CHS; Mike Touchette, AI. FBI file HH6A27, including a handwritten notation, "Gestalt Psychology?/ Encounter Groups?" ITT, 12/6/78, notes a connection to the confrontational therapeutic sect Synanon, and alludes to others. Mike Cartmell, q. in LAT News Service, in CDT, 11/25/78. Catharsis description: Patty Cartmell, "No Haloes Please," unpublished ms., ch. 17, CGA; cf. "Issues on the floor," 1972 unsigned journal on catharsis meetings, CHS. On the relatively benign character of early catharsis, see also Kilduff and Tracy (1979: 321–22); Jeannie Mills (1979); Thielmann and Merrill (1979: 81). Counseling, "court" procedures, the child's alienation, money-raising as punishment, the penitance assignment, Sandy Rozynko as a slave: Dale Parks, declaration for CAG/PT, CHS; member's journal, FBI file HH2, II, 114, 404–5, 393, 120, 117, 151, 143, 139; a letter describing the experience of "slavery," F255, CHS.

13. On "structure": Jones, cited by Bea Orsot, AI; PF, December 1976; and pp. 33ff., F156, CHS. Stephan Jones (1979: 86). Avoidance of physical violence with seniors, Jones's position described: member's journal, FBI file HH2, II, 401; only incident reported, Sally Stapleton, in MG, 7/21/77; Stapleton incident also described by Jeannie Mills (1979: 208–9), who places the date in 1973, but before defection of eight young Temple members; apparently the same incident, and Grace Stoen's role as head counselor, Kilduff and Tracy (1979: 322, 325). Origin of collective discipline: F156, CHS, with the supposed

precipitating incident described by Tish Leroy, Teri Buford, Jones. The incident appears to have been the same as one described in a letter by District Attorney Duncan James, 10/14/75, and a memo from Tim Stoen, F45, CHS, and discussed by Jones and Mendocino County Social Services Director Dennis Denny, on FBI tape Q710. Earlier events of corporal punishment are recorded in the member's journal, FBI file HH2, II, 92. Jones on "lesson givers" and matching comparable opponents: F156, CHS. Children's offenses deemed punishable: member's journal, FBI file HH2, II, 126, 136 (quotation), 143, 156, 161, 163, 164, 393; cf. p. 25, F156, CHS, for a case of teenager's lesbian relation, in which Jones's main concern is the involvement with someone outside the Temple. Adult offenses deemed punishable: member's journal, FBI file HH2, II, 80, 86, 161, 397, 400, 403, 406; Thielmann and Merrill (1979: 67). Ongoing account of paddlings and boxing matches, member's journal, FBI file HH2, esp. II, 401 (Jones's expressed opposition), 91–3 119, 119–20, 136, 142, 154, 156. On Linda Mertle's actions and paddling: F156, CHS, and her letter, and permission form signed by Elmer Mertle, Mertle file, CGA; her boxing, member's journal, FBI file HH2, II, 401. Unwritten rule against fighting back: Kilduff and Tracy (1979: 331). On social treatment of those disciplined, and Jones's receipt of physical punishment: member's journal, FBI file HH2, II, 93, 132; cf. Jeannie Mills, cited in SFE, 8/14/77; Jeannie Mills (1979: 135). Jones on being beaten: WP, 11/27/78; Baltimore *Sun*, 11/21/78, reprinted in CFA (385, 370).

14. Northeast Kingdom community: NYT, 6/23, 29/84; *Charisma* 1984: 68–79. The dry, matter-of-fact accounts in the Temple member's journal, FBI file HH2, underscore Erikson's view, for the Temple. See Erikson (1966: 189). For a case of banishment: member's journal, FBI file HH2, II, 401.

15. On sex roles in communal groups: Foster (1981). On Jones family: Theilmann and Merrill (1979:23–24, 68–69, 109); Pat Richartz, AI. Carolyn Moore Layton, letters, P9–4, P9–5, CHS. On relationships: Debbie Blakey, declaration for CAG/PT, CHS; Bea Orsot, AI. Jeannie Mills, AI. On the Stoen's marriage, interviews with each of them: SFB, 11/9/19. Note in the handwriting of Tim Stoen, 7/8/71, F101C, CHS. Grace Stoen's private access to Jones: Dale Parks, declaration for CAG/PT, CHS; cf. anonymous statement of Temple member, F95, CHS. John Stoen: "Certificate of live birth," informant, Grace Lucy Stoen, P2–2, CHS; "To whom it may concern," exhibit C–2, Complaint for temporary restraining order, PT/TOS, P2–8, CHS.

16. Martin Luther's solution to impotence cited by Lyman (1978: 70). Stoen's account of affidavit: Tim Stoen, declaration by defendant opposing application for preliminary injunction, PT/TOS, P2–19, CHS. Other (inconclusive) evidence concerning Grace Stoen's encounters with Jim Jones cited by Charles Garry and Patricia Richartz, Charles Garry, Interview, pp. 29–30, U.S. House of Representatives Committee on International Relations, (hereafter cited as CIR). Jones's claim, as early as 1973, to be biological father of John Stoen: Reiterman and Jacobs (1982: 222). Carolyn Layton caring for John Stoen: Moore (1985: 230). Lynetta Jones on John Stoen: "The tiniest disciple," c. 1975, F337, CHS. See also: SFB, 11/9/19; Sandy Bradshaw, AI; Kilduff and Tracy (1979: 325); Reiterman and Jacobs (1982: 286ff.). Handwritten consent form signed by Grace Stoen, agreeing to give up her son to Carolyn Layton by adoption: CHS 32.

17. Jesus, q. in Matthew 10: 35–36. Members distancing themselves from outside relatives: Moore (1985: 99–108); Steven Katsaris, AI; member's journal, FBI

file HH2, II, 410. Housing assignments: Mertle file, CGA; F241, CHS; Jeannie Mills (1979: 142ff., 170ff.). Theilmann and son: Theilmann and Merrill (1979: 67–68). Jones on marriages: member's journal, FBI file HH2, II, 401; Jones sermon, FBI tape Q1059, pt. 5; Mike Cartmell, LAT News Service, in CDT, 12/25/78; Thielmann and Merrill (1979: 90–92).

18. On the question of social control and family life in the modern era, with particular emphasis on the role played by modern social theory and practitioners of social work and psychotherapy, see Lasch (1977) and Donzelot (1979).

19. On the Houstons and Shaw: SFE, 11/13/77. Examples of other relational counseling: member's journal, FBI file HH2, passim. On "companionate" relationships: Rebecca Moore (1985: 175); cf. Debbie Blakey, declaration for CAG/PT, CHS; cf. Jim Jones and Grace Stoen, telephone conversation of 7/29/77, tape cassette, CGA. Mike Touchette, AI. Range of relationships: member's journal, FBI file HH2, II, 398 and passim; F156, CHS; Gerald Parks, declaration for CAG/PT, CHS.

20. Declaration of James Cobb, Jr. for *James Cobb, Jr.* vs. *Peoples Temple*, California Superior Court, San Francisco, case #739907 (hereafter cited as JC/PT), P12–1, CHS; Kilduff and Tracy (1979: 323); Christine Cobb Young, F189, CHS; Charles Touchette, Chris Kice, and Michael Cartmell, affidavits and depositions, PT/TOS file, CGA; Michael Cartmell, LAT News Service, in CDT, 12/25/78; Wayne Pietla, SFE, 8/14/77. On Jones halting paramilitary training: cf. Reiterman and Jacob (1979: 219ff.). Temple reaction to defection: Sandy Bradshaw, AI; Deanna Mertle, memo to Jim Jones, F240, CHS. Stoen's plan: Teri Buford, deposition for PT/TOS, P11–1, CHS; Reiterman and Jacobs (1982: 227–28). Phone conversation: tape cassette labeled "Wayne P.," CGA. Jones q. by Bea Orsot, AI; cf. Tim Stoen, on 1973 as the year Jones's attitude shifted, NYT, 11/26/78. Jones on bombing threat: Neva Sly, in NYT, 2/25/79; Wayne Pietla, SFE, 8/14/77. Rejection of terrorism: Jim Jones, FBI file O1A1f.

21. For a 1971 reference to the "socialist paradise" dream: Thielmann and Merrill (1979: 56). Strategies of sanctuary and hope of paradise: Jones sermon on FBI tape Q958. Redwood Valley as sanctuary from "emergency": Tim Stoen, letter, 2/15/71, F344, CHS. Migration plans: memo, "To Jim; From Tim S.," F159, CHS. Mission settlement and development resolutions and discussion, minutes, Peoples Temple board of directors, CHS. P.C. suicide talk: Jeannie Mills (1979: 231–32); Grace Stoen, NYT, 2/25/79, puts the first concrete talk of collective suicide two days before the defection of the eight young people, rather than immediately following it. Indianapolis rumor of Jones's suicide: Mrs. Jack Swinney, 5/22/65 letter to IR. Dog poisoning: SFE, 9/24/72. Jones on Jews, resettlement, plans: 1973 sermon, FBI tape Q958. Jones on martyrdom, May 1972 sermon: FBI tape Q967; paraphrasing of Jesus is from Matthew 24:28. Elmer Mertle, letter of 6/4/73, F237, CHS. Jones on defending people: sermon, FBI tape Q973. File on nonsuicidal persons, *U.S.A.* vs. *Peoples Temple*, Ex. 22, vol. III, 710–1085, CHS. "Suicide rehearsal" described by Reiterman and Jacobs (1979: 294–96), in part following Mills (1979: 300), who places the event sometime between January and August 1975—oddly enough, given Mills's efforts to discredit Jones, she does not mention the purported assertion that the wine was laced with poison; Grace Stoen, NYT, 2/25/79, places the event on New Year's Day, 1976, and in that article, she and Neva Sly both specifically describe Jones telling the group the wine was poisoned. It should be kept in

mind that Jeannie Mills and Grace Stoen were close friends after they defected in October 1975 and July 1976, respectively; Mills's account is the earlier one, but the two may have influenced each other's versions before either became public. Jones's talk of martyrdom: member's journal, FBI file HH2, 9/6/75, II, 154; 2/7/76, II, 398.

22. On the Black Panther party and the Black redemptive quest: Blair (1977: 90); Newton (1972; 1973). Meeting after January 27, 1977, between Jones and Huey Newton: mentioned by Reiterman and Jacob (1982: 284–85). Discussion of "revolutionary suicide" during Cuba meeting recounted by Huey Newton, in Naipaul (1981: 285ff.). The Black Panther party's "race-class line" and the Hoover quotation: Blair (1977: 94, 92).

23. Jones forcing out nonbelievers: sermon, FBI tape Q1016. Acceptance of suicide loyalty test: Neva Sly, NYT, 2/25/79. Requirements of leaving the Temple: member's journal, FBI file HH2, II, 412, 393, 127; cf. MG, 7/28/77. On intimidations: Steve Katsaris, AI. Survivor on thoughts of defection: Moore (1985: 161). Stephan Jones: in WP, 11/7/84. On Johnson girls: SFP, 7/31/77; SFE, 9/19, 20/72; cf. IS article shortly after 8/1/77 under headline, "Ex-disciple calls cult 'nightmare.'" Thielmann's departure: Thielmann and Merrill (1979: 93–95). Member's journal, FBI file HH2, passim. On high voluntary defection rates in new religious groups: Bird and Reimer (1982). On lack of terror for the average Temple member: Moore (1985: 140).

24. On social control in communal groups and other total institutions: Kanter (1972); Goffman (1961). On the tendency toward more extensive efforts at confinement among other-worldly sects: Hall (1983).

## Chapter 8: Politics and Public Relations

1. For an engaging discussion of these transformations, Boorstin (1962); a more wide-ranging discussion touching on similar issues, Goffman (1974); the "spectaclist" perspective, Debord (1977).

2. Case (1921: 30, 35, 78); Marston (1979: 112–13). A discussion of the way public relations has permeated religious organizations: Ross (1959: 203ff.). Phineas T. Barnum, q. in Boorstin (1962: 209).

3. Definition of manipulation: Arnold Kauffman, q. in Ross (1959: 182); Boorstin (1962: 204).

4. Unification Church member q.: Selengut (1983). On religions and plausibility structures: Berger (1967: ch. 6).

5. Carter q.: ITT, 12/6/78. On Black socialist preachers: Foner (1977: 150ff.); Wilmore (1983). New Republic, 12/2/78. Jones: FBI tape Q134 (transcript, FBI file O1A1–e).

6. Jones's religious references: e.g. FBI tape Q937. Example of Jones's recounting of warning to Blacks in Lynn: IR, 7/25/64; similar account, George Southworth, LCJ, 11/23/78; Reiterman and Jacobs (1982: 11). On similar usage of "poetic license" by Ronald Reagan in his 1984 campaign for presidential election: Nicholas Lemann, "Reagan's people," WPW, 10/22/84.

7. Jones advocating communalism: Reiterman and Jacobs (1982: 61); Guiana Graphic, 10/25/61, G3A14, CHS. Sermon topic, UDJ, 2/2/71; similar sermon, FBI tape Q1054, pt. 4. Proposal for Angela Davis exchange: UDJ, 1/1/71. SLA hostage offer: undated 1974 newspaper article in FBI file HH6A52; cf. SRPD,

2/14/74. Jones's eulogy on the Los Angeles police SWAT (Strategic Weapons and Tactics) Team shootout that killed the core of the SLA: FBI tape Q953. Talk in Jonestown on the Allende coup: FBI tape Q429.

8. Kathie Hunter report: UDJ, 7/26/65. Jones's civic positions: UDJ, 3/29/68. Cultivating law enforcement officials, donations: UDJ, 4/19/68, and advertisement, UDJ, 5/10/68. Letters and articles: UDJ, 3/7/69, 4/10/69, 6/5/69; cf. SFSR, 2/28/76. Fund for slain policeman's family: SFC, 9/4/70; and others, California *Sun-times* (a Temple front organization), 1/31/74, F320, CHS; SFC, 1/3/76.

9. Mack Hanan, lecture to American Management Association, 1960: q. in Boorstin (1962: 185). Motto revision: circa 1976–77, Jean Brown correspondence file, CGA. Rick Cordell: FBI file HH6A14, which corresponds to a press release printed in the UDJ, 12/2/66, and a laudatory article by Kathie Hunter, UDJ, 6/3/68. Gift of fudge: Louise Moseley, AI. Stoen-Katsaris correspondence, 4/11 and 4/13/73: P4-4, CHS. UDJ reports of Temple news: e.g. 10/11/68, 2/21/69, 4/25/69, 6/20/69, 6/30/69, 7/18/69. Pet items: UDJ, 12/16/69, 3/19/74; SFSR, 11/8/75. Undated UDJ Good Friday, 1966, photographs: FBI file HH6A40. Other antiwar story: UDJ, 10/14/69. Martin Luther King memorial services story: UDJ, 4/8/68. Nuclear war concern: UDJ, 3/29/68. Drug concern: UDJ, 4/11/69. Former drug users converted: UDJ, 7/3/69. "Statement that will hopefully bring understanding to the principle by Jim Jones and other concerned citizens inside and outside his parish": UDJ, 5/10/68. Nonmember advertisement: UDJ, 7/8/68. Hunter article: UDJ, 6/3/68.

10. The proselytizing media activities and publicity materials are described in detail in chapter 6. Lynetta Jones letter: F338C, CHS. Tim Stoen letter, 4/7/74: F232, CHS. Report of 400 letters: undated UDJ, G3A22, CHS. Letter-writing instructions: F442 and F488 (quotation), CHS. Report in *America*, 3/17/56, about Oral Roberts's letter campaign, in Temple files, F64, CHS. Mimeographed newsletters: F453, CHS. *The Living Word: An Apostolic Monthly* 1, no. 1 (July 1972), F457, CHS.

11. On the right- and left-wing appeal of "paranoid" political theory: Hofstadter (1979: 35). Mendocino Republican connections: Marjorie Boynton, letter, F467, CHS; Reiterman and Jacobs (1982: 152ff.). Brown elected: UDJ, 6/3/75. Sandy Bradshaw, AI.

12. Denomination citation: Temple pamphlet, circa 1973, F328, CHS. List of notable Disciples members: SFSR, 2/28/76. Note about using quotation: handwritten on letter to James Evans, from Oran Bollinger, a Disciples minister, 2/21/73, F445, CHS. Temple support for Irvin election: UDJ, 8/21/70. Other denominational background: Louise Moseley, AI; Barton Hunter, AI; Dorothy Hunter, AI; SFE, 4/8/79. Response to Kinsolving and Southern California affiliation: Disciples of Christ file, CGA; SFE, 4/8/79; Barton Hunter, AI; A. Dale Fiers, letter of 2/8/73, F375, CHS. Wade Rubick, "Memorandum," 4/22/74, F446, CHS.

13. Accounts of freedom of press donations: SFC, 1/17/73; SRPD, circa 1/17/73; Inter American Press Association *News* (Miami), February-March 1973; Jack Anderson returned the money and Karen Layton signed a letter answering Anderson's, 3/9/73, Mike Prokes file, CGA. *The Temple Reporter* 1, no. 1 (Summer 1973), F321, CHS. Other editorial communications: FBI file BB18Z50ff.; materials gathered for the magazine article are contained in FBI

files HH6 and BB18. Tim Stoen, F159, CHS; cf. Stoen's planned sketch of Jonestown for a "socialist" and "capitalist reading public," Legal—Stoen—correspondence and notes, CHS. Photo file labels and retouching: Slides and photos file, CGA; SFE, photo morgue. Example of California *Sun-times* news release letterhead: F320, CHS; other PR stories: *Independent Press-Telegram*, 2/15/75, G3A35, CHS; RPI, 4/6/75, G3A36, CHS; Berkeley *Barb*, 7/9/76; KGO-TV feature, 2/4/76. Temple PR materials: F70, F317, F328, F455, F462, F464, CHS. Jones's instructions to secretary: FBI tape Q622. Jones's press ridicule: FBI tape Q1054, pt. 4. Image projection instructions: Debbie Blakey, q. in Kilduff and Tracy (1979: 315).

14. Kinsolving transcript and related correspondence: F387–8, CHS. Account of Moore, the Temple and Kinsolving: Moore (1985: 131–37); cf. "Legal—media—libel," CHS. Kinsolving and congressional press corps censure: Tampa (Fla.) *Tribune*, 3/19/77; cf. member's journal, FBI file HH2, II, 105, 113 (quotation). On whether use of libel laws has undermined press and intellectual freedom: WPW, 3/26/84, 4/9/84. Hofstadter (1979: 3–4). 1975 resurgence of "conspiracy" motif: Bea Orsot, AI. Herb Caen note on Temple charity: SFC, 3/2/76. Julie Smith article: SFC, 4/26/76. Fresno *Bee*, 9/11/76, 9/19/76. Freedom of the Press Award: Napa (Calif.) *Register*, 6/17/77. Mike Prokes and KDKI radio man: FBI tape Q686.

15. Religion in American Life: F502, CHS. On heroes and celebrities: Boorstin (1962: 45ff.).

16. PF 1, no. 1 (April 1976), CHS; files of PF and Jean Brown correspondence, F363, F377, F434, CHS; Jean Brown correspondence file, Jim Jones correspondence file, PF correspondence file, CGA.

17. Jim Jones on San Francisco political relations: member's journal, FBI file HH2, II, 143 (8/30/75). A similar point about the limits of Jones's political influence in Mendocino County: Dennis Denny in UDJ, 3/9/79. Black Leadership Forum decision: SFSR, 2/10/77, 2/17/77. Williams complaint to police: Baltimore *Sun*, 12/28/78, for which District Attorney Joe Freitas later alleged Tim Stoen's interference, SFE, 1/21/79.

18. Donation to Seniors' Assistance Program: SFE, 1/21/76. Clinic support: SFSR, 11/1/75. Support for Dennis Banks: SFE, 2/28/76. Banks's decision to drop extradition struggle to face charges in Oregon: SFE, 3/30/76; cf. FBI tape Q614 with Jones seeking advice and support for Banks from Methodist John Moore, San Francisco Sheriff Richard Hongisto, and publisher Carlton Goodlett. Christmas party donation: Jones letter, 12/76, Jim Jones correspondence file, CGA. Efforts at alliance-building with the Temple: PF correspondence file, CGA, and letter to Hayden's organization, 6/24/78, general correspondence file, CGA.

19. SFC, 12/21/76. Jones on Angela Davis: FBI tape Q622. Eldridge Cleaver support: Oakland *Metro Reporter*, 6/20/77; Berkeley *Barb*, 7/9/76; SFC, 7/23/76. *Bakke* decision protest: SFE, 10/22/76. Rally with Socialist Workers party: SFC, 11/13/76; SFE, 11/13/76; *The Militant*, 12/3/76. Kimball Park rally: SFSR, 3/24/77. World Peace Council visit: SFSR, 4/21/77. Chileans: SFSR, 10/25/75, 12/31/76. Charles Garry: "Interview," CIR, CHS.

20. Defense alliance with Black Muslims: member's journal, FBI file HH2, II, 125, 135. Spiritual Jubilee: reported in the conservative digest, *Review of the News*, 7/21/76, F293, CHS, which quotes the leftist *Peoples' World* on the significance of the meeting; Wallace Muhammad was the successor to Elijah Muhammad,

who died around early 1975. Harriet Tropp memo on support of Jewish struggle: Mike Prokes correspondence file, CGA; San Francisco *Jewish Bulletin* 12/31/76, and Temple letter, general correspondence file, CHS. Temple support of orange juice boycott: SFC, 4/21/77. "Fight back against anti-gay campaign," F498, CHS. Jones q. Neimöller: Kansas City rally reported in UDJ, 10/8/76.

21. On the "above ground"/"underground" dilemma of the Left: Buttinger (1953). Jones on political strategy of Left: FBI tape Q622. Jones statement to Denny: FBI tape Q686. Dennis Denny q. in UDJ, 3/9/79. Letters from San Francisco Board of Supervisors members: Jean Brown correspondence file, CGA; F466, CHS. On Jones working the margins of Black and White: Major (1979: 22). San Francisco political power and voting fraud charges: NYT, 12/17/78. Lynetta Jones as Mendocino County deputy clerk for voter registration: Lynetta Jones file, CGA. Temple political workers suggested by Willie Brown, and number of Temple members registered for 1975 San Francisco election: Reiterman and Jacobs (1982: 266–67). Jones discussion of caucus organizing, with John Maher: FBI tape Q622. Jones's ally on party strategy: FBI tape Q622. Reiterman and Jacobs (1982: 267; cf. 585 note 36). Jeannie Mills: NYT, 12/17/78. Cf. Moore (1985: 169–74).

22. Jones with Rosalynn Carter, Walter Mondale: SFC, 9/15/76. "Thank you" note to Jones from local Carter campaign official: CHS 55; cf. Kilduff and Tracy (1979: 319). Letter from Rosalynn Carter: Baltimore *Sun*, 11/21/78, reprinted in CFA, 369. Letter quoted, from Mayor George Moscone: PF, 11/76. Other letters, F296; testimonial quotes, F516, CHS. NYT, 11/26/78, p. IV:1. Testimonial dinner: UDJ, 9/27/76. Proposition T: Oakland *Tribune*, 1/10/77. Repayment of political debts by Moscone: San Francisco political activist, AI. Stoen's appointment: UDJ, 5/18/76; NYT, 12/17/78; Reiterman and Jacobs (1982: 270). On voter fraud: NYT, 12/17/78; SFE, 1/21/79.

23. Jones's appointment: SFSR, 3/27/76; SFC, 10/19/76, 11/22/76. Peoples Temple redevelopment housing project: member's journal, FBI file HH2, II, 134. Swearing in: SFE, 12/1/76. On avoiding PF article on International Hotel: Gene Chaiken, 12/18/76 memo, F497, CHS. International Hotel: SFC, 1/8/77; SFE, 1/17/77; *Daily Californian* (Berkeley, Calif.), 1/17/77; Reiterman and Jacobs (1982: 282–83); SFC, 2/25/77.

## Chapter 9: From the Promised Land to the Promised Land

1. Martin Luther King birthday party "Programme": F428, CHS, and reported in undated San Francisco newspaper article, G3A53A, CHS, and SFSR, 1/20/77. Jones's denial of political ambitions: Oakland *Tribune*, 1/10/77. For a case study of a millennialist sect that has nevertheless accommodated to the established order: Beckford (1975). An example of Jones's pessimism without socialism: member's journal, FBI file HH2, II, 408 (2/13/77). Wright visit: SFSR, 11/11/76; cf. Jean F. Brown, letter to John Stennis, 11/16/76, F356A, CHS; Moore (1985: 177–78), who interviewed Committee on Foreign Affairs staffers and Dawsey. Assertion that the Wright incident was central to suspicions about a "conspiracy": F92, CHS; other accounts of incidents and surveillance, F30, F487, F303, CHS. On the promised land: cf. Cleage (1972: 203).

2. On Kilduff: Sandy Bradshaw, AI; Kevin Starr, letter of 2/15/77 to Marshall Kilduff, CHS, 36. Letters supporting Peoples Temple: Operations—correspon

dence—media—*New West*, CHS. Response to Richard Tropp's letter discouraging publication: James Turner, editor of *San Francisco*, 5/18/77, F425, CHS. On Tracy's interests: Berkeley *Barb*, 7/22/77. Tracy's two stories published in *New West*, 1/17, 3/28/77. His help from Barbagelata and the Moscone reaction: Weiss (1984: 175). On conservative opposition to the liberal political regime in San Francisco: SFC, 12/21/76; *The Sentinel* 4, no. 7, 3/24/77, G3A63; Barbagelata speech, SFC, 5/27/77; San Francisco Police Officers' Association, "Action bulletin 7," F432, CHS; San Francisco Police Commission meeting transcript, 6/8/77, CHS. Officers' Association support for Barbagelata: SFC, 6/9/77; SFC, 5/27/77; Joseph Freitas, letter to Tim Stoen, 6/1/77, F158, CHS.

3. General sources: Klineman, Butler, and Conn (1980: 246ff.); Oakland *Tribune*, 1/21/79; Jeannie Mills (1979: 25, 33, 36, 47–50); Carol McCoy, "Re: Mertles & picture stand, etc.," Legal—Mertle case, CHS; F364, CHS; Ross Case, AI. Deanna Mertle, F240, CHS, proposes a plan that effectively would marginalize Jones, leaving others to step in as leaders. On plan to send Mertles as missionaries: *Jeannie Mills et al.* vs. *Peoples Temple*, California Superior Court, San Francisco, case #727–517 (hereafter cited as JM/PT), suit, p. 6, and notes commenting on the suit's factual claims, Tish Leroy, F42, CHS. Jeannie Mills places the date of the missionary scheme as on or about February 1973; Leroy places the missionary date in late 1973 or early 1974. On mission work to get off projects: Deanna Mertle, F245, CHS.

4. On Deanna Mertle's power struggle with Jones: Lowell Streiker, AI, and Keith Harrari, AI (associates given accounts by Jeannie Mills [the former Deanna Mertle] after she founded Human Freedom Center). Harrari recalled Mills's saying she wanted to make the Temple live up to its ideals; Streiker remembered Mills's describing what he took to be a more opportunistic power play. Elmer Mertle, F129, CHS, questions punishment. Christine Lucientes, memo of 11/19/75 on Temple property in Mertles' house: F238, CHS. Linda Mertle, report on reasons for her parents' defection: F246, CHS. Temple internal communications about strategies for creating distrust among Zoe Kille and her children and former husband Mert: Mertle file, CGA; F238, F249, F256, CHS.

5. General sources: Klineman, Butler, and Conn (1980: 246ff.); Oakland *Tribune*, 1/21/79; Jeannie Mills (1979: 25, 33, 36, 47–50). Elmer Mertle: memo on intimate friendships, F352, CHS; Betty Carroll, affidavit, 9/23/77, CGA. Rita Tupper on Mertle connections: F99, CHS; Mertle file, CGA. Undated 1975 Mertle letter on exchange agreements: F65, CHS; cf. Deanna Mertle, letter to Jim Jones denying contacts, F259, CHS. Al and Jeannie Mills, "To whom it may concern," printed in Jeannie Mills (1979: 11–16). Grace Stoen's fears about group censure: "Tish," notes on defectors, Operations—correspondence—media—*New West*, CHS. On Grace Stoen's defection: Grace Stoen and Jim Jones, 7/29/76, telephone conversation cassette, CGA; Grace Stoen and Jim Jones, telephone call transcript, P3–1, CHS. Tim Stoen and Grace Stoen, Form 8, and Tim Stoen, power of attorney, F342, CHS. John Stoen to Guyana: memo exchange between Gene Chaiken and Tim Stoen, CHS 31; WP, 11/27/78; Charles Garry, "Interview," CIR, CHS; "Grace," tape cassette of telephone conversation between Grace Stoen and Tim Stoen, 1976, CGA. Buford's characterization of phone call between Grace and Tim as occurring before John Stoen was sent to Guyana: Lane (1980: 246–47). Zoanna Kille and Linda Mertle, mailgram to Jones indicating Linda's defection, 11/20/76: Mertle file, CGA. Jeannie and Al Mills's interest in "cults" described by Margaret Singer,

AI; Lowell Streiker, AI. Advice to Linda Mertle: Jeannie Mills (1979: 53). On the wider anticult movement: Bromley and Shupe (1981).

6. Klineman, Butler, and Conn (1980: 246ff.); Oakland *Tribune*, 1/21/79; Mills (1979: 56ff.). An early account based on interviews with the Millses, in Willits (Calif.) *News*, 8/31/77, says Temple defectors' revelations "prompted him [Klineman] to contact the Treasury Department and U.S. Customs to investigate," but in his book Klineman describes his meeting with a Treasury agent as a coincidence. U.S. Custom Service 1979 "Synopsis," Ex. 22, p. 39, and earlier "Background on Peoples Temple," Ex. 22, p. 12, both *U.S.* vs. *Peoples Temple*, CHS. Treasury agent meeting date, given in apparent Interpol report: F59A, CHS, summarized in F130, CHS. Steve Katsaris's mention of James Hubert, "affidavit," 4/4/78, reprinted in Kerns (1979: 257).

7. Banks's account of his encounter with David Conn: F84, CHS. Reiterman and Jacobs (1982: 587) mistakenly doubt that Banks informed the Temple of the Treasury investigation after his March 23 meeting with Conn, citing Banks's incorrect dating in his declaration. Klineman, Butler, and Conn (1980: 252–53) give the actual date of the meeting; their dating and the passing of intelligence by Banks are substantiated by a 4/11/77 discussion of the Temple's board of directors, CHS. Surveillance of Donna Conn's house reported by Teri Buford: Lane (1980: 235–38). Tim Stoen, "Go and be with them—make call now, it's urgent," undated notes, perhaps written in Guyana during an April "legal conference" there, P2-4-13, CHS. Letters to *New West* publisher Rupert Murdoch: Mike Prokes file, CGA.

8. SFC, 6/7/77; Klineman, Butler and Conn (1980: 258ff., 262 [quotation of Kilduff]); Jeannie Mills (1979: 63); Jeannie Mills, AI. *New West* break-in: SFC, 6/18/77; Captain John A. Mahoney, San Francisco Police Department intradepartmental memo, 6/29/77, F451, CHS. Temple characterization of burglary as publicity stunt: Sandy Bradshaw, AI. Contacts with Case: Klineman, Butler, and Conn (1980: 268); cf. MG, 7/21/77. The "hot phone," Kilduff's restraint, Klineman's request form, Tracy's photography, and Rosalie Wright: Klineman, Butler, and Conn (1980: 263, 264, 267, 270).

9. Kilduff and Tracy ([1977] 1979); *New West* publicity press conferences: SFE, 7/12/78; MG, 7/21/77, 7/28/77; SRPD, 7/27/77, 8/1/77; cf. SFP, 7/31/77, 8/3/77, 8/10/77; *Newsweek*, August 15, 1977; Berkeley *Barb*, 8/15/77; MG, 7/28/77; Tim Reiterman and Nancy Dooley, SFE, 8/14/77. First use of term *cult*: SRPD, 8/18/77; another news story with the brainwashing interpretation, MG, 7/28/77. On *cult* as a popular term and sociological concept, see chapter 1. Reiterman and Jacobs (1982: 586) attempt an "objective" definition of *cult* that nevertheless pejoratively alludes to the "arrogance" of the cult leader, the untestable nature of prophecies and revelations, and a tendency of the leader to create an "illusion of giving more to his people than he takes for himself."

10. Temple member's property sold: SFC, 8/19/77. Story on Harpe and Head deaths: SRPD, 8/9/77. Managing editor of SFE, letter to the editor, *Wall Street Journal*, 1/15/79, p. 21. Sociologist Stephen Warner of University of Illinois-Chicago recounted the Temple response in the Mendocino County area: personal communication with author. Agricultural mission stories: SFE, 6/9/77 (quotation); SFSR, 6/9/77. Temple affidavits on opponents: PT/TOS and other legal files, CGA. Temple response to *New West* article: PF 2, no. 4 (August 1, 1977). Cf. news articles and editorials that counter *New West* stories: SFSR, 7/21/77; UDJ, 7/22/77; *Bay Guardian*, 7/21/77. Authorization to confer with

lawyer: Peoples Temple board of directors, minutes, 6/29/77, CHS. Charles Garry: copy of 7/18/77 check, CGA; interview on KGO radio, 8/10/77; AI; SFP, 7/31/77; and Berkeley *Barb*, 9/23/77.

11. Gary Lambrev, q. on KNBR, 7/20/77: transcript, F61, CHS. Tracy, q. in *Bay Guardian*, 7/21/77, and Berkeley *Barb*, 7/22/77. George Moscone statement, 7/26/77: F88A, CHS; SFE, 7/26/77. Jones's departure for Guyana: Klineman, Butler, and Conn (1980: 274–75); Reiterman and Jacobs (1982: 326–27). Jones resignation: SFE, 8/4/77; report by columnist Herb Caen of its delay, SFC, 9/1/77; its early planning, Tim Stoen, notes, P2-4, CHS. Date of Jones's migration: Temple migration files, CHS. Lack of cases for prosecution: Reiterman and Jacobs (1982: 338). For an account of the assassinations of George Moscone and gay supervisor Harvey Milk by Dan White—an event that developed out of the same crosscurrents of San Francisco politics—see Weiss (1984).

12. On phases of British colonialism: Hechter (1975); Wolff (1974). The Puritans' interest in the Guianas and Sir Walter Raleigh's description: Dillon (1973: 112–13). On the border dispute with Venezuela, LAT News Service, in CDT, 9/28/82. On the working class in British Guiana: Rodney (1981). On ethnic, class and political cleavages in preindependence British Guiana: Despres (1973). Smuggling may be the subject of an obscure reference to gold by Tim Stoen during his stay in Guyana, P2-4-60, CGA; the present author discussed gold with the brother of a high-ranking government official during a 1979 trip to Guyana.

13. On the affinities between Jones, the Peoples Temple, and Guyana: *New Society* 49, no. 885 (1979): 607–10; CCR, 23. Complaint by Venezuela about settlement: CFA, 66, 133. British Guyana harboring of prison escapees: NYT, 12/24/78. On the House of Israel: SFE, 6/8/80; Jack Anderson, reprinted in CDT, 12/6/79; political observers requesting anonymity, Georgetown, Guyana, 1979, AI.

14. General sources on pioneering: Mike Touchette, AI; Charlie Touchette, AI; Debbie Touchette, AI; CHS 11. Naming of settlement: cf. Guyanese official Emerson Mitchell's denial he named the settlement, Reiterman and Jacobs (1982: 240). According to a U.S. embassy official, the settlement was not called Jonestown as late as May of 1976: CFA, 140. Krebs's visit: CFA, 135. May 1976 visit: CFA, 140–41. Temple in Georgetown: Debbie Touchette, AI; Steve Katsaris, AI. Amos replacing Adams: NYT, 12/13/78. On Paula Adams and Laurence Mann: CFAH, 44; CFA, 176. Temple report on Adams's conversation with Mann in Washington, D.C., and her willingness to "inform you of their content if you wish her to": FBI file MM8–9a. Loyalty to People's National Congress party (PNC) and government: Tim Stoen, notes, P2-4-23, CHS.

15. Wade Matthews, memo of 12/4/78: CFA, 140. The Cuban troop rumor and angry denial by the Guyana government: *Christian Science Monitor*, 3/11/76. CIA indication of its presence in Guyana obtained through Freedom of Information Act request by Rebecca Moore (1985: 418–24). On the CIA and U.S. foreign missions: overseas U.S. government employee requesting anonymity, AI; U.S. Department of State, "Organization of a mission" organizational chart, F700, CHS; cf. Agee (1975). Jones and Dymally itinerary: F499, CHS. McCoy meeting with Jones and Dymally: Georgetown, Guyana, U.S. embassy cable (hereafter cited as GUSEC; log number refers to State Department Peoples Temple Freedom of Information Act archive), 2637, 12/29/76, reprinted in

CFA, 147–49. On Guyanese government fears of U.S. "destabilization": letter of Laurence Mann, Guyanese ambassador to United States, NYT, 3/2/76; Miami *Herald*, 3/3/76; WP, 3/10/76; *Christian Science Monitor*, 3/11/76; GC, 5/2/76; ITT, 9/28/77. Jones newspaper quotation: CCR, 2.

16. Transfer of monies: Peoples Temple board of directors, minutes, CHS. IRS memo: Mike Prokes news clipping file, CGA. Temple payment of property taxes: e.g. "Real estate taxes due 12–10–75," Peoples Temple Finance—property tax, CHS. Establishment of Valley Enterprises: Peoples Temple board of directors, minutes, 5/10/76, CHS. Jones's complaint: FBI tape Q622; cf. Temple concerns evidenced by clipping on IRS probe: SFC, 11/18/74, in Temple files, CGA; PF 1, no. 2 (April 1976). Denial of tax exempt application: F491, CHS; see also F367, CHS. Temple memo: Gene Chaiken, 7/22/77, F349, CHS. Tim Carter, letter of 4/8/76: F28, CHS. Tim Stoen, letter draft to Stan Long and actual letter of 7/23/76 (ellipsis points in original): F117, F28, CHS. Stan Long, IRS, letter of 9/3/76: F28, CHS. Gene Chaiken, memo of 9/13/76: F28, CHS. Tim Stoen, letter to Stan Long, 9/22/76: F28, CHS. Tim Stoen, "Research project for legal dept," undated memo written after 8/1/75, and given contextual relevance, probably sometime during the tax crisis that emerged beginning with Tim Carter's 4/76 letter: F222, CHS.

17. Gene Chaiken, F66, CHS. "Feb. 1, 1977 Grace Stoen and Tim Stoen," tape cassette: CGA. On Jonestown: Tim Stoen, notes, F212, F220, CHS; Charlie Touchette, AI; Mike Touchette, AI. Jan Wilsey, probably embellished autobiographical sketch: F314, CHS.

18. Tim Stoen's account of defection based on homosexuality accusation: SFB, 11/9/79. On the other hand, Mills (1979: 305) reports that Stoen was subjected to similar scrutiny as early as August 1975. If the latter date is correct, it is unlikely that the scrutiny could serve as the basis for defection more than a year and a half later. But Mills's dates, as well as factuality, sometimes seem in doubt. Tim Stoen, calender: CGA. Copy of diary in London: CHS 27. Gene Chaiken, memo to Jim Jones, 12/18/76: F90, CHS. Joel Stoen, 2/16/77 letter to Tim Stoen: Legal—correspondence and notes, CHS. Stephen Sommerhalter, letter to Tim Stoen, 3/24/77, advising him on the New York bar exam: F229A, CHS. Stoen's notes, F220A; 3/25/77 telegram, P2-4-46; mention of "Bev" or "Beverley" in relation to attorney matters: P2-4-21, -27, CHS, and CHS 45. Klineman, Butler, and Conn (1980: 253) give the date of the Banks-Conn meeting, and they are the ones with the surest knowledge of it; Reiterman and Jacobs (1982: 587 n. 46) mistakenly assert that Jones did not know of the meeting at the time; they date Jones's collapse as a reaction to news about Stoen's disappearance, but this too is chronologically inaccurate (as is a reference, p. 319, to "Monday, March 29, 1977"!); Jones's collapse occurred "yesterday" according to the SFC, 3/25/77, article, and the telegram to Paula Adams was not sent until 2:56 P.M. on Friday, March 25, from Trinidad. Use of collapse as excuse for reduced public appearances by Jones: Jean Brown, letters to PF readers, PF correspondence file, CGA. Temple plane ticket records: F544, CHS; Sandy Bradshaw, AI; cf. Reiterman and Jacobs (1982: 318–20).

19. Jones compares Indiana and California migrations: FBI file 01b1b, p. 33. On U.S. embassy knowledge of Guyana's concerns over migration and embassy knowledge of migration interest: GUSEC 671, log 14, described in CFA, 90. Tim Stoen: notes after March trip to England, P2-4-25 to 26, CHS; "To: Jim Jones/ Re: Cde Codette," memo of 4/7/77, F220, CHS; P2-4-23, CHS. Reid's

encouragement and immigration processing: Tim Stoen, notes, P2–4–8 to 10, CHS. Reid's order to Mingo: NYT, 12/24/78. "JR Purifoy—treasury agent," tape cassette, CGA. Freedom of Information Act requests: Gene Chaiken correspondence file, CGA. Prokes meeting described in IRS letter of 4/25/77: FBI file MM.

20. April-May "legal conference": F87, F157, F195, F196, CHS. Temple awareness of anti-"cult" activities dates at least from a 12/7/75 SFC, article in Temple files; cf. Mike Prokes, letter to Daphne Greene, 12/8/75, F312, CHS; and other anti-"cult" clippings, SFC, 12/4–12/12/75, Mike Prokes news clipping file, CGA. Stoen's divorce plans: F91, P2–4–5, CHS. Visit to Grenada by the Temple leadership: F94, F198, F224, CHS. Given a subsequent coup and invasion by U.S. forces, Grenada hardly would have been the haven Jones sought. Tim Stoen, notes apparently during "legal conference" of April-May, 1977: F225, P2–4–14, –19, –49ff., F181, CHS. Mike Touchette, AI.

21. Jim Randolph, deposition for CAG/PT, CHS. Shipment records, purchase orders, and migration files: Jim Randolph file, CGA; Temple migration file, CGA; CHS 8–10, F106, F176, F343, CHS. Permission to import shotguns: Gene Chaiken, memo to Jean Brown, 2/21/75, U.S. vs. Peoples Temple, Ex. 22, vol. III, CHS. Customs distractions: Associated Press, in CDT, 12/5/78. Stoen preparation of guardianship forms: CAG, 10. Other details: member's journal, FBI file HH2, III, 2, 7, 10, 12, 20 (quotation), 27. Antisuicide demonstration: SFC, 5/31/77. Jones's meeting with Newton is discussed in greater detail in chapter 7. Date of Jones's departure: "Flights," CHS 30 and Temple migration records, CHS; Jones's passport, however, shows he did not enter Guyana until July 16, 1977; see CFA, 157. Jones's taped interjections: FBI tape Q358. Airline ticket purchases, bills: U.S. vs. Peoples Temple, Ex. 22, vol. III, CHS. Migration strategy: Sandy Bradshaw, AI. The existence of choice about migration is underscored in interviews conducted by court-appointed Peoples Temple receiver Robert Fabian, e.g. Thom Bogue, Vernon Gosney, Chuck Kirkendale, and Gerald Parks, CAG/PT, CHS.

22. Discussion of motivations for migration follows, in part, John V. Moore, "Peoples Temple and Jonestown, a statement," 12/16/78, F268, CGA. Temple news clipping file, CGA, contained 1974 and 1975 news clippings about the IRS and new religious groups, as well as a SFC, 11/18/74, story, "Secret IRS probe of moderates and radicals." Significantly, the Unification Church leader, the Reverend Sun Myung Moon, later went to prison after being convicted of tax evasion.

23. "Contagious paranoia": Reiterman and Jacobs (1982: 321). On the divisive controversies surrounding primitive Christianity: Meeks (1983). On the Puritans: Dillon (1973). The Swedish followers of Eric Jansson and the German Lutherans' migration to Missouri exhibit the dynamics of religious conflict and migration in almost classic form; see Elmen (1976: esp. 41, 100ff.) and Mikkelsen 1892). Janssonist martyrdom, from Swedish newspaper Norrlands-Poster, 1846, q. in Bishop Hill, Illinois, Museum. On the Missouri Lutherans: Forster (1953: esp. 35, 97, 153). On the development of the Missouri Lutheran Synod: Riddle (1981). On the Mormons: Ahlstrom (1972: 501–9); O'Dea (1957: 115).

*Chapter 10: The Concerned Relatives, the "Concentration Camp," and the "Conspiracy"*

1. On organizations, secrecy, and betrayal: Georg Simmel (1950: 305–76). On Jeannie Mills compensating for her actions within Peoples Temple: Lowell

Streiker, AI; Margaret Singer, AI (associates of Mills after she founded the Human Freedom Center in 1978). Fanaticism of opponents: MG, 7/28/77; cf. Disciples of Christ Peoples Temple Review Committee chairman, SFE, 3/8/79. The "paranoid style" (Hofstadter, 1979) is evoked by materials of both Jeannie Mills and Tim Stoen while they were Temple members: e.g. Mills's memo to Jim Jones after the "gang of eight defection," F240, CHS; Stoen's letter to a fellow lawyer, F344, CHS; Stoen's passing on of Children of God apocalyptic literature to Jim Jones, F366, CHS. Jeannie Mills quotation, AI.

2. Stoen on John Stoen in Guyana: SFE, 11/19/77. Tim Stoen's notes while in Guyana, P2–4, CHS, indicate full participation as a committed individual even as he was plotting his escape. Tim Stoen's Role Construct Repertory test: P2–4–15, CHS. Marceline Jones, P13–1, CHS; Jean Brown, Gene Chaiken, and June Crym, declarations of 8/20/77, CGA. Stoen's 1961 notes describing East Berlin: F210, CHS, and Arapahoe (County) *Herald*, 3/14/61, article, F216, CHS. Report on Stoen's briefcase: "To: JJ/From: TB," CHS 28. Typed transcript of diary: CHS 27. Stoen's conservative doubts about socialism: memo, 10/22/75, F211, CHS. Stoen accused as CIA agent: NYT, 12/7/78, 1/1/79. Paula (Adams), F229E, CHS. Stoen's concerns about prosecution: Stoen's notes, F225, P2–4–20, CHS.

3. Transcript of Stoen 7/13/77 message: F229B, CHS. Stoen's meeting with Grace Stoen and Peoples Temple defectors: Tim Stoen, deposition in opposition to injunction, 8/3/78, PT/TOS, P2–19, CHS; Grace Stoen, declaration filed 8/18/77, in GS/TOS; Jeannie Mills, AI. Stoen portrayed as afraid of Jones: Sally Stapleton, q. in MG, 7/21/77. Stoen's press interviews: UDJ, 8/23/77, in CFA, 327, and Jeannie Mills, AI. Press allegations: Kilduff and Tracy (1979); cf. SRPD, 8/9/77; SFE, 8/24, 8/25/77. On Joe Mazor: LAT 1/21/79. JM/PT named Tim Stoen as a defendant, and the request by plaintiffs for dismissal came only on 3/19/79, after the murders and mass suicide. In September of 1978 Temple attorney Charles Garry came to the conclusion that the defectors had blackmailed Stoen into cooperation, on the basis of their alleged knowledge that Stoen allegedly had embezzled over $1 million of Temple funds. The funds, Garry suggested, were used in turn to finance activities against Peoples Temple; see Charles Garry, "Interview," CIR, 37ff., CHS. Whatever the truth of this thesis, Stoen's turning toward the defectors can be explained as the action of a rational man confronted with other threats to his interests.

4. Investigations: SFE, 8/4/77; SFP, 8/3/77. "Big-name" connections influenced the social services investigation: CAG, 8, 30. Bob Graham, "Memo to: Joe Freitas/ Danny Weinstein/ Re: Peoples Temple," San Francisco District Attorney's Office, 8/28/77. U.S. Customs Service letter, 7/27/77: FBI file MM2–4. Genesis of the Customs investigation in the meetings of David Conn and defectors with reporter George Klineman: CFA, 90, 203–4. Crate loading: Jeannie Mills (1979: 63); *U.S.* vs. *Peoples Temple*, Ex. 22, pp. 12–13, 40, CHS. Customs search: CCR, 73–74; James Randolph, deposition of 9/29/77; F. J. Garmendia, "Reply-a-gram," 12/14/77, Garry letter and Customs response, FBI file MM2. Temple knowledge of Interpol report: CCR, 74; CFA, 25. Summary of Customs investigation: *U.S.* vs. *Peoples Temple*, Ex. 22, pp. 12–13, CHS; F653, CHS. Apparent copy of Interpol report: F59A, CHS, and memo summarizing it: "To: Martha Important/ Re; Interp. Report," F130, CHS.

5. Sharing of investigatory interest between S.F. police and FCC field officer: Rebecca Moore (1985: 294). "Paranoia" theory about Jim Jones: Reiterman and Jacobs (1982); CFA, 18, 20–21. The committee's report belies its own argu-

ment, by naming the individuals at whom Jones's supposed paranoia was directed, thus transferring the explanation from a psychological level to the level of social conflict.

6. On custody and abduction: SFP, 7/31/77, 8/10, 8/12, 8/14/77; SFC, 8/11, 8/12/77; NYT, 5/12/79. Investigation of abduction charges: Bob Graham, "Memo to Joe Freitas/ Danny Weinstein," San Francisco District Attorney's Office, 8/28/77. Mazor's contacts with relatives: Steve Katsaris, AI; LAT, 1/21/79. Mazor request to embassy, Department of State Peoples Temple Freedom of Information Act archive log (hereafter cited as DOS log) 15; CAG, 86–88. On Caroline Looman: U.S. State Department cable (hereafter cited as USSDC), DOS logs 18, 19; Caroline Looman, declaration, 9/2/77; Peoples Temple notes, F123, CHS. McCoy's discussions with Guyanese officials: DOS log 16, described in CCR, 3, 32ff. His visits to Jonestown: CCR, 3–4, 36ff.; CFA, 73–74; GUSEC, 1/18/78, DOS log 79; Richard McCoy, AI.

7. GS/TOS. Haas in Guyana: DOS logs 20, 26, 28, 35, 36, 37, 40, 41, 46, and transcript of tape recording by Charles Garry, 9/14/78, with references to Luckhoo's 1977 defense, F144, CHS. On the September crisis: "Jonestown, Tape 1–4, 9/10/77, 00–403, #15," CGA, and partial transcript of tapes, F311, CHS. Allegation that Ptolemy Reid interfered: "John Victor Stoen," publicity white paper distributed by Tim Stoen to Senator Frank Church, 1/31/78, DOS log 455. Charles Garry, "Interview," CIR, 66, 82, CHS; Garry q.: SFSR, 11/10/77.

8. On U.S. custody proceedings: Debbie Blakey, affidavit of 6/78, in CFA, 312; WP, 11/27/78; Bea Orsot, AI; Mike Touchette, AI; Pat Richartz, AI; Reiterman and Jacobs (1982: 361ff.). Rumors of Stoen's disillusionment: SRPD, 9/26/77; member's journal, FBI file HH2, III, 28 (9/22/77). Onset and tenor of Stoen's involvement with defectors: Steve Katsaris, AI; opponent requesting anonymity, AI. November custody decision: SFE, 11/19/77. Haas correspondence: DOS log 45. Freitas to Burton and reply: DOS logs 408, 410. Ryan to Vance, 12/8/77, and reply: DOS logs 413, 428. Freitas contact with Guyanese officials: SFE, 2/26/78. Leo Ryan and anticult movement: NYT, 11/24/78; Margaret Singer, AI; Shupe and Bromley (1980: 162, 213).

9. Ryan and Temple defectors: Associated Press, in CDT, 12/4/78. Houston story: SFE, 11/13/77, by Tim Reiterman; written Temple records of Reiterman's interview of Phyllis Houston, F41B, CHS and CHS 12; Reiterman and Jacobs (1982: 457). State Department reaction: Elizabeth Powers, memo, 12/8/77, DOS log 412. Other State Department assessment that legal outcome in doubt: GUSEC, 12/23/77, DOS log 54. Guyana custody proceedings: Richard McCoy, memo, 1/6/78, DOS log 449; GUSEC 2435, DOS log 40; GUSEC 3033, DOS log 46; USSDC 4065, DOS log 63; GUSEC 57, DOS log 64. Chronology of Stoen hearings: CCR, 7–8, 11. Account of 1/7/78 hearing, in which Haas believed judge was not unfairly influenced: Burke, GUSEC 57, 1/9/78, DOS log 64. 1/10/78 hearing: DOS log 66. Judge complaint of phone calls also reported in CFA, 129. Jones's paternity claim: GUSEC 201, DOS log 75; GUSEC 202, DOS log 76; GUSEC 270, DOS log 80.

10. Herb Caen: SFC, 1/27/78. Lenora Perkins, letter to John Burke, 1/24/78: DOS log 781. Transvestitism letter signed "G": CHS 13. Walter Duncan, Jr.: declaration prepared for PT/TOS, F85, CHS. Stoen's humiliation, assertions of paternity, assertion he signed a false document, and view of Temple motives: UDJ, 2/27/78; SRPD, 2/26/78; cf. SFE, 2/26/78.

11. On communal child rearing and biological parents: Berger (1981); Zicklin

(1983: ch. 4). California law described by Congressman Paul McCloskey: letter, 3/2/78, F360B, CHS. Carolyn Layton, q. in Rebecca Moore (1985: 286). Statistics on guardianships: CAG 80; Department of State list of deaths in Jonestown, analyzed in Wiencek (n.d.), F658, CHS.

12. "Dismantling": Steve Katsaris, AI. On Mazor, Stoen and real estate suits: SFE, 8/19, 8/24/77; LAT, 1/21/79; F118, CHS.

13. Embassy constraints: CCR, 20–23, 36. Debriefing after visits: CCR, 35. Blacken's memo suppressed: CFA, 127. On U.S. intelligence operations: Agee (1975). Dwyer is identified as having intelligence experience in the 1968 edition of the German publication *Who's Who in the CIA*; McCoy had served as a member of a U.S. Air Force counterintelligence team before joining the State Department; John Burke, a career diplomat who had served in trouble spots in Southeast Asia and the Caribbean before coming to Guyana as ambassador, was "detailed to the Intelligence Community Staff of the Directorate of Central Intelligence a year after the Jonestown tragedy"; information on intelligence community connections developed by Rebecca Moore (1985: 411–13). Avoidance of surveillance appearance: USSDC, 1/20/78, DOS log 81.

14. Oliver boys: interview transcripts, F15, CHS; declaration, 11/23/77, California Superior Court, San Francisco, case #97683; CCR, 7. Phone patch between Micki Touchette and Charlie Touchette, 12/3/77, F33, CHS; transcripts of children's interviews, 2/4/78, F74, CHS; letters to Charles Garry, F486, F495, F496, CHS. Donna Ponts letter: DOS log 566.

15. On Steve and Maria Katsaris: Steven Katsaris, affidavit, 4/4/78, reprinted in Kerns (1979: 252ff.); Steven Katsaris, AI; cf. Steve Katsaris, early conciliatory letter to Maria, 4/1/75, F154, CHS; Richard McCoy, memo to file, 9/19/77, DOS log 394; letter from Maria to Steve Katsaris before September trip, F358B, CHS. Stoen and Maria Katsaris conservatorship possibility: declarations of Harriet Tropp and Gene Chaiken, 10/10/78, F195, F196, CHS. Account of September visit of Katsaris: Richard McCoy, 9/29/77 memo, DOS log 397; Temple memo, F519, CHS; CCR, 6. Kidnapping effort: Steve Katsaris, AI.

16. Stoen's lobbying efforts and views on custody battle: SRPD, 2/26/78; "John Victor Stoen" white paper, 1/31/78, DOS log 455. Mailgram of Stoen noted: USSDC, 2/10/78, DOS log 90; State Department officer notes, "Stone [*sic*]/Katsaris," 1/27/78, CFA, 129; USSDC, 1/27, 2/4/78, DOS logs 82, 86; the embassy view on the proposed guarantee of custody-order enforcement is contained in a classified cable from Georgetown (either DOS log 84 or 85), and is inferred from the State Department response. Temple visitors to State Department: 2/16/78 memo, DOS log 501; Charles Garry, 2/10/78 letter, DOS log 484. Length of time for court decision and assurances of noninterference: DOS logs 92, 457, 494, 689, 784. State Department background briefing, 2/20/78: DOS log 503. Memo on information sheets, and information sheets, 2/78: DOS logs 508, 609. Stoen letters on repatriation, 3/2, 3/3/78, and GUSEC 5/6/67, DOS logs 521, 104, 521. Unreleased DOS cable traffic during March and April may shed further light on this matter.

17. Publicity efforts: Steve Katsaris, AI; SRPD, 4/12/78; (Concerned Relatives,) "Accusation of human rights violations by Rev. James Warren Jones . . . ," in Kerns (1979: 239ff.). Pamela Moton, letter to Congress, 3/14/77: DOS log 524. Concerned Relatives' statements publicly discussing mass suicide and mass murder, and Tim Stoen's recruiting efforts: Frances Muchnick, declaration, 5/8/78, F179, CHS; Mae Janaro, declaration, 10/9/78, for PT/TOS, F97, CHS.

Jessie McNeal and Tim Stoen, transcript of telephone conversation, around 5/30/78: F182, CHS. "Charles, these are questions to you from Jim," undated memo written no earlier than 5/78: F173, CHS. "Signatures of petitioners for elimination of human rights violations . . . ," in Kerns (1979: 275ff.). Statistics developed by comparison with Jonestown migration list, CHS, and Wooden (1981). According to CSS 14 and CAG 33, 54, 69, 80, 98, Wooden is incorrect in claims that large numbers of children were brought to Jonestown illegally. Steve Katsaris: q. in UDJ, 4/12/78.

18. On the suits: Steve Katsaris, AI; SRPD, 6/26/78; MG, 7/20/78; SK/JJ; JC/PT; *Wade and Mabel Medlock* vs. *Peoples Temple*, California Superior Court, Los Angeles, case #C243292 (hereafter cited as WM/JJ); cf. LAT, 6/9/78.

19. Temple essays and PR materials: "Dear Members of the [International Human Rights] Commission," unsigned draft, CHS 2A; Sharon Amos, "My experience of Jonestown," and undated revised version, printed in MG, F37, CHS; Richard Tropp, "The meaning of the Peoples Temple 'exposé': a viewpoint," 2/15/78, and "Notes from the last frontier," F334, F460, CHS. "Concerned parents . . ." leaflet, F128A, CHS. "Campaign mail" by members of Peoples Temple attained a visible profile in the State Department's overall mail tabulations; see "Public mail reports," DOS logs 623–29. Temple smear rumor: P1–1, CHS. Plan to lobby Congress: letters written by or on behalf of Peoples Temple, FBI file MM7–1 to 12a. Mercenary rumor: UDJ, 4/13/78.

20. Peoples Temple press releases: 4/18/78, 5/10/78, P1–2, –3, CHS. Press q. of press release: SRPD, 5/19/78. Temple frustration with press: Sandy Bradshaw, AI. "Documents which support allegations that Stoen acted as P.T. attorney," "These are things I would not necessarily want to use in court," and related court case responses: F94, F95, CHS. Garry's account of suit and allegation of embezzlement: "Interview," CIR, 39ff., and AI. Leaflet: (Concerned Relatives,) May 1978, F183, CHS. Tim Stoen: 8/3/78 declaration for PT/TOS, P2–8, CHS.

21. "Screening" statement by Jonestown staff: q. in Moore (1985: 255–56). Disciples committeeman q.: SFE, 4/8/79. Embassy views on conditions at Jonestown: Frank Tumminia, CFA, 137; McCoy assessment, 1/18/78, DOS log 79; Blacken view, CCR, 41–42. Tumminia thought many people "appeared drugged and robot-like in their reactions," but qualified his view as "a personal reaction probably influenced by what I had read about religious brainwashing." Comments on Stoen, and credibility problems: CCR, 31, 22, 47–48. McCoy, q. in Moore (1985: 368).

22. McCoy on work: CCR, 40. Crowding at Peace Missions: Weisbrot (1983: 127). On work, social organization of time, and diet at the Farm and other large-scale contemporary communities: Hall (1978). The compact, mostly public space design and physical crowding of Jonestown is described by Moore (1985: 73–77). Work organization: purchase orders, Jim Randolph file, CGA; Mike Touchette, AI; Laura Johnston, letter, circa 1979, F177, CHS. On diet: letters from Jonestown, F265–67, CHS; Madeline Brooks q.: Moore (1985: 202); Vern Gosney, Diane Louie, CAG/PT, CHS; Jim Bogue q.: *Newsweek*, December 4, 1978 (on Jonestown's efforts to deal with dietary difficiencies, see FBI file J3e). Visit of embassy staff, 11/7/78: CFA, 143; cf. notes on agriculture, "Guyana Coordinating Committee" file, CHS. The dull but adequate diet sounds neither better nor worse than I encountered in visits to the Krishna community in West Virginia and The Farm in Tennessee. Cottage industry schemes: Tim Stoen,

P2-4-55, CHS. Comparative references on self-sufficiency: Hall (1978: ch. 5); Bennett Berger (1981). On agricultural achievements, cash cropping and work: letters from Jonestown, CGA; P1, CHS; and Tropp's letter of transmittal, public relations file, CGA; AID officer q.: CCR, 38; Moore (1985: 201-4); Mike Touchette, AI. Viability of the site suggested by the interest, after the mass suicide, of Billy Graham, who wanted to use Jonestown to settle Laotian refugees: NYT, 3/30/80; Laurie Efrein, letter to the U.N., 4/22/80, F153, CHS.

23. Representative readings of the news and leftist analyses of international political economy: FBI tapes Q284, Q317, Q429, Q937. Attitude of seniors concerning news: Mike Touchette, AI. "Labor theory of value" question, Rebecca Moore, personal communication to author. Jones on solidarity: FBI tape Q937, probably recorded 12/77. Decline of faith healing and image of Jones as "god," and confinement conditions: Bea Orsot, AI; Mike Touchette, AI; Gerry Parks q. in SFE, 11/28/78; ITT, 12/13 and 12/20/78; CAG, 11; NYT, 11/22/78; Moore (1985: 220-21, 308-11). Estimate of number of people wanting to receive outside help to escape at less than 2 per cent: defector Gerald Parks, deposition for CAG/PT, CHS. Justification of monitoring: F98, CHS. Demand for monitoring: FBI tape Q284. An example of a call for solidarity: FBI tape Q284. Coaching of presentation to visitors: FBI tape Q317.

24. Preference for humiliation as punishment: FBI tape Q 937. Punishment of Tommy Bogue: account of Ron Crawford, CAG, 11. "Learning crew" roster: FBI file PP9-K1-2. New Brigade, greased rope pit, and other punishments: Stephan Jones (1979); FBI tape Q284; Vern Gosney, Dale Parks, Monica Bagby, Julius Evans, Gerald Parks, Chuck Kirkendale, Thom Bogue, all in depositions for CAG/PT, CHS. Punishment and pressures to mock religion: FBI tape Q597. Underground box and claim of exaggeration: Stephan Jones (1979); SFC, 6/15/78; Moore (1985: 309-10). Assessment of pharmacy: Dr. Leslie Mootoo, AI. Bonded pharmacy records: FBI file J1-3. Forms of punishment, rarity of physical punishment, use of "Extended Care Unit": Jones q. on "controls," Moore (1985: 310-11); Dale Parks, in NYT, 12/29/78; Monica Bagby, Dale Parks, depositions for CAG/PT, CHS; Dr. Leslie Mootoo, AI; Stephan Jones (1979); SFE, 8/30/81; Charles Garry, AI. Ryan, q. in Krause (1978: 21).

25. The Millses set up shortwave monitoring in April or May of 1977: Steve Katsaris, AI. About the same time, on the basis of amateur radio operators' complaints, the Federal Communications Commission began monitoring Temple transmissions; the FBI requested FCC monitoring on 9/11/77, when the Treasury investigation was at its peak; see CCR, 75; FBI file MM4-1 to 9; CFA, 207; Moore (1985: 296); FBI monitoring request on FCC released materials, G9, CHS. Leo Ryan, letter to Guy Young, 5/15/78: F209, CHS. On the Temple reaction to Ryan's letter: Mike Prokes, F116, CHS. On the 5/10/78 visit and embassy speculations about the collapse of Jonestown: CFA, 146; CCR, 25, 43. On Jones's drug use: Stephan Jones q., CDT, 11/22/78; WP, 11/7/83; Richard McCoy, cited by Moore (1985: 307). Blakey statement on suicide, 5/12/78: CFA, 304-5. Blakey defection and subsequent events: Blakey deposition for CAG/PT, CHS; Yee and Layton (1981: 235ff.); GUSEC, 5/15/78, DOS log 116; CCR, 50ff.; CFA, 68. Request to approach Guyanese government: John Burke GUSEC, 6/6/78, DOS log 126; reply, USSDC, 6/26/78, DOS log 130. Cable held misunderstood, CCR, 65. McCoy claim that cable was understood by State Department, Moore (1985: 371).

26. On Blakey's associations after defection: Yee and Layton (1981: 265ff.). Blakey

affidavit reprinted in Krause (1978: 187ff.); and another account by her, deposition for CAG/PT, CHS. Other accounts of suicide drill and reaction: Chuck Kirkendale, Thom Bogue, Dale Parks, Gerald Parks, depositions for CAG/PT, CHS; Mike Touchette, AI. The suicide drill Blakey saw, sources agree, was the only such event. Jeffrey Haas, letters to State Department: 6/15/78, DOS logs 573–75. State Department mishandling of Blakey affidavit: CCR, 55ff.

27. Blakey stories: SFC, 6/15/78; SRPD, 6/19, 6/22/78. SRPD arrangement for Hunter free-lance stories: John Riley, letter to Charles Garry, 6/15/78, F429, CHS. Hunter visit: UDJ, 5/26, 5/28, 5/29/78; SRPD, 5/28/78; SFE, 5/26, 5/27, 5/30/78; Hunter diary of visit, GC, 12/6/78; FBI tape Q284. KGO television story transcript on Hunter's return, 5/26/78, and other Temple materials on incident: F417, F132, F326, CHS. Rebuttal to Hunter charges, and Hunter's allegations of intimidating incidents in United States: SRPD, 6/27/78.

28. Charles Garry, letters to newspapers, 5/27, 6/17/78, F32, F40, CHS; cf. accusations by Lisa Layton, affidavit, 7/6/78, and others, legal files, CGA; F163, CHS. Reward advertisement: UDJ, 7/31/78; F394, CHS. Headline retraction: SRPD, 8/3/78. "Refutation of Deborah Blakey's affidavit," F92, CHS. Prokes on Temple as victim of conspiracy: q. in F297A, CHS. Other sources: Charles Garry, AI; Debbie Blakey, deposition for CAG/PT, CHS. Scientology documents on Interpol and the FBI: Mike Prokes news clipping file, CGA. Jones eulogy and doubts: FBI files O1B–14 and G1a–2f; grave marker, NYT, 10/11/79. On Blakey, and the changes at Jonestown around May and June 1978: FBI file G1a–2b; Mike Touchette, AI; Bea Orsot, AI; Sandy Bradshaw, AI.

29. Jeffrey Haas, letter to State Department, 6/15/78: DOS log 574. Embassy view of delays: Richard McCoy, letter of 5/2/78, DOS log 786. Judge's decision to step aside: GUSEC, 8/16, 8/18/78, DOS logs 135, 140. Temple strategies about the custody case, and possible departure of child from Guyana, possible return of Jones to the United States to face trial: F173, CHS. Temple initiatives on migration: FBI files G and GG; see especially a letter to "Charles," describing the political situation in Guyana, and Temple options, G1a–2a, and fears of U.S. pressure, FBI file MM8–10b. Continuing projects at Jonestown through early November 1978 are indicated by purchase orders for large quantities of food, medical equipment, and other supplies and equipment: Jim Randolph file, CGA; F136, CHS. Decline of agriculture: Mike Touchette, AI. Gordon Lindsay in Guyana: GUSEC, 6/20/78, DOS log 129, and interview with John Moore, 8/9/78, "Summary," F380, CHS. Temple wariness of press and overflight: F173, CHS; FBI file G1a–2c; cf. *National Enquirer* Freedom of Information request, CFA, 697.

30. Pat Richartz, in Charles Garry, "Interview," CIR, 57. Don Freed, Jonestown guestbook, 8/24/78: CFA, 104. Other inspirational remarks: "Two broadcasts of Don Freed—B10"; Freed speaking in Jonestown, tape cassettes, CGA. Mazor may have continued to work for Temple opponents on a clandestine basis after the fall of 1977, when various kidnapping projects were being considered or undertaken. He claimed so, and conceivably is the person identified as "J.M." described in handwritten notes, 2/9/78, as discrediting Peoples Temple and its leader; the notes were in possession of the embassy: DOS log 783. St. Francis Hotel meeting, 9/5/78: F118, CHS. Later, 10/17/78, Mazor executed an affidavit, F71, CHS, on Jones's paternity of John Stoen; its accuracy was disputed by Grace Stoen, in Reiterman and Jacobs (1982: 437). Donald Freed, "Confidential to Charles Garry and Jim Jones," 9/5/78: F43, CHS.

31. Charles Garry, transcript of tape cassette to Jim Jones, 9/14/78: F144, CHS, and AI. Mazor visit: GUSEC, 11/24/78, DOS log 278; Mike Touchette, AI. Lane's theories taken from St. Francis Hotel meeting, F118, CHS; cf. NYT, 2/4/79. "Mark Lane notes, 9/17/78," and Mark Lane, "Counter offensive": P7-1, CHS. Lane's Georgetown press conference, 9/19/78: GUSEC, 9/23, 9/29/78, DOS logs 142, 145; partial transcript, F140, CGA. Lane's subsequent San Francisco press conference: SFE, 10/4/78, SFC, 10/4/78, SFP, 10/4/78. Jim Jones, letter to Jimmie Carter, 9/25/78: F263, CHS; it is not clear whether the letter actually was sent. "B5," tape cassette of Mark Lane talk to San Francisco Peoples Temple on return from Jonestown, CGA.

## *Chapter 11: The Apocalypse at Jonestown*

1. Prokes: q. in SFC, 3/14/79. Children on death, and Jones illness: NYT, 2/25/79. Jones's ramblings: "Instructions given Monday, October 16, 1978," F126, CHS. Visitors' log: CFA, 103ff. Visit of Marceline Jones's parents for three weeks, through 11/12/78: RPI, 11/21/78. Alliance of youth: Mike Touchette, AI; Pat Richartz, AI; Charles Garry, AI; Stephan Jones, q. in WP, 11/7/83.
2. The Concerned Relatives and Ryan: Holly Morton, AI; Keith Harrari, AI; Lowell Streiker, AI; Margaret Singer, AI (Human Freedom Center staff and board members); Steve Katsaris, AI; Jackie Speier, deposition for CAG/PT, CHS. On Clare Bouquet's initial contact with Tim Stoen: Brian Bouquet, letter sent to SFE, 3/9/78, Peoples Temple, Legal—media—libel, CHS; Reiterman and Jacobs (1982: 411). Stoen passing information on morals charge to Ryan: LACA, 21–22. Stoen telegram, DOS log 588, and phone conversation, 10/3/78, DOS log 587, reported in USSDC, 10/6/78, DOS log 147. Ryan September meeting at State Department: Richard McCoy, briefing memo, 9/12/78, DOS log 586; 9/22/78 USSDC, DOS log 141; CCR, 76–77.
3. Further trip plans: CCR, 78ff.; GUSEC, 9/25, 9/26, 11/2, 11/5/78, and department cables, 10/10, 11/1/78 (2), DOS logs 143, 144, 158, 160, 149, 155, 156; CFA, pp. 43ff. Gordon Lindsay, Don Harris, and NBC crew: GC, 12/6/78; NYT, 2/4/79; Leigh Wilson, AI; Shirley Humphrey (wife of Don Harris) and Constance Brown (wife of Bob Brown), depositions for CAG/PT, CHS. Speier concern about Moon, Jones: State Department staff member notes, meeting of 11/9/78, DOS log 703. Leo Ryan, letter to Jim Jones, 11/1/78: CFA, 49. Buford's departure and Tim Carter infiltrating Concerned Relatives: Teri Buford, F171, CHS; Teri Buford, deposition for CAG/PT, CHS; Pat Richartz and Charles Garry in Charles Garry, "Interview," CIR, 86–88; Pat Richartz, AI; Charles Garry, AI; Steve Katsaris, AI; Tim Carter, q. in SFE, 11/28/78; NYT, 12/11/78. Pat Richartz: letter, 11/13/78, F125, CHS. NBC crew contact with Guyanese embassy in Washington sometime before 11/7: State Department memo, 11/7/78, DOS log 595.
4. On Lane: F167, CHS; radio traffic log and translation, and Jean Brown deposition, F300, CHS; Charles Garry, AI; FBI file NN. Ryan, Kilduff, and Brown: F302, CHS; SFC, 11/8/78. State Department knowledge of Derwinski's declining participation: USSDC, 11/1/78, DOS log 156. Don Edwards: q. in Moore (1985: 313). Mark Lane, 11/6/78 letter to Leo Ryan, and Ryan reply, 11/10/78: CFA, 52–56. Bonnie Thielmann's preparations and trip: Thielmann and Merrill (1979: 113ff.). Don Harris at Peoples Temple: F365B, CHS. Final State

Department briefing and anticipation of "friction," violence: DOS log 1779; CCR, 59, 82ff.; CFA, 24–25, 71; GUSEC, 11/2/78, DOS log 158.

5. General sources: CCR, 83ff., SFC, 11/15, 11/16, 11/17/78; SFE, 11/15, 11/16/78; Theilmann and Merrill (1979: 125). Consular visit to Jonestown: CFA, 143, 229ff. State Department-approved "press guidance" statement released by embassy, 11/15/78: DOS log 600. Temple press release, dated 11/13/78, apparently released 11/15/78: in GUSEC, 11/16/78, DOS log 168. Garry on Lane, contacts with Lamaha Gardens, Jonestown: F168, CHS; Charles Garry, AI; Pat Richartz, AI; Charles Garry, "Interview," CIR; Gene Chaiken, F141, CHS. Encounter between Dwyer and Ryan's aides coming in from airport, and Dwyer's account of logistics: USSDC, 12/16/78, giving text of State Department letter to Rep. Clement Zablocki, chair, U.S. House of Representatives Committee on Foreign Affairs, contained in Ex. 16–17 (vol. III), documents produced by United States in *U.S.* vs. *Peoples Temple*, CHS. Account of 11/16/78 meeting of Ambassador Burke with Concerned Relatives and threat of force: GUSEC, 11/17/78, DOS log 169. The embassy already had investigated the government checks issued a year earlier and found nothing illegal: CFA, 33–34, 710ff. Trip to Guyana police: Theilmann and Merrill (1979: 130). Steve Katsaris, AI; ticket given to Katsaris by Doug Ellice, 11/17/78: DOS log 789.

6. The account of the trip to Jonestown draws on Guyana Information Officer Neville Annibourne, "Saturday night horror," GC, 12/6/78; see also Charles Garry, "Interview," CIR, 82ff.; SFE, 11/21/78; depositions by Charles Garry, Vernon Gosney, Monica Bagby, Jackie Speier, Julius Evans, Diane Louie, Thom Bogue, Gerald Parks, for CAG/PT, CHS. Jones on evening of November 16, 1978, q. in SFE, 10/15/86. Jones overheard arguing with Sharon Amos: Monica Bagby, deposition for CAG/PT, CHS. Coaching by Jann Gurvitch and estimated number of Jonestown residents staging Ryan's visit: Vernon Gosney, deposition for CAG/PT, CHS. Rhoades and Wilson carrying footlocker, supposedly to a shed near Jones's cottage: Feinsod (1981: 180).

7. For general sources, see previous footnote. See also: Dale Parks, Vernon Gosney, Gerald Parks, Constance Brown, depositions for CAG/PT, CHS; Reiterman and Jacobs (1982: 524ff.).

8. Suicide rehearsal note: SFE, 12/17/78. Tape of last hour: Peoples Temple (1979). Jesus paraphrased: from John 10:17–18; a similar paraphrasing by Jones is to be found in a 1984 sermon on FBI tape Q1059 pt. 5. Reference to ancient Greece may allude to an incident during the Peloponnesian War; see chapter 12, note 4. Martin Luther King speech q.: NYT, 10/19/86, p. 6E. Certain details: Tim Carter, q. in SFE, 11/28/78; Charles Garry, deposition for CAG/PT, CHS; Dr. Leslie Mootoo, Guyanese forensic pathologist, AI; Odell Rhoades and Stanley Clayton, in Feinsod (1981: 187ff.); Reiterman and Jacobs (1982: 555ff.); Moore (1985: 329–38). Accounts by Mark Lane are not used because they fail to triangulate with details of disparate other accounts that basically agree with one another. Location of drugs, Fla-Vor-Aid, cyanide: Dale Parks, Gerald Parks, depositions for CAG/PT, CHS. Reiterman and Jacobs (1982: 474) indicate the cyanide was brought in by boat Wednesday, 11/15/78. Agreement with Soviet Union mentioned by Jones, 10/16/78: F126, CHS. "Udjara" as Don Sly: Feinsod (1981: 190). Annie Moore's note: Moore (1985: 336–38); cf. NYT, 12/18/78.

*Chapter 12: After Jonestown*

1. George Gallup: q. in Wooden (1981: 192). On the emergence of popular mass media interpretations: Weightman (1983: 165ff.). Discussion of mythology draws on Barthes (1972: 121ff.; quotation, 128). On the nonempirical truth in myth: Raglan (1958: 123). For a study that demonstrates methods for analyzing mythic structures and their historical presuppositions: Alker, Lehnert, and Schneider (1984).

2. Amos's murders and suicide: Bea Orsot, AI. Prokes's suicide: Mike Touchette, AI; SFC, 3/15/79. Survivors' reactions: Chuck Kirkendale, deposition for CAG/PT, CHS; Mike Touchette, AI; Bea Orsot, AI; Sandy Bradshaw, AI; Debbie Touchette, AI; Human Freedom Center psychologist Lowell Streiker, AI; Stephan Jones (1979); WP, 11/7/83.

3. Hit squads: Bea Orsot, AI; Steve Katsarsis, AI; CDT, 11/22/78, NYT, 12/22/78. Branham's death: Harrell (1975: 164). Certitude about Jones's death: CDT, 11/22/78, IS, 11/23/78. Death toll and jungle search: SFC, 11/22/78; LCJ, 11/22/78; NYT, 11/26/78. Firearms: LCJ, 11/21/78; Associated Press and WP News Services, respectively, in CDT, 12/5, 12/16/78. There are discrepancies in the total number of weapons, with the highest count at forty-five reportedly including five M-16 semiautomatic rifles and an AK-47 automatic rifle. The count cited is by the U.S. State Department. Elderly survivors, handling of the bodies, Jones's cremation, and ghost sighting: CDT, 11/25, 11/29/78; Steve Katsaris, AI; Rebecca Moore (1985: 29-50); IS, 11/25/78; member's journal, FBI file HH2, II, 155 (Jones prophecy about burial); RPI, 11/19/78; *National Enquirer*, 6/19/79. Disposition of Temple assets: SFC, 3/15/79, 3/23, 7/11/83, SFE, 11/22/81.

4. Jones's opposition to suicide: tape cassette B23, "Jim Jones and Grace Stoen" (1976), CGA; cf. Jones's participation in Golden Gate Bridge rally, discussed in chapter 9. Suicide: Durkheim (1952). People at Jonestown engage in a discussion of Durkheim's theories on FBI tape Q617. Thucydides's description of the mass suicide is described in a note, "Attorney—Tim Stoen/ from Lydia Schadan," undated, but presumably prior to Stoen's 1977 defection, CHS 5; cf. Thucydides (1959: III, 81). Martyrdom as suicide: Battin (1982: 67ff., esp. 71).

5. Frend (1967: esp. 41, 220). A recent study of Masada, with Josephus's history: Yadin (1966). Social control in early Christian martyrdom: Riddle (1931). Augustine and the martyrs: Battin (1982: 71).

6. Frend (1967: 57); cf. Lanternari (1963: 308). Weber (1977: 494).

7. Frend (1967: 58ff.); a more precise and detailed study, which offers a fascinating argument about Hellenistic influences, is that of Williams (1975).

8. Frend (1967: x); on charisma: Weber (1977: 1111ff.).

9. Ross Case, AI.

10. See, e.g., Cohn (1970); Lewy (1974).

11. Hall (1978: 206-7).

12. Lifton (1968).

13. Meerloo (1962: 67ff.) explores the psychological dynamics of such collective acts.

14. "Contingency conspiracy" theory described in CFA, 26.

15. Steve Katsaris, AI; Jim Jones, q. by Neville Annibourne, GC, 12/6/78.

16. Faction of Jonestown that wanted violence: Tim Carter, q. in SFE, 11/28/78.

## 358     Gone from the Promised Land

Survivors and observers believing Jones ordered airstrip attack: Mike Touchette, AI; Charles Touchette, AI; Debbie Touchette, AI. Larry Layton denial that
Jones ordered him to attack people at airport: WP, 12/14/78; CDT, 12/14/78;
LCJ, 12/21/78. Murder and suicide: West (1966). Old Believers: Crummey
(1970: 51); Tom Robbins was the one who first suggested the "Old Believers"
parallel to me in the early 1980s; after I had written the present chapter, he
showed me a draft of his subsequently published, much more extensive, comparison (1986).

17. Suicide meeting: Peoples Temple (1979). Annie Moore note: Moore (1986:
336–38); cf. NYT, 12/18/78.

18. Moses (1982).

19. Layton was acquitted of attempted murder charges in Guyana in 1980; he then
stood trial in the United States for conspiring to murder Leo Ryan, and a trial
completed in 1981 resulted in a hung jury and Layton's release. A third trial of
Layton in 1986 resulted in the conviction of Layton for conspiring to murder
Ryan; Sacramento *Bee*, 9/12/85, 10/15, 12/2/86; SFC, 5/23/80, 9/28, 10/2/81;
SFE, 8/10/83, 5/10/84, 10/15, 11/19/86; NYT, 9/21, 10/11, 11/19, 12/2/86;
WP 3/4/87. For commentary on the threat of "cults" in the aftermath of the
deaths: George Will, CDT, 11/25/78; *U.S. News and World Report*, December
4, 1978, pp. 23–24; William Randolph Hearst, in SFE, 12/10/78; WP, 12/16/78
news report about interdenominational reaction to "pseudo-religious cults."

20. Temple publicists who advanced their views include Richard Tropp, F334,
CHS, prior to November 1978, and Mike Prokes, F116, CHS.

21. Debbie Blakey: q. in SFC, 5/14/81. Parallels between Temple organization and
the operations at Human Freedom Center have been noted by Charles Garry,
AI; Lowell Streiker, AI. Jeannie Mills and her husband Al were murdered on
February 26, 1980, apparently in a development unconnected to Peoples Temple; suspicions focused on their son Edward, but charges were never brought for
lack of usable evidence; see SFC, 2/27, 2/29, 3/3, 3/11/80; NYT, 2/28, 2/29/80;
SFE, 8/10/83. The Temple notes by Lydia Schadan on Thucydides's account of
mass suicide, CHS 5, bear the handwritten notation: "Lydia—Do *not* pursue
this. See me. TOS." On Temple perceptions of Stoen's motives: for example,
Sandy Bradshaw, AI. Grace Stoen, National Public Radio, Washington, D.C.,
call-in program on Peoples Temple, 4/23/81.

22. The charges and countercharges between Garry and Lane center on the ethics
of Lane in various activities prior to November 18, 1978, and on revelations of
foreknowledge about the danger of poisoning in statements Lane allegedly
made to Garry and others after the suicides; see LAT, 12/4/78, SFC, 1/4/79,
NYT, 1/12, 2/4, 4/26/79, Hampton Roads (Va.) *Daily Press*, 12/26/79; Lane
(1980). The most direct criticism of Ryan came from Representative Don
Edwards (Calif.), q. in Moore (1985: 313) and a freelance consultant, David
Bradwell, letter to Congressman Edward Beard, F264, CHS.

23. On Dick Gregory: *The Black Panther*, 12/30/78; LAT News Service, in CDT,
4/20/80. CIA theories have been advanced (1) from the Left and Right and the
general public, e.g. *Workers World*, 12/13/78; *The Black Panther*, 12/30/78;
F29, F152, CHS; (2) by relatives and survivors of Peoples Temple, e.g. by Sandy
Bradshaw, AI, and Rebecca Moore (1985: ch. 16); and (3) by victims' relatives
and friends, e.g. Ryan's aide, Joe Holsinger, and Ryan's family, who brought
wrongful death suits against the U.S. government, *Christopher Ryan et al.* vs.
*U.S.A.*, U.S. Dist. Ct. No. Cal. C80–3137 and C81–4077 (SAW). Among possi-

ble CIA agents proposed are Jones, Phillip Blakey (who allegedly worked as a mercenary in the CIA effort in Angola before joining Peoples Temple), and Temple aide Paula Adams and her lover, Guyanese ambassador to the United States Laurance Mann; Temple suspicion may have centered on *National Enquirer* reporter Gordon Lindsay as well. State Department cable traffic shows that Mann passed information in all directions: to his own government, to the U.S. government and its embassy, and to Peoples Temple. In 1983 Mann murdered Adams, and then committed suicide; WP, 11/6/83.

24. The most succinct indictment of the deaths as murder occurs in a factually telescoped and erroneous flyer, "It was murder!" attributed to the Concerned Relatives, F278, CHS. The discussion of evil follows the social action perspective, looking to actors' definitions of evil, rather than attempting an "objective" definition. However, for a sociological definition of evil as the creation of alienation, see Becker (1968: 135ff.).

25. Steve Katsaris, AI; Reiterman and Jacobs (1982: 579–80, 592–93).

26. On *ressentiment* (resentment) of apostates, see Scheler (1961: 66ff.); Hofstadter (1979: 34) discusses the psychology of vicarious fantasy in "paranoid" political movements.

27. Steve Katsaris, AI.

28. For an exhaustive study of scapegoating as the transference of evil: Frazer (1935); see also Girard (1986). On the positive and negative cult: Durkheim (1947).

29. On the anticult movement: Bromley and Shupe (1981). The conversion of Shannon Ryan (who changed her name to Ma Amirta Pritam) is described in SFE, 4/26/81. Recently Bhagwan Shree Rajneesh revealed that purged members of his personal staff had engaged in monitoring and manipulation practices that he wished to disavow and he abruptly left the United States; see Seattle *Post-Intelligencer*, 9/21, 9/22, 9/29/85.

30. On the double psychology of resentment: Scheler (1961: 75).

31. See chapters 9 through 11. The Temple's opponents resemble other "counter-subversive movements" characterized by a "paranoid style"; see Hofstadter (1979: 33–34).

32. On scapegoating as cleansing: Frazer (1935).

33. Joseph Conrad (1967).

# Bibliography

Agee, Phillip. 1975. *Inside the Company*. New York: Stonehill.

Ahlberg, Sture. 1980. *Folkets Tempel*. Stockholm: Gummessons.

Ahlstrom, Sydney E. 1972. *A Religious History of the American People*. New Haven: Yale University Press.

Alker, Hayward R., Jr., Wendy G. Lehnert, and Daniel K. Schneider. 1984. "Two reinterpretations of Toynbee's Jesus: Explorations in computational hermeneutics." Department of Political Science, Massachusetts Institute of Technology.

Andrews, Edward D. 1972. *The Community Industries of the Shakers*. Charlestown, Mass.: Emporium (1933).

Anthony, Dick, and Thomas Robbins. 1981. "New religions, families, and "brainwashing." In *In Gods We Trust: New Patterns of Religious Pluralism in America*, edited by Thomas Robbins and Dick Anthony, pp. 263–74. New Brunswick, N.J.: Transaction Books.

Appel, Willa. 1983. *Cults in America: Programmed for Paradise*. New York: Holt, Rinehart & Winston.

Barthes, Roland. 1972. *Mythologies*. New York: Hill & Wang (1957).

Barzun, Jacques, and Henry F. Graff. 1985. *The Modern Researcher*. 4th ed. N.Y.: Harcourt Brace Jovanovitch.

Bastide, Roger. 1978. *The African Religions of Brazil*. Baltimore: Johns Hopkins University Press (1960).

Battin, M. Pabst. 1982. *Ethical Issues in Suicide*. Englewood Cliffs, N.J.: Prentice-Hall.

Becker, Ernest. 1975. *The Structure of Evil*. New York: Free Press.

Beckford, James A. 1975. *Trumpet of Prophecy: A Sociological Study of Jehovah's Witnesses*. Oxford: Basil Blackwell.

Bendix, Reinhard. 1974. *Work and Authority in Industry*. Berkeley: University of California Press (1956).

Benson, J. Kenneth. 1975. "The interorganizational network as a political economy." *Administrative Science Quarterly* 20: 229–49.

Berger, Bennett M. 1981. *The Survival of a Counterculture: Ideological Work and Everyday Life among Rural Communards*. Berkeley: University of California Press.

Berger, Peter. 1967. *The Sacred Canopy*. Garden City, N.Y.: Doubleday.

———. 1974. *The Homeless Mind*. New York: Vintage.

Berger, Peter, and Thomas Luckmann. 1966. *The Social Construction of Reality*. New York: Doubleday.

Bestor, Arthur. 1970. *Backwoods Utopias: The Sectarian Origins and*

*Owenite Phase of Communitarian Socialism in America, 1663–1829.*
2d ed. Philadelphia: University of Pennsylvania Press (1950).

Bird, Caroline. 1962. "Nine places to hide: The small world is getting smaller." *Esquire* 57 (January): 55–57, 128–32.

Bird, Frederick, and Bill Reimer. 1982. "Participation rates in new religious and para-religious movements." *Journal for the Scientific Study of Religion* 21: 1–14.

Bittle, William E., and Gilbert Geis. 1964. *The Longest Way Home.* Detroit: Wayne State University Press.

Blair, Thomas L. 1977. *Retreat to the Ghetto: The End of a Dream?.* New York: Hill & Wang.

Boorstin, Daniel J. 1962. *The Image, or What Happened to the American Dream.* New York: Atheneum.

Bromley, David G. 1982. "The archetypal cult: Conflict and the social construction of deviance." Paper presented at the annual meetings of the Society for the Scientific Study of Religion, Providence, R.I., November.

Bromley, David G., and Anson D. Shupe, Jr. 1981. *Strange Gods: The Great American Cult Scare.* Boston: Beacon.

Buley, R. Carlyle. 1950. *The Old Northwest: Pioneer Period, 1815–1840.* Indianapolis: Indiana Historical Society.

Burkett, Randall K. 1978. *Garveyism as a Religious Movement: The Institutionalization of a Black Civil Religion.* Metuchen, N.J.: Scarecrow Press and American Theological Library Association.

Buttinger, Joseph. 1953. *In the Twilight of Socialism.* New York: Praeger.

California Attorney General. 1980. "Report of investigation of People's Temple." Sacramento: State of California, April.

California Department of Social Services. 1979. "Investigation Report on Peoples Temple." Sacramento: State of California, November.

Canak, William. 1984. "The peripheral state debate: State capitalism and bureaucratic authoritarian regimes in Latin America." *Latin American Research Review* 19: 3–36.

Canetti, Elias. 1978. *Crowds and Power.* New York: Seabury (1960).

Case, Francis H. 1921. *Handbook of Church Advertising.* New York: Abingdon Press.

Childs, John Brown. 1980. *The Political Black Minister: A Study in Afro-American Politics and Religion.* Boston: G. H. Hall.

Chu, Franklin D., and Sharland Trotter. 1974. *The Madness Establishment: Ralph Nader's Study Group Report on the National Institute of Mental Health.* New York: Grossman.

Clark, Elmer T. 1949. *The Small Sects in America.* Rev. ed. New York: Abingdon-Cokesbury Press (1937).

Cleage, Alfred B., Jr. 1972. *Black Christian Nationalism: New Directions for the Black Church.* New York: Morrow.

Cohn, Norman. 1970. *The Pursuit of the Millennium: Revolutionary Mille-*

*narians and Mystical Anarchists of the Middle Ages.* New York: Oxford University Press (1957).

Committee on Foreign Affairs. 1979. *The Assassination of Representative Leo J. Ryan and the Jonestown, Guyana Tragedy.* U.S. House of Representatives, 96th Cong., 1st sess. Washington, D.C.: Government Printing Office, May 15.

Committee on Foreign Affairs Hearing. 1979. "The death of Representative Leo J. Ryan, People's Temple, and Jonestown: Understanding a tragedy." U.S. House of Representatives, 96th Cong., 1st sess. Washington, D.C.: Government Printing Office, May 15.

Conrad, Joseph. 1967. "Heart of darkness." In *Great Short Works of Joseph Conrad*, pp. 211–92. New York: Harper and Row (1899).

Coser, Lewis A. 1956. *The Functions of Social Conflict.* New York: Free Press.

_____. 1974. *Greedy Institutions: Patterns of Undivided Commitment.* New York: Free Press.

Crimmins, John Hugh, and Stanley S. Carpenter. 1979. "Study of the relationship between the People's Temple agricultural community in Guyana and the Department of State and the American embassy in Georgetown, Guyana prior to the incidents of November 18, 1978." Washington, D.C.: Department of State, May.

Crummey, Robert O. 1970. *The Old Believers and the World of Anti-Christ.* Madison: University of Wisconsin Press.

Debord, Guy. 1977. *Society of the Spectacle.* Detroit: Black & Red (1967).

Dem, Marc. 1979. *Jim Jones, le Demon de Guyana.* Paris: H. Veyrier.

Despres, Leo A. 1973. "The implications of nationalist politics in British Guiana for the development of cultural theory." In *State and Society*, edited by Reinhard Bendix et al., pp. 502–28. Berkeley: University of California Press (1964).

Dick, Robert C. 1974. *Black Protest: Issues and Tactics.* Westport, Conn.: Greenwood Press.

Dillon, Francis. 1973. *A Place for Habitation: The Pilgrim Fathers and Their Quest.* London: Hutchinson.

Divine, Mother. 1982. *The Peace Mission Movement.* Philadelphia: Imperial Press.

Donzelot, Jacques. 1979. *The Policing of Families.* New York: Pantheon (1977).

Dorough, C. Dwight. 1974. *The Bible Belt Mystique.* Philadelphia: Westminster Press.

Dunn, Jacob P. 1907. *The Word Hoosier.* Publication 4, #2. Indianapolis: Indiana Historical Society.

Durasoff, Steve. 1972. *Bright Wind of the Spirit: Pentecostalism Today.* Englewood Cliffs, N.J.: Prentice-Hall.

Durkheim, Emile. 1947. *The Elementary Forms of Religious Life.* Glencoe, Ill.: Free Press.

———. 1952. *Suicide*. New York: Free Press.

Edwards, Christopher. 1979. *Crazy for God: The Nightmare of Cult Life*. Englewood Cliffs, N.J.: Prentice-Hall.

Elmen, Paul. 1976. *Wheat Flower Messiah: Eric Jansson of Bishop Hill*. Carbondale: Southern Illinois University Press.

Engels, Frederick. 1964. "The peasant revolt in Germany." In *Karl Marx and Frederick Engels on Religion*, edited by Reinhold Niebuhr, pp. 97–118. New York: Schocken (1850).

Enroth, Ronald. 1977. *Youth, Brainwashing, and the Extremist Cults*. Grand Rapids, Mich.: Zondervan.

Erikson, Erik H. 1958. *Young Man Luther*. New York: Norton.

Erikson, Kai. 1966. *Wayward Puritans: A Study in the Sociology of Deviance*. New York: Wiley.

Eskin, George C. 1979. "Report concerning prosecution of James Warren Jones." Memorandum to Burt Pines, City Attorney. Los Angeles: City of Los Angeles, July 30.

Fallding, Harold. 1974. *The Sociology of Religion*. Toronto: McGraw-Hill Ryerson.

Feinsod, Ethan. 1981. *Awake in a Nightmare; Jonestown: The Only Eyewitness Account*. New York: Norton.

Foner, Philip S. 1977. *American Socialism and Black Americans: From the Age of Jackson to World War II*. Westport, Conn.: Greenwood Press.

Forster, Walter O. 1953. *Zion on the Mississippi: The Settlement of the Saxon Lutherans in Missouri, 1839–1841*. St. Louis: Concordia Publishing.

Foster, Lawrence. 1981. *Religion and Sexuality*. New York: Oxford University Press.

Foucault, Michel. 1965. *Madness and Civilization: A History of Insanity in the Age of Reason*. New York: Random House (1961).

———. 1973. *The Birth of the Clinic*. New York: Pantheon.

———. 1978. *The History of Sexuality*. New York: Pantheon.

———. 1979. *Discipline and Punish: The Birth of the Prison*. New York: Random House (1975).

Frazer, James G. 1935. *The Scapegoat*. Part VI of *The Golden Bough: A Study in Magic and Religion*. 3d ed. New York: Macmillan.

Frend, W. H. C. 1967. *Martyrdom and Persecution in the Early Church*. Garden City, N.Y.: Doubleday.

Gaines, Steven S. 1973. *Marjoe: The Life of Marjoe Gortner*. New York: Harper & Row.

General Accounting Office. 1980. *Guyana Tragedy Points to a Need for Better Care and Protection of Guardianship Children*. Washington, D.C.: General Accounting Office.

Girard, René. 1986. *The Scapegoat*. Baltimore: Johns Hopkins University Press (1982).

Glock, Charles Y., and Robert N. Bellah, eds. 1976. *The New Religious Consciousness*. Berkeley: University of California Press.

364     **Gone from the Promised Land**

Goffman, Erving. 1959. *The Presentation of Self in Everyday Life.* Garden City, N.Y.: Doubleday.
——. 1961. *Asylums.* Garden City, N.Y.: Doubleday.
——. 1974. *Frame Analysis.* New York: Harper & Row.
Hadden, Jeffrey K. and Charles E. Swanson. 1981. *Prime Time Preachers.* Reading, Mass.: Addison-Wesley.
Hall, John R. 1978. *The Ways Out: Utopian Communal Groups in an Age of Babylon.* Boston: Routledge & Kegan Paul.
——. 1979. "Apocalypse at Jonestown." *Society* 16: 52–61. Reprinted in Robbins and Anthony (1981), Levi (1982), and Zaniello (1987).
——. 1983. "Religion and commitment in nineteenth century communal groups." Paper presented at meetings of Society for the Scientific Study of Religion, Knoxville, November 5.
——. 1984. "World system holism and colonial Brazilian agriculture: A critical case study." *Latin American Research Review* 19: 43–69.
Harrell, David E. 1975. *All Things Are Possible.* Bloomington: Indiana University Press.
Harrington, Michael. 1962. *The Other America.* New York: Macmillan.
Harrison, Paul M. 1959. *Authority and Power in the Free Church Tradition.* Princeton: Princeton University Press.
Hechter, Michael. 1975. *Internal Colonialism.* Berkeley: University of California Press.
——. 1983. "A theory of group solidarity." In *The Micro-Foundations of Macro-Sociology,* edited by Michael Hechter, pp. 16–57. Philadelphia: Temple University Press.
——. 1984. "When actors comply: Monitoring costs and the production of social order." *Acta Sociologica* 27: 161–83.
Henry, W.E. 1908. *Some Elements of Indiana's Population.* Publication 4, #6: 388–89. Indianapolis: Indiana Historical Society.
Hofstadter, Richard. 1963. *Anti-intellectualism in American Life.* New York: Random House.
——. 1979. *"The Paranoid Style in American Politics" and Other Essays.* Chicago: University of Chicago Press (1964).
Hollenweger, W. J. 1972. *The Pentecostals: The Charismatic Movement in the Churches.* Minneapolis: Augsburg (1969).
Hoover, J. Edgar. 1958. *Masters of Deceit: The Story of Communism in America and How to Fight It.* New York: Holt.
Howe, Irving, and Lewis Coser. 1957. *The American Communist Party: A Critical History, 1919–1957.* Boston: Beacon Press.
Huberman, Leo, and Paul M. Sweezy. 1968. *Introduction to Socialism.* New York: Monthly Review Press.
Hunter, James Davison. 1983. *American Evangelicalism: Conservative Religion and the Quandry of Modernity.* Rutgers: Rutgers University Press.
Ingram, Larry C. 1983. "Ideology at personal and group levels: Testimonies

and conversion accounts at religious gatherings." Paper presented at the meetings of the Society for the Scientific Study of Religion, Knoxville, November.

James, William. 1929. *The Varieties of Religious Experience.* New York: Random House (1902).

Jones, Stephan. 1979. "Penthouse Interview." *Penthouse* (April): 85–88, 167–70.

Kanter, Rosabeth Moss. 1972. *Commitment and Community: Communes and Utopias in Sociological Perspective.* Cambridge: Harvard University Press.

Kern, Phil, and Doug Wead. 1979. *People's Temple; People's Tomb.* Plainfield, N.J.: Logos International.

Kilduff, Marshall, and Ron Javers. 1978. *The Suicide Cult: The Inside Story of the Peoples Temple Sect and the Massacre in Guyana.* New York: Bantam.

Kilduff, Marshall, and Phil Tracy. 1979. "Inside Peoples Temple." *New West* August 1, 1977, reprinted in CFA [source for pagination cited in notes].

Klineman, George, Sherman Butler, and David Conn. 1980. *The Cult That Died: The Tragedy of Jim Jones and the People's Temple.* New York: Putnam's.

Knollenberg, Bernhard. 1945. *Pioneer Sketches of the Upper Whitewater River Valley, Quaker Stronghold of the West.* Publication 15, #1. Indianapolis: Indiana Historical Society.

Knox, Ronald. 1956. *Enthusiasm, a Chapter in the History of Religion.* New York: Oxford University Press.

Krause, Charles, with Laurence M. Stern and Richard Harwood. 1978. *Guyana Massacre: The Eyewitness Account.* New York: Berkeley.

Lane, Mark. 1980. *The Strongest Poison.* New York: Hawthorne.

Lanternari, Vittorio. 1963. *The Religions of the Oppressed.* New York: Knopf.

Lasch, Christopher. 1977. *Haven in a Heartless World: The Family Beseiged.* New York: Basic Books.

Levi, Ken, ed. 1982. *Violence and Religious Commitment: Implications of Jim Jones's Peoples Temple Movement.* University Park: Pennsylvania State University Press.

Lewis, Gordon. 1979. "Gather with the saints at the river." Río Piedras: Institute for Caribbean Studies, University of Puerto Rico.

Lewis, Sinclair. 1927. *Elmer Gantry.* New York: Harcourt, Brace.

Lewy, Gunter. 1974. *Religion and Revolution.* New York: Oxford University Press.

Lifton, Robert J. 1968. *Revolutionary Immortality: Mao Tse-Tung and the Chinese Cultural Revolution.* New York: Vintage.

Lindesmith, Alfred R. 1947. *Opiate Addiction.* Bloomington, Ind.: Principia Press.

Lyman, Stanford M. 1978. *The Seven Deadly Sins*. New York: St. Martin's Press.

Maguire, John, and Mary Lee Dunn. 1978. *Hold Hands and Die*. New York: Dale.

Major, Reggie. 1979. "The twisted roots of Jonestown." *Mother Jones.* December.

Mannheim, Karl. 1936. *Ideology and Utopia*. New York: Harcourt, Brace & World.

Marcuse, Herbert. 1964. *One Dimensional Man*. Boston: Beacon Press.

Marks, C. R. 1906. "Monona County, Iowa, Mormons." *Annals of Iowa* 7 (April): 321–46.

Marshall, Gordon. 1982. *In Search of the Spirit of Capitalism*. New York: Columbia University Press.

Marston, John E. 1979. *Modern Public Relations*. New York: McGraw-Hill.

McKivigan, John R. 1984. *The War Against Proslavery Religion: Abolitionism and the Northern Churches, 1830–1865*. Ithaca: Cornell University Press.

Mead, Frank S. 1975. *Handbook of Denominations in the United States*. 6th ed. Nashville: Abingdon Press.

Meeks, Wayne A. 1983. *The First Urban Christians: The Social World of the Apostle Paul*. New Haven: Yale University Press.

Meerloo, Joost A. M. 1962. *Suicide and Mass Suicide*. New York: Grune & Stratton.

Mikkelsen, Michael A. 1892. "The Bishop Hill Colony." *Johns Hopkins University Studies in Historical and Political Science* 10: 11–80.

Miller, Floyd T. 1975. *The Search for a Black Nationality: Black Emigration and Colonization, 1787–1863*. Urbana: University of Illinois Press.

Mills, Jeannie. 1979. *Six Years with God: Life inside Rev. Jim Jones's Peoples Temple*. New York: A&W Publishers.

Moltmann, Gunter. 1983. "German migration as a social protest movement." Paper presented to the National Historic Communal Societies Association, New Harmony, Indiana, November.

Moore, Rebecca. 1985. *A Sympathetic History of Jonestown*. New York: Edwin Mellen.

Moses, William Jeremiah. 1982. *Black Messiahs and Uncle Toms: Social and Literary Manipulations of a Religious Myth*. University Park: Pennsylvania State University Press.

Naipaul, Shiva. 1981. *Journey to Nowhere: A New World Tragedy*. New York: Simon & Schuster (1980).

Newton, Huey P. 1972. *To Die for the People*. New York: Random House.

———. 1973. *Revolutionary Suicide*. New York: Harcourt, Brace, Jovanovich.

Nichols, Norma. 1979?. *Pot-pourri with a Taste of Cult*. Georgetown, Guyana: Autoprint.

Niebuhr, H. Reinhold. 1937. *The Kingdom of God in America.* New York: Harper.

Noyes, John Humphrey. 1966. *Strange Cults and Utopias of 19th Century America.* New York: Dover (1870).

Nugent, John Peer. 1979. *White Night: The Untold Story of What Happened Before—and Beyond—Jonestown.* New York: Rawson, Wade.

O'Dea, Thomas. 1957. *The Mormons.* Chicago: University of Chicago Press.

Olson, Mancur. 1968. *The Logic of Collective Action.* New York: Schocken.

O'Neill, John. 1972. *Sociology as a Skin Trade.* New York: Harper & Row.

Paris, Arthur E. 1982. *Black Pentecostalism: Southern Religion in an Urban World.* Amherst: University of Massachusetts Press.

Patrick, Ted, with Tom Dulack. 1976. *Let Our Children Go.* New York: Dutton.

Peoples Temple. 1979. "Jonestown tape." November 18, 1978, Jonestown pavilion suicide meeting, cassette tape. New York: Creative Arts Guild, copy at CHS, and transcription in Zaniello (1987: 412–27).

Piven, Frances Fox, and Richard A. Cloward. 1979. *Poor People's Movements: Why They Succeed, How They Fail.* New York: Vintage (1977).

Pope, Liston. 1942. *Millhands and Preachers.* New Haven: Yale University Press.

Quarles, Benjamin. 1969. *Black Abolitionist.* New York: Oxford University Press.

Raglan, Lord. 1958. "Myth and ritual." In *Myth: A Symposium,* edited by Thomas A. Sebeok, pp. 122–35. Bloomington: Indiana University Press.

Redkey, Edwin S. 1969. *The Black Exodus.* New Haven: Yale University Press.

Reiterman, Tim, and John Jacobs. 1982. *Raven: The Untold Story of the Rev. Jim Jones and His People.* New York: Dutton.

Reston, James, Jr. 1981. *Our Father Who Art in Hell.* New York: Times Books.

Reston, James, Jr., and Noah Adams. 1981. "Father cares: the last of Jonestown." Audio cassettes. Washington, D.C.: National Public Radio.

Riddle, Donald W. 1931. *The Martyrs: A Study in Social Control.* Chicago: University of Chicago Press.

Riddle, Richard A. 1981. "The 1974 Missouri Lutheran crisis: Historical and sociological sources of schism in a Protestant denomination." Master's thesis, University of Missouri - Columbia.

Robbins, Thomas. 1986. "Religious mass suicide before Jonestown: The Russian Old Believers." *Sociological Analysis* 47: 1–20.

Robbins, Tom, and Dick Anthony, eds. 1981. *In Gods We Trust.* New Brunswick, N.J.: Transaction Books.

Robbins, Tom, and Dick Anthony. 1982. "Deprogramming, brainwashing and the medicalization of deviant religious groups." *Social Problems* 39: 283–97.

Rodney, Walter. 1981. *A History of the Guyanese Working People, 1881–1905*. Baltimore: Johns Hopkins University Press.

Rodrigues, José Honorio. 1965. *Brazil and Africa*. Berkeley: University of California Press.

Rohrbough, Malcolm J. 1978. *The Trans-Appalachian Frontier: People, Societies, and Institutions, 1775–1850*. New York: Oxford University Press.

Rose, Steve. 1979. *Jesus and Jim Jones: Behind Jonestown*. New York: Pilgrim Press.

Ross, Irwin. 1959. *The Image Merchants: The Fabulous World of Public Relations*. Garden City, N.Y.: Doubleday.

Roth, Guenther. 1971. "Sociological typology and historical explanation." In *Scholarship and Partisanship: Essays on Max Weber*, by Reinhard Bendix and Guenther Roth, pp. 109–28. Berkeley: University of California Press.

———. 1976. "History and sociology in the work of Max Weber." *British Journal of Sociology* 27: 306–18.

Sanford, Charles L. 1961. *The Quest for Paradise: Europe and the American Moral Imagination*. Urbana: University of Illinois Press.

Santos, Manoel Hygino dos. 1979. *Sangue em Jonestown*. Belo Horizonte, Brazil: Edicoes Jupiter.

Scheler, Max. 1961. *Ressentiment*, edited by Lewis A. Coser. New York: Free Press (1915).

Segal, Steven P., and Uri Aviram. 1978. *The Mentally Ill in Community-Based Sheltered Care: A Study of Community Care and Social Integration*. New York: Wiley.

Selengut, Charles. 1983. "Insiders and outsiders: Presentation practices in cognitive minority religions." Paper presented at the meetings of the Society for the Scientific Study of Religion, Knoxville, November.

Selznick, Philip. 1952. *The Organizational Weapon: A Study of Bolshevik Strategy and Tactics*. New York: McGraw-Hill.

Shupe, Anson D., Jr., and David G. Bromley. 1980. *The New Vigilantes: Deprogrammers, Anti-Cultists, and the New Religions*. Beverly Hills, Calif.: Sage Publications.

Simmel, Georg. 1950. *The Sociology of George Simmel*. New York: Free Press.

Smith, Jonathan A. 1982. *Imagining Religion: From Babylon to Jonestown*. Chicago: University of Chicago Press.

Smith, John L. and Lee L. Driver. 1914. *Past and Present of Randolph County, Indiana*. Indianapolis: Bowen.

Smith, Morton. 1978. *Jesus the Magician*. New York: Harper & Row.

Smith, Rembert Gilman. 1950. *Moscow over Methodism*. Houston: University Press.

Smith, Timothy L. 1965. *Revivalism and Social Reform*. New York: Harper & Row (1957).

Snow, David A., and Richard Machalek. 1982. "On the presumed fragility of unconventional beliefs." *Journal for the Scientific Study of Religion* 21: 15–26.

Sorel, Georges. 1961. *Reflections on Violence*. New York: Collier-Macmillan.

Staudenraus, P. J. 1961. *The African Colonization Movement, 1816–1865*. New York: Columbia University Press.

Stowe, Harriet Beecher. 1981. *Uncle Tom's Cabin*. New York: New American Library (1851).

Swaggert, Jimmie. 1983. "What you should know about divine healing." *Evangelist* 15 (October).

Synon, Vinson. 1971. *The Holiness Pentecostal Movement in the United States*. Grand Rapids, Mich.: W.B. Eerdmans.

Syski, Jacek. 1980. *Swiatynia Zagady*. Warsaw: Ksiazka i Wiedza.

Tello, Antonio. 1979. *Los niños de Dios, el Templo del Pueblo u otras neuvas sectas*. Barcelona: Bruguera.

Thielmann, Bonnie, and Dean Merrill. 1979. *The Broken God*. Elgin, Ill.: David Cook.

Thompson, E. P. 1967. "Time, work-discipline, and industrial capitalism." *Past and Present* 38: 56–97.

Thornbrough, Emma Lou. 1957. *The Negro in Indiana*. Indianapolis: Indiana Historical Bureau.

Thucydides. 1959. *The Peloponnesian War*. Ann Arbor: University of Michigan Press (c. 400 B.C.).

Tipton, Steven M. 1982. *Getting Saved from the Sixties*. Berkeley: University of California Press.

Tucker, E. 1882. *A History of Randolph County, Indiana*. Chicago: A. L. Kingman.

U.S. Census. 1930. *Census of the Population*, vol. 5. Washington, D.C.: Government Printing Office.

Veyne, Paul. 1984. *Writing History*. Middletown, Conn.: Wesleyan University Press (1971).

Washington, Joseph R., Jr. 1967. *The Politics of God*. Boston: Beacon Press.

Weber, Max. 1958. *The Protestant Ethic and the Spirit of Capitalism*. New York: Scribner's (1905).

——. 1977. *Economy and Society*, edited by Guenther Roth and Claus Wittich. Berkeley: University of California Press.

Weightman, Judith. 1983. *Making Sense of the Jonestown Suicides*. New York: Edwin Mellen.

Weisbrot, Robert. 1983. *Father Divine and the Struggle for Racial Equality*. Urbana: University of Illinois Press.

Weiss, Mike. 1984. *Double Play: The San Francisco City Hall Killings*. Reading, Mass.: Addison Wesley.

West, Donald J. 1966. *Murder Followed by Suicide.* Cambridge: Harvard University Press.

White, Mel, Paul Scotchman, and Marguerite Shuster. 1979. *Deceived.* Old Tappen, N.J.: Spire.

Whitman, Lauris P., and Glenn W. Trimble. 1954–57. *Churches and Church Membership in the United States, 1951.* Series C, No. 13. New York: National Council of Churches.

Wiencek, David [Division of Continuing Education, University of Virginia]. N.d. "A demographic profile of Jonestown victims." Unpublished paper, F658, CHS.

Williams, Sam K. 1975. *Jesus' Death as Saving Event: The Background and Origin of a Concept.* Harvard Dissertations in Religion No. 2. Cambridge: Harvard Theological Review.

Wilmore, Gayraud S. 1983. *Black Religion and Black Radicals.* Maryknoll, N.Y.: Orbis.

Wilson, Colin. 1964. *Rasputin and the Fall of the Romanovs.* Secaucus, N.J.: Citadel Press.

Wilson, Edmund. 1940. *To the Finland Station: A Study in the Writing and Acting of History.* Garden City, N.Y.: Doubleday.

Wolff, Richard D. 1974. *The Economics of Colonialism: Britain and Kenya, 1870–1930.* New Haven: Yale University Press.

Wooden, Kenneth. 1981. *The Children of Jonestown.* New York: McGraw Hill.

Yadin, Yigael. 1966. *Masada: Herod's Fortress and the Zealots' Last Stand.* New York: Random House.

Yee, Min S., and Thomas N. Layton. 1981. *In My Father's House.* New York: Holt, Rinehart & Winston.

Zaniello, Thomas A. 1987. *Explorations in Reading and Writing.* New York: Random House.

Zaret, David. 1980. "Ideology and organization in the Puritan movement." *European Journal of Sociology* 21: 81–113.

Zicklin, Gilbert. 1983. *Countercultural Communes: A Sociological Perspective.* Westport, Conn.: Greenwood Press.

# Index

Adams, Paula, 133, 193, 194–95, 200, 204, 215, 225

Amos, Linda (Sharon), 65, 67, 81, 103, 194–95, 265, 266, 270, 290

Annibourne, Neville, 268, 269, 277

Anticult movements: atrocity tale usage, xiv–xviii; contemporary U.S., 107, 203, 220, 255, 259; historical examples, 208–9; and Temple, 73, 107, 181, 187, 213–14, 226, 303, 304, 309. *See also* Concerned Relatives; Peoples Temple opponents

Apostasy, 116, 137–38. *See also under* Peoples Temple

Augustine, Saint, 297

Aviram, Uri, 81

Bagby, Monica, 271, 273, 274, 278–79

Baldwin, Walter and Charlotte, 47, 293–94

Banks, Dennis: meeting with opponents, 182–83; reports to Temple, 197, 200–1, 207, 214, 215; Temple alliance with, 160, 162, 163

Barbagelata, John, 166, 169, 178, 184, 189

Barnes, W. E., 184–85

Barnum, Phineas T., 141

Barthes, Roland, 290

Bartolomie, Mendocino County, Calif., sheriff, 149

Bayh, Birch, 220

Beam, Jack, 24, 42–43, 44, 57, 59–60, 63, 119, 135, 279

Beam, Rheaviana, 43, 58, 60, 63

Bedford, George, 70–71

Beikman, Becky, 200

Benedict, Saint, 123

Berkeley *Barb*, 157, 189

Biddulph, John, 131–32

Bishop, Audrey, 249

Black Americans, xiv, 4, 70–71; messiahs and redemption of, 48–52, 135, 206, 302–3; ministers and churches, 9, 49, 62, 70–71, 97, 161–62; and socialist preachers, 25, 28, 144. *See also* Jones, Jim; Peoples Temple; United States, society

Black Muslims, 164

Black Panther party, 135–36, 163, 167, 189, 205, 237, 250, 281

Blacken, John, 221, 224

Blakey, Debbie Layton, 283, 304; assertions about Jonestown, 243–46 passim, 255–63 passim, 274; defection of, 243–49 passim, 280; in Temple, 68, 89, 93, 100, 219

Bogue, Jim, and family, 194, 236, 240, 273–74

Boorstin, Daniel, 140, 141

Boswell, Charles, 54

Bouquet, Clare, 255, 259, 268

Boyd, Carol, 268

Boynton, Marge, 153

Bradley, Tom, 164

Bradshaw, Sandy, 67, 68, 97, 99, 101, 153, 201

Branham, William, 111, 292

Breidenback, Wesley, 276, 278

Brightman, Lehman, 182–83

British Guiana, *See* Guyana

Broussard, Leon, 217

Brown, Amos, 162

Brown, Bob, 258, 277, 278–79

Brown, Jean, 153, 161, 204, 259, 261, 266

Brown, Jerry, 175

Brown, Willie, 163–69 passim

Buford, Teri, 67–68, 93; after Mark Lane employment, 252, 259, 261, 271; and Temple administration, 89, 96, 98, 99, 203; and Temple intelligence activities, 102, 119, 231

Burke, John, 224, 228, 244, 259, 260, 265, 267

Burnham, Forbes, 191, 193, 196, 227–32 passim, 247

**371**

Delancey Street Foundation, 167
Democratic party, 165, 166–68, 175, 220
Dennis, Ronnie, 278
Denny, Dennis, 71, 82–83, 84, 102, 165–66
Depression, Great, 3, 5, 8, 14, 25, 51
Derwinski, Ed, 258, 259, 261, 265
Disciples of Christ, 52–55, 62, 65, 115, 146, 155, 178, 182. *See also under* Peoples Temple
Divine, Father M. J., 176, 206; influence on Jones, 50–52, 72–73, 79, 80, 99, 146; parallels to Jones, 97, 163, 235. *See also* Peace Mission
Divine, Mother, 70
Dooley, Nancy, 187
Durkheim, Emile, 35, 294, 308
Dwyer, Richard, 224, 243, 244; and Jonestown expedition, 264–79 passim, 284
Dymally, Mervyn, 168, 184, 196

Edwards, Don, 261
Edwards, Irene, 285
Ellice, Doug, 264
Ellsberg, Daniel, 109
Erikson, Kai, 125
Evans, Julius, 272

Fabian, Robert, 90, 293
Faith healing, 17–24 passim, 35–36, 86. *See also under* Jones, Jim
Falwell, Jerry, 143
Family, 129, 139, 222, 234
Farm, The, 235
Fields, Mark, 254
Fiers, Dale, 154–55
Flick, Bob, 279
Foucault, Michel, 80, 106
Francois, Terry, 166
Freed, Don, 250–51, 252
Free-rider problem, 116–17, 242
Freitas, Joe, 164, 167, 169, 214, 220
Frend, W.H.C., 296–98
Fresno (Calif.) *Bee*, 159, 163, 168
Frost, Greg, 193

Gallup Poll, 289
Gantry, Elmer, fictional character, 252
Gardner, John, 124
Garry, Charles: and custody battles, 217,

227; early knowledge of mass suicide issue, 230, 305; and Jonestown expedition, 266–76 passim, 300; and mass suicide, 279–81, 287; as Temple lawyer in U.S., 163, 189, 215, 216, 224–25, 232, 248, 250; trips to Guyana, 219, 233, 238, 251–52
Garvey, Marcus, 49–51, 71, 72, 176, 206
Giamo, Robert, 220
Gieg, Clifford, 254
Gieg, Stanley, 278
Glide Memorial Methodist Church, 159, 161, 162, 170
Golden Rule Church, 64
Goodlett, Carlton, 162, 169, 189, 254
Goodspeed, Mr. and Mrs., couple at Jonestown, 264
Gortner, Marjoe, 43
Gosney, Vern, 271–74 passim, 278–79
Greece, ancient, 283, 295, 297, 302, 303, 304
Gregory, Dick, 305
Grenada, 203
Grubbs, Tom, 200, 241
Gurvitch, Jann, 270
Guyana, government of, 190–93; and Concerned Relatives, 220, 221, 227, 229–30, 255; and custody trial, 217, 218–19, 244, 249; and mass suicide, 277, 278, 285, 293; police, 215, 265, 268, 269, 276, 277, 294; Temple relations, 133, 194–95, 201–2, 205, 215, 216–17, 251; U.S. relations, 224, 228, 244–45, 305

Haas, Jeffrey, 217–21 passim, 227, 245–46
Halversen, David, 188
Harpe, Maxine, 102–3, 188
Harris, Don, 257–58, 262, 263, 268–74 passim, 279
Harris, Leanne, 225
Harris, Magnolia, 225
Harris, Sherwin, 268, 290
Hart, Steve, 186
Hayden, Tom, 163
Head, John, 103, 188
Hearst, Patricia, 148
Hofstadter, Richard, 158. *See also* Paranoid style
Holenwager, W. J., 9, 27
Hongisto, Richard, 167, 170